Journeys of Women
in Science
and Engineering

In the series *Labor and Social Change,*
edited by Paula Rayman and Carmen Sirianni

Susan A. Ambrose
Kristin L. Dunkle
Barbara B. Lazarus
Indira Nair
Deborah A. Harkus

Journeys of Women in Science and Engineering

No Universal Constants

Foreword by Lilli Hornig

Temple University Press
Philadelphia

Temple University Press, Philadelphia 19122
Copyright © 1997 by Temple University
All rights reserved
Published 1997
Printed in the United States of America

♾ The paper used in this publication meets the requirements of American National Standard for Information Sciences—Permanence of Paper for Printed Library Materials, ANSI Z39.48-1984

Interior design by Eliz. Anne O'Donnell

Library of Congress Cataloging-in-Publication Data

Journeys of women in science and engineering : no universal constants
    / Susan A. Ambrose ... [et al.].
        p.   cm. — (Labor and social change)
    Includes bibliographical references and index.
    ISBN 1-56639-527-5 (cloth : alk. paper)
    1. Women in science.   2. Women in engineering.   3. Women
scientists—Biography.   4. Women engineers—Biography.   I. Ambrose,
Susan A., 1958–   . II. Series.
Q130.J68   1997
508.2—dc21   96-50415

For the
next generation
of engineers
and scientists

❧

We all stand on
the shoulders of giants.

Contents

Foreword

Lilli Hornig

It is not often that a fresh look at a well-examined subject yields such illuminating results as this volume does. Women's careers in science and engineering have been investigated by many scholars from many different perspectives in the last two or three decades. None of the studies I know have managed to convey, as this one does, the sheer joy so many women take in their careers in the sciences and engineering, or the enormous range of the fields and activities that engage them.

The traditional studies fall into two general categories. One deals largely with statistics and analyses of girls' and women's participation at all levels of study and in the various fields, and with comparisons of their career attainments relative to those of men. This group also encompasses many historical studies that trace the trends in women's science education and careers over time. Studies of these types tend to focus on the institutional barriers, explicit or implicit, that kept women's numbers in science fields low and their achievements less illustrious. The second major category of studies has centered on women's psychological make-up, and on their attitudes toward careers in general and careers in the sciences in particular. Usually these analyses are especially concerned with how the ascribed feminine qualities of noncompetitiveness, nurturant inclinations, and desires to cooperate conflict with the needs for achievement motivation and for competitiveness in the sciences (or, for that matter, in other professional careers). These studies also often focus on whether females really have the requisite intellectual abilities for science. They tend to view women as "nonlinear thinkers,"

intuitive and empathic but not analytical. Both kinds of studies emphasize the conflicts that dedication to science must present for ordinary women, who generally want fulfilling personal relationships and normal family life along with their careers.

What all of these analyses seek to explain is the fact that women's participation in science, math, and engineering lags behind men's. The gaps are largest in the most quantitative fields and smallest in most social and biological sciences. Similarly, the differences in all fields are smallest at the lowest levels of study and employment and greatest at the top of each profession. In broad outline, the statistical and historical analyses tend to focus on the institutional constraints and barriers that have hampered women's full involvement in the past and that still do so in certain ways, in effect placing the blame for women's low participation at society's door. Conversely, the second group of studies, those focusing on women's inclinations, abilities, preferences, and "choices," result all too often in blaming the victim.

All of these approaches can be faulted for making science into such a special case. The sex differences we observe in science and engineering careers are replicated to some degree in every other profession, and tend to be lumped under the heading of the "glass ceiling." It is well to recognize that they also exist in female-dominated fields like teaching, nursing, and many kinds of administration, where the great majority of workers are women but the top positions are held predominantly by men. Since these hierarchies are so widespread, and since people at the top of a hierarchy often try to reinforce their position by claiming that it was superior ability that put them there, it is not surprising that women's absence from these upper reaches is often blamed on either their "preference" for family commitments or their inferior abilities. The latter explanation may be particularly appealing to scientists, who often believe themselves to be at the top of the intellectual heap and thus may feel a special need for bolstering their position.

Two aspects of this reasoning need further discussion: the ability issue and the matter of choice. The idea of an intellectual gender gap is not new. It has a long and dishonorable history among philosophers starting with Aristotle and, regrettably, among some scientists as well. During the nineteenth century the emerging fields of psychology and biology devoted much effort to demonstrating a hierarchy of intelligence that placed blacks and other nonwhite peoples at the bottom, white women next, and white men at the pinnacle of human abilities and accomplishments. Experimental evidence for such an ordering was scant, running mostly to measurements of cranial capacity which were readily modifiable to suit the expected results. In the twentieth century attention shifted to intelligence testing, which was developed largely in World War I to expedite assignment of military recruits. Unfairness in testing has been regarded by both women and minorities as a likely source of discrimination, though expert opinions continue to differ on the subject. At any rate, sex differences in testing are declining somewhat as women's educational profile grows to resemble men's.

The matter of women's choices is also viewed differently by different observers. Our educational and occupational system certainly does present a very wide range of choices, but that is not to say they are the same for everyone. It is quite clear by now that financial resources, for example, can limit these choices, sometimes disastrously. Similarly, until Title IX of the 1972 Education Amendments granted women equal access to and equal treatment in higher education, women's choices of professional training were severely limited by the admissions policies of graduate and professional schools. You could not be an engineer if engineering schools did not admit women; you were not likely to be a doctor or a lawyer if law and medical schools imposed quotas of 5 to 10 percent for women, as they all did; nor could you be a nuclear physicist or a mathematician if those graduate departments rarely admitted women. If you were a married woman, some institutions would not accept you as a student or hire you as a faculty member. It is useful to remember that while such policies no longer exist because they are illegal, many of the faculty members and administrators who instituted them are still in place. Remnants of restrictive practices and attitudes persist in some graduate science departments.

The choice to marry or to enter into other personal relationships, however, is what most observers focus on when analyzing the education and career decisions women make. It is most often also the issue that young women trying to decide what to do with their lives are most concerned about. The intuitive assumptions of most investigators are: (1) marriage (or a similar relationship) and children are more important to women than a career, (2) marriage inevitably has a deleterious effect on women's careers, (3) children further impair career success, and (4) presumably the effects of marriage and children will be the same no matter what the field. These questions have been examined in possibly hundreds of empirical studies in the last three decades. Taken as a whole, the results have not justified these assumptions.

The parameters of marriage decisions have changed for both women and men. Where once marriage was a woman's only certain means of adequate financial support and source of social status, careers can now fulfill both these ends. Nevertheless, as it became no longer possible to exclude women from education and careers simply because they were married, more women in careers in the sciences and elsewhere have married and more have children. But since men still earn more than women in all professions, the choices for married women become more complicated. When career moves come up, it is still most often the man's career that counts—logically so because, for the present, his will usually yield the best financial return for the family unit. Women must and do consider all these ramifications when they choose careers.

Interestingly, while one would expect the effects of marriage and children to be the same no matter what the field, this turns out not to be the case. Like other adverse effects such as greater difficulty in being hired, promoted, or paid equally, the disadvantage of family is generally less serious than an unfavorable labor market. When there are labor surpluses in a given field, men will have the advantage, but when there is a labor shortage, women will be hired more equally, regardless of marriage and children. Thus in engineering, for example, where full employment is currently the rule, women do significantly better in job status and salary than in chemistry, which has had an unfavorable labor market for several years. It is also the case, of course, that although men have not been shown to do significantly more family work than they used to, the greater availability of acceptable child care has greatly increased women's ability to pursue professional careers.

The marriage-career equation has thus undergone fundamental changes in recent years. Less discriminatory education has opened much better careers in general to women; and even though science careers have also become much more accessible, they are in competition with other equally desirable professions, notably medicine and law, which also discriminated heavily in the past. Women's professional careers, while still not quite the equal of men's, offer a degree of independence and achievement that women could not aspire to before. Lots of evidence suggests that as a result, decisions to marry have become much more selective.

The trend of the last two decades has quite clearly been toward increased equality for women in higher education, but the old patterns are still discernible. A little-recognized legacy of World War II and its GI Bill, offering veterans a free higher education, was the unintended consequence of displacing women from even those top universities that had previously admitted them. Women were therefore forced to attend lower-ranking colleges, mainly the state colleges that were emerging from the former teacher-training schools. Good as they are in many respects, many of these institutions do not offer adequate instruction in the sciences to this day, and their graduates are ill equipped for further study in science fields compared to the graduates of research universities or top-ranked colleges with whom they must compete. But attendance patterns that were set fifty years ago have not quite disappeared, and relatively high proportions of women still attend these lower-ranking colleges, thus effectively narrowing their occupational choices to nonscience fields. Many investigators believe that high school teachers and counselors still advise young women that such institutions are adequate for them, but that is generally not the case for women aiming for most professions.

The great growth in women's participation in higher education came about as the result of Title IX of the 1972 Education Amendments, which outlawed sex discrimination in a number of areas including recruitment, admissions standards, and access to educational programs or activities receiving federal funding. Women's share of baccalaureate degrees rose from 37 percent to over half in a decade, and from about one-tenth of doctorates to about 40 percent in the 1990s. The disproportion that persists between bachelor's and doctor's degrees is a measure both of remnants of discrimination and of the difficulty women see in reconciling the investment of time and money in an advanced degree with the demands of family life.

Women's increased interest in science and engineering was a part of this general movement toward greater similarity with men's choices. It came at an opportune time for universities. Women's participation rose rapidly just as men's was declining in these fields, and women helped to fill up the classes and laboratories that might have been sparsely populated without them. It is well to remember that as more men again turned to the sciences in the late 1980s, the rapid growth in women's participation leveled off. We cannot tell yet whether this signals a true shift of interests or subtle changes in admissions policies.

Title IX had another consequence that bears on the issue of women in nontraditional fields. That is the progressive opening of competitive sports to women. The scholars and advisers who worry that women are just not competitive enough to hold their own in science and engineering should take a hard look at the Olympic records of today's women athletes. Competitive sports, too, were once thought to be unsuitable for women—until Title IX forced colleges and universities to provide the necessary facilities and training. Women fought for these opportunities and then made good use of them.

Some philosophers of science have argued that the hard-driving competitive style of some areas of science, especially those at the cutting edge, is still one that women do not normally adopt and that they are predisposed to a more cooperative working style. The experience of women in sports demonstrates, however, that women are strong competitors when they have a reasonable chance at winning. Conversely, it can of course be argued that for men simply to declare women out of contention—whether by reason of inferior abilities, unwillingness to compete, or preference for other activities—is simply enlightened self-interest: it eliminates half the competition.

Even the most painstaking studies fall short of explaining the course of women's science careers fully. The volume before us now shows why: there is no adequate way to examine scientifically the myriad variables that make up a human life. People—male or female—simply do not fit into convenient boxes. Their personal histories and individual characteristics guide and inform their responses to education and opportunity in countless ways. Complex feedback loops make the various outcomes hard to analyze and compare in any rigorous way.

The tone of discussions about women's interests and abilities has also changed quite dramatically in these three decades. There seems little doubt any longer that, given a reasonable chance at access to education and a freer choice of fields, women's range of choices is very much more like men's than many scholars would have predicted. And although some fields—physics and engineering come to mind—continue to be much less popular with women than with men in the United States, the fact that many other countries show only small differences, if any, suggests that this situation could also change here.

There is one basic fact that young women considering careers in science or engineering need to know: they must enjoy studying these fields. They need not love every aspect—some people like crunching numbers, some do not; some like to play with theory, others want to apply science to human or social needs. But they have to love something about it and be willing to spend the time and effort to do it well. It is just as well to recognize at the outset that doing science is hard work. Even brilliant scientists may have to dig in to learn new material or master some field they have not yet had to work with.

Conventional wisdom to the contrary notwithstanding, that kind of dedication and occasional frustration at making slow progress is not unique to science and engineering fields. It happens in every profession at some time, and it is a mistake for young people considering various careers to believe that the sciences are substantially more demanding of time and effort than any other field in which one wants to excel. Getting to the top of any profession is what takes a special effort; just practicing science or engineering in an average way, which is what the vast majority of scientists and engineers do, is no more burdensome than carrying on any other calling in the same way. But it is especially important for young women not to be misled about the kind of ability and effort that is required to become an engineer or a scientist when they are making career choices. Painting science careers as requiring an all-out, tunnel-vision commitment gives pause to too many women who plan on having ordinary social and family lives while also pursuing their careers. This book should show them that many versions of such full and rewarding lives are indeed possible.

The myth of the scientist as superman is worth examining in a little more detail. The individual scientists about whom we hear the most are, by the nature of publicity, the ones who achieve important breakthroughs, make exciting discoveries, and garner Nobel prizes. They are indeed the ones who have always reached for the stars—who give to their work the kind of total commitment of time and energy and emotion that sets them apart from the crowd. Many of them have also had rewarding family lives, thanks largely to dedicated wives; some have seemed to care little for life outside of science. But all of them have had institutional backing—they were allowed to study at top institutions, to continue working there, and to benefit from their associations with other scientists.

It is also true that many people enjoy working in a particular field but do not really have the driving ambition to take them to the top. Some of the stories in this volume illustrate that point of view. Science and technology fields are just as open to this more laid-back approach as are other fields—the law, perhaps, or medicine or politics or journalism or business. The notion of success in science that is most commonly described may be the model of the Nobel laureate, but that is not the way most scientists live and work. That kind of ambition and dedication is not common; nor is it a realistic expectation for most practitioners. The vast majority of scientists and engineers practice their professions in quite ordinary ways. They work forty-hour weeks most of the time, and much longer ones when the pressure is on. So, of course, do lawyers or business people or high school teachers.

What, then, is the outlook for women in science and engineering? By any measure, these are inviting and rewarding fields for anyone with the ability and inclination to pursue them. The stories before us in this volume illustrate the countless ways in which individuals—some with exceptional talents and some with ordinary ones—have forged useful and rewarding lives in science. The stories, and the people who created them, bear testimony to the infinite possibilities in women's lives.

Preface

No Universal Constants?

In physics, there are certain values that are the same all over the physical universe. Among these are: the speed of light in vacuum, the gravitational constant, and Planck's constant. These are known as universal constants. *

I s it a parent or teacher who sparks a young woman's interest in science or engineering? Or is it a pure love of nature, a hunger for finding out how things work, the desire to help others, or a passion for numbers that starts a young scientist or engineer on her career path? The factors and circumstances are as diverse as the women profiled in our book. Though their paths have been diverse, their destinations are all the same: they are where they want to be, doing what they love.

In titling our book *Journeys of Women in Science and Engineering: No Universal Constants,* we are not questioning the existence or validity of certain physical truths about the universe. What we are seeking to do is to encourage people to question the unstated assumption that the practitioners of science and engineering have a uniform look and follow one particular path through life. The journeys of the eighty-eight women profiled in this book have no universal constants: committed, hardworking women of different races, ethnicities, socioeconomic backgrounds, sexual orientations, or those with disabilities, can find rewarding careers. It may be more challenging

for women, especially minority women, than for men. It may take more stamina to succeed, but women of all backgrounds are surviving and thriving as scientists and engineers.

Gathering the Stories

Our team of authors came together over several years. When anthropologist Barbara Lazarus, the daughter of a physicist and a community activist, arrived at Carnegie Mellon University from Wellesley College, she was struck by the dramatic differences between an educational environment oriented to women and a coeducational one. Susan Ambrose, social historian and director of Carnegie Mellon's Eberly Center for Teaching Excellence, was interested in women's lives and how class origin, sex, race and ethnicity, social conceptions of women, and other variables come together to influence women's life decisions and careers. Educated as a physicist and teaching in Carnegie Mellon's Department of Engineering and Public Policy, Indira Nair was interested in women students' attitudes toward science and engineering and factors that affect their success in these fields. Susan Ambrose, Barbara Lazarus, and Indira Nair collaborated for a number of years on a series of support programs for Carnegie Mellon women in engineering and science. When Barbara Lazarus suggested that a "field guide" to women working in science and engineering might be an important resource for women, they decided that they wanted to do something concrete to showcase the lives of many different women in these fields.

Deborah Harkus and Kristin Dunkle soon

*The complete set of universal constants are: the speed of light in vacuum, the permeability of space; the permitivity of space, the gravitational constant, and Planck's constant. See E. Richard Cohen and Barry N. Taylor, "The Fundamental Physical Constants," *Physics Today,* August 1995.

joined the team. Deborah, who had been working as Barbara's assistant, had been fascinated by the work from the beginning. A single mother and nontraditional undergraduate student, she was particularly interested in the alternative paths women can take to rewarding careers in male-dominated fields. Kristin Dunkle came on board as the project's research assistant, initially under a grant from the Alfred P. Sloan Foundation; but soon she became the team's anchor and the book's second author. She was interested in bridging her experience as a laboratory technician in neuropharmacology, her enthusiasm for writing, and her commitment to feminism and minority advocacy.

Together we were concerned about the difficulty women contemplating and pursuing science and engineering careers face in looking for effective role models—the fact that typically there are too few women in any one place to show the real richness of diversity. We found that the interplay of our collective expertise in history, physics and engineering, anthropology, writing, and biological science, as well as the different perspectives resulting from our varied life experiences, provided a good balance to address the challenge we set ourselves: to illustrate the varied paths taken by women working in science and engineering.

Rather than emphasize traditional markers of achievement, we wanted to focus in this book on how women define success for themselves. The reader will find here stories of individual women who have won Nobel Prizes and other distinctions, and many stories of women who have found satisfaction in engineering and science without becoming famous. These women also tell of other fulfilling life activities such as raising children, following a partner's career, and dedicating oneself to activism or public service. The diversity includes women who always knew they wanted to be scientists or engineers; women who had an interest in these fields, were discouraged from pursuing them, and later found their way back; and women who had lengthy careers in other fields altogether before choosing to start on the path to a technical career.

Our original inclination was to collect as many stories as possible and to showcase two hundred or more women in brief profiles organized by each woman's field of specialization. Although we planned to include "women of distinction" from throughout the twentieth century, we wanted our book to be more than a simple biographical dictionary: We wanted personal accounts of the experiences that had shaped these women's lives and careers. But as we began to conduct interviews, we were struck by the breadth and fullness of each woman's life. The richness of their individual stories convinced us that we needed to reduce dramatically the number of stories we planned to include so that we could treat each one in more depth. Although each woman's story could fill a book, we retained our commitment to presenting a large and diverse group of women; thus we compromised on shorter, but fuller, descriptions. We wanted to feature women who represented a range of backgrounds, experiences, and career trajectories, who were at different stages in their careers, who represented different races and ethnic backgrounds, who were both disabled and able bodied, and who identified themselves as straight, lesbian, or bisexual. We wanted to move beyond mere token representation to show how women from similar backgrounds, women working in the same fields, and women with anything else in common could still have very different, although equally valuable, experiences.

We are honored that so many different women have joined us in our work, but we do not expect or even advise that a young woman reading this book will find one person with whom to identify; rather, she will be able to assemble a composite picture of herself and—more importantly—of the scientist or engineer she wants to become.

Choosing whom to include was not easy. We began with the idea of balancing the fields and subfields in which our women were practicing while assuring that there was sufficient diversity in their backgrounds and lifestyles. To begin collecting this group, we solicited nominations from dozens of well-known professionals, as well as from students and younger women, to see whom they might have found particularly inspiring themselves. We also canvased special-interest and minority-affiliated Internet resources and organizations.

We received more than a thousand enthusiastic nominations, far more than we could possibly use. We owe a great debt of gratitude to everyone who took the time to send a nomination. For every woman included, there are hundreds who are not and who easily could have been.

In such a lengthy project, it was not possible to collect all the nominations before making some selections. Collecting nominations, making selections, and conducting interviews was an ongoing process for over three years; and as we listened to the women's stories, we realized that our initial two-dimensional conception of balance was not adequate to the task. Creating balance came instead to resemble assembling a patchwork quilt and needing to keep various colors in balance—or in this case, areas of specialty and employment sectors; socioeconomic background, race, and ethnicity; education; work experience; and families of origin and families of choice. We began actively seeking people whose lives were known to have critical dimensions (for example, welfare experience or in maintaining a long-distance relationship). This made our task much more complicated but the resulting product (we hope!) also much richer. It was a continuing juggling act.

The eighty-eight profiles in our book show how science and engineering have been and can be an integral part of many different women's lives. The core of each profile is a first-person narrative describing what originally attracted the woman to her field, her career decisions and experiences, successes and difficulties, and the roles of significant people or events in her life. Many profiles explore the day-to-day details of the woman's professional life: what excites her about her work, what her work environment is like, what is important about her work and her field from her own perspective, and why she remains committed to them. Of course, the precise balance of information presented varies from profile to profile, depending on what the woman emphasized in her interview and what seemed most appropriate to her story. Profiles range from 1,500 to 3,500 words in length, and they end with a listing of relevant biographical data including date of birth, colleges attended, and position currently held. These biographical synopses also include a sentence or two about the woman's household and/or family.

We originally intended to organize these profiles by field or specialty, but we changed our minds for two reasons. First, we began to see that no matter how broad our categories (biological science, physical science, and so forth), there were some women whose work simply would not fit into such arbitrary pigeonholes because women often tend to work in broader or interdisciplinary aspects of their fields. Our second impetus for change came from focus groups we conducted with high school students and middle school teachers, and from feedback we obtained from undergraduates, graduate students, and science and engineering faculty who read our drafts. Very few of our respondents felt that the book would be best organized by field, and many suggested that the juxtaposition of women from different fields would highlight both the common struggles and the unique experiences of women from different backgrounds or doing different work. We organized the profiles alphabetically, effectively creating an arbitrary mix.

The challenge in preparing each profile was to capture the woman's story as well as her voice. While a handful of women chose to draft their own stories (and their results are quite wonderful), we wrote the vast majority of the profiles ourselves based on lengthy interviews (conducted either face to face or, more frequently, over the phone) supplemented with e-mail correspondence. We generally structured the interviews to address three broad questions: "What do you do?" "How did you get there?" and "What challenges or obstacles did you face along the way?"

After interviewing each woman, we tried to piece together her life story in her own voice. Because we chose to write in the first person and wanted each woman to feel that her story and her voice were accurately reflected, we sent the first draft of each profile to the woman for feedback. Then, if it seemed advisable, we made one or more rounds of revisions, until the woman felt comfortable with her story as presented.

Because these stories represent a point in time, many things may have changed since they were written. We have written in what anthropologists call the "ethnographic present": the known "truth" at the time the data were collected.

One advantage of presenting the profiles as uninterrupted first-person narratives is that it allows the women to speak directly to the reader in an informal and often quite personal way. A disadvantage is that a book such as this constitutes public discourse, and some of our women needed to consider the personal and political ramifications of their statements. While we admire the honesty and candor of everyone featured, we must acknowledge that there are a few gaps in the narratives, especially around sensitive issues such as discrimination and abuse, which could only be filled by allowing anonymous presentation. Because anonymity would sacrifice the personal immediacy that is our purpose, we leave these matters to other authors and other books.

Assistance and Resistance

Parents, teachers, and mentors were crucial in encouraging the women we interviewed to explore engineering and the sciences. Many women spoke of parents who provided them with science kits, took them to museums, or fostered science-related discussion around the kitchen table. Others talked of parents who treated them almost like sons, teaching them how to use tools and fix things. Women who grew up on farms and ranches recall being outdoors and working with animals, crops, or equipment as being particularly good at fostering self-reliance and an ease with nature and the physical world. Others told how their parents simply encouraged them to follow their dreams and to believe that they could do anything they wanted to do. While some women had stories of parents who didn't encourage their educations, others spoke of the sacrifices their parents made to put them through college.

Many women told us how just one teacher or counselor who took time to urge them to study science or engineering had made the crucial difference in their choice of a college major. For others, finding a role model was as simple as reading a book about Marie Curie; having someone to emulate helped these young women envision themselves in careers in technical fields.

We also spoke with women who at some point had attended all-female high schools or colleges, and with others who had attended or worked at historically black colleges. Many recalled these environments as particularly supportive. Without the presence of men or white people, they were able to develop their talents and leadership skills without having to contend with sexism or racism.

Almost all the women have faced the loneliness, frustration, and self-doubt that often result from discrimination and the relative isolation of women in science and engineering. They have found support in a number of places. Some have done so by creating or joining professional networks. For example, a woman in a relatively obscure subspecialty created an electronic mailing list and newsletter to keep geographically dispersed colleagues in touch with each other. Another assembled a mailing list of scientists from a particular minority group in order to discuss common concerns. Many women have joined groups that are specifically for women in science and engineering, and many have served as mentors to young women.

Almost every woman had something to say

about integrating her career with her personal life. The women we interviewed frequently credited their spouses or partners with providing essential practical and emotional support for their careers—being willing to relocate, helping with the children, or being the at-home spouse. Mothers often spoke of the flexibility and encouragement of their children; others spoke of help from their own mothers and the importance of having supportive friends to talk to during a crisis. Many women discussed the importance of having hobbies or other interests ranging from dance or musical performance to social activism. We found a pervasive theme among the women of wanting to be useful to society or to the world.

Finally, some women developed specific strategies for dealing with difficult interactions. While none left science or engineering altogether, some did switch specialties. Others did not recognize what was going on at the time or actively chose to ignore it. Some women said they had learned to pick their fights carefully and not waste energy on battles they were unlikely to win. Others learned to use humor constructively to point out to colleagues when they were behaving unfairly or inconsiderately.

And then there are the women who have decided to handle these uneasy situations proactively, straightforwardly announcing, "Yes, I'm a woman; so what? Let's get to work."

Acknowledgments

Our book would not have been possible without the generous support of the Alfred P. Sloan Foundation and the Human Resources Development Division of the National Science Foundation (NSF).*

We are grateful to them not only for making the book possible but for their commitment to women in science and engineering. Ted Greenwood, Sloan Program Officer, and Lola Rogers, Program Director, Program for Women and Girls at NSF, deserve our special thanks.

We are enormously grateful to our colleagues at Carnegie Mellon University. Our Provost, Paul Christiano, believed in what we were trying to accomplish and supported our project each step of the way. We could not have done this work without his help or that of Susan Burkett, Associate Provost for Research and Administration. Our wonderful staffs, especially Michelle Pierson, Gwendolyne Wood, Victoria Massimino, Kathleen Minadeo Johnson, Rea Freeland, Jessie Ramey, and Peggy Heidish, and our incredible student staff were always there to help and to cheer us on. Jennifer Goetz wrote her mother's (Ann Grant) profile, did some research, and helped prepare the manuscript for

*The material is based upon work supported by the National Science Foundation under grant number HRD-99555832. Any opinions, findings, conclusions, or recommendations expressed in this publication are those of the author(s) and do not necessarily reflect the views of the National Science Foundation.

The ideas and opinions in this book are exclusively those of the authors and not necessarily those of the women featured, our sponsors, or Carnegie Mellon University.

publication. Shannon Gibney assisted with production; Juliette Park and Tara McDonald provided major clerical assistance. Barbara Pearson joined us in the middle of the project; her talent and hard work produced ten draft profiles in record time.

Lisa Ritter, who entered the project in its last year, was an invaluable part of the completion of this book. She took over unfinished work and wrote several wonderful profiles. Lisa edited the manuscript, wrote captions for the photos, and oversaw preparation of the manuscript. Her dedication and talent made an enormous difference. We owe her a great debt.

Our work on the book was continually informed and transformed by the eighty-eight women we profiled, by their stories as well as by their comments on our project and process. They served as the best possible colleagues and inspired us to write the book they deserved. We thank them for their time, their spirit of cooperation, and especially for their patience. We offer special thanks also to Bonnie Shulman and Priscilla Auchincloss, who are profiled in the book, and to Londa Schiebinger, Jane Margolis, Jessie Ramey, and Nancy Tobin, all six of whom provided invaluable comments on our editorial sections.

Many hundreds of nominators suggested these amazing women. Focus groups and others who reviewed the profiles—remarkable middle- and high-school students and teachers, and our own undergraduate and graduate students—were terrific readers. Special thanks go to high-school students and middle- and high-school teachers Bijal Amin, Marilyn Burstein, Tom Chacko, Cliff Chen, Marie Courtemanche, Jill Friedman, Victoria Gong, Rajeshwari Gopal, Ed Karsin, Toby Marriage,

Sally Martin, Leslie Mullins, Faruq Sabar, Nathan Steinwald, Elizabeth Stuart, and Anastasia Titarchuk. We loved that they loved the text, and we took their requests to reorganize and rethink the format seriously. The book is much stronger because we took their advice. Thanks also to Ruth Siegel, Laura Gault, Donna Riley, Jennifer Dunkle, David Lazarus, Jacqueline Rubin, Sarita Nair, and Nandita Nair for their thoughtful comments. Thanks especially to Sasha Wood for valuable conversation that helped us re-think a few key ideas and to Suzanne Brainard, whose guidance helped us to keep the work on track.

Many people must work together to make a book grow from an idea to a reality. Paula Rayman, our friend and a series editor for Temple University Press, and Michael Ames, our editor, have been of untold help. Paula Rayman sent us to Temple, believing in what we could do before we had begun. Michael Ames helped us transform our first visions of our profiles to fuller and livelier text. We are honored that Lilli Hornig, whose long commitment to gender equity in science and engineering and who is an inspiration for so many working in the field today, has written the Foreword. Charles Ault, Temple's production director, was always ready to answer our questions. Our copyeditor, Elizabeth Johns, and our production editor, Jennifer French, have added immeasurably to the quality of the manuscript. They were wonderful to work with.

Last but far from least we want to thank our friends and our families for their understanding and support, for standing by us for the past five-plus years. Five of our children have grown up with this book. We hope it will be a small part of transforming their futures.

*Journeys of Women
in Science
and Engineering*

Women, Science, Engineering, and Technology through the Ages

Queen Dido, who, according to Roman legend, founded the city of Carthage in the ninth century B.C., is the first person known to have solved an optimization problem. Originally from Phoenicia, she fled when her brother, King Pygmalion of Tyre, murdered her husband. She took her husband's money and sailed away, pretending to throw the money overboard to distract her pursuers. When she landed in North Africa, she offered to buy for a fixed sum as much land as could be enclosed by a bull's hide. She then cut the hide into thin strips, tied them end to end, and made a semi-circle bounded by the sea—thus solving the mathematical problem of enclosing maximum area in a fixed perimeter. Mathematical proof of this problem did not come until the nineteenth century, but in the meantime Dido had land for her new city.

—MARGARET ALIC, *HYPATIA'S HERITAGE*

❧

In our experience, far too few students of science and engineering are exposed to a sense of the past out of which current theories, ideas, and practice evolved. They get even less of a sense of the individual people who were the active agents in the past, especially when those people were either women or the members of a societal minority (for example, people of color or of the working class, disabled persons, or lesbians, bisexuals, and gays). Students who take a class in the history or philosophy of science may develop a sense of the human agency underlying technical knowledge, but few will encounter information about women's roles in the evolution of science and technology unless they venture into a women's studies course. Most of us find ourselves with knowledge of only a few famous women, who may be somewhat daunting as archetypes: Marie Curie, the super-genius and self-sacrificing heroine; Rosalind Franklin, whose X-ray crystallography data were used by James Watson and Francis Crick for one of the greatest discoveries of the century—the double-helical structure of DNA—without attribution to Franklin; or Barbara McClintock, whose unconventional findings regarding "jumping genes" (transposons) received little notice for years but finally won her the Nobel Prize (Curie 1938; Sayre 1975; Fox Keller 1983).

There is a common misconception that issues of women's presence or absence in science and engineering are new to this century, or even to recent decades. This is far from true. An overview of relevant history illustrates an historical tension between the presence in and exclusion of women from science, engineering, and technology and provides a helpful context for understanding the forces that influence the contemporary relationships of women working in these fields. For us, examining the history of women in science is useful not only for placing the present in context but also for illustrating how women have always been involved in science and technology. Knowing some of the contributions some Western women have made to science and engineering throughout the ages can provide a sense of historical place, and a knowledge that women are not encroaching into new territory but that they have always been there and always will be. But if examining history can provide a pride of place, it can also prove a source of frustration and anger: if women have always been active in these areas, why are access and acceptance still considered problematical for women in the fields of science and engineering? Feminist scholars have identified the repeated patterns of women's advances, setbacks, achievements, and marginalization; and while it can be infuriating to examine the stubborn persistence of discrimination against women through the ages, it can also help contemporary women begin to identify ways to transcend barriers. Awareness of what has and has not worked in the past can help women channel their frustration into constructive interventions.

Our discussion of history is limited to several salient strands that led to the development of Western science and engineering as it is practiced in the United States today. This is the core tradition that the women in our book have inherited and in which they do their work. Our review is drawn from generally accessible secondary sources and focuses on the history of white women in Europe and, more recently, the United States; we found little written about the many inventions and improvisations of slave, Native American, and other women of color in the United States. Our discussion concentrates on early history more than the very recent past, partly because the vast quantity of material available on recent history defies attempts at brief summary (and can be easily located by the interested reader in any event) and partly because we wish to make readers aware of the waxing and waning of women's participation in the formalized institutions of science and technology over centuries. As is the case with women in many fields, little is known about the true numbers of women who made contributions to science and technology over the ages.

A few caveats: we tell this story using a traditional model of history as a series of events and facts organized around "famous women," many of whom emerged from history recently uncovered by feminist scholars. In some cases, we include mythical and legendary women, or stories of women whose historical existence has been questioned, because we believe their stories have important symbolic meanings, and myths are often a reflection of reality. And be-

cause we are trying to balance what is known, not create a complete record of the doing of science and technology, our text focuses on the contributions of these known women, not women and men. We wish we could have told the historical story with the diversity represented in the contemporary stories in our book; but too many of those stories are lost. We have selected a few strands of history and commented along the way to suggest patterns that led to today's conditions and perceptions.

Defining Terms

Language—the use of words and their connotations—delineates societal prescriptions and boundaries in subtle ways, and it often contains unexamined assumptions. Exploring the history of words like *science, technology,* and *engineering* and looking at changes in their formal definitions provides useful information about who and what is or is not meant to be included. Examining old meanings of words can reveal otherwise hidden connotations.

In contemporary language, the distinctions between the terms *science, technology,* and *engineering* are often not clear. In everyday discourse, there is considerable overlap in both meaning and practice; indeed, these terms are sometimes used almost interchangeably. Where does science end and engineering begin? Is engineering merely "applied science," or is it something else? Is technology the product of one or both of the other two, or is it an entity unto itself? In the past, these distinctions were both different and, sometimes, clearer. The word *science* derives from the Latin *scientia,* knowledge, the present participle of *scire,* to know. It is thus different from *technology's* Greek predecessor, *teckne,* meaning skill, art, or craft, in that the latter is concerned with "methods for effecting certain results," according to the *Oxford English Dictionary* (OED). *Science* can be understood as a concern for universal truth—and a preoccupation with knowledge for its own sake—whereas *technology* is concerned with practical methods for creating or doing useful things. Thus it is not surprising that we find early science virtually indistinguishable from philosophy and sometimes religion, while early technology is firmly rooted in craft and guild traditions. Indeed, science was often known as "natural philosophy." Most women, and most men, were too busy eking out a living and working for the maintenance of family and economy to pursue knowledge systematically for its own sake.

The first science by today's definitions was what Aristotle named *physis* (which means "the nature of things"), study that did evolve into modern physics. Numerous other practices—including magic, witchcraft, alchemy, midwifery, and agriculture—had ties to science and technology in early history. Some of these are now entirely divorced from scientific enterprise while others remain intertwined.

Engineering (from the Latin *ingeniator,* contriver) is a more recent term than *science* or *technology;* it originated in the fifteenth century (OED) to describe the military endeavor of designing mechanical devices for warfare (Naples 1996). It was concerned with the application of universal scientific principles like vector analysis for practical purposes such as launching projectiles. About three centuries later, engineering would move into the civilian sphere (hence, "civil engineering") and begin to be tranformed into its present form.

Prehistory: Techne as Part of Daily Living

Many women in prehistoric times probably possessed what might now be considered technical knowledge. Women who gathered food for their families and tribes surely must have used some knowledge of time and astronomical events. Through observation and trial and error, they must have learned the nutritional value, medicinal properties, season, and methods of preparing and using various plant products. Eventually, they would have tried ways of deliberately cultivating the most

useful of these as agricultural products and of preserving them for later use. These early women could also have invented the tools they needed to perform these feats: sticks, levers, axes, flints, mortars and pestles, and others (Alic 1986).

Early women almost certainly devised ways of creating useful items such as clothing and storage containers from plant and animal products. They may have invented awls and needles and devised methods of sewing, weaving, and dyeing. They might have found ways of creating pottery and glazing and firing it. They probably domesticated animals, and there is considerable evidence to suggest that they served as healers (Alic 1986).

Myth and Legend: Women as Knowledge Bearers

If one accepts the premise that mythology mirrors the culture from which it originates— rather than the other way around—the centrality of women as keepers of knowledge in almost all of the ancient religions suggests that women may have held key roles in everyday life. It is interesting to note that goddesses from Mesopotamia, Sumeria, India, Egypt, Greece, and Rome were often identified as the sources of wisdom, learning, or technical innovation in the ancient world. While precise details of those myths are sometimes disputed, the credit given to goddesses as knowledge bearers is impressive.

Isis was the mother goddess of early Egypt who gave the people "religion, laws, writing and medicine" (Alic 1986, 15). She invented embalming and alchemy and taught agriculture; she was the patron of navigation and commerce and inventor of the sailing boat. She taught her people how to spin and weave and was sometimes credited with being the patron of astronomy. In Greece, Athena (Minerva to the Romans) was the goddess of agriculture who invented the plow and bridle and introduced the practice of yoking oxen and taming horses. Like Isis, she created spinning and weaving. She created olive trees and pressed the first olive oil. She was also the goddess of the crafts; she invented the cart, iron weapons, and armor. She also created numbers and made the first flute (Alic 1986).

There is a long-standing connection between women and the preservation of health. Accordingly, ancient goddesses usually held sway over health, birth, and death. The Greek goddess Ilthyia was goddess of childbirth; Hygeia and Panacea were goddesses of health, and their names persist into contemporary English. The temples of Hygeia and Panacea served as early hospitals and employed women as doctors (Alic 1986).

Some people have even suggested that some of these goddesses were not only reflections of women's roles in society but mortal women whose reputations attained divine proportions. For example, Ceres was the Roman goddess of grain and fertility, childbirth, and death. But Boccaccio would later claim that she had been a mortal queen of Sicily who invented agriculture, the plow and plowshare, domesticated oxen, and discovered a process to make leavened bread (Alic 1986).

Antiquity: Recorded History of Women Practitioners

According to Caroline Herzenberg (1990), we have historical evidence of specific individual women engaging in activity related to science or technology dating back about six thousand years. An early woman whose name has come down to us (many claim she is the earliest) is Merit Ptah (Herzenberg 1990; Herzenberg, Meschel, and Altena 1991; Alic 1986), a physician who worked in Egypt circa 2700 B.C. and whose picture is in a tomb in the Valley of the Kings. Medicine seems to have been a well-established field in Egypt, with many women working as doctors and surgeons (Herzenberg, Meschel, and Altena 1991). An inscription on the Temple of Sais reads: "I have come from the school of medicine at Heliopolis, and have studied at the women's school at Sais, where

the divine mothers have taught me how to cure disease" (Alic 1986, 20–21).

Another early woman known by name is Tapputi-Belatekallim, a perfume maker who worked in Babylon circa 1200 B.C. Today, she might be considered a chemical engineer, as she devised several new methods for preparing perfumes; the second half of her name indicates that she was regarded as chief chemist/engineer. Cuneiform records refer to another woman practicing in the perfume industry who wrote a text on perfume production, but her name is not known. This subject is reported to be the first known record of two women practicing in the same technological field at about the same time and the only such instance so far recorded in antiquity (Herzenberg 1990).

Around 600 B.C.E., Greek science began to flourish, and history recorded a much larger number of individual women in science and technology. Herzenberg points out that prior to this time, women appear in the recorded history at an average rate of one every two and a half centuries. After 600 B.C.E., women are found at a rate of twenty per century (Herzenberg 1990). The increase probably reflects the rise of the Pythagorean and Platonic schools of science and philosophy (remembering that, in this era, there was no real distinction between science and philosophy). Both schools encouraged the participation of women and treated them equally. Indeed, some scholars maintain that Pythagoras's young wife Theano ran the school after his death (Herzenberg 1990; Alic 1986).

A number of ancient women became quite distinguished, among them botanist Artemisia of Caria, physicist and philosopher Arete of Crete, and marine zoologist Pythias of Assos (as we would call them today) (Alic 1986). In Athens, where it was a capital crime for women to practice medicine, a woman named Agnodike (300 B.C.) dressed as a man and established a successful practice among aristocratic women. According to legend, when she revealed herself and was condemned to death, the women she had healed raised sufficient protest that her sentence was overturned and the law was changed to allow women to be physicians who treated only women (Giese 1992; Alic 1986; Herzenberg, Meschel, and Altena 1991).

The Greek period is especially important because of the great influence "the classics" would have throughout later centuries; citing the ancients would for years constitute proof in an argument. It is significant to note that where Plato tried to develop an inclusive system, Aristotle (384–322 B.C.), who is seen as the father of modern science, said that women possessed no logic or intelligence. Exclusion of women was an integral part of "scientific" thinking early on.

As the influence of the Hellenic Greek schools waned, the number of known women in science declined, apparently reaching the lowest levels in the West around 200 B.C. The center of intellectual activity in the Mediterranean shifted from Athens to Alexandria, where many women scientists and technologists lived and practiced. Miriam the Jewess (she is also known as Mary and Maria, although others claim she did not actually exist) was one of the most distinguished of a number of women alchemists from this era (Herzenberg 1990). Miriam appeared to have been most famous for inventing laboratory equipment, including a three-armed still and the waterbath, the latter of which is still found in modern laboratories. It is known in French as a *bain-marie* and in Spanish as a *baño de María* (Herzenberg 1990; Herzenberg, Meschel, and Altena 1991).

Hypatia (A.D. 370–415) is one of the best remembered of the pagan women scientists today. Educated by her father, Theon, an astronomer and mathematician, she was accomplished in mathematics, physics, astronomy, chemistry, and medicine and held a chair in philosophy at the University of Alexandria (Herzenberg, Meschel, and Altena 1991). She invented the astrolabe (for measuring the positions of celestial bodies), an apparatus for distilling water, and a hydrometer (for measuring the density of liquids). She appears also to have invented a form of planisphere (Tee 1983). Hypatia's death is almost as famous as her life. A prominent and powerful figure in Alexandrine society, she rejected Christianity and seems to have been particularly at odds with the Bishop Cyril. As she traveled from home one day, a mob of angry Christians seized her from her chariot, dragged her to a nearby empty warehouse, stripped her, tortured her to death, and finally burned her mutilated body. Hypatia's death, along with the burning of the Alexandrian Library, is generally considered to mark the end of pre-Christian civilization (Herzenberg, Meschel, and Altena 1991).

The Dark Ages and the Medieval Period

During the Dark Ages, documented participation by European women in science all but disappears. While women practitioners continued the practice of medicine and alchemy, much of what we call intellectual life in the West stagnated or came to a stop during this period. However, knowledge of science persisted in Arabic culture and elsewhere. Royal women in the Byzantine empire studied science and medicine with scholars in their courts, and there were women engineers in China (Giese 1992). Then, at the end of the eighth century, Charlemagne's brief Carolingian renaissance prompted the founding of many abbey schools, creating educational opportunities for women (Herzenberg 1990; Giese 1992).

Around 1000 A.D., European science began to grow and expand. This resurgence started in southern Italy, which had had the most peaceful dealings with Muslim and Byzantine culture, and slowly spread north (Herzenberg, Meschel, and Altena 1991). Much of the intellectual ferment of the time took place in the ever-expanding system of abbeys, and a number of German nuns achieved great prominence as scientists. Hildegard of Bingen (1098–1179?), a Benedictine abbess known as "the Sibyl of the Rhine," was probably the most famous and influential of these. A prophet acknowledged by the pope, she had visions and fits throughout her life. (Some have speculated that these might have been produced by migraines or epilepsy.) She also wrote music (the oldest music for masses composed by a woman) and numerous treatises on science including cosmology, medicine, botany, zoology, and geology. Her manuscripts, *Causae et curae* and *Physica,* are considered among the greatest scientific works of the Middle Ages, and she is the earliest woman scientist whose works have come down to us intact (Herzenberg 1990; Giese 1992; Alic 1986).

Another well-known scientist was Herrade of Landsberg, whose work *Hortus delicarium* records most of what is known of medieval technology. Héloïse of the famous Héloïse and Abelard romance was also an excellent mathematician and was reputed to be the most learned woman physician of France in her century (Herzenberg 1990).

This eleventh- and twelfth-century revival of learning was accompanied by the founding of the first universities. Although most church-affiliated universities would quickly become all-male bastions and remain so until the late 1800s (or even later), women were involved in founding and teaching at the earliest secular medical schools in Italy. The first such school was at Salerno, and one of its more famous faculty members was Trotula (also Trocte, Trottola, or Tortola). Her book, *Passionibus mulierum curandorum* (Diseases of Women), was a standard text for centuries (Herzenberg, Meschel, and Altena 1991). As Alic writes (1986, 51), "At times, Trotula's advice seems uncannily modern, emphasizing the importance of cleanliness, a balanced diet and exercise, and warning about the effects of anxiety and stress." Her husband and two of her sons also taught at Salerno.

The Renaissance: Waxing and Waning Participation

By 1200 more women were practicing science in Europe than at any previous time, due almost entirely to the rise of the convent system. Caroline Herzenberg calls the 1200s the Golden Age of Scholasticism. It overlapped and was followed by the Renaissance, which spread though Europe from the 1300s to the mid-1600s. Ironically, this great revival of art, science, and literature in Europe did not lead to an increase in known women scientists. While women of the noble or ruling classes could often exchange their social prestige for access to knowledge, or establish themselves as influential patrons of male scientists, the absolute numbers of women studying science, which rose rapidly from medieval times, abruptly leveled off and then dropped during the 1400s. This was all the more significant because the total numbers of people involved in science were simultaneously increasing. The number of documented women scientists did not begin to rise again until the 1600s (Herzenberg 1990).

There are many possible causes for this change. Bubonic plague killed between one-fourth and one-third of Europe's population during the 1300s. As we discussed earlier, science as the pursuit of pure knowledge required its participants to have the time for contemplation—something less likely to occur for women—especially during times of great crisis. The paranoia engendered by the "black death" in an era of relatively poor medical knowledge may have made many people hostile to anyone who broke with traditional (and religiously prescribed) gender roles. The closing of convents in Protestant countries following the Protestant Reformation in the 1500s greatly reduced opportunities for women to study science. As abbeys were closed in some countries, their property and resources were sometimes handed over to Catholic Church–affiliated universities that excluded women. In other cases, control was given to an abbot who was less likely to be supportive of women's education in science.

The greatest deterrent to women's involvement in scientific pursuits, however, was the witch hunts that swept across Europe between about 1300 and 1700. Accusations of witchcraft constituted the single largest peril faced by women physicians and alchemists. There are widely varying estimates of the number of women killed and tortured during these persecutions, some ranging into the millions (Herzenberg 1990; Giese 1992). The genocide was horrific: in each of two villages in Trier, France, all but one woman was killed, and four hundred women were murdered in one day in Toulouse (D. Noble 1992).

The Scientific Revolution: Science Formally Defined

The scientific revolution that began in the 1600s defined the systems of science and technology that exist to this day. The methodologies and precepts of modern science were being hammered out and set in place during the span of 1300 to 1700. Modern science was being defined as objective, rational, analytical, and detached. The role of women in this new endeavor was also being determined, albeit subtly. As Londa Schiebinger has argued, in the 1600s and 1700s, women's participation in science was very much an open question. The visions and writings of Descartes (1596–1650) in France and Francis Bacon (1561–1626) in England came to define the canon of science. Descartes declared that objective scientific theory requires a separation of logic (thinking) from emotion (feeling), a statement that has come to be known as the mind-body problem. Bacon defined the parameters of modern empirical science. According to him, reproducibility of observations is the condition for good science. In addition, he declared that the purpose of science was for man to conquer and control nature for his benefit. These two aspects, which then became part of the scientific culture—the positioning of man as separate from and above nature, and science as a way to control nature—have been blamed by some authors for alienating women from science (Fox Keller 1983; Merchant 1980).

It is instructive to think about the relationship between the formalizing of a system of knowledge like science and the exclusion of certain groups from that system. Historically, women's connections to knowledge have been its accumulation through practice in response to the needs of their daily lives. Formalization of this type of "tacit" knowledge involves establishment of rules, procedures, and standards, which in turn defined the system. The formalized knowledge then defines a profession with the prestige that accompanies professionalism. Often women have been left out of the new profession. Below are two examples that illustrate this phenomenon.

The Case of Midwifery

Until the 1600s, midwifery was developed and practiced almost exclusively by women. This craft was based on millennia of practical experience and innovation by those who actually gave birth. Women gained knowledge of midwifery through practice and tutelage. Then, beginning late in the 1600s and continuing into the 1700s, medical practitioners sought to upgrade their fields and break with tradespeople (surgeons from barbers, veterinarians from blacksmiths). It was at this time that obstetrics and gynecology were born as "scientific" male fields. As doctors and surgeons organized colleges and societies, they gained control of the right to license practitioners in these new fields. Unlike their female counterparts, "man midwives" had access to formal training in anatomy and the ability (both practical and legal) to use surgical instruments. While men could easily appropriate the millennia of women's accumulated experience, female midwives had no way to learn about new procedures and techniques developed by men. Some of these, such as the use of forceps, were actually helpful in particularly difficult births. Traditional female midwives, who began to be seen as less skilled, were slowly but steadily displaced. Although efforts were made both on the Continent and in England to gain for midwives the right to study formally and to license themselves, these drives were never successful. The man-midwives not only cost women jobs; because they were less willing to treat patients who were unable to pay, they also harmed poorer women's access to care. Most importantly, the men were unable or unwilling to dispense information about the many methods of fertility control known to midwives of the time, and their ascent was a severe blow to women's ability to regulate their own reproductive health (Schiebinger 1989).

The Guild Tradition

In the towns and feudal states of the thirteenth and fourteenth centuries, craft and merchant guilds established rules for training apprentices to carry on business. Guilds dealt with techniques for producing goods as well as tools and implements (Kirkup 1992). Craft and artisinal workshops, as family businesses, had traditionally welcomed women. Depending on the nature of the business, daughters would often serve as apprentices, and wives would assist their husbands as unpaid artisans. Indeed, in many places wives were considered so essential to the functioning of a workshop that each guild master was required by law to have one. In the event of a master's death, a wife could ensure the continuation of the business until the senior journeyman had advanced sufficiently to take over; or she might even retain control of it herself.

An excellent example of how "upgrading" and the dissolution of the craft tradition reduced women's access to technical careers is the case of Maria Winkelmann (1670–1720) and the Berlin Academy of Science. Astronomy, especially in Germany, was firmly rooted in the craft and guild traditions. Winkelmann was married to Gottfried Kirch, who was for many years the official astronomer of the Berlin Academy. He prepared catalogues of stars and, most importantly, the academy calendar. Winkelmann worked with him and, upon his death, requested to be allowed to stay on and carry out his duties, as she certainly appeared capable of doing. The position allowed for housing on academy grounds as well as a salary, and as a widow Winkelmann needed to support herself and her children. In applying to take over her husband's duties, Maria Winkelmann was asking for no more than was traditionally allowed to widows. But in order to avoid setting an uncomfortable precedent regarding the employment of women at the Berlin Academy, she was refused (Schiebinger 1989).

Science and Some Exceptional Women: Beginnings of Exclusion

Women working in craft-based traditions appear to have been integral contributors to their fields until male practitioners decided to upgrade and transform their fields into sciences. In institutions where "science" as knowledge for its own sake held sway from the beginning, women's participation was the exception rather than the rule, but women found many ways to slip inside. The Catholic Church was a central purveyor of literacy and knowledge for much of the Middle Ages, and, until their demise during the Protestant Reformation, some convents provided women a route to learning and power. Universities, by contrast, were created largely to teach theology, medicine, and law; these professions were closed to women, so there was no reason to admit females to formal training. Universities, in theory, were meant to transmit universal knowledge, although one might question whose universe was being considered. For the most part, women were completely excluded from European (and American) schools until the late 1800s. There were exceptions, particularly in Italy (as with Trotula, mentioned above) and in science and medicine, which were considered more appropriate topics for women than the classical studies that formed the basis of theology and law.

Maria Agnesi of Milan was among the exceptions (Schiebinger 1989). She wrote a textbook on differential and integral calculus that was published in 1748. She also studied

a cubic curve formulated by Euler that is still known as "the witch of Agnesi." Laura Bassi was a professor of physics at the University of Bologna. She received her doctorate in 1733 and did extensive work in mechanics. She became a member of the Bologna Academy of Science and was named on the university roster for forty-six years. Some people claimed she had twelve children. In allowing women to teach at its universities, Italy was the exception in Europe, but the few women who did make it onto the faculty were always carefully constructed exceptions. Bassi's chair, for example, was a specially created one set to terminate upon her retirement so she could not be replaced by another woman (Schiebinger 1989).

Universities, however, were not nearly as central to society as they are today. Throughout the 1600s and 1700s, there was no clear demarcation between popular or amateur science and the professional practice of science. Renaissance courts often supported inventors and scientists in addition to artists and explorers. While almost always consigned to play the intellectual inferior, women could wield considerable influence as patrons of science, if not always as its practitioners. Later, as the influence of the nobility waned and as the leisure classes passed from existence, women would have greater difficulty pulling rank to gain access to the knowledge they desired (Schiebinger 1989; Phillips 1990).

Another important Renaissance locus for science was the scientific society or academy. Scientific societies differed from universities in that it was less clear in the beginning that women would be excluded from them. Academies arose from both the universities and from royal patronage. To the extent that the influence of the universities prevailed, women's exclusion was a foregone conclusion; but in cases where the academics relied on royal (sometimes female) patronage, the case was far less clear. The very first academies in Italy (at Bologna, Padua, and Rome) did admit some women, but later academies in northern and western Europe, including the Académie Royale des Sciences in Paris (later the Académie des Sciences) and the Royal Society of London refused them admittance. Although few academies began with clear policies that forbade the admission of women, they rejected women whose names were submitted on a case-by-case basis; occasionally, these cases would lead to the formulation of a policy against female membership.

The Scientific Lady: Science as High Fashion and Parlor Game

An interesting case of a woman who was able to use her social rank to carve a niche for herself in scientific discourse was Margaret Cavendish, duchess of Newcastle (1623–73), known also as "Mad Madge." (Historians differ as to whether she merited this sobriquet.) She was beautiful, rich, flamboyant, and a well-known figure in London society. Her interest in science emerged after her marriage to the Duke of Newcastle. They found themselves on the wrong side in England's civil war and, during exile in Holland, were surrounded by a social circle that included many prominent scientific figures. Margaret Cavendish's emerging interest was thus fed by the ablest minds of the era. Science and the paraphernalia used to conduct it were enormously trendy and popular, and the most elegant homes sported at least a microscope and often a telescope or other devices. The Cavendishes were no exception (Phillips 1982).

Margaret Cavendish was exceptional, however, in her ability to popularize an interest in science among women. She was England's first prolific female author, penning over a dozen volumes that included plays, poetry, biography, romances, and several works on science (Phillips 1982). These latter were somewhat controversial. Margaret Cavendish was a staunch Cartesian in an era when Baconian empiricism was beginning to dominate. Fully aware of the flaws of early instruments, she felt that their imperfections rendered any experimental results suspect. She correctly argued that empiricism could lead to questionable

conclusions based on inaccurate or poorly understood observations. Neither her ideas nor her flamboyant and sometimes arrogant manner sat particularly well with prominent scientific minds of the day (Phillips 1982).

It was, however, less her ideas than her sex which engendered (literally) a great deal of hostility. Although much mocked and maligned, Margaret Cavendish considered herself an able intellectual and declared that she expected an invitation to visit the Royal Society of London, a declaration which put the all-male membership of that society in considerable distress. In the end, rank and influence prevailed, the invitation was secured, and the Duchess of Newcastle attended a meeting of the Royal Society in 1667; no other woman was admitted until 1945. The only female presence during the intervening time was a skeleton in the anatomy collection (Schiebinger 1989).

Margaret Cavendish has sometimes been designated as the first or even prototypical member of new breed known in these centuries as the "scientific lady." In her book on the rise of the scientific lady in England, Patricia Phillips notes that four intertwined trends produced this phenomenon: the primacy of classical study for "serious" (that is, male) scholars; the study of the natural world as a way to promote religious piety; the original nature of science as more parlor entertainment than intellectual pursuit; and, finally, the massive movement to popularize science (Phillips 1990).

Until the nineteenth century the primacy of classical education for serious scholars, nearly all of whom were men, was unrivaled and unquestioned. In the 1600s and 1700s, knowledge of Greek, Latin, and ancient philosophy held the highest status and served as a benchmark against which social status could be judged: it was reserved for white, upper-class men. Knowledge of classics was actually considered dangerous for women, whose weak moral characters would be unable to resist the temptations found in reading about the pre-Christian world; classical knowledge was also kept from the "rough classes" lest they attempt "social climbing." In this environment, scientific knowledge was considered somewhat base or trivial, and few felt threatened if women chose to acquire it (Phillips 1990).

Indeed, study of mathematics and science was considered beneficial for women, who would be less likely to be tempted into evil or mischief if they were busy studying. Contemplation of the natural world was also said to inspire an appreciation for the glory of God's creation (Phillips 1990). The study of mathematics was especially encouraged because it required no special equipment and was a particularly useful skill for a businessman's wife (Herzenberg, Meschel, and Altena 1991).

The nature of science with respect to popular culture in this era was another factor contributing to the rise of the scientific lady. Interest in science was frequently associated with anticlassical backlash sentiments. Many people felt that classical knowledge was arcane and impractical; scientific knowledge, on the other hand, was useful, particularly to businessmen and workers (surveyors, mariners, builders, and others) (Phillips 1990). Popular science writers who wished to reach this audience would therefore pitch their works so that those without classical training could understand them, and they wrote in the vernacular instead of Latin or Greek. Although women were not the intended beneficiaries of this accessibility, they certainly benefited from it (Phillips 1990).

Science found its way into the popular culture of the seventeenth, eighteenth, and nineteenth centuries through a number of routes. Science books for women written by both women and men authors were quite popular, but many other media were involved in popularizing science including journals, almanacs, public lectures, and the meetings of emerging professional societies. Women were (or in the case of professional societies, tried to be) avid consumers of and participants in all of these forums. Women were also a lucrative market for the expanding scientific paraphernalia trade (which dealt in such things as

microscopes, globes, and telescopes); additionally they formed an enthusiastic audience for scientific poetry, which became a popular genre.

Public lectures were a particularly popular method for bringing science to the people in England following their civil war. They were first delivered in 1650, and initially few women attended. Later, as lectures gained popularity, women were more encouraged and more inclined to go, and because the lecturers expected little basic knowledge from an audience, women could easily follow the discussion. Some venues even offered half-price admission for ladies. Many lecturers traveled, bringing science to most towns. Although women's attendance was not always condoned in more provincial areas, and attendance everywhere was confined mostly to genteel classes, working class women in larger communities would sometimes contrive to attend, especially if an indulgent lady of the house provided the ticket. Public lectures remained a popular and important medium through the late 1700s (Phillips 1990).

While popularization of science was important, women who wanted to pursue it as a profession needed teachers or tutors. Royal women could usually hire any tutor they wanted, and their interest surely encouraged interest among those of slightly lower rank. But the middle and upper classes had to find other opportunities, and for them the role of tutor was usually filled by a male relative or friend of the family. A significant impediment to women's studying seriously was their communal obligations during the daytime. Often the only private time they had to study was late at night or early in the morning. If several women shared an interest, one might read aloud while others embroidered or engaged in similar tasks. This kind of activity, however, did not necessarily lead to significant work in science (Phillips 1990).

Some women from the "lower" classes, however, contrived to earn a living through practical field work. For example, Mary Anning began working as a "fossilist" at age

twelve when her father died. She found the first complete skeleton of an ichthyosaur and also discovered the skeletons of a plesiosaur (in 1821) and a pterodactyl. Not only was she able to earn a living and support her family, she brought fossil hunting to the attention of the general public and eventually became an honorary fellow of the Geological Society (Phillips 1990; Alic 1986).

Mary Anning was an exception, however. Throughout the 1700s and 1800s, it slowly became more essential to have certification to practice science as a professional, and women were left with two basic options: they could attempt to obtain public instruction and earn degrees (attempts that were largely unsuccessful until the mid- to late 1800s) or they could remain the largely invisible assistants of male counterparts (husbands, fathers, brothers, uncles). Many took the latter route.

The fact that some women were making attempts to secure degrees suggests that not all were prepared to settle for the role of invisible supporter. In 1721, an English writer known as "Sophia" traced arguments for the superiority of women. She claimed that women were "born to teach and practice physic" (as used here, "physic" meant medicine) (Phillips 1990) and that women must be responsible for their own emancipation. She called on women to study physic and chemistry as preparation for occupying positions in government, earning a salary, and obtaining political and social prestige. Though her arguments were extreme for the time, she was not alone in calling for women to be educated to support themselves and fill leadership roles. Mary Wollstonecraft's groundbreaking *Vindication of the Rights of Woman* would appear in 1792.

The Industrial Revolution (1750–1850): Technology outside of "Woman's Sphere"

Mary Wollstonecraft wrote out of frustration with the limited roles available to women of her day. Throughout the 1700s and 1800s, the doctrine of "separate spheres" gained prominence and popularity. This code of mores dictated that a man's proper sphere was the public realm of business and politics while a woman's domain was the personal, private, and domestic. Simultaneously, the Industrial Revolution was occurring, and the advent of mass production struck a near-fatal blow to home-based craft and technology. Mass production became the engine of economic power, and it took place in the public, male sphere. Women were thus effectively ousted from technology's craft tradition, which had been their traditional strong suit.

The power of the aristocracy was also beginning to break down, and well-born women began to lose their access to and influence upon science. The trend toward professionalization made it harder for amateurs of either sex to influence science, a trend that was complete by the end of the 1800s (Schiebinger 1989). The economic philosophy most closely identified with the revolution was the theory of Adam Smith (1723–90), which became the basis of capitalism and included the division of production into capital and labor. Women and children, when they entered the world of production, were used merely as labor.

The United States: The Colonial Period and Beyond

While women of color were no doubt involved in "science" and "technology" long before, during, and after the colonial period, we have little documentation of their contributions. We do know there were a great number of similarities in the positions of white women with scientific interests in the colonies and those in England and the rest of Europe. The colonies had their share of scientific ladies, and, perhaps to a greater extent than in Europe, there were women who practiced "physick and chirurgery" in addition to midwifery. Joan Hoff Wilson credits the relative shortage of medical practitioners with creating an environment in which "doctoresses"

were accepted. She notes that, although these women seem to have been numerous, their names have not come down to us, possibly because their work did not contribute to scientific advancement in ways that men of their time or later historians would recognize (Wilson 1973).

Despite the historical neglect of colonial women in the medical profession, there are a number of women of the time whose interest in and contributions to science have become part of the historical record. Like European scientific ladies, these women were all members of the upper class (by birth, marriage, or both), and they justified their scientific interests not out of a serious interest in "progress" but as a way of avoiding vice or idleness. Their work was confined to fields considered fit for women, such as agronomy or botany (Wilson 1973). As with their European female contemporaries, these American women were dependent on the indulgence of a close male, almost always a relative, for the resources and permission to pursue their interest.

The most widely known of the colonial women is Jane Colden Farquher (1724–66), the daughter of Cadwallader Colden, a prominent New York politician who pursued many scientific interests on the side. He was a regular correspondent with Linnaeus, the "father of plant classification," and encouraged his daughter to study botany, which he regarded as particularly suitable for women: "their natural curiosity and pleasure they take in the beauty and variety of dress seems to fit them for it" (Wilson 1973, 226). He translated the Linnaen system from Latin to English for her, apparently believing that she could not learn the necessary Latin. Jane Colden Farquher made considerable contributions to the taxonomic classification of more than three hundred local plants and even discovered an entirely new genus, the gardenia. However, despite the pull toward popularization of science, much scientific research was still reported in Latin, and women like Jane Colden Farquher who did not receive any formal training could not communicate their discoveries to the scientific community. All of Farquher's findings were presented through her father or his friends. Although these men commented favorably on her skill and contributions, their observations, like those made about so many other women scientists, often included extraneous remarks, on the order of "what good cheese she made, in order 'to palliate and excuse so much feminine scientific knowledge'" (Wilson 1973, 227). As is the case with many other women, we will never know the extent of the contributions Jane Colden Farquher could have made to science, as her career came to a halt after her marriage.

Other American women who achieved some distinction in this era included horticulturists Martha Laures Ramolives (1759–1811), who worked on growing and preserving olives; Martha Daniell Logan (1702–79), who wrote a standard reference on gardening in South Carolina; and agronomist Eliza Lucas Pickney (1723–93), who perfected the cultivation of indigo (Wilson 1973). Sibilla Masters became the first American inventor to get an English patent (registered in her husband's name) for a method of cleaning and curing maize. In keeping with the unwritten dictum that women's technological contributions should have acceptable practical applications, Sibilla recommended the resulting product for "consumptive and sickly persons" (Wilson 1973, 229), but the real beneficiary was the mill she and her husband had outside Philadelphia.

The Birth of Engineering

As mentioned above, although the term *engineering* arose from the Latin word "to contrive," it was used beginning in the fifteenth century to denote the design of devices for warfare. The engineer was a military man who employed skills learned in apprenticeships to build machines of war. The progress of systematic science in the seventeenth and eighteenth centuries, and the beginning of the Industrial Revolution in the mid-eighteenth century, made it evident that scientific knowl-

edge could be systematically applied to make a discipline of designing that would be superior to the earlier methods that relied primarily on trial and error. In 1747, the École Nationale des Ponts et Chaussées (National School of Bridges and Roads) was established as the first formal school of engineering, although there had been previous courses of study in engineering in France.

Engineering had its origins neither in the upper-class, intellectual sphere of science, nor in the craft and guild traditions, but rather in the military, which meant it automatically excluded women. It was only around 1794 that engineering acquired the aspect of a discipline and the qualifier "civil" to denote that it could have nonmilitary applications.

In the United States, the first engineering school was the United States Military Academy at West Point, New York, established in 1802 to educate engineers. The first "civil" engineering school patterned after West Point was the Scientific and Military Academy at Norwich, Vermont, which offered military and civil engineering degrees in 1821. This school closed down because of financial problems in 1832. The oldest existing nonmilitary engineering school in the United States is the Rensselaer Polytechnic Institute in Troy, New York, which was established as the Rensselaer School in 1824 "to qualify teachers for instructing the sons and daughters of farmers" (Grayson 1977).

Engineering as an academic discipline rose from the realization that there were common principles to building roads and bridges and catapults; it prescribed a series of steps to be taken and formulas to be followed in the devising of things. Although it strongly resembled the craft tradition, women found no place in this new field. As discussed earlier, the Industrial Revolution had largely removed women from leadership roles in production, and engineering's roots in the military meant that women's exclusion was de facto. It appears to us that as the discipline of engineering formally entered the academy, it looked for an educational model and found that it looked most like mathematics and science since it employed their principles. As a result, engineering as an academic discipline inherited the cultural and philosophical tenets of mathematics and science—and the tradition of excluding women from any role except as labor for mills and factories.

General Observations on the 1800s

Throughout the 1800s, women were very much dependent on men for access to scientific and technical careers. In a discussion of nineteenth-century American botanists, Nancy G. Slack observed (1987) that a woman's career was largely dependent on her husband's or other male relative's access to knowledge and power and his willingness to share it. Spinsterhood was not a very respectable choice, and women without male sponsors could encounter considerable difficulty. Women with intellectual aspirations seemed to have three options: stop work after marriage, be lucky enough to find a supportive and encouraging husband, or become a widow. Of the three, widowhood may have been easiest (assuming the woman was not left destitute): widows were allowed the greatest degree of self-determination and possessed the respectability that came with marriage (and motherhood).

Science, although rapidly transforming, was not fully professionalized; it could still be pursued as a home-based endeavor in which women could contribute through family links. Most frequently, these involved husband-wife teams. As Marilyn Bailey Ogilvie suggests, these pairs were usually perceived as husband-creator/wife-executor, an acceptable arrangement because it left the intellectual work safely in male hands. How many pairs actually conformed to this paradigm and in how many the wives made greater contributions will never be determined. There are many examples of such women partners in a wide range of fields: Hertha Ayrton (physicist and electrical engineer), Elizabeth Britton (botanist), Mary Buckland (geologist), Amalie Dietrich (entomolo-

gist), Margaret Huggins (astronomer), Mary Lyell (conchologist), Marie Pasteur (biologist), Eliza Sullivan (botanist), and, in early in the twentieth century, Lillian Gilbreth (industrial engineer). Although many of these collaborations must have been based on genuine cooperation, one should not suppose that all were: Amalie Deitrich's husband, for example, was reportedly quite abusive. She left him to become successful independently (Ogilvie 1987).

Although it was difficult for a woman to have a professional career without a supportive male figure in her life, it was certainly not impossible. As Regina Morantz-Sanchez has detailed in her 1987 essay on nineteenth- and early twentieth-century women physicians, some women, determined to pursue their careers, did not bother looking for supportive husbands but instead found ways to create their own families. These women sometimes adopted children as single mothers or formed bonds and households with other women. Lillian Welsh, a graduate of the Women's Medical College of Pennsylvania, met Dr. Mary Sherwood after her graduation. They studied pathology together in Zurich for a year and then moved to Baltimore in 1890, where they shared a home and medical practice until Dr. Sherwood's death forty-five years later. Dr. Emily Blackwell, dean of the Woman's Medical College of the New York Infirmary, enjoyed a long relationship with Dr. Elizabeth Cushier, regarding whom a colleague wrote to Blackwell's sister in 1888, "She is in fact a remarkable woman, spirited, unselfish, generous and intelligent. I do not know what Dr. Emily would do without her. She absolutely basks in her presence; and seems as if she had been waiting for her for a lifetime" (Morantz-Sanchez 1987, 57).

Increasing Access to Higher Education

Although few women, with the possible exception of Jane Colden Farquher, achieved professional distinction in the United States during the late 1700s and early 1800s, most daughters of the upper class (merchants, planters, politicians) received basic science training in everything from mechanics and astronomy to botany, mineralogy, and chemistry (Johnson 1936). Higher education for women was a relatively new concept. For many years, educating women had been discouraged, but "by 1820 . . . the traditional belief . . . that denying women an education would assure their virtue and make them better wives and mothers had not proven correct" (Rossiter 1982, 4).

During the turn of the century, however, reformers began to promote education as making women better able to perform their duties as mothers by giving them needed information and skills to raise their sons to be good citizens. Accordingly, dame schools began to proliferate, and many of these included science in their curriculum along with or even instead of the traditional "accomplishments." These schools would often advertise the size and quality of their scientific instruction materials as well as the caliber of the (male) faculty who taught the courses (Johnson 1936; Warner 1978).

Organized scientific instruction for women that might lead to careers in science was still largely unavailable. The Georgia Female College at Macon, which opened in 1836—two hundred years after the first school for men (Harvard)—was the first institution of any sort to grant degrees to women in the United States; among its required courses were chemistry, mineralogy, and astronomy. With a dearth of formal options, some women organized to teach themselves. In 1817 more than fifty women in Charleston got together to study botany; in Georgia City, local women formed the Caroline Herschel Society and raised five hundred dollars to buy themselves a telescope (Johnson 1936).

A few women during this period did manage to have careers in science. Almira Hart Lincoln Phelps joined the by-now established tradition of women as authors of scientific textbooks, writing a number of popular and widely utilized books on botany, chemistry,

and natural philosophy. She was the second woman elected to the American Association for the Advancement of Science (Slack 1987), and she eventually grew quite wealthy from the success of her publications. She also ran the Patapsco Female Institute with her husband.

Formal higher education for women came with the founding of Mount Holyoke in 1837. Oberlin opened in 1833 as a coeducational college, and the Cherokee National Female Seminary in Park Hill, Oklahoma—the first such institution for women west of the Mississippi—opened in 1851. Women's colleges proliferated following the Civil War, beginning with Vassar in 1865, and soon including Smith, Wellesley, Bryn Mawr, Barnard, and Goucher, among others.

One of the more important of the early women professors at these schools was astronomer Maria Mitchell (1818–1889). Trained by her father, she discovered a comet in 1847 and for this achievement won a gold medal from the king of Denmark. She subsequently became the first American woman elected to the American Academy of Arts and Sciences and the first woman member of the American Association for the Advancement of Science. Appointed to Vassar in 1865, she became a strong early advocate for women's participation in science. She aided the formation in the mid-1870s of the Association for the Advancement of Women (AAW), an umbrella group addressing the interests of women professionals of which she was later president (Kohlstedt 1978).

Gaining Entrance to Graduate School

As education for women became more popular, women's colleges began seeking to hire women with doctorates, which meant that women had to obtain them if they wanted the positions. Initially no American institutions would grant graduate degrees to women, and many women went to great lengths to attend prestigious German schools. As Margaret Rossiter details, the movement to obtain doctorates had three phases: Before 1890, women could only gain admission to American graduate programs as "special" (usually nondegree) students. Between 1890 and 1892, women were admitted to six major graduate schools: Yale and the University of Pennsylvania, which admitted women as graduate students but not as undergraduates; Columbia and Brown, which also formed coordinate colleges for women undergraduates; and Stanford and the University of Chicago, which became fully coeducational (Rossiter 1982). Beginning in 1893, several other schools finally gave in to changing sentiments and "peer pressure."

The women's colleges might have been an option for doctoral programs, but only a few had the money to develop them. Few professors at these schools favored segregated education at the graduate level. Shortly after the war between the states (the Civil War), when women began applying for graduate degrees, most received a standard response: "no precedent." Some schools were willing to make exceptions under certain circumstances, but they then went to considerable effort to ensure they set no legal precedent. When mathematician Christine Ladd (later Ladd-Franklin) was admitted to Johns Hopkins in 1878, it was with the stipulations that she would not be listed in the course catalog and that her case would set no precedent (Rossiter 1982). Although she was allowed to attend classes and she produced a dissertation, the Board of Trustees refused to grant her a degree when she submitted her dissertation in 1882 (Rossiter 1982). Finally, in 1926, at the fiftieth anniversary of the inauguration of its first president, Johns Hopkins awarded the Ph.D. to the seventy-eight-year-old Ladd-Franklin, forty-four years after she earned it (Green and LaDuke 1990).

Margaret Rossiter suggests that two strategies, used in combination, eventually undermined this pattern. The first was "guerrilla warfare," whereby individual women sought to test repressive systems on as many fronts as possible and evaded rules informally; when enough women had done this, a push for a change in policy could be initiated quietly. The second was "creative philanthropy," with women endowing chairs or giving huge gifts to universities contingent upon their admitting women (Rossiter 1982).

Women also founded such organizations as the Naples Table Association (NTA), in existence from 1897 to 1933, to provide fellowships for women and promote women's interests. The NTA persuaded several women's colleges and some wealthy individuals to give fifty dollars apiece each year so that the total annual fee of five hundred dollars could be raised to secure a "table" for a talented woman to work for a year at the Naples Zoological Station in Italy. The table was actually a research bench at the station, and payment of the fee entitled a researcher to use it and the facilities of the station. The association was later able to sponsor a second table and a more general research fellowship for women (Rossiter 1982). By the early twentieth century, women were accepted at most graduate schools and had begun establishing their own fellowships for postgraduate education.

By allowing more women to study science systematically and by increasing jobs for future generations, the rise of higher education for women succeeded in bringing more women into the profession at various levels. Although the early women's colleges and some co-ed schools provided employment, working conditions were still not ideal. These teaching jobs were among the very few opportunities afforded to single women to practice science; indeed, women faculty were expected to be "of good Christian character, and not only single but in no danger of marrying" (Rossiter 1982, 15). Male faculty, conversely, were expected to be married.

The logic of these rules went largely unquestioned and unarticulated. In 1906, Harriet Brooks, a physicist at Barnard, announced that she would be marrying and that she intended to continue teaching. The case caused a furor in the college, which eventually concluded that Brooks should "dignify her home making into a profession, and not assume that she can carry two full professions at a time . . . [because] the college cannot afford to have a woman on the staff to whom the college work is secondary; [yet] the college is not willing to stamp with approval a woman whose self-elected home duties can be secondary" (Rossiter 1982, 16).

It is interesting to note that when efforts to gain higher education for women met with success or even approval, it was for fields that were considered "more genteel." This might explain why there was no concerted push to gain admittance for women to engineering programs; engineering still usually involved handling heavy equipment and "getting your hands dirty." However, since experimental science could also involve considerable physical labor, the lack of interest in engineering may have been a side-effect of the fact that most women able to pursue higher education and professional careers were white women from middle- or upper-class backgrounds who may have been uninterested in a pursuit that still resembled a rough trade.

Entering the Professions: The Invention of "Women's Work"

The growing number of female Ph.D.'s wanted jobs. They were extremely intelligent, highly trained, and used to fighting for a place in the professional world. Nevertheless, resistance to allowing women to compete directly with men for jobs was extreme; most jobs were strongly sex typed, and women simply were not permitted to undertake "men's jobs." This was a continuation of attitudes set in place through the scientific revolution: men would not permit women to undertake the work they themselves wanted and regarded as important. The only alternative for women was to accept jobs that men found undesirable.

Margaret Rossiter has traced how a separate labor market for women scientists began

to emerge in the 1880s and 1890s and became entrenched by the early 1900s. The changing structure of the scientific establishment allowed the creation of jobs that might be said to use women's "special talents" and "unique skills." First, there was the rise of "big science," particularly at observatories. These were projects with large budgets and a great need for support staff, jobs for which women were doubly suited because they would do less interesting work for lower pay than the men. Second, a growing concern for social problems, especially in large urban areas, led to the creation of programs to "solve" them; women could become involved in social work, counseling, or nutrition. Finally, land grant colleges were being established, and the need for faculty and personnel was great enough that some women could find employment (Rossiter 1982).

The jobs thus created for women were of two types: so low ranking or low paying that men were not interested (these jobs often required docility or great attention to detail), or in social service working with the poor, women, and children. The classic example of the first type was the Harvard College Observatory. Reportedly, one day in 1881 Edward Pickering, the newly elected director of the observatory, became so disgruntled with the ineptitude of his male assistant that he proclaimed that his maid could do a better job. Accordingly, he set Williamina P. Flemming, a divorced single mother in his employ, to copying and computing. She became a well-known astronomer and eventually supervised a staff of nearly twenty other women engaged in the business of sorting and cataloging photographs of stellar phenomena (Rossiter 1982; see also Kass-Simon and Farnes 1990).

While work for women in "big science" was tedious and low ranking, women could attain some distinction as long as they stayed in sex-typed work involving science applications in the home or on behalf of those less socially advantaged. Home economics, a field dominated almost exclusively by women for decades, was basically invented by Ellen Swallow Richards (Rossiter 1982). Alice Hamilton more or less single-handedly created the field of industrial medicine after living in Jane Addams's settlement house among the working poor of Chicago. When Harvard's medical school went looking for a specialist in industrial medicine in the early 1920s, Hamilton was the only sufficiently distinguished person available. She was appointed the first woman on the medical school faculty with the stipulations that she could not use the Faculty Club, obtain football tickets, or march in the commencement procession (Glazer and Slater 1987).

Seeking Professional Standing and Collegial Respect

If women's work did not often win the respect of employers, neither did it gain them standing with their peers practicing in the same fields. In the latter half of the 1800s, science was consciously trying to transform itself into a profession and, as part of that quest, scientific societies were formed. These groups rarely welcomed women. They were formed largely for the purpose of excluding "mere amateurs," and, as we have noted, prestige, professionalism, and status were all very closely tied with masculinity. Those organizations that did admit women often imposed stiffer membership requirements on them than for the men (requiring them to have more degrees, for example) or restricted them to lower levels of membership (Rossiter 1982).

Sometimes the cold shoulder given to women was the result of reorganization efforts specifically aimed at increasing prestige. An inner circle of "fellows" might be created that excluded women, or rules might be rewritten in such a way that women could not be admitted. Some membership requirements were also harder on women. For example, a stipulation that members be visible practitioners in their fields would have excluded all

but those women who held professorships. The meetings themselves often involved misogynist entertainments, making women feel further out of place. Women's recourse was to form and strengthen their own clubs, but there were rarely enough women practicing to make this a truly viable option, and the top women were cut off from interaction with their male peers (Rossiter 1982). This formal communication as a central value of science and scientific discourse was denied to women.

First-Wave Feminism and the Fight for Suffrage

Women's systematic exclusion from scientific societies is less surprising when one considers that around 1900 "everyone knew" that women were biologically inferior to men, both on questions of physical strength and of intellect. Then, in 1898, Helen Thompson Woolley had the temerity to point out that no one had ever actually tested this assumption experimentally (Rossiter 1982). Woolley conducted her own experiments and found only minor differences between the sexes. Surprisingly for the time, she attributed these to differences in social conditioning.

It was no accident that such feminist research began appearing around the turn of the century. First-wave feminism was in full swing, and the suffrage movement was gaining momentum. Women scientists contributed to these movements by conducting research, especially in psychology and anthropology; by beginning for the first time to protest publicly about women's low status, lack of opportunities, and lack of recognition in the scientific community; by actively working in the suffrage movement; and finally, when the United States entered World War I, by joining the war effort. Women's war contributions were usually in "feminine" fields such as home economics and social service, but many also took over industrial positions left vacant by men.

The Twentieth Century: War, Boom, Bust, and Civil Rights

After the war, the right to suffrage was finally gained, a victory that Margaret Rossiter credits at least partially to society's gratitude for women's contributions in wartime. Unfortunately, postwar gratitude did not extend to allowing women to keep their new jobs or continue exercising their newly proven talents. They were expected to cede their places gracefully to the returning men. As one newsletter stated, "The women chemists of the Illinois Steel Company not only made good as chemists but showed their fine spirits by resigning to make places for men returning from war work" (Rossiter 1982, 118, and 354 n. 36).

World War I thus established a pattern that would be repeated during and after World War II: there was a boom in the employment of women in science as men left for the prestigious and essential work of soldiering. When the men returned, there was a backlash against the employed women as men reasserted themselves in their old territory. Although women had indisputably proven themselves capable of doing "men's work," they were not allowed to continue doing it—at least not on equal footing with the men. Although women scientists and engineers got better and better at generating statistics to prove they were being treated unfairly, they were unable to persuade any institutions to rectify the problem. Thousands of women were now employed in women's colleges, at co-ed institutions, in government, and in industry, but they were unable to advance as men did. With territorial and hierarchical segregation still in force, women were channeled into certain fields, kept in lower ranks, and paid lower salaries by employers who minimized their contributions while blaming them for not doing more.

The experience of one of the greatest scientists of the time, who happened to be a woman, offers valuable insight into the double standards applied to women who ventured into men's fields. In 1921 Marie Curie came to the United States on a publicity and fundraising tour organized by reporter Marie Meloney of New York City. During the three weeks she spent traveling, she was awarded twenty honorary degrees and given one gram of radium (worth $100,000), funds for which had been raised by committees of wealthy philanthropists assembled by Meloney (McGrayne 1992). This was a triumphal moment for women in science, but it had a double edge: Madame Curie, despite being the world's first female Nobelist and the only double Nobelist in science (physics, 1903; chemistry, 1911), was in a desperate situation financially. Unable to raise funds in battered postwar France, she was dependent on American charity to continue her research. Ironically, the publicity around Curie was all laudatory, and an opportunity was lost that could have been used to point out the absurdity of the barriers still faced by a female scientist of Curie's stature. She could not get into the Académie Française or the U.S. National Academy, and Harvard and Princeton refused to grant her honorary degrees. Madame Curie was certainly living proof that women could achieve remarkably in science but, as Margaret Rossiter has pointed out (1982), depressingly few people were questioning why this still needed to be proven. Indeed, Marie Curie created a new double bind for women scientists. Her success could have laid open many opportunities for women in its wake, but instead it was used to set an impossible standard: no woman scientist was considered worthy unless she promised to be another Marie Curie. Of course, no similar standard was applied to men (Rossiter 1982; McGrayne 1992).

It is impossible to say what might have happened had there been no stock market crash in 1929; but it is certain that during the Great Depression, the few jobs available were very unlikely to go to women, and young women starting their careers encountered nearly insurmountable barriers. (Note the stories of Eleanor Baum, Gertrude Elion,

Thelma Estrin, Esther Hopkins, Salome Waelsch, and Rosalyn Yalow in this volume.) The combined effects of a slow economy and enduring discrimination left women with very few options, and many adapted a conservative strategy defined by Margaret Rossiter as "deliberate overqualification and personal stoicism" (1982, 129). In other words, they internalized and accepted the double standards decreeing that they had to be more qualified, smarter, better trained, and still accept lower paying, less interesting work—frequently at the cost of having a family (Rossiter 1982).

Despite dramatic fluctuations in the national economy, the years between 1920 and 1940 were a time of very little overall change for women in science. Women began earning a higher percentage of the doctorates, and there was some expansion of employment opportunities. A few prominent figures like anthropologists Ruth Benedict and Margaret Mead made headlines, and a few women became presidents of professional groups or members of honorary societies, but overall things were not any better in 1940 than they had been in 1920. Apart from suffrage, all the gains made by women during World War I seemed to have evaporated (Rossiter 1982).

World War II

During World War II, the national rhetoric claimed that women scientists were a valuable commodity, but in actuality they were only welcome in certain fields and there rarely permitted above entry-level positions. Men were promoted, and women were brought in to fill the lower-level positions. At universities, anti-nepotism rules forbidding the employment of members of the same family (almost always to the detriment of qualified faculty wives) were temporarily suspended, and women were brought in to fill vacant teaching positions. Some women, like Thelma Estrin, were hastily trained as aides or assistants, and overall the number or women in science and engineering doubled in about four years—though

many of these women were at the baccalaureate level or below (Rossiter 1995).

However, despite much public lament about the shortage of technical talent, industry proved largely unwilling to employ women, blacks, or older nontraditional workers in other than the lowest-level work, if they were willing to employ them at all.

Women fared a little better in government, although they were still largely confined to certain fields. As home economists, women helped plan wartime rationing and contributed advice on nutritional needs, and they helped establish the nutritional guidelines known as the U.S. Recommended Daily Allowance (USRDA). Woman anthropologists were able to carve out a niche in the Office of War Information, providing information on other cultures. Outside these relatively sex-typed endeavors, women had less success. The Office of Strategic Research and Development, which handled the big wartime science projects, employed very few women scientists. Although women did participate in all of the major research projects, including the development of penicillin and radar and the Manhattan Project, they were rarely placed in positions of authority, and their contributions were seldom credited in the historical record.

At least eighty-five women scientists and engineers were involved in the Manhattan Project, the war's most impressive technological effort. Among them were Lilli Hornig (author of the Foreword to our book), who helped to develop the high-explosive lenses used in the implosion bomb; Leona Woods, who helped construct detectors that would monitor the flux of neutrons from an atomic "pile"; Maria Goeppert-Mayer (Nobelist in physics, 1963), who studied uranium hexafluoride gas and the energy emitted by a nuclear explosion; Ella Anderson, who prepared the first sample of nearly pure uranium 235 for use at Los Alamos; Elizabeth Riddle Graves, who helped monitor the Trinity test; and Joan Hinton, who helped build the first reactor at Los Alamos (Herzenberg and Howes 1993). After the war, some of these women, like

Goeppert-Mayer, went on to distinguished careers, but many of them, no longer needed or encouraged in their fields, dropped out of science altogether. Although they and many other women made important and visible contributions to science during the war, in the immediate postwar era they lost a lot of ground. They were expected to retire to make room for the returning men, and many did.

After the War: Returning to "Normal"

As the war came to an end, 7.8 million veterans, mostly male, returned home, and the nation attempted to return to what it thought was normal. Women who had been eagerly encouraged to join the technical workforce in support of the war effort were now urged to return home and devote themselves to the emotional support of returning war heroes (Hartmann 1978). As with the women chemists of Illinois Steel after World War I, they were expected to cheerfully cede their jobs to former GI's and devote themselves to homemaking and child rearing, and in fact most did. Those who preferred to keep their jobs were sometimes able to, but often they could not. Regardless, the employment of women scientists dropped about 10 percent almost immediately after the war (Rossiter 1995).

The impact of the returning men on the workforce was delayed slightly by the GI Bill, which provided funds for education and led to many veterans entering the universities. As Lilli Hornig pointedly writes in the Foreword, this had an enormous impact; schools that had been underutilized during the war were suddenly flooded with men. Female enrollment at some co-ed schools had reached as high as 50 percent during the war; but as the demand for slots increased, many institutions reintroduced—or even introduced for the first time—quotas or caps on female enrollment. Despite record postwar enrollments and rapid expansion, the female faculty who

had filled in during the war were steadily pushed out; nepotism rules were reintroduced, and many women who married lost their jobs. Discrimination against women was as bad as ever, but as Senator McCarthy's hearings ("witch hunts" against suspected Communists and Communist sympathizers) progressed, nobody was particularly eager to critique American society (Rossiter 1995).

Women were being systematically pushed out of science and engineering just as the economy was booming and the technology sector was poised for rapid expansion. When one considers that individual institutions typically see expansion as an opportunity for upgrading, the exclusion of women seems even less surprising. As we have noted, increasing prestige has often implicitly or explicitly included masculinization. Expanding research budgets meant that higher-ranking scientists could afford to employ large numbers of research associates. Women were largely confined to these junior positions and prevented from climbing higher, even when they were clearly qualified or overqualified. Rules against nepotism were particularly insidious in keeping women from employment commensurate with their skills. At the University of Kansas, for example, Beatrice Wright, a psychologist and internationally known expert on persons with disabilities, was barred from working on the basis of her marriage to Professor Herbert Wright. The university resisted changing their rules until she pointed out that they were using her textbook, *Physical Disability: A Psychological Approach,* in a class she herself was barred from teaching (Rossiter 1995, 141).

During this period of upgrading, expansion, and masculinization, home economics, the traditional women's field, faced enormous and sometimes insurmountable challenges. From the late 1940s to the early 1960s, the field was under external attack from central administrations for being out of date, insufficiently serious, and too vocationally oriented. It was also under internal attack from male practitioners who were beginning to enter the field, calling their work things like "nutritional science" or "human ecology." Not wanting to rank low in the department or to be supervised by female deans, these new male faculty, with the support of university administrations, often took over and renamed or dissolved "home economics" departments (Rossiter 1995).

As the Cold War progressed, government officials began to voice concern about anticipated shortages of trained technical personnel, and women were officially encouraged to study science. These efforts intensified after the former Soviet Union launched Sputnik, the first satellite in space, in 1957. As Susan Henry, Sue Rosser, and Mary Shaw note later in this volume, Sputnik set off a flurry of programs to encourage all students toward science. But highly trained women again had difficulty finding jobs comparable to those held by their male counterparts, ending up instead as assistants and technicians. And while women were attending graduate school in record numbers, they were also dropping out at depressingly high rates. Most programs skeptically assumed that women would drop out, failed to offer them adequate financial or emotional support, and then blamed these students for the failure that had been expected of them in the first place (Rossiter 1995).

The Feminine Mystique, Consciousness Raising, and Legal Challenges

By the early 1960s, there was a growing sense of malaise among many upper- and middle-class white women regarding their place in American society—a feeling transmuted into concrete action following the 1963 publication of Betty Friedan's groundbreaking book, *The Feminine Mystique*. The book touched a nerve with the middle-class white women who were to become the vanguard of the women's liberation movement, and second-wave feminism was born. The National Organization for Women was established in 1966 and, beginning in 1968, academic and professional

women, including scientists, began to organize formally to lobby on their own behalf.

The groundswell of popular support for women's rights led eventually to a number of national-level legal reforms. The Civil Rights Act of 1964 barred discrimination in employment, although it exempted educational institutions. Then, in October 1967, President Johnson signed Executive Order 11375, which created the Federal Women's Program and outlawed sex discrimination in employment by the federal government and its contractors, effective in October 1968. As most colleges and universities received federal monies, this order provided grounds for numerous antidiscrimination lawsuits against schools. While this strategy proved a reasonably effective publicity tool, the government was disappointingly unwilling to enforce the terms of the order. Pressure for more effective legislation mounted. Finally, in 1972, the House and Senate passed, and President Nixon signed, the Equal Employment Opportunity Act, which updated the Civil Rights Act of 1964 and removed the exemption for educational institutions. In the same year, the Equal Rights Amendment passed Congress, although it was never fully ratified by the states and so failed to become a constitutional amendment (Rossiter 1995; Rossi 1971).

Amid the larger context of the women's movement, women in science and engineering had their own agenda. In particular, they were interested in overturning antinepotism rules as de facto discrimination against women since their practical effect was almost always to prevent qualified wives from obtaining employment. They also advocated the creation of part-time positions that would better accommodate working mothers, better maternity leave policies, and affirmative action. At colleges and universities, women lobbied for better gynecological services, women's studies courses, on-campus child care, and the creation of women's centers (Rossi 1971). In this renewed push for equity in women's education, the question of women's participation in engineering entered public discourse: women began demanding access to training as well as equitable treatment in the field. It has not been an easy fight, and we note that, as of 1997, only the repeal of antinepotism rules has been widely achieved.

The Most Recent Quarter Century

Although much work remains to be done, the women's movement for equality that began in the late 1970s had a profound impact, and the last twenty-five to thirty years have seen considerable progress in the participation of women in science and engineering. As the Foreword to our book noted, there was a dramatic increase in the percentage and numbers of women practicing in science and engineering during the 1970s and 1980s. Because affirmative action introduced accountability, institutions began keeping better information and statistics, and women were better able to track their progress or lack thereof in various fields, institutions, and departments.

Figures 1 and 2 (pp. 24, 25) illustrate the fluctuations in women's participation in various science and engineering fields over time. Figure 1 shows the percentage of all science and engineering bachelor's degrees awarded to women from 1950 to the present. The significant features of this graph are the way the steeper increases in engineering that began in the 1970s leveled off in the 1980s; how both the physical and life sciences experienced increases; but how, after years of steady increases, numbers of degrees awarded in mathematics began to drop in the late 1970s. Figure 2 shows the percentage of science and engineering doctoral degrees awarded to women in various fields since the 1920s. This graph dramatically illustrates that the number of doctorates awarded to women in engineering, mathematics, and the physical and life sciences were higher in the 1920s than in the 1950s, after which they began a steady rise, reversing the setbacks of the Depression and post–World War II era.

How did the present situation evolve and what must we do to progress further? These are complicated questions with several overlapping answers. During the mid-1980s the focus of the debate around women's participation in science and engineering shifted away from questions of equality and was recast in economic terms. Science and engineering policy makers became concerned about keeping a competitive edge in technological innovation and production in an international market. A shortage of highly trained technical personnel was widely expected. The American workforce was changing to include more women and minorities. Because of these changing demographics, it was necessary to pay attention to recruitment and retention of women and minorities in science and engineering. While the anticipated shortage of scientists and engineers has not materialized, it led at the time to lots of attention by various government and private agencies and cast women's participation in science and engineering as one of economic necessity. In 1988, Sheila Widnall, then president of the American Association for the Advancement of Sciences, devoted her presidential address to analyzing the apparent reasons that women's participation in science was curtailed relative to that of men. Concurrently, the National Science Foundation (NSF) started numerous initiatives to help increase women's involvement in science and engineering, including offering graduate scholarships and visiting professorships for women, keeping accurate records of the numbers of women receiving degrees and gaining employment, and creating a Program for Women and Girls in the Human Resources Division. The NSF also required research institutions and universities receiving funding to show the number of women involved in the projects, and explicitly asked NSF-funded research centers to increase the recruitment of women. Agencies such as NSF and the National Institutes of Health (NIH) also recruited women for work on panels that evaluate proposals. At the same time, a number of colleges and universities started special support programs for women, some of which have already had a profound impact—often dependent on the level of institutional support they received. Private

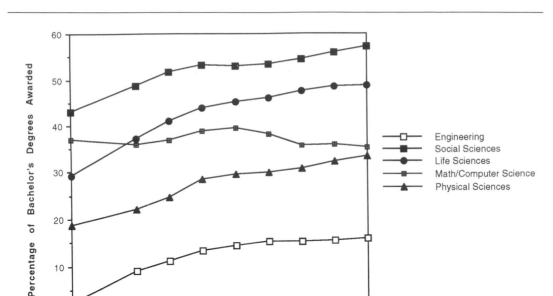

Figure 1. *Percentages of Bachelor Degrees Awarded to Women by Field*

Sources: *American Statistics Index* (Washington, D.C.: Congressional Information Service, 1951–91); National Center for Education Statistics, *Digest of Education Statistics* (Washington, D.C.: Education Division, Department of Health, Education, and Welfare); National Center for Education Statistics, "Earned Degrees Conferred, 1969–70: Part A, Summary Data," Circular OE-54010 (Washington, D.C.: Education Division, Department of Health, Education, and Welfare); Federal Security Agency, "Advance Report, Survey of Earned Degrees Granted during Year 1958–59," Circular 282a, "Earned Degrees Conferred by Higher Education Institutions" (Washington, D.C.: U.S. Office of Education).

funding agencies like the Alfred P. Sloan Foundation and the Intel Foundation made issues of woman's equality central to their funding awards and created special programs for projects around women's participation in science and engineering. National associations such as American Women in Science (AWIS) and Women in Engineering Program Advocates Network (WEPAN) were formed for the purpose of facilitating the participation of women in science and engineering.

Why So Few?

While, despite all of these efforts, the rate of increase of women in science and engineering has slowed, the considerable attention paid to ques-

tions of gender equity in these fields has been effective in identifying some of the important remaining barriers to women's full participation, and this is a crucial step toward reform. We agree with those researchers who suggest that fewer women than men are successful in engineering and science for a number of reasons:

- Gender-role socialization and internalized stereotypes may lead women to believe that they are not capable of becoming scientists or engineers, or that it is inappropriate for them to do so.
- The low numbers of women in these fields suggest that individual women may face discouraging isolation (including a lack of role models).
- The culture of science was evolved largely

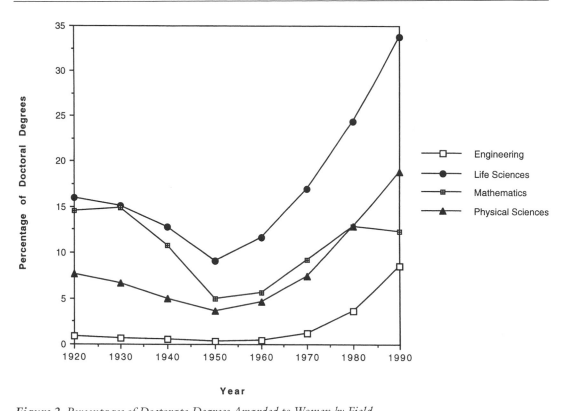

Figure 2. *Percentages of Doctorate Degrees Awarded to Women by Field*

Sources: National Science Board, "Science and Engineering Indicators—1996," NSB 96–21 (Washington, D.C.: National Science Board, 1996), appendix table 2–18; National Center for Education Statistics, "Earned Degrees and Completion Surveys," Washington, D.C.: U.S. Department of Education; National Research Council, U.S. Committee on the Education and Employment of Women in Science and Engineering, *Climbing the Academic Ladder: Doctoral Women Scientists in Academe* (Washington, D.C.: National Academy of Sciences, 1979), table 2.1, p. 20; National Research Council, doctorate records file.

by able-bodied heterosexual white men, and people who do not fit this mold may encounter discrimination ranging from the subtle to the overt; "outsiders" may not be able to integrate easily with—or may simply dislike—the dominant culture.

• Women in science and engineering must contend with the same sexism that confronts professional women in all fields.

The women profiled in this book illustrate that women journey through various phases to find their niches in science or engineering. As Lilli Hornig also outlines in the Foreword, the factors listed above, among others, pose obstacles of various kinds and at various points in these journeys.

Socialization

Children are not born with sexist, racist, ethnocentric, homophobic, classist, able-ist, or other prejudiced attitudes; they learn these from their environment, including their parents, teachers, peers, and the popular media. And as they grow up, they may begin consciously or unconsciously mistreating members of other groups because they have learned that such behavior is acceptable and even encouraged. More insidious, however, is the way in which people can internalize negative or discouraging messages about groups to which they belong. Many factors conspire to encourage girls and women to believe that science and engineering are not appropriate fields for them, and to sabotage their confidence in their ability to succeed at science and mathematics.

As we discuss socialization, we focus primarily on gender roles because our book is about women. It is important, however, to keep in mind that gender-role socialization varies by racial and ethnic cultural group as well as by socioeconomic class, so while we paint with a broad brush, there will be considerable shades and contrasts in individual experiences. It is further important to remember that everyone is also learning and internalizing information about racism, ethnocentrism, classism, homophobia, and other forms of prejudice in addition to gender stereotypes.

Parents

Parents are among the first people to influence a child and, unfortunately, are often the first to discriminate against their daughters, especially if they also have sons (Mullis and Jenkins 1988). Research has shown that parents interact differently with newborn infant girls and boys (Sadker and Sadker 1994). Parents are generally more physically active with boys (Huston 1983; Lewis 1972; Parke 1976) and provide boys with more spatially complex toys and more opportunity to interact with the physical world (Baenninger and Newcombe 1989; C. L. Miller 1987; Serbin and Connor 1979). The result is that most children enter kindergarten with attitudes about "science" and "math" that are already differentially socialized. Girls who do well in science and math classes may find that their parents praise their *hard work;* boys are more likely to be congratulated for having *talent* (Keynes 1989). The result is that girls are less likely to believe that they possess an aptitude for math and science. However, girls with one or both parents working in a technical field are much more likely to be encouraged to pursue these fields themselves. And regardless of their occupations, parents who praise and

encourage their children can have a huge positive influence.

Teachers and Counselors

Teachers also play a large role in socializing children as they move through the educational system. Much research has shown that teachers of both sexes discriminate in the classroom, even if they believe that they are not doing so (Sadker and Sadker 1994). Boys tend to dominate discussion and teacher attention (Lee, Marks, and Byrd 1994) to the point that, on average, teachers spend 56 percent of their time with boys and only 44 percent with girls (Kelly 1988). As Kahle (1996) notes, "classroom patterns involve more frequent interactions with boys, fewer challenging questions posed to girls, fewer opportunities for girls to use manipulative equipment, and more examples and exemplars related to masculine activities" (Davis 1996, 64–65). Kahle (1996, 60, citing Kahle and Lakes 1983) notes further that "boys generally have more opportunity than girls to use scientific equipment, to perform experiments, and to take science related field trips."

Like parents, teachers may praise girls for neat performance or hard work when they do well in math but imply that they are not bright if they fail. Boys who fail, in contrast, are taken to task for not working harder, and boys who succeed are praised for their ability (Dweck 1986; Dweck et al. 1978; Stockard 1980).

The influence of instructors and advisers continues well past high school. Although many people opt out of science or engineering before they reach college, some who do begin college-level programs in these fields fail to complete them. The level of support and encouragement they receive during the undergraduate years makes a big difference. For women, these years are too often accompanied by a drop in confidence, especially in their ability in science and math. Just one discouraging professor can have a major impact, especially during the uncertainty of the first year.

In addition to neglect and sometimes overt

discouragement from instructors and counselors, young women encounter fewer female role models and have fewer opportunities for same-sex mentoring. This is compounded by the fact that women in the scientific community tend to occupy the lower ranks and so may be less able to offer advice or entrées into power-sharing networks.

Peers

The very notable drop in the number of girls pursuing science in junior high and high school may be related to the gender role behavior expected by adolescent culture. Peer group influence persists through college. According to Astin (1993, 398), "The student's peer group is the single most important source of influence on growth and development during the undergraduate years." "Women in college science and engineering classes have a mostly male peer group who may make them feel unwelcome in many ways" (Seymour and Hewitt 1994).

Loss of Math Confidence

An unsurprising result of all these interactions is that girls may begin to lose confidence in themselves, and especially in their ability to do math. A 1992 report issued by the American Association of University Women (AAUW) found that preteen girls are equal to boys in their confidence and performance in math, but that girls' confidence erodes steadily through secondary school. Other studies have found that girls often end up internalizing the messages from their parents and teachers and will attribute any success in mathematics to effort and blame a lack of ability for failure. Boys who fail, by contrast, tend to assume in general that they did not work hard enough, not that they do not have the ability (Eccles, Kaczala, and Meece 1982; Fennema and Sherman 1978).

It is particularly interesting to note that this drop in confidence does not parallel any actual drop in ability or even necessarily lower grades. Several studies have shown that girls and women tend to express lower opinions of their own math and science ability even when their performance is higher than that of boys and men (DeBoer 1986; Marsh, Smith, and Barnes 1985; Sax 1995; Sherman 1983). Boys and men, in turn, are more likely to believe themselves to be good at math and science even when their grades are the same or lower than girls' or women's. Indeed, in a comparison of undergraduate GPA's for bachelor's recipients, women averaged 3.17 in engineering and computer science to men's 2.96, and women's science and math GPA averaged 3.18 to men's 2.98 (Adelman 1991).

While it may not have a direct impact on grades earned, math confidence is still very important because "independent of ability, men and women with higher levels of mathematics confidence earn higher grades in college, earn higher GRE Quantitative test scores, and are more likely to pursue careers in science" (Astin and Sax 1996, 106).

Girls and young women who lack confidence in their ability to do math may shy away from math courses in high school and college. This this can be a serious setback to their progress because math skills are absolutely critical to successfully completing the journey toward a career in science and engineering (among other fields). Almost all undergraduate and graduate-level science and engineering programs require a minimum level of math skill for admission. Although it is challenging to do so, it is possible to pursue science and engineering by taking these courses later, as some of the women in this book did.

In many ways, appropriate socialization is required to equip people for their journey in science and engineering, and it should be clear that not everyone starts on equal footing. Many factors influence women in science and engineering once they decide they want to enter those fields, all of which overlap and influence each other, but it seems to us that there are a few categories of challenges that can be usefully identified.

The Lack of Critical Mass

Members of a minority group—and the group itself—are easily marginalized when their numerical presence in a given situation is low. In theory, as the size of the minority group increases, the quality of its relationship with the majority changes; eventually, the minority is able to organize, ensure its own continued presence in the situation, and have that presence accepted by the majority. Some claim that this shift occurs when the minority's numbers rise to at least 15 percent of the group in question. In practice, the dynamics of a small minority presence *are* different from a larger one, but it is rarely a smooth or simple transition to acceptance with increasing size (Etzkowitz et al., 1994).

The challenges accompanying minority status exist regardless of the relative position of the minority and majority groups in the wider society (for example, men in nursing might have these difficulties), but the problems are exacerbated when the group with low numbers is a traditional target of discrimination. Minority members may find themselves subject to increased visibility and scrutiny, but this extra attention rarely means added support. In contemporary American culture, minority members often face accusations of tokenism and—especially if they belong to a "protected class"—suggestions that their success results merely from affirmative action and not from individual merit.

Individuals belonging to a severely underrepresented group may also need to cope with feelings of isolation within the dominant culture. Isolation can be severely compounded for people who are "different" in more than one way—in terms of gender, race or ethnicity, age, socioeconomic background, sexual orientation, physical ability, and any other factor.

Individual reactions to isolation vary considerably. Some find it easiest to assimilate and mimic the dominant culture; others try fighting to be accepted for who they are, a response that may leave them with few resources to do the professional work they might like to do. Still others, like closeted lesbians, bisexuals, and gays, must spend enormous amounts of energy hiding their true identities and worrying about being discovered.

A lack of critical mass also means that members of a minority will lack a collective voice to urge changes in unfriendly policies. The dominant group, which frequently has an interest in maintaining the status quo, can steamroll over any reform effort that seems too threatening as long as those agitating for reform are present in only small numbers. Even when the members of a minority group are sufficiently numerous to exceed the critical threshold, its members may not have a large enough presence to tolerate internal diversity. No group of people is totally homogeneous. But to cultivate change effectively in an environment, a minority group must be large enough to accommodate differences in individual reactions to that environment and various ideas about how to best effect reform.

Discrimination against "Outsiders"

Although women and members of other minority groups have historically made many contributions to science and engineering, they have frequently done so from the margins and not as central, accepted players in their fields. The culture of science and engineering was developed by heterosexual white men, and those—including women—who do not fit the image that this dominant culture holds of itself are likely to encounter discrimination, even (and in some cases especially) if they are present in more than token numbers.

Science and engineering are highly social activities, and often a group of people will work together on a single project or several related ones. Everyone in a lab group, department, or institution may share the same physical resources, such as laboratory space and expensive equipment, and they often share funding from the same sources as well. When it comes time to start a new project, it is much easier to call on the person down the hall who has been using a needed technique on a different problem. Perhaps most importantly, colleagues provide an intellectual synergy that helps foster creativity.

This kind of interaction, of course, presupposes a certain level of cooperation and goodwill among the parties that unfortunately is not always forthcoming. Science can be very competitive, and those who do not mesh well with the dominant paradigms often have a harder time of it. As with the critical-mass problem, those who fall into more than one minority category may face compounded difficulties.

These can range from what Mary Rowe (1977) called "micro-inequities" to outright discrimination in hiring, salary awards, and promotions. The force of micro-inequities should not be underestimated. These are small day-to-day encounters and slights that, taken individually, seem barely worth fussing over but when compounded over time can become quite draining. Rowe also termed this the "mosquito bite problem." One mosquito bite is a small annoyance; a hundred mosquito bites become agonizing.

Women and other minorities may also be unable to find anyone willing to share hidden and rarely articulated information and norms of behavior that are nonetheless important (for example, how to get on the department head's good side, which journals to publish in, with whom to network, and what conferences to attend). The result can be that they do not find out about important events or funding sources or that they have no one to make introductions and help them establish necessary connections with colleagues. As Hollenshead et al. note (1996, 134), "significantly fewer women than men in science programs said they came to know one or more male faculty members well, or that at least one male faculty member treated them as a junior colleague." In many other ways, women and other minority members can be left out of the small day-to-day personal interactions that foster collegial alliances.

Getting due recognition for one's work can also be challenging. The difficulties are similar to those encountered in networking but also have a lot to do with cultural misunderstandings; those in power may not recognize success achieved by models different from their own. Peer evaluation is part of the culture of science, and lack of tolerance for a different style may be justified or rationalized by casting doubts on the value of work itself.

Differences in cultural expectations for different groups can lead to double standards where one person is penalized for the same action for which another is rewarded. For example, men who like to joke at work may be considered "great guys" while a woman engaging in the same behavior is considered flippant and incapable of being serious.

Double standards also apply when different groups receive very different rewards for the same actions. For example, the lack of domestic-partner benefits at many institutions means that lesbians, bisexuals, and gay men who have same-sex life partners are actually paid less than married heterosexual employees through the receipt of much smaller benefits packages. The discrepancy becomes worse if the employee's same-sex partner also has children who cannot be covered, as would be the case for the adopted children or stepchildren of heterosexual employees.

The latter example, of course, also shows how outgroup discrimination can operate in ways that are not at all subtle and can result in very real and tangible differences in the way different groups are treated, how much they earn, and where they can work.

Sexism

Women also face problems in the workplace simply because they are women; sexism also affects the lives of women in science and engineering. We could construct a parallel discussion about any other "-ism" (racism, heterosexism, able-ism, classism, and so on) that also impacts women. The gender-based problems women encounter in the workplace result from two main conflicts: the tension between social and sexual roles and professional interactions; and the conflict between women's perceived familial roles and their careers.

Women face many problems in trying to conduct collegial relationships with men who may view them as potential romantic partners or even as simple sex objects. The resulting difficulties range from simple misunderstandings through sexual harassment. Men may misinterpret normal collegial interaction as romantic or sexual overtures, or they may take an undue or inappropriate interest in a female colleague's personal life or sexual behavior.

These dynamics are quite different for lesbian and bisexual women. Depending on the level of sensitivity and understanding in their workplace, lesbians may find that their male colleagues do not relate to them as potential romantic or sexual partners, or, conversely, that they are singled out for harassment by men who find their lesbianism threatening and insist they "just haven't met the right man yet." (Usually the "right man" means the speaker.) Both lesbians and bisexual women may be subject to inappropriate curiosity about their sexual habits and practices, and bisexual women in particular may have to confront stereotypes about promiscuity from those who wrongly think that an openness to relationships with persons of either gender means "anything goes." All of this, of course, comes in addition to more general forms of homophobic discrimination.

Sexual harassment occurs when a coworker or superior makes unwanted and unwelcome sexual advances, and is particularly vicious when it involves elements of blackmail and unequal power. Sexual harassment can be a very isolating experience, rife with selfdoubt, especially when the victim must decide whether to pursue a formal complaint.

Women also face a greater risk of sexual assault than their male colleagues and so can be put at a disadvantage by work that requires them to tend experiments late at night in locations where building or grounds security is poor. They may also face more risk than men when doing fieldwork in remote or dangerous

locations. Unfortunately, the dangers involved in working in isolated environments can just as easily come from co-workers; there are accounts of harassment and even rape at remote field locations and aboard ocean research vessels—and to compound the problem, these incidents are sometimes used as justification for excluding women from these environments altogether.

Despite the fact that women can no longer be fired from their jobs simply for getting married or becoming pregnant, and despite changing attitudes about who should do what around the house, women are still viewed as primary caregivers for children and as primarily responsible for taking care of their homes. This creates several kinds of difficulty: First, some employers are still reluctant to hire or promote women with families on the assumption that their home commitments will make them less productive or less committed than male workers. Second, since many women *do* actually have greater needs for flexibility in balancing their professional and personal lives, they are put at a disadvantage by employers who do not have family-friendly policies. And there is the internal conflict and confusion about roles that women themselves must contend with as they attempt the necessary juggling acts.

Discouragement about the possibility of having both career and family can begin in the undergraduate years or even earlier, as young women encounter few role models to show them how it can be done. In graduate school, discouragement can become more overt, especially if women are trying to get married or have children as they pursue their degrees. As Etzkowitz et al. note (1992, 167), "marriage and children are generally viewed by male faculty as impediments to a scientific career for women." Once in the world of work, women may encounter odd misperceptions and double standards. Interestingly, although many employers still worry that women will get married or pregnant and quit, there is still no research showing that women voluntarily change employers more often than men (Vetter 1996).

Most professional women are married to other professionals, but only some men are in such marriages (Fox 1996). This means that women are much less likely than their male colleagues to have someone at home playing a supportive role, and instead are likely to assume primary housekeeping and childrearing duties themselves. Many women put in a full day at their workplace and then head home to put in more hours of hard work there. Women are also more likely than men to need time off to care for children, parents, or spouses; they certainly need time off for childbirth. They may be more interested in options such as part-time work, flextime, alternate tenure tracks, telecommuting, and other family-friendly work options, and be put at a disadvantage by employers who frown on such policies. Clearly women are not to blame for the fact that they face these challenges more often than men for in a truly equitable society, men would be equally responsible for family and work commitments.

Women may also suffer from guilt or confusion as they try to juggle careers and families. They may get a message from the workplace that having a family implies lack of commitment to the job; society often suggests that professional women make bad mothers. Although there is no evidence to support either claim, the myths surrounding them are pervasive.

While women in science and engineering confront many problems, most of these result from a single conflict: the fact that our culture's attitudes toward science and engineering and toward women have traditionally been incompatible. Not surprisingly, the culture of science and engineering has evolved as an inhospitable place for women. To date most efforts to change the situation have focused on helping women adjust to the "chilly climate." The slower progress of reform in recent years may suggest that this strategy has reached the limits of its usefulness. What we must do now is focus on institutional change—transforming the culture of educational and professional institutions so that all women, as well as all men, may easily find a home in science and engineering if they choose to do so.

While the challenges have been great throughout this century, many women have managed to have productive and fulfilling careers in science and engineering. The women in our book are among them. Indeed, the presence of women has expanded the knowledge base in some fields. In primatology, women's work redefined our understanding of behavior patterns from a focus on male-female or male-male relationships to a more inclusive perspective. In medicine, women's research has expanded to include women's health as a unique field of study. The numbers of women participating in these fields are still notably low and far from parity with men, but numerous women have transcended the odds to become scientists and engineers. We present many of their stories in our book. In those diverse journeys, however different their paths, difficult or easy, direct or tortuous, the predominant theme is one of the joy of doing the work, the satisfaction of intellectual challenge and achievement, the excitement of discovery, creation, and service, and the fulfillment of a good life's work.

Priscilla Auchincloss

Director, Program for Women in Science and Engineering,
and Research Associate, Department of Physics and Astronomy
UNIVERSITY OF ROCHESTER

Priscilla Auchincloss's current job reflects the family from which she came: her father was a medical researcher and physician, her mother a community leader in civil rights and feminist issues. Her Ph.D. in physics from Columbia University and her concern with women and climate issues in physics have led her down an alternate path from where she began—to what she finds is a more integrated and balanced life.

❧

My current position is twofold: I am director of the Program for Women in Science and Engineering at the University of Rochester and a research associate in the physics department. My professional background is in experimental high-energy physics. In my day-to-day work, much of my energy goes to women in science—teaching, advising, giving talks, writing grant proposals, and doing various funded and nonfunded projects. I want to help create the type of professional community that women want to join, and stay in, in order to enhance their lives. My interest is in revealing the "culture" of science—what we take for granted: its everyday interactions, professional practices and customs, unstated beliefs and myths— particularly as it affects the climate for women. I realize, however, that I could not do this work if I were not a physicist.

One of my earliest influences to go into science was my father, a medical doctor and researcher. My father thought of physics as "a beautiful subject." I recall how, in eighth or ninth grade, all the students in my class had to choose between Latin and science. Although my father never spoke to me about this, I believed that he wanted and expected me to take science, which I did. He often talked about his work in a reflective, philosophical way, and, through the example of his own life, he instilled in me a sense of responsibility to do meaningful work.

When later I pursued physics in college and graduate school, I was choosing my father's world over my mother's. My mother was actively involved in social issues, following in the footsteps of *her* mother, who had been a

Priscilla Auchincloss in her office at the Department of Physics and Astronomy at the University of Rochester, October 1995
PHOTO BY JAMES MONTANUS

feminist—an advocate of family planning and a community leader in upstate New York. My mother (along with my father) was intensely involved in the civil rights movement in Syracuse during the sixties. She was one of the few people there who bridged the gap between white upper-middle-class liberals and the African American community. A few years ago, she received public recognition for her contributions to the community. As a child, I couldn't understand what my mother did as a meaningful form of *work*. It was only much later that I understood the importance of my mother's efforts and her positive influence on my life. Now, after once making a decision not to do the sorts of things that women in my family had done, I find myself involved in the same issues. I have three sisters (no brothers), and we all carry this strong, female legacy though we work in very different areas.

When I started out in physics, I never envisioned myself doing what I'm doing now. But when I finished high school I didn't envision myself getting a Ph.D. in physics either. I studied modern dance intensively for several years, then writing, environmental science, and anthropology, and then gained a general (premedical) science background, before deciding to major in physics. Physics initially attracted me as a way of using my mind. I recognized that this was something that I wouldn't learn on my own and that it challenged me mentally. I think it also sparked in me an intense fascination with logical, analytical problem solving and held out the possibility of understanding how things really are at the most fundamental levels. In explaining what physics has meant to me I often return to an image of gazing upon "truth," simple, unadorned, gleaming, and beautiful. I felt my mind somehow at home in that place.

This was in college. At a certain point in graduate school, I began to feel that I was not really using my mind in physics, at least not creatively. I seemed (or felt myself to be) unable to achieve the level of mastery—of the concepts, the math, the jargon—that I thought would make my work and interac-

tions flow more easily. My long doctoral research project involved repeating a very fundamental measurement in particle physics, the rate at which neutrinos interact with protons and neutrons, revealing the inner quark structure of matter. I had a research adviser whom I respected, as well as a lively and friendly research collaboration. But I was a little older than my peers, my background was complicated and different (I was actually in the process of divorcing my first husband), and I was the only woman graduate student in my research group. On some level I was isolated; I just could not be "one of the guys." Now I can understand this in terms of the very male-identified culture of physics. I was fortunate to have women friends in other fields to talk to who could reflect back to me my strengths. And I was compelled to do a great deal of thinking about my situation; this is when I first began to analyze the culture of physics and how it might relate to the low numbers of women in science.

I received my Ph.D. from Columbia University in 1987 and began a postdoctoral fellowship working on the Collider Detector at Fermi National Accelerated Laboratory (CDF). During this period, I worked in the Level Three Trigger subgroup of CDF, developing an online parallel-processing component of the data acquisition apparatus. But I felt that I had reached a kind of dead end. The disjuncture between my image of attaining the "truth" in physics and the reality of my day-to-day life had become so great that there seemed to be no relation between them. I had lost the thread of why I was doing physics. I spent a great deal of time thinking and writing, researching my own life for clues to what was important to me and what work I wanted to do in the world. I also came into contact with other women who were asking the same questions, and also with several wise women who helped me begin to sort out the answers. Eventually I understood that I had made a great personal investment in physics, but I needed to take it in a different direction than pure research.

I came to the University of Rochester as a

research associate in January 1989. I managed the high-energy physics group's computer system, and the following fall I resurrected and taught a physics course called Energy and Environment. I also began meeting with a group of graduate women. They were interested in articulating the larger issues behind some of the demoralizing experiences they were encountering in graduate school, like speaking up in class and being ignored, and then having a male student say exactly the same thing and receive an enthusiastic response from the professor. From these discussions we began to identify a set of issues, and, with input from the college's intercessor on sexual harassment, we discovered that they fit a pattern that even had a label, as the "chilly climate" for women. Working with the graduate women, the intercessor, and Arie Bodek (chair of the physics department's teaching-assistant training committee), I coordinated a classroom-climate workshop that was integrated into the department's annual teaching assistant (TA) training program. This workshop was one of the first anywhere to try to raise instructors' awareness of the classroom climate; the theory was being applied in a practical setting. Working with graduate women has continued to be one of the most productive aspects of my work, and I have witnessed how women have been helped to survive graduate school by discussing their issues in a group.

The following year, I applied for and won a Congressional Science Fellowship from the American Physical Society (APS). This came as the fulfillment of a wish to take my physics background in the direction of social issues. I moved with my fiancé and two of his three then-teenaged children to Washington, D.C., and worked for one year on the staff of Representative Louise Slaughter, Democrat from the New York congressional district that includes most of Rochester. I was particularly interested in energy policy, which brought physics together with environmental, security, and economic issues. The year 1991 turned out to be very active for energy issues, from the Persian Gulf War and burning oil

fields to major energy legislation that tried to balance coal and oil industry interests, taxpayer opposition to gasoline taxes, wilderness protection, and global warming concerns. In Slaughter's office, I also covered telecommunications, animal issues, and technological competitiveness, all new areas for me, as well as the Superconducting Supercollider, to which opposition was beginning to rise. The fellowship provided an amazing opportunity to observe the U.S. government at close range, and from this experience I learned many valuable lessons about politics—in government, in the office, and in life generally. Having been a fellow has brought opportunities of its own, such as serving on the APS Panel on Public Affairs.

When I returned to Rochester, I received a grant from the National Science Foundation (NSF) for a project called "Improving Academic Climate for Women in Science and Engineering." I had the sense that my women-and-science work was taking on a life of its own; that was what people wanted to hear more about and where they wanted to see more happen. The main objectives of the project were to expand the TA training program, to "export" the climate training to other science departments, and to figure out how to work with science faculty on climate issues. The work sponsored by the grant yielded long-term results: the climate (now also called "gender equity") workshop was permanently integrated into the TA training program, the TA program was expanded, and the Program for Women in Science and Engineering was established. There were intangible results from the experience as well. In this first grant, things didn't always go the way I thought they would, and I learned a great deal from the varied forms of resistance I encountered.

Not surprisingly, my experiences with women and climate issues in physics and science also took me in the direction of women's studies. In the spring of 1992, an English professor, Lisa Cartwright, and I began jointly to create a course called Science, Gender, and Culture, which we taught in spring 1993.

Working on this course was my first exposure to feminist approaches to science. Feminist scholars weren't asking, "Why aren't there more women in science?" but rather, "Is science truly gender neutral?" This question disturbed me because of my long "indoctrination" into the world of physics. Like most physicists, I believed that the neutrality (closely related to the objectivity) of science was beyond question, and I tended to view any suggestion that science was not neutral as either misunderstanding science or simply antiscience. But the question also intrigued me as an opening to a perspective that might explain parts of my experience. So a transformation in my thinking began to take place. Now, after a few years of reading and teaching in women's studies—I currently teach Women and Gender in the History of Science, which evolved from the original course—I can still think like a physicist, but I cannot help but be aware of and question the human choices and value judgments guiding what physicists look at and how they think. Scientists tend to think that they are simply posing questions to nature and reporting nature's replies; they disown the human agency and the possibility of a human agenda in science. Feminist and other social studies of science have shown how very problematic the idea of the objective position or method really is. I believe that scientists can use this perspective to examine critically some of the ideas about science that have been taken for granted, and the links to such human agendas as power and control. It is through this kind of questioning, I think, that science will develop and grow.

A student of mine once wrote in a letter that she was amazed that a person of my intellectual breadth could focus all of it into one specialized area. It was a very insightful remark. An older woman whom I regard as a mentor once told me something similar: "You are very interdisciplinary." She also encouraged me to explore women and science. I've often felt that her belief in me allowed me to take steps into this territory before I knew that there would be ground under my feet.

If I had to say why it is necessary—not only for women, but maybe especially for women—to pay attention to the culture and climate of science, it comes down to this: to the extent that you can truly be yourself, at home in mind, body, and soul, that is the extent to which you can access all your creativity. And that is the extent to which you can contribute and be productive and engaged. This applies in work and relationships, and it's a lesson that I've had to learn several times, in different ways. In spite of my original wish to focus all my energy in physics, my experience was not one of being "at home" there. When posed as a question of how much of myself I would have had to leave behind in order to do only pure physics, my choices have become clearer. In taking a different path, I have had a sense of reclaiming my mind and using it creatively. Women's studies has enabled me to see the same human imagination and artfulness running through the sciences as well as the humanities; these divisions might be labeled the scientific and humanistic "arts."

My husband, Arie Bodek, has helped me tremendously to maintain a very complex and interesting life both professionally and at home, where I have been a stepmother to his children and now am mother to our son, Avi. My husband, a professor of physics, and I work in the same department and often on the same projects. He has always supported the work I've done with women in science, usually by getting involved and incorporating the ideas into projects to make the department stronger, like the TA training program. At home, we share equally in the cooking, housework, and raising of Avi (now three and a half). Dual careers coupled with responsibility for a small child is stressful by definition, but I love having a child and learn so much from him, and from the experience of being a mother.

At this stage of my life and career, I look behind me and see my path stretching backward and there is much physics in it. But this woman on the path, is she a scientist? If so, it must be of a different kind from what I thought I would become when I started on this path, the kind I looked up to and learned from and meant to model myself after. The task seems to be to integrate the different parts of my life that sometimes seem to pull me in different directions—a search for nature's "truth," the necessity of attending to issues of gender, the reality of being a mother and wanting to spend time with my son.

I can see the values that my parents shared and continue to cultivate. They didn't talk about personal integration, though now I can see the balance my father has maintained in his life along with the focused dedication to his patients and research that I remember from my childhood. He is an accomplished pianist who has practiced and played all his life, and in retirement he has taken up the lute. He keeps up with politics and continues to reflect deeply on world events. My mother reads broadly and remains as active in women's rights as she can. As I look at my parents today, the integration seems to lie in finding ways to live out what they believed was important or necessary. My parents passed their personal values—their choices about what was important and necessary—along to me, together with something about defining values through patient cultivation and lived, real-life involvement. And this is something that I hope to pass along to my child.

PRESENT POSITION: Research Associate, Department of Physics and Astronomy, and Director, Program for Women in Science and Engineering, University of Rochester

FIELDS: Experimental high-energy physics; women in science

RESEARCH AREAS: Neutrino physics, programs for women in science

EDUCATION: B.A. in Physics (1977), New York University; Ph.D. in Physics (1987), Columbia University

DATE/PLACE OF BIRTH: March 8, 1952/Syracuse, New York

Priscilla Auchincloss lives in Rochester, New York, with her husband, Arie Bodek, and three-year-old son, Avi, and with intermittent visits from Arie's three children, Haim, Esther, and Aviva.

INTERVIEW DATE: January 1995

W. Lena Austin

Associate Professor of Microbiology, College of Medicine
HOWARD UNIVERSITY

Lena Austin married and had a child at fifteen, lost her husband at twenty-six, and earned a Ph.D. in botany and mycology at thirty-five. She specializes in diseases caused by fungi. Austin calls her mother her inspiration and credits her success in large part to a family who always supported and believed in her. It was her mother who taught her not to focus on racism or sexism, and who encouraged her to follow her dreams.

❧

Most people have never heard of my area of expertise. I am a medical mycologist—I specialize in diseases that are caused by fungi. Many of the diseases I study or observe are found in young people, and they sometimes cause aesthetically displeasing results: fungal infections such as ringworm of the scalp, ringworm of the feet or athlete's foot, jock itch, cutaneous fungal infections of the toenails and fingernails, and *tinea versicola,* a disease that causes spots on the face or other parts of the body. When fungal diseases afflict persons with AIDS, they become life threatening.

My research focuses on spore-wall development in one group of fungi called the ascomycetes. The name of the particular organism is *neurospora*. The spore wall has several components, including ribs (raised off the surface) and veins (valleys). I'm studying the rib-vein component of the ascospore wall of neurospora to determine development forces that cause the ribs and the veins to form. We've done the critical observations using brightfield scanning and transmission electron microscopy. The wall of the spore is made up of more than the rib and vein layer; we're now trying to determine when the other walls form and then get into the molecular biology of spore-wall formation. At one point we also studied the spore wall in an organism that causes meningitis, *Cryptococcus neoformans*. This organism is an opportunistic pathogen that can survive in vivo for long periods.

I am a teacher as well as a researcher, and I function as a teacher at various levels. I currently have a grant from the National Science

Lena Austin, 1995

Foundation that funds a Young Scholars Program for thirty gender-paired eighth and ninth graders from Prince Georges County, Maryland. We introduce the students to medicine, microbiology, and medical mycology. They spend time in the microbiology lab at the Medical College here at Howard University, they have experiences in the computer lab, they are introduced to methods of research, and they go on field trips to places such as the laboratories at the National Zoo and the U.S. Department of Agriculture. Recently we took the students on a field trip to see where and how the American hot-weather cow is bred. This animal is a cross between a Jersey cow (a good milk producer) and a Brahma bull (which can withstand heat); it can both withstand heat and give milk. We have completed the second year of the program, so we now have sixty students. We recently held a symposium supported by the National Institute of Immunology and Aging called "Science in Our Lives," in which all sixty children participated. The topics ranged from ethnic diseases like type II diabetes to genetic disorders like Tay-Sachs disease. Many of my colleagues at Howard give generously of their time to talk with these students and show them their labs. The students have also visited the Franklin Institute in Philadelphia. We plan to keep in touch with these students throughout their high school careers. In addition to my precollege program, I also have a program for teachers. We train mentor teachers to help others who teach science in grades four through eight. And, of course, in any given semester I teach medical mycology to pharmacy, nursing, and medical students.

I was always interested in science. I grew up in MacClenny, Florida, surrounded by farms and farm animals, and became interested in animal behavior at an early age. I used to feed horses and cows, and they would follow me because of that. Even though I swore to my mother that I wasn't feeding them, she knew that I was because of the animals' behavior when I was around. As I grew older, I became more curious. My mother was always

my inspiration. When I was in fourth or fifth grade and learned about the planets, I would say, "When I get up to Mars, the people there won't look horrible because I'll be the best doctor," and my mom would say, "Yes, you'll be the best doctor." I was the oldest in the family, and my mom encouraged me, my two sisters, and my brother to do well academically. My sister is the director of music at a high school in Jacksonville, Florida; my brother is an astrophysical engineer; and my other sister, who died, was a playwright and thespian. My mother believed in me, and she was always my most tenacious supporter. I had my first child at age fifteen, and this did not stop my mother from continuing to say what she had always said: "You can" and "You will." She never took no for an answer. My family had no great financial legacy to give us, but they gave us everything else!

My mother always worked outside the home. I remember her leaving for work at 4 A.M. to clean offices, coming home to get us off to school, and then going to her other job at Sears, Roebuck and Company. My father had very little education, but he was a very, very smart man. He worked construction, and he could do more with a level or trowel than my brother could do with all his fancy equipment. My father became a foreman when he was almost sixty, and they always called him when things needed to be done. He never got the recognition he deserved, probably because he was a black man. That's just the way it was then. Thank goodness, my parents survived through all of the adversity they had to endure to give us a lasting legacy.

My maternal grandmother was also a remarkable woman. She was blind, but she taught us to read. Her parents were slaves, and she was born right after slavery. She was the youngest child and part of the first generation of black people to go to school. She learned to read from a book called the *Blue Back Speller,* a book that has been passed down through the generations in my family. It used phonics to teach spelling. She remembered the stories in the book and taught us to

Lena Austin being presented the Kaiser Permanente Outstanding Teacher Award by Charles H. Epps, Jr., M.D., Dean of the College of Medicine, Howard University, November 1992

PHOTO BY JEFFREY JOHN FEARING

read from it. She, too, was a great inspiration in my life. My paternal grandmother made me feel like I was a princess all of the time. I think I was richer than most; I had love and encouragement.

All of my teachers were encouraging. I was a highly motivated student, and they responded in kind. My sixth-grade math teacher stands out in my mind. She's the reason I like science and math today. I had many women teachers who served as inspirations to me, and since teaching was an acceptable profession for black women in the South, originally that was my plan. I attended Florida Agricultural and Mechanical University (Florida A & M) and earned degrees in biology and chemistry, thinking that eventually I might go to medical school. After college I taught algebra, chemistry, and biology for a few years and earned a medical technologist degree to make money to fund my graduate education. I couldn't be in the regular program because I was black; I had to do all my work at a predominantly black hospital. However, the pathologist, Lela Wells, was a white woman who gave me the same lectures individually that she gave the white students. She was a good person, and I've never forgotten her generosity.

I remember once, when I was working in Dr. Wells's lab, saying that I'd like to go to graduate school. One of the lab technicians said to me, "I think you're making about as much money as you'll ever make being a black woman, so you might as well stay here." Well, there was the challenge. That technician did more for me than anyone else, without even knowing it! The one graduation notice I sent out when I finished my Ph.D. was to that technician.

I received the Ph.D. from Atlanta University in Atlanta, Georgia. My postdoctoral experiences include two years of specialty training in medical mycology at the Medical College of Virginia in Richmond, three years as a fellow in the National Institute of Dental Research (a part of the National Institutes of Health) specializing in teratogenesis of mycotoxins, and follow-up postdoctoral work at the U.S. Army Institute of Chemical Defense in Edgewood, Maryland. I came to Howard University for the second time in 1983 as an associate professor. The professor with whom I worked more closely, Lafayette Frederick, was, in a word, wonderful; he had patience and truly believed in my ability. He reminded me of my mother; he had expectations of me, and I rose to those. I simply didn't have a choice. At times graduate school was difficult, and I used to think that no matter what I'd do in life, when I died I'd go to heaven because it couldn't get any worse than this. Ann Frederick, Dr. Frederick's wife, was so very kind to me and the children. She really made things pleasant. She was a kind of mother away from home.

I was married at fifteen, and my husband died when I was twenty-six. He drowned in a river in which we had played all our lives. One of his friends accidentally dropped his wallet in the river, and my husband, of course, tried to help the friend by diving into the water to get the wallet. What he didn't know was that there were several underwater cables in that area; his feet got entangled in the cables, and he drowned before he could be rescued.

My husband and I had one child together. I raised our child throughout high school and college, with the help of my mother. Then, when I was in graduate school, my sister died and I raised her child as well. When I look back at what I accomplished under those circumstances, I realize how young and naive I was. The thought of it scares me now, but it didn't at the time. Our vacations consisted of taking the kids to scientific meetings where I would be giving a research paper. I'd put them in the back of the old car I had at the time and drive to wherever the meeting was. I do the same thing now with my grandchildren. I have two grandchildren in a school of performing arts who have appeared at the Kennedy Center.

I would be naive to say that prejudices because of my sex and race haven't had some impact on my life. But my feeling has always been that prejudice is the other person's problem, not mine. I once told an entomology professor of mine, who was white, that I would not

have lasted long as a slave: I would have used all of my energy and wit to outsmart the slave owner. That's my personality. I'm not going to let anyone deter me from anything I want to do. I can't linger on things like racism and sexism; my mother taught us that focusing on this was unhealthy and counterproductive. I wasn't going to let those kinds of attitudes stop me from achieving my goals. I'm from a small southern town, and while we knew there were certain things we couldn't do, we often got around them. In fact, it made us smarter with a seventh sense. There was a park in town that blacks couldn't go to when I was a little girl, but my mother used to dress us up in our finest clothes and we'd walk around the park looking at the flowers. It was her way of saying you are more beautiful than any flower that could be grown in that park. I believe her more today than yesterday.

I enjoy working at Howard. I'm a southerner through and through. I only wandered from the South once, when I spent a winter in Massachusetts—and that was enough! Besides the weather, I was not comfortable with the hypocrisy. In the South I know what I'm up against, and I can fight fires that I can see.

PRESENT POSITION: Associate Professor of Microbiology, College of Medicine, Howard University

FIELD: Medical mycology

RESEARCH AREAS: Spore wall development in the sordariaceous fungi, teratogenicity of mycotoxins

EDUCATION: B.S. in Biology and Chemistry (1960), Florida Agricultural and Mechanical University; Ph.D. in Botany and Mycology (1973), Atlanta University

DATE/PLACE OF BIRTH: March 24, 1938/ MacClenny, Florida

Lena Austin currently lives in Pepper Mill Village, Maryland.

INTERVIEW DATE: October 1995

Judith Badner

Fellow, Psychiatric Genetics
NATIONAL INSTITUTE OF MENTAL HEALTH

Judith Badner works both as a practicing psychiatrist and as a researcher, using statistics to look for genes that contribute to the development of psychiatric conditions. Her initial interest in genetics arose from reading about her own genetic condition— achondroplastic dwarfism—in junior high school. She attended MIT as an undergraduate and earned M.S. and Ph.D. degrees in genetics and an M.D. from the University of Pittsburgh.

☙

I was born in Washington, D.C., in 1960, the third of three children. My father was a meteorologist, and he worked for the government; my mother was a weather observer before they were married and stayed home once she had children. I was born with achondroplastic dwarfism and had numerous developmental delays growing up—slow to walk, slow to talk. I am forty-seven inches tall and appear very different because of my unusual proportions—large head, short arms and legs, and average-sized trunk. I don't have any current medical problems related to my dwarfism, but as a child I had multiple surgeries on my ears and some on my legs as well. I attended the Easter Seal Center and then a Montessori school from ages four through nine; the rest of my education was in the Montgomery County (Maryland) public school system. While at the Easter Seal Center, I was diagnosed as mentally retarded. They rescinded the diagnosis as my hearing problems were corrected and my development progressed.

As a child I read a lot. My interest in science was heightened in junior high when I de-cided I wanted to learn more about my dwarfism. I started reading books on genetics and medicine. The form of dwarfism I have is genetic, although I am the only dwarf in my family. If I chose to have biological children, there is a 50 percent chance I would pass the dwarfism on. As a result of my reading, I knew I wanted some kind of career in science.

I went to MIT for my undergraduate degree in biology. I chose MIT because at the time I wanted to study both math and genetics and MIT had very good programs in both. I also knew several people who went to MIT, and they recommended it highly. But I was very nervous when I arrived. I heard someone say that "90 percent of MIT freshmen believe they are going to be in the top 10 percent of their class." Well, I was one of the 10 percent who did not believe that. College was difficult, but I got through with a pretty average

Judith Badner at age two, 1962
PHOTO BY JULIUS BADNER

*Judith Badner in her office at the National
Institute of Mental Health, 1995*
PHOTO BY ELIOT GERSHON, M.D.

(for MIT) performance. I did better in terms of grades in graduate school.

I applied to go to medical school after college, but I didn't get in the first time, probably due to my college grades but also perhaps due to my dwarfism. At the time there was only one other dwarf who had gone to medical school. I then decided to go to graduate school to study genetics, and I enrolled in the master's program at the University of Pittsburgh. In my second year of graduate school, I reapplied to medical school and was accepted by the University of Pittsburgh. I completed my M.S. degree in human genetics in two years and started medical school. Initially, I was in the straight M.D. program. I did want to go back to graduate school and get my Ph.D., but I didn't think I could afford it; I was taking out a lot of loans for medical school, and at that time, the Pittsburgh M.D./Ph.D program was not funded. But I unexpectedly received a large inheritance and substantial assistance from Pennsylvania Vocational Rehabilitation. The combi-

nation paid for my last three years of medical school. So, after my second year of medical school, I went back to graduate school for two years and completed my Ph.D. in human genetics, and then I completed my last two years of medical school. This all occurred between 1984 and 1990.

All of the institutions I attended were very supportive of women, including the hospital where I served my residency. There were lots of women in my classes, and so I never felt isolated or at a disadvantage because I was a woman. There were times when my dwarfism was a disadvantage, like doing surgery in medical school when everything I needed was out of reach, but in general the schools I attended and the National Institute of Mental Health (NIMH), where I now work, have been very accommodating. NIMH recently redesigned my office because initially everything I needed was stored in high places; now everything is much more accessible. My workplace and my apartment have been adapted to my height with a lot of low furniture and stepstools. I have also found most people to be very positive and accepting.

The focus of my research is statistical genetics. I work with derivation of equations and statistical analysis. My thesis project was studying Hirschsprung's disease, which is aganglionic megacolon. The disease is a lack of nerve cells in the large intestine and occasionally in the small intestine, a condition that is present at birth and reduces gut motility, causing severe constipation. Surgery is frequently required to correct this condition, which can be fatal if untreated. I studied how the condition was transmitted within families and how many genes might be involved in its development. After I finished my degrees, I did a four-year psychiatry residency at McLean Hospital, a Harvard-affiliated hospital in Boston. I wanted to do medicine because I loved science, but I also wanted to work with people, and psychiatry fit the bill. Psychiatric genetics—the genetics of psychiatric conditions—was a relatively new field at this time, and it looked exciting to me.

After residency I joined the National Institute of Mental Health, where I am a senior staff fellow. There are multiple branches within NIMH; I am in the clinical neurogenetics branch, which is made up of several different divisions: the statistical division (where I work), two molecular genetics labs, and a social work division, which does the patient recruiting and interviewing. I work both as a psychiatrist—seeing patients, doing therapy, prescribing medications—and as a researcher on the statistical aspects of looking for genes that contribute to the development of psychiatric conditions. We study families where several members are affected with the same psychiatric condition like bipolar disorder, schizophrenia, or panic. We interview as many members of the family as possible, make diagnoses, and then collect blood specimens. We look at their DNA to see whether there is any association between the genes they are transmitting and their condition.

Prior to my coming to work with this group, they found evidence of a linkage between one of the genes contributing to the development of bipolar disorder and chromosome 18. The actual gene was not found. My work uses statistical methods to try to narrow down the region on chromosome 18 where the actual gene might be. I have also been involved in looking at other chromosomes to identify regions where other genes contributing to the development of bipolar disorder might be.

A lot of my work is independent, but it is carried out in collaboration with others. For example, other people obtain the molecular data, and I do the statistical analysis. Sometimes I use computer programs that someone else has written to do formal analysis or, if there isn't a computer program to do what I want it to do, I write my own.

My work days run from about nine o'clock in the morning to five-thirty or six o'clock at night. On the weekends I spend a lot of time with my family, especially my nieces and nephews. My mother and both my siblings and their families live in the area. When my nieces visit me, we play computer games, watch videos, paint, and draw. My nine-year-old niece is high-functioning autistic, and she often likes to play the same games over and over again. My seven-year-old niece is extremely creative and likes to do a lot of role playing or acting things out with dolls. With the rest of the family, we go shopping together and out to restaurants. My sister (the mother of my nieces and sixteen-year-old nephew) and I are very active on computer lists for autism and have made friends with quite a few autistic adults. Periodically, one of them will come to visit, and my sister and I will entertain them.

I still read a lot, especially fiction. I used to read for information; now I read for escape. I particularly like John Irving, Anne Tyler, Stephen King, Anne Rice, and Erica Jong. I also like reading about disability issues and patients' rights.

In the very near future I plan to adopt a child, hopefully a child with dwarfism. Little People America has an adoption committee that identifies children with dwarfism who are available. I have always wanted children and sometime when I was a teenager decided I would rather adopt a child with dwarfism than have biological children. I decided now would be a good time to consider adoption because I am more financially secure than I have ever been. I believe I could be a very nurturing and supportive parent, especially to a child with dwarfism. Balancing a career with parenting will be difficult, but I know many women who have been successful at it, so it is doable. The place I work now is very supportive of people raising children. I'm hopeful and excited about the prospect of having a child.

PRESENT POSITION: Fellow, Psychiatric Genetics, National Institute of Mental Health

FIELD: Psychiatric genetics

RESEARCH AREAS: Statistical aspects of psychiatric conditions; genetic epidemiology of psychiatric conditions

EDUCATION: B.S. in Biology (1982), Massachusetts Institute of Technology; M.S. in Human Genetics (1985), University of Pittsburgh; Ph.D. in Human Genetics (1988), University of Pittsburgh; M.D. (1990), University of Pittsburgh; Psychiatry Residency (1990–94), McLean Hospital, Boston.

DATE/PLACE OF BIRTH: May 22, 1960/Washington, D.C.

Judith Badner currently lives in Silver Spring, Maryland.

INTERVIEW DATE: November 1995

Eleanor Baum

Dean of Engineering
THE COOPER UNION

Eleanor Baum rebelled against societal norms dictating very limited career choices for young women: secretary, teacher, or nurse. She became an electrical engineer, despite her mother's alarm that "no one will marry you" and her guidance counselor's warning that "no one will hire you." Neither fate materialized: Baum married and worked in the aerospace industry after earning her Ph.D.; she then moved into academe at the Pratt Institute, where she was a faculty member, department head, and dean. In 1987 she became dean of engineering at The Cooper Union in New York City.

❧

I was born in Poland; my family left at the beginning of World War II. My father owned a rubber factory in the part of Poland that had been invaded by the Russians. Through strategically placed bribes, he found out when the Russians were coming to arrest "the capitalist." Arrest would have meant being sent to Siberia, and it was impossible to get visas to other countries due to the war. So my father sat down with an atlas, identified a small and distant country, made a stamp, and created a visa in order to leave Poland. He picked Curaçao, hoping that the border guards would have never seen a visa from there and wouldn't question the authenticity of the document. He also picked Curaçao because he spoke French, having gone to college in France. He didn't realize that Curaçao was Dutch, but neither did the border guards. We couldn't travel through Europe because we are Jewish and the Nazis had already begun their push across the continent, so we headed toward Russia. We sneaked out of Poland in the middle of the night, crossing the border in a farmer's wagon covered with hay; they had me, an infant, drugged so I wouldn't cry. My father was wanted by the communists. We traveled first to Vladivostok and then to Japan, where my father was able to get visas to Canada; ours was the last ship of refugees to leave Japan before Pearl Harbor. We ended up in Quebec because my parents knew French, and we stayed there until they learned English. I was three years old when we came to New York. We were very lucky, and luck has followed me my whole life.

Eleanor Baum in her lab at The Cooper Union for the Advancement of Science and Art, August 1987
PHOTO BY GREG SCHALER

Although I was an infant and toddler throughout the ordeal, this history affects the way I think and the way I am. My parents taught me never to take things for granted, that the world can turn upside down in a minute, and that, whatever happens, I should be independent, strong, and able to take care of myself. It's always been very important for me to know that I can take care of myself and my family.

I went through the New York public school system and was a very good student. When I was a senior in high school, the choices for girls were clear: you were supposed to become a secretary, or go to college and become a teacher or a nurse. Young women didn't think in terms of careers but in terms of getting a job until you got married and pregnant. Then you spent the rest of your life taking care of your husband and children, deriving your pleasure from their achievements. That's the way it was supposed to be. I took some advanced math and science courses in high school because they sounded kind of interesting; I didn't find them particularly easy, but I did well. The guys in the class talked about becoming engineers. I had always been a good kid, a rule follower; but my mother was driving me crazy with notes on my pillow about the joys of motherhood and the benefits of becoming a school teacher. One day I rebelled and announced that I was going to be an engineer. My mother turned green and said, "You can't do that; no one will marry you!" When I told the school guidance counselor the same thing, his answer was, "No one will hire you; that's not a job for women." I resolved at that moment that someone would hire me because I was going to be a very good engineer.

I went to City College in New York because my father thought it was foolish to pay tuition at a private school when City College was free and had a good reputation. I liked the idea of engineering not only because it provided a form of rebellion but because I would be able to work in the field after four years, and I wasn't all that crazy about school. Actually, the program was a five-year program, but I took classes in the summers to get

out as fast as I could. My college experience was not terrific: the school at the time was insensitive and unsupportive, I felt very conspicuous, and was made to feel that way. I was the only woman in most of my electrical engineering classes. The examples used in many of my classes to explain concepts were based on things that I didn't relate to at all: a lot of explanations centered around how cars work. The assumption was that everyone had worked with their hands and knew how machinery operated. If I didn't understand something, the teachers generalized it to "all women" and concluded that there were certain things women didn't understand and that was why they shouldn't be engineers. Everyone was always overly interested in what grades I was getting.

When I graduated in 1959 I got a job in the aerospace industry on Long Island, but I was quickly bored with the job. Those were the days of cost-plus contracts when companies hired engineers to do work for which they were overqualified because the government paid their salaries. I sat with red and yellow pencils making drawing changes; it was ghastly. I decided to go back to graduate school to get a master's degree and be assured of interesting engineering work.

I went back to graduate school at City College, and soon after they got a call from what was then Brooklyn Polytechnic University; Brooklyn Polytech had just received new fellowship and scholarship money through the National Defense Education Act. They had already given out existing fellowships and scholarships to everyone who qualified, and they needed a recommendation of people to whom to award new scholarships. None of the faculty were around, but the secretary who answered the inquiry remembered me and gave them my name, and I received a fellowship. To my surprise, I discovered it was a fellowship to work toward a Ph.D.; I had never thought in terms of getting a doctorate, but I figured what the heck. My mother was very concerned about my pursuing a Ph.D.; not only was I an engineer but now, in her mind, I was becoming overeducated and the pool of suitable men was decreasing fast.

Tony Giordano, a wonderful mentor and friend, was the dean of the graduate school at Brooklyn Poly during my graduate years. One of the things he did that really changed my life was to insist that graduate students teach a course. Up to this point I had rebelled and suffered in order *not* to teach, but when I got up in front of a class I absolutely loved it.

A few Poly faculty members adopted the attitude that I was taking away the place of some man because they assumed I would never use my degree, and they were discouraging, even vicious; but others compensated for them by being incredibly supportive and encouraging. All in all, graduate school was a positive experience for me, and I even proved my mother wrong: I *did* find someone to marry. Paul was getting a Ph.D. in physics from the University of Illinois, so we had a long-distance romance. He finished before I did, moved to New York, got a job in the aerospace industry, and we married while I was still in graduate school. I was very pregnant when I walked across the stage to receive my Ph.D.

Paul had no problem with my working; he always knew it was what I had planned to do. But his mother was quite upset. She felt it was embarrassing, that it sent a message to the whole world that Paul couldn't support me. She also believed that it was a terrible thing to do to children. I had a great housekeeper who stayed with us almost eighteen years, and she made my life much easier. But I lived with guilt for many years, guilt that was reinforced, or maybe precipitated by, societal standards reflected in magazines, newspapers, television, and people's attitudes. I was made to feel like a terrible person. Part of the way I dealt with my guilt was to overcompensate. When I came home I didn't even read the newspaper because I needed to spend as much time as possible with my two daughters. Interestingly enough, both of my adult daughters feel that their childhoods were wonderful and don't ever remember resenting my work.

Happily, the women's movement came along, and suddenly a new level of consciousness was raised by many of the women I knew who were at-home moms or worked in traditional jobs. The women's movement caused marital upheavals for some of our friends; there were a lot of divorces at the time. For me, this period was much easier because I had been working and our marriage was already more of a partnership.

I spent a few years in the aerospace industry after my Ph.D., working on classified research, mostly inertial guidance systems. Electrical engineering is a wonderfully diverse field: I started off doing control guidance systems for airplanes, moved to clean-air electric vehicles, and then to electric power generation. One of my biggest concerns has always been giving this technological society what it needs in a way that doesn't harm the environment.

Eventually both Paul and I wound up at universities—I at Pratt Institute and Paul at Queens College. We actually halved our salaries to do this, but I loved teaching and we both liked the flexibility of university life—we had two kids at this time. Together we were able to stagger our hours and handle crises with the children. In those days, I took summers off to spend with the girls.

The School of Engineering at Pratt was small, and at the time we did wonderful things in minority education. Pratt is located in New York City, just outside of the Bedford-Stuyvesant neighborhood. The school had a very deep commitment to helping disadvantaged New York City students escape poverty by becoming engineers. We took a chance on students with low high school GPAs—nurturing, tutoring, helping in any way we could; and we did retain a lot of students, many of whom became fine engineers. This was one of the best things I've done in my professional life. I was at Pratt for nearly twenty years, rising from assistant professor to department head to dean, and I loved the school; I used to think that the only way I'd leave Pratt was in a white pine box, but it didn't happen that way. In 1987, I was convinced to accept the position of dean at The Cooper Union.

The Cooper Union is a fully endowed university with free tuition. Every student who comes here, independent of need, gets a full scholarship. When I started in 1987, we had about 7 percent women students; we are now up to 30 percent. We've also gone from almost no minority students to 11 percent. I'm very proud of this accomplishment. Diversity in engineering is important, not only because it's the right thing to do but because it enhances creativity to mix different kinds of people together on a team. That's why design today is done by teams of people who often represent different disciplines. We also focus strongly on clarifying the connection between engineering and the condition of society. We're involved in a lot of interdisciplinary projects that focus on improving life in New York City: biomedical, infrastructure, and environmental projects, for example. This is what makes engineering so wonderful—it's more than just an intellectual puzzle; you have an opportunity to make the world a bit better.

As a dean, I have varying responsibilities: I oversee the college's education and research programs, I am an ambassador for my institution to the outside world, I serve on corporate boards, and I travel a lot. I have traveled to Australia to advise colleges and universities on how to encourage more women to consider engineering and science careers, to Russia as part of a National Science Foundation team to look for potential areas for joint university research and cooperation, to China on a task force on reciprocity in credentialing engineers, and to Japan to discuss U.S.-Japan engineering education. I draw on many skills in my current job (some of which engineering students often don't view as important): problem solving, writing, speaking, and, at times, my "mommy" skills. I don't manage so much as establish partnerships with people; that, I think, is one of my strengths. I also use humor a lot to diffuse potentially explosive situations.

There have always been fundamental things that are more important to me than money and promotions: personal happiness, my children, my husband, and doing something useful for society. I'm very tied to New York City because my mother and Paul's, both in their eighties, and my children live here. I love this city and find it a vibrant, exciting place to work and live.

Neither of my daughters was interested in science or engineering: one has a degree in anthropology and works in the hotel management business, and the other teaches first grade. She married right out of college and then decided to get a master's degree in education so that she could teach and be home at three o'clock for her children. It's funny how the world goes around: I rebelled against that exact scenario when there weren't many acceptable career options for women, and she choose it as one of many.

PRESENT POSITION: Dean of Engineering, Cooper Union

FIELD: Electrical engineering

SPECIALTY: Systems and controls

EDUCATION: B.S. in Electrical Engineering, City University of New York; Ph.D. in Electrical Engineering, Brooklyn Polytechnic University

PLACE OF BIRTH: Vilna, Poland (now Vilnius, Lithuania)

Eleanor Baum lives with her husband, Paul, in New York City.

INTERVIEW DATE: July 1995

Susan H. Brawley

Professor of Plant Biology
UNIVERSITY OF MAINE

As a little girl growing up on a farm in Charlotte, North Carolina, Susan Brawley developed a love of plants. She created her own museum and chemistry lab in her attic. A seventh grade field trip to a marine biology lab secured her interest in marine biology. Today, she studies seaweeds and marine fertilization success in waters off the coasts of Maine and Sweden.

❧

My research is done in two fields, developmental biology and marine ecology. The organisms that I am most interested in are the marine algae (seaweeds), and I use them as much as possible in my ecological and developmental studies. For example, there has been continued controversy about how successful external fertilization is in marine organisms, most of which utilize this form of reproduction. The prevailing view has been that few eggs are fertilized because the often-turbulent conditions in the intertidal and subtidal zones would quickly dilute sperm and prevent fertilization. However, it has been difficult to determine natural levels of fertilization or to do experiments to understand the factors that affect fertilization success because most scientists have worked with marine animals that have long periods of larval life after fertilization. Their larvae literally float out to sea.

The advantages of using seaweeds to study this question include the fact that the embryos settle onto the sea bottom immediately after fertilization; therefore I don't have to chase their larvae! Six years ago I began to use intertidal brown algae called fucoid algae to examine how factors such as water motion af-

fect fertilization success. These algae are often the most abundant seaweeds on rocky, temperate shores throughout the world. Anyone who has ever walked as a child (or with a child) on such a shore will know these algae because they have air bladders that are fun to pop. Two postdoctoral fellows, two graduate students, five undergraduates, and three other professors—especially Drs. Ladd Johnson, Gareth Pearson, and Ester Serrao—collaborated in this research. We have studied marine communities from the California coast to the Baltic Sea in Europe. Our overall finding is that nearly 100 percent of the eggs released

Susan Brawley diving at Discovery Bay, Jamaica, in 1974, just after her first year in grad school. She was taking a course in coral reef ecology given by the Organization for Tropical Studies.

into the sea are fertilized, in large part because adults can sense high levels of water motion and don't release their eggs and sperm except during periods of calm water. We are now investigating the biochemical and physiological basis by which the seaweeds can tell how rough the sea is.

I like working on problems that take me back and forth between the laboratory and the field. In the laboratory, I work with electron microscopes, preamplifiers, and oscilloscopes; analyzing cells and organisms with this equipment always creates a sense of magical discovery in me because they let me see the world on a scale that my eyes cannot. However, working in the field as an ecologist puts my lab work into perspective. As I scuba dive underwater, I don't just think, "Gee, why are there so many animals here that eat seaweeds?" I'm also thinking, "What are the structures or chemicals or other factors that allow my seaweeds to live in this stormy, cold place, and to survive being eaten by all of these animals?" I enjoy the holistic view of my favorite organisms that I get from doing both lab and field work.

Another problem that we are studying is the difficulty marine species may have in reproducing under brackish conditions. Brackish means low salinity, and brackish regions include any estuary (places where rivers meet the sea). The reason this interests me is that marine eggs of many plants and animals require sodium ions at fertilization to block a second sperm from fertilizing the egg. If more than one sperm fertilizes an egg, a condition called polyspermy occurs and the egg dies. This means that it is just as important for an egg to be fertilized only once as to be fertilized at all! The fascinating question becomes: How do marine organisms reproduce in brackish conditions where sodium ions aren't plentiful? Estuaries, such as at the mouth of the Penobscot River in Maine, are one good place for my research because some marine species have clearly adapted enough to live in areas where the river and ocean mix in a tidal cycle. However, the Baltic Sea, the largest body of brackish water in the world, is the best place for my studies. The Baltic was very salty, just like the ocean, about three thousand to seventy-five hundred years ago; then the connection to the Atlantic narrowed as uplift of the land occurred. This reduced the flow of ocean water into the Baltic, and the Baltic is now as much like a lake as an ocean because of the many rivers that drain into it. Most marine animals and plants retreated into the North Sea as the salinity change occurred, but a few species have adapted to the nearly freshwater conditions. One of these is a fucoid alga, *Fucus vesiculosus,* but there are six closely related fucoids in the North Sea that barely enter or are absent from the modern Baltic. Why has *Fucus vesiculosus* been successful there? I think the reason might be a change in its polyspermy block to make it less dependent upon sodium ions. *Fucus vesiculosus* is also one of the seaweeds that penetrates farthest up estuaries in both Europe and North America, but there is an interesting difference in the two habitats. Estuaries are tidal, so there are regular fluctuations in their level of salinity. At some points in the tidal cycle, the seaweed is exposed to water that is almost as salty as the ocean. However, the Baltic lacks tides and is a very large body of water with constantly low salinities. We may find that the same species has adapted differently to low salinity because of this difference in the two habitats. This aspect of our studies of external fertilization involves a wonderful biogeographic problem, and our work will help us to understand how species are able to adapt to rapid environmental changes.

There are lots of perks to my job. For example, I love to travel. Even in a more mundane kind of research, scientists go to meetings all over the country, and they will usually attend some international meetings during their careers. I enjoy different cultures and different kinds of people; however, I didn't know ahead of time whether I would enjoy my four-year-long project in Sweden. When I was in high school, I was an exchange student in Norway. Norwegians and Swedes have a love-hate relationship with each other. After I

Susan Brawley showing University of Maine Ph.D. students Rui Lui and Ester Serrão how to record an egg's membrane potential

had almost finished the first year of my project in Sweden, I visited my exchange family in Norway. I laughed when I told them that I had made an important discovery several weeks before: That my concern about working in Sweden was rooted in the Norwegian prejudices against the Swedes, which I had picked up as an exchange student, a prejudice I now realized was very unfair!

Sweden was clearly the place I needed to go for this research. The fucoid seaweeds in the Baltic are very important economically because they provide the framework for the community in which economically important fish such as herring obtain shelter and food as young fish. This fact coupled with a general love of nature have prompted local people at our field sites to respond very warmly and generously to our work. On a recent dive in August, the water temperature was 3°C, and even with a dry suit on, I was cold by the end of the dive. When we came out of the water with our seaweed, a couple living nearby had prepared hot drinks and lunch for us. At another of our field sites, a high school teacher took his boat out to help us set up our equipment underwater, and he took my students fishing and berry picking many times during the summer. Very enduring friendships can be made through these kinds of experiences. I have also done research in Japan, China, Ja-

maica, and Great Britain, and I was standing at the Berlin Wall only three months before it fell, the result of an invitation to a scientific meeting in Germany.

I work year round, with an appointment that allocates half my time to research and half to teaching. The courses that I teach at the University of Maine include introductory biology, introductory marine biology, and, at our marine laboratory, the ecology of rocky shores. I enjoy teaching most of the time. When you teach, you really learn things yourself! For example, as a college student, I really disliked portions of courses on metabolism because there were so many biochemical reactions to memorize. Then, when I taught cell biology at Vanderbilt University, I was asked by my chair to revise the laboratories on respiration in the introductory course. By the time I finished, I was fascinated with photosynthesis and respiration, and I find that I still love to teach these subjects. However, with my own college experience in mind, I emphasize the elegance of the many checks and balances in metabolism rather than memorization of equations. I also find that I am asked questions by students that make me rethink my ideas about biology in ways that enrich my research. The disappointing side of teaching is when one encounters students whose study habits aren't mature enough for college-level work; every professor has this experience to varying degrees.

I always loved plants and animals. I grew up on a farm in Charlotte, North Carolina. Both sides of my family had been in farming for about two centuries. My dad always took me out into the fields with him, and frequently I would ride all day long with him on the tractor. I was always out of doors and watching things. I went on nature walks with my mother from the time I was a toddler. My mother was an excellent English teacher who loved literature and words, but she also loved to hunt and identify plants. Growing up on a farm fostered my interest in biology. My parents let me have a museum and chemistry lab in our attic. I loved having a place of my own to do experiments and display my collections. Charlotte had an excellent Children's Nature Museum that my parents frequently took me to. Both of my parents were very supportive; my family valued education. If I had been a boy, my parents probably would have wanted me to take over the farm. But at that time, farming was not a career that a woman could easily pursue. My parents didn't push me in any one direction; they simply wanted me to do something that I liked at which I could be successful.

When I was in the seventh grade, I went on a marine biology trip over the weekend to the Duke University marine labs. This trip was led by Harold Humm, a professor at Queens College in Charlotte and formerly an acting director of the marine lab at Duke. It was a fantastic trip. For my first introductory marine biology course at the University of Maine, I constructed a laboratory on bioluminescent marine bacteria from some of the notes that I had kept from this field trip! In addition to marine microbiology, Dr. Humm was very interested in marine algae and was considered one of the leading authorities on them. After the trip, he asked if I would like to work in his lab on Saturdays. For almost a year when I was in the eighth grade, my parents took me to his lab once a week, and he taught me about extracting agar from seaweeds and how to cul-

ture different kinds of marine bacteria. I would take things home and work on them, transferring cultures in my attic laboratory throughout the week. Dr. Humm left Charlotte a year after I met him, but he continued to be my mentor by mail. I was already predisposed to be interested in plants, and these experiences secured my interest in marine algae.

When I went to college, I chose Wellesley because of its strong academic reputation and its location near, but not in, Boston. Coming from a farm, I didn't want to be in a city, so Wellesley was a perfect alternative. I had read a book in the fourth grade that created an image of Boston as a wonderful city. I can still remember the picture of the swan boats in the park. In my senior year of high school, I visited one of my former high school debate partners at Wellesley. It was during the peak of autumn, and I decided there couldn't be a more glorious place to spend four years of one's life. Helen Padykula, the second woman president of the American Society of Cell Biology, became my undergraduate thesis adviser. When I first approached her about doing a thesis, I told her that I wanted to do it on marine algae. She laughed and said, "Susan, you'd better do a topic I know something about." I would bring in buckets of marine algae from the coast and use her nice research microscope to look at them; however, following orders, my thesis was on opossum reproduction at an ultrastructural level, which was one of Helen's specialties. I left college with an interest in cellular structure and function and went to graduate school still intent on going into marine botany.

I went to the best place in the United States at the time to study marine botany, the University of California at Berkeley. The fusion of my two interests, marine biology and cell biology, led me to focus on fertilization and embryogenesis in algae. At Berkeley, I met a wonderful retired professor who was still very active, a taxonomist named G. F. Papenfuss. He was very supportive of what I wanted to do. Just before I started graduate school, while I was taking a course at the Marine Biological

Laboratory in Woods Hole, Massachusetts, I also met Ralph Quatrano from Oregon State, and his interests were similar to mine. He eventually became the outside member of my dissertation committee. My interactions with him and several other professors were very important during graduate school and thereafter; most people in science can point to at least one person who has had a strong effect on their training. Science is very much an apprenticeship because it's a blue collar and white collar job rolled into one. You not only have to sit at your desk and think up exciting experiments that someone is going to be interested in funding, but you have to know how to do simple repairs of equipment, solder wiring, fix plumbing, and haul your diving gear all over the shore. You acquire practical training from your mentors that makes the experience an apprenticeship rather than just scholarly criticism of your work. My postdoctoral advisers were also excellent: Walter Adey at the Smithsonian Institution, with whom I did coral reef biology; and Ken Robinson, then at the University of Connecticut Health Center, from whom I learned cell physiology. I still have fun talking with Ken about science and politics. All of my mentors were very well-rounded individuals, which made them a lot of fun.

In general, my professional experiences have been positive, and my professional accomplishments have been recognized and rewarded. I have held elective national offices in professional societies in my field, have received grants from private and public agencies for my research, and have received tenure (twice) as a professor. I haven't encountered much discrimination against me as a woman in science. When I was at Vanderbilt, I was the only woman in my department. I was often aware at faculty meetings that if I hadn't been there, issues concerning women students would have been decided differently. Just one woman on the faculty made a difference. Once, when we were considering new faculty at Vanderbilt, three people were on our short list—two men and one woman, and the woman had children. Just after she had finished interviewing, my de-

partment chair, who is a wonderful person and scientist, came to me and asked, "Susan, what do you think of candidate X?" I said, "It seems as if she's going to have a great career. She gave a really good seminar, and she seems to have good research ideas." He responded, "But you know, she has two young children." I smiled and replied, "Don't *you* have two children?" He realized, of course, what I meant, and later he thanked me.

The issue of children is one that many women scientists have faced when searching for a job, and it happened to me, too. I had been invited to interview for a position in the botany department of a very large university in Texas. Shortly after the interview started, one of the faculty asked me how many children I planned to have. I was so surprised that I cannot even remember how I answered him, but he launched into a discussion about how children damage women's careers. This happened more than once during the interviews; the faculty were much less interested in my professional accomplishments and plans than my present and intended family tree. To cap the experience, they telephoned a male candidate before I even returned home, and they never contacted me to indicate they had offered him the position. My interview had obviously been a sham.

Of course, when I married and had a child, I found that my work *was* affected. For one thing, you can't bounce around the world with an infant. However, my four-year-old daughter has now spent three summers in Sweden, and she loves it! Combining parenting with my career works for me because I spend a substantial amount of my salary on a nanny to take care of my daughter while I'm at work. Good child care is a fundamental necessity for women scientists, and I am particularly sensitive to this now that I am divorced. Having a postdoc and graduate students to work with me while my daughter is young has also made a huge difference. My laboratory group is lots of fun, and they continue the work when I can't, especially at night. I hire baby-sitters on weekends and at night during critical periods in our work, but I rarely work more than sixty-five hours a week now, even with a home computer to help. When Anne is older, I'll have more flexibility, especially because she already likes going on field trips to help collect seaweed—"Mommy, you don't have to show me how to take care of the seaweed; I know what to do!"

I have mixed views about the demands of an academic job. There are times, especially as a graduate student, that you have to be around a hundred hours a week or you can't get the job done. There has to be, at least in some intervals, a real commitment to time on a project. However, it is a mistake for people to put their personal lives on hold. I came from a family where people traditionally marry late and have children later, so I never felt the "biological clock" pressure that many young women experience between developing a career and starting a family. I had so many things I wanted to do before I was ready to settle down and have a family, and I did them. However, age and reproductive potential are real issues for young women, and I think a better model is to integrate one's personal and professional lives, much as the Swedes do on a routine basis. In the Swedish system, graduate students are paid professional salaries, and many marry and have children as graduate students, taking as much as eight years to finish a Ph.D. in order to spend enough time with their children. Supportive spouses and academic and societal conditions that make it possible to be a woman scientist with a family are increasingly available in the United States, but we remain a long way from the ideal. Nevertheless, it is important for young women to realize that they can have families and still be very successful scientists.

I was promoted to full professor two years ago, and I have apprentices of my own. As I find myself in an increasingly senior position, I want to help expand the opportunities for young people in my field. As I continue my research on fertilization, I am also working with other scientists in New England and China to nurture a seaweed mariculture industry off the Maine coast. So I may finally become a farmer, too.

PRESENT POSITION: Professor of Plant Biology, University of Maine

FIELD: Marine biology

RESEARCH AREA: Marine fertilization success

EDUCATION: B.A. in Biology (1973), Wellesley College; Ph.D. in Botany (1978), University of California–Berkeley

DATE/PLACE OF BIRTH: October 6, 1951/Charlotte, North Carolina

Susan Brawley lives with her daughter, Anne, in Eddington, Maine.

INTERVIEW DATE: February 1995

Aida Casiano-Colón

Director, Microbiology Laboratory
GENESEE HOSPITAL

As a child in Puerto Rico, Aida Casiano-Colón had two serious interests—biology and theater—and she has pursued both. She earned a Ph.D. in microbiology and directs a clinical microbiology laboratory; in 1990 she starred in the play called Rosa de Dos Aromas *in Rochester, New York. In between working full time and parenting three children, Casiano-Colón is also taking acting classes and plans to continue to pursue a part-time theater career. She believes that, with the support of a great partner and relentless personal perseverance, a woman should be able to "seize the day" and have it all.*

❧

I was born the youngest of three children of a humble and loving family in Mayagüez, Puerto Rico, in 1958. A mechanic most of his life, my father was an honest and stern man.

My mother, however, was the strong one in the family; she was quiet and submissive on the outside, but behind the scenes she ran the show. My mom always worked to make extra money, usually as a seamstress in a factory, which enabled us to have a decent life. My mom had a great influence on me and my siblings, always talking to us about our futures "when" we became professionals, not "if" we became professionals. I always thought juggling a career and a family was simply a part of life. Knowing that she could do it with limited resources helped me to believe that I also could do it when the time came. I always knew that she would be there when I needed her and never felt cheated because she worked.

I was very focused as a child. I had many interests, but a few of them ran very deep. I was always torn between the arts and the sciences. I loved biology: I loved when we cut up a chicken in school to look at its organs. As a

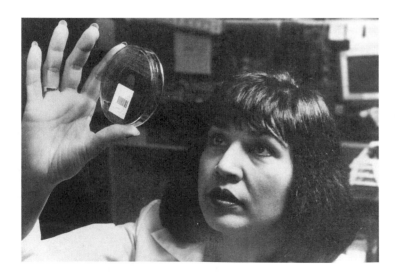

Aida Casiano-Colón identifying colony morphologies in her lab at the Genesee Hospital, 1996
PHOTO BY DAVID W. BURNHAM, THE
GENESEE HOSPITAL

youngster I wanted to be a surgeon; I was very interested in the anatomy of living things, especially the human body. But I was also interested in theater. I didn't have the opportunity to go to the theater much, but I routinely performed in school plays and on local television. I was a pretty confident little girl, always active and on the go. My parents were encouraging and proud of my accomplishments. Sadly, my father died shortly after I completed by postdoctoral residency and was ready to begin my current job. This left me with an empty feeling inside. My best memories of my father are of learning to dance with him when I was very young. He was always so proud of his children.

I was very different from my siblings. As a child my older sister preferred to stay home and read. My sister was one of my earliest role models: she always wanted to be a lawyer and fight for people's rights, and she did it. She inspired me to go after what I wanted. My brother went to college for engineering, and although he didn't complete his degree at the time, now in his forties, he is back in school finishing his bachelor's degree and getting all A's, and he is ready to begin working on his master's degree.

I started college at the University of Puerto Rico—Mayagüez is a college town. There was never a question that I would go to college; it was as natural to me as was going from middle school to high school. I was there for three years and transferred when my future husband, Fermín Colón, a chemical engineer, was hired by the Eastman Kodak Company in Rochester, New York. I moved to Rochester with him and completed my microbiology degree at the University of Rochester. I graduated in May 1981, and Fermín and I married in Puerto Rico around Christmas of the same year. Nine months later, Ambar Lorena, our first child, was born.

I got a job right after graduation as a technician in the microbiology lab at Eastman Kodak, although Fermín and I had already decided that we would both pursue master's degrees, I in microbiology and he in chemical engineering. We took evening classes and juggled school, work, and parenting. It took us four years to finish our masters' degrees, but we did it and graduated at the same time. To this day our friends talk about the great party we had to celebrate our simultaneous graduations.

Then I decided to go on for a Ph.D., and I took a leave of absence from Eastman Kodak. This was a turning point in my life, and it was influenced heavily by Dr. Marilyn Menegus, who was and still is a very important mentor to me. Marilyn is the director of the microbiology lab at Strong Memorial Hospital, the hospital associated with the University of Rochester. She is one of the few women to obtain a full professorship at the University of Rochester, and she was doing exactly what I wanted to do. I met her when I worked in the lab while finishing my undergraduate degree. I didn't know much about diagnostic microbiology, but I learned a lot in the lab. I remember the day Marilyn stopped me in the hall and said, "We're going to turn you into a microbiologist." That was the beginning of a very important relationship. After that, I always consulted with Marilyn when I had to make a major decision in my life. I still remember telling her that I was thinking about pursuing a Ph.D. in microbiology. She said, "That's a great idea," which was all it took for me to move ahead.

I started my Ph.D. immediately after I finished my master's degree. In 1988, while I was working on my Ph.D., we had twin boys, Adriel and Ulyses. I think graduate school is the best time to have kids: your time is very flexible. I took all my summers off to be with my children. I was never concerned about someone viewing this negatively; I was focused when I worked, and the hours I spent in the lab were very productive. My adviser was also a wonderful mentor: he knew I was committed and focused, and he also had strong family commitments. So as long as the work got done, he didn't care how I used my time. The experience of working full-time, going to school part-time to earn a master's,

Aida Casiano-Colón, husband Fermín, daughter Ambar Lorena, and twin sons, Adriel and Ulyses, November 1995
PHOTO BY MINH DANG, TIMELESS PHOTOGRAPHY

and raising a child made the shift to doctoral study a breeze—I was focusing on my graduate work, my husband and our kids, and that was all!

During my graduate work I focused on dental caries. We were working with a bacterial organism that normally colonizes the oral cavity. I was working with a pathway for arginine degradation with base production trying to create a strain of a streptococcal hyperproducer of ammonia from arginine. Theoretically, this strain would then be implanted in the mouth and create a way to counteract the effects of acidity that actually dissolves the tooth enamel and creates caries. Mine was a very biochemically oriented project, working mostly with the isolated enzymes—trying to describe the enzymes or pathways, the activity of the enzymes, and trying to come up with their optimal activity in the presence of different metabolites such as cobalt or harsh conditions of extreme temperature or acidity. I don't have very strong feelings for my Ph.D. research: it was something I had to do to get to where I wanted to be.

What I really wanted to do was diagnostic microbiology; that was my goal from the time I started working in the microbiology lab as an undergraduate. And that's where I ended up doing my postdoctoral training, in medical and public-health microbiology at the Uni-

versity of Rochester Medical Center. Luckily, there was a program like this in Rochester, so I didn't have to make choices about moving my family or finding another niche.

The focus of my postdoc and subsequent work has been to look at a disease and determine the cause; that's what diagnostic microbiologists do. We get specimens from patients who are sick, culture them for viruses or bacteria, come up with a causative infectious agent for the illness, and report to the doctor both the identity of the pathogen and also what to treat the patient with to be most successful. On the side, we generate a lot of statistics from the laboratory that we can provide to doctors—for example, on the prevalence of specific diseases and trends in susceptibility. Ours is a very service-oriented profession, meeting the needs of physicians and other health care professionals.

We deal with a lot of common problems like urinary tract infections, but the job becomes much more interesting when we deal with difficult and complicated patients like those with autoimmune deficiency or cancer. It's like detective work when we get patients who have been exposed to many different organisms and we need to determine what's going on. We don't use just bacteriology but also virology (culturing viruses), mycology (culturing different fungi), mycobacteriology (culturing organisms such as those that cause tuberculosis), serology, and immunology. I often work very closely with physicians, even to the extent of visiting patients. As head of the lab, I can become fully involved with the difficult and challenging cases, which are usually more time consuming, while the staff handles the more routine matters. I have about twenty-five people working in my lab, most of whom are seasoned microbiology technologists with many years of experience. I am also lucky to have Barbara Hulbert as my right-hand woman; she supervises the lab and handles the day-to-day matters and works very closely with me to direct the lab and move it forward.

My specific research interest right now lies in clinically relevant, cost-effective microbiology. In an era of managed care, there is less and less money for the laboratory to do all the things we want to do, so we have to use our resources wisely. We have to be savvy in allocating our labor and reagent expenses; and that's part of my role as director, knowing when it's important to do a full workup on a clinical specimen and when minimum information is all the physician needs to treat the patient.

The key reason I've been able to maintain my career is that my husband and I are an incredible team. For a Puerto Rican man, he is very modern in his beliefs. He has always been very supportive of me. He is a wonderful husband and father, and we split the parenting job fifty-fifty. We prioritize together and if, at times, things don't get done, we always keep our goals in sight. We were lucky to find a woman who stayed with us for ten years to help take care of the kids; she was a blessing, as was my mother, who always helped when things got rough. When the twins were one, I was in the middle of my Ph.D. thesis, experiments were running all night long, and I needed to be there. Fermín was running himself ragged. My mother's response was that it was time to leave her work for a while, and she came and lived with us for one year. She's currently living with us again, after retirement.

My mother is my best friend. She has a great sense of humor and is a lot of fun to have around. We are so blessed that the children get to know their wonderful grandmother.

I have had a terrific support system—nobody can do this alone. I was always very committed not to give up on what I wanted, and I wanted it all—a career and a family. So Fermín and I worked together to find ways to make it happen.

Every time I experienced a roadblock in my life, I became more adamant that I would persevere. And I used being Hispanic in my favor. I don't think being a woman was an issue because there were always a lot of women in biology with whom I interacted. I think being Hispanic among mostly white Anglo-Saxons helped me; people needed to fill their quotas and I just "seized the day." I knew I was smart and could use the system that afforded opportunities to non-Anglos. But I never abused the system.

Besides directing the lab, I teach microbiology to second-year medical students, and I enjoy teaching for a couple of reasons: I like to interact with young people and share my passion with them, and I love to perform—the classroom is my forum. I did have an opportunity to do theater a few years ago when I finished my Ph.D. in 1990 and before I started my postdoctoral training. Luck played a major role. I answered an ad for an audition from a very well-known Puerto Rican director who was coming to Rochester to produce a play and needed two Hispanic women in their late twenties or early thirties. I auditioned and got the lead role. It was an interesting experience—the play was performed in both English and Spanish, so we had to learn our parts in both languages. He wanted to attract the Spanish-speaking audience in Rochester and at the same time expose the English-speaking audience to a Hispanic play. The play was a comedy called *Rose of Two Aromas,* or *Rosa de Dos Aromas.* The rehearsals were intense but a lot of fun. This was my celebration and gift to myself for finishing my Ph.D. I am currently taking acting classes and would love to pursue theater when time permits. I don't think there are many roles for Hispanic women, but I still enjoy it.

Throughout my life luck has always been on my side. I finished my postdoc in 1992 and was in the right place at the right time. The head of the microbiology lab at Genesee Hospital was retiring and they needed to replace him. I had consulted with them for a while, so they knew me and my work, and I was offered the job. I have been here ever since and I love it.

We're very happy in Rochester. Rochester has a fairly large Hispanic community, many of whom work as engineers and scientists for Eastman Kodak or Xerox. When we left Puerto Rico, three other couples from our university were also hired at Kodak, and we all came to Rochester as a group. They are our family here. We helped each other settle in and watched one another's children grow, and we travel on vacations and celebrate holidays together. When we're together, we do our favorite thing: we talk about Puerto Rico and what it was like to grow up in that beautiful land. We also love to dance. Dance is a very important part of Hispanic culture.

My children speak Spanish fluently, and we talk to them about what it was like growing up in Puerto Rico. We take them there for visits as often as possible and maintain close contact with their grandparents, even if by phone.

Fermín's parents are also a very important presence in our kids' lives. Many people, especially professionals, leave the island, but it never leaves us; Puerto Rico and its culture and traditions remain very important to us. My husband is active in the Hispanic community in Rochester, and so our children are surrounded somewhat by their culture. There is also a group within Kodak for Hispanic professionals.

As I consider my own life I see three themes: I never compromised what I wanted or what was important to me; I focused, focused, focused; and I aimed very high. It seems to have paid off.

PRESENT POSITION: Director, Microbiology Laboratory, Genesee Hospital

FIELD: Diagnostic microbiology

RESEARCH AREA: Clinically relevant, cost-effective microbiology

EDUCATION: B.S. in Microbiology (1981), University of Rochester; M.S. in Microbiology (1985); University of Rochester; Ph.D. in Microbiology (1990), University of Rochester

DATE/PLACE OF BIRTH: September 21, 1958/ Mayagüez, Puerto Rico

Aida Casiano-Colón lives in Rochester, New York, with her husband, Fermín, their three children, and Milagros Sepúlveda, Aida's mom.

INTERVIEW DATE: November 1995

Martha A. Chavez

Research and Development Project Manager
HEWLETT PACKARD

Martha Chavez never considered going to college until a high school counselor inspired and encouraged her. Thinking she would like to help other kids the way he had helped her, she started off to become a guidance counselor but was discouraged by the prospect of master's degree work. After trying several majors, she settled on electrical engineering as the most challenging and most interesting—and ended up with a master's degree after all. Working creatively to overcome the challenge of being a single working mom, she has had a successful career at Hewlett Packard and enjoys working with young people in her community.

❧

I was raised in Albuquerque, New Mexico, as the youngest of nine children—two brothers, six sisters, and me. My mom and my dad come from El Paso, Texas, and the five older children were born there; the four youngest were born in Albuquerque. As a family we had extremely limited financial resources, and we learned the importance of hard work from our parents. People often ask me if I'm spoiled because I'm the youngest child in a large family, but when there are nine kids and not a lot of money, you don't get spoiled.

Of the nine children, I'm the only one with a college degree. That is not to say that I'm the smartest. We are all smart, but we had different access to education and different opportunities to use our native talents. When my parents were growing up, getting an education took second place to helping the family make ends meet. My mom finished third grade and my dad went through seventh grade. While my parents do not have much formal education,

they are both very smart. My mom is a great money manager; she can make a dollar go further than any financial guru. My dad is also extremely creative; he devises solutions out of the most unexpected materials and methods.

My parents expected their children to work hard and to do their best. However, the school system I went through failed to challenge me and the other students in the same manner. My friends and I were from the poorer part of town, and most of us were Hispanic; we all went to elementary, junior high, and high school together. Looking back, it seems to me that we weren't pushed to work hard at school or to do our best. For example, in sixth grade, I was good at math, but instead of encouraging me, if I got the first few questions of the daily test right, they let me go do arts and crafts.

Martha Chavez reviewing the current status of the development project she manages—an electronic imaging desktop scanner, 1995

In junior high, we took aptitude tests, and then counselors came to tell us what we should be doing in high school. They tended to expect little from us and directed us to traditional occupations. They told me that since I was doing really well in math, I didn't have to take any more math classes to graduate from high school. Instead, I was encouraged to take classes that would prepare me to be a secretary; a Hispanic girl was pretty much expected to get married or take a service job. Nobody ever pushed us in high school, and we never pushed ourselves. Our teachers had preconceived notions of what we could do and couldn't do. By my senior year, we didn't have a whole lot of respect for the teachers, and they didn't have much respect for us either. Fortunately, a very important, positive thing happened to me in high school. An excellent high school counselor, Mr. Archibeque, started saying to me, "Why don't you go to college? You can do more than you are doing now!" His belief in me really made an impression. It was the first time anybody at school had asked me to be more. I decided that I wanted to be a counselor and change kids' lives like he had changed mine.

Thanks to his influence, in the middle of my senior year of high school, I decided to go to college. I enrolled at the University of New Mexico. I started out in psychology and took one of those Psych 101 classes with hundreds of people in it. A few years earlier, I hadn't even known there was a university in my city, and now there I was, taking classes amongst hundreds of people, wondering what I was doing there and thinking everyone was smarter than I was. There were so many people that I figured I would need a master's degree to get a counseling position in the school system. Since I could barely imagine myself getting a bachelor's degree, I began looking for other careers to pursue that I thought would require only a bachelor's degree. I tried history, and then political science with the thought of going to law school. During this time, I also took an engineering course, and it was the hardest course I'd ever taken. I

thought everybody knew what they were doing except for me. I had to study a lot and felt I was in way over my head. But I found it very interesting, so I changed my major to electrical engineering. As I was finishing my bachelor's degree, my senior adviser urged me to apply for a fellowship for graduate studies. I was awarded the fellowship and went on to get my master's degree.

I put myself through college with scholarships, grants, loans, and summer jobs. I applied for every available source of financial aid. I also tutored math during the school year and worked every summer saving money to apply it toward the following year's tuition.

As I started college, I found out that it was important to spend my time with people who were focused on studying. I lived at home for the better part of my bachelor's degree, an arrangement that had many advantages over living in the dorms. However, I discovered that my family didn't understand the amount of work required to go through college. For example, I would spend a lot of time studying at the library and my family would tease me that I must be visiting a boyfriend instead. It became a joke around the house that every time I went to the library I must be going out on a date. I soon found that I would get distracted from my studies if I spent time with friends who were not in college and had full-time jobs. I would need to study, and they would want to go out after they got off work. While I was spending money on my tuition, they were able to buy cars and other things I could not afford at the time. It made me question whether I should stay in college or get a full-time job. Fortunately, I realized that, given the extremely competitive job market, people without college degrees typically have a lower earning potential, so I stayed in college. Back then my friends seemed to have so much more than I, but it doesn't seem so now.

While I was in college I worked during the summers at various places: Rockwell, Hewlett Packard, Bell Labs, IBM. I got good experience along with exposure to the different companies' styles. Hewlett Packard's style suited me best, so I came to work here after I got my master's degree and I've been here since. There are different functional areas in all HP divisions: Marketing, Research and Development (R&D), Product Development, Manufacturing, and so on. I started out as an engineer in R&D, working on the design and development of products. I worked on reel-to-reel tape drives, 3½ inch floppy disk drives, and hard disk drives. As an engineer, I was responsible for a part of a whole design. For example, on a typical design you might have one engineer working on the power system, another working on the controller system, a third working on the mechanical system, and so on. As part of the design team you must make sure that your design works correctly not only by itself but also within the whole design. Working within a design team requires not only technical know-how but also good teamwork and communication skills.

After a few years, I decided to take an opportunity in Marketing as a product manager. Product Development has a counterpart in Marketing that determines the product's features and then introduces the product when it is completed. I worked in Marketing for a year and a half. It was at that time that I gave birth to my son and decided that working in Marketing required too much business travel; I decided to return to R&D.

For the next three years I focused on working with other companies to help them integrate their products into HP products. I then became the Engineering Services manager for the H. P. Greeley site. This involved managing all the support services for two R&D labs, including the printed-circuit layout shop, the mechanical prototype shop, and labstock. These groups support the engineers during the development cycle. After a few more years, I became a project manager in R&D. Today, I continue in the project manager position with my group working on desktop scanners.

On a typical day, I check my voicemail before I go into the office. I then drive to work and review what I must get accomplished dur-

ing the day. I keep a list of my tasks and meetings. As a project manager, my job is to focus the development team on the project goals and to ensure all the project activities are getting done on schedule. This primarily includes the work for which the development engineers are responsible. Another part of my job is to ensure communication between the various functional areas. I meet with cross-functional members of the team to ensure the different parts are coming together. This is important because a product will only satisfy customers' needs if it has all the various solution components from each functional area.

I like managing people and having a technical background. I get to do people management and technical management at the same time. If someone is having a technical problem, we can all help to solve it. I believe the synergy of a team will always be stronger and better than that of individual people.

Being in a nontraditional occupation has its positives and its negatives. The biggest advantage is that I am doing what I really enjoy, and I work with high-energy, creative people. Of course, in a nontraditional occupation I tend to work with a lot of people with whom I don't have much in common. There are still people from the "old school" who have a problem working with people who don't look like them. This creates problems that do weigh me down, but things are improving every year. For example, when I started at HP in 1983 I was the only woman in R&D; today there are many of us.

Some people will always credit my advancement to affirmative action, and they have confronted me directly with this. The first time I got a promotion, one of my peers said, "Well, we know why you got a promotion; you're a woman and a minority." You have to be careful not to be drawn into their views because the old self-doubts will start creeping back into your mind. You must fight these doubts and remind yourself that you are in this position because of your skills, hard work, and contributions. Several studies have shown that many, many people in business doubt themselves, but it's especially bad to have that linked to your being a member of a minority. It is very important during college and during your career to find a network of supporters who will help you during these times.

Following my high school counselor's example, I try to help others set high expectations for themselves. I have gone to local elementary schools with large Hispanic populations to do science tricks with magnets and such—things that look fun. I try to get the kids interested in science and math. I want them to know that here is a person who grew up much like they are growing up and who has gone to college. My purpose is to provide them with a role model and to broaden their horizons.

For the last three years, I've also coached my son's soccer team. I felt this provided a perfect opportunity to build a child's self-esteem while enjoying soccer. This has been very rewarding for me. When I see some of the kids from my team now, they come over and give me a hug even though they're getting older.

I am the single mom of an eight-year-old boy, Kyle. The hardest thing about being a single mom and working is business travel. If I have an overnight trip, I have to make arrangements for my son. I really hate this part of my job and avoid it as much as possible. Longer business trips, like overseas, require that I ask my mom to come from out of town to help. Hewlett Packard has been fairly flexible about this; I try to conduct as much business from the office as possible to reduce business travel. Some people say that by limiting my business travel I am limiting my career growth. My pri-

orities are my son first, all else second. I've started a new strategy this year to have more time with him. He leaves for school at 8:30 and comes back at 3:30, so those are my office hours, and I work at home the rest of the time. There is a risk that I'm going to pay a price for this new work schedule because people who see me leaving early might get the wrong impression. While this bothers me, I strongly think this arrangement is best for me and my son. I believe it's easier and better to raise a child right than to fix an adult. I'll pour my life into my son now, so he will grow to be a confident and self-sufficient adult. Work comes and goes, but family is always there for me.

My hope is that I am providing my son and other kids with an example of the benefits of hard work and that I can serve as a role model for others in similar situations with a desire to reach for their own dreams. I hope I can show them that they do not have to let their dreams be stifled by other people's low expectations. Hard work and perseverance can accomplish so much.

PRESENT POSITION: Research and Development Project Manager, Hewlett Packard

FIELD: Electrical engineering

SPECIALTY: Product development

EDUCATION: B.S. (1981) and M.S. (1982) in Electrical Engineering, University of New Mexico

DATE/PLACE OF BIRTH: July 26, 1958/Albuquerque, New Mexico

Martha Chavez lives in Greeley, Colorado, with her son, Kyle.

INTERVIEW DATE: August 1995

Yvonne Y. Clark

Associate Professor of Mechanical Engineering
TENNESSEE STATE UNIVERSITY

As a child Yvonne Clark loved to fix things around the house. Her later interest in airplanes steered her toward the engineering field, and in 1952 she became the first woman to receive a degree in mechanical engineering from Howard University. She went on to become the first female faculty member—and department head—in the College of Engineering and Technology at Tennessee State University. In 1972 she was the first woman to receive an M.S. in engineering management from Vanderbilt University.

❧

I grew up in Louisville, Kentucky. My daddy was a physician and surgeon; he graduated from Fisk University and Meharry Medical College in Nashville. (Fisk is a liberal arts college that was established in 1866 to educate the newly freed slaves.) Mom also graduated from Fisk; she was a librarian, a journalist with the Louisville *Defender,* and a Latin teacher. Her mom was a teacher in Houston, Texas. My brother, C. Milton Young III, graduated from the University of Louisville and Meharry Medical College and is now a physician in Louisville specializing in rheumatoid arthritis.

I have always used my hands to build things. When I was a child you could put something in front of me and say, "Put this together," and I loved it. I had Erector sets and things like that when I was a kid. And I fixed things around the house. But I also had a doll.

I didn't have many role models when I was growing up. My mom was a teacher, a librarian, and a journalist, but none of those possibilities moved me.

Back in those days if you wanted to go to college, you had to have a well-rounded background. I took a year of Latin and a year of Spanish. You were also required to have two years of science to graduate, and I had three—a year each in chemistry, physics, and aeronautics. In aeronautics class, we'd build planes, fly them off the fire escape at school, and let them crash.

I don't remember whether I was the only girl in those classes; I don't think so. But I do remember that I couldn't take mechanical drawing because I was a girl. When I came back to visit my high school after my freshman year at Howard, I went to see Mr. Adams, who taught the class, and told him, "If a girl wants

Yvonne Clark as a college freshman, 1947

to take this course, you'd better let her have it." I had gone in cold for a drafting class at Howard and could have done much better if I'd been allowed to take a semester of mechanical drawing in high school. Girls do take the class now.

I was a squad leader in my high school's chapter of the Civil Air Patrol. Adult Civil Air Patrol members were our advisers. The Civil Air Patrol today does search and rescue. We marched, we had classes, and we learned how to shoot a rifle and a gun at the armory—I was Annie Oakley. They also taught us how to fly in the link trainer, which simulates the experience of being in an airplane. I'd always wanted to fly an airplane, and I especially wanted to ferry planes across the Atlantic Ocean to England. I thought—but didn't know and didn't ask—that you had to be an engineer to do it.

I had just turned sixteen when I graduated from high school in 1945. Mom and Dad thought that was too young for me to go to college. They thought I'd waste my time and might not do my best. Mom had started a library at Camp Lejeune, a Marine base in North Carolina, and she knew some of the officers there. She asked two colonels what they thought about my going up north to get some more education, learn how to get around, and become more responsible before I went to college. So I went up to Boston and stayed with one colonel's family for a year and with the other colonel's family for a second year. I went to Girls' Latin School for my first year, where they considered my high school education to be about on a par with what their sophomore class was learning. I took Latin—my high school Latin came in handy—and math and French; I also played field hockey and swam. In my second year in Boston, I went to Roxbury Memorial High School for Girls; I was known as a person who was just learning more, waiting to go to college.

I broke the family tradition of going to Fisk University because Fisk didn't offer courses in engineering. And because I was south of the Mason-Dixon line, I could not attend the University of Louisville. Wrong race. So the state paid for my tuition at Howard University. I had originally planned to go to the University of Illinois to study aeronautical engineering. I was accepted there but could not get into the dormitory, and I wanted to live on campus. I applied to Howard and got into the dorms. I planned on transferring from Howard to Illinois after two years, after I had taken the basic engineering courses, but I liked mechanical engineering so well I got my degree in it.

When I was at Howard I was the only female in mechanical engineering, the first woman to get a degree in it. They did have female graduates in electrical engineering before I got there. Electrical engineering and chemical engineering didn't have the stigma that mechanical engineering did—that you're out there getting dirty. And yet there was nobody around who hated getting their hands dirty more than I did. I asked one of the teachers in the machine shop, "Is there something I can put on my hands so that when I use soap that it will just wash off and my hands won't be dirty and grimy?" And they said yes, and that's where we started.

At Howard they did not discourage me. And it has always seemed to me that if you're not discouraged, your own motivation will take you wherever you want to go. They told me that I might have a hard time, but if I was prepared nobody could stop me.

As a senior, when I interviewed with companies that came to campus, one interviewer said that his company brought in their engineers at the bottom level so that they would know how the machinery works and then could work their way up. I said OK. Then he said, Well, we can't hire you. I asked why not, and he said I didn't have the muscles to break down the machinery. I said OK, no problem, but don't use my lack of strength as your reason for not hiring me; just say it's because I'm female and move on. But the Navy *did* say that. There was a superstition that if a woman was on a ship that it was bad luck, and even as an engineer I'd be required to go on a shakedown cruise. So that knocked me out of the Navy. Most of the interviewers seemed to have some reason not to hire me, but I finally got a job.

My first job was at Frankford Arsenal–Gage Laboratories in Philadelphia, designing gages and making final drawings. My next job was at RCA's Tube Division in Harrison, New Jersey. At RCA, I designed equipment to be used in that factory or other RCA plants. It was great talking to a person who needed something, trying to fill his needs, and then seeing the piece of equipment made in the shop and shipped out to the plant to be used. I worked there for three years.

Then I said "I do" and moved down south. My husband, Bill Clark, Jr., who was from Raleigh, North Carolina, had been friends with my first cousins in Nashville, so we probably met each other in the early forties. I'd see him when I came to see my cousins in the summertime. He graduated from Fisk and started teaching biochemistry at Meharry Medical College in Nashville. I was in New Jersey at that point. We started dating, talking on the telephone. We "agreed to agree," and I moved down to Nashville.

I started teaching after working in industry because that's all I could do in Nashville. I had tried to get into industry when I first came to Tennessee, but they had no use for me. Those were the words that they used. I don't think it was sexism, I think it was racism. It was not until President Kennedy said "Let there be color" that things started to change.

I was the first female faculty member in the College of Engineering and Technology at Tennessee State. I started as an instructor and worked my way up to associate professor and then was made department head of mechanical engineering. I was also the first female department head in the college.

I worked during the summers as an engineer, to learn what was out there and bring the information back to the classroom. Plus I needed the money. I went back to Frankford Arsenal for a few summers, working on recoilless weapons. I also worked at NASA in Huntsville, Alabama, where I investigated Saturn 5 engines for hot spots. Another summer I was at the NASA Manned Spacecraft Center in Houston, where I worked on containers for returning moon samples to earth. I also worked one summer at Westinghouse's Defense and Space Center in Baltimore, where I was part of an interdisciplinary team of engineers and sociologists that helped revitalize and modernize an old section of inner-city Baltimore.

I stepped down as department head in 1970 to take a two-year leave of absence to go back to school for my master's degree in engineering management. The Kellogg Foundation gave Tennessee State some money for development over a period of five years, and I was lucky enough to apply and get it and that's how I got to Vanderbilt.

I had begun teaching at Tennessee State because nothing had been available for me in private industry. But now I had to get a job to collect data for my master's thesis. The supervisor of plant engineering at Ford Glass plant in Nashville was on the advisory committee for my program at Vanderbilt. He also knew me as a professional engineer because we were both in the Tennessee Society of Professional Engineers—we had seen each other once a month at the meetings since 1964. When he found out that everyone in the program had an industry job but me, he asked if I would like to work at Ford Glass. I said I'd be glad to work there but didn't know whether I would fit in. I explained about what happened when I first came south in 1956 and the company had told me, "We have no use for you." He checked with the company, then came back and told me I had a job in industry like everyone else for the year I needed to get data for my master's thesis.

I was the first female engineer in the plant; I broke the ice, and they hired female engineers from Tennessee State after I left. One has been promoted up to headquarters, and the other is still at the plant.

While I was at Ford, I was invited to a luncheon where the managers were honoring the employees. Now, mind you, I was the only black at this occasion. One of the white men

Yvonne Clark teaching an engineering computer graphics class at Tennessee State University, 1995

got up and left the table. Everybody else was upset because they knew why the man got up—because I was sitting there—but I said, "Oh, he's going to miss a good meal—this steak looks good." Why should I damn the man because he was a racist or whatever his reason was? It was his reason; it wasn't mine. I sat there and enjoyed my steak. This is why I really think I've succeeded: I try not to wear anyone else's troubles.

I had no problem combining my career with having children. My son was born in 1956, my daughter in 1968. I was lucky enough to have a leave for the fall quarter when my son was born. He was born in October and they asked me to come back in December, so he was at least two months old when I returned to work. My daughter was somewhere between six weeks to two months old when I went back to school. My husband and a housekeeper helped take care of the kids. I was lucky.

Both of my kids are married, and my son has made me a grandmom. My grandson, Junior, will be seven years old in June. My son, Milton, lives in Louisville, Kentucky. My daughter, Carol, and her husband live about twenty-two miles outside of Nashville in Antioch. Milton

went to the University of Louisville and majored in computer science; my daughter was a management major at Hampton University. My son is a computer analyst, and my daughter is claims manager at Phoenix Healthcare in Nashville.

When my son was young, I got involved in the Boy Scouts. Technically, I was a master in the Boy Scouts, but I wouldn't let them call me a master. I was one of just a few women to receive the Boy Scouts' Long Rifle Award, which is given for volunteer service. I never got involved with the Girl Scouts because my daughter would go along to the Boy Scouts with me. I was just one of the boys. I stayed with the Boy Scouts even after my son went to college, helping boys become men and keeping them out of trouble. Because I was an engineer, some of the boys are engineers now.

I'm not with the Boy Scouts anymore, but I'm dedicated to doing other work in my community. I've been a member of and have held offices in the Hendersonville area chapter of the Links, Inc., a national nonprofit service organization, and the Nashville alumnae chapter of Delta Sigma Theta, a public-service sorority that has established a thousand-dollar annual scholarship in my name for a rising in-state mechanical engineering junior at Tennessee State. I've also volunteered for many years at the Eighteenth Avenue Family Enrichment Center and at a local television station's UNICEF Telethon.

I have always enjoyed participating in professional organizations as well. I've been a member of the Society of Women Engineers since 1952. I also maintain membership in many other organizations, including the National Education Association and the Tennessee Education Association, the American Society of Engineering Education, the National Society of Professional Engineers, the Tennessee Society of Professional Engineers, the American Society of Heating, Refrigerating and Air-Conditioning Engineers, the American Society of Mechanical Engineers, and the Order of the Engineer.

I just completed my fortieth year at Tennessee State. At the present time I'm teaching

Introduction to Engineering to freshmen. I also teach a computer graphics course using the program AutoCAD Release 13. I've been involved in computer graphics since 1988, when AT&T donated a lab to the department.

I currently have a grant from the Department of Energy for applied research dealing with refrigerants. The Montreal Protocol says that we can no longer make R-12 and R-22, or Freon, so we are testing alternative refrigerants. I've been doing that since 1987. Between 1984 and 1987, I conducted research for the Department of Energy to see what ran up an electric bill. Was it how a house was constructed—whether the insulation had been put in properly, and so forth—or the activities of its occupants? We found out that the occupants were the ones who caused the peak of electricity use.

I really enjoy teaching. I like seeing my students mature. Right now I'm dealing with freshmen and trying to cut the umbilical cord. I'm making them account for their actions, making them responsible. And to see them go on, graduate, get their master's, and tell me, "I'm getting my Ph.D. in May"—that just makes you pop buttons. They'll say, "I passed my professional engineer's license exam," and you pop some more buttons. These are the things that are meaningful.

I look at the student as a full being. Each student is a warm body, has a personality, and is teachable. I make sure that the student understands and that the class isn't boring, even though there are problems to do. I ask the students if they are comfortable where they're sitting and if they mind remaining in those chairs for the rest of the semester so I can get to know their names and their faces. They can feel that I'm interested in their learning my subject. And in computer graphics, one of my sayings is "Everybody has an A." You tell kids they've got an A, they're going to try and keep that A. It's psychology: you're psyching them into learning. If you work, you learn. And if you learn, you succeed.

Tennessee State's College of Engineering and Technology is about 25 percent female. It has taken me a long time to get them to come, but they're coming. I went to career days in the high schools, did volunteer work—that helped. You have to go where the kids are and try to catch them young. You have to give them information on what they need to take. The main thing is to try to get the kids to take the courses that everyone says are hard. They are hard if you don't understand; but they are easy if you understand and aren't afraid of them. And that's the bottom line.

I'm looking forward to seeing some of my classmates from Howard at a reunion luncheon this May. I had planned to take a week to attend all of the reunion affairs, but it's on the same weekend we're having graduation at Tennessee State. So I'll fly up just for the luncheon and be back for graduation. You don't hold your students' hands for four years and then not watch them walk across the stage.

PRESENT POSITION: Associate Professor of Mechanical Engineering, Tennessee State University

FIELD: Mechanical engineering

RESEARCH AREA: Alternative refrigerants

EDUCATION: B.S. in Mechanical Engineering (1951), Howard University; M.S. in Engineering Management (1972), Vanderbilt University

DATE/PLACE OF BIRTH: April 13, 1929/Houston, Texas

Yvonne Clark is now widowed and lives in Nashville. She enjoys getting away on weekends to her "hideaway" cabin in Monticello, Kentucky.

INTERVIEW DATE: January 1996

Jewel Plummer Cobb

President and Professor Emerita of Biological Science
CALIFORNIA STATE UNIVERSITY AT FULLERTON

Trustee Professor
CALIFORNIA STATE UNIVERSITY AT LOS ANGELES

Through examples set by her physician father, her teacher and social activist mother, and other African Americans she met only in books, Jewel Plummer Cobb grew up in a world full of possibilities. Her experience at the University of Michigan in 1941 could have changed all that: at Michigan in the 1940s, black students were not permitted in certain campus hangouts, and women could not enter the student union by the front door. But Cobb reframed her optimism and persisted. Her long and prestigious career has included the presidency of California State University at Fullerton.

Through my parents I was exposed early on to the importance of education, the wonders of science, and strong women. My parents taught me first-hand about the importance of education; my father was a physician and my mother was a teacher. She had started college but quit when I was born. She went back later in her life, so that she received her bachelor's degree in philosophy the same year I received mine in biology. During my early years, my mother was quite active in many civic activities. For example, she served on a cinema review board for the city of Chicago, which evaluated whether films were suitable for children. She also did some substitute teaching. There was a lot of reading material around my house—both scientific journals and books as well as material about black Americans. The possibilities seemed endless.

I became interested in science in ninth grade when my biology teacher, Miss Hymen,

put a microscope in front of me. That experience literally opened up a whole new world for me. Soon after I read Paul Dekruif's book *Microbe Hunters,* which was a detective story written for teenagers about the lives of several famous scientists like Pasteur and Lister. That book really heightened my interest in biology. I was encouraged by my parents, teachers, and friends to pursue my love of biology, and so from ninth grade on I planned to teach it. Since my two high school biology teachers were women, I had wonderful role models.

I went to the University of Michigan in 1941, but I only stayed for three semesters.

Jewel Plummer Cobb in her office at California State University at Los Angeles

The academic exposure was fine, but at that time the University of Michigan was an extremely racist place. There was no support system for black students, and the dormitories were segregated (this was true for all the Big Ten schools at the time), so we were relegated to a house on the very edge of campus. Black students weren't permitted in the Pretzel Bell or Beer Parlor, where everyone else went after the football games. The university was sexist as well—women couldn't walk in the front door of the men's union building. So in June 1942 I transferred to Talladega College, a warm and friendly school with a strong academic reputation. Talladega was a liberal arts college founded by the American Missionary Society just after the abolition of slavery, and it has proportionally more Ph.D. alumni than any other black college of its size. I graduated in 1944 and enrolled in New York University to work on a master's degree so that I could teach high school. After my first year I received a teaching fellowship and was paid to teach biology at the college level. At the same time I did some substitute teaching at a high school in New York City and found it to be a very unpleasant experience. I spent more time on discipline than teaching. Since I was having a great time in graduate school, and enjoying my research and teaching-assistant responsibilities, I decided I might as well continue and get my Ph.D., which I completed in 1950.

My research in graduate school was in cell physiology, and I worked with a biochemistry professor. After that, I had a postdoctoral fellowship from the National Cancer Institute and worked at Harlem Hospital's Cancer Research Foundation. I grew human tumors and learned how to conduct tissue culture, a procedure where the cells you want to study are grown in laboratory dishes under carefully controlled conditions. I did a lot of cutting-edge work in the field, exploring promising new cancer chemotherapy agents. It was a very exciting time. After two years, I took a position at the University of Illinois Medical School. I met my husband, we married, and I moved back to his home in New York in 1954. In 1957 we had our first and only child, a boy. Balancing work and family was possible when I was married because my husband did things like the grocery shopping; we shared housework and child-care responsibilities equally. I continued to work in cancer research—our group moved to New York University's Post-Graduate Medical School. I was a part-time instructor and a full-time researcher with grants from the National Cancer Institute, the Damon Runyon Foundation, and the American Cancer Society. I had a very active research lab with a marvelous research assistant and a couple of other doctoral people.

In 1960, with a three-year-old son, I left full-time research at NYU to become a faculty member at Sarah Lawrence College. I was there for nine years. I took my research with me, which now focused on melanin, a brown or black pigment that colors skin. I was interested in melanin's ability to shield human skin from ultraviolet rays and worked mostly with melanoma, an abnormal pigment formation in cancer cells that results in a malignant tumor on the skin. Because Sarah Lawrence was an undergraduate institution, I didn't have graduate students working in my lab. I hired a research assistant and funded several undergraduate biology students as research assistants through a grant from the National Science Foundation.

When I moved to Connecticut College in 1969 (a year after it became coed) to become dean, I found myself doing administrative work, teaching, and research. My husband and I had divorced in 1967, so I was a single parent of a twelve-year-old boy. I kept him busy so that he wouldn't "hang out" and get into trouble. Before we moved in 1969 he went to a structured program every day after school, the best one being the YMHA (Young Men's Hebrew Association) in Mount Vernon, where we lived. We lived in a Jewish community with wonderful public schools, so he had excellent academic and social experiences. On weekends in Connecticut I often took my son skiing. It was a full and interesting life.

One of my proudest accomplishments occurred while I was at Connecticut College. I founded a program called the Postgraduate Premedical and Predental Program for Minority Students. We awarded six recently graduated minority students each year a scholarship to do intensive preparation for dental or medical school. The program was very successful—over 80 percent of the forty students in our program got into the professional school of their choice and are now practicing medicine or dentistry. While I'm saddened that the program no longer exists at Connecticut College, I am pleased that other colleges across the country have developed similar programs.

In 1976 I became dean of Douglass College, which is the women's division of Rutgers University. We had a strong science faculty and a wonderful women's studies program with women like Adrienne Rich, Catharine Stimpson, and Mary Hartman. It was a great place to be. The list of colleges where I worked may deceive someone into thinking that I chose these colleges because they were women's colleges. Not true. I never sought to teach at or lead a women's college; it just evolved that way—Sarah Lawrence, Connecticut College, which was still predominantly a women's school when I was there, and then Douglass College. Being dean of Douglass was like being president—we had our own faculty, our own students, and our own campus. I was the chief administrative officer, so I had to give up my research, although I did teach a course periodically.

Between 1974 and 1980 I was also on the National Science Board, which controls and directs what happens at the National Science Foundation. I chaired the Committee on Women and Minorities in Science, and we initiated several exciting national programs for women despite the meager budget assigned by Congress.

When I became president at California State University at Fullerton in 1981, I im-

mediately asked about their women in science and other academic programs. When I found out they didn't have any women's programs, I moved to create one. There were quite a few differences moving to a coed institution, especially as the president. There was some skepticism about whether I could handle it all, especially aspects like intercollegiate sports. In fact, athletics assumed a major role in my administrative activities because Fullerton was a Division I-A school, which meant they were in the top-ranking group of athletic organizations. Only two or three women headed universities with Division I-A teams. But I'm a strong supporter of sports, and, much to the surprise of many people, I was a strong advocate for athletics. I did have to negotiate heavy-handedly when they tried to hire a woman basketball coach at a different salary than the male coach, even though she had an equivalent amount of experience. I had to constantly monitor the whole machismo issue in sports, and I did.

I retired from the presidency in 1990 and assumed a CSU trustee professorship. After a sabbatical year I took up residency in Los Angeles and was asked to direct the ACCESS Center, one of fifteen comprehensive regional centers for minority education at the CSU–Los Angeles campus. The center is funded by the NSF. We work at the K–12 level, especially in middle schools and high schools, to get underrepresented minorities interested in careers in science and math. We have programs in three categories: direct student intervention with Saturday science academies, summer science programs, or intensive residential math and science programs; university prep programs in high school; and teacher in-service training, including institutes on new ways to teach math and summer science academies.

I know that I was at a constant disadvantage because I was both black and a woman, but I used that as a drive to work hard and succeed. This was the world we lived in; who knows where I would have gone if I had been a white woman, or a white man? I was always optimistic about what I wanted to do and never thought anything was impossible. I always kept focused. I advise young women and minority students today that a long-term goal requires immediate and short-term actions, literally day by day. And that they should always keep their "eye on the prize."

PRESENT POSITIONS: President and Professor Emerita of Biological Science, California State University at Fullerton; Trustee Professor, California State University at Los Angeles

FIELD: Biology

RESEARCH AREAS: Factors influencing growth, morphology, and genetic expression of normal and neoplastic pigment cells; in vitro growth of mammalian neoplastic cells; changes produced in vitro by cancer chemotherapeutic agents, by hormones, and by other agents known to disrupt cell division

EDUCATION: B.A. in Biology (1944), Talladega College; M.S. in Cell Physiology (1947), New York University; Ph.D. in Physiology (1950), New York University

DATE/PLACE OF BIRTH: January 17, 1924/Chicago, Illinois

Jewel Plummer Cobb lives in Los Angeles, California.

INTERVIEW DATE: February 1995

Theo Colborn

Senior Scientist
WORLD WILDLIFE FUND

Theo Colborn began her professional life sharing a pharmacy business with her husband in northern New Jersey. The family later moved to a sheep farm in Colorado, where they lived an idyllic life until an enormous deposit of coal was discovered near their land during the energy crisis of the 1970s. In response to the increased mining activity that followed, Colborn became an environmental activist, working as a private citizen until frustration at not being taken seriously because she lacked the "right" credentials motivated her to enter graduate school at age fifty-one. Her current work focuses on examining the long-term and delayed effects of chemicals on developing embryos.

∾

The first thing I remember from my childhood is standing in a creek near the farmhouse where we lived, playing in the water, turning over rocks, catching crayfish, wondering about the other animals crawling on the rocks, and enjoying the sunshine. My mother loved birds and flowers and gardening, and I learned to love them too. I had a pet crow my brother caught for me, and it followed me around wherever I went. Being outdoors was a very important part of my life.

In high school, I discovered that I really loved biology and chemistry. I graduated during World War II, and although my family did not have the money to send me to college, I had a couple of options. I had a Navy scholarship to study mechanical drawing at a university in the Midwest, but I was fairly certain I wasn't interested in that. And there was a chance that I could go to the Juilliard School of Music on a piano scholarship, but I knew I would never be a concert pianist. Then a wonderful registrar at our high school insisted that I look at pharmacy. She had a good friend at the Rutgers College of Pharmacy in Newark, New Jersey. At that time, we lived in East Orange, which was only a train station away. So I went to the college to look it over, and I loved what I saw.

Theo Colborn by the Gunnison River in Colorado, 1976

I think being a child of the Depression made me want something that would give me a sense of security, and I thought pharmacy could. I loved it from the minute I walked in the door. In those days, we studied pharmacognosy (the study of crude drugs) and learned the genus and species names of all the medicinal plants. The curriculum was quite different from what it is today. I attended college on a four-year scholarship from the Vick Chemical Company, and was fascinated by everything I learned.

I met my husband, who was a war veteran, when he was finishing up his college training in pharmacy. We had our first child the day he was taking his final exam for his degree. We moved to northern New Jersey, where we eventually owned three pharmacies. I enjoyed it but always felt there was more to life. I served on the local school board and started a junior Audubon group. We built one of the first bluebird box trails in the country.

Then my husband became quite ill, and my children were reaching the age where we wanted them to have more of an outdoor experience. My husband and I also wanted more time together as a family, and we were concerned about pollution. Bedroom communities were moving farther and farther out from New York City, and air pollution was becoming a problem. So we packed up and moved to Boulder, Colorado. We attended graduate school at the University of Colorado for about a year, but my husband was not satisfied with that either. He wanted to try to raise beef on the western slope of the Rockies. I was not willing to buy a big ranch but agreed to try a smaller place. We bought a small sheep farm, which I ended up running with my daughter.

For a while we had an idyllic life, and then the world's largest lode of low-sulfur, high-BTU coal was found under our valley and very near our land. It was during the energy crisis of the 1970s, and it precipitated a turning point in my life. I became what is now called an environmental activist, trying to educate people about the government's decision to sacrifice our valley for the energy crisis. The valley was already overextended in coal leases,

and there wasn't enough water to supply the people already living in the valley, let alone the people who would be attracted if more mines were opened. But the government proceeded to issue more leases, and that's when several friends and I formed the Western Slope Energy Research Center and started fighting back with well-researched information.

About that time, my oldest daughter graduated from college and got a job working for a consulting firm doing water-quality work in our valley, where a new coal mine was being developed. She had also applied for a job in Alaska, and when the Alaska job came through she didn't want to miss the opportunity. I said, "You go to Alaska, I'll do your water quality work." Because I'd worked in the control laboratory of a pharmaceutical manufacturer while I was in college, practiced pharmacy ever since, and had been following the chemistry involved in water quality monitoring because of my activist work, the consultants were willing to hire me. I worked as a field technician, collecting water samples. I knew the area, the birds, the vegetation; this was my life. I soon got very interested in what was happening to invertebrates in streams, and I began to realize that invertebrates living below mines have more toxic metals in their exoskeletons than those living above mines.

As a private citizen, I could testify at federal hearings on coal leasing, land use, energy development, and minerals mining activity; but I was always the last on the agenda, and no one paid any attention to me. It made me mad because I was better informed than many of the people hired to speak at the hearings. I knew the lay of the land, I knew what they were talking about, and it made me furious that no one took me seriously because I didn't have the "right" credentials. So when my youngest daughter graduated from veterinary school and offered to take the sheep, I decided to go back to college. I was curious anyway; I've always been a scholar at heart. I also wanted an excuse to get off the farm in the summers, climb around the mountains, spend more time bird watching, and learn to iden-

*Theo Colborn in her office at the
World Wildlife Fund*
PHOTO BY SAM KITTNER

tify the wildlife and plant species, many of which I learned about in pharmacy school.

I was fifty-one when I started my master's work at Western State College of Colorado. My research focused on invertebrates in high-altitude streams, measuring the concentrations of toxic trace metals that they picked up in their exoskeletons above and below mine adits. I also worked out of Rocky Mountain Biological Laboratory (RMBL), where graduate students are mentored by some of the top scientists in the world. Like my high school adviser and other friends, people were again helping me. I was very fortunate; RMBL was a marvelous experience.

I went on to the University of Wisconsin for my Ph.D. in zoology under Dr. Stanley Dodson, one of the professors at RMBL. He wanted me to take distributed minors in epidemiology, water chemistry, and toxicology, which allowed me to catch up in disciplines relevant to questions I kept asking because of my global perspective. The most challenging part about going back to school was learning the advances in genetics, computers, and biochemistry. For years, I never had the time to read a novel or go to the movies. I was busy reading textbooks and scientific journals, and taking courses on evolution and ecology, which were not taught when I was in college. There was a lot of catching up to do.

After I got my degree, I was fortunate to be offered a congressional fellowship to work at the Office of Technology Assessment in Washington, D.C. That was the experience of a lifetime, especially for someone my age who had never been to Washington in her life. After two years, I moved to the Conservation Foundation (later absorbed by the World Wildlife Fund) to work with five public-policy people on a book about the state of the environment in the Great Lakes. It was up to me to provide an analysis of the health status of the wildlife and people living in the basin as well as the health of the ecosystem itself. That's how I became involved in the work I am doing today.

As I began collecting information on the wildlife, it became obvious that something was wrong. Many animals in the Great Lakes Basin were reproducing, but their offspring were not thriving. Even though the ecosystem seemed to have been cleaned up since the unregulated dumping of the 1950s and 1960s, and the concentration of chemicals in the system had dropped significantly, many animals still weren't thriving as they should. This problem continues today.

Thank goodness for computers! With computer storage and spreadsheet capabilities to organize information, it became obvious that effects on the endocrine system might be responsible for the myriad problems seen in the offspring. In almost every animal in the contaminated ecosystems around the world—the

Baltic, the North Sea, and the Mediterranean as well as the Great Lakes—there is evidence that the vital systems, including the endocrine system, are being affected. The same suite of persistent chemicals are found in the animals in these systems, although perhaps in different ratios. The endocrine system is closely involved with the development of the immune system and the brain, and thus has an impact on disease susceptibility and behavior. Damage to the endocrine system seemed to explain both the loss of reproductive capability and the embryonic and early mortality reported in the animals. It was becoming evident that chemicals in the environment were disrupting the chemical messengers that actually control development and control life.

I then began to worry about what was happening to humans in the Great Lakes region because humans take longer to reach reproductive age, live longer than the wild animals, and might therefore take longer to express some of the effects of chemical exposure. There was less literature available on the health of the people in the Great Lakes region than on the animals. My coauthor and I were particularly concerned because the chemicals we were finding in all animal tissue, including human tissue, had been tested quite thoroughly and they seemed to have passed the test for cancer. In our book *Great Lakes, Great Legacy,* we pointed out that the old risk-assessment paradigm based on cancer was not as protective as we thought it was and that it needed to be expanded. We needed a much more encompassing standard, such as species survival: Can an animal produce an offspring that's capable of reproducing?

I was certainly not a prominent scientist, and I knew there was no way for me to say, "Hey, I think I've discovered something that we should pay attention to" and get a response. So I decided to share my ideas with other people who were experts in their fields and see what they thought. With financial support and a great deal of encouragement from the W. Walton Jones Foundation and others, I brought together twenty-one scientists from seventeen different disciplines to discuss the topic of "Chemically Induced Alterations in Sexual Development: The Wildlife/Human Connection." By the end of the work session, the participants reached a consensus that there was a problem. They agreed that synthetic chemicals widely distributed in the environment, and thus in our bodies, compete for the same receptor sites that tell us how to develop and how to function.

That was a turning point. Since then people have been generous with their encouragement. I wouldn't be doing what I'm doing today if it hadn't been for hundreds of people supporting me and saying, "Don't stop" and "We need this." Researchers in academia and government laboratories also felt that this work was very important because it answered some key questions about wildlife and human health changes since the midcentury. Previously, clinical diseases, cancer, and mortality were the focus of health concerns. Here was a new paradigm that said disrupted gene expression—not genetic damage—could lead to functional deficits that undermine such human potential as reproductive success, behavior, intelligence, and susceptibility to disease.

I'm sixty-eight. I should be getting feeble, but in some ways I actually feel better now than I've felt in years. I love discovery, and every day there's something new in my mailbox. Every day I think I'm going to come to work and finish something, and every day there's an interruption. My team and I sit at the hub of a new idea.

As I look around my office at what's on my desk and floor, there are messages requesting our attendance at various meetings. I have an in-house staff meeting coming up in an hour to review our plan for the next three years. We're writing three proposals that are due in a few weeks. We're looking at budgets for each grant. I'm going to be a keynote speaker at three major conferences; there are little notes scattered over my desk about what I want to say and what kinds of slides I want to make. My most pressing commitment right now is a book I'm working on in collaboration with Dianne Dumanoski and Pete Myers. I'm working with the artist who's doing work for the book, and every three or four hours I get a new drawing by fax. I work late into the night and on weekends and holidays to do my major writing. There's never peace here; it's unbelievably stimulating and sometimes overwhelming.

Many people depend on us. Without planning it, we started a movement, and, unfortunately, the movement has gotten ahead of us. We haven't built the support to keep up with the demand on our time. I believe we have enough evidence to be concerned about what's happening to our children's behavior and intelligence. New studies continue to support the observation that human sperm counts have dropped at a million sperm per milliliter per year for the last fifty years. The fact that we only recognized it three years ago is an example of how insidious these effects are, and so it's critical for us to keep going. Believe me, there are those who do not want this information to become general knowledge. They are trying to stay ahead of the literature so that they can preempt what's breaking in the news with material to confuse people or deny what's happening. How I wish industry and its trade associations would pitch in and try to solve the problem instead of expending their resources and energy on denial!

I think we are making an impact. I know our work is changing basic attitudes, but more needs to be done. Toxicologists have got to stop thinking solely about single-chemical, high-dose testing, cancer, and "kill-'em-and-count-'em" assays. We need a new toxicology that incorporates ecological considerations. We need to rethink epidemiology as well. Epidemiology was designed to work with communicable disease, and it works well with rare problems. But when there are across-the-board subtle effects in a population, it does not work as well. There are many chemicals in the environment now that have the same effects on everyone, as well as different effects depending on the age of the individual at the time of exposure. It is futile to expect that a direct causal link will be made between a single chemical and an adverse health effect. As we are beginning to understand so well, the delay between exposure and effect is long. Epidemiology must take ecology more into consideration, and in the case of chemicals that disrupt the endocrine system, epidemiologists must start looking at the exposure of the mother of their victims before she became pregnant and while they were in the womb. In other words, we must look at the health of the offspring of directly exposed individuals. It could be years from the time a woman is exposed before her male child reaches age twenty and discovers his sperm numbers are low. Extensive work must accompany these changes at the laboratory level to replay actual environmental exposure and identify the biochemical and physiological processes driving the change.

I think the fact that I was out of science for so many years working as a pharmacist, a mother, and a farmer is actually an advantage in that I did not get locked into using scientific jargon. I find it easier than some scientists to find a word to describe something that the people at the street level can understand. While I worry constantly about sacrificing scientific accuracy, the ability to communicate in lay language has been valuable in outreach and education.

I have been fortunate. I started over again at fifty-one and have done many wonderful things that I had never done before. I'm very happy that I did. I have no regrets, and I never feel lonely. I am too busy. I've reached the point where the world is my home.

PRESENT POSITION: Senior Scientist at the World Wildlife Fund

FIELD: Environmental health

RESEARCH AREA: Long-term and delayed effects of contemporary chemicals on the developing embryo

EDUCATION: B.S. in Pharmacy (1947), Rutgers College of Pharmacy; M.A. in Science (1981), Western State College of Colorado; Ph.D. in Zoology (1985), University of Wisconsin–Madison

DATE/PLACE OF BIRTH: March 28, 1927/Plainfield, New Jersey

Theo Colborn lives and works in Washington, D.C., and has a home in Paonia, Colorado.

INTERVIEW DATE: August 1995

Lizabeth Coller

Software Verification Engineer
INDEPENDENT CONTRACTOR

A TV show on computer-generated special effects sparked Lizabeth Coller's interest in a technical career. She earned degrees in electrical and software engineering and spent eleven years working conventional full-time jobs. She now works as an independent contractor, enjoying the freedom and variability self-employment offers. Outside of work, she is active in the Seattle bisexual community and is a member of Digital Queers.

I'm a third-generation electrical engineer: my paternal grandfather specialized in power and worked for a public utility. My dad is an electrical engineer who started in power but moved into structures and building. I've always been into the computer end of things. When I told my mother my plans to become an engineer, she said, "Oh, no, you'll be just like your father!" Now she's really proud of my ability to take care of myself. I enjoy what I do, make good money, and I can do the things I like to do. She knows I won't have the same problems she had; she was very young when she married and had three kids by the time she was twenty-two. She was thirty when she finished college.

I currently do software verification as an independent contractor. Right now I'm working for a company that makes ultrasound machines. Last year I was working with electrocardiogram monitors and before that on radio frequency communication systems. I take the documented specifications and requirements for a product and write tests to verify that the functions and performance issues are actually met by the end product. For example, if the specification says, "The greymap display of the image can be reversed," I will write a test that looks for the control that does this, and check that the control actually causes a reverse image

Lizabeth Coller updating software verification specifications based on new requirements, 1996

of the original. If I find inconsistencies in the series of documents I use, I write up problem reports. This traceability is required both by good software process and by the various agencies that act as watchdogs over the medical-equipment companies such as the Food and Drug Administration.

What really excites me about my work is learning new things. Since I contract, I'm usually at a company for six months or a year, and I don't have time to get bored. I started contracting three years ago, after being an employee at various places for eleven years. I interview for a position, and usually the manager makes a decision in a day or two. I'm expected to go into a situation, pick up on things quickly, and do a good job. I like the flexibility: I can work a job and then take as much time off as I can afford. I like the pay—at least 50 percent over what I'd make otherwise. And since I'm not a direct employee, when things are slow I work less, and when things are busy I work more. And of course, I get paid overtime! The lack of stability doesn't bother me.

After eleven years of regular jobs in development, I burned out. I felt that my education and all the time I spent trying to do things the right way were really hurting my career because management just wanted me to have something done by the deadline and didn't really care if it was done right. I was working in various fields, doing real-time embedded systems. Some companies were better about setting up processes and procedures and allowing people the time and resources to follow these. But mostly I found managers being pushed by higher-ups to "just get it done." It became very frustrating for me to have a project almost finished and then have the requirements changed and still be expected to meet the original completion date. I found listening to marketing types proselytize about the marketplace just made me think less of them, not of the customers. When the customers are doctors, nurses, and other health-care providers, you know their level of intelligence and knowledge is not low.

Companies that bring me in as a contrac-

tor also pay my agency a large amount of money for my time, so they don't bring people like me in unless they have a big commitment to improving their work processes. Frequently they are places that want to do international business and so need to be ISO 9000 certified, which means they will be audited on this commitment by a third party. ISO 9000 certification requires that businesses adhere to quality standards set by the International Organization for Standardization. I'm much happier working for companies that want things done right; and being at the end of the path—doing the final check on the product—allows me to be very involved all along the way and still have some control over the quality of the work done.

At my current site, I work in a building with five hundred other people; I have my own nine-by-eight cube equipped with a very comfortable chair and my own Xterminal. I have a lot of personal things around, like pictures, cartoons, and some toys: a spinning top and colored blocks. I have a phone too, but I can turn it off.

At the beginning of a new job or product evaluation, I spend a lot of time reading the documentation and then talking with people about any questions I have. I may find missing requirements or direct contradictions that need to be taken care of. If I'm at a new company, I need to learn their processes and understand how they want me to do my job. I talk with marketing people about what they think the customer wants in the product. I'll sometimes talk with end users, in this case sonographers, about their experiences. I like to have as much knowledge as possible about who is using the equipment I'm working on so I have a better understanding of what they want. I'll talk to the systems people, who write detailed descriptions of what the underlying functions should do, and the software people who write the code that executes these. I end up getting to know everyone.

My day is really based on what phase of the project we're in. In the beginning I read a lot! I might try to talk with the different authors and search out other people with information that will be helpful to my understanding of the product. As the project goes on, I start to write tests. These can be as simple as "Step 1: Push this button. Verify the display at row X column Y is updated to value Z." Or I might write instructions for the automated test tool and then run the test.

On other days I work with the testers who execute the tests I've written. They may have corrections I need to make, or clarifications, or ideas to increase the usefulness of the tests. In crunch time I will work as a tester myself, executing tests, noting errors, and writing problem reports. Then I need to spend time with specific engineers to try to fix the problems. On the side, I also get involved in code walk-throughs, formal inspections, document reviews, and auditing of internal processes. In general, I spend a large part of the day talking with others.

My interest in engineering was actually sparked by Steven Spielberg. I was watching a special on TV many years ago about how he used computers to control the cameras in the filming of special effects. I asked my dad what kind of schooling I'd need to get into that type of work. He suggested electrical engineering, and since he was an electrical engineer himself I believed him. He was right. I have found my background to be a bigger asset than I could imagine. Everyone wants a coder who can read a schematic, read a data sheet, or help debug a board.

When I started college at Syracuse University, it was hard for me. I had been the top student in my high school, but I wasn't really challenged there, and I hadn't learned to study. At college I wasn't on top any more; my teachers didn't know me and expected me to perform at a low level. It took years to adjust.

One of the first engineers I met at school was surprised that I'd never seen a resistor or a chip, so he brought in a box from his car and gave me my first chance to see what I was getting into. Unfortunately, not everyone has been so helpful. I've had several really bad experiences with sexual harassment. I have had

to learn to trust myself and my abilities and not to allow anyone to make themselves feel superior at my expense.

For example, one year near the Christmas holidays I was sitting in my boss's office with him and another engineer. After the business part of the meeting was over, my boss started to ask me about any holiday parties I might be having, and whether there would be mistletoe, and if I'd do a lot of kissing. This line of questioning made me very uncomfortable, so I ignored him and talked about starting on the action items right away. Afterwards I talked with the other engineer who had been there, a man, and asked what he thought. He had been so appalled he hadn't known what to say. I also asked another woman about it, and she said I must have misunderstood the questions. Much later I realized the man was a pig.

Another time I had a boss who would stand in the doorway to my office and ask me to do something that required me to leave the office. When I would try to go through the doorway he would not move away. I always felt he wanted to get a cheap thrill by my having to rub against him on my way out; I was too timid to ask him to move: he was my boss, after all, and I must be too sensitive if this was bothering me. In retrospect, I see I've had problems dealing with men who have power over me, who held my job in their hands. But because I'm not small and cute, others can't believe that I would be sexually harassed. Even my father had to be hit over the head with these examples before he would believe me.

Fortunately, I don't have problems with my peers. If someone says or does something I don't like, I try to talk to them about it, about how it makes me uncomfortable. I also tell them if they continue the behavior in question I can report them. I have only needed to do that once. Off company time (at lunch) and off company grounds (out walking), a co-worker started to talk crudely about a young woman who was walking in front of us. I tried to tell him jokingly he was off base, and he started to tell me I was being judgmental by not accepting his opinion of this woman. The encounter ended very badly. My agency asked me to report it to the Human Resources Department, and I did. A short time later the man was laid off; it seems there were several complaints against him as well as problems with his job performance. I initially felt some guilt over my part in his dismissal, but I realized it was his problem and that I didn't have to be a part of his agenda.

I'm a strong woman, and this causes problems in my relationships with men, particularly those men who try to control me. If a man expects me to be passive, to take his direction without question, we're in trouble. But if he appreciates my experience and capabilities, and can give me a framework to work in, we do really well.

I've had to learn to tone down some of my opinions and not take things so personally. I once worked for someone who thought all women were first-level engineers and only men could be higher-level engineers. The problem was that I was a senior-level engineer. I now see I should have talked more with him, given him a better sense of what I was doing and how I did it, instead of taking the position that "I know my job; just leave me to do it." His attitude came from his background, his culture, and had little to do with me.

I was once hired just after the yearly raises had been given out, at a salary higher than anyone else in the department was getting. At the half-year mark, one of the male engineers was given a promotion and raise, not because he had worked for it but because he had found out I made more money than he did and he threatened to quit. Now, as a contractor, I make enough for me to be satisfied, and I don't discuss the differences with my coworkers. Why become angry? I don't need to go looking for more things to make my life hard.

I get a lot of social support from work. Since I spend so much time talking with people at work, we end up sharing things about our personal lives. It helps make a better work environment if I know why someone is having a bad day. At times I've found myself working very long hours, and I then make efforts to see people outside of work, even if it's a lunch date. I've been attracted to some people I worked with, but I've only dated one or two and never for long. I generally don't think it's a good idea. I have always made special efforts to meet the wives of the guys I worked with, to show them I had no intentions of snagging their husbands. I recognize that I may spend more time in a day with the guy than they do, and I respect their place in his life.

Now that I'm contracting, I am very active in the bisexual community in Seattle, and I'm pretty out to people in my work environments. I have a rainbow flag on my car, I wear a rainbow-colored necklace to hang my picture ID on, and I talk quite openly about my life and the groups I support. It helps that in my current work group three out of nine of us are queer. Overall, this place is very tolerant. Last week at a going-away lunch the man who was leaving brought his boyfriend, introduced him to everyone, and held his hand under the table. And no one said anything, even later. I'm sure not everyone was comfortable with it, but when the majority of folks are clearly tolerant, it makes it harder for those who aren't to cause problems.

Being out of the closet at work is a function of how confident you are, how good you are at what you do, and reading the signs. If I go somewhere with a lot of bumper stickers for right-wing groups or causes in the parking lot, that's a big warning. My general philosophy these days is if I don't fit in somewhere, I don't want to work there. This is not always easy to do if you live in an area with limited work opportunities, but it's definitely worth thinking about.

I also belong to a fairly new group called Digital Queers. They act as fund-raisers for queer nonprofit groups, helping them get computerized, on-line, and networked. My involvement allows me to work with other high-tech people and give something worthwhile to my community.

I like knowing I have the skills that are in demand. My current boss tells me all the time how much my skills are needed. And he is helping me continue to gain more so I'm marketable after this job. This is a perfect situation, and it won't be like this everywhere. But I'm enjoying it while I'm here.

PRESENT POSITION: Software Verification Engineer

FIELD: Software engineering

SPECIALTIES: Software verification and validation, human-computer interface

EDUCATION: B.S. in Electrical Engineering (1981), Syracuse University; Master of Software Engineering (1992), Seattle University

DATE/PLACE OF BIRTH: September 21, 1960/ Pottsville, Pennsylvania

Lizabeth Coller lives in Seattle, Washington, with her partner of two years, four cats, and one dog. Nonwork activities include reading, movies, music, hiking, and travel. They hope to add children to the family soon.

INTERVIEW DATE: September 1995

Margarita H. Colmenares

Director, Corporate Liaison
U.S. DEPARTMENT OF EDUCATION

Margarita Colmenares excelled in math and science through junior high but was detoured into high school secretarial courses after being told by a counselor she wasn't "smart enough" to take algebra. As a high school student, she was employed by Xerox Corporation, where her business mentors encouraged her to explore all opportunities. During college, she discovered engineering by accident and went on to graduate with an engineering degree from Stanford. Colmenares was the first female to be elected president of the Society of Hispanic Professional Engineers, and she is a former White House Fellow. At the U.S. Department of Education, she draws on her experience in the private sector and her work in community service to make "better education everybody's business."

∽

I grew up in a low-income, working-class neighborhood in Sacramento, the eldest of five. My parents immigrated to the United States from Mexico in the 1950s in search of new opportunities for themselves and the family they were planning to have. They settled in Alkali Flats, the oldest residential neighborhood in the heart of the city and within walking distance of the state capitol. My neighborhood was always in a constant state of flux—families arriving, families leaving. It was the primary entry point for immigrant and migrant families that came to the fertile Sacramento Valley to pick almonds, peaches, tomatoes, and asparagus. My father's first job was picking crops; later he took a job at a canning and warehouse facility while my mother worked in a department store. Even though

both parents worked, our family needed to generate extra income, so we would all pitch in to help my brothers deliver more than four hundred newspapers throughout downtown Sacramento each day. We were all expected to work and to do well in school.

The houses on our block didn't have big, grassy backyards, so we used to entertain ourselves by playing badminton or soccer in the alleys. Sometimes we would simply chase each other up and down the sidewalks, between and behind the houses. From one summer to the next, we never had the same group of children to play with. It was always very sad at the end of every summer, as our newfound play-

Margarita Colmenares at age seventeen

mates moved away with their migrant families to go pick the next season of crops in Kansas, Texas, or Nebraska.

In the evenings, my dad would sit down and read the paper, and my sister and brothers and I would go get our books and read along with him. Since we lived within walking distance of the city library, it wasn't unusual to see the Colmenares kids hauling cartloads of books to and from the library. It was a big deal to get a library card and have the privilege of borrowing books. I loved to read so much, I made my poor eyesight worse because I refused to put a book down until I finished it, even if it meant continuing to read by moonlight or with a flashlight under the covers.

My love for reading spilled over to other subjects. In the second grade I was very proud to be selected to help tutor other children in reading. I was very competitive, and there was no boy who could beat me at math or spelling. As the smartest girl in my eighth grade science class, I had high expectations upon entering high school. It's not surprising that when people expect you to be smart, you are. When people expect you to be dumb, either you prove them wrong or end up meeting those low expectations as well. Even though I had straight A's and B's going into high school, I did not do well on a placement exam and ended up in typing, shorthand, and adding-machine classes. I was advised by my counselor that I wasn't "smart enough" to take algebra. Not to be outdone, I became the fastest typist and quickest shorthand taker. This was little consolation when, at a schoolwide awards ceremony, I was recognized for my typing and shorthand skills while others were recognized for their math and science prowess.

The summer after my sophomore year I had an opportunity that provided new challenges for me. I was hired by the local branch of Xerox Corporation, which had started a community outreach program to hire four inner-city youths. In contrast to my high school experience, Xerox gave me significant and ever-increasing responsibilities. By the age of seventeen, I was entrusted to develop a customer

care program; I developed a process to survey and track customer satisfaction levels, which was then shared with management. My Xerox colleagues quickly recognized my potential and reaffirmed my desire to go to college.

Because I was so frustrated with what was going on in high school, I wanted to finish early. I started attending summer school and taking night classes and finished my high school requirements by my junior year. Since my counselors thought I was too young to graduate and "find a job," they allowed me to enroll half time in high school and half time in community college. By the second half of my senior year, I was attending the community college full time. As soon as I met the admission requirements, I transferred to California State University–Sacramento, where I enrolled as a business major.

As I entered my second year of taking college courses, I discovered engineering by accident. I was on a study date in the library. My boyfriend had all his books spread out and was so totally absorbed that I leaned over to see what he was studying. I read a word problem that required determining the thrust and acceleration of a space shuttle rocket. I flipped the cover of the book and naively asked, "What is physics?" He explained to me that physics was one of the courses required for engineering. My next question was, "What is engineering?"

By the next school day, I had resolved to switch my major from business to engineering and made an appointment with the dean of the School of Engineering. Even though I hadn't taken chemistry, physics, or calculus in high school, I convinced him in our meeting that I really wanted to pursue an engineering degree. After some contemplation, he said, "OK, let's sign you up and see how you do." Much later I discovered that this dean had initiated the Chicanito Science Project, which introduced science-related careers to sixth and seventh graders. Perhaps when I walked into his office that day, he thought, "Better late than never."

I signed up for chemistry, physics, and other introductory engineering classes. It took a lot of work to get A's and B's, but I was

Margarita Colmenares in front of the White House, Washington, D.C., 1996
PHOTO BY LUIS FERNANDEZ

ing stations, and dams, massive amounts of water are moved from the northern part of the state to the south. I did structural inspections, interpreted data, and wrote technical reports. It was a terrific experience because I was able to see what was expected of engineers. It gave me a lot of confidence as I approached the theoretical course work at school. As I realized how something was going to be used, I became more interested in learning it.

I was preparing to enroll at the University of California–Davis (which was within commuting distance of my home in Sacramento) when I was accepted by Stanford University as a transfer student. I was ecstatic, incredulous, and full of trepidation. I wondered if I was going to be out of my league. I was so scared during my first quarter at Stanford that I didn't get involved in any extracurricular activities for fear that it would affect my grades.

Even though I was doing well in school, I started to feel unhappy. My life wasn't balanced. I have always tried to maintain a balance between working and community service. My parents have always been very involved in the community: they would help newly arrived immigrants enroll their children in school or tell them how to get their driver's license. We were always the first family in our neighborhood with a yard sign. On election day, my dad has been known to get out a bullhorn and drive around the neighborhood, reminding people to vote. We all grew up with the confidence that we could help or influence others. In my early teens, I tutored younger kids in math, writing, and reading at the local neighborhood center. And in my later teens, my sister and I started a Mexican folk dance group which performed at neighborhood festivals, nursing homes, weddings, and schools.

As I regained confidence in my academic ability, I eased my way back into extracurricular activities. I tutored, mentored, and taught young children who lived in East Palo Alto, an area of high poverty and high unemployment that was adjacent to the university. I also became a resident assistant in my dorm and organized political, cultural, and community

challenged and excited. I returned to the community college the following semester, lured by the prospect of competing for the General Electric Scholarship for Women and Minorities, which paid up to 80 percent of tuition and books, depending on financial need. Ultimately, I was awarded several scholarships and grants, from both the private and public sectors; but I still had to work part-time during college to make ends meet.

I loved my engineering course work but wanted to confirm my enthusiasm, so I talked my way into a position as an engineering student assistant at the California Department of Water Resources. I worked after school and full-time during the summer and school breaks. I was part of a surveillance team assigned to assess the structural integrity of the California aqueduct system immediately following an earthquake as well as at regular intervals. Through a series of aqueducts, pump-

events for the dorm and surrounding community.

In 1981, I graduated from Stanford with a civil engineering degree and went to work at Chevron. My job required me to remain fairly mobile, and over a span of ten years I lived in six cities. While based in Salt Lake City, I managed construction crews in Utah, Nevada, Idaho, and Wyoming. At company headquarters in San Francisco, I coordinated and developed training assignments for engineers from companies worldwide that did business with Chevron. In Houston, I managed our environmental and safety compliance efforts with local and state regulators in Texas, Louisiana, Arkansas, Oklahoma, and New Mexico. In Los Angeles, I supervised a multimillion dollar environmental clean-up project and later, as an air quality specialist, I worked with regulatory agencies to reduce air emissions into the Los Angeles basin.

I also continued my involvement with community service. Immediately following my college graduation, I organized and was elected founding president of the San Francisco chapter of the Society of Hispanic Professional Engineers (SHPE), a nonprofit volunteer organization. SHPE provides role models, financial assistance, and inspiration to aspiring engineering students. For the next ten years, I served in various leadership capacities. Eventually I was elected national president, the first female to head this nonprofit organization of more than ten thousand volunteers.

As national president, I met thousands of engineering students, parents, counselors, and corporate representatives. One time I spoke to a group of parents in Denver at an "Expanding Your Horizons" conference for young women. Following my remarks, a mother in the audience stood up and said, "My teenager is always reading *Cosmopolitan* and *Seventeen;* she's really into this glamour thing. How do I get her interested in engineering? There's such a nerdy stereotype of engineers." I had on a very chic red suit that day, so I stepped from behind the podium into their full view and asked, "Do I look like an engineer?" They all

started laughing, and we agreed then that we need to change people's concepts of what engineers look like.

All my life I've encountered people who are either surprised or curious that I'm an engineer. One such incident occurred at a construction site across the street from Golden Gate Park in San Francisco. I was supervising a crew that was replacing steel underground storage tanks with fiberglass tanks. Local fire and safety regulations required sign-offs by the fire marshal before the job was completed. I was waiting for the fire marshal, who was late, when all of a sudden a red car screeched onto the site. A rather large man emerged and started walking very quickly past me, even though I was standing at the edge of this very large hole in the ground. He moved toward an older man standing by the office, yelling out, "Where's the engineer?" The other man pointed to me and said, "She's right there." He wheeled around on his heels and exclaimed, "*You're* the engineer?!"

In other instances, it has been necessary to gain the confidence of my colleagues. When one of my job assignments took me to Utah, on the plane ride over from Colorado my male colleague turned to me halfway through the flight and said, "You know, I just don't understand why they're sending you to replace me." When I naively asked, "What do you mean?" he replied, "Well, you're a woman and you're Hispanic." Up to that point, I don't think I had given it any real consideration, but his comment made me realize that I probably would be the first minority female engineer sent to supervise construction crews in the Rocky Mountain region.

Sure enough, the construction crews were quick to size me up. They tried to get away with shortcuts on the specs, but I held my ground. On a job in Chubbuck, Idaho, I stuck through a small blizzard well past midnight while the crew worked overtime to finish securing an underground tank. They were impressed that I didn't retire to the comfortable confines of my hotel room until the job was finished and simply wait to be called out for the final inspection. My field assignment was to have lasted nine months, but because of cooperation with the various crews we were done in seven months, ahead of schedule and below budget. When it was time for me to return to California, the crews called up my bosses in Denver and told them they didn't want me to leave.

When I was in school, IBM was extremely visible at various college campuses around the country through their executive-on-loan program. IBM executives were allowed to take a one-year sabbatical to work in education. It was this program that inspired me to ask Chevron to put me on loan full-time to SHPE. I wrote a proposal describing the need for the company to make an investment in human capital, comparing it to the company's current investments in oil fields—vast amounts of money—to yield future long-term dividends. I stressed that it was imperative that the company devote resources in populations that would make up a greater percentage of the future workforce. My proposal was ultimately approved by the board of directors, and I became a Chevron executive-on-loan, enabling me to work full-time for SHPE while being reimbursed by Chevron for salary and travel expenses.

Following my second year as SHPE national president, I applied for and was selected as a White House Fellow. Fellows are selected for "outstanding leadership ability, professional excellence, intellectual ability, character, and commitment to community and national service" and are given one-year assignments at the White House or a cabinet agency. By a wonderful coincidence, I was assigned to work with David Kearns, then Deputy Secretary of Education and former CEO of Xerox Corporation. I shared with him the significant role that Xerox had played in preparing me for the workplace and broadening my horizons; my experience at Xerox had helped me develop my communication, presentation, and teamwork skills. We were both delighted that our lives intersected through the White House Fellow program. He shared with me that it was under his leadership as CEO of Xerox,

some twenty years earlier, that the company initiated the Community Involvement Program, which brought me into the corporate environment as a high school student.

As a White House Fellow I was assigned to work with an interagency council on math and science education. The council's purpose was to review and coordinate federal spending on math and science education by sixteen federal agencies including NASA, the National Science Foundation, the Smithsonian Institution, and the Department of Education. After my one-year stint in Washington, D.C., I returned to Chevron to take on an international marketing assignment in Latin America. The summer following President Clinton's election, I was invited to apply for my current position.

As Director of Corporate Liaison for the U.S. Department of Education, I work with business leaders and organizations from around the country to engage their support for education. There is an incredible need to help young people understand what awaits them in the working world. During a visit to a high school calculus class, I shared examples of engineering projects I had managed. As we talked through some of the problems I solved as an engineer, one of the students suddenly waved his arms excitedly as he pointed to all the math equations on the classroom walls and proclaimed, "So that's why we need to learn all this stuff!" As I was leaving, the teacher asked me to come back more often to his classroom. It's because this scene has been repeated so often that I'm convinced employers should be encouraged to give their employees time to be involved in classrooms as resources for teachers and mentors for students.

I believe it's never too early to introduce kids to what awaits them. For example, at a school in Vermont, fourth graders visited a local manufacturing plant that makes diapers. The kids were given a plant tour of the entire operation. At the conclusion, a voice came over the loudspeaker and announced, "You are now all employees of the company. We just found out that we are losing our market share to China. Each of you will have to pick a job and figure out how to get it back." This experience showed the students how they could use what they're learning in school to solve real-life problems.

In my job, one of my activities is to work with business leaders who have committed their organizations to family-friendly practices. There is no shortage of examples: John Hancock has an on-site child care facility, GTE Corporation provides information to employees and their children on the college admissions and financial aid process, and Southern California Edison conducts parenting seminars for their employees. Through publications, speeches, and satellite town meetings, the Department of Education shares the ideas and programs that are working.

More than thirty years of research findings show that a caring adult can make all the difference in a child's learning. In my own home, my parents were constantly saying, "Tú vas a ir al colegio!"—"You're going to go to college!"—even though they had never been to college themselves. I am a product of the "whole village" working together to educate a child. Without all of the components working together—my parents, caring teachers, business mentors, and my community activities—I would not be where I am today.

I enjoy keeping in shape, and dance has continued to be a constant in my life. Over the years, I've tried jazz, country, shag, tango, and East and West Coast swing. I absolutely love dancing! I believe that the performing arts have made me a more poised, confident, and well-rounded individual. Currently, I'm in the process of helping to organize a dance group in Washington. We will teach adults and eventually, I hope, children. I also love to travel and have been to Israel, Poland, Germany, Ukraine, Russia, France, Mexico, Guatemala, El Salvador, Nicaragua, Colombia, and to the Amazon. I would love to take four to six months off and travel throughout the Pacific Rim. Within the next year, I will need to decide whether to go back to school, work in the nonprofit sector, or find a job that marries my international and environmental engineering interests.

PRESENT POSITION: Director of Corporate Liaison, U.S. Department of Education

FIELD: Environmental engineering

SPECIALTY: International marketing and private-public partnerships

EDUCATION: B.S. in Civil Engineering (1981), Stanford University

DATE/PLACE OF BIRTH: July 20, 1957/Sacramento, California

Margarita H. Colmenares loves old buildings and lives in a quaint apartment with hardwood floors in the Adams-Morgan section of Washington, D.C., the most ethnically diverse area of the city.

INTERVIEW DATE: February 1996

Esther Marly Conwell

Research Fellow
XEROX CORPORATION

Adjunct Professor
UNIVERSITY OF ROCHESTER

Esther Conwell's perseverance has paid off. She faced many challenges early in her career: At her first job, her salary was reduced when the company discovered there was no payroll classification for women in her position, and in one of her first post-Ph.D. interviews, another company said it had a rule against hiring married women. Nevertheless, she ended up with a successful career at GTE and later Xerox. At seventy-three, she continues to work, although she is unavailable on Tuesday and Friday mornings, when she attends ballet classes.

I first took physics at Brooklyn College before it was completely coed. The school had been created by combining a men's college and a women's college, and I had my elementary physics in an all-women's class, a very good way to start. When the teacher gave sailboat problems, requiring the use of vectors of forces, for instance, he'd ask, "When the wind is blowing this way, how do you put the sail?" As city girls, we simply hadn't had the experience of sailing that boys might have. So the teacher had to explain how vectors of forces applied to the problem in a way we could understand, and that helped me feel I could cope with the assigned problems. It gave me and the others a measure of confidence.

Although I was thinking of majoring in chemistry, and physics was only an elective, I found physics suited my temperament better. I was more interested in concepts—general descriptions of nature and physical systems—than in lab work. I did end up as a theoretical physicist, the kind who doesn't handle equipment, probably because, as a woman, I never had experience handling tools until I went to graduate school. My family lived in an apartment, and there was no occasion or need for me, or even for my father, to learn any such skills.

My parents were immigrants who did not have a chance for much of an education. But they were very insistent that my two sisters and I get a good education. In elementary school, I skipped five times, and would complete half of each grade. So I was quite young—only nineteen—when I finished college. In the late 1930s and early 1940s, it wasn't typical for

Esther Conwell, 1994

women to go to graduate school either. However, in college, one member of the physics department—Professor Kurrelmeyer—encouraged me to go to graduate school, told me where to apply, and helped me a lot with information and his positive attitude.

Overall, I believe it's better to go to a school where they have women on the faculty and a special appreciation for women's differences and problems. For instance, Purdue has a special program for women engineers; but in general, few schools offer such things. Women's colleges, insofar as they offer science, are serious about it and educate their women well. Most research universities have too few women on their faculties and certainly could do much more to improve the situation for women.

Throughout the years—even while employed with major corporations—I always believed it was important to be part of academe. I taught at Brooklyn College from 1946 until 1951; and I have been a visiting professor at the École Normale Supérieure, University of Paris, France; a staff member with the Department of Applied Physics at Stanford University; and the Abby Rockefeller Mauze Professor at MIT. Since 1990 I have been an adjunct professor of chemistry with the University of Rochester.

In general in the United States, it's not typical for women to go into physics. When I was starting out, something like 3 percent of the American Physical Society were women. Now it's increased somewhat—maybe up to 7 percent. The low percentage seems to be particularly characteristic of the United States. Many European countries have a higher proportion of women physicists. That's something the Committee on Women in Science and Engineering of the National Research Council, of which I was a member, wants to study. Obviously, the sociology and the attitude toward women in science in the United States is different, and not always supportive. But science is a good career opportunity area for women.

The first job I had was a summer job while still in graduate school. They hired me as an assistant engineer at Western Electric, on the basis of experience equivalent to a master's degree. A couple of weeks after I was hired, my boss told me they had discovered there was no such payroll classification for women. They made me an engineer's assistant and reduced my salary.

A few years after that, when I was looking for my first full-time job, I was interviewed by IBM. Finally they told me they couldn't hire me because IBM had a rule against hiring married women. Of course, that was a long time ago, and I know they've changed their policy and now have women in the research labs and even as vice presidents. Those were some of my early experiences. I get the most credit for perseverance! My first regular industrial job was with Sylvania, which became General Telephone and Electronics. For twenty years, I had a number of positions with GTE: member of the technical staff, manager of the Electronic Materials Program, and manager of the physics department. My fundamental studies there were in the properties of semiconductors, especially transport, acoustoelectric effect, and integrated optics.

Today some companies are trying hard to do right by women. Some businesses offer a situation for women that is better than that in academic life; of course the other end of the scale exists in industry as well—some companies are worse for women than academe. I believe one of the good companies is my own—Xerox Corporation. I've been with Xerox since 1972. I began there as a principal scientist and during part of that time was also manager of the Electrooptics Program; I've been a research fellow there since 1981. In 1983 I was also a member of the American Physical Society Council Executive Committee.

A woman today can probably see pretty quickly what a company offers, how it treats women, and whether it intends to give her the same kind of professional career as it would a man. A book that talks about which companies are good for women is *Best Companies for Women* by Baila Zeitz and Lorraine Dusky, published by Simon and Schuster in 1988. In addition, I recommend talking with women who currently work in a company. They could speak off the record, first hand, to someone considering employment.

When I was younger, I'm sure my efforts to balance career and family were very typical. It was important for me to have a supportive husband who was interested in my career. Fortunately, I also made enough money to afford a full-time housekeeper. After having my son, I went back to work part-time in three months and full-time in six months. But housekeepers could be a problem, and at times I didn't know whether I would have child-care coverage the following Monday—that was stressful.

My husband, Abraham Rothberg, is a writer. He's had many careers—he holds a Ph.D. in English literature, has been a teacher, and writes fiction and nonfiction. Some of Abe's books are in the local library. I recommend a "portable husband," which a writer is. I also recommend, if possible, marrying outside of your field because it's hard to find two jobs in the same place with the same specialty.

My son, Lewis, is a physicist and to some extent works in the same field I do. He's been at AT&T Bell Labs for ten years and is a distinguished member of the technical staff. It's nice having a son you can discuss your work with. Sometimes we give papers on the same program and go to the same conferences. That's worth a lot to me and gives me enormous satisfaction.

If women really want to succeed today, they will have to work extraordinarily hard. I know I had to. I am author of one book, *High Field Transport in Semiconductors,* have edited several other books, and have written more than two hundred technical publications in condensed matter physics, electrical engineering, and physical chemistry. I'm proud to say I hold several patents as well—for a microwave power detector, externally controllable miniature lasers, elastomer waveguide optical modulators, and a waveguide imaging system.

Even though at times it was tough, and I had to call up an enormous amount of energy, I have served on over forty professional and government service committees throughout my career, including the American Physical Society's Committee on Women in Physics; the Committee on the Education and Employment of Women in Science and Engineering of the National Research Council (NRC) Commission on Human Resources; and the NRC Committee on Women's Employment and Related Social Issues. Because of my technical work and contributions, I am a member of seven honorary academies and societies, among them the New York Academy of Sciences, the American Academy of Arts and Sciences, and the National Academies of Science and Engineering. While all of this has kept me—and still keeps me—extremely busy, currently, on Tuesday and Friday mornings I'm definitely unavailable. That's when I attend my ballet classes!

PRESENT POSITIONS: Research Fellow, Xerox Corporation, and Adjunct Professor, University of Rochester

FIELD: Physical science

RESEARCH AREA: Solid state physics

EDUCATION: B.A. in Physics (1942), Brooklyn College; M.S. in Physics (1945), University of Rochester; Ph.D. in Physics (1948), University of Chicago

DATE/PLACE OF BIRTH: May 23, 1922/New York, New York

Esther Conwell lives in Brighton, New York, with her husband.

INTERVIEW DATE: May 1995

Debbie C. Crans

Associate Professor of Organic Chemistry
COLORADO STATE UNIVERSITY

Debbie Crans grew up in Denmark as an only child. Her mother was never afraid to do things that other people wouldn't even dream of, and she passed this trait along to Debbie, who applied to (and attended) Harvard because she could not have faced herself if she had failed to apply "for fear of being turned down." She earned her Ph.D. in organic chemistry and currently works on the chemistry and biochemistry of vanadium compounds, which she hopes will eventually lead to oral substitutes for insulin injections.

❧

As a biological chemist I am interested in biological problems that require an in-depth and detailed understanding and application of chemistry. When I became an assistant professor in 1987, I began with an interest in studying how enzymes worked. Enzymes are proteins that do most of the metabolic conversions in the body; they are responsible for the conversion of food to energy. Specifically, I was interested in how enzymes recognize substrates, the compounds on which the enzymes act (for example, nutrients or drug molecules). Many substrates consist of an organic uncharged part and an inorganic charged part. When I began my research program, most recognition studies focused on the organic uncharged part. I was interested in studying enzyme recognition of charged substrates, and as I explored various ways of studying this question, I became familiar with vanadium chemistry. Vanadate, one form of vanadium, could potentially replace the inorganic portion of a substrate. Furthermore, I learned that the vanadium chemistry I was considering had im-

plications of relevance to diabetes. Although I never lose sight of the fundamental problem under study, I do enjoy working on problems that may have real, practical importance. I now only work on a problem if I can see a future benefit to humanity. Currently, my research focuses on the chemistry and biochemistry of vanadium compounds. Last year two vanadium compounds were tested as oral substitutes for insulin in humans. If such compounds are effective, they will eventually relieve diabetes patients from daily insulin injections.

The frustrating part of the vanadium compounds story is the amount of time it took to reach this point. The insulin effect was first ob-

Debbie Crans in her lab in the Department of Chemistry at Colorado State University

served in 1980 in a test tube, but it wasn't until five years later that another research group took these compounds and determined that they also worked in rats. And it was nine more years (1994) before there was a study in humans. There are two major reasons for the slow progress. First, the researchers saw some toxicity in some of the animals, partly because the M.D.'s and toxicologists working on this project didn't understand the importance of the chemistry, so the experiments were not performed consistently. As a result, different laboratories had problems repeating each other's experiments. For example, when a compound is administered to an animal in drinking water, it matters what the pH of the water is and what other compounds are added to the water. If a compound is used in a form that results in a high pH, the animal may resist drinking the fluid simply because of this higher pH, which gives it a "soapy" taste. Alternatively, if a compound such as citric acid is added to decrease the pH, a new vanadium compound having different biological activity can form.

What the research project needed was a molecular scientist bridging chemistry and biochemistry to determine why the different laboratories were obtaining different results. Simply understanding the chemistry relevant to biological conditions allows us to understand how these materials would interact with proteins, which explains many of the reported discrepancies. Perhaps even some of the toxic effects can be explained by these side reactions, a problem we are now examining. I may not be the scientist who discovers the vanadium compound that will become an insulin replacement, but there is no doubt in my mind that my work is helping to pioneer this field and is an important stepping stone for what happens in the future.

Even though I am an organic chemist by training and teach organic chemistry, many people believe I am an inorganic chemist. I am comfortable interacting and making contributions in three different fields: bioinorganic chemistry, bioorganic chemistry, and biochemistry (enzymology). Quite frankly, this kind of cross-disciplinary approach to science is common for many women. Women often choose problems that are relevant to the real world, and such problems in science are often interdisciplinary and less likely to fit the classical ways science disciplines are defined.

I attribute much of my creativity and perseverance to my mother. She was never afraid to do things that other people wouldn't even dream of, and she passed this trait on to me. I was raised in Denmark as an only child. My mother was always my best friend and most ardent supporter. She had little formal schooling but spoke eight languages fluently. She was raised in Holland and had been taken out of school during World War II to work in show business. She was an artist, an acrobat, and a model who stopped working when she married at twenty-one and began working again in her thirties. She took classes to improve her promotion possibilities and worked her way up to a librarian in Nationalbanken (the bank printing currency in Denmark), quite an accomplishment for someone who never completed high school. No matter what she did, she always had time for me and supported all of my educational choices. Her attitude was different from my grandmother's idea that "it doesn't matter if she's good in school, she's a girl." My mother was and will continue to be a major influence in my life even though she passed away several years ago.

I became interested in science in high school. Throughout high school and junior college I was intrigued by two fields: psychology and chemistry. I thought that if I went into psychology I would never do chemistry as a hobby, but if I went into chemistry I would maintain my interest in people. I didn't know that if I went into chemistry I wouldn't have time for anything else for quite a while, but I have never regretted my choice. I majored in biochemistry at the University of Copenhagen because I was interested in chemistry as it applied to biology. When I was close to graduating with the candidate of sciences degree, which is equivalent to a master's degree in the United States, there was a hiring freeze on academic jobs in Denmark. I knew that if I wanted to land an academic job, I was better off going abroad to earn a Ph.D.

There was an American professor named James P. Snyder at the University of Copenhagen with whom I had done research during my undergraduate years. He was my first real mentor and encouraged me to apply to the top universities in the United States, England, and Germany. I was accepted into all the universities to which I applied, including Berkeley, MIT, Harvard, Columbia, Cornell, and California Institute of Technology.

I'd always thought of myself as an average person intellectually. I was never number one in my class, even in grade school. I never really expected to get into most of the universities to which I applied, especially Harvard. However, I was determined; I applied because I couldn't have faced myself if I didn't try for fear of being turned down. When I was accepted to Harvard I thought it was a mistake, particularly since my mentor wanted me to attend one of his alma maters, Columbia or Cornell. It was a difficult decision. I surveyed all of my professors; everyone suggested the universities they knew something about (usually because they visited there) *and* Harvard. So in 1980 I entered Harvard as a graduate student.

I have always thought of myself as creative, persistent, stubborn, smart, and hardworking. However, I felt completely lost when I arrived at Harvard. Many of the graduate students had attended schools like MIT, Princeton, and Berkeley as undergraduates, and most of them were sharp as nails. I immediately formed a study and support group with two other students; we worked together on problems and helped each other. I never looked upon myself as the strongest of the three. When the first exam was returned, I had expected to be at the bottom of the heap. When I realized that I had one of the top scores in the class, I was so shocked I couldn't speak. I think that many women lack the confidence that many men have. My two friends said, "Don't worry, Debbie, we'll work harder and get through this together"; they had scored with the bottom half of the class.

Debbie Crans, her husband, Christopher Roberts, and their twin daughters, Gerrie and Patricia
PHOTO BY STAN KERNS, CONTEMPORARY STUDIOS

My success in graduate school was helped by the right choice of a research adviser, George M. Whitesides; he understood my creativity and personality. Although he interacted very little with me, he, more than anyone else, toughened me up and prepared me for what was to come in the future. Harvard was a rough place to be, but it's a fantastic place to have been if you survive it intact.

I did my two-year postdoc at UCLA. I wanted to work with a "real" biochemist, but I knew if I did a postdoc with a biochemist it would be difficult to get a job in a chemistry department. So I opted for a joint postdoc with a chemist and a biochemist. Most of my laboratory work at UCLA felt like a nightmare. My two professors were philosophically far apart and agreed on very little. When one thought I was making progress, the other was unhappy with me, and vice versa. Even though I did not accomplish much for my advisers, I learned a lot, especially about the importance of effective communication across fields and disciplines, and I made some life-long friends in the process.

Since I arrived at Colorado State University in January 1987, I have mentored many women as well as men. I never had a woman science professor, let alone a woman mentor, during my undergraduate years; but I did interact in graduate school with a female physical chemist, Sine Sarsen, who was a collaborator of my mentor. She showed me that a delightful female with a husband and kids could make it in the field of chemistry. I want to do the same for my students and have been running a Women in Science program at Colorado State University. This program was created by the dean of natural sciences, John C. Raich, to improve the environment for women at Colorado State. During the two years I have been director, we have sponsored many programs for faculty, graduate, and undergraduate women. I try to organize events to facilitate the development of these women. It is important that a support network is available and that the wonderful aspects of science are shared and made available for young women to see and experience.

I find myself occasionally talking with my male colleagues about their women students because it seems that they are either too supportive or not supportive enough. I think one is just as harmful as the other. A distinguished colleague of mine had an extremely talented woman student who went to Stanford for her postdoc. She was so used to being catered to and emotionally supported by a research adviser, who treated her like a daughter, that she could not take the increased pressures in a more competitive environment with a less nurturing adviser. She ended up changing careers.

I married at thirty-five after receiving tenure. I married late because I didn't feel able to handle marriage and a career while working toward tenure, and I was not willing to make compromises early in my life and career. I needed time to mature. Had I married one of the men I dated when I was younger, it would have been catastrophic. I waited instead and hit the jackpot on the first try. My husband and I had known each other for many years; he was my lab partner and friend throughout graduate school. He went off to do his postdoc in Colorado when I left for UCLA. Destiny placed me at Colorado State University and put us together when we both were ready for a lasting commitment. My spouse, Christopher R. Roberts, is also a chemist and he works in industry. He supports me both emotionally and intellectually. He doesn't like the amount of travel I must do, but he accepts it. We have a wonderful marriage. I think it's vitally important for young women to be careful to choose someone who won't be intimidated by their intellect and success and who understands the nature of their work. Most men I dated couldn't understand that I couldn't stop a reaction when it was running in the lab. If it meant being there twenty hours straight, that's what was necessary. They couldn't understand that it didn't have anything to do with my feelings toward them. Another chemist understands this better. Chris and I had twin daughters in August 1995. One of the girls is named Gerrie, after my mother, and the other is named Patricia. Their arrival has enriched and complicated our lives.

When I think about what it takes for women to be successful as scientists, four categories come to mind into which most successful women scientists fall: some are oblivious to negative feedback; some are stubborn, and the more they hear "you can't do this," the harder they try; others are very creative and take unusual paths in both their careers and personal lives; and a few are simply incredibly brilliant. Most women fall into the first three categories, and there is room for all types of personalities. I consider myself part of the "stubborn" category. I've always found science fun and stimulating. For me it is important to remember the wonderful aspects of it even when I experience unpleasantness. After all, life is not all fun.

PRESENT POSITION: Associate Professor of Organic Chemistry at Colorado State University

FIELD: Biological chemistry

RESEARCH AREAS: Chemistry and biochemistry of vanadium compounds, mechanism of the insulin action of vanadium compounds, model studies, probing the mechanisms of phosphatases and kinases, seed germination

EDUCATION: Partial completion of the Candidate of Science degree in Organic Chemistry/Biochemistry (1980), University of Copenhagen; Ph.D. in Organic Chemistry (1985), Harvard University

DATE/PLACE OF BIRTH: August 13, 1955/Copenhagen, Denmark

Debbie Crans lives with her husband and twin daughters in the foothills of Colorado. They live on 118 acres of land located halfway between Fort Collins and Boulder (their respective work places) outside a small town called Berthoud.

INTERVIEW DATE: March 1995

Fay Dansby

Product Marketing Manager
DELPHI AUTOMOTIVE SYSTEMS, GENERAL MOTORS CORPORATION

A love of math and the direction of a caring guidance counselor led Fay Dansby to choose industrial engineering as her college major. A college co-op job and an attraction to the automotive industry led her to a career at General Motors. She has had many interesting experiences before facing her greatest challenges and rewards as a professional and single parent.

❧

At the time I grew up, neither of my parents were "typical" African Americans. They each had advanced degrees. My father has a degree in veterinary medicine from Tuskegee University, and my mother has a master's degree in nursing administration from Ball State University. My mom was always a working professional. My family didn't force it upon us, but my siblings and I knew that we were going to do more than just get through high school and go to work. My parents exposed us to a lot of things. We traveled quite a bit. My father worked with the federal government and traveled to Brazil, Russia, and China. He always brought back slides of his trips. My parents' lives gave me higher expectations than the norm. To this day I feel that I'm just average in comparison to what they have achieved.

I grew up in Anderson, Indiana. During high school, I worked summers in a co-op program. The director of that program was a guidance counselor named Mr. Forest. When I told him I wanted to go into law, he told me that I had to start with an undergraduate degree. I had a straight-A average, and since math and science were easy for me, I was a perfect candidate for engineering. Mr. Forest said that engineering would be a wide-open field for women, and since Purdue University, which had an excellent engineering program, was in our state, he suggested I investigate it. Although I had no clue what an engineer did, I researched it and thought that it wouldn't be so bad. I chose to study industrial engineering because I enjoy solving problems, which in my current job helps the company be more cost effective and productive. Now that I'm an industrial engineer, I have Mr. Forest to thank for his good advice.

When I got to Purdue, there were many other women in engineering. Purdue has a support office for women in engineering that

Fay Dansby in her graduation photo from Purdue University, May 1984

really helped. Without them, I probably would have switched majors or dropped out. The women at Purdue could take a one-credit course on women in engineering. I also became a member of the Society of Women Engineers (SWE) and the Society of Black Engineers. SWE did a phenomenal job at hosting seminars where women speakers offered advice. It was inspiring and encouraging to hear older women, some of whom were the first women engineers in their field, tell you that if they could do it at the time they became engineers, anyone could. After I graduated in 1984, and my friends and I went our separate ways into industry, I found myself thinking: "Where is everybody? Where are the women?" Out in the workforce, I often feel alone. I have no peers with similar backgrounds. Fortunately, quite a few of my Purdue friends have kept in touch, and we still support one another. I also use prayer a lot. Being a divorced single parent with a toddler makes it even more difficult to find someone like me to relate to.

I began employment with Delco Remy as a co-op student while still at Purdue. Delco Remy is a division of General Motors known for the manufacture of generators, though we make other products as well. After I graduated, I decided to take a position with this division full time. I was interested in the automotive industry from the beginning, maybe because it's such a visible industry. I worked in Albany, Georgia, on a six-month assignment. The pace in Albany was slower than I had been accustomed to, but I worked with a younger group of engineers and I really enjoyed it.

After I returned to Indiana, I worked full-time for three years on flexible manufacturing systems in the plant. As my experience grew, I began to want to get more involved with the decision-making process instead of trying to improve upon a system that someone else had purchased. I felt that getting a master's in business administration would allow me more career options. I was also tired of the Midwest and felt ready for a change, so I went to Columbia University with the idea of becoming an investment banker in New York City.

My experience at Columbia University was something I couldn't have imagined beforehand. There was a lot going on in business at the time. The stock market crashed, and I was at the heart of all those dynamics. In the city skin color didn't matter, but money did. If you didn't have the money, there were certain places you couldn't go. And it was so diverse: you could hear ten languages in ten blocks. The people seemed colder, but their energy level was phenomenal. Then I interviewed a man who was trading with one of the investment banks, and I realized that it was not the life for me. My interests continued to be more product oriented. It was an expensive experience but worth every penny. Still, if I had remained single, I think I might have stayed. Instead, I returned to General Motors as an account manager in Troy, Michigan—with all of GM trucks and GM midsize cars as my customers.

Now I'm back in Indiana at Delphi-E (the result of a merger) working on a team that's helping to increase our generator business beyond General Motors. While Delphi-E is still owned by GM, our relationship is far different from the way it was because we try to function as a stand-alone business. Today, we have to compete with other firms for GM's accounts. We can also sell our products to Chrysler, Ford, other automotive companies, and to the automotive service suppliers.

Normally, my team consists of four to ten engineers. If I have an idea, I get feedback and support from the team, or someone helps me modify it, before I present it to management. This way I get more buy-in. I work closely with the product-engineering group. We also work with the finance organization, the manufacturing engineering group, and industrial engineering. I like the challenge of positioning our products to be the best in the world.

Right now I'm assessing projects that we're working on in China and Mexico. We're considering working with some other automakers in 1998 and 1999. The project entails a lot of planning and projecting what the market is going to do. We forecast what, besides just a basic small vehicle, people in a particular market

Fay Dansby and her daughter, Alexandrea

will want. It involves determining whether disposable income is increasing, whether a certain percentage of the population will be able to afford a vehicle, and if so, in what year there will be a demand for X volume of vehicles. To determine the generator market, we need to forecast how many people will want air-conditioning and similar options. We have to offer a higher-output generator to handle all the power those features require. Though we may not have any reason to interact with a particular auto manufacturer today, we need to establish a relationship with them so that in the year 2000, we'll be the supplier they choose for their vehicles.

Because of my industrial engineering background, I know the different types of manufacturing systems available and what they're capable of producing. I can analyze what systems are in place in a particular part of a country and estimate whether they're going to produce fifty thousand or a hundred thousand vehicles. Our team can then recommend whether our company should have a plant constructed near a particular automaker or should ship our parts from another country where we already have manufacturing facilities. Sometimes we recommend finding a partner in that country who is in the same business. My engineering background also helps me understand the mechanics of the product. I have more credibility when talking to the people who are going to make the deal happen because of my engineering background.

Although my team has a good working relationship, I notice that there are times when I'm not heard. I'll make a recommendation or a suggestion and have to throw it out two or three times to get someone's attention. I'm one of the few women in these meetings, and sometimes I think the men need to work on their listening skills. But I also find support in the closeness of my immediate team. It's one of the reasons that I decided to stay in the industry.

My number one accomplishment, however, is my daughter, Alexandrea. If I had to give up everything—my degrees, my career, whatever—to have her, I would do it. I could never have imagined the joy a child brings. It's like learning about life all over again.

I keep a binder for my daughter containing clippings about women who have done non-traditional things. Someday she'll be able to look at it and see examples of women who did what they wanted and no one stopped them even though they were women. It's important to me that she know she has options. I don't think we expose our kids to enough career options, and often they get directed into a field they don't really want to pursue. I'm active with a sorority, Alpha Kappa Alpha, which helps kids look at options for college. We take them to a college fair in Indianapolis every fall. We're planning to start a young girls' group, too. We're going to do a career day with women from several different types of backgrounds to talk about their professions. Education is so powerful. It's important that kids know they have a choice in their education.

At the time I had my daughter, I was married and we had agreed how we would manage our responsibilities. I thought we had it pretty well balanced, but when it fell through I knew I had to come up with another game plan and that, in the short term, my daughter came first. I'll have my career until my health fails or I die, but she's only going to be my direct responsibility from age two to eighteen. I didn't want to miss her elementary years. I didn't want to miss the field trips. I'm very family oriented. Right now we're living with my parents in their home, and it's a phenomenal situation for everyone. My daughter is their only grandchild, and I'm enjoying the fact that she's getting to spend her formative years with her grandparents.

GM offers an outside service called Work and Family Directions as a resource, which has helped me. I am fortunate to be a part of a company that is working to modify the workplace to be more family friendly. They offer flextime and dependent-care leave time. In the magazine *Working Woman,* GM was listed among the top one hundred companies for working mothers based on their child-care centers and other benefits. Yet at some level, I still feel that there may not be as much opportunity for me as there could be, whether it's because I'm a woman, African American, or a single parent. And while at this time I'm not seeking advancement, I'm not sure there will be other paths for me in the future.

At some point in time I would like to go into teaching. I used to tutor algebra in college, and I envy people who have been a lecturer, an author, or a teacher. I'd like my biography to list a diversity of accomplishments. A hero of mine, Dave Hall, first had a military career, retired as a brigadier general, and took an executive position with General Motors. Now he's teaching in Michigan. I would like to pattern my life after his. I know another man, a minister, who got a Ph.D. at forty-eight. They prove to me that you don't have to rush your career. Most people focus on one career path for thirty years, then retire. I can't imagine "retiring" to Florida. People who continue to work are more active and able to interact with their peers as well as younger people. I would like to continue learning and growing. I think teaching would keep me young.

PRESENT POSITION: Product Marketing Manager, Delphi Automotive Systems, General Motors Corporation

FIELD: Industrial engineering in the automotive industry

RESEARCH AREA: Product marketing

EDUCATION: B.S. in Industrial Engineering (1984), Purdue University; M.B.A. (1989), Columbia University

DATE/PLACE OF BIRTH: March 16, 1961/ Milwaukee, Wisconsin

Fay Dansby lives with her daughter, Alexandrea, and both of her parents in her hometown of Anderson, Indiana.

INTERVIEW DATE: August 1995

Jane Dillehay

Dean of the College of Arts and Sciences
GALLAUDET UNIVERSITY

Jane Dillehay's self-reliance and motivation, which she attributes in part to her deafness and in part to her family's strong interest in science and technology, helped her to aspire to and earn a Ph.D. in molecular biology. She always believed her deafness was inconsequential to doing science; overcoming people's assumptions about deafness was far more difficult. Today she helps others as a professor and dean of the College of Arts and Sciences at Gallaudet University.

M y earliest interest in science arose from my parents' love of learning. The Depression had frustrated their ambitions to go to college, and they transferred their high expectations to me and my two brothers. With their guidance, we were the first generation in our family to attend college. My brothers became mechanical engineers, and I went on to earn a graduate degree in biology. Our parents believed that we all had equal potential, so I grew up knowing that women and men both deserve the opportunity for higher education.

Although they never earned college degrees, my parents had a great interest in science and technology. My family subscribed to *Popular Science* and *Popular Mechanics,* and my brothers and I raced to be the first to read them when they arrived in the mail. Family discussions around the dinner table frequently became arguments about the how and why of the latest scientific discovery. Often we would incorporate dinner utensils and food into our discussion on the effect of air resistance on falling objects, or wedge two forks together to illustrate the stability of an object with a low center of gravity. Our demonstrations left the table in chaos!

My parents showed me how to observe and enjoy science through their own hobbies. I learned about nature with my parents from watching animals in our backyard, from frequent trips to the zoo and farms, and from visits to national parks. My mother and I grew flowers and vegetables under various weather conditions. My father was a bird watcher, so we would have long discussions about the way

Jane Dillehay in a recent photo
PHOTO COURTESY OF GALLAUDET UNIVERSITY

birds behaved around our feeder. I have a lasting memory of helping my father in his workshops; he had two, one for woodworking and one for electronics. Here my brothers and I learned to solder, turn a lathe, and use an oscilloscope. Regular visits to Pittsburgh's Carnegie Museum were another highlight of our childhoods. Although our parents conscientiously tried to show us the fine arts, we always headed straight for the dinosaur bones and the technology exhibits.

I have been profoundly deaf from birth. Initially I depended on a hearing aid and lip reading to communicate with people. I'm sure that many people had difficulty understanding my speech as a child. My main ambition growing up was to fit in with the other children, to avoid appearing to be different! I basically fended for myself in public school and college with some weekly speech instruction. This was well before the days of "mainstreaming" or interpreter support in the classroom. My strategies were to depend completely on lip reading, sit at the front of the class so I could watch the teacher closely, and read like mad in the library to stay ahead of the class.

At the time, I was convinced that I was doing a super job of "passing for normal," but now I wonder how successful I really was. As a teenager, I loved to watch old movies like *Casablanca*. Now many of these movies are available on tape with closed captioning, and I am discovering how much dialogue and plot I missed: "Oh, is that what he said?! Oh, is that what started the fight?!" I am sure that a lot of what was happening around me in high school and college also went right by me. And I wonder if people thought I was strange when I responded inappropriately or did not respond at all when I should have.

As a child, I enjoyed reading and my brothers loved music, but my parents focused us on interests that would lead to practical careers. Throughout high school I took all the math and science courses that were offered, partially because I was preparing for college and a science career but also because I enjoyed science. I loved the intellectual challenge of proving

geometric theorems, and Mr. Fails, my chemistry teacher, stimulated my curiosity with experiments and his enthusiasm.

In college I enjoyed the intellectual challenge of science courses but missed out on the social nature of science, projects, and internships because my deafness made it hard for me to interact with people. As a result of my independence from other students, I became self-reliant and self-motivating about what I wanted to learn. My teachers did not teach me; I taught myself.

It was not until graduate school at Carnegie Mellon University that I had my first interpreters so that I could better follow seminars. It was wonderful to know exactly what everyone was saying and, even better, to be able to sit in the last row of the lecture room with my interpreter, where I could leave discreetly rather than be trapped up front! My graduate adviser in the Department of Biological Sciences created a social community of undergraduates, graduate students, postdoctoral fellows, and lab technicians that I was able to join. For the first time I began to appreciate the social nature of scientific research: the importance of bouncing ideas off one another, the excitement of sharing new hypotheses, demonstrating proofs, and finding interesting but unexpected results.

For my graduate work I researched DNA polymerase I, a repair enzyme that corrects errors in transcription of DNA. The gene for this enzyme is called pol A. There is a group of pol A mutations that render the bacterial strain more sensitive to chromosomal damage. In my thesis project, I selected one of those pol A mutant strains and introduced secondary mutations in the pol A gene (by localized mutagenesis through hydroxylamine treatment of the pol A gene carried on a transducing bacteriophage, P1). As a result of secondary mutations, I was able to collect two groups of bacterial strains. One group had greatly increased mutator behavior by DNA polymerase I, and the other group had antimutator behavior because of increased fidelity of copying the DNA. I partially characterized the mutant enzymes from these strains. The long-range goal was to determine how the enzymatic structure matched with increased or decreased accuracy in copying the DNA.

I did not use an interpreter for lab work since lab discussions were carried out one-on-one and I could get immediate correction and feedback if I misunderstood anything. I discovered that group-discussion dynamics work against the interpreter. I was and still am deeply appreciative that I had an interpreter to help me understand 100 percent of the group discussion, but using an interpreter made it impossible to participate in that discussion: you can't take your turn when taking turns is controlled by eye contact and split-second timing. If I am watching the interpreter and not the speaker, I cannot indicate that I wish to join the discussion; because the interpreter is always one beat behind in the interpreting, I cannot find the opening to seize the discussion. In effect, I become invisible within the group while the interpreter is highly visible because of his or her signing. Frequently afterwards people flock to ask the interpreter questions while I am ignored. Again, this is not the fault of the interpreter or the group participants; it occurs because the dynamics of hearing-group interactions do not accommodate the communication needs of deaf attendees.

My adviser was very supportive of me, but I found the scientific community to be less so. This community was highly dependent on communication via phones—which in the late 1970s and early 1980s automatically excluded me—and meetings, none of which provided interpreters. As a result, the community was inaccessible and not particularly welcoming to me. Today, especially with e-mail, the rules of the game have changed, and I am in correspondence with people across the world.

Deafness itself was not a handicap—it did not interfere with my lab work or research; communication was the problem. I always felt that my deafness was inconsequential, not a valid reason to excuse myself from doing something, but that the real problem was other people. *They* created the difficulties that I had to learn to cope with. I never felt limited in pursuing any area of science or technology that interested me; the only barrier was other people and their assumptions that deaf people were impossible to communicate with or teach or work with.

After completing my thesis work, I accepted a position as an assistant professor in the biology department at Gallaudet University, the only liberal arts university for the deaf in the United States. Coming to Gallaudet was a shock because my entire graduate experience had been oriented toward research, and Gallaudet is primarily a teaching institution without facilities for biological research. For a time, I kept up my research as a visiting professor at Lawrence Livermore Laboratories in California in the summer and at George Washington University Medical School during the school year, but after a while I became very involved in the demands of effective teaching.

My husband, whom I met when we shared an office at Lawrence Livermore Laboratories one summer, is an associate professor at Johns Hopkins University Oncology Center and has always been very supportive of my career. We share equally in both the responsibilities and joys of raising our two boys. However, with two small children I felt that the cost of doing and having it all became too high. Now I take a more realistic view: life is about trade-offs, and there will be time later to pursue research. So instead of becoming Superwoman, I am setting active research aside for the years while our boys are growing up. Working women need to develop a long-term perspective: Children may require your concentration for fifteen years or so, but we still have twenty to thirty years of productive life after the children are grown and gone.

Between teaching, marriage, and two children, I was not able to take advantage of research opportunities that were offered at the National Institutes of Health and at the University of Michigan. Now that I am an administrator, I realize that I am moving further away from my original interests in both re-

Jane Dillehay, left, and Audrey Grissom, coordinator of the summer institute and a former high school science teacher, discussing preparations for the physiology rotation of Gallaudet's Summer Institute in Biology for high school science teachers of deaf students

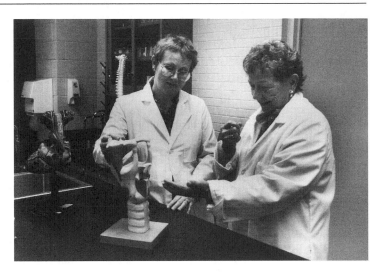

search and education. I do not envision myself staying permanently in administration. In the future I want to return to research, but I know that I am falling behind on what is current in some scientific areas. At some point, I will apply for a sabbatical and return to the lab for a refresher course in research techniques.

For now, I have refocused my research interests toward science-education issues, such as the effect of reading strategies on course performance, the assessment of tools for measuring lab skills, and the improvement of writing skills. I am presently managing two National Science Foundation science-education grants. One grant provides life sciences educational software to deaf and hearing high school students and also entails their evaluations of that software. The other grant funds four years of summer institutes in biology for high school and middle school science teachers of deaf students.

Precollege science education is one of the National Science Foundation's priorities, as is the recruitment of minorities, including deaf students, into science and technical careers. At Gallaudet University, we have found that our freshmen arrive unprepared to deal with college-level science courses. We believe that one key reason for their lack of preparation is that their teachers themselves have little back-

ground in the sciences. Their teaching degrees tend to be in special or deaf education.

The Summer Institute in Biology offers graduate credit for a five-week summer course for middle- and high-school teachers of deaf students. The program will run for four years, involve twenty-four teachers each year, and provide follow-up activities after the teachers return to their home schools. The topics covered are genetics, physiology, and environmental studies; and the program involves organizations such as the U.S. Fish and Wildlife Service, the National Biological Survey, the Smithsonian Environmental Research Center, and the Genetics Services Center of Gallaudet, as well as guest faculty from area universities and medical centers. We hope to improve the teachers' knowledge of some areas of biology and give them hands-on lab ideas to take to their home schools.

The HIBIOS (High School Biology Software) project provides educational software in the life and environmental sciences to teachers across the country for use in their classrooms free of charge in return for evaluating the teaching effectiveness of the software. In addition to giving students access to a wide variety of educational programs, we hope to help the software companies improve the instructional methods used in the software they develop. We are in the last year of a four-year grant for this project. I supervise a staff of four people—two project coordinators, a secretary, and a research assistant—in running the two projects.

As a teacher, I find it very satisfying to motivate students to understand basic biological principles, to apply them to their own lives, and to become excited about the knowledge they are acquiring. I have always had the attitude that no one, including myself, ever stops learning, so I continually seek out new ways to teach and encourage my faculty and students to do the same. In general, I have three types of students and I have created goals for each type. For students who are taking biology to meet a general education requirement, I try to instill excitement about science, background knowledge so that they can become informed citizens, and the confidence that they can understand the basic concepts of scientific discoveries. For students who are planning to become teachers, I teach those same concepts along with a sense of the importance of passing on this knowledge to the next generation of children. I encourage students who major in biology to learn the basics of scientific experimentation, and I aim them either at lab technical careers or at graduate school.

Remembering my interactive graduate career, I design my classes to provide the opportunity for creative brainstorming, for bouncing ideas off one another, for the stimulation of differing viewpoints, and for the give and take of discussion of apparently unsolvable problems. Discoveries have no meaning unless they are shared with other people because science is a collaborative process. I have been attempting to go against the traditional way of teaching through the lecture format by introducing the cooperative approach in the classroom. I pose problems and ask the class to break up into groups to analyze these problems, and report back to the class their solutions. From the students' answers I can see where there are deficiencies in their reasoning that have to be corrected with further instruction. The results of such activities can be surprising. When students work together, they begin to see that people tend to interpret things from their own point of view. They learn the valuable lesson that people don't all think or reason in the same way.

Today I am more proficient at setting hearing people at ease in professional meetings. I help people understand that my interpreter needs time to relay the message; that the fact I'm looking at the interpreter doesn't mean that I'm ignoring the hearing person; that lip reading, note writing, and e-mail are all valid forms of communication; that the visual environment (glare from lights or a window, for example) can have an effect on communication; and that a hearing person can understand me once he or she adjusts to my "deaf" voice. And I pack all of this instruction into the first few minutes of a meeting!

PRESENT POSITION: Dean of the College of Arts and Sciences, Gallaudet University

FIELD: Biology

RESEARCH AREAS: Molecular biology and science education

EDUCATION: B.S. in Biology (1971), Allegheny College; Ph.D. in Molecular Biology (1980), Carnegie Mellon University

DATE/PLACE OF BIRTH: August 29, 1949/Hazeltown, Pennsylvania

Jane Dillehay lives with her husband, Larry, who is a faculty member at Johns Hopkins Oncology Center, and their two sons, Matthew and Andrew.

INTERVIEW DATE: February 1995

Mildred Dresselhaus

Institute Professor of Physics
MASSACHUSETTS INSTITUTE OF TECHNOLOGY

She thought she was destined for a traditional woman's career in the 1950s—teaching elementary school—but a college mentor convinced Mildred Dresselhaus to consider a career in science. She earned a Ph.D. in physics from the University of Chicago and worked at Lincoln Lab until she accepted a one-year fellowship at MIT, enticed by the flexibility of faculty life because of her four young children. She never left; in fact, Mildred Dresselhaus became the first woman tenured in the School of Engineering at MIT, and in 1985 became the first woman to be honored as an institute professor because of her accomplishments.

My parents were immigrants: my father came from Poland and my mother from Holland. Neither of them had high levels of education, and they were always busy just trying to help the family survive. They did encourage us in a general sense to work hard and succeed, but they didn't get involved in my or my brother's studies because they had neither the background nor the time to do so. My mother worked twelve-hour days in an orphanage, and my father was a laborer. My mother's job was steady, although her wages were very low. I lived in a poor neighborhood and didn't really know any professionals beyond my own teachers and the medical doctors we visited when I was sick. I did meet some professionals through music school, but they were different from the teachers and doctors.

I was the younger of two children. My brother, three years older than I, was a child prodigy. He taught himself to read by the age of three, and at age four he was awarded a music scholarship. There weren't many books around our house, but we did get the newspaper because my father was an avid newspaper reader; so my brother read the *New York Times* daily. When he began school he skipped a few grades because he was so advanced intellectually. It was through him that I received my own scholarship for music training through one of the New York settlement houses. I could read music by age four. I used to tag along with my brother to his music lessons, and the teachers assumed that I was going to be another prodigy. I was a pretty

Mildred Dresselhaus in a recent photo
PHOTO COPYRIGHT 1996 DONNA COVENEY/MIT

good music student, but I wasn't in his league, partly because I didn't have the motivation he had. Still, he was always a source of inspiration to me.

I was always interested in science. I didn't think of it as a career possibility in the early days but did it instead out of sheer enjoyment. I explored a lot on my own. When I was about ten years old I read Paul DeKruif's *The Microbe Hunters* and was very intrigued with the scientific work he discussed in the book and the people behind the work. At twelve, I became especially interested in math and began to teach myself what my teachers weren't addressing; I was, however, interested in a broad range of subjects. What opened up the world for me, and what triggered my own self-study program, was the possibility of going to Hunter High School, a special school in New York City for talented girls. I found out about Hunter from children at my music school and was quite excited by the prospect. The school required entrance exams, so I wrote asking for sample copies. I started working through the exams and realized that my formal schooling wasn't adequate—I couldn't answer many of the questions. I spent many, many hours learning on my own those things on the exams that I didn't know; my teachers weren't interested in helping me. This led to a lifelong habit of self-directed study.

I was accepted and went to Hunter, which was a great experience. The teachers there encouraged us to work on our own, and so I continued to teach myself things that interested me. Our brother school was Stuyvesant High School, which was a boys' school. Stuyvesant had more math focus than Hunter, and I was introduced to different topics from my contact with the boys. After I identified new topics, I proceeded to learn them on my own. Now and then the boys would show me some things— they liked to show off—but essentially I taught myself. The advisers at Hunter High School were pretty practical at that time, and they knew there weren't a lot of careers open to women. So they encouraged me to become a grade school teacher, which seemed reasonable to me.

I went on to Hunter College, the mecca for schoolteaching. I took a broad spectrum of courses and early on, in taking science courses, I met faculty who encouraged me to major in science-related subjects. This was immediately after World War II, and everyone felt that science had won the war and was therefore important. But it was a confusing time for me because I was really good in a variety of fields and many of the faculty were encouraging me to pursue different avenues. In the end I did focus on the sciences: I completed majors in physics and math and almost completed one in chemistry. Hunter College had a lot of required courses because it was a liberal arts school, so the number of electives I had was pretty small.

One of my advisers at Hunter College was Rosalyn Yalow, later a Nobel laureate in medicine and a Hunter alumna herself. She was very influential in my life. She gave me a lot of individual attention because there were very few students seriously interested in physics at that time. She encouraged me to pursue a career in physics because of my ability and interest. I got from Rosalyn Yalow and others the message that elementary school teaching was only one of many career options for me. I considered a career in science as an alternative to teaching school.

When I finished Hunter College I wasn't sure what I wanted to do, and the level of science training I had received was pretty low compared to what was available at the top private schools. I simply didn't know enough science to be competitive in graduate school. I thought about going to graduate school in mathematics, and had been accepted at MIT in applied mathematics to work on the Whirlwind, a very early computer. I didn't do that in the end because I received a Fulbright scholarship in physics, which took me to Cambridge, England. I was excited to study abroad and to study physics; the experience really solidified my interest in physics as a career. The year in Cambridge also gave me a background equivalent to that of graduates of the Big Ten schools. I was happy to see that I could handle all that came my way—the rigorous school-work, the new environment, the different culture. I figured that if I could handle Cambridge, I could handle graduate study.

I returned to the States and began graduate school at age twenty-one. I spent one year at Harvard, passed all the examinations, and then did my thesis at the University of Chicago. I had enough encouragement through graduate school that I wasn't discouraged, and the early inspiration I had at Hunter College and then at Cambridge sustained me. I really believed that I could do anything I wanted academically. There were barriers in graduate school, but I went around them. My adviser wasn't supportive of careers for women; he was upset when I received fellowship support because he fundamentally and philosophically believed that women shouldn't be supported for graduate school because they would never contribute much to their fields. I stayed away from him as much as possible! He wasn't a serious obstacle—I simply plodded along, hoping for a chance to do what I wanted to do. I had no idea whether my career would be easy, difficult, or great; I just knew I'd be happy pursuing my love of physics.

In graduate school my thesis focused on microwave properties of superconductors. This approach allowed me to observe the electromagnetic response of superconductors in the superconducting state. Normally materials in the superconducting state have no resistivity, so there's nothing to measure; it's zero. That's not very interesting. But if you look at higher frequencies there are losses that can be measured, and the effect of magnetic fields on those losses can also be measured. I was doing studies as a function of the magnitude and direction of magnetic fields and mapping the effects as the material approached the normal state. I found some unusual phenomena that surprised a lot of folks. In simple terms, you would expect the magnetic field to continuously suppress the superconducting effect in going from the superconducting to the normal state as the magnetic field was increased. But under some conditions it appeared that the superconductor in a magnetic field became even more superconducting than with no field. This effect had to do with an interesting interplay between field patterns in the skin depth of the superconductor in the normal and superconducting states. This phenomenon couldn't be explained by the newly proposed theory of superconductivity.

Several external and unpredictable factors helped me and my career. First, the fundamental theory for superconductivity was published a year before I submitted my Ph.D. thesis, and superconductivity became a very important topic. I was in the right field at the right time, and I found an effect that the theory couldn't explain. This got people very interested in my work. The second thing that helped my career was the launching of Sputnik in 1957, just as I was finishing my thesis. All of a sudden there was a lot of national interest in science and in training more scientists, and there I was.

I completed my Ph.D. and married another physicist in 1958. Like today, finding career opportunities for two people in the same place was difficult. What helped us initially was that I had an NSF postdoctoral fellowship that I could take anyplace; so for two years I joined my husband at Cornell, where he had a faculty position. Then the real world caught up with me and I had to find a job. My husband gave up his job at Cornell, and we both got jobs in 1960 in the same place, as staff members at Lincoln Lab. Lincoln Lab was part of MIT and was set up as a defense lab. Unlike today, that era saw many job opportunities in science and in research.

When I was hired at Lincoln Lab, it was with the understanding that I could work on a very broad range of topics in solid state physics (which at that time was an up-and-coming field) but not in superconductivity. So I had to change fields. The discontinuity in topics was fine with me—I liked the idea of moving around within the field and becoming good in other areas. It broadened my understanding and appreciation of physics. I was able to turn what some people would have viewed as a negative into a plus; I moved into working with high magnetic fields and semiconductors. Later, when I joined the faculty at MIT, I branched into many other areas. While at Lincoln, I looked at the electronic properties of graphite and other semimetals. My studies on graphite led me to a new appreciation of column four of the periodic table, which is very important for the semiconductor industry. I always tell my graduate students when they finish their Ph.D.'s that the best thing they can do is learn a second field. It gives them a lot more room to maneuver. To have a successful career it's important to know a couple of things really well and then to gain breadth.

By the mid-1960s I had four little kids and a full-time job. One of my biggest problems was in getting to work on time. Work started at 8:30 in the morning, but I usually arrived at 9:00 or 9:15 because my baby-sitter couldn't come any earlier. I was harassed about my lateness; even though my productivity and the quality of my work were never questioned, the bureaucrats couldn't handle my tardiness. In 1967 I had an opportunity to come down to the MIT campus for a year, and I figured that in a year the kids would be a little older and maybe my life would become a bit simpler. MIT had received a large endowment from the Rockefeller family to pursue the scholarship of women. My visiting professorship allowed me to spend a year on campus thanks to the Rockefeller endowment. I was the second woman to hold this position. Although I only intended to be at MIT for one year, I never actually went back to Lincoln Lab. So the difficulty of getting to work on time turned into an advantage. I would not have actively sought another position, but I recognized that the flexibility that accompanied a faculty position would be wonderful.

When I came to MIT the student body was only 4 percent women, and the percentage was even smaller in my field. I worked hard to support the women students in electrical engineering, the department in which I initially had an appointment. I did a lot of networking with the women students, I tried to support them when they had problems with their advisers, and I tried to help them find jobs. I was the first tenured woman faculty member in the MIT engineering school; at that time we had very few women faculty at MIT overall. I really wanted to help make MIT a more responsive place for women to study and be successful. I would not have predicted at that time the success we've had in more recent years with women students. Today women students almost never question that they should have equal treatment. When I first came to MIT, women were extremely tentative about their place; I've seen incredible progress in the opportunities for women in science and engineering in the last thirty years.

While there was prejudice against women at the time I was entering the job market, there were at least a lot of job opportunities within those confines. The opportunities today for both men and women are much more limited. Life for me has always had unexpected twists and turns and opportunities. I took advantage of the opportunities, and I went with the twists and turns, and somehow it all worked out. Nobody that I knew in the early years at Hunter focused on money, power, or fame; that wasn't what was important to students in the inner-city environment. We were more interested in serving society to repay our free public education and simply happy to have the opportunity to do the work that we wanted so much to do.

PRESENT POSITION: Institute Professor of Physics, Massachusetts Institute of Technology

FIELD: Physics

RESEARCH AREAS: Physics of solids

EDUCATION: A.B. in Physics and Math (1951), Hunter College; Ph.D. in Physics (1958), University of Chicago.

DATE/PLACE OF BIRTH: November 11, 1930/ Brooklyn, New York

Mildred Dresselhaus lives in Arlington, Massachusetts.

INTERVIEW DATE: March 1995

Barbara Duhl-Emswiler

Director of Chemical Development
PROCYTE CORPORATION

Barbara Duhl-Emswiler is an organic chemist who currently works for a small biopharmaceutical company; she is also an accomplished harpist who specializes in Scottish traditional music. As a bench chemist her work involved large-scale peptide synthesis. She worked at several companies before accepting a position at ProCyte and working her way up to her current position.

❧

I am an organic chemist and have chosen to spend my career in the pharmaceutical industry. At present I am the director of chemical development and manufacturing for a small company. I am also a freelance professional musician; I compose and perform on Celtic harp and specialize in Scottish traditional musical styles. When I look at what my current job encompasses, I am amazed! I would never have imagined myself doing all this when I set out on the road to becoming a chemist.

I've always wanted a career in chemistry, from the time I learned what chemistry was. In seventh grade we learned about the structure of DNA and the discovery of new elements, and when I read Marie Curie's biography I knew what I wanted to do. I spent the summer between seventh and eighth grades memorizing the elements, reading about science, and building "molecular models" from Tinkertoys.

I grew up as an "army brat" and spent eighth, ninth, and tenth grades in Germany. My school in Garmisch was small and progressive enough to provide very special programs for gifted students. An experimental in-dependent-study program allowed six or eight of us to focus on subjects that interested us, in my case math and science. Joyce Mattson, who taught the science courses, was a treasure; she scrounged high school chemistry books and lab equipment and taught a chemistry course for us. She also told me about the National Science Foundation's sponsored summer programs for high school students. "When you get back to the States," she said, "you need to find one." So I did.

Between my junior and senior years of high

Barbara Duhl-Emswiler by the shore at Lerwick, the Shetland Islands, August 1989. She is playing her small wire-strung harp during a study trip to the islands to learn traditional Shetland music.
PHOTO BY JOHN EMSWILER

109

school, I participated in an NSF chemistry program at Northern Illinois University. It was the pivotal point in my education. What a wonderful summer that was, living with other kids who shared my interest, taking a chemistry class, and working on research projects with a faculty member. I had the privilege of working with Dr. Laurine LaPlanche Graham, who served as my role model. She had a life that I wanted very much for myself—poise, confidence, an exciting research career, publications, and marriage to a fellow chemist. I chose to go to college at Michigan State University, with its large research-oriented chemistry department, based at least partly on the fact that she had done her Ph.D. work there. In a nice bit of circle-closing, her major professor was a member of my Ph.D. thesis committee.

I never doubted that I would continue in school and earn a Ph.D. Three years of undergraduate research in Professor Donald Farnum's lab, working with his graduate students on synthesis projects, paved the way. When I became allergic to the first compound I worked with, the brightest graduate student in the group, Alfred Hagedorn, took me on his project and became my mentor and friend. I learned an incredible amount of laboratory technique from him; Al had a wonderful knack with difficult, delicate synthesis. But more important, I learned how to think like a scientist: ways to design experiments and approach problem-solving and, behind it all, a set of ethical values.

Just after I made the decision to go to graduate school at the University of Wisconsin, I met the person with whom I wanted to spend the rest of my life. John had just started as a graduate student in chemistry at MSU during my senior year, and we shared an intense spring term before I went to Wisconsin for a year. I had taken most of the MSU graduate organic chemistry courses as an undergraduate, and I wanted some different exposure. I returned to MSU after that, and John and I were married on campus surrounded by our friends. I rejoined the Farnum group and

did my Ph.D. thesis research on a synthesis of the gypsy moth pheromone.

I remember graduate school, for the most part, fondly. With John and me on assistantships and living in (horrible!) student housing, we had adequate income for our needs and enough free time to grow a vegetable garden and take weekend trips. The camaraderie in our groups was fun, and we practically lived in the lab.

I knew I wanted to work for a pharmaceutical company once I finished my graduate work, but I wasn't certain that I'd be able to find a position in that competitive industry. However, I got an industrial postdoctoral position where I could broaden my research experience in preparation for a permanent position. My postdoc at McNeil Pharmaceutical was a chance to see the pharmaceutical industry from the inside and to do some exciting and publishable work in synthetic chemistry. My manager was an outstanding scientist who stressed the need to present our work publicly, and provided plenty of opportunities to do so. It was a time of intense concentration on science, with little life outside the lab, but it was a chance to discover some of my strengths and to identify things I enjoyed doing.

I chose to specialize in chemical development. This differs from basic discovery research in that it is not focused on making a lot of new potential drug molecules but rather on a good process for making a chosen compound on a large scale, cost effectively. It also involves considerations of safety and environmental responsibility in the choice of reactants and solvents to use. I liked the fact that I was much closer in research development to the final marketed product.

My first few years as a bench chemist in a large company were spent learning my craft, the art of developing a good process. This is not something taught in school. My graduate work had trained me for it a little, since we had prepared quantities of the pheromone I had studied for USDA field testing as part of our grant obligation, but this was unusual. One learns process chemistry by doing it and from working with more experienced people. Some excellent lab chemists never quite "get it"—that is, they never develop the deep instinct for what should be improved about a reaction to make it an efficient process.

The work that I did for the first eight years of my career involved large-scale peptide synthesis. I had never intended to become a peptide specialist, but it turned out to be a skill that was in high demand. Peptides are chains of amino acids, the building blocks of proteins. Large peptides and proteins are made most efficiently by recombinant DNA methods, but small peptides can be treated just like any other small molecule—that is, synthesized chemically. When I started very few people had ever done any work with making hundreds of kilograms of peptides—in fact, hundreds of grams was considered a major achievement. Our process-development group devised a synthesis for making a pentapeptide (five amino acids linked together) on commercial scale. It involved twelve steps, and we developed some unique technology to do it in good yield and with high purity so as not to require an expensive purification step at the very end.

I probably didn't appreciate the significance of what we had done at the time; I felt like my career was stalling, and rebelled against the politics and bureaucracy of a large company. My work and supervisory styles were very different from those of my boss, resulting in inevitable conflicts. I am collaborative by nature, and prefer to get people to buy into things I want them to do rather than issue directives. What I saw as the ability to compromise when necessary was viewed as weak and waffling.

During this time I realized that I needed to get back to the rest of my life. I had been expecting my job to meet all of my needs for accomplishment and recognition, and finally it became apparent that it would not. I picked up some new hobbies; John and I took weaving classes together, and I started designing and weaving scarves and accessories that I sold at craft shows.

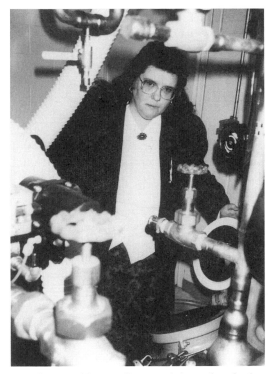

Barbara Duhl-Emswiler examining a hundred-gallon reaction vessel between production campaigns in the Primary Manufacturing Facility, ProCyte Corporation, Redmond, Washington, January 1996
PHOTO BY JOHN EMSWILER

I also needed to get back to music. Some of my earliest memories are of songs and tunes I heard as a child, and I've always played one instrument or another, from piano to recorder to mountain dulcimer. It had been a long-time dream of mine to play the harp, so I bought my first harp and started taking lessons. It was as if I had found the missing piece of my life, the element that would link all of the rest of the parts together. I started performing informally within a year or so. I was very drawn to Scottish music, and I did well at Scottish harp competitions, starting at the beginner level. I traveled with a small harp on business trips; my first trip to Scotland was tacked onto the end of a trip to Belgium to observe the scale-up of a step of my peptide process.

In learning to be comfortable as a performer, I gained an enormous amount of confidence that I had never felt before. The feedback is immediate—you learn to read your audience and play to them. This translated into a much-improved degree of comfort with presentations and public seminars at work. I won the national amateur competition in 1988 and the professional title the next year. My prize was a study trip to Scotland, which I chose to use to study the fiddle music of the Shetland Islands at a summer school.

Three months before my trip, the entire process group was laid off, the result of a business decision involving our products. I consider it the best thing that ever happened to my career, since the outplacement support gave me the necessary kick to move on to something where I'd be happier. After the initial shock wore off, I realized that the most important and enduring things in life are your friendships. There is no security in companies; don't expect it, learn what you can while you're there, and move on.

I learned about my next job by networking. The person who hired me was an old friend with whom I'd been mostly out of touch—Al Hagedorn, the graduate student with whom I had worked as an undergraduate at MSU. Small world, but here was someone who believed in my ability. My new position utilized some of my specialized peptide knowledge; I was to establish a peptide synthesis group in support of a discovery research effort. While I had supervised one assistant in my previous position, this was a chance to set up my own lab, hire a staff, and learn the business of running a group (with budgets, planning, and all the rest of it).

Before I started the job, John and I made the trip to the Shetland Islands for my music course. It turned out to be an incredibly rejuvenating three weeks. How long it had been since I'd had no responsibilities but to get up in the morning and make music! It was a hauntingly beautiful place; my harp was welcome among all the fiddles, and for the first time in my life, I had the experience of making music with other people as part of an ensemble.

I spent three years with Berlex Laboratories until they decided to move R&D operations to the West Coast. During that time, I developed a thriving freelance harp business, performing almost every weekend for weddings or parties. It was a good experience building up the business, learning about things like advertising and contracts, and I loved working with the diverse client base I built.

Staying in New Jersey proved impossible; it was not a good time to find a new midlevel-management or principal-scientist job because pharmaceutical companies were all laying people off. Networking again, I was invited to interview for my present company in the Seattle area, based on my large-scale peptide process development work. My husband, amazingly, was able to arrange a transfer within his company, so we moved cross-country.

I started at ProCyte Corporation in 1992 as manager of process development, with one assistant. The company employed approximately forty-five people then. It had no products on the market yet, but our first drug was going into phase-three clinical trials as a wound-healing agent. The drug, a small peptide, was being purchased from an overseas manufacturer, which wasn't going to be cost effective commercially. One of my responsibilities was to evaluate the need for building a manufacturing facility of our own versus contracting out the work. To ensure a steady supply of high-quality product at a reasonable cost as the organization continued to grow, we eventually chose to build a chemical manufacturing plant.

I was deeply involved in the design and construction of that facility, one of the most exciting projects I've ever participated in. It required design decisions about things that I hadn't realized I knew or cared so much about! These were things I had picked up in those long early years at my first job without consciously realizing that I was learning them. The plant was completed two years after I joined the company; we held our annual shareholders' meeting there amid great festivity.

In a small company people must be versatile enough to fill many roles. One side of that is that everyone works very hard, but the other side is that individual contributions in any area are valued. When the director of finance (and facilities) showed up in jeans to change the lightbulbs in my fume hood shortly after I started, I knew this was my kind of place. One of my frustrations in a big company was that no one cared about what I knew or could do outside of my narrow job description. At a small company, the things I did and said made a difference that I could see. It's a much bigger responsibility because you aren't going to be second- or third-guessed, so you'd better be right most of the time.

The manager who hired me became the most influential mentor I've ever had. Ron not only believed in what I was doing but shared with me his thinking about how he did his job. There was a deep trust between us, and I learned a lot about how to manage a project or a department from our candid discussions. He helped me to see that maybe I was limiting myself by viewing my advancement in terms of a career as a chemist. From this mentoring relationship I drew the confidence to look higher and wider, and I suggested to our CEO that I would be a good choice for Ron's position as director after he was promoted. I have often felt that the hardest thing to do is to ask for what you need for yourself, but in this case that assertiveness was what got me the job.

By the time I was named director of chemical development, my current position, my mentor had chosen to leave the company for family reasons and I was truly on my own. My process group had grown to five people, and I also became responsible for an analytical chemistry group, a dosage-form manufacturing group, and the drug substance manufacturing plant—a total of twenty-five people by the end of our phase-three trials. I had done analytical chemistry in my process development life, but the rest was new to me. Fortunately, the people I hired to manage those operations are talented, strong people, and I have a good rapport with them.

It's a very different challenge, accomplishing science though other people rather than directly with my own hands. I miss being in the lab doing the experiments, and I do occasionally slip into the lab to help out in a crunch. I think that a great deal of my success in managing this diverse group is based on my technical knowledge: I can suggest experiments when someone is up against a brick wall, or stand back to evaluate data from a big-picture point of view. Equally challenging is knowing when to let go and let people do their jobs. It's a delicate balance, and you have to read people well. My job is to see the corporate big picture and help shape it, and to fit all the details into it so that things happen on time and within budget.

As all too often happens in the pharmaceutical industry, our wound-healing drug did not perform up to expectations in the phase-three clinical trials, meaning that we would not be able to get Food and Drug Administration approval to market it. This was a major setback that led to an inevitable need to regroup as a company with our other therapeutic programs. We had to downsize by one-third, a layoff of twenty-five people. That was the hardest thing I've ever had to do in my life; it was actually much easier when I was the one being laid off.

My greatest challenge right now is establishing a contract manufacturing business that will make effective use of our manufacturing plant, equipment, and staff expertise. It's exciting; we're basically starting a new business—advertising, talking to potential clients, and quoting on jobs. Bringing our first paying customer on board was a thrill equal to any in my career because I know how much effort went into accomplishing it. Every customer has new and different projects to evaluate. I've had to do some quick learning—you don't learn much about finance, contracts, marketing plans, or shipping regulations in graduate school in chemistry! I'm fortunate to have colleagues in those areas who are great about sharing their thought processes so that I can learn as we go.

It's hard to balance my life right now—this

job takes an inordinate amount of my time and energy. But I've decided that there are different times in life to focus on different things; this is a time for concentrating on my career. There will be time again for performing music frequently. Right now, I'm afraid to schedule a performance at a wedding that is months away because I might have to travel on business that weekend.

My husband has been incredibly supportive of my choices. After nearly twenty years of marriage, he's still my best friend; as a chemist he is also a valued sounding board for my chemistry conundrums and ideas. He once told me he never expected to be "herding bridesmaids" at the weddings I was doing. Recently he said he never thought he'd see copies of *Packaging Digest* and *Creating a Business Plan* sitting around the house alongside *Chemical and Engineering News* and the *Folk Harp Journal*. That's OK. It's certain that my career has evolved quite a distance from where I started. I'm excited and pleased to be where I am, living in a beautiful part of the country, developing and commercializing new drug therapies, and making music.

PRESENT POSITION: Director of Chemical Development, ProCyte Corporation
FIELD: Organic chemistry
RESEARCH AREA: Large-scale peptide synthesis
EDUCATION: B.S. in Chemistry (1974), Michigan State University; Ph.D. in Organic Chemistry (1979), Michigan State University
DATE/PLACE OF BIRTH: October 13, 1952/Fort Knox, Kentucky

Barbara Duhl-Emswiler lives with her husband, John Emswiler, in Renton, Washington, southeast of Seattle, with a glorious view of Mount Rainier!

INTERVIEW DATE: July 1995

Bonnie J. Dunbar

Astronaut
NATIONAL AERONAUTICS AND SPACE ADMINISTRATION

Growing up on a farm in Washington state, Bonnie Dunbar frequented the bookmobile, helped her father fix tractors, played with Erector sets, and belonged to 4-H. Her interest in becoming an astronaut surfaced as early as high school but was not taken seriously by those around her. Before she was selected to join the astronaut corps, she worked on the thermal protection system for the space shuttle both as an undergraduate and in her job at Rockwell International's Space Division. It was during her time at Rockwell that she also earned her pilot's license. Her first space flight was in 1985, and she's flown three others since then.

❧

I grew up in a farming-ranching community called Outlook in the state of Washington. My mother had grown up in Montana and my father in Oregon; they met in Oregon and married and homesteaded in Washington after World War II, when some of the federal lands were opened up to homesteading. My mother and father farmed about forty acres of land and leased pasture land for Hereford cattle, which we raised. I had two younger brothers and a younger sister. We lived far enough out in the country that I really only played with my brothers and sister. My family very much loved and encouraged learning; my father would have gone to the University of Oregon on a scholarship but didn't because of World War II. My mother's family were sheep ranchers in Montana, and she worked with her eight brothers and sisters on the ranch. Going to school meant riding a horse into the nearest town and boarding there for a week at time. She had to quit school at sixteen when

it became too expensive to board so far away from home.

There were always books around my house. My grandfather, who lived with us for a short time, had brought books with him when he emigrated from Scotland, and his were some of the earliest books I read. During the summers we were pretty much confined to the farm, but the bookmobile would come around periodically and I'd check out my ten books. I was a classic tomboy and classic bookworm. I was also interested in mechanics; my father used to let me work with him on the tractors. I played with Erector sets much more than dolls, belonged to 4-H and played sports, but I also

Astronaut Bonnie Dunbar
PHOTO COURTESY OF THE NATIONAL AERONAUTICS AND SPACE ADMINISTRATION

studied hard because my parents insisted on well-roundedness.

I rode a bus about thirty minutes to a little country school until I was in eighth grade; there were twenty-two kids in my class throughout those eight years. I became interested in science fiction and space somewhere around the fourth or fifth grade. A teacher read to us aloud from a book called *The Angry Red Planet* about a mission to Mars, and I was fascinated.

I had an incredible physics and chemistry teacher in high school—Mr. Anderson. It was he who introduced me to engineering as a discipline and a career. I didn't know any engineers and I didn't have any idea what engineers did, but I was enamored with space and collected rocks. I thought that college would be like high school and that I could study a whole bunch of different things. I was very interested in the romantic poets—Byron, Shelley, Keats—and planned to study those as well as science and engineering. Mr. Anderson encouraged me to major in engineering because I could pursue my literary interests on the side, but if I majored in literature he warned that I couldn't really pursue engineering on the side. By high school I had learned that saying I wanted to be an astronaut lost me credibility—people thought it was just outrageous—so I kept that ambition to myself.

I tried to apply to the astronaut corps when I was eighteen. NASA responded with a very nice letter that indicated I really needed a college degree. So I went off to the University of Washington, a naive little farm girl in the big city of Seattle. I had done well in high school, I had taken math and physics, and I was considered an "all-American girl"—a cheerleader and part of the prom royalty. I showed up on campus to find out that in my freshmen class within the engineering college alone there were two thousand students—and only six women! That was a surprise, but I think my naïveté worked for me—I just plugged along working hard and never focused on the occasional professor who thought women shouldn't be in the field. My parents had raised me to be confident and believe in myself, and so I never

took sexism personally. I thought it was the other person's problem, not mine.

My undergraduate degree is in ceramic engineering, which is an element of materials engineering. Ceramic engineering includes everything that's not a metal and not a plastic—it ranges from semiconductors to nuclear fuels to glass and brick. It's really high-temperature inorganic chemistry. I started college in 1967 planning to major in aeronautical engineering, but I was introduced to Dr. Jim Mueller, whom everyone called Doc, the chairman of the ceramic engineering department. He had heard of my interest in space and showed me some pictures of the space shuttle. At that time, the University of Washington had a NASA grant to perform research related to the thermal-protection system on the space shuttle. The space shuttle at this time was simply a concept. I saw the diagrams and the reentry heating profiles and decided to become a ceramic engineer and work with him on the project.

Periodically the research review teams from NASA would come to the university to review the progress of the research, and Doc would introduce me to these engineers. This reinforced my yearning to become an astronaut and my interest in pursuing an advanced degree.

I accepted a graduate fellowship in biomedical engineering at the University of Illinois at Champaign-Urbana but didn't stay there long. While I was in college my brother, who was sixteen months younger than I, was killed in Vietnam. I ended up coming home to be with my family during a very difficult time in all our lives. I took a job in Seattle with Boeing as a computer systems analyst, waiting until a position in materials engineering opened up. I was there about two years when Doc called and suggested I apply for a graduate NASA grant in the department to do research on space applications, this time on high-energy-density batteries. So I went back for my master's degree. My yearning to be an astronaut was still strong, but I was a realist and kept my options open. I knew a lot of other factors had to materialize if I were ever

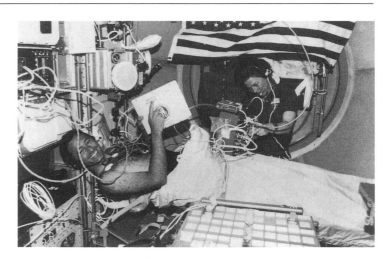

Astronaut Bonnie J. Dunbar, payload commander, monitors a test being run on payload specialist Lawrence J. DeLucas in the lower-body negative-pressure apparatus in the science module aboard the Earth-orbiting space shuttle Columbia.
PHOTO COURTESY OF THE NATIONAL AERONAUTICS AND SPACE ADMINISTRATION

to be an astronaut: NASA had to start choosing astronauts again, the canceled Apollo program needed to be revived (the shuttle was still just an idea on paper), and NASA had to start selecting women, which they hadn't yet done.

After I finished my master's degree, my adviser, Dr. Suren Sarian, arranged for a research science exchange to Harwell Laboratories in Oxford, England, for three months. My work involved the wetting behavior of liquids on solid substrates. Before I left for England, I applied to the Rockwell International Space Division in Downy, California, and secured a position as a senior research engineer in production operations upon my return. When I returned from England I worked on the thermal protection system for the shuttle, the same system I had been working on as an undergraduate at the University of Washington. It was a wonderful position. I was there for two years working out in Palmdale on the actual production of space shuttle tiles and various process developments. I loved being in the desert, and I loved the excitement of being in a test facility. I started flying and received my license while working at Rockwell. In late 1977, while I was at Rockwell, the first application call for space shuttle astronauts came. I applied and was accepted for an interview—Rockwell was very supportive of this—but I didn't make the final cut. However, I

was offered a job with NASA, and the management at Rockwell encouraged me to take the position to enhance my qualifications for later selection. They indicated that if I wanted to return to Rockwell the door would always be open.

I started out at NASA in July 1978 as a *Skylab* guidance and navigation engineer in Mission Control. The *Skylab* space station was in orbit at the time but unmanned after having supported three crews that set the U.S. space-duration record (eighty-four days). We had three teams controlling the spacecraft on rotating shifts. Each team had people who operated different systems, such as the electrical system or the computer system. My job was related to the guidance system, which controlled the orientation and navigation of the craft—the part that tells the spacecraft its location and position in space. It was an excellent learning experience in operations. I worked on *Skylab* for nine months, until it deorbited and burned up. Part of our job was to make sure that the part of *Skylab* that survived reentry came down in an uninhabited portion of the world, so we picked the Indian Ocean. We did have some small pieces land in Australia, which thrilled the Australians, but all in all things went smoothly.

I also was in the payload operations group, which was formed to support future space shuttle payloads. *Payload* is a generic term that means anything you put on the space shuttle that isn't part of the shuttle; it can be an experiment or a satellite. We had to develop very complex drawings, called operational drawings, that required you to know the electrical systems of the payload, the mechanical interfaces, the commands that were sent to it from the ground or from the crew, and the data or telemetry sent from it to the ground or the crew. We would develop these very complex drawings for use during an actual mission.

Part of my agreement with NASA when I came to work for them was that I could pursue my Ph.D. at night. I already knew what I wanted to do for my dissertation research: I was interested in the effects of space flight on bone strength and calcium. From 1978 to 1980 I worked full-time and attended class at the University of Houston at night. I finished most of my course work by the time I was selected as an astronaut. NASA agreed to support me while I finished my Ph.D.—I was also in training at the time and had to do my job—and I had lab space both at the Johnson Space Center and at the University of Houston. Because I was a materials engineer and in past work had looked at mechanical strengths of different materials, I was interested in knowing whether the calcium loss attributed to space flight that we measured on *Skylab* also led to any mechanical differences in load-bearing bones. I used an animal model to do the research and simulate space flight. I used rats and put them in a harness for thirty days to simulate bed rest; they could use their front paws, but their back legs were suspended. After a month I evaluated the blood chemistry for the hormones, sacrificed the rats, and looked at bone strength. For the population I looked at there *was* a change in bone strength, a definite shift in metabolism. This research was interesting not only to NASA but to the medical community at large because of the high incidence of osteoporosis in older women. I finished my Ph.D. in 1983.

I went from being a guidance and navigation engineer to training to work in Mission Control as a payload officer for space shuttle launch. Meanwhile, NASA had put out a call for the 1980 astronaut class; I reapplied and was selected for that class. In May 1980 I began training with eighteen other U.S. citizens and two Europeans. We began our candidacy year with classroom lectures; the year allows the candidate to determine if this is what he or she really wants to do, and it allows management to ascertain if they made the right selection. During that year we became familiar with flying the T-38 jet, we were scuba certified, and we did water and land survival. We studied an overview of the shuttle systems and of nineteen different science disciplines—the stars, the effects of space flight on the human body, material science, and geology. The second year of training included simulator training for the shuttle. Three years is about the amount of time it takes to train as an astronaut, and typically once you are assigned to a flight it takes another year or year and a half to train for that flight. The first shuttle flight was in 1981; two missions were planned for that year and four for the next, so we all knew our turn would come within a few years.

My first flight, in October 1985, was a joint mission with the Germans; we carried the *Spacelab* that was built by the European Space Agency. The German government bought the flight for their experiments. We provided most of the crew, although three of the crew members were European (two Germans and one Dutch). I was the only woman. My job was to operate the *Spacelab* and its experiments; to do that I spent about seven months training in Germany. While conducting the experiments in space, I was the hands, eyes, and ears of about a hundred different investigators.

There is no earthbound experience to compare space flight to. Looking down at the earth from 150 nautical miles out, rotating around the earth every ninety minutes and seeing the planet from that perspective, is amazing. Weightlessness is a great equalizer: it doesn't matter how strong you are or how short; weight is meaningless in an environment where there is only mass. I like working in crews—

NASA looks for real team players because that's a vital component to the success of any mission.

I have flown four flights since 1985: STS-61A, STS-32, STS-50, and STS-71. Crews were selected by the chief of the astronaut office and his boss, the director of flight-crew operations. Many factors go into selecting a crew. Two pilots and at least three mission specialists are assigned to every crew. The mission specialists are selected based on the payload, the objective of the mission, and their availability. I have performed hundreds of experiments, launched satellites, operated the shuttle's robotic arm, trained for spacewalks, and docked to the Russian space station, *Mir*. My job has taken me around the world and to thousands of students. When I'm not flying, I have a technical job to support. We rotate through jobs, often to introduce us to areas we are not familiar with. It's in NASA's interest to have people fairly broad-based, and it's one of the things that keeps the job so stimulating.

My husband, Ron, was a professor of electrical engineering at the University of Colorado, Colorado Springs, when I met him at an electrical engineering meeting in 1987. He was interested in the space program; he had been an Air Force pilot and had taught at the Air Force Academy in Colorado Springs. We married in 1988 and were a commuter couple for two years. He applied for the 1990 astronaut class, and in January 1990, when I was on orbit with my second flight, NASA faxed us the list of the newest astronaut class and my husband was on it. He flew his first flight in January 1994 and is currently training for his second.

NASA has been very supportive of women in the workplace since long before it was a trend. When I first came, I was only the second woman to work in the Mission Control front room. But beginning with the selection of women in the first astronaut class in 1978, there was an intellectual push in this agency to encourage the best and the brightest; race and gender didn't matter. NASA's been a leader in the federal government in this respect. I think NASA is a great place for women; it provides a lot of opportunity for creativeness because we're developing for the future. We can't compete with industry in terms of salary, so the people who come to work here really believe in what they're doing and what this does for the nation.

I attribute my success in large part to my parents, who always taught me to be the best I could be, and to my grandfather, who taught me that "a horse never wins a race it doesn't enter." He came to this country at age nineteen with no money, and worked his way from New York through Colorado to Oregon, where he homesteaded. I learned from him and my parents that failure is a part of life, but if you never try, you can never succeed. I learned to ride horses before I could walk, and my parents immediately put me back on the horse when I fell off so that I would not develop a fear of riding. Most of the performance fences I see built are built by individuals around themselves: they say "I can't learn that" or "It's too hard." I've heard women say they can't do chemistry but then I see them create a recipe; or they say they can't do engineering but they create their own dress patterns. They are just words—the principles are the same.

PRESENT POSITION: NASA Astronaut

FIELD: Ceramic and biomedical engineering

RESEARCH AREA: Microgravity research; materials science and physiology

EDUCATION: B.S. in Ceramic Engineering (1971), University of Washington; M.S. in Ceramic Engineering (1975), University of Washington; Ph.D. in Biomedical Engineering (1983), University of Houston

DATE/PLACE OF BIRTH: March 3, 1949/Sunnyside, Washington

Bonnie Dunbar lives with her husband, Ron, in Seabrook, Texas. In their free time they enjoy flying, sports, and the mountains of Colorado, and it isn't unusual for them to visit air and space museums!

INTERVIEW DATE: August 1995

Cynthia Dusel-Bacon

Geologist

U.S. GEOLOGICAL SURVEY, DEPARTMENT OF THE INTERIOR

Cynthia Dusel-Bacon's interest in science was never encouraged when she was a girl. In college she majored in Spanish; it was while taking a geology course to fulfill her science requirement that her fascination with rocks began. Though she went on to teach junior high school Spanish after graduation, her interest in rocks eventually brought her back to school to get a second bachelor's degree, this time in geology. In her third summer working in Alaska with the U.S. Geological Survey, she had an accident that changed her life—she was attacked by a black bear and lost both of her arms as a result of her injuries. Although her graduate work was disrupted by the accident, the Survey has been committed to allowing her to reach her potential as a researcher. Now a mother, she continues to do research in metamorphic petrology and is entering a new research area in geology.

When I was young and told my mother that I was interested in science, she suggested that someday I could marry a scientist. My family was never really able to envision me doing science myself. My father was an English professor, and my mother had briefly taught high school English. Early in my college career, the furthest I ventured from their example was to get a degree in Spanish and a secondary-school teaching credential.

My interest in geology came from an undergraduate science requirement at the University of California at Santa Barbara. I took geology my junior year and loved it. The class went on a field trip to the hills above Santa Barbara and found a fish fossil. I was astounded. I couldn't believe that the hill I was standing on was once under water. The lectures and labs really interested me and, though it was a difficult course, I did very well. After that, road cuts along highways were never the

Cynthia Dusel-Bacon at age twelve, conducting a study of molds for a sixth-grade science class project, Saratoga Grammar School, Saratoga, California, May 1958

same for me: I always studied them to see if I could read a story in the rocks. But the die was cast for me to graduate in Spanish and spend my senior year in Spain; I wasn't about to change my plans.

When I came back from Spain, I spent a year getting a secondary-school teaching credential. The following year, I took a position teaching Spanish to junior high school students. I also began backpacking as a hobby and would buy a book on the geology of an area and look at the rocks. I made the decision to become a geologist while backpacking in the Canadian Rockies. Not long afterwards, I met a geologist at a gas station in the town where I was teaching. We became friends and often talked about geology. Soon afterwards, I discovered that nearby Sonoma State University offered a geology course for teachers and I took it. I loved every minute of it. At the same time, I had a friend who had decided to go back to school for a master's degree in zoology. I was envious of the work she was doing. As much as I loved interacting with the kids, I felt I was teaching what I already knew and that the students really weren't interested. These events influenced my decision to get a degree in geology.

When I first told my parents of my decision to go back to school, they were exasperated. My mother felt that a bachelor's degree and a job put a woman in a holding pattern to be independent from her parents until she married. She felt I was already successful in the first two things and just needed to wait for a husband to come along. Neither of my parents thought I could ever get a job in geology, and they made it clear to me that they were not going to give me money for school or support me. So I continued teaching for a year to save money before starting, and I taught night school, waitressed, and occasionally worked as a substitute to put myself through school. Because I didn't have a math or science background, I had to begin all over to get my bachelor's degree in geology. It took me three and a half years.

I think of geologists as being rock detectives. I'm fascinated with finding out about events that happened hundreds of millions of years ago. It requires piecing together different types of data, working with other people, combining information, and being imaginative about envisioning a hypothesis that takes all of this information into account. I enjoy the outdoor aspect of the work when it meets my own conditions of safety. It's also the kind of job that requires a lot of different talents. It involves development of a research strategy, data collection and analysis, collaboration, travel, writing up the results of your research, and communicating your findings at conferences. It's a really exciting field, and I can't imagine doing anything else.

I'm in a mineral resource assessment group at the U.S. Geological Survey. My primary focus has been metamorphosed rocks in Alaska. Metamorphosed rocks are sedimentary rocks, lavas, or crystalline rocks, such as granites, that have recrystallized under high temperatures and pressures deep within the earth over the course of millions of years. It takes millions of years for some of these rocks to cool. The mineral constituents of metamorphosed rocks generally align themselves in a way that reflects the stresses that they underwent as they recrystallized. Minerals have certain stabilities and want to get to their equilibrium state, so they transform in a solid state to a new mineral. Certain minerals, like garnet, will change composition as they grow under evolving conditions. Using an instrument called an electron microprobe, I can measure the composition of the garnet at the core and as it added onto itself sequentially toward the rim in order to determine the pressure and temperature that caused the change to occur. Then, because of what I know about the earth's crust, I can trace the pressure and temperature path that the rock underwent while it metamorphosed and subsequently cooled and uplifted. Was it near the surface and then buried, and was it rapidly brought to the surface by moving faults? This type of research is geothermobarometry, one of many aspects of petrology. Petrology is the study of rock history, and geothermobarometry is the study of temperatures and pressures that affected metamorphic rocks.

Over a period of about five years, I compiled and published maps of all the metamorphic rocks of Alaska, which comprise over half of the rocks exposed at the surface. I devised map units based on pressure and temperature conditions and the age of the metamorphic events, and wrote descriptive and interpretive texts to accompany the maps. The metamorphic map that I did of Alaska also will be used as a component of a complete metamorphic map of the world currently being compiled by geologists in other countries.

I work with other people who date the timing of metamorphic events by measuring the radioactive decay of certain elements contained in minerals that are present in the rocks I collect during fieldwork. I also work with another woman who studies the deformation of the rocks that occurred while they were being metamorphosed. My work needs to be done in conjunction with these other studies so we get the whole picture of the deformation and recrystallization of the rocks, including when it happened. Not only do I analyze what happened to the rocks during metamorphism, I also try to look through the metamorphism to understand what the rocks were before. It isn't that easy to look at a metamorphic rock and know if it began as a sediment or lava. It requires experience and knowledge of chemistry and primary textural features in a variety of rock types. This type of information has direct practical applications. Different types of mineral deposits are more likely to occur in certain kinds of rocks and under certain metamorphic temperatures. For example, volcanic rocks that have never been heated above about 500°C have the potential to contain low-sulfide gold-quartz veins.

The results of my work are twofold. By dating and determining what the rocks were before metamorphism, I contribute to a body of knowledge that helps the scientific community determine where different parts of Alaska originated—whether they were parts of seabeds or different continents and how old the rocks are.

By combining geologic data with geophysical and geochemical information, we can predict what mineral resources may lie beneath the surface. Alaska is different from the rest of the lower forty-eight states in that 57 percent of the state is federally owned, and 63 percent of it has not been studied in any detail. Congress passed a bill to have the Secretary of the Interior assess the mineral and energy resources of all the public lands in Alaska. If a section of land contains a major mineral deposit, the government wants to be able to compare the value of that deposit with the value of the other uses of the land. Because a large portion of the jobs in Alaska are mineral related, minerals are an important part of their economy.

I'm now moving away from metamorphic study because it is viewed as esoteric and it is hard to fund. There's been a major downsizing at the U.S. Geological Survey resulting from cutbacks in the government. Sixty percent of the people in the minerals office in Menlo Park, where I work, lost their jobs. In order to make my work more relevant, I've moved into research in a new field that has more direct application to societal problems. There are rocks in Canada, much like the ones I've been studying in Alaska, that contain massive sulfide deposits related to volcanic activity. These deposits are accumulations of polymetallic sulfide-rich rock formed on or near the sea floor by convection of hydrothermal fluids through submarine volcanic and sedimentary rocks. I'm going to visit the local geologists in western Canada to learn more about where these deposits occur and then try to look for similar potential in the rocks in Alaska. I'm planning to collaborate with a geologist from the University of British Columbia.

Alaska's field season is only the summer months. During my first summer there, I put in four grueling months out in the field. When I tried to do fieldwork in 1975, I was informally advised by a Geological Survey geologist that my only chance to get experience was to go out with another woman. Most geologists were men, so my opportunities were severely limited. There were only three female project chiefs at the Geological Survey's Western Center at the time I was looking for a job. It just so happened that the woman I went out with worked harder than most geologists at the Survey. She was also afraid of using guns in the field, so as her assistant I was denied the opportunity to carry a gun. Maintaining her field practices set me up for a situation that changed my life.

We were mapping a six-thousand-square-mile area in east-central Alaska. In 1977, my third summer of working in the Yukon-Tanana Upland of Alaska, there was a lot of money for fieldwork, and we had three months of helicopter time. Nowadays, I feel very lucky if I get five to ten days of helicopter use the whole summer, but back then the helicopter would fly around every day, dropping off each field team member at a different ridge to map the geology. Usually there were five geologists and, for part of the time, a group of geochemists who studied stream sediments, and geophysicists. The whole team consisted of as many as ten scientists. With a helicopter, flying from place to place is really fast, so the geologists would be spaced up to ten or twenty miles apart from each other. We would hike during the day, collecting samples, recording the location of the samples on a topographical map, and writing notes that were keyed to the same numbers as each sample, describing the rocks and any sorts of faults or features we observed. At a prearranged time and place, we would be picked up. Because we each had to cover ten to fourteen miles during the day, we had to work quickly.

On August 13, 1977, I was descending a ridge that I was mapping, breaking off rock samples from outcrops along the way, and putting them in my pack—when I heard a noise in the undergrowth below. I looked up to see a black bear emerging out of the brush about ten feet away from me. I had encountered bears before during my fieldwork, but always at a greater distance. Twice the bears hadn't seen me, and another one had been startled by my presence and run away. From my reading and discussions, I knew that some bears could be intimidated. I didn't want this

Geologist Cynthia Dusel-Bacon about to board a helicopter that will take her to examine rocks in a remote area of east-central Alaska, 1981

bear to know that I was afraid, so I clapped my hands and waved my arms to scare it off. For about a minute, my strategy seemed to be working. The bear had been below me, and it slowly circled to higher ground. When it was level with me, it looked up the trail I was on and then looked back at me; I knew it was trying to decide whether to run away or attack. I took a little step up on an outcrop. Perhaps that seemed like a more aggressive move or it flipped the mental coin in the bear's head. It turned around and attacked. It happened so fast there was never an opportunity for me to run or to fight it off. One moment the bear was ten feet away, and the next it had run around behind me, knocked me down, and had its teeth in the back of my head.

From that point on, the bear was either biting my head, biting my shoulder, or ripping the flesh off my side and arms. I deliberately played dead, remembering that an attacking bear would supposedly lose interest and go away once the threat to it was removed. But this bear seemed determined to consume me. Over the course of half an hour, the bear dragged me by my right shoulder through the brush. At one point, the bear stepped away from me and lay down to rest, and I was able to use my uninjured left arm to stealthily get into my backpack and retrieve my walkie-talkie. Talking as loudly as I dared, I radioed the helicopter pilot that I was being eaten by a bear. I tried to inform him of my location, but before I could be certain that my message had been received, the bear lunged at me, savagely attacking my left arm and knocking the radio away. The bear continued to tear at my arms and shoulders, licking my blood from my wounds, stopping only to rip apart the contents of my backpack. I thought about my husband of five months, Charlie, and how much I wanted to live.

About ten minutes later, I heard a helicopter make a pass over a nearby ridge. The helicopter left, leaving me to wonder if my radio call had been heard. After another ten minutes, it passed directly over me, this time scaring the bear away. Eventually the helicopter landed nearby, and I was rescued. They flew me to Fort Greeley Army Base in Delta Junction, an hour away. Emergency measures were taken to stabilize my condition before I was flown to a Fairbanks Army hospital, where I was immediately rushed into surgery. Within twenty-four hours I was flown to San Francisco for further medical treatment.

My left arm had to be amputated halfway between my elbow and shoulder, but the doctors tried to save my right arm by grafting a vein from my leg. After a week, the infected tissue in the right arm lost blood circulation and, knowing that the dying arm was endangering my life, the doctors amputated at the shoulder. After four months of recovery, I was fitted with artificial arms. It was to be another six months before I got artificial arms that actually worked for me. My left stump has a wide range of motion. I've continued to work at the Geological Survey and have done fieldwork with the assistance of my husband, who is also a geologist for the Geological Survey.

Safety practices have changed since my accident, and everyone who wants it now receives gun training. I have friends whose lives have been saved because they knew how to shoot. My husband and I don't go into the field in Alaska without a gun.

At my computer, I use a modified mouse set on the floor that I operate with my foot. I have a peg much like a golf tee glued to the mouse so I can slip my toes around it and curl them to click the button and then lift up to move the mouse around the pad. I am still restricted in that I can only plunk out one key at a time with one arm. The microscope that I occasionally use was modified by engineers and a machinist at the Survey. I also use a speaker phone a lot so that I can take notes. Because I haven't had an assistant for the last two years, things have been slower and harder for me. It makes a big difference in my efficiency when I have someone to help me with things that are particularly time consuming or hard to do.

Though my master's degree schooling was interrupted by my accident, the Survey has been committed to providing opportunities for me to develop as a scientist. The standard way to become a full-blown research geologist is to get a Ph.D. in geology. When it wasn't feasible for me to go back to school, I was assigned to work on a metamorphic compilation project and given my own research project to see what I could do. I have continued to produce and have been promoted on the basis of my work, not my education. I'm living proof that independent research can be done without an advanced degree.

I've rarely felt disadvantaged for being a woman in this field, but I feel that I don't get recognition for being someone with a significant disability. Other than having hooks for hands, my appearance is so normal that most people aren't aware of how much longer it takes for me to do things and how much struggle is involved. When I was invited to talk at the Smithsonian on my disability, one of my colleagues asked me, "Why are they having you speak?" When I replied that I do have a disability, he said, "I don't think of you as disabled." It's nice that people perceive me as an able-bodied person, but I feel that I'm missing recognition for the added effort, frustration, and creativity that I'm forced to contribute to be able to do my work.

In 1986, after years of working as a full-time geologist, I went to part-time status to care for my newborn son. He was the result of three tries with in vitro fertilization. My infertility was due to my using the Dalkon Shield intrauterine device as a birth control method in the 1970s. In many ways, infertility was harder to deal with than the loss of my arms because I felt it was completely out of my control. I could learn how to do things with my artificial arms, use my feet, or get modifications to cope with my disability. My husband and I were in control of reversing those devastating effects; but in trying to get pregnant, I was up against the wall. Nothing worked. After five years, we decided to try in vitro and went all the way to Norfolk, Virginia, for the procedure. I was thirty-eight at that point and really couldn't wait any longer. Having a child has been a wonderful experience, and it has opened up a whole new level of experiences. We're a very close family, and family is important to me. I credit my parents with giving me the self-confidence, presence of mind, and determination to accomplish what I have, starting with saving my own life.

I would never tell young women that they can't do science and have a family. Sometimes you have to make a decision about the extent to which you're going to get involved in a career. I've found that you can lessen the degree a bit and still be taken seriously as a significant player in the field. It was more important for me to fulfill different aspects of my life than to focus strictly on my research. I don't think having a family has held me back that much. Most people don't even know that I work part-time because you wouldn't guess it from reading my monthly report. It's what you produce, not how long it's taken you. If you're productive, that's what's important.

PRESENT POSITION: Geologist, U.S. Geological Survey, Department of the Interior

FIELD: Geology

RESEARCH AREA: Metamorphic petrology, Alaskan regional geology

EDUCATION: B.A. in Spanish (1968), University of California, Santa Barbara; Secondary Education Credential in Spanish (1969), San Jose State University; B.A. in Geology (1975), San Jose State University.

DATE/PLACE OF BIRTH: August 16, 1946/San Jose, California

Cynthia Dusel-Bacon lives in Menlo Park with her geologist husband, Charlie, and their son, Ian, who is now old enough to go with them to do fieldwork.

INTERVIEW DATE: January 1996

Kathryn Edwards

Professor of Biology
KENYON COLLEGE

Kathryn Edwards grew up in New Jersey, Texas, and Kenya. She came back to the States for college, intending to become a veterinarian. She has ended up as a plant physiologist, teaching biology and women's studies at Kenyon College. She is very active in the lesbian community and owns a kennel where she raises Jack Russell terriers and boxers.

I've always had an interest in science. As a child, I would do experiments with bumblebees or with my mother's plant cuttings. My mother is a retired surgical nurse, and my father is a retired but consulting economist; they were always supportive of my experiments and of anything I was interested in. When I was young, we lived in Princeton, New Jersey, and then moved to Houston, Texas. When I was fifteen my father was hired as an economic adviser to the Kenyan government, and we moved to Africa. My parents still live in Nairobi.

My biggest challenge growing up was working out my own feelings of inferiority. My mother often told me that my younger sister was smarter than I and that my father was a genius. I have no idea what our actual IQ scores are, but I do know that I felt I wasn't as smart as others in my family. Very early on, I started comparing myself to everyone else and feeling like I didn't have an original thought. My feelings were reinforced at the end of high school when my application to Oberlin College was rejected. A month later I got another letter from Oberlin saying I was accepted; I took it to my parents, asking

"Now, why would this happen?" It turned out that my father had called friends of his there, and they got me in. My parents had been very concerned that, because I had attended British colonial school in Nairobi and was not prepared for SAT exams like most students in U.S. schools, U.S. colleges might not take my application seriously. They felt they had put my career in jeopardy by moving to Africa and were simply trying to look out for my welfare. But it made me feel like I wasn't really worthy of going to Oberlin, although, in the end, I did just fine there. By my senior year I was a straight-A student in science.

Getting into plant physiology was a fluke. As an undergraduate, I was pre-vet; I thought plant science was not "true" science and avoided all plant courses. Then during my se-

Kathryn Edwards, 1969

nior year I had to satisfy a college sociology requirement, which conflicted with the few remaining animal courses, and I had to take a plant course. I took plant physiology, and I was so intrigued that I did honors research in the area.

In the meantime, the Vietnam War was raging, and I was somewhat involved in anti-war activities. I knew full well that men were draft-exempt if they went to medical or veterinary school, so I decided not to go to vet school until the war ended. In the interim I considered graduate programs in ecology because it was a form of applied science that could help the world. The summer after graduation I received an offer to do graduate study on elephant migration in Africa. Then I got a call from the professor who had supervised my undergraduate research. He had left Oberlin to become head of the botany department at the University of North Carolina, and he asked me to apply there. I wasn't too sure about it since I'd only had one course in plants—his. Besides, I was still planning to go to vet school someday. But I needed something to do in the meantime, so I applied. A few weeks later the department came back and offered me a lot of money. I thought, "For a year, what the heck?" I went, got hooked, and never did go to veterinary school.

When I graduated with my Ph.D. in 1974, I felt torn. I wanted a job, but my mentor wanted me to do a postdoc. I did a two-year postdoc at Yale and then applied for jobs in industry, at big universities, and at small colleges. One of the things that I disliked about the big universities was their emphasis on "publish or perish; get your grant money in or forget it." That's harder to do in botanical fields, where funding is scarce unless you are focused on agriculture. Also, I just wasn't sure I wanted to compete in that male environment. When I interviewed for industrial positions, I found that they too were more agriculturally oriented than I wanted to be, and I really didn't like the lack of academic freedom or the male fraternity that I saw. I had come from a small-college environment with a long

tradition of dedication to undergraduate education. A lot of Oberlin alumni go on in education, and I too made the decision that I wanted to be at a small liberal arts college. I found such a position first at Rollins College and now at Kenyon.

I see my work at Kenyon as threefold: research in science, teaching science, and work in women's studies. Teaching is my primary focus; I keep an active role in research in order to be a good teacher of science. For me, science and women's studies overlap in many ways, but they can also be disparate. I like to keep the two halves of my professional life separated. It reflects the fact my life isn't fully integrated: when I publish in science, I publish under the name "Kathryn Edwards"; in the women's community I publish as "Ryn Edwards."

My scientific research first focused on acid-induced growth and hormone transport in higher plants, particularly corn roots. A number of years ago, funding constraints encouraged me to switch my focus to how plants respond to gravity and the underlying cellular mechanisms controlling that response. Many plants and fungi respond to gravity asymmetrically, which means that growth rates vary across the responding organ (shoot, root, sporangiophore) causing "bending" either toward or away from the gravitational force. I am presently working with a fungus called *Phycomyces*. It produces a large single cell called a sporangiophore that bears a vegetative reproductive structure, the sporangium. This long single cell responds to gravity in a negative way—it grows away from gravity, or upwards. It intrigues me that within a single cell we have the mechanisms for both the detection of gravity and the response to gravity. This is different from what is usually found in multicellular higher plants. In my lab, we are looking at the cytoskeleton as a possible means for the detection of gravity. We're also trying to understand components of second-messenger systems that would coordinate between the detection of gravity and the asymmetrical growth response. We are working to discover what genes may be expressed when this fungus is stressed in the gravitational field.

My lab consists of two to four undergraduate students and me. My students generally work full-time over the summer and two or three afternoons a week during the school year. The work is funded in part by NASA and in part by our biology department. NASA is interested in knowing how they might best grow plants in space, particularly whether they'll have to provide a gravity field. My work contributes to a ground-based understanding of how plants respond to gravity, which can help us better understand the role gravity plays in plant productivity.

Teaching is my primary duty as described by the college, and it is where I focus most of my energy. In addition to directing my research students, I teach two courses and an introductory lab each semester. I have been broadly trained, so I can teach everything from genetics to biochemistry, from animal anatomy to plant physiology. Currently, I am teaching an introductory course for majors called From Cell to Organism, a plant physiology course, and a one-year introductory experimental biology course. I also teach an interdisciplinary course for nonmajors called the Biology of Female Sexuality.

The interdisciplinary course is really a women's health class. We consider how and what science understands about the biology of women and look at feminist critiques of that science. We consider perspectives from as many different American women as possible. For every issue we consider, we talk about how it impacts black women, Native American women, other women of color, disabled women, lesbian women, and elderly women. We consider sexuality and related health issues, including everything from body image to sexually transmitted diseases; we look at AIDS, reproduction, reproductive technology, and health-care alternatives. One of my goals for the class is to assist students in developing their abilities to read scientific writings related to health issues. I focus particu-

larly on cancer because many of us will have to face it sometime in our lives, and whatever health issue we face, we may want to be able to assess the literature for ourselves. My second goal is to provide and create new tools for communication that respects different positions on issues, and show how policies that serve one subpopulation may not serve another. For example: Why is so much money being put into reproductive technology when we aren't spending money to serve the basic health-care needs of the poor? Why is so much money poured into osteoporosis when comparable moneys aren't spent on the other problems of black women, who are not prone to osteoporosis? It is implied in workshops I've attended and in ads I see on TV for calcium products to stop or slow osteoporosis that the disease is a problem for all women. The problem is not in the disease but rather that our government, researchers, and pharmaceutical companies spend more money and time on the health problems of white folks and little is directed for problems predominant in women in the black community. I try to teach students to recognize their ignorance of "others," identify their assumptions of others, and to commit to a lifelong endeavor to diminish ignorance in positive ways.

When I began my career, I was very focused on my professional development in plant physiology, but then I began to get frustrated with the politics and sexism of professional meetings. I started a women's caucus in the American Society of Plant Physiology, which was recognized in 1984. My big awakening was in 1980, when a librarian friend told me that I should go to the National Women's Studies Conference. I did and was totally transformed. It was such a different kind of conference from any professional science conference I'd ever been to. It made me realize what was really missing in my professional meetings: a sense of self in the organization, a sense of self in the "being a scientist" (a male concept), and true camaraderie. I realized that I kept my female and lesbian self out of the professional arena; I wasn't whole.

Kathryn Edwards in her lab at Kenyon College, July 1991
PHOTO BY TED RICE, COURTESY OF KENYON COLLEGE

I could be a whole, "real" person at the National Women's Studies meetings. They and the Midwest Society for Women in Philosophy meetings began my transformation to "radical," and I dove deep into women's studies.

Like most women, I know I faced discrimination throughout my education. I had a professor at Oberlin who once told a group of his female students over dinner that we shouldn't get married if we were going to graduate school. He said that the only way to have a professional life as a woman in science was to remain single, not have children, and to dedicate yourself to your career. I know now that it's untrue, but it was discouraging at the time to see that *he* could have career, a wife, and children. Then, in graduate school, the male graduate students were paid more for the same job than female graduate students.

Being a lesbian has sometimes influenced how seriously people take my opinion—both positively and negatively. Although I had my first female lover when I was sixteen, it wasn't until I was in graduate school that I realized that I was, in fact, a lesbian. I spent about five years being celibate and learning to be happy with who I was; I also came out to my family and friends. When I first took my position at Kenyon, the college administration and many

of the faculty knew, but I didn't push it in my department. Once I had tenure, I made sure I was clear with everyone about who I was. Now I'm completely out: my partner is listed in the college directory, and "lesbian power and community" is listed as one of my research interests under my photo in the department directory—where everyone, including prospective students, can see it. I don't feel that I have run into much overt discrimination on the job because of being a lesbian, although there have been a few problems. There was one serious incident in the women's studies program where I had a disagreement with some other women, and they said annoying things like, "You're only doing this because you're a dyke." I ended up resigning from the committee until it blew over. But I haven't had any serious problems with students—I get far more positive feedback than negative. The course I teach on female sexuality is quite popular with students who are uncovering or discovering their own identities, and I think that some of the young lesbians find it helpful to see an out lesbian as a senior faculty member.

Balancing my personal life with my work is hard. I have learned to carve out a space for my personal life, and I try to set aside a half a day or a day on the weekend. My partner complains that it isn't enough time! I've had to learn to say no and to prioritize better. I've also learned to let other people do some of the work, a skill I developed during my three years as department chair.

Outside of work, I'm into dogs and country living. I have a kennel where I raise Jack Russell terriers and boxers. My partner and I also have three cats. We spend a lot of time with the dogs. It's a good outlet. I don't have to talk shop with them. I get to bark and yell; it gets out all sorts of frustrations, and they, of course, listen intently or don't give a hoot, as the case may be. They make me laugh a lot!

I also do some work in the lesbian community. I'm a member of the Lesbian Business Association in Columbus, Ohio, because of my kennel business. They are responsible for putting on the Ohio Lesbian Festival, and I've served as promotions manager for that. The festival is part of the reason I became involved in the group; I think it's one of the greatest things they've done for this area. However, the LBA is a mostly white organization, and I have been trying to find ways to broaden the support system to include black women's businesses. My partner and I helped start a group called Second Wave to put on more inclusive events for the community. We've had some very successful events, but the LBA boycotted them. We don't want to be divisive; that isn't the point. It's a struggle and we're still working on it.

One of the things I do to bridge my lesbian-community and professional interests is to coordinate a 300-member lesbians-in-science (LIS) electronic mailing list, which allows lesbian scientists worldwide to discuss common issues and concerns and to network and share information. The idea for the list was born one summer at the Michigan Womyn's Music Festival (one of the largest annual gatherings of lesbian, bisexual, and feminist women in the United States) and was put into actual practice in 1991 at the University of Wisconsin–Madison by a physicist, E. J. Zita. I've been maintaining the list for a while now. I think that it's important for women in science to network with each other because there aren't enough women mentors.

When women come into science, especially at the large universities where they gain most of their experience, they find that most of the technicians are women and most of the faculty are men. We need to find ways to encourage women students not to think of themselves as limited by what they see around them, but to go for what they dream of being. This is why I so much enjoy being with students. There's so much energy there, and so much potential for them to make a difference. I know I will have done a good teaching job if I have helped them to be grounded in themselves, to go for what they want, and to understand and work for the diversity of humanity.

PRESENT POSITION: Professor of Biology, Kenyon College

FIELD: Plant physiology

RESEARCH AREAS: Gravitropism and lesbian issues

EDUCATION: A.B. in Biology (1969), Oberlin College; Ph.D. in Botany (1974), University of North Carolina

DATE/PLACE OF BIRTH: May 8, 1947/Washington, Pennsylvania

Kathryn Edwards lives in Mount Vernon, Ohio, with her partner of thirteen years, Marianne Perine, and with ten dogs, puppies of assorted ages, three cats, two computers, and many artworks.

INTERVIEW DATE: March 1995

M. Joycelyn Elders

Professor of Pediatrics
THE UNIVERSITY OF ARKANSAS FOR MEDICAL SCIENCES

Dr. Joycelyn Elders was in the public spotlight for voicing what she believed as the Surgeon General of the United States. A desire to help people was always her motivation, and she used every opportunity to get a medical degree at a time when black women did not do such things. Now as a physician, professor, and a speaker on public health issues, Joycelyn Elders continues her crusade to speak out for the people.

❧

I am a physician. I am concerned with the health and welfare of people. Even as a little girl, when I was chopping cotton all day in a field in Arkansas, getting an education to help people was a great dream, even though it seemed impossible, even though becoming a physician was then beyond my wildest dreams. Over the years so many impossible things have happened in my life that I no longer believe in impossibilities. Some things seem highly unlikely, even impossible, but I have learned the important life lesson that nothing is impossible.

Every week I see children who are my patients in the endocrinology clinic at Arkansas Children's Hospital. Many of them are children of poor families. Having been a black child from a poor rural family in Arkansas, I identify strongly with them. It is important to me that each person is treated with the same dignity and deference as a multimillionaire. At Arkansas Children's Hospital, I give lectures to students, make rounds, am on call—everything a physician at a teaching hospital does, I do. I have a small office at the Arkansas Children's Hospital with space for only a desk and one extra chair, so I do not generally see people in my office but use it to dictate charts, take calls, and sign correspondence and charts.

I speak to people and groups around the country, at colleges and universities, meetings, associations, seminars, on television shows, and radio shows. Every weekday I do the "Dr. Joycelyn Elders Show" on radio, on which I speak about current social and political issues and health care and health concerns and take calls from the listeners. I have an agent who arranges my speaking engagements around the country and takes care of organizing the necessary travel.

Official portrait of M. Joycelyn Elders as U.S. Surgeon General

It is exciting and humbling for me to be able to speak to groups, and my goal, my challenge is always the same—to stimulate people to think about the issues. Knowledge through education is a wondrous gift, but knowledge seen through the paradigms, the filters of scholarship, experience, reason, and tradition develops wisdom. That is what I am searching for in myself and in others. Many people of all opinions are smart, but intelligence without integrity is something I have never craved. No matter how much trouble stating my beliefs gets me into, I am unwilling to cower in the face of the way I see a thing to be. Frequently I am told something like, "Dr. Elders, I disagree with absolutely everything you say and everything you stand for, but I know you don't lie." I like that. It's exciting to me and energizing that people understand that. I hope it also helps them in some way.

In addition to my work as a physician, each weekday I prepare for the next day's radio show early in the morning. One of the reasons daily preparation is necessary is that I try to have something that is pertinent and prominent in the news, so it is usually not possible to prepare too far in advance. I also travel several days of the week, so I spend a lot of time on airplanes. I use this time in the air to write speeches and to sleep.

I do most of my own cleaning, housekeeping and cooking, gardening, and shopping. These prove to be times that are doubly productive because I use them as an opportunity to meditate. My husband and I have a large garden with a variety of vegetables. We maintain our grounds of about fourteen acres mostly by ourselves with some help. We also work together on the rental property that we own; we do everything from making sure that it is rented to keeping all the toilets working at once. Of all the things I do around the house, I enjoy cooking the most. The things I do at home are so different from what I do in my work as a pediatrician and as a speaker on public health that they seem more like recreation.

I was the first of eight children born to sharecropper parents in rural Arkansas. My par-

ents were loving and hard-working, spiritual people. Although my mother stressed the importance of a good education, we all had to work in the fields. That was just the way life was. My mother taught me to read by the light of a kerosene lantern, and she instilled in me the love for education.

My brothers and sisters and I attended a one-room school house, and I was concerned that our education was not up to par. However, when my family lived in California for a short time, I was tested to determine my grade level and was placed three grades above my standing in Arkansas. When we returned to Arkansas this enabled me to graduate from high school three years early.

In my high school—a black school because segregation was still the law—all of the young women were taught to be maids. This was quite rigorous training, and it made sense because that was about all a black woman could do in those times. I have always been pleased that I had this training because it has helped me to understand what keeping a house is all about and to appreciate those who do it.

It was always a dream of mine to go to college, but I could not imagine how this might be possible. Then one day a woman from United Methodist Women came to speak at our church about their college scholarships. I applied and was awarded a scholarship to attend Philander Smith, an African American Methodist college in Little Rock. The scholarship paid for my tuition, but I had to work for my room, board, books, and clothes, and my family helped me all they could.

I graduated from college at age eighteen and found that there was nothing for a black eighteen-year-old college graduate to do. I wanted to go to medical school, but I knew that I would not be able to do that, so I joined the Army and became a physical therapist.

After my tour of duty in the Army, I realized that I could go to medical school on the GI Bill, and there was already a black female at the University of Arkansas Medical School. I had heard Edith Erby Jones speak. She was the first black student to attend the University of Arkansas Medical School and is now an internist in Houston, Texas. She was so very inspiring that I knew I must go ahead with my dreams for becoming a physician. I applied and entered there in 1956. All the black people at the university had to eat separately in the cafeteria, and so I was able to meet the housekeeping staff and heard and saw their problems and aspirations.

After graduating I did a pediatric internship in Minnesota, then returned to Arkansas for a pediatric endocrinology residency. Dr. Theo Panos, the head of the Department of Pediatrics, and Dr. Edwin Hughes were especially encouraging and helpful to me in my development and in wanting me to always aim higher. There have always been people around me who were encouraging and strengthening to my personal and professional life.

I have always believed that when one door is shut to me, it means that God has something else in mind for my life, and I do not spend much time fretting about the fish that got away. Certainly there have been many obstacles to face in my life—sexism, racism—however, these are nothing but challenges that provide the opportunity for spiritual, personal, and professional growth. It has been my experience that honest, plain speaking, courage, a large serving of faith, and unrelenting perseverance is what it takes to overcome all the "isms" that face us in life, whatever they are.

Many seem to think that being fired by President Clinton from my position as surgeon general was devastating to me. On the contrary, I believe that I am in very good company in being fired by powerful people. The theologian Reverend Matthew Fox was fired by the pope; Ram Dass was fired by Harvard University. The list of outstanding people who have been fired by presidents of the United States is very long.

When President Clinton set me loose, my voice for the people was set loose. I had thought the Office of the Surgeon General was not a political one, but it seems rather obvious to me now that all of Washington, D.C., is political.

M. Joycelyn Elders in a recent photograph

Now I can speak freely without regard to politics, and I believe that this is a positive step in my life's work.

All it takes to age is not to die, but long life is not a worthy goal in and of itself. Saging—not only aging—is what we can strive for in our lives. To grow old does not make one wise; rather, it must be a purposeful endeavor just as exercising to develop one's muscles is. If you have been given opportunities in your life, it is necessary for you to pass on your wisdom to others. This is saging. There were those who helped each of us, and so we must be the ones to help others along their path.

There were many people along my path, and still are, who help me to keep my focus, and whom I know I can lean on if the need arises. I want to give this back to them by giving it to someone else. My family has always been paramount in my life and in the use of my time. No one makes it on their own; rather, we are each a part of some community, a family. I consider it of utmost importance to be a friend and to make friends, and to nurture those friendships.

I would not presume to give generic advice concerning the advancement of women's professional careers. My method of dealing with life is forthright and head-on, which has worked for me but admittedly might not work in someone else's case. Each person must find her own way. There is no formula that fits everyone. I do believe that we each need to mentor others, to be sages for others, and that we can help one another in a personal way. A person's life is so unique that even though we face many of the same difficulties and obstacles in life, our circumstances are very different. Mentoring must be personal; and, while it is enormously time consuming, it is our responsibility to one another and to the future. It is not only a duty, but to be a mentor or a sage to another is also one of life's greatest gifts. We can encourage one another at all times and be faithful to one another in our unending story of perseverance. Many times all it takes for a person to "keep on keeping on" is the comfort they have in knowing that there is someone who is backing them, cheering them on, caring so that they do not feel alone. If you need a mentor and have not found one, start searching; be intentional and persistent.

The Bible story about Peter walking on the water is a story of focus for me. Peter wanted to walk on the water, and Jesus told him to come on and step out of the boat. When he did, at first he was exhilarated; then he noticed the storm around him, and he realized that this was impossible. He took his eye off his goal, and he sank. We must have the courage to step out of the boat if we want to walk on water. Then we must keep our eye on the goal and ignore the chaos around us. There is nothing in life that can take the place of risk. It is not only exhilarating but necessary for a full and vital life.

I view myself as an ordinary person who has been given extraordinary opportunities to speak out for the ordinary people in our community. As long as there is one child who is not cared for properly, nurtured lovingly, educated wisely, or one teen who commits suicide; as long as there is one adult who is without health care, without friends, without community; as long as there is one elderly person without medical care, without shelter and food, we cannot stop working to raise consciousness. Somehow, in spite of great improbabilities, I find myself in a position to speak for the people who are forgotten, and I will never stop.

PRESENT POSITION: Professor of Pediatrics, The University of Arkansas for Medical Sciences

FIELDS: Medicine, public health, pediatrics, endocrinology

RESEARCH AREA: Endocrinology, growth, and metabolism

EDUCATION: B.S. (1951), Philander Smith College; M.D. (1960), University of Arkansas Medical School; M.S. in Biochemistry (1967), University of Arkansas

DATE/PLACE OF BIRTH: August 13, 1933/Schaal, Arkansas

Joycelyn Elders lives with her husband, Oliver B. Elders, in Little Rock, Arkansas.

INTERVIEW DATE: February 1996

Gertrude Belle Elion

Scientist Emeritus
BURROUGHS WELLCOME COMPANY
Medical Research Professor
DUKE UNIVERSITY

Gertrude Elion was one of three winners of the 1988 Nobel Prize for Physiology or Medicine for "introducing a more rational approach [to drug development] based on the understanding of basic biochemical and physiological process." She is only the ninth woman to have won a Nobel Prize in science; she is also one of very few people from industry or without a Ph.D. to have done so. During her career, she helped develop drugs for treating leukemia, for preventing rejection of transplanted organs, and for treating gout and herpes virus infections.

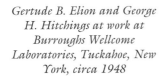

I've always been very clear about my motivation for doing science, although when I tell people they sometimes think I've made it up. I was a student who was very good at almost everything in high school, and I was re-
ally in a dilemma about what to pursue. I had no real desire to be a teacher, so I was looking for other opportunities. At that crucial time—the summer before I entered college—my grandfather died of stomach cancer. In those days, there was really nothing that could have been done for him. We were very close, and I used to visit him in the hospital. And then suddenly it came to me that maybe there was something I could do about cancer, that maybe I should become a scientist. Since being a doctor was almost impossible for a woman in those days, I decided I'd be a chemist. That way maybe I would discover a drug that would treat cancer. I did not know then that my mother would also die of cancer years later.

It was a rash decision, really. There weren't very many jobs for research scientists in those days, and there were none for women. I don't think I anticipated the trouble that was awaiting me. But I was determined to try anyway

Gertude B. Elion and George H. Hitchings at work at Burroughs Wellcome Laboratories, Tuckahoe, New York, circa 1948

and having made my decision, I never wavered. I loved science. It was clear that there was no going back.

My father had lost all his money in the stock market crash, and so I couldn't afford to go to a private college. Fortunately, we were living in New York, where Hunter College (for women) and the College of the City of New York (for men; now the coeducational City College of the City University of New York) were free to anyone whose high school grades were good enough. My brother and I might never have gone to college otherwise. Getting out of college in the midst of a Depression in 1937 was a real shock. There were very few jobs or graduate school assistantships available, and what few there were certainly were not available to women.

I spent an unsuccessful summer hunting for a job. For reasons I don't understand today, I wasn't angry about it. I was mostly just disappointed and frustrated, especially when a prospective employer told me, "You're qualified, but we have never had a woman in the laboratory. We think you would be a distracting influence." I was determined that it couldn't be what they were telling me—that it would have to change and that I just had to be patient. At one point I enrolled in secretarial school, figuring that I had better learn something useful. Fortunately, I was then offered a temporary job helping to teach a biochemistry course to nursing students. It was only for three months, but I didn't hesitate; my secretarial career was over. Soon after that position ended, I obtained a job in a lab working for free for a chemist I had met socially. After six months, he was able to pay me a salary, and by the time I left a year after that, I was earning twenty dollars per week and had enough money to start graduate school at New York University. I worked on my thesis part-time while teaching chemistry and physics in the public schools.

I never intended not to get married. It wasn't a distinct decision. About the time I graduated from college, I had fallen very much in love with a young man. He was still in college, and he was a statistics major. When he graduated, he went to work for Merrill Lynch, and we were planning to get married. And then he died of subacute bacterial endocarditis, which was the result of his having had rheumatic fever as a child. Two years later, with the advent of penicillin, he could have been saved. It reinforced in my mind the importance of scientific discovery, that it really was a matter of life and death to find treatments for diseases that hadn't been cured before.

After that I became immersed in my work, and since I was also trying to go to school part-time, I didn't really have time to look for relationships. I went out with a number of people, but the comparison was always there: "He's not as great as the other fellow; I don't want to spend the rest of my life with this person. If I had to choose between him and what I'm doing, I would choose what I'm doing." The right person just never showed up again. Maybe I didn't look, but there wasn't that much chance to look; I was really wedded to what I was doing in the sense that I worked nights and I worked weekends.

This was also a time when women couldn't have both a family and career very easily. I don't think that's true now: I see women who have both. In those days it would have been very much frowned on for a married woman to be working, or to come back to the lab if she had a child. Nowadays, nobody thinks twice about taking maternity leave and coming back. I don't advise people one way or the other. I've been quite happy, but I probably would have been quite happy the other way too.

My family was very supportive. My mother was a housewife. She married when she was very young. She didn't have a college education, and she never had any opportunities, but she was very, very supportive of my having any career that I wanted. My father was a professional person, a dentist, and certainly very eager to have me go to college. If he'd been able to afford it, he would have sent me to graduate school. For many years when I couldn't find a research job because of sex discrimination, they supported me financially and never

Gertrude B. Elion in her lab at Burroughs Wellcome, 1989
PHOTO COPYRIGHT 1989 BY WILL AND DENI MCINTYRE

suggested that I should abandon my goals or get married. They never made me feel that I wasn't welcome to stay as long as I wanted. Without their support, I would have been unable to continue.

There's no question in my mind that I might never have gotten a research job if it hadn't been for World War II. With all the men in the armed forces, jobs were finally open to women. I worked first as a quality-control chemist in a food laboratory, measuring the color of mayonnaise and testing the acidity of pickles. It wasn't glamorous, but I was earning money and learning a lot about instrumentation. When I felt I had learned all I could, I moved on to a job at Johnson and Johnson synthesizing sulfonamides. Then they reorganized and terminated the program, so I went job hunting again.

The real turning point was when I interviewed with Dr. George Hitchings for my job at Burroughs Wellcome. During the interview, he explained his research to me. I didn't know much about nucleic acids, but the idea that one might interfere with cell division by making antimetabolites of structural bases sounded exciting. I held off on other job offers until I heard back from him, and I started work with Burroughs Wellcome on June 14, 1944. I loved the job because I was allowed to advance at my own rate. I could do as much as

I wanted to do, and that was tremendous because in many other places I would have been told, "This is as far as you can go" or "You're a chemist; why do you want to be an immunologist? Why are you interested in virology?" There was never any barrier to my jumping into a field in which I had no formal training. That was a very enlightened attitude on the part of Dr. Hitchings and the company.

My big frustration during this time was that I couldn't figure out how I was going to get a Ph.D. and continue working at the same time. I couldn't afford to drop the work, and I didn't want to. For a number of years I felt that I hadn't done my job because I hadn't gone ahead and gotten a doctorate. I tried attending graduate school part-time by taking night classes at the Brooklyn Polytechnic Institute. For two years I commuted from Tuckahoe to Brooklyn during rush hour. After class, I rode the subway home to the Bronx, which took an hour. Then the dean called me into his office and told me that I would have to start full-time. I told him I couldn't give up my job; I'd worked too hard to get there. He told me that I clearly wasn't "serious" enough, so that was the end of my attempt to get a Ph.D. It wasn't until a couple of years after I achieved real professional success that I could say, "Oh, who cares?" But I did care, and I knew that if I lost my job at Burroughs

Wellcome and went looking for another job, it would make a big difference in the kind of job that I would be able to get. For years, I really felt the lack of that degree; now I consider it a badge of honor. When I meet young women who want to go into science, and they say, "But of course I could never do it without a Ph.D.," I say, "But of course you can." I hired a young lady in the early eighties who had only a master's degree, and now she's head of a group with about five Ph.D.'s in it. It can be done.

Of course, it was a number of years before I really reached that level of success. My relationship with Dr. Hitchings and with the company was really an evolution. At the beginning I was definitely his assistant. He had one other assistant when I joined him, and the three of us were the whole department. He told me what he wanted done, and it was up to me to determine the best way to proceed, and then do it. He would give me whatever help he could, but often it was something I had to get or derive from the literature. As time went on, he let me have more autonomy within a field. In other words, if I was to make a whole bunch of derivatives of 6-mercaptopurine, which ones I made and how I made them was my problem. He always allowed me to write my own papers, and eventually I published quite extensively. As I began to do more work in related fields like biochemistry and pharmacology, I would get an assistant to help me in this and an assistant to help me in that. Pretty soon I had a good-sized group, and it grew as the department grew. As Dr. Hitchings advanced toward being a vice president, he had less and less contact with what was going on in the laboratory, although I still consulted with him. By the time I was made head of the Department of External Therapy, I had been with the company twenty-three years and was really working on my own.

As head of the laboratory, I allowed everybody to do the best they could. I never held them back, and I gave them as much encouragement as possible. I think it really did work

because most of those people are still here, still doing excellent work. I made it a principle not to take credit for everything that they did. I think there was a feeling years ago that the head of a department had to have his name on every paper. Well, I broke that; I didn't think it was the way it should be. If I didn't make any real contribution to a particular project, I didn't want any more than a sentence of acknowledgment thanking me for my interest or advice. This was unusual in those days, but eventually the idea spread that you don't have to have your name on the paper of everyone in your group.

In the beginning, we were working on a theory that was not very popular, namely, that we could interfere with DNA synthesis of cells by making antimetabolites—compounds that looked so much like the natural constituents of DNA that the cell would be fooled into taking them up, incorporating them, and killing itself. This idea had been introduced by a couple of scientists who found that sulfonamides worked on bacteria by interfering with one of the nutrients that bacteria needed and that people didn't need, so the bacteria starved to death while the person was relatively unaffected. We thought that maybe we could do this with cancer cells by making what I think we used to call "rubber donuts"—modifications of natural DNA bases—that the cell would take up and incorporate, and really do its own job of killing itself. And we were successful with this approach. We developed an antileukemic drug, 6-mercaptopurine (6-MP), which was a very simple change from one of the naturally occurring bases in DNA.

Later we found that a derivative of 6-MP (Imuran) had immunosuppressive properties that would prevent rejection of transplanted kidneys from unrelated donors. Our studies on the metabolism of 6-MP also led to the development of a compound that is effective against gout.

In 1968 we turned our attention to antiviral chemotherapy. We had ventured into that field in 1949 with some of our antimetabolites, but we had found that those compounds that were active on viruses were too toxic to be used as therapy. This time we began to look at changes in the sugars attached to the DNA bases rather than at the bases themselves. Out of this research came acyclovir, which inhibits the replication of herpes simplex virus, types 1 and 2, and varicella zoster virus. Unlike previous antiviral agents, acyclovir was highly selective and nontoxic to the host animal. It was the first major success with antiviral chemotherapy, and it came at a fortuitous time. Shortly after we presented our work, all the major pharmaceutical companies geared up for antiviral work. A few years later, when the AIDS epidemic broke, scientists were prepared to think about antiviral chemotherapy. Indeed, in 1984, the year after I retired from being department head, I had the pleasure of watching my former group discover that another antimetabolite, azidothymidine (AZT), was effective against HIV.

The Nobel Prize that I was awarded in 1988 with Dr. Hitchings and Sir James Black came as a complete surprise. When the first reporter called to ask me about it, I told him I thought he was joking. I can honestly say I never thought about it; I certainly never used it as a goal. Most times, people get the prize for some one thing they've done, and usually in the middle of their career; for us it was for a whole lifetime of work. At first I thought it would all be over after a few weeks, but the honors came in a steady stream. I was elected to the National Academy of Sciences, the National Inventor's Hall of Fame, and the National Women's Hall of Fame, and I received the National Medal of Science. I find now that I'm very much in demand to speak, particularly to students with the idea that maybe my life will inspire them. It's a peculiar sensation to be held up as a role model for the first time in my life.

People frequently ask me what my most exciting discovery was, and I always answer in the same way: I don't discriminate amongst my children. Each one came along at a different time, and each one was terribly exciting

from the beginning until it came to fruition. Later on they were grown up and out in the world, but I never abandoned one afterwards; it was still my child. No drug is perfect, but no child is perfect either, and that doesn't keep you from loving them. In the early days, when I began to realize what was possible, I was on a high most of the time. Having an effect on the length of life of children with leukemia, or on the ability of surgeons to transplant organs because our drug would prevent rejection, finding a treatment for serious gout, finding a drug that is effective against the herpes virus in all of its manifestations—how could I possibly choose between them?

Outside of science, I'm a great opera lover. Of course, since Burroughs Wellcome relocated to North Carolina it's a little more difficult, but I do go up to New York City. I've kept my subscription to the Metropolitan Opera all these years. I go to concerts a lot; I like chamber music. I also love photography. I used to do a lot more of it—I used to do a lot of printing and enlarging in the days of black and white. When I started taking color photos, that passed; there just wasn't time to set up that kind of darkroom. I especially love to travel. I have always, whenever possible, taken a vacation which involved travel. Last month I went to Antarctica; next week I am going to Geneva. There is no place I don't want to go.

Through it all, my motivation never changed, although later on it did broaden. I realized that cancer was not the only problem in the world. When my first successful compound was an antileukemic drug, that fortified me and said, "You're on the right track. You are in the cancer field." One way or another, I've stayed in that field all these years, often treating other diseases, but diseases that are common to cancer patients. I was very active in the American Association for Cancer Research and was its president in 1983, and I was on the National Cancer Advisory Board. For twenty years I served on various committees at the National Cancer Institute. I was never divorced from it, even though some of my work wandered off in other directions.

I think my greatest frustration is that we still are not very far along in curing solid tumors. We think we know how to proceed, and we make some progress, but we just haven't had the same success with lung and colon cancer that we have had with leukemia. I continue to read and go to meetings, and I try to give advice to people here and at the National Cancer Institute. Now I look upon myself more as someone who transfers information to other people so they can do something with it, and that is very satisfying.

It's a wonderful life; I don't think I could have chosen anything that would have made me happier. I don't think people emphasize that enough—they think about the scientist as someone stuck away in the laboratory and oblivious to the rest of the world. That's the farthest thing from the truth. I feel as though I've made a contribution with my life. Every time I give a talk at a university or medical school, someone will come up to me afterwards and say, "I want you to know that I've had a kidney transplant for twenty years thanks to your drug," or, "My child who had leukemia is graduating from college." There isn't anything that can give you greater satisfaction than that.

PRESENT POSITIONS: Scientist Emeritus at Burroughs Wellcome Company; Medical Research Professor at Duke University

FIELD: Chemistry

RESEARCH AREA: Drug development

EDUCATION: B.S. in Chemistry (1937), Hunter College; M.S. in Chemistry (1941), New York University. Dr. Elion received honorary Ph.D.'s from George Washington University and Brown University in 1969, one from the University of Michigan in 1983, and seventeen others after she received the Nobel Prize.

DATE/PLACE OF BIRTH: January 23, 1918/New York City, New York

Gertrude Elion lives and works in Research Triangle Park, North Carolina.

INTERVIEW DATE: February 1995

Patricia L. Eng

Senior Transportation Project Officer
U.S. NUCLEAR REGULATORY COMMISSION

Patricia Eng switched from physics to engineering because she viewed engineering as less abstract and more practical, which better suited her interests and personality. Her first job included working at a construction site supervising the installation of radiation shielding material that she helped develop for a nuclear reactor. She quickly realized that she loved seeing her designs and ideas turned into reality.

❧

I wasn't always interested in science. As a child in Chicago, I wanted to be a ballerina. I wanted to wear the beautiful chiffon dresses that the dancers wore and listen to beautiful music all day long, so I enrolled in ballet classes. At the end of each class, we always stretched out and worked on simple tumbling skills like cartwheels and handsprings. I had trouble with cartwheels—I couldn't quite seem to get my balance and I fell down a lot.

When I reached the third grade, I was lucky to have a teacher—Loretta Moran—who enjoyed teaching. Her method was simple—she posed a question and then involved students in reasoning out the answers. One day I asked her why a ball bounced, just to see if she could answer the question. She did, but not in the way I expected. She told me that if I wanted to know why things did what they did, such as why balls bounced or, better yet, how to do a good cartwheel without falling down, I should take physics when I got to high school.

Well, I did just that and found that I liked math and science. It was more interesting to figure things out than memorize the capitals of all the countries in the world. I also realized that my third grade teacher was right: in physics we actually studied why things worked. I particularly enjoyed the classes where we learned about wave theory and studied how water and sound traveled. Although I didn't think anything of it at the time, I was the only female in my physics class. It didn't matter—all of us were studying and trying to learn as much as we could; gender was not an issue.

That spirit of inquiry continued throughout college. I spent one year at Smith College, a liberal arts college, where I was one of two physics

Patricia Eng in a recent photograph

majors. At the end of that year, I transferred to the University of Illinois to major in physics because it had one of the best physics departments in the country. What a shock, to go from a small women's college of 2,700 to a school of 55,000 that was much more competitive. I found the environment very stressful, and I was not a straight-A student, although, even as the material got harder, somehow I managed. As I progressed through college, I noticed that there were fewer women than men in my classes. Eventually, the women in my classes got together and formed a study group, and we became friends. I spent my years at Illinois just trying to survive.

In my junior year in college I noticed that most physicists had Ph.D.'s, and I knew that I didn't want to take the time to pursue a Ph.D. I also noticed that many engineers were able to find employment without a Ph.D., and so I switched my major from physics to nuclear engineering. Physics deals a lot with subatomic particles, energy, and matter; when I switched to engineering I still wanted to stay with subatomic phenomena. There are only a couple of really fun things you can play with in nuclear engineering, and I was interested in the interaction of radiation with inanimate matter. So I wound up specializing in radiation shielding—protecting people and equipment from the effects of radiation.

I found engineering a little easier and a lot more practical. While physics studies why things are and is somewhat abstract, engineering applies that knowledge to make things safer, better, and more economical. I liked the engineering focus much better.

I graduated in 1976 and received several job offers. I chose to begin my career at Westinghouse Hanford, a research and development facility where I worked on optimizing radiation shielding for a prototype nuclear reactor. This job required working at the construction site to supervise the installation of shielding material once it was fabricated. I felt a great deal of satisfaction and pride when I saw my designs and ideas turned into reality. This was the best job ever: people believed in

me right off the bat—in fact the only one who doubted my abilities was me. I was on the cutting edge of technology; the lab facilities were wonderful; and they put me in a two-year development training program, which meant I rotated from job to job until we found a match. I worked in the lab, I worked with plutonium, I worked with chemicals, I worked in construction, and I did some computer analysis. I left Westinghouse Hanford in part because the construction phase was ending and they were going into systems testing; I wasn't ready to go into something that would be so highly structured and rigorous in that way. The thought of sitting and watching a pressure gauge for hours on end trying to figure out what was determining the response of the system did not thrill me. So when another opportunity arose, I took advantage of it.

I went on to several different types of jobs, including developing a material assessment system, conducting pipe stress analysis, and performance testing of new machine designs. Each was interesting and I learned a lot. In most cases, I found myself working with intelligent, hard-working people who were committed to doing a good job. At one point I did run into overt sexism, which, until that time, was completely and totally foreign to me. No one had ever told me I couldn't do something because I was a woman or because I was Asian, so I didn't know how to respond. I remember laughing at my antagonist and telling him that I hoped no one told his children about their ethnic and gender limitations; if so, he might fail in his role as a parent. I learned a lot about myself and how the world works, and I didn't stay in that particular job long. I also took the professional engineer's exam and obtained my license from the state of California in the area of mechanical engineering.

After several years in the private sector, I joined the federal government. I got a job with the Nuclear Regulatory Commission (NRC) by answering a newspaper ad. I began in 1983 as the first female reactor inspector in the NRC's Region 3 offices, inspecting com-

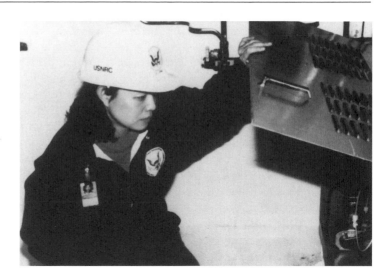

Patricia Eng inspecting an air radiation monitor at the Zion Nuclear Power Plant
PHOTO COURTESY OF THE NUCLEAR REGULATORY COMMISSION

ponents in power plant safety systems. I also authored the procedure currently used by NRC inspectors for inspecting pumps and valves in critical safety systems. After that I held a number of positions: I was the NRC resident inspector at the Zion Nuclear Power Plant, where I reviewed and inspected testing, maintenance, operations, and quality control activities to ensure that the plant was being operated safely and in compliance with federal regulations. I then served as a project manager for the NRC, which involved reviewing and evaluating licensing and operational activities associated with commercial nuclear power plants. I worked as technical assistant to NRC's commissioner, E. Gail de Planque, advising her on matters regarding the formulation of NRC policies and programs and evaluating proposed agency activities. I then moved to a position as senior operations engineer for the Human Factors Assessment Branch, where I examined the role of human performance in nuclear power plant operations.

I am currently a senior transportation project officer in the Office of Nuclear Materials Safety and Safeguards of the NRC. I am responsible for the development and implementation of the inspection program for the storage of radioactive materials at commercial sites. I also develop and review domestic and international regulations regarding the storage and transportation of radioactive materials and ensure that radioactive material containers are properly designed, reviewed, and certified in accordance with federal regulations. Although I am not directly involved in system design, I identify potential concerns during the systems design review prior to fabrication and installation of equipment. My previous industry experience has helped prepare me for my current job. In short, I believe in what I'm doing, I find my job meaningful, and I enjoy my career as an engineer.

Of course, I have borne the brunt of the occasional denigrating remark regarding my ancestry or gender, but generally I don't hear such remarks anymore. It seems to me that the comments of this nature that one receives is a function of how one carries herself in the workplace. I firmly believe that, for the most part, one's career is dependent on the technical content and accuracy of one's work, the quality of one's character, and, most important of all, the ability to communicate verbally and in writing.

I have been fortunate to benefit from the experiences of many women throughout my career. There have been times when a male colleague would say something of a questionable nature and I wouldn't be sure what he meant or how to handle the situation. Often, my women mentors provided insight on how to handle awkward situations, such as being asked to make coffee for a meeting or to answer the phones so that the men in the group could take the secretary out for Secretary's Day. I don't get those kinds of requests anymore. Even today I turn to women who are more experienced. Their willingness to share their observations, past experiences, and counsel have been invaluable.

Organizations such as the Society of Women Engineers (SWE), the Association for Women in Science (AWIS), and the American Association of University Women (AAUW) have also provided much support and guidance as I progressed through my career. I've received a lot of practical advice on how to handle tricky situations from many women in these organizations. SWE and AWIS, in particular, also provide a safe place to develop and enhance managerial and leadership skills. Many young women develop these skills by becoming actively involved in the local chapters of these organizations. Some go on to hone their skills by continued participation at the regional and national levels. Although SWE is composed primarily of engineers and AWIS of women scientists, both have a common goal and demonstrate that there are many pathways to success. I am sure that my active involvement with these women's organizations has directly contributed to my success as an engineer.

My parents' influence has also contributed greatly to my success. My father had very little formal education; but while he isn't "book learned," he is one of the sharpest people on the planet. He spent most of his life in the restaurant business and gained a lot of street smarts. He took a small, dinky restaurant on the west side of Chicago and turned it into a very successful restaurant that boasts patrons like the first Mayor Richard Daley. He taught me a lot about people and about myself. My mother came to the States from China during World War II. After she had gone through the trials of assimilating into a new culture, with the burden of learning a new language and looking different, she eventually met and married my father. She finished her high school degree and began college part-time when I was in the third grade. She kept changing majors and finally graduated from college six months before I did. She's a real Renaissance woman; in order to get rid of her Chinese accent she initially majored in medieval English literature. I used to help Mom with her homework when she would memorize quotes from Shakespeare; I'm probably one of the more literate engineers in my group as a result. Both of my parents have always seen potential and possibilities in every situation; they encouraged me to work hard and repeatedly told me that I could do anything that I set my mind to.

I was kind of a bookworm growing up. The first real book I read was Edith Hamilton's *Mythology;* she sparked my interest in astronomy because all of the people in her stories were visible up in the sky as constellations. I was also a physically active child—I studied ballet on and off until about two years ago. I enjoy both the physical activity and the physics of dancing. I participated in competitive gymnastics in high school and have always been fascinated by the limits of what the human body can do.

All of the men I've dated for any length of time have been engineers. I used to wish for someone without a technical background so that I could expand my knowledge and learn new things. But the truth of the matter is, it all resides in me. If I want to learn something new I can do it on my own; I don't need someone else to do it for me. The advantage of a significant other with a technical background is that I can talk about my work with him. Engineers tend to be analytical and think along the same lines. We tend to understand each other's problems and why we are concerned about specific issues. On occasion I have found myself walking with my partner hand in hand on a moonlit beach, listening to the waves lapping on the sand, sipping champagne, and discussing why tailpipe temperatures on pressurizer relief lines are not necessarily the best indicator of a system leak (the instrument could be faulty)! It may not be terribly romantic, but somehow I find it acknowledges that I am a whole person—an engineer and a woman.

PRESENT POSITION: Senior Transportation Project Officer, U.S. Nuclear Regulatory Commission

FIELD: Nuclear engineering

SPECIALTY: Nuclear materials safety

EDUCATION: B.S. in Nuclear Engineering (1976), University of Illinois

DATE/PLACE OF BIRTH: March 11, 1955/Oak Park, Illinois

Patricia Eng lives in Chevy Chase, Maryland.

INTERVIEW DATE: July 1995

Deborah Estrin

Associate Professor, Computer Science Department
UNIVERSITY OF SOUTHERN CALIFORNIA

Deborah Estrin does her best work sitting in a café with her ever-present laptop and pager, two essential pieces of technology. Estrin's research is on designing routing protocols, which direct data from their source to their destination, a task that becomes more complicated as the Internet expands from hundreds of thousands to many millions of computers. She loves the messiness of her work (its large scale and heterogeneity), the craft aspect of the design process, and the fact that the work she does uses technology she has helped to develop.

❧

I do research in the area of computer networking, spend a lot of time advising doctoral students on their dissertation research, and work collaboratively with both students and colleagues in my field from around the world.

The focus of my work is protocol design.

Computer networks operate based on rules they follow to send or exchange data, and those rules are called a protocol. If you think of two computers communicating, or your own personal computer communicating with some bulletin board or a larger host system you have dialed into, the protocol is relatively simple. But the Internet has thousands and thousands of different types of machines, all interconnected and able to communicate flexibly with each other, under complex operating rules. The emphasis of my work has always been on scaling and heterogeneity—how to develop protocols for a network like the Internet so it can continue to operate as it grows from thousands, to hundreds of thousands, to millions, to many millions of computers. When any system grows to that size, a lot of what changes is how decentralized it is and how heterogeneous it becomes. With anything that grows that big, it's more and more likely you can't impose homogeneity or centralized control.

Deborah Estrin describing a network protocol concept to her doctoral students

In my work, I help define the important problems that need to be solved in order for Internet technology to serve communications needs five to ten years from now, on a worldwide scale. My particular emphasis has been on designing routing protocols, which let data get from their source to their destination, and most recently on having the Internet support multimedia communications—not just data but also real-time voice, video, and graphics delivery. This is for use by all kinds of people, not just for academics. In the past five to ten years the Internet has had very wide commercial and government use, and in the last few years it's been proliferating among residential and small business users as well.

What excites me about my work is, in part, the messiness of it. The problems are those of very large scale and heterogeneity, defining what's important, and figuring out the key design issues and design constraints. When building a system this big, you can't optimize everything without making a lot of fundamental design trade-offs and judgments.

The craft part of the design process interests me, and so does the fact that the work itself uses the technology we're developing. In the last fifteen years, use of the Internet as a collaborative infrastructure has been essential. We've been able to see the fruits of our labor deployed, and have ourselves used what formerly was an experimental and is now an operational facility. There's the continual possibility of the work becoming so real you get to see it—or at least some of the concepts—put into practice. Collaborative designs are some of the positive offshoots. Almost everything I do involves collaboration with other people— a stimulating and rewarding process. Those people aren't just my colleagues who work in the office next door; they are, in fact, most often people who live in other cities and even on other continents. Our particular focuses coincide in different ways. We have small working groups and weekly meetings via the Internet and a lot of e-mail exchanges in between. This diverse group of colleagues and I codesign and coauthor papers and also cosupervise my graduate students. In the summer I send a lot of my students out—early in their doctoral studies—just to get the increased exposure of internships.

In general, I work in three places: I teach and meet with students on the USC campus; I also hold a lot of research meetings and conferences with colleagues at an office in Marina del Rey at USC's Information Sciences Institute (ISI); but I do my best work sitting in a café with my ever-present laptop and my pager, those two essential pieces of technology! A typical day for me is either a teaching-and-meeting day or a thinking day. I may be in my office for two-thirds of the day, and then spend a couple of hours in a café trying to think or write.

My mother, Thelma, and father, Gerald, are academics; both are electrical engineers and computer scientists. [See Thelma Estrin's profile on page 154.] As I grew up, that made being an engineer not something that I had to do but certainly something on the menu. I was able to start out—as a lot of women in my generation weren't able to do—with engineering as a career option. Math and science were always highly respected in my household. My parents actually discussed academic politics more than they did technical things at the kitchen table. But without question much dialogue was about science and mathematics, with a lot of respect shown for those fields.

My parents never told me what I had to do, but for one reason or another I only considered doing something related to science or math. I never questioned having a career in an area that was engaging to me—that was an essential part of a rewarding life. Obviously, having a mother in the field was very important to me, but having a father who was never gender biased also made an enormous difference. They both always taught my sister and me to strive to fulfill ourselves. Their impact on me had a lot to do with what they had accomplished as well as the types of people they knew and respected.

What steered me into working with computers were math and science, but also an enormous respect for creativity, for doing something special. As a young child, someone asked me what I wanted to do, and I remember saying I wanted to invent something. As an undergraduate at Berkeley, I was in electrical engineering and computer science. I took a theory of communications course, which is not really what I do now, but it gave me an interest in that general field.

I had more trouble with gender bias as an undergraduate than at any other time in my career. I don't think I've ever experienced overt discrimination but rather something which Mary Rowe has described as the "mosquito bite problem," small negative interactions with men, each one individually not very significant, but combined they drain positive, productive energy away. When you get just one mosquito bite it's not a problem, but when your body is covered with mosquito bites, you become obsessed with scratching. Interactions with people—negative interactions that weren't about the reasons I was studying—sometimes distracted me from learning. These were just the random, social, inappropriate attentions of male graduate students and some faculty. By the time I reached graduate school at MIT I understood the issues better and was able to deal with them more maturely. In fact, while I was at MIT I coauthored, with several other graduate women in computer science, what became a quite well known report about this kind of discrimination.

At MIT my master's degree was an interdisciplinary one in technology policy, a rich area that integrated technology with social and policy issues. After completing a master's that involved both design and some social policy analysis, I decided I really wanted to stay in the area of engineering design, as opposed to pursuing an academic research career on the political science side.

However, I then went on to work mostly on the technical side—I think you don't always move in your career in a systematic manner—and that's how I got channeled in a technical direction. At the time, there was a very rich community—I think there still is—

in the MIT computer science laboratories. Both Jerry Seltzer and Dave Clark were working in internetwork protocol development. This was in the early to mid-1980s, an exciting era to be working in Internetworking in that stimulating community.

Today I am the only woman professor in my department, and I'm usually one of the only women in the smaller academic groups I participate in. I work mostly with men, but I have a few women colleagues. The number of women is small, but I'd say it's growing—it makes a lot of difference that I'm not the only woman. Earlier in my career, I felt it more. Now, I'd say I go many months at a time where it never crosses my mind; when I was younger I had daily, maybe weekly, experiences that reminded me I was different. Of course I look forward to a time when there are more women in academia.

One of the biggest challenges I've encountered later in my career has been balancing family and work. The pulls to become involved in an academic community that isn't just local and can include enormous amounts of travel and substantial commitments are tough, particularly in a collaborative field like mine. And if you collaborate well, an enormous number of both administrative and technical committees can eat up your time. As each invitation comes—to conferences, workshops, and meetings—it's very hard to assess which ones are really worth the commitment. You must find enough time to balance work with family and still leave time to think. When I don't get that breathing room, I lose the reason for doing what I do. You can't make a commitment and then, when the time comes, cancel. It's a real struggle.

Balancing family and work requires a lot of extra thought and much better use of your time than it does for your colleagues who don't have young families. You recognize you have to pick and choose more among opportunities, whereas colleagues who don't have those constraints can go to all the meetings; they'll be at the right ones as well as the ones that wasted their time. I made a lot more work-oriented compromises before tenure, and then was able to gain a little more control over my priorities after my tenure in May 1992.

I had my son, Joshua, early in my career, which worked very well for me. I was able to take more time with him in the very early years and still put in a surge of work and time later, which I hadn't wanted to do when he was very young. I believe that unless you're superhuman, you can't get tenure on forty hours a week. Having my son early gave me time with him before he was older and needed me less; and then a few years later, I had more time to devote to teaching and research before tenure evaluation. It's essential to have a very good support structure, be it a significant other or your family. What we need in society today is a respect for how family plays into one's work life. We need more flexibility to allow people to take longer to do things—whether it's sharing jobs or tasks—and the facilitation of good-quality child care.

In my career I've learned that it's important to find a focus, an area where you can make a definable and discernible contribution. It sounds sort of cheap to say "something that's yours and that you can put your name on," but it really is gratifying. There's less time for accomplishments because you're juggling family and career. Each of the blocks you put in place counts. You don't know on each project you start what its outcome is going to be, and so you have to pay more attention to which projects you get involved in. I had to focus carefully and not get distracted by other projects and other obligations, more so than people who didn't have family demands on their time. I also realized what I could and couldn't do. The trade-off is that you can't necessarily learn all the latest tools, or every new software package, or keep all your papers filed. You learn to accept those kinds of constraints.

I highly recommend becoming part of a support group. I always had some form of women's group all through my studies. At Berkeley one woman helped facilitate a Women in Computer Science and Engineering subgroup. But a couple of women reentry students, who were quite mature, also recognized that a women's group would be beneficial. They helped us realize that some of these issues should not be taken personally but were part of a social phenomenon. In graduate school a number of women formed a group to create the MIT report that let us articulate some of the social and professional issues women face in academe. I think the MIT report helped us constructively channel what would have otherwise been more personally destructive interaction. Having women in the upper parts of the hierarchy definitely facilitates support groups. Institutions can also foster support groups—which doesn't always happen—and must not interfere with their formation.

PRESENT POSITION: Associate Professor, Computer Science Department, University of Southern California

FIELD: Computer science

SPECIALTY: Computer networking and Internetworking

EDUCATION: B.S. in Electrical Engineering/Computer Science (1980), University of California at Berkeley; Master's in Technology Policy (1982) and Ph.D. in Electrical Engineering/Computer Science (1985) from the Massachusetts Institute of Technology

DATE/PLACE OF BIRTH: December 6, 1959/Los Angeles, California

Deborah Estrin lives in Pacific Palisades, California, with her son, Joshua.

INTERVIEW DATE: March 1995

Judy Estrin

Chief Executive Officer
PRECEPT SOFTWARE, INC.

Judy Estrin never questioned whether a woman could do whatever she wanted: she grew up with a mother who had a Ph.D. in electrical engineering and a father who respected and supported his wife and her career. She realized early on that she preferred application to theory and has spent her career as an entrepreneur, starting three successful companies with her husband, Bill. She loves the risk involved in the entrepreneurial path, thrives on the building process, and is happy not to fight the infrastructure of established organizations. Judy Estrin has built her own house without a glass ceiling.

❧

A big difference between my career and those of most other women is that I decided early on to become an entrepreneur. Together with my husband, Bill Carrico, I have started three companies. The first was Bridge Communications, formed in 1981 to build local-area networking products. Bridge reached $70 million in revenues before merging with 3Com Corporation in 1987. A year later, we left to launch a second company, Network Computing Devices, which develops Xterminals and electronic-mail software; NCD grew to $160 million in sales in 1994. Last September, after thirteen years building and running start-ups, Bill and I decided we needed a break. I replaced myself as CEO at NCD and took six months off, much of which was spent with our five-year-old son, David. In March 1995, we started our third company, Precept Software, which is developing Internet- and multimedia-oriented products.

One downside of the entrepreneurial path is that it is far more consuming than a traditional job. As an entrepreneur you have no one to fall back on; everyone falls back on you. But I love the building process and even the certain risk. And when you create a business yourself, you're not fighting an already existing infrastructure, including the so-called "glass ceiling." I think I've built my house without the glass ceiling. I've had incredible support in that process from Bill, who started out as my boss, was later my business partner, and became my husband in 1987. Working as a team has made starting—and running—companies much easier.

If you had told my parents or anyone who knew me in high school that I would someday

Judy Estrin in her office at Network Computing Devices

be CEO of my own company, they would have reacted with disbelief. Though I liked people, I wasn't aggressive and didn't consider myself a leader. Furthermore, my aspirations lay strictly on the technical side. My undergraduate degree from UCLA and my master's from Stanford were both in technical areas; at Stanford, I worked with Vint Cerf and his team on the TCP/IP protocols, now known as the fundamental technology of the Internet. Preferring to apply what I had learned rather than be a theoretician or academic, I opted not to go on for a Ph.D. I saw myself becoming an engineer and perhaps later a project manager.

After graduating from Stanford in 1976, I turned down job offers from Xerox and Hewlett Packard because I worried about being pigeonholed in a narrowly focused discipline. Instead I chose a fifty-person start-up company called Zilog that I thought would give me broader business exposure and possibly let me move more quickly into management. While such a small company posed some risks, making the right career decision sometimes means sticking your neck out and knowing when to take advantage of a good opportunity. In my case joining a dynamic, innovative, small company paid off. After only two years as an individual contributor I moved into engineering management at Zilog.

The idea for Bridge Communications— developing products for the then-emerging local-area-network market—was Bill's and mine; we saw a need in the market, wrote a business plan, raised money ($1.8 million), and hired a team. Bill, with his business experience, was CEO; I started out as VP of engineering. But because of the technical nature of our product, I began dealing with customers on a regular basis and found that I actually liked it! So when, several years later, our sales vice president left the company, I became executive vice president running sales and marketing, the first major shift in my career. While I remained involved in the technology and product architecture, I had given up the actual management of the engineering effort.

Following a 1985 public offering, Bridge merged with 3Com Corporation in 1987. While this was strategically a good move, it didn't work out quite as we had planned. A serious difference of opinion with 3Com management over company direction led Bill and me to leave in 1988. Planning to take six months off and then decide what to do next, we were persuaded almost immediately to join a small team developing a new type of desktop display, the Xterminal. On the fast track once more, we raised the funding for Network Computing Devices that year, had 1989 sales of $13 million, took the company public in 1992, and built it into a $140 million entity by 1993.

While I oversaw NCD's technology direction and product planning from a high level, my real area of responsibility was marketing and sales. Though I've never seen myself as a pure salesperson—I hate cold-calling and could never sell people something they don't need—I've been told by my salespeople that I'm very effective because of my ability to bridge the gap between technology and sales. Engineers often have trouble moving into marketing roles because they want to tell "the whole truth." But sometimes too much detail can be irrelevant, even confusing, to the customer. Once I recognized this, I found that one of the things I enjoy most is meeting with customers, understanding their problems, and explaining why and how what we offer solves those problems. People may not view that as a technology or engineering function, but without a deep understanding of the technology underlying your products, you can't be successful at selling these products in different environments.

In our last year at NCD, Bill and I decided that I would move into the CEO role while he would work part-time and pursue outside interests. Finally I would not only get exposure to all aspects of the business but also have responsibility and authority for it. After a year in this position, and after crafting a plan for NCD's future direction, I decided to step down.

Judy Estrin in her office at Precept Software, Inc.

This time Bill and I really did take our six-month hiatus. For the first three months we relaxed. The following three were spent thinking about our next venture. By this time we realized we were true start-up people—willing to work broadly on all aspects of a project and able to deal, at least for a time, without infrastructure. We didn't need the comfort and security of a big company, where you're set up with an office and a computer and handed an already-defined project to implement. On the contrary, our initial team at Precept had the flexibility to define what our company would do and react to this fast-changing industry.

I'm positive that much of my success stems from my family environment. My parents, both computer professionals in academia, taught me and my two sisters how to think for ourselves from the beginning. My father wouldn't tell me how to spell a word, he'd show me how to look it up in the dictionary. They exposed us to problem solving in a sci-

entific way, making it fun at the same time. And they both enjoyed—in fact, really loved—working, so I never saw work as something you had to do.

It's a running joke in our family that I'm the only one without a Ph.D. My older sister, Margo, realized early on that she wasn't into math or computers, that instead she was very people oriented; she became a doctor. My younger sister, Deborah, has a Ph.D. in computer science. Deborah is on Precept's board of directors because she's doing research at USC that's relevant to our product development focus. [See Deborah Estrin's profile on page 146.]

In my family it was never a question of whether a woman could or couldn't do something. I was raised thinking I could do whatever I wanted. I had a mother with a Ph.D. in electrical engineering and a father who respected her and that environment. Instilled with the confidence to learn and achieve, I didn't come out of school with a chip on my shoulder or a self-esteem problem. I meet a lot of women today who focus on all the negative things that can happen. I tend to be more optimistic, which is probably why I have a lot of tolerance for people's combination of strengths and weaknesses. I tend to view a person as a package. If someone is basically a good person who respects me for what I'm doing but who makes a sexist remark from time to time, I'm likely to ignore it. But like many women, I've run into the male co-worker or boss who clearly would have stifled my career; you've got to get away from that kind of person because you're never going to change the package.

Though I've had to work hard to get where I am today, I've probably faced fewer obstacles than many other women in science. Silicon Valley has created a young and progressive high-technology environment in which to work. It was also critical that I established a strong set of technical credentials early on; you don't get to be somebody just through affirmative action, and you don't get somewhere because of luck. Those prejudices that I have encountered have had less to do with my gender than with my age. I was only twenty-six when Bill and I started Bridge, and people were asking, "Who is this guy and his girlfriend? What makes them think they can start a company?"

With regard to the dilemma of career versus family, I firmly believe that having children is a matter of individual choice. If a woman doesn't feel the driving need to have a family, she shouldn't feel pressured to do so. But she should pay close attention to that feeling inside her and not pass up having children because of a career issue. It may be a matter of timing. I could not have built my first two companies with a young child at home; I was too involved in every customer situation, and I traveled far too much. So I built those companies first, and then, once the snooze button broke on my biological alarm clock, we had a child. By then I had invested enough years and energy in my career that I could make some tradeoffs and compromises. I also was able to

afford a nanny, which I needed to make it all work. My son, who will soon be five, knows I work, he knows Mommy and Daddy have a company, and he doesn't yet differentiate between us with regard to work. We tend to sacrifice other aspects of our social life to spend more time with him. The point is that you can do both career and family and make it work.

PRESENT POSITION: Chief Executive Officer, Precept Software, Inc.; Member of the Boards of Directors for FedEx, Rockwell International, and Sun Microsystems

FIELD: Networking software, computer networking

EDUCATION: B.S. in Math and Computer Science (1975), UCLA; M.S. in Electrical Engineering (1976), Stanford University

DATE/PLACE OF BIRTH: November 17, 1954/Tel Aviv, Israel

Judy Estrin lives in Los Altos, California, with her husband, Bill Carrico, and their son, David.

INTERVIEW DATE: June 1995

Thelma Estrin

Professor Emerita
UNIVERSITY OF CALIFORNIA AT LOS ANGELES

Thelma Estrin married at age eighteen during World War II. Because women were in great demand in the factories, she worked in a tool and model shop and later assembled test equipment and repaired radio transmitters. In 1945 she and her husband moved to Madison, Wisconsin, and in six years she earned B.S., M.S., and Ph.D. degrees in electrical engineering. Her entire research career focused on using mathematical methods, via computers, to analyze the activity of the brain. Today she devotes herself to increasing equity in her field.

∂

Although my entire career has been spent in biomedical engineering, it is not what I now work on. At this stage of my career, although I'm active in a number of engineering organizations, I'm primarily interested in women's studies and the differences in learning between men and women. Science is always portrayed as an abstract and objective entity, but I believe it envelops a whole area of learning that's intuitive, that's below what's abstract, and that involves a person's feelings and the environment. I've witnessed a lot of this in computer science. It's been said that when some girls experiment with the computer, they do so the way a person might play an instrument. I think a number of people in computing, especially the hackers, use that kind of approach. They play and fiddle around, as opposed to just thinking things out abstractly and then proceeding. I'm interested in that kind of learning because of the way it affects women, and also because, with today's math programs, we really need to ed-

ucate our girls well to move them into the information age.

My current interests could not have been formed without my long career in electrical and biomedical engineering. I grew up in Brooklyn, New York, as an only child, which I believe made me more outgoing. At Abraham Lincoln High School, I was good in math and always had an opinion about something; my teachers listened to me and encouraged me to give my opinion. That was my environment and what I was born with. My

Thelma Estrin as a machinist's helper, circa 1943

154

mother was a liberal woman for the times. Before she was married, when automobiles first came out, she drove a car and owned her own business—a small auto parts shop. She was active in the Democratic Party in our neighborhood, and was very interested in my getting a good education and in my future career. She died when I was only seventeen, but I inherited her spirit. She never told me, "Your father will do this" or "A man will do that." She was independent.

I chose science by chance; originally I wanted to be a lawyer. I attended City College of New York's Baruch School of Business, which only admitted seventy-five women students each semester. With my mother having died, and my father dying shortly thereafter, friends advised me to take something that would be useful. I planned to study Spanish and be a Spanish/English secretary, but then I met my future husband, Gerald Estrin, and married before I was eighteen. World War II broke out right after that and changed my destiny. My husband joined the Army, and I needed a job. Women were in great demand in the factories, and so I took an exam at the Stevens War Industries Training School in New York. They advised me not to go into engineering because I had done well in the verbal part of the exam but poorly in spatial visualization. Undaunted, I completed a three-month engineering-assistant course and got a job at Radio Receptor Company, a tool and model shop. I worked with lathes, shapers, and surface grinders and later assembled test equipment and repaired radio transmitters. I attended evening classes in engineering at City College and eventually worked as a radio technician for the Army Air Force. While I was gifted at mathematics, visualization was much harder for me—drafting was difficult—until I finally caught on. Later in my career, I actually taught a course in mechanical drawing.

In 1945 Jerry and I moved to Madison, Wisconsin, where we both entered the undergraduate electrical engineering program at the University of Wisconsin. With eighteen-hour days and a lot of hard work, I completed my

B.S., M.S., and Ph.D. by 1951. My mentor and thesis adviser during this time was Professor Thomas "T. J." Higgins, an authority on numerical methods as employed in electrical engineering. He was and still is very open: I'm now seventy-one and he's in his early eighties, and we still keep in touch. My being a woman was no issue to him. At the time I wanted to go into analytical work because I thought if I went into something experimental I might not be able to get or keep a job while raising a family. I knew I was going to go wherever Jerry went, wherever his job was. There wasn't any talk of us choosing equal jobs; we just didn't think of life that way.

While in college, I read George Orwell's book *1984*, which portrayed a technological society in which people lose their human qualities and act like robots. That idea got me interested in the brain; and so did the concept that you could record brain activity from electrical signals on the top of the scalp. As an electrical engineer, I had an idea to try to do something with that someday.

Upon completing school, my husband got a job on one of the first computers, at the Institute for Advanced Study (IAS) in Princeton. I also worked at IAS for a couple of months, testing and documenting the arithmetic unit of the machine. But I wanted to work on my own. Through a friend working at Columbia, I got a job at the Neurological Institute of Columbia Presbyterian Hospital in the electroencephalography department, where I began studying electrical signals. I had the idea that computers could be used to study this kind of activity, and that's what I did for my entire research career: I used mathematical methods, but via computers, to analyze the activity of the brain. I look at two kinds of electrical activity: one where electrodes are implanted to look at the nerve impulse, and one where electrodes are pasted on the scalp to look at the EEG. At that time what we did was really very primitive; biomedical engineering did not even exist.

In the early 1950s, Jerry and I moved to Tel Aviv, Israel, where he was asked to head an electronic computer project at the Weizmann Institute of Science in Rehovot. We took along with us our newest arrival, our baby Margo; our second daughter, Judith, was born not long after. [See Judy Estrin's profile on page 150.] During this period I was also a principal member of Jerry's engineering group, working on the WEIZAC computer. We returned to the United States in 1955, where I became a part-time mathematics instructor with Douglass College at Rutgers University. By 1956 my husband's new position with UCLA took us to Los Angeles; the school's nepotism rules prevented me from also being hired by the School of Engineering. I taught at Valley College and had my daughter Deborah late in 1959. [See Deborah Estrin's profile on page 146.]

In the early 1960s, the Brain Research Institute (BRI) of UCLA Medical School hired me because of my work at Columbia on electroencephalography. At the BRI I had the funding to design and build an analog-to-digital conversion (ADC) system that could be used either to convert an analog tape to a digital tape or to convert analog signals from recording instruments to digital signals for immediate input to a computer. It was one of the first ADC systems for biomedical data.

My work at the BRI was an important chapter of my life, with many accomplishments. I did some of the first research work with minicomputers, designed one of the first time-sharing systems, became head of the Data Processing Laboratory, taught a course in electronics for neuroscience, and pioneered the use of interactive graphics as a tool for neuroscientists and neurosurgeons. I helped speed and facilitate the use of the first microcomputers—today called personal computers—and also helped many researchers make use of computers in their studies.

While working at BRI, I became a proponent of medical informatics—the application of computers to medical research and treatment—but I was not able to get funding for research in that area. By 1980 I turned much of my attention to trying to get women into

engineering. At that time, the whole status of computing was changing and funds were drying up. With nepotism rules no longer in effect, I became professor in residence in the computer science department of the School of Engineering and Applied Science at UCLA, where I introduced courses on computers in medicine and computers for nonscience majors.

In 1982 the National Science Foundation offered me a rotating position in Washington, D.C., as division director for electrical, computer, and systems engineering, which I accepted. I oversaw more than four hundred grants totaling $30 million annually and established a new program, Bioengineering and Research for the Handicapped. By 1984 I was back at UCLA as director of the Extension Department of Engineering and Science, which, although challenging, did not allow me to be entrepreneurial. In my last years before retiring from UCLA in 1991, I introduced courses in technology and society and women in engineering, of which I'm particularly proud.

I was able to balance my work and personal life because for thirty years I lived right across the street from the university. My girls went to school in the same neighborhood, so there was no commuting problem; and if something happened, I was always able to come home. For part of that time I also had live-in help. What also assisted me was sheer energy—being used to doing a million things, fast! Jerry was a very supportive husband; but I took care of most of the household responsibilities. Still, my children are my three greatest contributions. I know many women can be happy without children, but I definitely recommend having a family—it gives you insight.

Through the years, I have been active in academic organizations. I was chair of the American Association for the Advancement of Science (AAAS) Group on Information, Computing, and Communications, which attends the AAAS Conference each year and puts on sessions. I'm also a member of Women in

Technology, which is concerned with women in management. I'm interested in how technical people go into or can become leaders through management. I believe women make very good managers; I think they're skilled, and their aptitude and home life before they begin an engineering career teaches them to make decisions, deal with a lot of people, do several things at one time, be personable—all attributes that make good managers. I'm also active in the Center for the Study of Women and am a member of its committee on Gender Studies of Science, Technologies, and Medicine. I'm an honorary member of the Los Angeles Women in Business organization, which is also for entrepreneurial women. And I'm writing several papers on the history of a number of the women in bioengineering. In my free time, Jerry and I still like to go to movies, plays, musicals, and operas, and to entertain. I go to the gym every morning; and when possible we enjoy Israeli folk dancing.

My husband has always been an influence—not so much on my career but that I should have a career and do what I wanted. Although we're in the same field, we don't work together, and our methods are very different. But he greatly supported me. One woman in the Biomedical Engineering Society of the Institute of Electrical and Electronics Engineers (IEEE), Julia Apter, also had an influence on me: in the mid-1970s she asked me to head the Committee for Professional Opportunities for Women. This really gave me a chance to help increase the number of women in engineering. I really liked working in that group of IEEE, and became the president of the Engineering in Medicine and Biology Society—one of the thirty societies of IEEE, which now has three hundred thousand members. I helped publish the journal, was very active in national activities of the IEEE, and was the first woman to run for executive vice president in their national election. I have been active on about a dozen committees with IEEE for more than twenty years; in 1977, they honored my research contributions by appointing me a fellow. I

Thelma Estrin in a recent photo

was the sixth woman to become a fellow, at a time when there were not a lot of women members.

Although I have accomplished a lot, throughout my career I've been covertly discriminated against. I remember once being the only person to get an A on an electronics exam, and the professor saying to the class, "The person who got an A will certainly know how to fix an iron!" I didn't get an Alumni Association fellowship because they didn't think I would pursue a career. To make their point they told me that many women had taken valuable places in medical schools but were not practicing physicians. At that time it seemed like a logical argument. During my junior year, my husband, Jerry—who was blond, quiet, and had less of a New York accent than I—got into Tau Beta Pi, the engineering honor society, while I didn't. Jerry discovered this was because I was not of northern European descent. I realize now, years later, that it was probably also because I was a woman. Jerry went to the dean, and as a result I gained membership the next year. It is interesting that I did receive an honorary doctor of science degree from the University of Wisconsin in 1990 for my contributions to biomedical engineering and health research.

A number of times I was not considered for a position, or taken seriously, because I was a woman. I was interviewed for the position of dean at a number of schools, and sometimes wasn't even responded to afterwards because the interviews were just a formality. Unequal treatment can take many forms. In my years at UCLA, I tried to get support for a biomedical institute for which the school had funding. They looked for a director for five or six years and finally found one who turned out to be inadequate, so UCLA took the funds away from Engineering and gave it to the School of Medicine. If I had been a man, I would have had that position and been able to build a biomedical engineering institute. That was a big disappointment to me—and eventually helped push me out of the field.

Young women today need a lot of energy. My advice is, if you choose to go into engineering and you decide to marry, it should be to a supportive partner who believes in your having a technical career. Many positions in engineering can be a good career choice because there are jobs all over the country and you can mold what you have learned to a job. Biomedical engineering is a good field. The computerization of medical records and the integration of computers and electronics in hospitals will be rich areas. Brain research will also present some wonderful opportunities in the next twenty to thirty years. If you're interested in a nine-to-five job, then engineering is a good field to consider. If you want to climb the ladder, or live in Silicon Valley and join a new firm, you will be expected to work probably sixty hours per week. You must decide what you want in relation to your energy and lifestyle. If you have a lot of ambition and plan to be president of the company, you need the energy and the supportive husband to go with it.

PRESENT POSITION: Professor Emerita, University of California at Los Angeles

FIELD: Biomedical Engineering

RESEARCH AREA: Electrical activity of the nervous system, use of computers in medical practice

EDUCATION: B.S. in Electrical Engineering (1948), M.S. in Electrical Engineering (1949), Ph.D. in Electrical Engineering (1951), University of Wisconsin

DATE/PLACE OF BIRTH: February 21, 1924/New York, New York

Thelma Estrin has been happily married to Jerry Estrin for fifty-three years. They live in Santa Monica, California, and have three grown daughters: Margo, a successful physician with her own practice; Judy, CEO of Precept Software; and Deborah, Associate Professor of Computer Science at the University of Southern California.

INTERVIEW DATE: August 1995

Anne Fausto-Sterling

*Professor of Medical Science, Department of
Molecular, Biochemical, and Cellular Biology*
BROWN UNIVERSITY

*Complexity is the hallmark of problems that
attract Anne Fausto-Sterling. She looks to find
the pieces of the puzzle, whether in
developmental biology or in social studies of
science, two diverse fields to which she has made
eminent contributions. She was encouraged by
her parents and her upbringing to think
globally, to look for fundamental causes of
problems, and to find one's own truth. The
questions and the search in science are more
important to her than the solutions or the
applications.*

☙

My interest in science comes from my
family. I am a "red diaper baby," a child
of Marxist parents. My brother and I grew up
in what could be called alternate educational
modes, reading and thinking in an environment that encouraged us to look conceptually
for fundamental causes and to think globally in
analytical, theoretical frameworks. I love complex, global problems and trying to arrive at an
overarching theory; I am impatient with details, or with viewing science primarily as a
means to technology, and I've always maintained a commitment to political action and
social change.

As children, my brother and I gathered material for our mother's books on natural history for children. Mom encouraged us to observe nature. We searched the woods for
specimens. When she wrote *Caterpillars!* we
found them, fed them, and watched them
metamorphose. My parents valued science and
had tremendous respect for scientific knowledge, broadly construed. After all, Marxists
considered their version of socialism to be the
scientific version. My brother and I joined a
reading group that read Marx and Engels, including Engels's *Dialectics of Nature* and *Socialism, Utopian and Scientific*. Our parents
and their adult friends studied and discussed

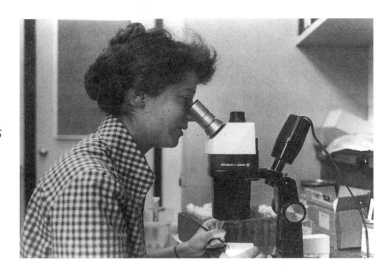

*Anne Fausto-Sterling sorting
fruit flies in her laboratory, 1975*
PHOTO BY JOHN FORASTE, BROWN
UNIVERSITY

Marxism as science and we grew up with these discussions, trying to understand dialectics as a scientific way of seeing the world and how the scientific approach enabled one to think objectively about the world.

The United States in the 1950s suffered from extreme political repression. Mere membership in the Communist Party was cause for criminal prosecution, fines, and long prison terms. Family friends were jailed for their beliefs. Because of this ever-present danger, we led a schizophrenic life in terms of our public and private identities. My parents' work on black history and culture and on women's history has influenced and informed me in incalculable ways, and the roots of my work on gender and science certainly lie there.

In college I majored in zoology. Developmental biology interested me. I remember being thrilled by the time-lapse films of gastrulation. I am attracted to complexity; I don't know why. I go for problems that look too hard to solve. If it is simple, it bores me. Right now I am looking at pieces of the puzzle of development and evolution. I am less interested in the solution than in the process of working through the problem. My goal is not to build an embryo in a test tube.

In my graduate work at Brown, I started off studying the developmental genetics of *Drosophila* (the fruit fly). These were the early days of molecular biology. I did what is routine now but was new then, looking for mutations that affect development. After getting my Ph.D. in developmental genetics, I joined the faculty at Brown. I worked with fruit fly genetics for twelve to fifteen years. The field became extremely crowded during this time. The molecular biology revolution was on, and genetics was taking its present shape. Geneticists began to unravel gene structure. I do understand why these activities are important in the study of development: these techniques have led to incredibly interesting new information. However, I left the field for two reasons: one, I wasn't interested in doing this type of work myself, and two, the field became highly competitive, very macho, and

quite unpleasant to be in, because I don't do well under high-pressure, competitive situations. So I became less and less happy doing that work.

After I got tenure at Brown based on my *Drosophila* work, I took a sabbatical leave to work on my book, *Myths of Gender*. After this, I took time to write about development and to figure out why I was unhappy with the direction that the field of *Drosophila* development was taking. In this process of reflection and searching, I came across a new—actually an old—developmental system that had been out of favor, but one in which I could ask some simple biological questions using unsophisticated technology. Furthermore, it would be cheap; I wouldn't need large grants to do the work. The granting process was getting more and more competitive, and people in my field were spending huge amounts of time applying over and over again until their proposal passed the study section, the process used by the National Institutes of Health to evaluate grant applications. I couldn't bear doing that. I ended up deciding not to close my lab but to begin the new research project. I decided also to continue to do more of the social studies of science that had started with *Myths of Gender* and that I was becoming more and more involved in.

That was about six years ago. Then I began a new research project that fused studies in development with studies in evolution. The organisms I use are little freshwater flatworms known as *Planaria*. I realized I could ask some very simple questions. In the late 1800s and early 1900s, Thomas Hunt Morgan studied how planarians regenerate, that is, how they grow back after they are cut into pieces. But he felt unable to progress and gave up, turning instead to fruit flies, where his success, as we know, was unparalleled.

Now, however, we can rely on some conceptual tools that were unavailable in Morgan's time. I thought I could start by asking some simple questions. If regeneration evolved—and it must have, because we see it today—the question is: was regeneration itself the trait that was

Anne Fausto-Sterling speaking about her work on gender and science, circa 1992

selected for, or was it the byproduct of some other suite of traits? A simple starting point would be to examine the natural variation in the ability to regenerate. If population and species were invariant with respect to regeneration (that is, if they all regenerated in the same way), you couldn't have natural selection, which must act on a variable population. So I took advantage of the fact that planarians regenerate to do genetics with them. It wasn't the classical chromosomal genetics. From every individual planarian you isolate from the wild, you could raise up a clone colony of genetically identical worms, if the type was one that regenerates. (There are planarians that do not regenerate.) If the clones differed in regenerative ability, that would provide evidence for genetic variability for the trait of regeneration.

Planarians have five different modes of reproduction; three modes are asexual and two are sexual. All modes do not occur in every species. An evolution of this degree of life-cycle variation interests me. I use an old approach from population genetics for my work. If you take a hundred planarians out of the river and you propagate each worm separately via asexual reproduction, you can produce a genetically identical line of planarians from each original worm. Then you can ask if different lines have different regenerative capacities. (The short answer is "yes.") I have been

remiss in not publishing this work yet; I am just beginning to. I do all this work with undergraduate students.

My daily lab work is really low-tech, simple observations under the microscope and some chromosome studies. It's old-fashioned biology. I have identified different "races" of planarians in different ponds and rivers. Some of them are completely asexual, showing vegetative reproduction. That is, they split into two organisms; the top half grows out the missing tail, and the bottom half grows out the missing head! There are ponds in which the organisms are completely sexual. They are hermaphrodites, both sexes in the same worm, and after they mate, each member of the mating pair will lay eggs, fertilized by the sperm of its mating partner. Among the egg layers, however, there is also a parthenogenetic group—that is, eggs that don't need sperm. This kind of asexuality differs from the vegetative type.

A number of my approaches belong to the field of population genetics. I am now doing two types of large experiments with my populations. In one, we look at something called the "norm of reaction," that is, how genotypically identical worms express a particular phenotype in different environments. So I have an experiment that takes the same species from different ponds and with different modes of reproduction and looks at how fast they regenerate at different temperatures. This shows how the same genes have evolved different expressions depending on their environmental settings. This is a massive experiment, with a lot of statistics to arrive at conclusions.

The second experiment deals with a phenomenon called fluctuating asymmetry. No bilaterally symmetrical organism is truly bilaterally symmetrical. Even though the two halves have identical genes—they are genetically symmetrical—they don't quite develop the same way. The degree to which there is an asymmetry is a measure of how tightly controlled developmental pathways are. From only studies on clonal variation in regeneration, I found something that is surprising. The current dogma in population biology is that sexual reproduction is so widespread because it provides variation. It turns out that the asexually reproducing populations show much greater variability in their regenerative responses, for better and for worse, than the sexually reproducing ones. From these results, I hypothesize that, in reality, vegetatively reproducing worms can tolerate more error. Asexually regenerated organisms start with half an organism containing a large number of cells, whereas in sexual reproduction you have to build up the organism from a single initial cell. If a mistake occurs at the two-cell level, the organism dies. But starting with many cells, a mistake in a couple of cells is not fatal. If I am right, I predict we will find less fluctuating asymmetry in my egg-laying planarian populations than in the sexually reproducing populations.

To test this, we are looking at newly hatched planarians to see how asymmetric they are immediately following embryogenesis, growing them up, cutting them in half to look at asymmetry in the regenerated worm. This study is also a way of looking at systems that constrain developmental pathways. So it is still a developmental question using a population biology approach and low-tech methods. We take photographs and make measurements of various morphological features such as eye size. I have large data sets and have to learn a lot about the statistical analysis involved. I am collaborating

with my colleagues in evolutionary biology. I am quite happy wandering through lakes, looking for the worms, and doing science that asks complex but basic questions. I am really a born-again nineteenth-century biologist applying late-twentieth-century ideas to biology.

The other work I do in the field of science studies is also very compelling for me. It took me about ten years to study this whole new field, but with these two diverse areas of research, I constantly feel that I am doing too much. I can't get any one thing done. I often fear that I have too many irons in the fire, and I never quite finish shaping any one of them. I often contemplate the possibility of concentrating in science studies and leaving the lab work, but I feel bereft at the thought of not doing some form of direct science. I am working on a book now. It's about biological experimentation and the construction of sexuality. It has a tentative title, *Body Building: How Biologists Construct Sexuality*. I examine how science is influenced by social beliefs. For example, steroid hormones affect both sexes. But how did the historical act of naming them "sex hormones"—testosterone as the male hormone and estrogen as the female hormone—affect scientists' subsequent discoveries? I teach a course in the history of genetics that is a comfortable mixture of history and science. After this book I plan to work on another area, this time to explore how social and political beliefs affect the science in the case of E. G. Conklin's work on cell lineage.

My personal life has been simple in one sense. Right out of college, I married a very nice man, a research scientist who was originally from Brazil. That is how I came to graduate school at Brown and ended up staying there. He is several years older than I am. We were married for twenty-two years and did not have children. We drifted apart, and I ended up developing primary relationships with women. After our marriage broke up, I met a woman with whom I am now in a committed relationship. I have developed a whole second life. It is a different way of living one's life than as a married woman, and I am extremely happy. I maintain a close relationship with my ex-husband. He has remarried, and we are extended family to one another.

Young people have the idea that when you choose a pathway in life that it's forever. There is nothing wrong with that. But a life cycle is a long time, and people's interests and emotional states change. My switching from a primarily heterosexual affiliation to a primarily homosexual one reflected a change in my emotional state that was deep and real. I don't understand exactly how or why it happened. It is one that I was open to follow partly because the women's movement presented a set of possibilities that seemed neither wrong nor scary to me. By the time I ended up in a primary relationship with a woman, I was in my forties. I liked myself, wasn't worried about other people's views, and I had a clear idea of who I was as a person. I skipped the agonies that young people go through when they come out with a minority sexuality. Young people need to know that life takes different twists and turns. You can't predict or control them, but you can decide to live with them and learn from them. One may follow unusual roads and be happier in the long run than one might have expected.

It is also really important to know that in science there are different kinds of women doing different kinds of things in different kinds of institutions. There is a great effort now to encourage young women to go into science by showing that you can be a "gender-normal" person and still do science. This has led to a narrowness of presentation about the sorts of people who become scientists. You can, of course, lead a conventional heterosexual life, but women of all sorts can and do become scientists.

Science is really many subcultures, not a single culture. Subcultures in the same field change over time as I have seen *Drosophila* genetics do. Like any other field with a diversity of people in it, science has places where you can work in a highly collaborative way and places that are highly competitive; places where knowledge is treated as something to be shared, and places where knowledge is something to keep secret for a variety of reasons—marketing or to get the credit or prize. My advice to young people is to look around and find the field and style that is compatible with who you are, how you are, and how you work best. When you are starting out, you are apt to believe what a more advanced person in the field says, instead of evaluating and looking for examples. Did Rachel Carson have a Ph.D., or Betty Friedan, people who changed the world with a single book?

I had an advantage starting out because our family was so outside the mainstream. What I heard at home was completely different from what my teachers taught in school—about communism, for example. I grew up with the "Question Authority" bumper-sticker slogan integrated into my daily life. As students become mature adults, they need to come to a point where they know what their personal truths are and can reject the authority's truth if the two clash. Then one can search for the niche where one belongs. If one believes, for example, that one can't be a scientist unless one has a competitive urge, you will stop trying if you hate competition. Instead, one should get one's self to a place that values collaboration. So young people should see science as an enormously diverse set of worlds in which it is possible to find a comfortable place if one works hard enough and doesn't believe everything grown-ups say!

PRESENT POSITION: Professor of Medical Science, Department of Molecular, Biochemical, and Cellular Biology, Brown University

FIELDS: Developmental biology; science studies

RESEARCH AREAS: Developmental genetics, social construction of science

EDUCATION: B.A. in Zoology (1965), University of Wisconsin; Ph.D. in Developmental Genetics (1970), Brown University

DATE/PLACE OF BIRTH: July 30, 1944/New York City

Anne Fausto-Sterling lives in Providence, Rhode Island, with her partner, Paula Vogel, who is a playwright and teaches playwriting in the creative writing graduate program at Brown University.

INTERVIEW DATE: May 1996

Eden Fisher

Senior Business Adviser
ALUMINUM COMPANY OF AMERICA (ALCOA)

Using science and engineering to help in planning, Eden Fisher blends her interests in technology, social problems, and communications. She works on problems that have to be posed and solved within the constraints of organizations and policies and communicated to policy makers to be of value in decision making.

❧

Although I work in strategic planning, I smile when I recall that I came to this career without formally planning to be here. I have found challenging work that I really enjoy through a combination of my interests, education, and experience, and through fortunate choices along the way.

In 1979 I was working as an analytical chemist in New Jersey. Because I was getting married and my husband planned to be in graduate school at Carnegie Mellon University's Department of Computer Science, I thought about what I would most like to do with a chance to start something new. My work in the analytical laboratory was interesting but limited; this was a chance to broaden what I did. A description of Carnegie Mellon's doctoral program in Engineering and Public Policy (EPP) caught my attention, and I was intrigued about working at the interface of science and society.

After I requested information, I almost talked myself out of applying. I believed there were interesting interdisciplinary questions to study, but EPP was an "engineering" program and I had a chemistry degree; I guessed that they wouldn't want me. (Although I had taken some chemical engineering courses as an undergraduate at Princeton, I had chosen to major in chemistry to have the freedom to study more of the broad range of subjects that were available to liberal arts majors.) I was also sure that I would not be able to afford EPP; it sounded like one of those graduate programs that were too much fun to offer students full assistance. So, with no data, I concluded that EPP was probably a program for engineers with independent means of support.

Indira Nair, the associate department head of Engineering and Public Policy, called to

Eden Fisher (when she was Eden Steiger) working on her senior thesis, "The Effects of Laser Excitation on the Heterogeneous Decomposition of Formic Acid Vapor," in the chemistry laboratory at Princeton University, 1978
PHOTO COURTESY OF FRED H. STEIGER

encourage me to visit Carnegie Mellon, and I learned that I might well qualify for both admission and financial assistance. Still, I had some lingering uncertainty about whether I could do something useful with this new, nontraditional graduate program. Fortunately, Indira helped me recognize that EPP was a good step for me at that time in my life. Indira Nair is a scientist, teacher, and adviser with a special gift for helping others recognize what is important; it is a talent that I very much admire.

My doctoral studies introduced me to a number of technology-policy issues, especially concerning the environment, and provided me with a foundation in formal analysis and decision making tools. In addition, the program gave me the experience of managing fifty students and faculty in a one-semester technology-policy "project course"; this provided some intense real-time learning about organizational decision making.

Through Carnegie Mellon I was also introduced to interesting opportunities outside of academia. I spent one summer studying risk assessment as a Young Scientist at the International Institute for Applied Systems Analysis near Vienna, Austria; it's a "think tank" where researchers from seventeen countries study issues that cross national boundaries, including environment and population. The year I completed my Ph.D. I was a postdoctoral fellow at the U.S. Environmental Protection Agency (EPA), helping the Office of Toxic Substances understand how expert systems might be used for assessing new chemical hazards.

After my fellowship at the EPA, I returned to Pittsburgh to work as a planner in private industry. This move surprised some of my friends from Engineering and Public Policy. For me, however, there were strong connections between the issues and approaches that I had studied and those that would be important in my new position at ALCOA. In both EPP and in planning at ALCOA, there is a real interest in helping decision makers—in the public or private sector—understand the implications of technology. This is vital because there is often a translation problem in society. Scientists are perceived as not speaking the same language as decision makers. I see EPP as providing a bridge between technical issues and the public policy community, and I see strategic analysis and planning, as we do it in ALCOA, as connecting opportunities offered through technology with the business decisions to be made.

Because ALCOA is a large company, with many different business units, planning at the corporate level offered me an opportunity to work with a variety of technical areas and to consider a wide range of policy implications that all are part of a connected system. I could have broad involvement with a number of very real issues. Moreover, the technology planning methodology that Keith Turnbull and his staff at ALCOA were developing is particularly powerful, and I was excited to be able to join them in this work.

Planning is making a decision about how to act to achieve a desired future state. One approach to planning is simply to observe the present situation, identify a future state that is more desirable, and declare "Get there." Another approach to planning involves looking at the past and observing, "Well, if it was like this in the past and it's like this now, then perhaps we can extrapolate to where we will be in the future." Limitations of these approaches are that the target for the future might be either too aggressive (not possible) or too timid (considerably more progress could have been achieved). In addition, neither approach provides much help with *how* one might reach the desired future state.

The approach that the strategic analysis and planning group developed uses science and engineering principles to set appropriate targets and identify the important "how-to's." When we are helping an organization plan the future performance of a process, we establish a context that helps decision makers make better plans and prepares the organization to act to reach the targeted performance levels. The context includes past and present performance but also considers the theoretical limits for a process. In a sense, we ask what could *not* happen. We do this by helping the organization consider the underlying fundamental scientific principles of why it could not happen. For example, two people in a standard automobile could not travel from Pittsburgh to Los Angeles on one gallon of gasoline. The process that has been defined could not achieve this because the combustion energy of the fuel could not move that much weight that far, even with perfectly efficient use of the energy. However, by thinking about the limiting factors (the quantity of fuel, the energy content of the fuel, the weight of the vehicle, the efficiency of the vehicle), we begin to identify ways that we could change the process to improve performance. We look at the scientific possibilities and the engineering limits as well as the available technologies and benchmarks of what others are achieving in similar processes.

It was very exciting for me the first time I heard this approach described; I was instantly intrigued by the thought that plans could be based on interpolation (between current performance and an identified limit) rather than on extrapolation. By understanding the range and the fundamental principles you are dealing with, you can identify actions that will capture an opportunity.

We look at processes when we do planning. For example, consider the process of recycling aluminum beverage cans. Today that process brings back about 65 percent of the aluminum beverage cans that are used. I have historical data on how the number has climbed since the aluminum can was introduced. But in our approach to planning, we consider the gap between the actual situation and the theoretical limit. What is the theoretical limit? In this case it is 100 percent of the cans that are produced. That's our starting point; it could never be more than that. Once we've bounded the problem, we can focus on the remaining gap. What are the reasons for that gap? One hundred percent would mean that every time anyone uses an aluminum beverage can, it is put into the recycling system. A way to approach this limit would be to

have a recycling system that reached every consumer, wherever they have a beverage can.

Thinking about problems in this way helps people identify opportunities for process improvement. The planning method is powerful because people reach conclusions for themselves once they recognize what the opportunities are and what could be done. They are then in a position to act upon their conclusions. In strategic analysis, we try to structure our analyses so that the decision makers discover the opportunities and convince themselves about what is really important. We work to include appropriate technical experts in the discussions so that these discoveries are possible.

I have an office, but I spend a lot of time traveling to meet with people in our business units because we do planning work with them on a unit-by-unit level. My assignments have included working with our automotive wiring harness business, our closures business (which produces plastic bottle caps), and our building products business (which produces aluminum and vinyl siding). I enjoy working with different people, learning about different technologies, and working on things that are a tangible part of our world. Although strategic analysis and planning can be somewhat abstract, I am usually able to describe my work to my children by associating it with specific products.

My husband and I have two children. I started working at ALCOA before our first child was born. I have heard from other people that when a woman tells her supervisor that she is going to have a baby, she does not always receive an encouraging reaction. I was fortunate that Keith Turnbull was very positive and supportive. A father of five, he told me that I was going to learn some important things about management from being a mother. I found his prediction to be perfectly true, but I don't know that many supervisors offer that useful perspective when they are told that an employee is going to have a baby.

I returned to work full-time two months after our son was born. At that time, most of my work was in the office near home. Just before our daughter was born five years later, I was finishing a project with a business unit hundreds of miles from home. I was doing a lot of traveling and I felt that I wasn't going to be able to keep up the same kind of schedule with a new baby and a five year old who was just starting kindergarten. I still planned to return to work after a two-month leave, but this time I asked to come back on a part-time schedule. Initially, I came back as a "60 percent" employee, which I intended to be three days a week. I found, however, that work wasn't something I could easily turn on and off. I was soon coming in almost every day. Over a period of about a year, I increased my hours back to full time again. Although I did not do it for very long, this experience gave me an appreciation for the flexibility of part-time work. I developed an even greater appreciation for my husband, Allan, as we worked as a team to defy the popular bumper sticker "2 kids + 2 jobs = 2 much!"

While I was working part time, I had the opportunity to do a different type of work than I usually did. Specifically, I was offered an assignment to prepare a paper for the National Academy of Engineering about ALCOA's planning methodology. Up to that time, our group had not put much emphasis on formally documenting our processes or communicating outside of ALCOA. Keith Turnbull had been asked to present our work to the National Academy of Engineering as part of a study entitled *Manufacturing Systems: Foundations of World-Class Practice;* I was asked to do the actual writing. Preparing a formal paper was different from the interactive work I had been doing, but it was valuable to bring together the thoughts and experiences of our planning organization. It was a chance to think through and document our process and present it to an insightful audience who would give us feedback on what we do. When the work was presented, I was pleased that audience members from academia commented that our methodology had clearly gained richness from being developed through our real experiences with businesses over a number of years.

Eden S. Fisher, 1995
PHOTO COURTESY OF ALCOA

I am particularly interested in the societal implications of what we do. I think that most people are. We each play different roles in the world, but the big-picture issues affect everybody. I look for ways that what I do can make a positive impact.

For the past two years, I have worked with our environmental affairs department on product life-cycle assessment; we study the resource consumption and environmental emissions associated with a product from "cradle to grave." In this work, I've linked some ideas and approaches we've used for business strategic analysis and planning to explore the total environmental potential of aluminum in products such as automobiles. I believe that by combining life-cycle analysis with our planning methodology, decision makers can be better prepared to improve a product's environmental impact.

I have been interested in some kind of technical work with concrete application as far back as I can remember. My father is a chemist who has developed consumer products, so I am aware of how exciting it can be to use science to help make something. My father is also very interested in photography, and he introduced me to his hobby when I was quite small. I was initially drawn to photography by the art, but I soon was fascinated by the science as well. Photography and developing pictures were the start of my thinking about technology as a way to achieving something myself. When I was thirteen, I won two prizes in a photography contest sponsored by *Scholastic Magazine* and Kodak. As a result, I had some wonderful experiences. I went to New York City to meet some of the other winners; I was interviewed on "Voice of America"; I visited *Life* magazine. All of that was very exciting. Photography kept me interested in lab work as a teenager and helped build my confidence in my ability to make contributions that others would appreciate.

My hobby stayed with me through college, where I was a photographer for the college newspaper. Photojournalism gave me the opportunity to cover a wide range of stories, which I found very appealing. Reporters spend a good deal of time on each story, but photographers can quickly capture what's happening in a single picture and then move on to another story. When you are successful, the images that you capture are as powerful as the words in the accompanying text. Although you might never know you made a difference, a very powerful photograph can have an important impact on people's thoughts and actions.

I believe that some of the most significant impacts you can have occur because you have communicated something to other people, who then act on their new insight. My mother was a teacher, and I am always impressed when I consider how she has touched so many people's lives, both directly through her teaching and indirectly through her students' work.

When I work with others to help catalyze thoughts into action, I feel some of the power of being a teacher.

Sometimes I am asked whether I will try to encourage my daughter to become interested in science, but I'm a little afraid of imposing expectations that aren't necessarily right for her. However, I have been involved in some local programs that help teachers encourage girls in math and science. I believe that if you help the system, indirectly you help your daughter and many other people.

Ideally, I would like my children to be able to make the important choices about their futures without being constrained by arbitrary or artificial barriers, and I do believe there are fewer of those now than once existed. During a campus visit when I was very young, I decided that I wanted to attend Princeton University. At the time I first voiced that aspiration, Princeton was still an all-male college. My parents didn't emphasize that point to me, and I didn't notice it. I was fortunate that by the time I was ready for college, the barrier that would have prevented me from studying at Princeton had been removed. I hope that my children find it easy to devote their talents and energy to whatever they would like.

PRESENT POSITION: Senior Business Adviser, Aluminum Company of America (ALCOA)

FIELD: Engineering and public policy

RESEARCH AREA: Strategic analysis and planning

EDUCATION: A.B. in Chemistry (1978), Princeton University; Ph.D. in Engineering and Public Policy (1984), Carnegie Mellon University

DATE/PLACE OF BIRTH: July 20, 1956/Philadelphia, Pennsylvania

Eden Fisher lives in Pittsburgh with her husband, Allen, Associate Dean of Computer Science at Carnegie Mellon University, and their children, Clark and Miranda.

INTERVIEW DATE: August 1995

Kathy Hardis Fraeman

Study Manager/Staff Scientist
WESTAT, INC.

A high school chemistry teacher inspired Kathy Fraeman to pursue a degree in science at MIT. A summer job at OSHA sealed her interest in industrial hygiene. She went on to receive her master's degree in industrial hygiene from Harvard and to work in that field for several years. Her career path changed, however, when she decided to become a full-time mother; she has recently reentered her field after a ten-year hiatus. Her daughters, Dora and Abigail, now ages eleven and eight, say they are very proud of their mom.

❧

I don't remember when I became interested in math and science. I know it wasn't in the eighth grade when the students considered to be good in math were placed in Algebra I. My teacher put me in a slower math class. It wasn't until I grew out of my adolescent awkwardness and became more self-confident that I started to like math and do extremely well in those classes. I would like to tell my junior high school math teacher that by the time I graduated from high school I had completed multivariate calculus.

I went to Montgomery Blair High School in Silver Spring, Maryland, now nationally known for its magnet program in math and science. When I was a student there in the early seventies, we didn't have that program; we did, however, have Mrs. Abramson. Mrs. Abramson taught Advanced Chemistry, and she inspired lots of her students—many of them girls—to pursue careers in science. Her class was my favorite, and I spent many afternoons in her classroom mixing chemicals to-

gether, testing hypotheses, and on occasion causing minor explosions or destroying things that should have remained intact. She nominated me to be the school's delegate to a statewide science symposium and helped me get a National Science Foundation grant at a local university to do summer research. She and my very supportive parents also encouraged me to apply to the Massachusetts Institute of Technology (MIT). I was accepted as one of about two hundred women in a class of more than a thousand students.

Inspired by the teaching of Mrs. Abram-

Kathy Hardis working under a National Science Foundation program in the chemistry department at the American University in Washington, D.C., summer 1973

son, I wanted to be a chemistry major. But at MIT I learned that—as the old saying goes—at the college level, chemistry is really physics and biology is really chemistry. Quickly realizing the truth to that adage, I switched to the biology department and concentrated in molecular biology and biochemistry.

During my first two years at MIT, I never questioned my decision to be a biology major. However, by my junior year I had entered a new phase in my life and started questioning what I was doing and why I was doing it. Most of my fellow majors had plans to go on to medical school or pursue a career in laboratory research. In my case, medical school was out: I tend to get light-headed and queasy at the sight of blood and hypodermic needles. I spent the second semester of my junior year doing a bachelor's thesis in a biochemistry research laboratory and found myself practically living in the lab, along with many postdoctoral students. Laboratory research work had its interesting and exciting moments, but I also realized that I didn't want to be a laboratory researcher. After considering and rejecting the two most common career options of the other biology majors, I was at a loss for other alternatives.

While looking for a summer job, I saw a notice in the career planning and placement office requesting applicants for a federal summer internship at the Occupational Safety and Health Administration (OSHA). Because they were looking for students with a background in biology and statistics, I applied, got nominated by MIT, and was selected among students from all over the country. My ultimate career choice was influenced by that job.

At OSHA I became involved in scientific and regulatory work on the toxic effects of chemical pesticides. The work coincided with the discovery of a serious and widely publicized health problem involving a pesticide called DBCP. Workers exposed to the chemical were unable to conceive children. My group at OSHA reviewed an abundance of toxicological and epidemiological literature, directly briefed the directors of OSHA and the Environmental Protection Agency (EPA), and wrote the scientific justification of the emergency health standard published in the Federal Register. By the end of the summer of 1977, I was sure about the career I wanted to pursue.

After graduating from MIT in 1978, I went on to get a master's degree from the Harvard University School of Public Health in the Department of Environmental Health Sciences. Because of my experiences at OSHA, I concentrated in industrial hygiene, a multidisciplinary field devoted to understanding, evaluating, and controlling occupational hazards to reduce the incidence of occupation-related illness and injury. Industrial hygiene was rated as one of the top career choices for women in a 1995 issue of *Working Woman* magazine.

After graduating from Harvard in 1980, I spent a year working for a consulting firm in Washington, D.C., helping the EPA administer the Toxic Substances Control Act. At that time, however, government regulation of toxic substances was not politically popular. Concerned about both the future and the effectiveness of that job, I started working at a company called Westat in 1981.

Westat is a contract research firm located outside of Washington, D.C. My group in the company provided support for a broad range of health and epidemiological studies sponsored by such agencies as the National Cancer Institute, the Centers for Disease Control, and the Veterans Administration. These studies examined the effects of various environmental exposures such as radiation and industrial chemicals on the incidence of cancer, birth defects, and other diseases. Because I had always been—to use MIT parlance—a computer hacker, Westat hired me as a systems analyst, a fancy phrase for a computer programmer. I designed, developed, and maintained the large computer databases containing disease and exposure information for the many thousands of people in these studies.

At this point, my story took an unexpected turn—different from many other educated, professional women in technical fields. On

Kathy Hardis Fraeman at home with her daughters, Dora and Abigail
PHOTO BY MARTIN FRAEMAN

December 6, 1984, I became a mother for the first time. After my maternity leave ran out in January 1985, I quit work. And I didn't go back for ten years.

I thoroughly enjoyed being home with my two daughters—the second was born in 1987—and I feel very lucky that our family was able to live on just my husband's salary. I put the same enthusiasm and energy into being a mother as I put into my academics and career. I did everything with my daughters and loved every (well, almost every!) minute with them. I never regretted my decision to stop working.

During those ten years, my brain didn't atrophy. I became the head of a citizen's technical committee involved in local environmental issues, read a lot, developed many interests in nontechnical subjects, and became a prize-winning, published quilter. I was attracted to quilting because of my fascination with the geometry of quilt designs, and I began using my Macintosh computer to design and produce quilt patterns. Involvement in quilting also became a social activity that led me to meet and develop friendships with other women.

In August 1994, I received two unsolicited job offers in one week. The first came from a fabric shop, wanting me to promote their store to quilters; I turned that down. The second offer came from a friend and colleague from my days at Westat, wanting to know if I was available to return to work. Westat had gotten a contract uniquely suited to my background, and my friend wanted to know if I was interested in coming back to work on the project.

The contract was with the National Institute of Occupational Safety and Health and involved designing and developing a large computer database to manage and maintain air sampling data collected in occupational settings. Westat clearly didn't hire me on the basis of my up-to-date computer skills; they needed someone who understood both the science of the project and principles of database design. The project sounded extremely interesting, and, after a series of many discussions with Westat and my family, I went back part-time in November 1994, working directly with many of the same people I'd left ten years earlier.

I have been back at Westat for over a year, and our project is almost completed. Our work has gone extremely well, and from it we produced a paper that we submitted for publication in a technical journal. However, I can't leave the impression that my return to work after a ten-year hiatus was smooth and easy, although the project was a success. Ten years is a long time, and I, my company, and technology had all changed. We took a while to get caught up with each other.

As a computer programmer, I had to learn new technologies very quickly. In 1984 I did all my programming on a large IBM mainframe computer in a style called top-down, structured programming. I came back to an environment in which work is done using a network of linked personal computers. Programming is now done with event-driven, object-oriented languages. I enjoyed getting caught up with the scientific aspects of our project; I spent a lot of time reading books and journals and was pleased to realize I remembered much from graduate school.

When I first worked at Westat, programmers were often hired because of their academic backgrounds and their technical understanding of the projects on which they worked. Now, because programming has gotten so specialized with many different computer platforms and programming languages, programmers are often hired for their specific computer skills. Although I initially returned to my prior position of systems analyst, I have subsequently moved to the project management side of the organization where emphasis will be placed on industrial hygiene and my primary interest in the health sciences.

Although the issue was never raised explicitly, I could sense some skepticism about my ability to return to work after such a long absence. People who had previously worked with me did not share these concerns, but not everyone currently at Westat was there when I left. Their concerns were indirectly reflected in my salary, my employment status, and subtle ways in which I was treated. I had to work very hard to prove myself and, after having done that, had to work equally hard and stand up for myself to get my salary and status upgraded. I am now doing what I want to do and feel I am being treated fairly for doing it.

And, hopefully, I have gained some professional respect in the process.

I have often thought about that junior high school math teacher, the one who didn't think I was a strong math student. I developed the self-confidence to prove her wrong, and that was the same self-confidence I used to return to work and prove I could be a successful, productive professional after ten years of full-time motherhood. Someone once said to me that I set a bad example for my daughters by not working outside of the home, especially with all my education. I disagree. I hope I have taught them to make their own choices, to believe in themselves, and not to always accept what other people say or think about them. I hope they have learned the value of self-confidence. The story of my career in the sciences isn't over; a new chapter is just beginning, and I'm excited to see where this new, comeback phase of my life will lead me.

PRESENT POSITION: Study Manager/Staff Scientist, Westat, Inc.

FIELD: Industrial hygiene, occupational epidemiology

RESEARCH AREA: Quantitative exposure assessment in occupational epidemiological studies

EDUCATION: S.B. in Life Sciences (1978), Massachusetts Institute of Technology; S.M. in Environmental Health Sciences (Industrial Hygiene) (1980), Harvard University School of Public Health

DATE/PLACE OF BIRTH: March 30, 1956/ Washington, D.C.

Kathy Fraeman lives in Olney, Maryland, with her daughters and husband, Marty (MIT '73), an electrical engineer at the Johns Hopkins University Applied Physics Laboratory who designs integrated circuits for applications in outer space. The Fraemans' house is also full of Kathy's original quilts.

INTERVIEW DATE: February 1996

Judy R. Franz

Executive Officer
AMERICAN PHYSICAL SOCIETY
Professor of Physics
UNIVERSITY OF ALABAMA, HUNTSVILLE

Judy Franz has an unusually strong research record in both experimental and theoretical physics. She finds discovering something new— whether an experimental result or a new theoretical explanation for a phenomenon— very exciting. By her own admission, one of the biggest challenges she has faced has been learning how to promote her work, since often people do not receive recognition and respect for doing good work alone. She has dedicated much of her professional life to promoting institutional change, particularly for women in science.

❦

I came to physics through a love of mathematics, an infatuation that began as a small child. My interest in problem solving and math puzzles predated school but was further bolstered by a fourth-grade teacher. Once a week she had students in my class compete against each other on our math tests for the honor of sitting according to test scores. I often found myself sitting in the first chair. While this strategy was probably debilitating for students with less ability, it reinforced my confidence in my math ability and my love of the subject.

My interest in math was further enhanced by my mother and father, both of whom have Ph.D.'s in physical chemistry. My father was much more influential than my mother in my early years for a couple of reasons. I had unwittingly internalized society's habit of downplaying women's roles as professionals and so did not fully appreciate my mother's work. Also, since there were no boys in the family, my father spent time with me and instilled

some of the values and qualities that might have gone to his son had there been one. My discussions with him about science and math further heightened my interest in these fields. Finally, my father seemed to do "real" chemistry as an industrial chemist, while my mother was a faculty member in the chemistry department at Drexel University and was given mostly introductory courses to teach.

I felt my mother's influence later in my career. When people asked whether I thought it

Judy Franz at the University of Alabama in Huntsville
PHOTO COURTESY OF THE UNIVERSITY OF ALABAMA IN HUNTSVILLE

"unfeminine" to be in physics, I thought of my mother and could honestly answer "no." When people chastised me for competing with my husband in terms of career aspirations, I looked to my parents and found such comments bizarre. Since these questions and attitudes didn't mesh with my experience, I never internalized them. Despite the fact that the people making these comments implied that I should feel strange or different, I didn't. Finally, when I became a mother myself, it was natural to continue to work because my mother worked throughout my very happy childhood.

I began studying physics in my sophomore year at Cornell University. After graduation I entered a doctoral program in physics at the University of Illinois at Urbana-Champaign and received my degree in 1965. I then spent two years in Zurich, Switzerland, as a postdoctoral research physicist at an IBM Research Laboratory. My son, Eric, was born during this time, and when I returned to the United States, I began my university career as a part-time faculty member at Indiana University as a young mother. From 1967 to 1968, I was a part-time assistant professor at Indiana University. I became a full-time faculty member in 1970 and full professor in 1979, a position I maintained until 1987. I was also associate dean of the College of Arts and Sciences at Indiana from 1980 to 1982 and a visiting professor at the Technical University of Munich, Germany, from 1979 to 1980 and at Cornell University from 1985 to 1986.

I started out as an experimental physicist and my work was focused in the lab. We carried out experiments in high magnetic fields, which sometimes meant that we had to use a superconducting magnet. This had to be cooled by liquid helium, which was quite expensive. Once we had filled the dewar flask with helium, we worked until it all evaporated, even if that meant working all night.

After a sabbatical leave, I switched to working predominantly on theoretical physics. This work is done on paper and with a computer terminal in an office rather than in a labora-tory. It is unusual to work as both a theorist and an experimentalist, but the combination has worked well for me.

The most exciting moments in my work have come when I've discovered something new—a new experimental result or a new theoretical explanation for a phenomenon someone else has observed. The important and thrilling moment is to see or understand something that no one else has seen or understood before. Of course, sometimes I found out later that my explanation was wrong, but that is part of science.

My career has involved more geographic moves than the typical professor of physics because I moved with my husband as his career presented major new challenges. (Frank rose from dean at Indiana University to provost at West Virginia University and is now president at the University of Alabama, Huntsville.) I served as a faculty member and on major committees at all of these institutions. After working at Indiana University, I moved with Frank to West Virginia University in 1987, where we stayed until 1991 (with brief times for me as visiting professor of physics at Cornell in the spring of 1988 and 1990). I have been a professor of physics at the University of Alabama, Huntsville, since 1991 and, in addition since 1994, on leave as the executive officer of the American Physical Society, the world's largest organization of physicists, with over forty thousand members.

Much of my work has been done with one or two graduate students, although some of the time I work alone. This pattern was not by choice but dictated by where I was and the people who happened to be around me. I particularly enjoyed the time I spent as a visiting professor at Cornell because there were many people with whom I could "talk physics" on a daily basis, and many more faculty and postdocs with whom I could work. It is always thrilling to work with students and watch them develop and become more independent over the course of a semester or year.

As is the case for most faculty members, a typical day in my office contains variety. Once I no longer worked as an experimentalist in a lab, much of my work was done in my office, even on evenings and weekends, so that I did not have to carry things home with me. Since I have spent most of my career at universities with large teaching assignments, it is rare for a day to go by without my spending several hours either lecturing, preparing lectures, grading papers, working with students on an individual basis, writing letters of recommendation for students, working on new demonstrations, or teaching labs. I also typically spend an hour or two with a graduate student who is doing research with me, reviewing their progress or helping them to plan or write a research talk or paper.

I have served on numerous university and national committees, so a typical day involves at least one committee meeting. I have been president of the American Association of Physics Teachers, a large national organization of university, college, and high school teachers of physics. I have been chair of the American Physical Society Division of Condensed Matter Physics, a member of the governing board of the American Institute of Physics, a member of the Council of the Association of Women in Science, and a member of the advisory committee of the National Science Foundation Division of Materials Research. This kind of committee work requires me to spend a large amount of time on the phone or reading and composing e-mail, often answering questions or planning conferences.

I almost always have at least one paper or research proposal waiting for me to review for a journal or funding agency, and these take time and effort. I also write quite extensively myself on electronic properties of disordered materials for both theoretical and condensed matter physics journals. After all my other work and if any time remains, I try to catch up on reading recent articles in my field, planning new research, reviewing the financial accounts of my grant or contract, or writing grant proposals and grantor contract reports. For a number of years I have been invited around the country and the world to speak on physics research and education. I always try to find time to work in local schools and small col-

leges. I enjoy talking about my research, particularly to people who are obviously interested and ask good questions. It's wonderful to feel that you are an expert and have something substantial to offer science.

I have dedicated a major part of my professional life to my belief that institutions must change. Departments hiring new faculty must be committed to doing what it takes to help junior members succeed. They must provide training to improve teaching skills instead of simply evaluating teaching. They must ensure that all faculty know that research funds are available and distribute funds equitably even though male faculty members may be more aggressive in seeking them.

I believe that young women interested in science cannot underestimate the importance of developing self-confidence and self-esteem and of not letting others deflate them as they go through the system. I always tell them never to doubt their value and worth as individuals and to surround themselves with people who believe in them and will build them up, because there are so many things that knock you down on a daily basis. Having a good support system—a spouse, a partner, friends—who constantly remind you that you are good at what you do, that your work is worthwhile and important, and that you can succeed despite others' perceptions is crucial. My husband played this role for me exceptionally well. I believe good mentors are also an important part of this support group. They can provide crucial understanding and advice that others cannot.

The biggest challenge I have faced as a physicist was self-imposed, albeit a result of socialization. For a long time I never quite took myself seriously as a physicist. During the time I was raised and educated, few women had any type of career; those who did were, for the most part, not taken seriously. I never saw a woman physicist until I was twenty-five and almost finished with my Ph.D.! Women in the fifties and sixties were supposed to marry, stay home, and take care of children. Even though both my mother and I deviated from the norm, I didn't think of myself in terms of my career, not even when I first became a faculty member.

Compounding my view of myself as a professional was my belief that if I simply did good work, I would receive recognition and respect. It was a long time before I realized that not only must you do good work, but you must learn to promote yourself, defend your work, put yourself in the right place at the right time, and remind people of what you're doing. In essence, you must learn to "play the game." This realization came slowly and painfully, but it did come, and I have learned much of what is necessary to receive recognition and respect.

PRESENT POSITIONS: Executive Officer of the American Physical Society; Professor of Physics, University of Alabama, Huntsville

FIELD: Condensed matter physics

RESEARCH AREAS: Theory of electronic properties of disordered materials

EDUCATION: B.A. in Physics (1959), Cornell University; M.S. and Ph.D. in Physics (1965), University of Illinois

DATE/PLACE OF BIRTH: May 3, 1938/Chicago, Illinois

Judy Franz lives in Washington, D.C., and Huntsville, Alabama, with her husband. Her son, Eric, is in his mid-twenties.

INTERVIEW DATE: May 1994

Cynthia Friend

Professor of Chemistry
HARVARD UNIVERSITY

Cynthia Friend's definition of good research is that it raises more questions than it answers. She takes pleasure in the little steps—the details—that eventually synthesize into a bigger picture. Her work focuses on reactions that occur on solid surfaces, and she enjoys collaborating with colleagues currently as far away as Sweden and Holland. She finds strength in cross-disciplinary research because each person brings something different to the table.

❧

M y work is in surface chemistry; my students and staff and I study reactions that occur on solid surfaces. We're motivated by an interest in several different technological problems, one being a field called heterogeneous catalysis—for example, understanding catalytic reactions that are made to go faster and in which you favor some reactions over others. If a molecule reacts in several different ways, you might want to favor a particular product, and in a good catalyst you will favor the product you want. An example of important catalysts are catalytic converters in cars. But catalysts are also used widely in a variety of different commercial chemical processes. In our work, we try to understand fundamental aspects of surface reactions that might be important in a particular catalytic process, and in so doing we develop general principles that govern surface reactions. By looking at specific systems, we develop a very broad understanding or picture that could apply to many different, related systems.

Our work is not at the stage where it could be commercialized, and it's done under very idealized conditions. Our approach is to make model catalysts, which are usually very complicated materials, using simpler, more well-defined systems. For example, we have much better control over the structural arrangement

Cynthia Friend studying surface chemistry using the vacuum systems in the lab at Harvard University's Department of Chemistry, 1988
PHOTO BY JANE REED, HARVARD UNIVERSITY NEWS OFFICE

of atoms on a crystalline surface than we would in a real catalytic material, and we have better control over the reactants that go into our surface. This way we can pick apart the reactions that occur. We don't do the practical part but rather try to develop concepts that can be used in other areas by someone like an engineer designing a process. Many of my students eventually work in industry and in actual practical applications of catalysis.

Another aspect of my work in research is teaching—one-on-one teaching of graduate students and postdoctoral fellows. Traditionally there are more men than women in the physical sciences, and so I've had more male than female graduate students; but if you compare my group to the average, I've had a larger fraction of women students than in other research groups.

In academics one has to juggle a lot of balls: I teach in traditional settings such as classes, work with graduate students, oversee undergraduates who work in the research laboratory, and work on various university committees. I regularly give lectures at other places on my research, either at meetings, at companies, or at other universities, which means I travel a reasonable amount. And of course I write grant proposals and technical papers. One of the fun elements is that there's a lot of variety and no such thing as a typical day. I've seen people who are my peers, or a little older, becoming bored with what they do. Since I do a lot of different types of work, have control over the kinds of things I do, and am doing research, my job is never boring.

I collaborate, usually with someone who has a common interest and a particular capability I don't have. For example, I have an ongoing collaboration with a colleague on the faculty at Lund University in Sweden, and I'm also just starting a collaboration with a group in Holland. At Lund we've been doing studies to try to use spectroscopy, which is the study of light interacting with molecules, to try to determine molecular structures and changes in how molecules are bound together. My collaborator in Sweden has access to a fa-

cility called a synchrotron, which is a very special light source. Because he's a physicist, he has a different technical approach to the work we do. As a chemist, I've found it useful to collaborate because we each bring something different to the table. We mostly communicate over the Internet—clearly the easiest method for this kind of collaboration because of the time change. Both fax and Internet are invaluable. We travel back and forth—he comes here one or two times per year—and I occasionally go to Sweden. Our goal is to try to understand certain systems: right now we're working on the spectroscopy of oxygen-containing molecules on metal surfaces.

In science, if you learn one thing you also learn about several other things that you don't understand. Often you hadn't even thought about these issues until you learned about the first. The characteristic of a good research project is that it raises more questions than it answers. That may sound self-defeating, but it's not. Maybe a way to characterize it is that you have a door and you don't know what's behind it; you open it up and discover a big panorama in front of you that you couldn't have imagined before.

If you're interested in science, you must enjoy learning about little details, and research and teaching are in many ways like solving little puzzles. You have to be able to take pleasure in little steps because you generally do not solve major problems in one fell swoop; it's a series of many small steps. If you take pride in those details, and try to synthesize them into a bigger picture at every point, it's really fascinating!

Throughout my life, a lot of people have encouraged me in the sciences. My parents thought science was something important to know about and a good career to pursue. They were always very encouraging, and I learned to do a lot of practical tasks when I was really young. My dad was really handy, and my parents often did remodeling work around the house. I developed a lot of skills that have been helpful in my research from working around the house. Even though I have an older brother, I never felt excluded. As I got older, I had an interest in autos and worked on cars, and that kind of practical experience has also been helpful in what I do now.

In high school I had several mentors in my biology and chemistry teachers who encouraged me. I also had an after-school prep lab job where I helped set up and make solutions for the experiments students were doing in classes. In college I was able to do undergraduate research from a very early point on, and my work-study adviser—Professor Verne Mendel—helped me learn about science, kept me excited, and gave me a lot of opportunities.

Over the course of my undergraduate career I moved more toward the physical sciences: I liked being able to put things together as quantitatively and mathematically as possible. My undergraduate work-study job was in animal physiology, and I started out thinking I was going to be a biochemistry major. My important turning point occurred when I had a really excellent teacher in physical chemistry. The experience was completely unexpected: when I first showed up at college, I was told by a junior that physical chemistry was extremely difficult, and I went into the class thinking I'd be lucky to get a C; but I did well and loved it! It showed me that I shouldn't believe everything I heard—I could have been deterred completely from taking the course by what one person told me.

Everybody faces challenges independent of gender. There are turning points in anyone's career: a co-worker or boss may try to tell you that you can't do something, or discourage you, or be overly competitive. I have ignored these things and forged forward: that's my particular personality trait. People ask me whether I was harassed when I was younger, and my gut-level response is "No." But if I go back and think about certain instances, I didn't pay any attention to some prejudices, and I flew past them. The best argument against someone giving you a hard time is to prove them wrong and be successful. Sometimes you may need to seek official help, but such actions should only be used if absolutely necessary.

I know that I was fortunate not to have to deal with a number of problems because women preceded me and made changes that I have benefited from. One thing I would convey to younger women is an appreciation for how much has changed in so little time because women pushed the system, put pressure on it to make things change. Women today have to keep pushing for additional change and be vigilant about not letting things revert back. I have been fortunate. I've had people throughout my life really trying to help me and further my career. I've benefited from people taking an interest in me and helping me out.

My advice to young women is don't be afraid to ask questions: if you don't understand something, make sure it's explained to you. Chances are that other people don't understand it either. Don't be afraid to be assertive and aggressive; instilling that fear is another kind of manipulation used against women. By being too submissive, or going along with the system, you're not going to help yourself. Being a "good girl" and just going along with what other people say doesn't pay professionally.

My advice to institutions is to continue to hire and promote women as faculty members and researchers. Role models are extremely important for many young women, and when young women see a woman in a position, it may help them envision themselves doing similar work. It's important not to have just one woman in a department, which is the situation I'm in. Maybe I'm not the person a particular student can envision herself as being. In my work it's important to have groups at various levels—research groups, classes, and positions—that contain a critical mass of women. In research groups we've seen the atmosphere change when they contain at least 25 percent women; and to get full participation, the more representation the better.

I have two children—my daughter, Ayse Gurdal-Friend, and my son, Kurt Gurdal-Friend. I don't push my children toward science; they're both in middle school now, so they have a way to go. I've certainly found it challenging balancing home life and professional life. Having primary responsibility for the children as a single parent makes it difficult to have as much free time as you'd like. And the surprises are hard—a snow day, for example. In a workplace population dominated by older white men, most of my colleagues can't relate to these kinds of issues. Most institutions don't have programs in place to accommodate work-family issues. It's getting better, but it's been an uphill battle.

One of the advantages of being a parent is that it forces you to prioritize and decide what it is you really need and want to do. If you're asked to give a lecture, is it really worth it to go someplace to do it? Is it worth it to serve on a certain committee? You must decide what comes first and what fraction of your time you want to allot to various tasks. You definitely need to get help at home and keep your responsibilities as simple as possible. My goal is to maintain simplicity and recognize I can't do everything. I just can't be a mother who drives on school trips; I really appreciate those people who do, but I can't make myself feel bad because I don't have the time for it. My children say they're really happy that I have a career and I don't just stay at home. They're proud of what I do.

Don't buy into the idea that you have to work twenty-four hours a day or you're not doing your job. To have some time outside and take a break from everything is good, and it helps creativity. You can devote all of your time to your work, but that doesn't necessarily make you a very good scientist. You may not be able to stop and look around you, and you'll miss many opportunities. When I was younger, my career alternative was golf, and I've recently started to play that again. My father taught me how to play when I was very small and coached me through competitions. Since I started so young, when I went back it was not so difficult. I had played competitively toward the end of high school, and then—not quite young enough to have benefited from Title IX—had to decide if I was going to get an education, or play golf. I chose an education. Now I play competitively in tournaments at the state level. This year I'm going to try to qualify for the National Amateur competition. It makes me feel good that I'm out there with a bunch of college-age women who play golf all the time.

Young women may not think of science as being particularly glamorous, but I've traveled all over the world, met all kinds of people, and have done interesting things because of my career and the life it allows me to lead. The most exciting aspect is that I continue to learn, and a new challenge is always waiting. I find that very stimulating.

PRESENT POSITION: Professor of Chemistry, Harvard University

FIELD: Chemistry

RESEARCH AREA: Surface chemistry

EDUCATION: B.S. in Chemistry (1977), University of California; Ph.D. in Chemistry (1981), University of California

DATE/PLACE OF BIRTH: March 16, 1955/Hastings, Nebraska

Cynthia Friend lives in Lexington, Massachusetts, with her two children.

INTERVIEW DATE: June 1995

Beatrice Fu

Director of Microcomputer Software Labs
INTEL CORPORATION

In her current position, Beatrice Fu manages about two hundred engineers in four locations. She is most concerned with product development, and she supervises software engineering development teams. She has changed careers within the computer industry several times, and credits her excellent "basic training" at CalTech and Berkeley with her ability to adapt easily to new work situations.

⁓

I grew up in a middle-class family in Hong Kong. My father was a sales manager for a British trading company and my mother was a homemaker. I was the youngest of four children; I have two brothers and a sister. It was acceptable within my culture that boys go to college but not girls. However, my father believed that education was important and wanted to give all of us that gift. There is only one university in Hong Kong, and it is very difficult to get into it. I was accepted, but I decided to come to the United States anyway. My parents supported my decision to leave Hong Kong, as they did my brothers' decisions to leave before me, despite the financial strain it put on them.

Like many engineers, I was good in math and science throughout my schooling; I was never very good in the liberal arts. I wanted to pursue some field of engineering, but I didn't know which one since I had never been exposed to engineering or engineers. I'm not sure that being flexible helped me to choose a career, but it has certainly given great variety to my work. Every time I accomplish something in a new area, I become fascinated by the work.

I majored in engineering at the California Institute of Technology. As an undergraduate I studied quite a bit of aerodynamics and applied math. There weren't many women students at CalTech: I think about 10 percent of the student population was women, but most of them were in biology. When people told me that engineering was not appropriate for women, I always took that as a challenge. I knew I was smart and always did well in school; there was never a doubt in my mind that I would be successful in my chosen field. When I graduated I went to Berkeley and studied aerodynamics and heat transfer in the Department of Mechanical

Beatrice Fu, 1993
PHOTO BY C & I PHOTOGRAPHY

Engineering. At Berkeley there was a big project related to the space shuttle, so I found myself studying the inflammation material used on the outside of the shuttle.

I left Berkeley with my master's degree after a year, and I joined Intel, where my husband was already working. He and I had met in college and married; he is also an engineer and originally from Hong Kong. I stumbled into the computer industry with some background but not a lot, so my husband helped me out. He told me what books to read and what areas were new and exciting. He provided enormous guidance the first couple of years; he's really the only mentor I've ever had.

At Intel I discovered, after the initial hurdle of learning new buzzwords, that all the engineering sciences are quite similar: the fundamental training, problem solving, and basic technical skills are all the same. I was happy that CalTech had put a lot of emphasis on basic training because I had the building blocks to learn any science and ended up doing quite well in the company.

I joined Intel in the early 1980s when the computer industry was booming, and I knew that if I stayed, I'd have a promising career. At first I was in semiconductor fabrication, part of the manufacturing group. Fabricating a semiconductor chip involves a lot of complicated machinery and chemicals, and of course you have to design on top of that. My first job was to understand the process and characterize the behavior of the transistor.

I moved from there to component design, where I did microprocessor and microcontroller design for several years, and then I found myself in software development. Now I supervise several software engineering development teams, where I have dozens of responsibilities. I'm mostly concerned with product development. One of my development projects is a software compiler —a software development tool that translates the high-level computer language that software engineers code with to low-level machine code that a computer can execute. There's an integration team and a test team that puts the product out the door. I work on a high level of the project, making staffing decisions, figuring out what kind of schedule we should try to follow, and judging what kind of content we will put into the software product. As problems arise, I'm responsible for resolving them. As a manager, I am also responsible for communicating to the senior management of the company. We discuss the direction of the products and periodically do strategic planning, not about the work we're doing now but what we plan to work on a few years down the road and where we see the industry going.

I manage about two hundred engineers in four locations. There are the actual engineers whom I work with to review product schedules and to resolve problems and two levels of managers who report to me. I also interface with other organizations like the hardware design group; I talk to them about our products to get in sync with their development, to make sure that the products are consistent and in the same program, so that the development of the company is consistent.

Seventy percent of my time is spent in meetings. Half of those meetings are one-on-one with my developers or with people from other departments. Developers report to me on a regular basis, and I meet with other departments just to keep the communication lines open. The other half of my meetings are in groups—for example, status review and strategic planning.

I have found it difficult to balance my career and personal life, but I have managed. Everyone finds an equilibrium point. A couple of my friends quit their jobs and are at home full-time; they tell me they're still busy. It doesn't seem to get any easier if you decide to leave a career in industry for one at home.

I have two sons, ages six and eight. I had been working at Intel for six years when my first child was born. I had decided to work for a while before having children, although I realized early on that there was never really a "good time" to do so. I was actually working the day my first child was born because he was early! I was off for only six weeks before I returned to full-time work. When my second child was born, I had timed my sabbatical just right, and with maternity leave could stay home for six months. That helped the transition. I'm also fortunate that my parents now live nearby; they helped out quite a bit, especially when my children were infants. They moved to the States when my father retired because they wanted to be close to their children and grandchildren. Three of the four of their children live in California.

Everyone has a unique turning point at which they figure out how to make things work. End results are really the most important element of success. But many people expect you to work in a certain style and will not accept you if you deviate from that style. Throughout my career and education, I've been surrounded by white men who have particular ideas about how things should be done. Many have their own style, their own way of doing things, and you're expected to display a similar style to be successful. When I demonstrate what I can do in my own style, I risk not being understood.

I have generally found men more confrontational than women. They are more abrupt, more direct, more reactionary. I find women more likely to diffuse their anger, to explore and understand the cause of their anger, and to be sensitive about their actions. Although I've never experienced any conscious discrimination, I have found that the higher I move, the more difficult it is for me to advance. I think the difficulty is this different style of expression. In this industry you are judged by a group of Caucasian males, so you have to be able to communicate with them in order to advance. I would tell other Asian women in America to be more assertive, more confrontational. Our culture discourages confrontation, especially open confrontation, but I think you have to accept that feature of American business if you want to succeed in it.

Within the computing industry I have changed my career a couple of times, from technology development, processing, fabrication, and manufacturing technology to component design and hardware design, and now to software development. All these occupations were

Beatrice Fu and Liz Kolowitz (Beatrice's administrative assistant) at the Intel winter party, 1995

within Intel. I think what helped the most was the basic training I received in school. Solving one problem in a course isn't practical because the industry and the world are changing, so you never know what new technology will be next. A good basic training is very important.

I am truly happy with a career in management because I enjoy solving problems at a high level rather than at the actual coding or design level. When you find a solution, you get things done. I enjoy that. I believe it is important to do something you enjoy and that you do well. When I find a strength, I try to develop it. If I use my strength to make a positive impact for the company, I almost always get rewarded for it, which makes me feel great.

PRESENT POSITION: Director of Microcomputer Software Labs, Intel Corporation

FIELD: Computer Science

SPECIALTY: Very large scale integration (VLSI) design, software development, and management

EDUCATION: B.S. in Engineering (1980), California Institute of Technology; M.S. in Engineering (1981), University of California at Berkeley

DATE/PLACE OF BIRTH: April 20, 1958/Hong Kong

Beatrice Fu lives with her husband and two sons in Los Altos Hills, California.

INTERVIEW DATE: October 1995

Diana Garcia-Prichard

Research Scientist
EASTMAN KODAK COMPANY

Young Diana's curiosity got her into trouble many times for tearing things apart to see how they worked. In school she was bored and read books in the library instead of going to class. At twenty-seven, she was a divorced welfare mother with two small children and little formalized training. Her life seemed without direction until she found her emancipation through education and embarked on a discovery process that led to a Ph.D. in chemical physics. Now a scientist at Eastman Kodak, she proudly represents the Latina community as a spokeswoman and education advocate.

❧

I grew up in Hunter's Point, a housing project in San Francisco, California. My father was born in Texas and came to California to work for the federal government; my mother immigrated to this country from Nicaragua. Her father had come to the United States first and then my mother joined him. Together they worked to earn enough money to bring her mother and five siblings here. I often wondered how my grandfather found the courage to come here alone, postwar, but my family strongly believed that in the United States everyone is equal. That made the struggle worthwhile. They believed that the Constitution, not how much money you have, defines citizen rights. These family values contributed to my conviction that things can happen if you want them to.

I often pretended that I was doing experiments when I was a child. It was the Sputnik era, and many television programs talked about scientific discovery. I remember my first scien-

tific experiment because I got into trouble for it. I was less than four years old. My aunt, who was my age, had one of those little toy cans that had pictures of cows around the outside. When you turned it upside down, it mooed. My curiosity tortured me into finding out how it worked, so I opened it to find the mechanism that made the noise. It was the first of many times that I got into trouble for taking things apart. Adults thought that I was destructive, but I can see in retrospect that I had a curiosity that was based upon intellect and that no one knew how to channel my behavior into a positive force. Perhaps if someone had, I would have had an earlier start in science.

I was extremely bored in school and as a re-

Diana Garcia's high school graduation photo, 1967

sult was an unmotivated, poor achiever. But by the age of twelve I was reading books by authors like Faulkner and Steinbeck. I would spend time in the library at school reading and not go to class. When I graduated from high school at age seventeen, I took a friend's advice and chose to go to nursing school. I didn't understand study methods and my only goal was completing the program, so I didn't explore other opportunities that were there. I graduated eighteen months later and started working as a nurse. I liked the "helping people" aspect of the job, but my intellect was not being stimulated and I felt unfulfilled. Nursing made me feel like I had no ownership of knowledge, that I couldn't think independently. Nursing was a career dominated by women but managed by men. I found it stifling.

Still, my life moved forward and I got married, had children, and worked part-time. When I got divorced, my future didn't look too bright. I was on welfare, and the prospect of going to work full-time wasn't appealing. Since I was a licensed vocational nurse and not able to practice high-level nursing, the pay was not very good. I felt I was too old and had too much work just to support my children to go back for more training. But my brother David said something very wise to me. First, he asked me my age; I was twenty-seven. Then he asked how old I would be when I graduated from college if I started right then, and I told him thirty-one. Then he asked how old I would be in four years if I didn't go to college. And it clicked in my mind that, one way or another, I would get older. I could get older while getting my college degree, or I could let the years just go by. I knew then that I wouldn't go back on welfare.

I applied to California State University at Hayward but, due to my poor high school grades, wasn't accepted immediately. After talking with someone in the administration, I was admitted conditionally as an economically disadvantaged student. He told me something that I've carried with me for a long time: "The best thing you can do for your community is to graduate." At the time they were powerful words, but it never occurred to me just how powerful until I graduated, years later, as a Latina with a Ph.D. in chemical physics.

When I started to apply myself, things began to happen. My algebra instructor would give us a quiz every week, and before he finished handing it out, I would be finished and score 100 percent. I had positive reinforcement elsewhere as well. My chemistry course was so incredibly enlightening. Something clicked and I knew that this was what I should be doing. I took a lot of history of science courses and saw characteristics in other scientists that matched my own. The low self-esteem that I had from being out of sync with the world and not understanding why began to fade away. I was finally learning things that were important to me. I was emancipated through education.

A female physics teacher at Hayward, Dr. Whitehead, began to take an interest in me. She asked me to apply for the Associated Western Universities Research Award. It's a competitive program and I was accepted. The program sent the recipients to the University of California at Berkeley to do undergraduate research and interact with a mentor. He talked to us about science and the philosophy of graduate school. We had the opportunity to talk with graduate students and hear about their research. For the first time, I felt that I was viewed as a potential scientist, not as a woman and not as a Latina. After that experience, I knew I was destined for graduate school.

I returned to Hayward more focused and decided to major in chemistry and minor in physics. My new husband, who was majoring in physics, and I both wanted to go to graduate school. We applied to three schools and both got into Boston University and the University of Rochester. The University of Rochester seemed to fit our requirements, so we moved east.

My transition to graduate school was not easy. Right before we moved to Rochester, I was diagnosed with diabetes. On top of that, only my junior high school–aged daughter was willing to move with us immediately, and then she hated Rochester. My son stayed in California with his dad for two years because he didn't want to leave his high school. I was not prepared for the cultural shock of the East Coast. I had left my extended family and all of my support systems behind. Though I passed all my courses, I didn't get straight A's, which was discouraging because I had been at the top in my undergraduate classes. Fortunately, I had been advised by Dr. Whitehead that by the time you get to graduate school, you've proven yourself smart enough. My research work eventually brought me the rewards that made it all worthwhile.

When I first arrived, I picked a lab to work in and was faced with the first person who ever discriminated against me as a woman. I was later thankful that he didn't choose me to work with him. His lab was fraught with problems because of his treatment of women. I had him removed from my thesis committee because of his sexist behavior. He felt that he should be rougher on women because they needed to be taught what it's really like "out there." Another professor told me that the reason family values were degrading in the country was because of women like me who, instead of staying home taking care of their kids, were in college. It was a good thing that I wasn't a younger woman; it could have been devastating. It's hard to believe those things were still occurring in 1985.

I managed to get set up in a lab and immerse myself in research. My specialty became absorption infrared spectroscopy of weakly bound species called van der Waal clusters. I constructed a quantitative mechanical model for measuring energy that comes in discrete packages. Molecules vibrate and rotate at certain frequencies that are very characteristic, like fingerprints. I would point infrared light from a laser at a molecule so that it would vibrate at a certain frequency. As it absorbed that frequency, it would vibrate and rotate, absorbing energy. I could then use the quantitative mechanical model to look at the energy. I would start the experiment knowing something about both the monomeric molecule's vibrational-rotational energy and about the infrared laser energy. The first molecule that we looked at was perplexing because we thought that it was asymmetric but it didn't behave that way. The symmetries associated with molecules absorb light at characteristic frequencies with a regular pattern. What we found out subsequently was that the original molecule cluster that we were looking at was not the cluster we thought. It turned out to be a symmetric, trimer cluster molecule with an oblique, symmetric top. We had performed the first trimer high-resolution infrared spectroscopy on a van der Waal cluster. We subsequently presented one of the first papers on this topic, which now has more than a hundred citations. It became part of my adviser's, John Muenter's, key focus. He taught me a lot and exposed me to exciting research. He was understanding and very supportive.

Though much of the work I did was thrilling, I had my own personal breakthrough, which was unlike any experience I've ever felt. A group of us were collaborating on an experiment with some people from Oxford University and over a period of two days hadn't found anything. It was a very difficult, high-resolution spectroscopy experiment. At the last moment, on the last day, my adviser and the Oxford professor went off to discuss what the problem was. I looked at a graph, saw the signals recorded there, and thought that I would try just one more experiment. I moved and calibrated everything to do the particular experiment I had in mind. Then these huge spectroscopic absorptions came on that were off the scale. They were high resolutions that no one thought existed. Every time a reading hit the top and went off the scale, I experienced an incredible feeling of discovery. It was like riding a roller coaster and was enormously fun. I could not believe the readings were so large and that my intuition had led to the discovery of them. I was alone when I did the experiment, but when the group came back we had champagne to celebrate. I've had subsequent discoveries, but the first one has always been the most memorable.

My husband had graduated and gotten a job at the University of Rochester. We decided that I would apply to Eastman Kodak when I graduated and if I didn't get a position we would move back to California. I applied and got hired. They hired me because I was a woman, but this didn't bother me because I was very qualified and I had gotten my foot in the door. It helped make me a role model for the community. After I got hired, I remained because I had something to contribute. I think we get too caught up in the affirmative action controversy, but if it gets you in, it allows you to make a difference.

At Eastman Kodak, I manage and do research with a team of engineers and scientists. We use fundamental principles of thermal dynamics, chemical kinetics, and engineering processes to understand the scale-up process when interfacing with the solid state of silver halide crystal. It's helpful that the team is made up of people with a variety of backgrounds because we get different perspectives on the research. What I try to do in this cross-functional situation is to maintain the long-term view of what the company wants to be able to do in the year 2002. But it's easy to lose sight of long-term goals because our research is so focused. My work is valued by the company. I have several internal publications and two patent applications thus far.

What I like about industry is the flexibility. If you decide you don't like research the day after tomorrow, you have the option of changing focus. Eastman Kodak Company has treated me more than fairly and has allowed me to do a lot of things that aren't necessarily part of my job description. Specifically, I work with the National Science Foundation and the National Committee on Science and Technology. We're looking at the importance of educational reform for science, engineering, mathematics, and technology. I have been involved in many aspects of these committees and was included as an initial participant with the science and technology clus-

Diana Garcia-Prichard at the Rochester Institute of Technology, where she was a Hispanic representative on a career panel for Black History Month, 1996

ter of the Clinton-Gore transition team. Technology affects everyone. Technological companies such as Eastman Kodak have to create a technically literate citizenship not only to work for them but to buy their products. It's a very worthwhile cause for all of us.

I also work with a local group called Latinas Unidas, and I'm on the board of trustees for a number of other groups. Latinas Unidas focuses on Hispanic and Latin women from all walks of life and on cultural identity and strengthening self-esteem. It's a grassroots movement to enhance the skills of these women as a way to improve their own quality of life and to give our community a voice. One of our first goals is to get Latinas into boardrooms.

My biggest struggle since I graduated has been with my diabetes. When I'm stressed, I have a hard time controlling it. The diabetes makes me sick, which causes more stress. There are days I think I can't take off because I have deadlines and have to keep going. It isn't something I talk about much because it's hard for people to understand. Under the Americans with Disabilities Act, I'm considered disabled, but no one would know it to look at me. Sometimes my husband doesn't even understand, but he's beginning to learn. He's been the continual driving force for me because he believed that I could do anything that I set my mind to. It has made our relationship special.

Both of my children have moved back to California, where I had raised them with a really great support system. They both decided that, since I'm so busy all the time, they're happier in the support structure in California than in Rochester. They call me often. My son, Erik, has tried college three times but doesn't like it. I've told him that he can always try again later. After all, I was two years older than he is now when I actually began college. My daughter, Andrea, is very interested in children and wants to be a special education teacher. Both of my children have begun to give back to the community. Your success is one thing, but you have to be happy in what you do—and you can't forget about the people who may not be as happy as you. My kids have been good that way and are very proud of who they are. That is very important to me.

When I first began working, I found it difficult to assimilate into the corporate environment. It's hard for mainstream scientists but even more so for a Latina. My style was quite different from those of my peers. I've found support in well-chosen mentors and in networking with other Latinas. I've often wondered if I would have pursued the same path had I known the rarity of a Latina with the type of degree I earned. The satisfaction and sense of accomplishment I feel when I'm asked about my credentials and I reply, "I've got a Ph.D. in chemical physics" tells me that there could have been no other choice.

PRESENT POSITION: Research Scientist, Eastman Kodak Company

FIELD: Chemical physics

RESEARCH AREA: Photo science

EDUCATION: Licensed Vocational Nurse (1968), San Mateo County Community College; B.S. in Chemistry (1983), California State University at Hayward; M.S. in Physical Chemistry (1985) and Ph.D. in Chemical Physics (1988), University of Rochester

DATE/PLACE OF BIRTH: October 27, 1949/San Francisco, California

Diana Garcia-Prichard lives in Rochester, New York, with her husband, Mark, an optical engineer at Eastman Kodak.

INTERVIEW DATE: November 1995

Rhea L. Graham

Director of the Bureau of Mines
U.S. DEPARTMENT OF THE INTERIOR

Rhea Graham has had a distinguished and varied career: she has held positions in industry and government and worked as an independent consultant. She has found that the ability to work with her hands and carry her weight, which she learned while growing up on a farm in Indiana, helps in getting people past racist and sexist prejudices. In 1994 she became the first woman and the first African American to serve as director of the federal government's Bureau of Mines.

❦

I grew up on a farm in Sullivan County, Indiana, one of the largest coal-producing areas of the Illinois Basin. My mother's father was born into a family of freed slaves. He moved his own family from Ohio County, Kentucky, to Sullivan County because he wanted public schooling for his children that would not be subject to the vagaries of coal-mine closures. Both he and his wife were schoolteachers. Unfortunately, the two children for whom they had made this move died of tuberculosis; but happily, my mother was born afterwards. She carried on the family tradition of education—she has more college degrees than the rest of us. Unfortunately, when she graduated, the employment potential of African Americans was quite low, and she was unable to follow her math-major classmates to lucrative positions at places like IBM.

My father was also college educated, and so I grew up with a strong family emphasis on education. From the time I was seven years old, I knew I would go to college; it was just a question of where. Because we lived on a farm, cash flow was often a problem; and al-

though we certainly had enough to eat, we didn't have opportunities for things that required a lot of money. Still, my parents always made sure that my brother and I had opportunities to learn. They took us to the library for new books every other day in the summer, and they always encouraged us to learn more than was taught in the classroom, not to stop at what the teacher said was the assignment.

When I started college, I thought I might

Rhea Graham, director of the U.S. Bureau of Mines, 1994
PHOTO COURTESY OF THE U.S. BUREAU OF MINES

be a foreign language major. Then I found out that they usually study literature in advanced-level courses. In all honesty, I felt that if I really wanted to read literature, I could do so without going to classes. I was at Bryn Mawr, an expensive private college for women, and I thought I wouldn't get my money's worth as a foreign language major, so I switched to geology. A number of factors influenced my decision: I like to travel, and to be a good geologist you have to go out in the field. Geology also requires chemistry, which was another field I liked; but most of the chemistry majors were premed, and I just wasn't interested in that. Geology also seemed like it would be a good ticket into oceanography, which I was very interested in pursuing—and I did indeed go on to get a master's degree in oceanography.

I went straight from undergraduate to graduate school. That was a very conscious decision. I felt that I wasn't mature enough intellectually to go into the workforce. I knew what I wanted to learn, but I didn't know enough to start applying things. Oceanography appealed to me because I had always liked the idea of being a naturalist, and an oceanographer is sort of a marine naturalist: You have to study physics and chemistry and geology and biology because everything is mixed together in the ocean; there are no hard boundaries. Ultimately, my oceanography training has been most useful to me and has helped me with bridging as new things evolve in my field, particularly environmental issues.

When I graduated, the petroleum industry was one of the major employers of earth scientists, and they actually conducted interviews on campus. I ended up accepting a position with Exxon in onshore exploration in the Gulf Coast division. It was in Houston, Texas. It was my first real job, and I learned a lot, but the work wasn't completely satisfying to me personally because there wasn't much opportunity for fieldwork. I worked on the geophysics side of exploration, and it tended to be the geologists who got to go out in the field. A friend at work advised me that I might

be happier working in engineering geology; a friend of his had gone to work for an engineering firm and said it fit his personality much better. I had heard good things about a consulting firm called CH2M Hill, and I got a job with them in Portland, Oregon.

It was an interesting time to make such a career move because at that time engineering jobs paid a lot less than the oil industry jobs. I think everyone has to decide at some point whether it is more important to make money or to be happy with your choice of work. I chose to be happy but, as it turned out, I had made a smart career move. Shortly after that the number of jobs in the oil industry started declining, but the work I was doing with engineering firms—environmental compliance and remediation—turned out to be a growing field.

Although there was general growth in my area, I was living in Oregon, where the state economy fluctuates a lot with the timber and wood-products industry, and I was laid off during one of the down times. So I began working with the U.S. Forest Service, first as a volunteer and then as an employee. I was doing a lot of research, which turned out to be personally rewarding in the long run; I made a lot of contacts and expanded my knowledge base. I was fortunate that I was married by that time and that my husband was working too, so we didn't struggle financially.

Eventually, we moved to New Mexico because my husband had been offered a tenure-track position at a university. Moving to New Mexico was good for me because there were a lot more opportunities for geologists than in Oregon. Initially, I took a management position with a small company doing environmental work. I learned a lot there; when you're with a small firm everyone shares in the nuts and bolts of the operation regardless of position. I also did some consulting on my own for a while. By then I had realized that one of the disadvantages of a small company is limited financial stability. I thought I would go for some stability—especially because we were having our children then. I went to a large company, Science Applications International Corporation (SAIC). I didn't play a huge administrative role at SAIC, but I enjoyed the work. I had a lot more fun being a specialized expert and working on interesting projects.

While there, I took a leave to fill an appointed position as director of the Mining and Minerals Division for the New Mexico state government. I discovered that public service could be very rewarding. I met many "faceless bureaucrats" who were in reality committed, qualified, and dedicated individuals who cared about their country and the public good. I promised myself that I would never allow to go unchallenged the rhetoric common in the science profession that certain employment arenas, such as teaching and government service, are for less dedicated scientists.

Throughout my career, I have had to deal with both sexism and racial discrimination. One thing I've found helpful is to gravitate to areas where there are fewer people with real expertise; as long as you are technically competent and capable, your race and sex will be less of an issue because there is less competition. At some point, people have to decide, "Are we going to get on with this project or not?" Certainly there have been times when I've gone out in the field on a project, and when I show up the people look at me as if to say, "Surely you jest." I simply tell them that the packaging is incidental. It helps that I grew up on a farm and am used to working with my hands. Once I show people that I can carry my own weight, they tend to forget the physical traits that they might see as barriers. I think if people thought I'd grown up in an urban area, it would have been more difficult for me to work in this field.

I was appointed to my position as director of the Bureau of Mines by President Clinton in 1994. Because the functioning of the agency affects the national good, I was also confirmed in the post by the Senate. My job is to run the bureau according to the philosophy of the administration and to carry out the wishes of elected officials, including the president and the Congress.

I was fortunate that the Clinton administration was looking for a person who was technically competent and administratively skilled; they weren't seeking to reward someone for political contributions. They found candidates by consulting groups like the National Academy of Science to see who was considered good in a nonpartisan way. That attracted me because it meant that peers and colleagues I trusted had input in the process, and that regardless of what happened politically while I held the post, I would still have professional respect. If the appointment hadn't been based on those values, I wouldn't have been interested in pursuing it. I don't think that it's good for an agency that depends on the technical and professional qualities of the staff to have a leader who doesn't embrace those same qualities.

The Bureau of Mines has roughly two thousand employees and four regional research centers in addition to our headquarters in Washington, D.C. This year we're operating on a budget of $150 million. Our mission is to ensure that the nation has access to the minerals it needs in as cost effective and environmentally sound a manner as possible. We conduct research on worker health and safety and address issues where the government is really the only agency that can fill the research role necessary for the public good.

For example, we have a problem with acid mine drainage caused by past mining practices. The Bureau is looking at ways to treat the source of such drainage so that we don't need continually operating treatment plants. This is called passive treatment—building a system that will work naturally by itself. We also look at recycling. For example, we developed a technology for recovering precious metals from catalytic converters. Again, it's a way of increasing the public good by not using a material like platinum just once and then discarding it—which, clearly, with its high price, is not a smart practice in the long term.

We also try to ensure that we do mining in efficient and low-risk ways. For example, we're looking at in-situ leaching as a way of mining some copper ores. When the rock containing the ore was formed, there was a small pathway of liquids that traveled down and essentially caused the mineralization. We've found ways to drill wells and then add liquids much like the acids that are used on rock that is dug from an open pit mine and then broken up. This process instead extracts the ore "in place"; the liquid is then propelled to collection wells and taken to the surface. This allows you to pinpoint what you're interested in instead of taking everything out and then deciding, "Well, this is what we want" and leaving the rest as spoil that has to be dealt with. This is a big leap from current technology and there are lots of uncertainties. Our research has focused on getting the technology to the point where industry can say, "Yes, this looks like something that has potential," and then work to develop it further.

The Bureau is also a source of information. We collect data on where and how minerals are being used in society—we have information for about one hundred common minerals used worldwide. Materials that were formerly used in applications such as jet engines or communications cables are being replaced, and the role being played by minerals removed from the earth is changing more quickly than ever before. We provide this information for decision makers in government and industry, and we also help provide succinct explanations and analysis of its importance. We also provide industry with information on what people have tried in the past and what worked for environmental protection and compliance. Sometimes the land management agencies of the federal government and the states use our research to determine the best way to evaluate operating permits and to make land use decisions. Environmental groups have also found our information useful because they learn more about what our options are when we decide to use the mineral potential of land. This is part of the investment that society makes in our government so that information is always available to decision makers and to the public.

Mine workers are also our customers: we do a lot of health and safety research. I can recall the grieving in my childhood community when miners were trapped by "bad air" between their location and the mine opening. Mine fatalities have been reduced to about one hundred annually, but workers in underground coal mines still have an injury rate twice the average of other industries. We work on technological advances that will reduce risk factors.

This is a fairly exciting time in the government because we're trying to become more efficient. We're making a lot of progress in changing our organizational structure. For example, decisions no longer have to be "stovepiped" up through so many layers of administration. I spend a lot of time making sure that people feel comfortable with the change and understand that they have my support to do it. I'm the only person who changes when the administration changes in the executive branch. The real work gets done by career employees. They've usually been with the bureau a lot longer than I (or anyone else in this administration for that matter), and I try to balance their experience with the reinvention of government and efforts to make decision making more efficient so that when we marry the two we get real results and not just a lot of tension.

I do a lot of political work as well, especially this year, because in addition to the reinvention of government there are significant challenges to government spending. I'm responsible for providing testimony on these issues to congressional committees. It's very unusual to have reinvention and a detailed budget scrutiny going on simultaneously, and it's quite a bit to manage. I spend about 60 percent of my time trying to manage those issues; I spend the rest of it getting feedback from the bureau's employees. I have a deputy director who handles most of the administrative work; I couldn't be this involved in policy issues if I had to manage the operations.

I enjoy my job. The employees are very thoughtful, energetic, and caring people, many of whom have been with the bureau their whole career. I've seen a lot more change in my career than they usually have because it really is new to have this much shake-up in government. I enjoy helping people understand what it means and how to cope when something potentially traumatic is proposed.

I do go out into the field some, but not very frequently. I don't really get to do the "real" work anymore, but I do get to look at it. In positions like this, you make a lot of decisions based on other people's data. To do that well, I think you have to be able to go back to where someone did the analysis in the field or at the bench. I think it's important for scientists who believe that scientists can also be policy leaders to not get so far away from the experimental work that you can't sit down, do a literature search, construct an experiment, carry it out, and analyze the results. I think too many people consider scientific re-

search a luxury that the government shouldn't pay for. Part of my reason for taking this job was to challenge that notion and help ensure that there would be opportunities in the future for people to do this kind of work.

PRESENT POSITION: Director of the U.S. Bureau of Mines

FIELDS: Geology, oceanography, mining

EDUCATION: A.B. in Geology (1974), Bryn Mawr College; M.A. in Oceanography (1977), Oregon State University

DATE/PLACE OF BIRTH: August 11, 1952/Terre Haute, Indiana

Rhea Graham lives with her husband, Cliff Dahm, and their daughters, Katharine and Kristina, in Vienna, Virginia. She considers herself a resident of New Mexico.

INTERVIEW DATE: March 1995

Temple Grandin

Owner
GRANDIN LIVESTOCK HANDLING SYSTEMS
Assistant Professor
COLORADO STATE UNIVERSITY

Temple Grandin is one of the world's foremost authorities on the design of livestock handling equipment and systems. She is also an authority on autism and has written several autobiographical works on the topic.

❧

I don't think in language; I think in pictures. I'm an autistic person, and this is just how my brain works. Thinking in pictures is very helpful to me in my work: designing ways to handle livestock. Some people say that maybe cattle and other animals don't think, but I've always thought they do. Some of the scientists out there who tend to deny animals' thinking are highly verbal people. People who think primarily in language have a hard time imagining how animals might think. But I can picture myself as a cow and imagine what equipment would feel like if I were put into it. I can empathize easily with the cattle because in many ways my emotions are more like those of cattle than people. Fear is one of the primary emotions in people with autism, and when I was younger I was very nervous and fearful. The things that made me afraid as an autistic child are the same things that make cattle afraid: sudden motion, loud noises, high-pitched noises, and confusing distractions.

Cattle just are not scared of the same things people are scared of, and they don't understand the world in the same way. When most people look at cattle going into a meat plant they think the animals know they're going to die. Animals don't know they're going to die. People are often frightened by blood, but I've seen cattle walk into blood, lick it, drink it—they couldn't care less about blood. However, if you leave a little chain hanging down in the chute that jiggles, they won't go by it; if there's air hissing, they won't go by that either. If you drop a coffee cup in the chute, they won't walk over it; you can just about shut a plant down with a coffee cup. It's little distractions that upset cattle. The cow can only remember his previous experiences; he doesn't know he's in a slaughterhouse. He knows he's in a chute, and I think that if the cattle are thinking anything, they probably think they're on a giant truck ramp because that's what it looks like.

When I first started out working on cattle handling, I was out in feedyards in Arizona

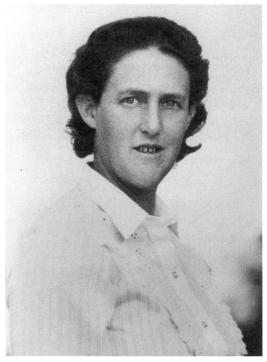

Temple Grandin

working on my master's degree. I noticed that sometimes some cattle would go through a facility just fine but other cattle wouldn't go through. At some feedyards everything worked just fine, and at others the same things didn't work. My immediate reaction was, "Well, I need to get down in the chute and see what the cattle are seeing." I got my camera, went down in the chute, and took pictures. I saw that cattle will balk at things like a person walking in front of the chute, shadows, puddles on the ground, or reflections. Nobody had ever bothered to look this way before; some people thought it was kind of weird to get in the chute and look, but it seemed to me the obvious thing to do.

The first thing I designed was a ramp-and-chute system for moving cattle through a meat packing plant. My second design was a large corral for handling cattle up in Oregon. What I did that was unique was to apply the principles of layout that I had learned for feedyards to the ranch—nobody had ever done that before. For example, I set up a system of curved chutes. Why do you use curves? Well, because you don't want the cattle looking down the alleyway and seeing all the people at the end. Since then, I've laid out systems of one sort or another for most of the biggest companies. I also do a lot of consulting work for people on how to handle their animals better. I don't necessarily design any new equipment for them, but I show them how to move cattle more efficiently without using prods and how to move them quietly without getting them excited.

One of the biggest projects that I've worked on was developing a thing called the center-track restrainer system, which is a conveyer system for restraining cattle at the meat packing plant. I was hired to work on it in 1986 by the Council for Livestock Protection, a consortium of animal welfare groups. There were many things I took into account in designing the system that people hadn't necessarily thought of before. I made sure the device didn't have any pressure points that were going to dig into the cattle. Restraint de-

vices must also hold the animal with the correct pressure. People always want to hold the animal too hard, and if it struggles they just want to squish it tighter. But that's not the way to do it; there's an optimal pressure. I also made sure no part of the device moved in a sudden, jerky motion; that kind of motion excites the animal whereas smooth, steady motion has a soothing effect. The system also blocks their vision so that the cattle don't see people too close to them. Cattle have a flight zone, and they don't like people right on top of them. Finally, the system uses careful lighting. Cattle won't walk into dark holes, and they don't like shadows; it won't work if your lighting is wrong. With the center-track restrainer system, the animals will walk through very, very quietly and easily and not get scared. A third of all the cattle in North America are now handled on this system.

In addition to my work on livestock handling, I do a lot of lectures on autism. Parents with young autistic children need information. For many years people never recognized the sensory problems in autism: autistic children can have super-sensitive hearing where loud sounds hurt the ears, super-sensitive eyes where bright light hurts the eyes, super-sensitive touch where being touched hurts. It's like having bionic senses. Well, bionic senses are not all that great; you get overwhelmed with too much sensation. Autistic children often withdraw to shut out this intolerable bombardment of stimulation, but if they withdraw there's a good chance of secondary damage to the brain. We all know that if an animal in the zoo paces and does stereotypies for years, you'll get an animal you can't rehabilitate. Pacing back and forth all the time damages the brain; brains need a certain amount of input in order to function. If an autistic kid just sits there and does stereotypies, he blocks everything from coming in. He can't learn anything—he's just like a lion in a zoo cage. Autistic children need to be protected from excess stimulation, but they must also be kept constantly engaged.

There are different types of autistic kids.

Fortunately, I was the type who could pay attention when someone told me to. Even though I could be snapped out of withdrawing, I still had to be protected from certain loud noises that hurt my ears; when the school bell went off, it hurt. The most important thing in preventing a child from withdrawing, though, is to have a lot of intensive one-on-one engagement. That was done with me.

When autistics reach adulthood, about half of them need to be on medication. An autistic's nervous system is in a constant state of overarousal. It's as if the nervous system is activated to fight off a lion even though there's no lion there. When I was younger, my nerves acted as a motivator. I wouldn't have wanted to take all the energy away. As I got older, however, the nervousness got worse and worse; in my early thirties it started ripping me apart. I once believed that the nervousness was purely psychological, but I later discovered from reading medical journals that it has a purely biological basis and can be treated. I've been taking low doses of tricyclic antidepressants for the last fourteen years. What an improvement that makes!

I always liked science. My grandfather invented the automatic pilot for airplanes, and when I was a little kid I used to go visit him and ask him all kinds of questions. Why is the sky blue? Why do the tides go in and out? I can remember saying, "When I grow up, I want to be a scientist." But, largely because of the autism, I was not the greatest student. Fortunately, when I got to high school, I had a really wonderful science teacher, Mr. Carlock, who gave me the opportunity to do all kinds of interesting things. He got me in the library using psychological abstracts and the *Index Medicus,* reading journals, getting into the things that the real scientists use. He gave me a reason to want to study in school. I learned that if I wanted to be able to do research on interesting things, I had to study some boring things as well.

When I was going into puberty, I started having severe anxiety attacks; it felt like constant stage fright. Of course, I wanted to get rid of it; it really was horrible to feel that way. During the summer after my junior year of high school, I was out on my aunt's ranch, and I noticed that when some of the cattle went through the squeeze chute for their vaccinations, they seemed to relax. I wondered if I'd relax if I got into it, so I tried it. It did relax me, and that's where I got the idea for building a squeeze machine for myself. My first model was kind of crude and made of wood; later versions were padded and had a pneumatic cylinder to operate the squeeze sides. At first, a lot of people thought my squeeze machine was strange and bad; they thought my using it was an unhealthy compulsion and wanted to take it away from me. Mr. Carlock told me that if I wanted to change people's minds about my squeeze machine, I should look for scientific reasons for why it relaxed me. I began reading through all the scientific literature on the sensory system and how it works. When I got to college, I actually conducted experiments on nonautistic students to see how they reacted to being in the squeeze machine; 60 percent of them found it relaxing. Today, unlike thirty years ago, it's known that physical pressure can relax people and that lots of people with autism are pressure seekers.

I did my undergraduate degree in psychology at Franklin Pierce College, and then began working on a master's in psychology at Arizona State University. While working on my degree, I started working cattle in local feedyards. I realized that I was most interested in cattle behavior, so I switched my major to animal science and did my master's thesis on cattle handling in feedyards, focusing on the use of various kinds of squeeze chutes.

After I got my master's degree, I was livestock editor for the *Arizona Farmer Ranchman* magazine for seven years. I got that job by walking up to the publisher at a rodeo and asking him if he'd be interested in an article on my squeeze-chute research. He said he would be, and he published the article. Soon, I started writing something every month, and eventually they hired me as livestock editor.

Temple Grandin demonstrating to a worker at a packing plant how to turn a steer without getting him excited
PHOTO ROSALIE WINARD 1994

That job was really crucial in helping me get started because I got to visit all of the ranches and farms around Arizona, and to go to meetings and make contacts. Eventually, I got a job designing equipment at a feedlot construction company. A year and a half later, when the company started asking me to participate in some questionable business practices, I quit and started my own consulting and design business.

Until recently, most people I worked with didn't know I was autistic. I've never felt that I've been discriminated against for it, although I have been discriminated against because I was a woman. It was worse when I started out than it is now. When I was a student, I got kicked out of a feedyard simply because I was a woman. The manager said the cowboys' wives didn't like having me there. I was the first woman to work in the dairy at the Arizona State University; they had said a woman couldn't do the job because she wasn't strong enough to lift the full milk jugs. Well, I figured out a way around that; I just put the empty milk jugs on the cart and milked the cows into them. Later, there was one plant where I was told I couldn't set foot inside. They complained to the company I was working for that the system didn't work, and I simply said, "I can't fix equipment that I'm not allowed to see." That plant had made

some very major, stupid mistakes, and they ended up going broke.

After a number of years running my business, I decided to pursue my Ph.D. in animal science at the University of Illinois. I finished my degree in 1989. Now, in addition to my business, I'm an assistant professor of animal science at Colorado State University in Fort Collins. My students are both graduates and undergraduates. I have a two-week short course that I teach each semester on cattle behavior and the design of the facilities. I have students actually lay out and design the facilities. It's a very different experience for them; students are used to just spitting up answers on the final exam, but in this they really have to think. A lot of the students have a very hard time with this work because they can't visualize at all.

I give lectures for a number of other classes: in the veterinary college on basic cattle handling and behavior; in the meat science course on humane slaughtering; and in nutrition class on nutrition and behavior. I also give lectures in the horse behavior class, in an ethics class, and in a research methods class.

My business work is more independent. A plant will call me for help, and I typically work with that plant's engineering department. In some cases I have to go to the plant; in other cases, they can send me the drawings and I can work on them without having to go to the plant—especially if I've been there before and know what it looks like.

I work to reform and improve the meat industry, but I don't want to get rid of it. People sometimes ask me how I can care about cattle but be involved with slaughtering them. A lot of people who are interested in animals feel that we should get rid of meat plants. That's not the way I approach it. I keep in mind that everything dies—someday I'm going to die. I believe our relationship with animals should be symbiotic, a mutually beneficial relationship between two different organisms. We breed cattle, we feed them, and in return they're going to give us food and fiber, but we owe those animals a decent life and a humane death. If we do otherwise, our relationship will not be symbiotic but exploitative. I feel I can improve the systems, improve how animals are handled, and it's going to make things more humane. I like my work. I feel strongly that I want to do something positive with my life, and I know there are a lot of animals that suffer a lot less because of the work I have done.

PRESENT POSITIONS: Owner, Grandin Livestock Handling Systems; Assistant Professor, Colorado State University

FIELD: Animal science

RESEARCH AREA: Livestock handling equipment and systems

EDUCATION: B.A. in Psychology (1970), Franklin Pierce College; M.S. in Animal Science (1975), Arizona State University; Ph.D. in Animal Science (1989), University of Illinois

DATE/PLACE OF BIRTH: August 29, 1947/Boston, Massachusetts

Temple Grandin lives in Fort Collins, Colorado.

INTERVIEW DATE: June 1995

Ann Grant

Senior Director, Pharmaceutical Process Development
ROCHE CAROLINA, INC.

*Ann Grant's career in the pharmaceutical
industry could not have been successful without
her Ph.D. in physical chemistry. But it is her
untaught managerial skills that allow her to
keep track of the laboratories, pilot plant, and
process development department housed in the
PharmaTech Center she runs for Roche
Carolina, Inc. She believes the key to happiness
is to accept that it is neither possible nor
necessary to be the perfect wife, mother, and
career woman at all times.*

❧

I work for Roche Carolina, Inc. (RCI), which
is a newly formed subsidiary of the Swiss
pharmaceutical company Hoffmann-LaRoche.
The American headquarters of Hoffmann-
LaRoche are based in my home state of New
Jersey, where I worked for the past fifteen years
and lived almost all of my life. RCI is based in
Florence, South Carolina, and holds an entirely
new work and cultural experience for me. My
department is physically the same size, about
fifty people, but our significance in the company is greater. Although my title is the same as
before, director of pharmaceutical process
development, my role in the company has
changed drastically. We are one of two facilities
worldwide that are responsible for process development for Hoffmann-LaRoche's compounds. I am also now in charge of the PharmaTech Center on the RCI site, which houses
both my own department and Quality Control.
The site is focused entirely on the development
and launch of new pharmaceutical compounds.
I am involved directly in site management and
have more responsibility for setting policies for
personnel, administration, strategic planning,
and resource utilization. The laboratories and
pilot plant do scale-up work, where we take
processes from the small experimental level to

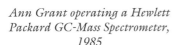

*Ann Grant operating a Hewlett
Packard GC-Mass Spectrometer,
1985*

the full manufacturing scale. The pilot plant is a small-scale manufacturing plant where processes are demonstrated on the manufacturing level and data are gathered so they can be installed in the manufacturing plants. In these stages, we also work to improve efficiency and lower production costs.

My day typically involves meeting informally with the three people who are the heads of the groups in my department. We discuss issues related to experimental work going on in the labs, on a compound; we talk about start-up progress and issues, and sometimes we tackle administrative or personnel issues. I might have a larger meeting with all the personnel to go over policies, procedures, or decisions generated at the corporate level that we had to implement. I like to keep in close touch with all of the scientists, engineers, and pilot plant workers; this way people feel free to come to me when problems arise.

About one in fifty thousand compounds tested by pharmaceutical companies actually make it out to market. By the time a compound reaches my department, it has passed many tests and its chances have increased to one in twenty to thirty. By improving our work processes we've been able to streamline our activities so they are done in two to three years, with the entire drug-development process taking about six years, compared to the industry standard of ten to fourteen years. I think what keeps us all going is that we know sooner or later we will have a successful compound and that we will get to file a new drug application and install a new compound in a plant. It is a very exciting experience to see all of your work and planning come to fruition. The people who work in this field are not doing it primarily because of the money; they do it because they love their work and they find it challenging.

I became interested in science because it can make order out of chaos and explain the world in a rational way. That is somewhat ironic because what I am doing right now, mostly managing people, is the messiest and most chaotic thing anyone could possibly be

doing. I only use chemistry and chemical principles in about 30 percent of my current work. I enjoy doing the chemistry as an escape to an orderly world—one that I can still understand. The other skills that I have had to learn are finance and budgeting, project management, personnel management, leadership, and long-range and strategic planning. I don't think it would be possible for someone to manage a technical department such as mine without a technical background because much of my job is providing a bridge between the technical professionals and upper management.

My father was not very enthusiastic about sending me to college. As a matter of fact, he felt that education was wasted on a girl because all she was going to do was get married and have children. Although he respected and admired educated people, I believe he was envious of them because he hadn't had the same opportunity. My mother had gone to college and gotten her degree in English and French, but she never used it because of the custom of the time. Women were not encouraged to pursue careers. After she got married she stayed home, had kids, and took care of the family. I guess it was the fifties thing.

Still, my mother was the reason that I went to college. She encouraged me from a young age to work hard despite my problems in reading and math. Although it was not identified at the time, I believe I was dyslexic, and without her I probably would have been lost in the system. I often inverted letters and numbers, so my mother trained me to see things as they were "supposed to look." When I wanted to go to college she argued with my father on the subject and convinced him I should go.

In 1961 I went to Douglass College, which was a women's college with an excellent chemistry department. There were feminists at Douglass before feminism was popular. The school was very egalitarian and proactive in promoting women, and all the professors were very supportive of women pursuing their careers. In fact, it was assumed that we would become professionals. At school I found

Ann Grant awarding a prize to a poster presentation, December 1993

plenty of positive role models because half of the professors in the chemistry department were women. Although they supported us, we were not coddled at all. The head of the department used to say that you have to be good and you have to be tough because you are going out there with two strikes against you.

Despite the warnings of my professors, I had a Pollyanna attitude early on in my career and I simply did not recognize discrimination; therefore, I did not have to deal with it consciously. I went along blithely and ignored it; it was easier just to keep going than fight every little battle. Later on, when I saw that things hadn't changed in twenty years, I became more sensitized to the issue. One thing that helped my awareness was that I saw discrimination was not only affecting me, it was also affecting women who worked for me. I often noticed this in comments that male managers made about women, and about whether they should be promoted because they were women. In many cases it was subtle, but in some cases it was very blatant. I remember one manager speaking of a pregnant employee: "Should we really be giving her a promotion if she is just going to end up staying home and taking care of her baby?"

Things like this were said in front of me, and sometimes the men didn't understand how insensitive they were, so we had some fights. When I felt that they were discriminating I told them so, but they often didn't understand where I was coming from. I had to educate them about many issues, and to some extent I developed a reputation for being very difficult to deal with on this subject. In reality all I was doing was reminding them of their responsibilities to treat everyone equally.

More than my father or discrimination in the workplace, however, my worst enemy was often myself. I had this perception that I had to do it all—have an incredible career, be a wonderful mother for my children, be the perfect wife, and take care of my home. I wanted to be "Superwoman" and nothing less. It began when I returned to school at Rutgers University to pursue my Ph.D. in physical chemistry. Between 1969 and 1979 I pursued my graduate work, taught part-time, and bore and raised two toddlers. Because of the graduate study, research, and teaching, I was able to be extremely flexible in my hours, and I arranged for child care by combining part-time baby-sitters, my husband (who was also a student at the time), my mother, and myself.

Even when I resumed full-time work in 1979, I somehow could not give up the ideal of the mother that I was supposed to have been. I would leave at 6:30 in the morning so that I could get home in the afternoon and be with my children as soon as possible. I felt guilty every moment I was away from them. Every day when I came home from work I cooked dinner and cleaned. I made "family days" a mandatory part of every weekend and planned an event so the girls wouldn't mind being with their parents too much. Especially when the girls were young, I went all out for holidays and birthdays. At Christmas I baked dozens upon dozens of cookies, pies, and even fruitcake. I made sure my daughters, husband, and entire extended family all had the perfect presents. In the very beginning, I even knitted all the girls' presents: hats, gloves, and sweaters. I admit that I took great joy in this and in the happiness it brought my children, but the problem was that I never saw it as a choice. I simply believed that all of these things were necessary.

I ended up just getting really tired. The sheer physical challenge of what I felt needed to be done was not possible. Despite the time I spent with them, I felt extremely guilty for not being there for my children all the time. At times I even (briefly) considered ending my career to take care of them. More recently I have rescinded my duties as "career woman/homemaker/most dedicated mother in the world" and taken up trying to be content with what I have accomplished rather than worrying about what I have not.

I think that American industry has to change. It is already changing in some positive ways—becoming less individually competitive and rewarding of the efforts of people who work in teams. I think that women really are more in tune with other people and they try to make things go smoothly, whereas men are taught to be more competitive. I think that women have a lot of social skills that serve them very well in modern industry and the direction it is taking; but like the head of my chemistry department used to say, you still need the technical skills.

To anyone entering chemistry, or any career path, my advice is to make sure to do whatever you are doing because you love it. If you are not happy with what you are doing, then maybe it's not the right career for you. You need to have a vision of the future—it doesn't have to be really specific—it could just be "I want to become a chemist." But you also need measurable goals and objectives along the way to fall back on when you get discouraged, which you will. You need to follow those goals and reassess as you go along. I have a road map, and I have to check it from time to time: Am I following that map and getting to where I want to be?

PRESENT POSITION: Senior Director, Pharmaceutical Process Development, Roche Carolina, Inc.

FIELD: Pharmaceutical industry

RESEARCH AREA: Chemical process development

EDUCATION: A.B. in Chemistry (1965), Douglass College; Ph.D. in Physical Chemistry (1976), Rutgers University

DATE/PLACE OF BIRTH: December 21, 1943/ Perth Amboy, New Jersey

Ann Grant recently moved to Florence, South Carolina. Her daughter Jennifer is attending Carnegie Mellon University, and her daughter Annemarie is a senior in high school in Maplewood, New Jersey.

INTERVIEW DATE: February 1995

Deborah Lynn Grubbe

Director of Engineering
E. I. DuPont de Nemours and Company

As director of engineering, Deborah Grubbe manages about five hundred people; she's come a long way since she started at DuPont in 1977 as an assistant to operations, where she wrote operating manuals and trained operators to run particular units. She attributes her success to many factors: wonderful mentors, the positive working environment at DuPont, and her own work philosophy. She believes her job is to set the vision, point her management team in the right direction, give them the tools and help they need, cheerlead, and say thank you along the way.

❧

I am the only child of second-generation immigrants. I was born and raised in suburban Chicago. My mother's parents and two of her older sisters were born in Italy; my father's heritage is German, and his family emigrated around the turn of the century. Neither of my parents went to college—I was the first in my family. My father was an electrical lineman for Commonwealth Edison, and my mother worked from the time I was five in a bank in downtown Chicago. I always knew I would work, just like my mother; she was my earliest role model. She worked because she wanted to be able to afford more things. I remember watching a neighbor go through a divorce when I was in high school; her standard of living went from pretty good to pretty lousy because she had no skills. I remember her sitting at our kitchen table crying and asking what she was going to do, and I vowed I would never be put in the situation where I had to depend so totally on someone else.

Schooling was stressed in my family despite my parents' lack of it. I went to a Catholic school for eight years and then to a public high school. I was always good in math; I had some independent-study math classes in seventh and eighth grades, so that when I got to high school I coasted for a year. I had a wonderful high school math teacher who directed me toward engineering as a career. In my junior year he asked what I wanted to be when I grew up, and I said I wanted to be a math teacher. He told

Deborah Grubbe preparing to sample a reactor in the 1980s
Photo courtesy of E. I. du Pont de Nemours and Company

me that was a bad idea because there wouldn't be many jobs by the time I graduated from college. He then suggested I think about becoming an engineer, and I asked what an engineer was. He gave me information that intrigued me enough to go and see the guidance counselor, who promptly told me I would never make it as an engineer. I trusted the math teacher over the guidance counselor and pursued engineering. I am still in touch with my high school math teacher—last year he was one of twelve finalists for Illinois state teacher of the year.

My father's first reaction to my idea of becoming an engineer was, "You want to be a what?" but my mother reminded him that I was very bright and should be whatever I wanted to be. Part of his reaction came from the fact that I was the only child; he never wanted me to leave home.

I started out at Purdue wanting to major in biomedical engineering, but in my third semester I changed to chemical engineering, partly because biomedical engineering was still so undefined as a field and it seemed like you needed a Ph.D. to do anything. I knew by that time I didn't want to pursue a Ph.D. There were about 110 graduates in my class and 9 of us were women. There was some sexism in college, but I knew I was good and I tried not to let it get in my way. I tried not to let myself fall victim to the fact that I'm a woman.

I had technical summer jobs all through college. There weren't many women in technical fields in the early seventies, and as soon as I went looking for a job I found one. I had good grades and was able to secure really interesting summer work, and that helped me to understand what I wanted to do when I graduated. I initially thought I wanted to do research, but after some summer experiences with research I knew it wasn't for me. I realized I needed more immediate feedback on my performance.

After I graduated in May 1977, I began working for DuPont at their facility in east Chicago. DuPont is a manufacturing organization involved in many markets; it builds manufacturing facilities all around the world.

I was at DuPont for a few months when I took a year's leave of absence to accept a Winston Churchill fellowship to study chemical engineering at Cambridge University in England. I headed to Europe in the fall of 1977. I learned a lot from this experience—a little chemical engineering and a lot about living in other cultures and about life—probably more than I could ever have learned by going to graduate school in the United States. It was a real growth experience for me, and a few years later it helped me to get a job at a facility DuPont was building in Northern Ireland.

When I returned to the States I went back to DuPont and was transferred to Delaware, where I've been ever since, working in a number of different jobs. I began as an assistant to operations, which entailed writing operating instructions and training operators on how to run a particular unit. I then moved to an environmental assignment where I worked at an environmental plant site—different chemistry, different product, a different market, and a whole set of different technical problems. My third assignment was in construction, and that's where I found out that I really liked project work. I managed chemical plant construction projects for DuPont. Construction provided very immediate feedback: when I received a performance review at the end of every day, I realized I had found my calling. One of my first assignments was to take down an old distillation column and put up a new one. In college I learned how a distillation column ran, but that wasn't important now. I was looking at the problem from a very different perspective. It was a fascinating growth experience. I had to relate to many different kinds of people: laborers, carpenters, pipe fitters, managers, and researchers in the building where we were working. I spent four years doing construction management work at various locations in Delaware and New Jersey.

I moved from construction to design and worked in an office with people designing a Kevlar® facility in Europe. Kevlar® is a fiber that goes into bullet-proof vests. I became a frequent traveler to Northern Ireland and

London. For the last year of the job I was the lead engineer. There were no other women working on the plant in Northern Ireland except secretaries, but I didn't allow that to become an issue. People respect competence, and I've always worked hard to make sure that I am competent in whatever job I'm doing. This experience also enabled me to grow professionally.

My next job was my first pseudo-management job; I was a staff assistant to an engineering director for fourteen months. I was given special assignments that enabled management to look me over, and then I was promoted to a human resource manager. After a year I moved into a project manager's job, a lateral move that gave me more exposure and enabled me to work on developing people. I then moved to a regional office where I managed a group of 208 people in small project design. I interfaced with many different plants and many different types of people and worked on budgets. Then I became a business engineering manager for our specialty chemical business for two years, and in February 1995 became a director of engineering.

I currently manage about five hundred people and am responsible for capital investment, core competencies, process engineering, environmental engineering, energy engineering, and process safety engineering; I also have liaison responsibilities in construction and in small project design for the northeastern part of the United States and international liaison responsibility for Mexico and South America. My schedule varies from day to day and week to week. For example, I might spend a week in Brazil to make sure that we are set up to do engineering work for our businesses down there. Or I might spend time with the capital investment group, which advises DuPont on how much it costs to build things. When some of our businesses want to expand and perhaps build a new facility, we need to know what it's going to cost from a capital and noncapital standpoint. The core investment group is responsible for making sure that we keep track of and give the right guidance around those kinds of issues. My days start early and end late, but the job is fascinating and energizing.

It's very important to be able to relate to people wherever they're at, meet them there, and take them somewhere they may or may not want to go. Warren Bennis identifies that as an important characteristic of a leader. I am a high-activity manager; I'm open and honest with people; I don't micro-manage; I always do things with a business focus; and I try to build support with people. My job is to make the management team the best they can be—

set the vision, point them in the right direction, give them the tools and help they need, cheerlead, and say thank you along the way. My past work at DuPont has helped me to build a bond and a bridge to people in the organization.

I have been blessed with many mentors over the years who trusted me and exercised good judgment in placement. My first real mentors showed up about four years into my career. Some of them are retired now; some are dead; some are still around; some are outside of DuPont; and most are men. My mentors at DuPont placed me in environments where there were always one or two key people who really wanted to help me grow and learn. And I always approached new tasks or jobs as learning experiences: I didn't come in pretending to have all the answers but instead expecting to learn a lot. I found that people were more than willing to teach me. One thing about project work—you know when your piece of the job is done and you move on to another job. I proved my competence and earned the respect of certain people, managers who knew my work and my capabilities. When I became available, they said, "Hey, I'd like her working for me on this project." Without the help of people like that, it doesn't happen.

I made it known early on that I was serious about my career and interested in being promoted. I got my professional engineer's license and purposefully hung it on the wall in my office so people would know. Early on I had to tell managers that I was serious about my career so they'd give me opportunities to prove myself; I don't need to do that anymore. And I always did more than the job required so that people could see that I could handle more and was capable of contributing at a higher level.

The working environment at DuPont has been very positive for women. I have been offered jobs for more money elsewhere, but I stay because of the environment. DuPont allows people who are business focused and have skills to contribute to work outside of

their box. In 1986, before it was popular—before diversity became a buzzword—we set up internal women's networks and discussed gender issues in the workplace. DuPont has had enlightened leadership for many years; they had enough on the ball to realize the value of diversity. Since 1980 about 50 percent of new hires have been women and people of color, and there are now critical masses at certain salary levels and below. We don't have parity at management levels yet, but we are making progress.

I adopted an attitude early on that if it's to be, it's up to me. Many times we blame other people for the problems we have, and while some of the obstacles are external, I always ask what I'm doing to contribute to the situation. And I try to stop doing that. Some people are stuck in victim mode and identify the source of their problem as everyone else—they don't take any responsibility for themselves. I think people often have more power than they think they do, and more women have to understand that.

I view myself as a businessperson first who happens to be an engineer and happens to be a woman. I've stood in front of many groups consisting of men who are often older than I and said, "I stand before you born into a female-type package. DuPont is not paying me or you for the package; rather they are paying us for how we use the gray matter between our ears."

I don't let work consume me totally or I'd end up performing poorly. I need to get away to bring the right perspective back to work. I have a boat and enjoy water-skiing and spending time at the beach; those are the things I use as an escape to rejuvenate myself. I also spend a lot of time with the Girl Scout organization; I think it's important to give back to the community, and this is one way to do so. Nonprofit community volunteer activities are actually an excellent way for young women to develop leadership skills in a very low-risk environment, skills they can bring back into the workplace.

I am also involved in a serious and happy relationship with a man who works for DuPont and was trained as a chemical engineer. I have dated men who didn't want me to travel or were intimidated because I made more money than they did, but he doesn't feel the need to change me in any way.

The good thing for women today is that we have choices; the bad thing is that we're not used to it and we don't always take advantage of the choices we have. I believe that women can have it all, even if we can't have it all at the same time. I took care of the career first; now I'm taking care of my personal life.

PRESENT POSITION: Director of Engineering, E. I. DuPont de Nemours and Company

FIELD: Chemical engineering

RESEARCH AREA: Women engineers in the workplace

EDUCATION: B.S. in Chemical Engineering (1977), Purdue University; Certificate of Post Graduate Study in Chemical Engineering (1978), University of Cambridge, England

DATE/PLACE OF BIRTH: April 10, 1955/Chicago, Illinois

Deborah Grubbe lives in Wilmington, Delaware.

INTERVIEW DATE: July 1995

Susan Armstrong Henry

Dean of the Mellon College of Science and Professor of Biological Sciences
CARNEGIE MELLON UNIVERSITY

Susan Henry comes from a long line of strong women. Her grandmother taught her to cook, sew, and garden, encouraged her interest in nature, and instilled in her the importance of being able to stand on her own two feet. After earning a Ph.D. in genetics from Berkeley, she has worked continuously on a single problem—in a virtually linear progression of derivative problems based on an initial set of experiments—since 1968. She attributes her success, in part, to a husband who gave her extraordinary support.

❧

I am often asked why there are so few women in the upper ranks of academic science. I point out that building an academic career in most scientific disciplines requires that an individual pursue a very long and linear course, starting with college, continuing through graduate training and often postdoctoral research, culminating in an academic appointment. It generally takes an additional ten years or more to achieve the rank of full professor, the minimum qualification for most subsequent administrative appointments. Any time out for family or other personal reasons will lengthen the process or derail it entirely. This is, no doubt, one of the principle reasons that women are so underrepresented in the upper ranks of academic science. Women, more often than men, find it necessary to rearrange their careers due to family considerations.

I have been very fortunate in making rapid progress along the career track of an academic scientist. I did not have to take any detours or time out to meet my family obligations, largely due to the support I received from my husband, Peter Henry. He was willing, on numerous occasions, to rearrange his own professional activities to ensure that our family life did not suffer due to my demanding schedule. Without his support and encouragement, I am sure that I would not be where I am today. Many men, but few women, get this level of family support.

My Ph.D. is in genetics, but I consider myself to be a biochemist, a molecular biologist, and a microbiologist as well as a geneticist. The work I do is interdisciplinary, and for that

Susan Armstrong Henry on the campus of the University of Maryland, circa 1966–67

reason I don't feel completely comfortable with any one label. I studied genetics in graduate school, but I also employed biochemistry in my Ph.D. thesis research. My postdoctoral fellowship was given for studies in microbiology and molecular biology, but I did a lot of biochemistry in that research as well. The disciplines of genetics, microbiology, molecular biology, and biochemistry have all contributed tools that I use in my work to solve particular problems.

My research is unusual because I've worked continuously on a single problem since I started my Ph.D. thesis project at Berkeley. I began working on this problem in 1968 and, in one way or another, have continued in a virtually linear fashion on derivative problems based on that initial set of experiments. I have never really changed direction—there have been detours and deflections, but the overall problem has had continuity over time. I have had a single source of funding from the National Institutes of Health (NIH) from 1972 to the present time, without any interruption. This situation is almost unheard of in the current funding climate.

As an undergraduate, I became interested in the question of how cells synthesize their membranes. The membrane is the boundary between the inside and the outside of a cell and it has a distinct chemical composition. The membrane provides a selective barrier between the cell interior and the outside world. It allows in only those things that the cell needs. It must also keep the internal cellular contents, with the exception of waste products, from leaking out. In the cells of higher (eukaryotic) organisms, in addition to the outer (plasma) membrane there are multiple intracellular compartments that have membrane boundaries. The membrane is made up of lipids (fats) and proteins and some other molecules. Some of the membrane-associated proteins are responsible for the active transport mechanisms that selectively take compounds from the extracellular environment and bring them to the interior of the cell. The cell can also modify the properties and func-

tion of the membrane by changing the species of proteins or lipids from which it is composed. Modifications of this sort can occur through metabolic regulation of the biosynthetic pathways responsible for synthesis of the membrane components. The question I asked was: How does the cell regulate the synthesis of the various lipids and how does this synthesis change in response to environmental cues?

At the time I started this research, many other people were studying membranes in different ways, for example, looking at the biochemical and biophysical properties of biological membranes. Other laboratories were exploring the mechanisms by which proteins get into the membranes. I chose to study the synthesis of the lipid components of membranes using biochemical as well as genetic techniques. Using the tools of genetics, biochemistry, and ultimately molecular biology, I asked how the cell regulated the synthesis of the hydrophobic (that is, lipid) components of the membrane.

To do these studies, I had to choose an organism that is easy to analyze and manipulate genetically. People had done successful studies of the sort I envisioned using bacteria, which are easy to work with because they are microorganisms, reproduce rapidly, and are easy to manipulate genetically. Bacteria, however, are prokaryotic organisms and have a relatively primitive cell structure, lacking intracellular compartments. Bacteria also synthesize different membrane lipid components than those found in cells of eukaryotic organisms like ourselves. I wanted to work with a eukaryotic microorganism, and so I chose baker's yeast. At the time I began my research, a great deal of biochemistry had been done on yeast. Furthermore, yeast had been studied classically by geneticists since the earlier part of the century. Because of the extensive genetic analyses that had been done with yeast, many mutants were already available and could be obtained from other laboratories. However, no mutants had been isolated that appeared to have genetic lesions in the enzymes of the pathways I was interested in exploring.

Yeast was, therefore, the obvious choice for the research that I planned. It is a simple unicellular organism that is well characterized, both biochemically and genetically, and it is inexpensive to grow. It is also nonpathogenic and therefore safe and easy to use in a laboratory where students of all levels are working. I set out to exploit those properties to generate a collection of mutants that would define the major enzymatic activities in the pathways of lipid biosynthesis. The first group of mutants I worked on for my thesis were defective in the synthesis of fatty acids. During my postdoctoral research at Brandeis University and my first appointment as an assistant professor at the Albert Einstein College of Medicine, I continued to be interested in lipid synthesis. Over the years, this work has continued and, together with my students, I have been able to define in significant detail the regulation of a key set of reactions leading to the synthesis of membrane lipids in yeast.

Science has been an important part of my life for a very long time. My interest in science emerged in early childhood, and my family encouraged it. I was very close to my paternal grandmother, who was in many respects an old-fashioned "lady." She believed that women should know how to cook, sew, and garden, and she taught me all of these skills and more. She was widowed as a relatively young woman, as were her mother and grandmother. She told me that women had to be able to stand on their own two feet. She had been a teacher before her marriage and was an amateur naturalist, a veritable font of information about the ecology, flora, and fauna of the New England woodlands. She encouraged my interest in nature, calmly identifying all the frogs, snakes, and beetles that I brought home. She never reacted negatively to any of these creatures or implied that young ladies shouldn't collect snakes or insects.

My interest in science continued throughout my schooling, and my father also encouraged me. I went through several stages of interest in science, progressing through botany, astronomy, paleontology, and medicine. My father bought me books about any subject in which I expressed interest, and I spent many hours reading. He also helped me with projects, like building a bubble chamber. He never told me there were things that girls shouldn't do. When the Soviets launched Sputnik, my father took me out to look at the satellite pass overhead. He talked to me about orbits and gravity as well as the politics of science.

I was a part of the "Sputnik generation." After Sputnik, the government and society in general became concerned that American schools were lagging behind the Soviets in math and science. As a result, the government provided more money for school science programs and for research experiences for young people, and I was a beneficiary of this increased funding. One such government-funded science program was given at the NIH in Bethesda, Maryland, near where I lived, in the winter of 1962–63. It involved a special series of lectures on heart disease that were open to high school students. I attended these lectures along with hundreds of other students. Famous scientists and doctors lectured on consecutive Saturdays, and at the end of the program a competitive exam was given. The top ten students were awarded stipends to do summer research in a medical laboratory. I won one of these awards and spent the summer between my junior and senior years doing research in an immunology laboratory at the National Navy Medical Center in Bethesda. There I did skin transplants between groups of inbred strains of mice, trying to work out the genetics of tissue rejection. The specific question I studied was: Were there differences of tissue incompatibility determined by genetic factors carried on the Y (male sex determining) chromosome?

I loved lab work, and I realized that I wanted to pursue a career in medical research. Originally I thought I would become a medical doctor and do research, but I altered my path as a result of several experiences. In 1964 I enrolled at the University of Maryland as a premedical student majoring in zoology. The premedical adviser quickly gave me the facts: very few women were then being admitted to medical school. He told me that a few special schools accepted women and that the major medical schools did admit a few very talented women. The University of Maryland, for example, had admitted a couple of women a year to medical school throughout the last decade. At that time, it was still legal to discriminate against women, and most academics—and the rest of society as well—believed there were good reasons to do so. They believed that women got married, had babies, and wouldn't make use of a professional education. Therefore, why waste a slot in medical school on a person who might never pursue a full career?

After receiving this advice, I reevaluated my situation. I wanted to do medical research and thought perhaps I could find an alternate route. I talked to a number of professors and they suggested graduate school. They told me there was still discrimination in admission to graduate school, but it was not as difficult for a woman to gain admission to graduate school as to medical school. These same professors suggested that I would have a better chance of being admitted to graduate school if I had research experience, so I applied for, and received, an undergraduate National Science Foundation (NSF) grant to do summer research. I worked continuously in the same lab all the way through my undergraduate years with NSF support. For my NSF project, I worked on blood proteins of salamander species and studied their evolutionary relationships under the direction of a zoology professor.

All of the science professors at the University of Maryland during my undergraduate years were men—there were only a few women as instructors and graduate students. However, all of my professors were highly supportive and told me that I had talent for research. Most of the students in my science and math classes were also men. I remember one math class in which there were about two hundred students and I was the only woman.

Susan Henry in her laboratory at Carnegie Mellon University, 1993
PHOTO COURTESY OF CARNEGIE MELLON UNIVERSITY

The professor came in every day and began his lecture by addressing the class, "Lady and gentlemen." I also remember a comparative anatomy lab that I took as a sophomore; I was the only woman in my section, and none of the men wanted to be my lab partner. The man who was assigned to be my partner continually made caustic comments about how I was occupying a spot in the class that could have gone to a man who would go to medical school and ultimately support a family. The teaching assistant for the class addressed the men by their first names, but he referred to me as "Miss Armstrong." One of the men in this same class approached my boyfriend and offered him fifty dollars to get me to drop the class because I was wrecking the curve.

However, these occurrences were minimal irritants. I loved lab work, excelled academically, and received a lot of support and advice from my professors. I decided I would attend graduate school in molecular genetics. During the interview process at one prestigious graduate school, I encountered faculty members who questioned me about my intentions with respect to marriage. Such questions of women applicants were routine at that time. At this same university, a distinguished faculty member told me that he was only interviewing me because of "this damned [Vietnam] war." He said, "We'll only be able to recruit the lame, the halt, the blind, and the women." I did not accept the offer to attend that university; instead I went on to graduate school at the University of California at Berkeley in 1968 with an NSF graduate fellowship. Once enrolled at Berkeley in the genetics Ph.D. program, I never encountered any active discrimination. No one ever made comments on the fact that I was a woman or that I was married. (I had gotten married in the summer of 1968, just before I started graduate studies at Berkeley).

There is a misconception in society that science is carried out by eccentric loners. As a scientist, I've never worked by myself, and in fact most science is done collaboratively. In graduate school many students work on subsets of a bigger problem, and frequently there is collaboration among the students themselves and between laboratories. Science is a very social process that involves sharing equipment, facilities, ideas, and expertise. In the past, I've typically had about a dozen people working in my lab, including graduate students, postdoctoral fellows, a senior technician, and often a number of undergraduate students. The size of my laboratory has decreased since I've become dean because I cannot offer the individual attention required for the training of graduate students, particularly those students in initial stages of thesis research. For this reason, I haven't taken any new Ph.D. students since I became dean of the College of Science.

It's very difficult for any professional person, male or female, to balance all of life's responsibilities. This is not true just for the academic profession. Because of flexibility in scheduling, academic careers are more amenable to family life than some other professions. Basically, the only obligatory thing on my schedule when I was a young professor was teaching my classes. My research schedule was extremely flexible, and other than those days and times when I taught, I could rearrange my schedule at will.

I have always believed that it is important to choose the thing that interests you, something that you are good at, and to do the best you can in pursuing it. I never viewed my education as a bridge to the rest of my life but rather as part of my life that I was going to enjoy. The most important thing that I learned during my formal education was how to keep learning. I have continued to ask questions and to learn new skills throughout my career, and that continues to be exciting.

PRESENT POSITION: Dean of the Mellon College of Science and Professor of Biological Sciences, Carnegie Mellon University

FIELD: Molecular biology

RESEARCH AREA: Molecular genetics of yeast, lipid biochemistry

EDUCATION: B.S. in Zoology (1968), University of Maryland; Ph.D. in Genetics (1971), University of California at Berkeley

DATE/PLACE OF BIRTH: June 27, 1946/Alexandria, Virginia

Susan Henry lives in Pittsburgh, Pennsylvania, with her husband. She has a daughter and a son.

INTERVIEW DATE: July 1994

Esther A. H. Hopkins

Deputy General Counsel
MASSACHUSETTS DEPARTMENT OF ENVIRONMENTAL PROTECTION

Esther A. H. Hopkins transcended poverty, racism, and an early marriage that tried to mold her into a traditional role, before earning a Ph.D. in biophysical chemistry from Yale University and a law degree from Suffolk University. She worked as a scientist for Polaroid Corporation, as a patent attorney, and as a liaison between the company's patent department and the engineers and scientists working on project development before accepting a new position as chief fiscal counsel to the Massachusetts State Department of Environmental Protection.

❧

I was born in Stamford, Connecticut. My family was poor: My mother worked in domestic service, and my dad was a chauffeur for a number of years and then a custodian at a church. My father never finished high school and my mother didn't complete primary school, and they very much wanted education for their children. I have two brothers, one older and one younger. I started school at the same time as my older brother. I accompanied my mother to register my brother for kindergarten, and the teacher suggested—I think because I was physically bigger than he was—that if I took and passed a test I could also start school. I passed the test and at three and a half entered kindergarten. My brother and I went through all of elementary school together.

In junior high boys and girls were separated, but there was only one high school in the town at the time, so everyone came back together for those years. I was in the precollege track taking chemistry, biology, and physics because I knew as early as junior high

that I wanted to be a brain surgeon. There was a woman doctor in Stamford who had an office in one of the buildings my father cleaned. She was a physician and a graduate of Boston University Medical School. I wanted to be just like her, so I took as many science courses as I could and hoped someday to attend Boston University.

Thankfully my older brother wasn't as interested in school as I was. My parents could only scrape together enough money to send

Esther A. H. Hopkins in a recent photo
PHOTO COPYRIGHT 1995 BY C.A.K. MAINFRAME
PHOTOGRAPHICS

one of us to college, and had he wanted to go, he would have been the one sent because he was older and he was a boy. His lack of interest provided a great opportunity for me.

I spent a lot of time at the YWCA during my teenage years, although those are not all fond memories. The guidance teachers there did not encourage black children to study anything of significance; in fact, they actively discouraged us. I remember being at a YWCA banquet when a woman guidance counselor asked what I was interested in doing with my life. I told her that I wanted to be a brain surgeon; she totally ignored my response and suggested that I look into hair dressing. I was flabbergasted and hurt, but comments like that didn't discourage me from pursuing my dream.

I applied to Boston University in the premed program and was accepted; I remember my mother scrubbing people's toilets so that we could afford the tuition. When I arrived on campus in the fall of 1943 and the dean of women realized that I was black, she told me that there was no room in the dormitories for me, so I lived off campus.

I remember the day that I was in an organic chemistry class and decided to major in chemistry rather than in biology. I liked the reasoning in chemistry; in those days biology was a descriptive science that involved more memorization than reasoning. So I majored in chemistry and applied to medical schools when the war was over. However, medical schools were admitting mostly men and people with master's degrees, and so I didn't get in. I must have cried for a week, until a woman graduate student said, "So, you didn't get in; what *are* you going to do with yourself?" That really shook me up, and I decided to go to graduate school in chemistry.

I entered a master's program in physical organic chemistry at Howard University in 1947. When I finished my degree I got a job at the Howard Medical School in physiology. That's when I found out that I wouldn't have made such a good doctor. Some of my work required me to interact with people in the

clinic instead of working with test tubes, as I had been doing. One research project required preparing electrolyte solutions to administer to people with certain conditions. These were real, live people, and I found the situation fraught with emotional tension. I remember the looks of the patients when you'd come into the room wearing a lab coat (they didn't know who was a doctor and who wasn't); they looked at you as if you were God. But I understood how little the doctors really knew: this was before sulfa drugs, and there were very few things that physicians could actually cure. The emotional pressure was more than I could have taken. I learned that what happens to you often happens for the best, although sometimes I wonder if that's my rationalization for not getting into medical school.

After the medical school job, I accepted a job teaching chemistry at Virginia State College in Petersburg, Virginia, then a historically black college. I was moving farther and farther south into environments that were vastly different from what I had grown up with. It really was culture shock. Until I came to Howard, I had never been in an environment that was mostly black. The state college and the community of Petersburg were also predominantly black. For the first time in my life my race was not the first thing people noticed about me. It was wonderful to be in situations where there were a lot of black people, especially black women.

I married for the first time right after I left Virginia State. My first husband was Liberian, and we had a daughter. Although I met my husband when we were in graduate school together at Boston University, he really wanted a wife who was more domestic than I—willing to stay home and care for the children and the house. When he finished his graduate work he wanted me to go back to Africa with him, and I simply wasn't interested.

In 1953 I returned to Stamford, Connecticut, where I worked in a variety of settings: a small pharmaceutical chemistry plant, a hospital, a medical research institute in

Ridgefield, Connecticut, and then a research lab at Cyanamid Corporation. It soon became obvious that having only a master's degree in chemistry was a problem for me: companies wouldn't hire me at a bachelor's level because they didn't want to pay me more, nor would they hire me at a Ph.D. level without the degree. I decided to earn a Ph.D. in chemistry and I went off to Yale.

I received a traineeship (tuition plus a small stipend) for my first year of study from the U.S. Public Health Service and began working for Dr. Wang. At that time, I had a daughter in the sixth grade and a son in preschool. I always think of my son and myself as Yale's oddest couple: he went to the nursery school, and I was in graduate school. The nursery school was housed in the School of Theology, and their philosophy was to show young children that adults in addition to their parents loved them. It was a wonderful environment, and I never worried about my son's welfare. My son grew up thinking that fathers went to work and mothers went to school.

My current husband, whom I married in 1959, was working as a social worker for the city of New Haven when I was at Yale. We had the two children and lived on the same budget that most of my husband's welfare clients lived on. Thankfully I received a scholarship from the Negro Business and Professional Women's Club, which helped us out financially. Shortly after I began at Yale, the university reexamined the amount of stipends awarded to graduate students for traineeships and teaching and research fellowships and increased the amounts. We were no longer the single, just out of college, graduate students of earlier days.

There were eight women in my graduate class of thirty at Yale; many people thought that was a lot. Yale had always had women in the graduate school, but they had almost always been foreign women. The women in my class were mostly American. There were some faculty members who felt we were taking slots away from men and that we wouldn't stick it out. They fussed a lot, but that didn't influ-ence me. The next year, however, Yale accepted fewer women into the graduate program. The undergraduate program went coed during my graduate studies, so women were becoming more and more a part of the culture at Yale.

My graduate research was in biophysical chemistry. I was interested in a chemical model for an active site for an enzyme and the kinetics of a model enzymatic reaction. I worked in a polar nonaqueous medium using alkaline metals to catalyze a reaction. The work involved measuring the energy released with spectrophotometry; it took advantage of using luciferase from lightning bugs because of their production of adenosine triphosphate (ATP).

There were no women academics in the chemistry department at Yale when I was there. I had been very active with the American Chemical Society during my graduate years, and at one point we did a survey of women chemists in the academy: we found very few. I thought carefully about my alternatives. For all of my professional life I had been a woman in a male-dominated environment and a black person in a white-dominated environment, and I didn't want to do that anymore. I also didn't want to work as a Ph.D. in a hospital where M.D.'s ran the show. So I decided to accept an offer from Polaroid Corporation in Massachusetts.

One of the vice presidents at Polaroid Corporation was familiar with my work. They were interviewing Yale graduate students, and this was also a time when a number of companies were particularly looking for black professionals. Here was a black woman professional with a Ph.D. from Yale saying, "I'd like to come and work here." It didn't take much for them to hire me. I ended up working at Polaroid for twenty-two years. I worked in the analytical lab, a part of the research laboratories, and supervised a small group in the emulsion lab, where we did various kinds of photographic coatings.

One day I ran into a colleague whom I hadn't seen in a long time, and he mentioned that he was in law school. I recall hearing myself reply that if I had it to do all over again, I would go to law school. I had been interested in patent law for some time because I could combine scientific work with my legal interests. So I applied to law school and was accepted into a night program at Suffolk. At the same time I applied for a "career exposure" program where I could spend nine months working in a different field within Polaroid; I was transferred to the patent department and worked closely with the people in the research labs where I had previously worked. Because I spoke their language, I found the work satisfying. Life was hectic working full-time and going to school at night. I wanted to maintain some of my extracurricular activities, so I gave up housekeeping. I firmly believed, and still do, that the washing machine, dishwasher, and vacuum cleaner don't care about the sex of the person pushing the button. My husband was very understanding and helpful, as were my children, who were used to a working mother.

I stayed at Polaroid for eleven years after I completed law school, working in a business development group within the film division. I served as a liaison between the lawyers in the patent office and the engineers and scientists who were working on new products. It was the best of all worlds for me; but when Polaroid downsized, the division was eliminated and I retired after twenty-two years.

About six months later I interviewed with the Massachusetts Department of Environmental Protection. They were looking for two lawyers, one who knew environmental law and one who was interested in contracts and fiscal matters. I have worked here since 1989. I have responsibilities for contracts, grants, and trusts; I advise on conflict-of-interest issues; and I handle various personnel matters.

I've grown to know my strengths. I'm best at refining, editing, elaborating on, and amending others' ideas and looking for ramifications of other people's work. That's been a constant in all of my careers—as a chemist, a patent lawyer, and as chief fiscal counsel. I have also always known how important it is to maintain balance in my life. Religion and music have provided this balance for me: I sang with the Choral Arts Society as an undergraduate; I was an organist at a church when I was working at the medical school; and I ran a men and boy's choir in Petersburg when I was at Virginia State. Currently I serve in the choir, play the organ and the piano, and even preach sermons when asked. I am a trustee at Boston University, and I've also worked with the local and national board of the YWCA and the alumni association at Boston University. In October 1995 I received the Boston University General Alumni Association Award for Distinguished Service to the Alma Mater. I have a hard time saying no, but I have a full and rich life. I only wish I could find more time for sleep!

PRESENT POSITION: Deputy General Counsel, Massachusetts Department of Environmental Protection

FIELDS: Chemistry, law

SPECIALTY: Patent law

EDUCATION: A.B. in Chemistry (1947), Boston University; M.S. in Physical Organic Chemistry (1948), Howard University; M.S. in Biophysical Chemistry (1962), Yale University; Ph.D. in Biophysical Chemistry (1967), Yale University; J.D. (1977), Suffolk University.

DATE/PLACE OF BIRTH: September 18, 1926/Stamford, Connecticut

Esther Hopkins lives with her husband in Framingham, Massachusetts.

INTERVIEW DATE: May 1995

Wen-Ling Hsu

Information Systems Research Scientist
Bell Laboratories, AT&T

Wen-Ling Hsu's mother provided a strong model: she worked as a teacher in Taiwan at a time when most women didn't work, and she raised seven children, kept house, cooked meals, and maintained a beautiful garden. Hsu ignored the warnings of those around her who said that science wasn't appropriate for women, confident that the person who is good at her work will not be discriminated against. She earned a B.S. in computer science and a Ph.D. in management information systems, and learned that it's not necessarily true that good work speaks for itself. Her mother now helps her to balance her career and family.

❧

Growing up as the youngest in a family of seven children—five girls and two boys, with an eighteen-year age difference between me and my oldest sister—I've always had the luxury of strong family support, plenty of at-tention, and the opportunity to be independent. This unusual combination contributed to the strong sense of security I feel today.

I grew up in Taiwan, where the educational system is quite different from that in the United States. In Taiwan, women were tradi-tionally discouraged from entering the sciences and engineering and channeled instead into more "feminine" fields such as art, the human-ities, and home economics. In tenth grade, every student has to decide between two cur-ricular paths: science and engineering, or arts and humanities. Prior to taking the college-entrance examination, each student also has to rank all the departments in all the universities according to interest. Unfortunately, the de-mand for jobs often takes precedence over the student's personal interests when he or she fills out the preference list. The list and the stu-dent's score in the national college examina-tion determine the university and department where the student will study. The difference of

Wen-Ling Hsu in her office at Bell Labs, Murray Hill, New Jersey

a quarter point may result in a major in physics instead of one in textile engineering. Transferring at any stage in college is no trivial matter either.

Having made up my mind to become a scientist at a very young age, I consider myself lucky to have actually become one, although not the white-lab-coat kind I had envisioned as a child. As it turned out, I was admitted as a computer science major to National Chiao-Tung University (an absolutely "geeky" school). Only 59 other women were there among the 2,300 students on campus; 12 women were in my class year. I was lucky that there was one other female member in my major class.

Naturally, the sixty of us attracted a lot of attention. In the Taiwanese educational system, men and women attend different high schools, so my male classmates hadn't dealt with women socially in schools. Most of them fell into two categories: they were either buddy-buddy and treated me as though I were one of the guys, or they thought I was a strange species. It was tough at first trying to be friends with my colleagues—being able to blend in but keeping my female identity. I will never forget my first day on campus. I was really into swimming laps in those days, so the first place I checked out was the pool. Upon finishing my laps, I looked up and saw the high-rise dormitories with their windows surrounding the pool. Hundreds of men had flocked to the windows to look at a woman swimming in the pool!

Still, I never felt discriminated against in school. As a whole, women were treated well. Seats were always reserved for us in class—in the front row. There were only two women in computer science, so neither of us could cut class—it would be conspicuous even without the reserved seats. Membership fees for societies on campus were always waived for women. Women were escorted door to door at every event. Learning to live with such attention was not easy, but the skill of learning to be at ease under pressure benefited me tremendously in later years. I never felt threatened by prejudice or stereotyping throughout my years in undergraduate or graduate school.

My choice of graduate school was really chance. I had applied to several master's and doctoral programs in the field of computer science. I had chosen to go to the University of Illinois but decided to defer admission for a year, partly for financial reasons and partly for personal reasons: I wanted to spend some time with my parents while working as a computer engineer in a pulp factory in my hometown. During that year, I went to a conference and met Andrew Whinston, a professor of management information systems at Purdue University, who single-handedly changed my career destiny. After I talked to Andy and completed all the graduate school application procedures, Krannert School of Business at Purdue University offered me a full scholarship for Ph.D. study in information systems. I turned down Illinois, accepted Purdue's offer, and Andy became my graduate adviser.

Although Andy was supervising a dozen or so doctoral students, he somehow was able to meet with every one of us individually at least every other day. He would give us research papers to read daily on top of our course work. Because I didn't have a degree or background in business and management, I had to take all the business prerequisite courses along with the required courses in the Ph.D. program. I chose a minor field in econometrics since the language barrier is much smaller in mathematics. Meeting with Andy on weekends to discuss research was a routine. For three and a half years of graduate school I did not distinguish between weekends and weekdays. Learning to focus and concentrate has helped me achieve many goals.

I planned to finish graduate school in three or four years and gain some teaching experience. I also wanted other experiences along the way, and was drawn to work as a staff resident in the graduate hall. Staff residents help newer graduate-student residents settle in, provide counseling when needed, and hold social activities for them. In return, a staff resident receives free room and board. It was unusual for a foreign student to become a staff resident; however, it was an excellent opportunity for me to meet people, socialize, and learn about American as well as international culture. Good fortune looked after me again, and I got the job. It turned out to be one of the most enjoyable experiences and responsibilities I've ever had in my life. Even today, I encourage foreign students in the United States to learn about American culture as much as possible—it's important to know about the country you're living in.

It's almost painful to think about my thesis topic: designing a programming language for decision support systems. I came up with a language paradigm called "Functional, Logic, Object-Oriented Language" or FLOO. (I thought FOOL would have been a cute name, but my adviser didn't agree!) The reason it's painful to think about is because I did not pursue this area any further, and object-oriented programming really took off and became widely used a decade later!

After graduation I took a faculty position in management information systems at Carnegie Mellon University for seven years (the last two years were spent on leave at Siemens Corporate Research). Life at CMU was challenging, interesting, and intellectual. There were few boundaries between the different schools, which encouraged all sorts of multidisciplinary research activity. There was information system–related research in just about every department at the time. Research in the field of information systems is especially fertile in such an environment.

I started out doing research in scheduling systems for manufacturing environments. A factory is a dynamic environment. Traditional optimization approaches break down when dealing with reality in a dynamic environment. Human experts' simple heuristics often replace complicated mathematical modeling in shop-floor scheduling. My challenge at the time was to create an approach that integrated operations research, artificial intelligence, and human computer interface techniques for decision support. My colleague and I built a decision support framework that included modeling human problem solving, improving the performance of problem solving algorithmi-

cally, and incorporating a friendly interface that "coincides" with human thinking. The buzzword we created was "coincident problem spaces." In plain words, it means that the interface is intuitive to human users, and the software system and humans think alike. When our system was deployed and used by an expert human scheduler successfully, my sense of accomplishment was definitely more than publishing a paper!

Being a faculty member is equivalent to holding two full-time jobs: one for research and the other for teaching. Although I truly had fun doing research, it took me a few years to learn the skills of running research projects and reenergizing the continuing research. (Unless you are a true genius, no one can deny that funding support helps tremendously in keeping research momentum going.) I also enjoyed being a teacher. Some of my own teachers have had a great influence on me, and I've always looked up to them as my role models. Being a professor at a very young age made me enjoy my students even more. In one of the first classes I taught, I was the youngest person in the class. Still, they were all my "kids."

Just about everyone in my family is or was a teacher—my sister, my mother, even my in-laws. One of my sisters was a professor when I was an undergraduate. I always aspired to the great balance of work and family that she had. Unfortunately, I did not time my life right—I left academia before I started my family.

Meeting Guy and getting married all seemed natural to me, although it might have appeared unusual to an observer. He was a graduate student in computer science while I was a faculty member at CMU. He was a Jewish American who grew up in the heart of Brooklyn, and I was from a rural town in Taiwan. Yet somehow we never seemed foreign to each other. When his career path led us to New Jersey, I thought I would try working in an industrial research laboratory and took a two-year leave from my faculty position. I spent my two-year leave at Siemens Corporate Research (SCR) as a research scientist in the

Wen-Ling Hsu (on right), her daughter, Kira Wei-Hsin, husband, Guy Jacobson, and mother, Amei Yang, on a cruise in 1995

Department of Factory Automation Research, and later in the Department of Machine Learning. Most of my research at SCR related to manufacturing decision support systems and distributed systems. In one of our projects, we designed distributed intelligent agents that automatically built a conceptual model of the factory environment (for example, average processing time throughout), and these agents used this model to monitor and control the shop floor. In another project, we designed and implemented a prototype power distribution system that allowed power sources to negotiate and coordinate with each other whenever there was a problem with the power supply.

At SCR I began to change; I found myself becoming very practical when viewing research, interested in how an idea or a concept would be used or applied. Although I liked the intellectual environment, the individual thinking, and the freedom of research in an academic setting, I also liked working in an applied lab where I had to deal directly with problems and applications. I was happy to rid myself of the worries about resources to fund my research when I made a decision to leave my tenure-track position in the university and stay in industry.

I now work for AT&T Bell Labs as a full-time member of the technical staff (their title for research scientists). I work in the consumer lab, which specializes in consumer research and new service concept testing and analysis. In one of my early assignments, I participated in a project requested by the U.S. Treasury Department to create a depreciation model for telecommunications plants. It's easy to price a used car; there is always a blue book that can tell you the resale market value. But telephone networks and equipment are more like computers; the technology evolves very quickly and there is no resale market for old networks. Our job was to create a methodology that would help the government to determine the value of telecommunications plants; it was a challenging task. On top of that, we had a difficult hurdle to overcome: in a company as large as AT&T, detailed data aren't always readily available. The telephone network is vast and complex and involves many different components of different technology of many versions. Factoring in all the elements of the network is nearly impossible. In the end, our team was able to come up with an aggregated approach to model the network. We all felt proud of our accomplishment.

Virtually every project I work on now is

done in a team. The number of people on each team can vary from two to twenty (or more), depending on the scope and complexity of the project. Most of the time, people from AT&T business units are involved because they often bring to us the applications. If we are lucky, an application will come along with existing problem statements, data, and associated processes. Otherwise, we'll only have a story or a mission, and then the team needs to articulate a goal statement and determine an approach to accomplish that goal. Problem solving includes not only how to use technology but also how to coordinate organizational issues, deal with existing processes, obtain data for analysis, and create approaches to the solution. Solving a problem can take weeks to months and sometimes even years.

Most of my days are spent in meetings with others. I spend my remaining time reading and, if possible, writing. Sometimes meetings will take up all of my time, and then I have to complete the rest of my work at home. Reading and thinking are best done alone, quietly; then I can bring ideas back to the group for discussion. Following ongoing research is fun, especially in the field I currently focus on: the Internet. I enjoy bridging the gap between research and applications: identifying potential applications for research and searching for research results or ongoing research that meet the needs of business problems. Problem solving is challenging and rewarding. For me the most exciting part is "structuring the unstructured." More often than not, we are given a problem in the form of a bunch of unstructured information. The true challenge lies in finding a way to organize thoughts and structure the information so that it becomes useful and relevant. At that point, a plan for problem solving can be made. Problems don't get solved in meetings. A meeting is a place where you can exchange thoughts with your peers, identify issues, and brainstorm. The real work happens after meetings when one can do his or her own thinking.

I first began thinking about issues of women in science when I was working at Siemens.

Again, I was only one of a handful of female scientists out of a group of about a hundred. My major career change came when I joined Bell Labs. In our lab, there are more people with multidisciplinary backgrounds, and the ratio of women is substantially higher than that in a computer science lab. For the first time in my life I've discovered the joy of chatting with others about the daily-life issues a woman faces—especially after the birth of my daughter, Kira Wei-Hsin. After Kira was born I found that there are many things that women are forced to think about concerning their careers. I chose to work part-time for a while, but I was driving myself crazy by constantly working close to full-time hours and still feeling behind in my work. I didn't want to be a part-time mother or a part-time worker; I couldn't give up either one. With a live-in nanny and the help of my mother, I returned to a full-time schedule. Still, I am struggling to find a way to balance my family and my career.

I feel very lucky to have had my mother's influence in my life. In her own quiet way she has always been supportive to my whole family. She is now seventy-nine years old and can boast of having a career herself—quite unusual for a woman of her generation in Taiwan. She was a schoolteacher for forty-odd years and successfully raised seven children. It was more difficult in her generation because she was unequivocally expected to care for the household. In the morning, she would get up at 5:00 A.M. to make breakfast for everyone and pack lunch boxes for us children—not merely sandwiches—a Chinese lunch box is a full meal. She would also come home to make lunch for my father and herself, and then go back to work. Returning home around 5:30, she'd have our entire family dinner ready at 6:30 sharp. On top of this she kept a beautiful garden and allowed us to keep a variety of pets. She managed her time miraculously well and was always prepared. Although she was a determined person herself, she never imposed her ways on my siblings or me. Her open-minded and supportive nature also made her the most popular mother among all of our friends. It was no surprise to us that in 1980 Taiwan's president, Deng Huei Li, presented her with the National Mother's Award.

When I decided on a career in technology, she was worried, but she never said I couldn't do it. Although I heard a hint of objection, I was allowed to make my own decisions. There was never any doubt in my mind what I wanted to do. I was surprised when other people told me it was not appropriate for a woman to study science or engineering. A friend of my brother's even sent me a long letter explaining how difficult it would be for a female to be in engineering or science. Certainly these people acted out of good intentions. Still, I followed my heart and went ahead.

I have always believed that as long as an individual could compete, it didn't matter whether you were female or male. As long as you were good at your work, you wouldn't be discriminated against. As I grew older, I learned that this is not necessarily true, but the belief gave me the momentum I needed to get where I am today.

PRESENT POSITION: Member of technical staff, Bell Laboratories, AT&T

FIELD: Information systems

RESEARCH AREA: Internet dynamics, distributed artificial intelligence, manufacturing information systems

EDUCATION: B.S. in Computer Science (1982), National Chiao-Tung University; Ph.D. in Management Information Systems (1986), Purdue University

DATE/PLACE OF BIRTH: February 2, 1960/Hualien, Taiwan

Wen-Ling Hsu lives with her husband, daughter, and mother in New Jersey.

INTERVIEW DATE: April 1995

Linda Huff

President
HUFF AND HUFF, INC.

Inspired by a high school chemistry teacher and encouraged by her parents, Linda Huff entered Purdue as the only woman in her chemical engineering class. Treated equally by her classmates and the faculty, she first encountered sexism when she began interviewing for jobs. Even those attitudes didn't affect her: she realized the men weren't judging her as an individual and that, given the opportunity, she could change their opinions. Luckily she didn't need to; she was hired by a firm where being a woman wasn't an issue. When she and her husband decided they wanted more flexibility in both family and career, they founded their own environmental consulting firm.

&

I am a chemical engineer and the president of Huff and Huff, Inc., a sixteen-person environmental consulting firm. We work with a variety of clients ranging from industry and transportation to individual communities and private developers. Our project area extends from the Mississippi River to the eastern part of the United States, although we also do some work in California. We focus on all types of environmental problems: air emissions, underground storage tanks, ground water and soil remediation, hazardous waste management, training of industrial personnel in hazardous waste and hazardous materials regulations, and measurement and abatement of noise. Besides my chemical engineer husband and myself, we employ a biologist, a geologist, a hydrologist, a historian, four civil engineers, a mechanical engineer, and another chemical engineer. For a small firm, we have great diversity in both personnel and projects.

One of our current projects involves a municipality concerned with the impact of ammonia in a stream. They've reduced the concentration as low as possible but question whether what's left is still affecting the stream. We collect samples to determine the quality of the water. We also conduct biological surveys where we collect aquatic insects and fish, not-

Linda Huff leaning on part of a soil vapor extraction unit
PHOTO COURTESY OF HUFF AND HUFF, INC.

ing the types of diversity and how they change as you go downstream. We've set up various sampling stations above and below the discharge. If there's a big difference between upstream and downstream locations and other conditions are equal, this helps in our analysis of the impact of the pollutant on the stream.

One of our more interesting projects involved roadwork on Chicago's Lakeshore Drive, along Lake Michigan. Our job was to find out as much as we could about the material that was used to fill in the lakeshore to create the roadbed. Among other things, we had to research historical records like park district meeting notes to determine the source of the fill material. It turned out some areas contained ashes from the Chicago fire of 1871. The variety of projects keeps me engaged and excited about my work even after sixteen years of owning my own firm.

I am a middle child with one sister and one brother. I grew up in a rural area outside of Columbus, Ohio, and spent a lot of time reading, especially in the summer, because there wasn't much else to do. We had a large vegetable garden and I sold vegetables, which I absolutely hated because I was very shy as a child.

I remember getting my first chemistry set at age nine, but my real interest in chemical engineering was sparked by a wonderful high school chemistry teacher. She inspired many of us, and eventually she went back for her Ph.D. I was intrigued by the subject, even though I remember her telling us that it was really hard to make a living in chemistry. Neither of my parents had a college degree, but both worked in the aeronautical industry with a lot of engineers. I was always good at math and science, and my parents encouraged each of us to do whatever we wanted to do. My father kept telling me that engineering was a wonderful field full of opportunities. Because I liked chemistry, I became interested in chemical engineering. I had never met a chemical engineer until I went to college. What's funny is that I took a test in high school that indicated that I'd do pretty well in most areas, but engineering

was last on the list. So of course I picked engineering. I've always risen to challenges.

I was the only woman in my chemical engineering classes at Purdue. It didn't hit me during my freshman year because the core math and science classes included females from other majors. But the first chemical engineering class in my sophomore year was interesting—everyone who came in sat at least one seat away from me. I ended up in this little isolated island. That didn't last long, and eventually I felt like I had a hundred brothers. I never felt that my peers viewed me as any less able than they. I never had a woman engineering professor; I saw my first women chemical engineers when I began interviewing for jobs.

That's also when I ran into my first experience with sexism. An interviewer with one company told me they didn't hire single women for their research facilities. Another told me they wouldn't hire me because in three years I'd be married and pregnant and they'd be left high and dry. When I told my male classmates this, they actually created a petition because they were so upset that someone would even think, let alone say, these types of things. Despite these negative experiences, I realized that the interviewers weren't really judging me as an individual because they didn't know me. I was insulted by the way they viewed women, but I always felt that, given an opportunity to prove myself, these types of opinions would change.

My first job was with Procter and Gamble in food product research. It was a wonderful job—both creative and technical, at a really dynamic firm. I never felt that being a woman in this company was detrimental to my work.

Jim and I married in April 1971, a year after I graduated, when I was working for Procter and Gamble in Cincinnati and Jim was working on his master's degree at Purdue. We didn't want to live apart, so I went to personnel and asked if I could work three or four days a week so that I could commute between West Lafayette, Indiana, and Cincinnati, Ohio. They couldn't imagine my position being part-time

Linda Huff digging soil pits during wetland delineation
PHOTO COURTESY OF HUFF AND HUFF, INC.

(remember, this was the early seventies), and I understood their concern. So I did the "traditional" thing and left Procter and Gamble and moved back to Purdue to be with my husband. I helped Jim with his master's degree; I did some of his literature review and helped with the lab tests so that we could get him out of school sooner. After his graduation, we decided to live in the Chicago area, and because of my interest in environmental engineering, I ended up accepting a job in the first regional office of the newly formed U.S. Environmental Protection Agency. Basically, my section consisted of five people in a warehouse. I was in the water division, developing permit regulations for industrial water pollution discharges. I evaluated industrial discharges of pollutants to determine levels that would be acceptable to drinking-water quality of streams in Indiana and Illinois. I stayed with the EPA for three years, working part-time in the last year while pursuing an M.B.A. full-time at the University of Chicago.

I decided to go back for an M.B.A. for a number of reasons. My job was losing its challenge; as the staff grew it had become increasingly bureaucratic with a lot of paperwork. I had also become interested in economics as a result of my job, seeing the economic effect of pollution laws on different people and industrial sectors. Finally, the state of Illinois was interested in developing regulations that required economic evaluations of all their environmental laws as they passed them. I decided that I wanted to specialize in the economic effects of environmental regulations. While the M.B.A program didn't offer exactly what I wanted, the school offered courses related to the effects of industrial organizations and the economic effects of regulations in general. It looked like a great field to enter at an opportune time.

Another factor that prompted my leaving the EPA and entering the M.B.A. program was that Jim and I sat on opposite sides of the table, literally, because he was with Mobil Oil at the time. I'd brief my boss, he'd brief his boss, and then we'd all meet. It wasn't adversarial, but it was uncomfortable, and we decided that we'd rather work on the same side. It was at this point that we thought we'd try to find jobs together, and we took each other's résumé when one of us had a job interview outside the Chicago area. We met with considerable resistance over a husband-wife combination. One company in Connecticut wanted to hire us, but specifically not in the same department. They were worried about what might happen if we had an argument on the way to work, or the effects of one of us becoming the boss and the other the subordinate. We didn't think these scenarios would be issues between us, but the personnel department didn't agree. (The one offer we both received from the same company was to work in a plant in Texas, but that didn't appeal to either of us.)

By this time Jim had left Mobil Oil and was working at the ITT Research Institute, a not-for-profit organization that performs research on industrial and governmental projects. When Jim told his boss that I was graduating and suggested that his department could benefit from my expertise in the environmental area, they hired me on a part-time basis. The part-time work allowed me an opportunity to attempt to market myself for smaller projects. Then Jim and I decided that this was the perfect time to begin a family, hoping that we could job-share one position. When I became pregnant, Jim's boss said the personnel department couldn't accept such an arrangement because of insurance and benefits complications, so he offered to give Jim leave as requested and I would continue to work on a part-time basis. We would have taken him up on this flexible arrangement if a really great job hadn't cropped up for Jim at an industrial chemical company. I stayed with my part-time job at ITT Research Institute through the eighth month of pregnancy.

Laura was born November 6, 1976, the day that Purdue beat Michigan in football, and for the next three years I worked on my own. It was the perfect situation: I worked when Laura napped. Three years later our son was born, and Jim and I incorporated as Huff and Huff, Inc., the same month. The reason we joined forces and incorporated was that I was getting more and more work, primarily from the state of Illinois, and with a second child I would either have to stop working or we would have to do the work together. Jim agreed and told his boss that I had made him an offer he couldn't refuse.

I became president because I had spent three years building the clientele. We found office space, moved the business out of our house, and hired a baby-sitter. We worked when we had work, and we played when there wasn't any work. We always let the work come to us; we didn't do any marketing, and we didn't make any cold calls. We never really worried much about failure because we figured that if the company didn't make it we could always get jobs somewhere else. We never really got frantic when there wasn't anything to do; we figured something would come up sooner or later. Our firm basically grew at the rate of about a person a year. We were not trying to grow; our goals were to be involved professionally, build and maintain a good reputation, and have time for our kids. We took turns going on field trips and helping with things like the scouting troops, Indian Guides, T-ball, and soccer. It was a very relaxed life until about 1991, when the environmental area exploded. It's much more work now.

Jim and I find that, as our company has become larger and taken on more complex projects, it is harder to leave work behind at the end of the day. The kids know a lot about the business, which I've decided isn't so good because often it's the problems that we bring home and discuss. I don't want them to see only the difficulties and not realize how much fun we have had and continue to have in our careers. Also, they only remember the last few years when things have gotten really busy, not the early years that allowed us to spend so much time with them. I'd like them to understand how good our lives have been and continue to be because I believe that family history has a real impact on future life. My mother and Jim's mother worked, so we both expected women to have careers and families. Furthermore, because Jim grew up in a family with four boys and a working mother, he was used to doing domestic chores. This has been very important to our marriage.

I am in a field (consulting) that is still male dominated, especially at the partner level. I am the first woman on the board of directors for the Consulting Engineering Council of Illinois. I am usually the only woman at the meetings, unless my colleagues bring their wives. Not many women have their own consulting firms, although it's an area that's ideal for women because the independence allows a mixing of personal and professional goals. Women will catch up—there are increasing numbers of women in the environmental and consulting fields; we just need to get them into the executive positions. I believe that demographics in these fields will look very different in another ten years!

PRESENT POSITION: President, Huff and Huff, Inc.

FIELD: Chemical engineering, environmental engineering

RESEARCH AREA: Environmental assessments, economic impact and risk assessment

EDUCATION: B.S. in Chemical Engineering (1970), Purdue University; M.B.A. (1975), University of Chicago

DATE/PLACE OF BIRTH: August 1948/Columbus, Ohio

Linda Huff lives with her husband, Jim, and son, Tim, who is a sophomore in high school. Her daughter, Laura, is currently enrolled at Rice University and is majoring in chemical engineering, English, and Spanish.

INTERVIEW DATE: July 1995

Shirley Ann Jackson

Chairman
NUCLEAR REGULATORY COMMISSION

Shirley Jackson's life is full of firsts: she was the first African American woman to earn a doctorate in any field from the Massachusetts Institute of Technology, and she is the first woman and the first African American to serve as chairman of the Nuclear Regulatory Commission (NRC). She is a theoretical physicist who has worked in both industry and academe.

❧

I was sworn in as a commissioner of the Nuclear Regulatory Commission in May 1995 and then, two months later, appointed by President Clinton as its chairman. The NRC regulates the uses of nuclear materials and technology throughout the United States to ensure the protection of public health, safety, and the environment. That is our overarching mission. Specifically, our responsibility includes regulation of more than one hundred commercial nuclear power plants, about a dozen fuel cycle facilities, and more than seven thousand licensees of nuclear materials used in medicine, research, and industrial applications. And finally, the agency has an additional responsibility to ensure the safe storage, transport, and disposal of nuclear materials and waste.

Several issues are currently at the forefront of my job. One involves aging nuclear power plants, specifically ensuring that licensees pinpoint potential problem areas and address and correct them promptly. Another involves the anticipated deregulation of all electric utilities, which will in time transform the power industry as we know it. There will be increased price competition from a variety of generation sources. Already energy compa-

nies are restructuring or merging in order to position themselves for a more competitive environment. Some nuclear power plants, in the face of strong competition, may close down short of the forty years permitted by their NRC licenses. In those instances, it is our job to ensure that they have the funds to decommission their plants safely.

Other nuclear plant owners are considering applying to the NRC to extend their licenses

Shirley Jackson, chairman of the Nuclear Regulatory Commission, 1995
PHOTO COURTESY OF THE NUCLEAR REGULATORY COMMISSION

for an additional twenty years, in which case we must make sure they take whatever prudent steps are necessary to assure continued safe operations.

Another complex issue arises over the question of disposal of spent reactor fuel (high-level nuclear waste). By law, the Department of Energy has the task of developing a permanent repository for nuclear waste, with the NRC providing a license upon a determination that the disposal can be effected in a manner that protects public health and safety. As you can imagine, a good deal of controversy surrounds the question of where and how to dispose of nuclear waste.

So, as this sampling demonstrates, the issues I must confront each working day are technically challenging and politically sensitive, and they also have cost implications that we cannot lose sight of. Nuclear energy provides about 20 percent of the nation's electricity. Nuclear materials in the hands of skillful physicians save lives and in industrial applications help promote a healthy economy. But everything we do at the NRC is consistent with our primary mandate to protect the public health and safety and the environment.

You would not be surprised, then, to learn that my workday typically runs twelve to thirteen hours? That includes a quick sandwich at my desk at lunchtime. I do get out of the office—as when I go up to Capitol Hill to testify before a congressional committee or discuss legislative matters with the members of Congress. At other times, I meet with executive branch officials on matters of mutual interest. Sometimes I attend a working dinner or diplomatic function. I also visit facilities we regulate all over the country, especially those grappling with issues of common concern such as storage of spent fuel. Then, too, there are trips abroad where I am the official U.S. nuclear safety representative, addressing international conferences and discussing safety issues with other governments, as in the former Soviet Union.

Every step I've taken in my professional life has involved changes and different challenges

but, fortunately, all have come together to prepare me for the challenges I face in this post. For example, the research and development work that I've done has given me the technical base and analytical skills to deal with the highly technical issues that arise at the NRC. I have done research management and served on a number of corporate boards and scientific commissions, which have provided management oversight experience. I have been involved with financial institutions and in managing, developing, and overseeing budgets, important to me now that I oversee a government agency with about three thousand employees and an annual budget of approximately half a billion dollars. Appointments by various New Jersey governors (where I lived) to public commissions, where I dealt with state legislators and gubernatorial officials over policy issues, helped to prepare me for the policy arena in the nation's capital.

My training is in theoretical physics. I earned a B.S. in physics in 1968 and a Ph.D. in theoretical particle physics in 1973, both from MIT. I was the first African American woman to earn a Ph.D. there in any subject. When I entered MIT as a freshman, there were only about ten African Americans in the entire student body of eight thousand, and only forty-three women in my freshman class of nine hundred. At first, my undergraduate experience was isolating. I was shunned by my classmates, even by some young white females. But as we got to know one another, I developed a number of good friends. People came to judge me on my merits. There also is a certain ironic advantage to standing out among others—people tend to remember who one is.

I worked for AT&T Bell Laboratories for fifteen years, conducting research in theoretical physics, solid state and quantum physics, and optical physics. One area of research I have focused on is known as polaron physics—polaronic aspects of electrons on the surface of a liquid helium film. This research relates to the electronic and optical properties of VLSI (very large scale integration of integrated cir-

Chairman Jackson touring the Dresden Nuclear Power Plant
PHOTO COURTESY OF THE NUCLEAR REGULATORY COMMISSION

cuits) type systems, which are the basis for a lot of the information revolution. If you look at electrons on the surface of a liquid helium film, due to the dielectric properties of the film, the electrons behave as if they see image charges in the film and in the substrate that the film rests on. These image charges attract the electron. When that happens, we say the electron falls into "image potential bound states," which restrict the motion of the electron perpendicular to the surface of the film. This means that the electrons tend to move freely on the surface or just above the surface of the film; they go from being fully three-dimensional particles to being quasi two-dimensional particles where most of their activity takes place in a plane. They are free except for interaction with surface excitations known as capillary gravity waves.

Electrons in semiconductors—which is what this research relates to—are affected by and affect the movement of atoms in an atomic lattice from their regular position. The movement or vibration of these atoms is expressed in terms of normal modes of distortion, or phonons; the analog of the phonons for the electrons on the surface of the films are the capillary gravity waves or riplons. My work focused

on the electron surface-distortion interaction, or the electron-riplon interaction, in order to make predictions about what the behavior of the system would be. It turns out, depending on the strength of that interaction, to look like a "polaron." A polaron is a particle that "digs its own grave": it moves through its environment, and as it moves it affects or distorts its environment, and that distortion then acts back on the particle and affects its ability to move. If there is a strong enough interaction, this self-induced distortion can cause the particle to effectively plunk down under certain conditions. It is a very important effect if you are looking at an electron-phonon system because it controls what happens to the electronic properties as a function of temperature, as well as a function of the geometry of the surface. If you want to model electronic devices, you have to know how the electrons move around in two dimensions.

I developed a basic model for treating these interactions within a path integral framework—it is a mathematical methodology for treating certain kinds of interactions when you have a large number of particles. I extended the use of that apparatus for this system, and I was able to show that these electrons on the liquid helium film behaved like "acoustic" polarons. I worked on this research for many years at AT&T Bell Labs and was elected a fellow of the American Physical Society as a consequence of this work. It also formed the basis of work I did later on at Rutgers: I studied the electronic and optical properties of low-dimensional systems, primarily two-dimensional or quasi-two-dimensional systems, looking at other kinds of excitations and how they affect the properties of electrons. I looked particularly at spin fluctuations and how they affect the electronic and optical properties of electrons in two-dimensional semiconductors.

I joined the faculty at Rutgers University in 1991, when I was made an offer I couldn't refuse. However, I continued my relationship with the AT&T Bell Labs as a part-time employee and consultant. In fact, I kept my same office and worked there once a week. Making the move from an industrial research lab to academe was quite an experience. Academe offered a fulfilling opportunity to interact with bright young students, to stimulate their imagination. It also gave me the luxury of having a group of graduate and postdoctoral students work solely on my ideas, while I helped to sharpen their research skills and encourage their intellectual growth. I loved the flexibility of academic life; while there are a lot of responsibilities, a professor determines how to meet them. I was intrigued by the collegial decision-making process, in contrast to the top-down managerial process in industry. Both experiences help me enormously today.

I grew up in Washington, D.C., with two sisters and a brother. My mother was a social worker and my father a postal worker. Both parents encouraged us to study hard and excel. One of my sisters, a lawyer, is a senior official at a federal agency; the other, a historian, is a dean at a major West Coast university. My brother is deceased. My parents were the biggest influences in my life—they were my ultimate role models in the way they lived their lives and dealt with adversity, and in the solid values they imparted to us.

I was always a strong student and a curious child, eager to understand how things worked. My younger sister and I built soapbox go-carts, and I conducted a number of scientific experiments. For a time I collected live bumblebees in jars and fed them sugar to see how diets and environments affected their behavior.

Like many others of my generation, I benefited from the U.S. response to Sputnik, the Soviet satellite that beat us into space in 1957. I participated in one of the many accelerated educational programs as the country tried to nurture its scientific talent. I got into the honors program in the seventh grade, finished the high school curriculum early, and then took college-level courses in my senior year. Interestingly, it was the assistant principal for boys who took notice of my mathematical ability and encouraged me to apply to MIT. In 1964 I graduated from Roosevelt High School as class valedictorian and set off for MIT in Cambridge, Massachusetts.

I met my husband, Morris A. Washington, while working at the AT&T Bell Labs; he too is a physicist. We have a son who was born in 1981. In my view, childbearing is a life decision. I have been able to manage both family and a career because I had a very supportive husband, a healthy and well-balanced child, good friends, great early child care, and focus. Without all of this, balancing my personal and professional life would have been very difficult.

My career has evolved in terms of opportunities offered and seized, but I always had a career plan generally aimed in a particular direction. I had an early interest in math and science, and physics allowed me to combine the two. I became interested in research as a result of my undergraduate experiences at MIT and that pointed me to graduate school. Once in graduate school, there was a natural progression to a career in research. I was always interested in scholarly pursuits, but I was also interested in the role science and technology play in public policy, particularly in economic development. Now I am in a policy role, built on a science and technology base, where the focus is public health and safety. I have always tried to contribute at the highest level of any activity I have been engaged in, and this focus has paid dividends throughout my life.

PRESENT POSITION: Chairman, Nuclear Regulatory Commission

FIELD: Theoretical elementary particle physics

RESEARCH AREAS: Theoretical physics, solid state and quantum physics, and optical physics

EDUCATION: B.S. in Physics (1968), Massachusetts Institute of Technology; Ph.D. in Theoretical Elementary Particle Physics (1973), Massachusetts Institute of Technology

DATE/PLACE OF BIRTH: August 5, 1946/ Washington, D.C.

INTERVIEW DATE: November 1995

Elizabeth Jones

Professor of Biological Sciences
CARNEGIE MELLON UNIVERSITY

In one way or another, science has always been a part of Elizabeth Jones's life. She grew up in an isolated part of the Cascade Mountains of Washington state, with a father who was an avid bird-watcher and a mother intrigued with plants and flowers; the importance and beauty of nature formed a backdrop to her childhood. Her interest in nature took her from a one-room schoolhouse to the University of Washington, where she earned a Ph.D. in genetics.

❧

I do genetics of yeast. I use yeast as a model organism, hoping that our findings can be extrapolated to humans or at least allow us to better formulate questions to ask in experiments on human cells.

When we began this work, many biologists hoped that what we found out about yeast would transfer to humans because both yeast and humans are eukaryotes—their cells are complicated with subcompartments and are more complex than bacterial cells, which have a much simpler structure. This hope was realized beyond our wildest dreams because it turns out that evolution has been obsessively conservative with respect to the proteins and genes that organisms carry. Many of the genes that encode proteins for fundamental processes are actually exchangeable between cells of different species. In yeast we have the great opportunity to remove, with ease, any gene selectively and replace it with another gene—with a human gene or yeast gene or gene from any organism to see if it will work. What we find is that we can often replace the yeast gene with the human gene and the human gene will function perfectly well and the cell will be perfectly normal. We can do the reverse experiment as well—that is, supply a yeast gene to an animal cell and often—not always—it will work and satisfy the function.

More specifically, we're interested in find-

Elizabeth Jones in her office in the Department of Biological Sciences at Carnegie Mellon University, 1996
PHOTO BY KEN ANDREYO

ing out how one of the subcompartments in yeast functions and how it is assembled. This subcompartment is called the lysosome; it's a very important structure in both yeast and animal cells. Defective functions in this compartment are responsible for human metabolic diseases like Tay-Sachs and Sandhoff's disease, where the cell, and therefore the organism, has lost the capacity to degrade proteins that it no longer wants or needs. These diseases are fatal in early childhood. So it's an important organelle, absolutely crucial for the life of humans.

Many people are doing this kind of research all over the world, and there is a constantly updated computer database that includes the sequences for all known genes and proteins. We can submit our entry and see if another gene like it has been found in any organism under study; it takes about a minute. We commonly find that no one has found genes like ours, and so we're exploring new territory. Sometimes that's not true, and we find that the gene we're studying is related to another gene that somebody else is working on. For example, one of the first genes that we studied turned out to have a very strong resemblance to one of the proteins that's in your stomach and is responsible for digesting proteins that you eat. But more commonly that's not the case. We're finding a lot of proteins that somehow are on the membrane of this lysosomal compartment and must therefore contribute both to its assembly and function. No one has ever found anything similar to these. We're now in the process of trying to figure out what these proteins do. It is hard, but this is where the excitement of science is found—in finding out what was previously unknown.

I do my research with students who are at various stages in their education: half a dozen graduate students, between six and ten undergraduates, and sometimes postdoctoral fellows. Doing science is very social—it's an interactive and collaborative process. Those working in my lab meet weekly; people bring in their results and we discuss the implications. But what's far more important is that they bring in their experimental problems—things they can't get to work or can't figure out—and as a group we try to figure out where the problem is and how it can be overcome or what it may mean. The interplay of many minds often leads us to places that we couldn't get to by ourselves.

In one way or another, science has always been a part of my life. Both my parents have always had interests in nature: my father is an avid bird-watcher and my mother has always been intrigued with plants and flowers. During my childhood they were always taking us places throughout the West—Yellowstone, Bryce Canyon, Grand Canyon, Mesa Verde, Crater Lake, many places in Washington, Oregon, California, Utah, Colorado, Texas, Arizona, New Mexico, and Wyoming. Somehow we skipped most of Idaho and Nevada, and I got to Montana on my own later. Many of these trips entailed looking at the scenery and natural history, but we also visited lots of museums, missions, dams, locks, forts, and churches. My parents indulged their hobbies and took us along for the ride, much to our advantage and delight. My elder sister became a zoologist. Unlike her, I never followed either of my parents' interests directly, but they provided a background of heightened awareness of things around me that fed my curiosity. I grew up in a very isolated area, high in the Cascade Mountains of Washington. I was always up to my ears in the out-of-doors—forest, lakes, animals. All of this formed a backdrop to my childhood.

I had an inclination, perhaps in part because of my environment, to be a tomboy and do things like climbing trees, fishing, hiking, and camping (long before their recent surge in popularity). Furthermore, my father, in a mental sense, raised me as a son. Although he had southern roots, he did not subscribe to stereotypical "boy things" and "girl things"; rather he expected me to do well in whatever I did and to seek out and make the most of opportunities. Also contributing to this "masculine orientation" was the fact that the other three children in my "grade" at the one-room schoolhouse I attended were boys, and I played with them, doing all the physical things that little boys do.

In high school I intended to become an organic chemist and work in industry. When I went to college, I realized that I wasn't very talented in chemistry and so I started looking for alternatives (although I did graduate in 1960 with a degree in chemistry). While an undergraduate, I was very lucky to get a job doing lab dishes for a geneticist named Herschel Roman. I became interested in his research and discovered that my mind worked very well in genetics. I've ended up walking the border between biochemistry and genetics, and more recently the border between genetics and cell biology—but it's always been genetics.

I never really thought much about what I wanted to do in the long term; I always lived in the moment. In college I initially had no idea there was such a thing as graduate school. Herschel Roman and his wife, Caryl, began to open my eyes, and I learned more about graduate school and what it was all about. I entered the genetics Ph.D. program at the University of Washington, but even then I didn't think about what I wanted to do with it. Continuing my education might have been in part a deferral of a decision. One of the few legitimate career options for women at the time was teaching, and I was being pushed pretty hard in that direction by my parents, my teachers, and by everyone I encountered. My decision to be a chemist and then a geneticist was perhaps one way of resisting having my decisions made for me. My parents were opposed to my going to graduate school, though they never voiced their opposition. I knew it, they knew it, but we never talked about it. But it wasn't a question of trying to restrict my options. It was some years later that my mother said she had been opposed to my decision because she didn't think I would be happy. She had come to realize, by the time of this conversation, that she was wrong: it was clear to her that I was extremely happy with my career.

Herschel Roman, the man in whose lab I worked as an undergraduate, opened my eyes to other possibilities. I was a very good student and clearly interested in genetics. I graduated from the University of Washington in 1960 with a B.S. in chemistry—the genetics department had been created the year before, and Roman was the head of it. He and other people encouraged me to stay and attend graduate school at the University of Washington (they didn't encourage me to apply to other graduate schools). As a matter of fact, I never took GRE's or got a letter of recommendation—to my knowledge I never even applied to graduate school! It almost seemed to be the path of least resistance—I could do genetics, I did it well, and the doors were opened in front of me. I ended up being the first Ph.D. graduate of the genetics department at the university.

Caryl Roman was also a very important influence in my life. She noticed that I didn't have much dimension beyond science and decided to help broaden my perspective. She began bringing in books and novels that she thought I'd find interesting—she started me off with Mary Renault's novels about ancient Greece. She had perfect taste for knowing what I would and wouldn't like. And so, during my graduate years, I started reading more broadly. Both she and Herschel remained supporters and confidants throughout my career, but she was especially important in my early years as a faculty member when I began to question my decision. She always talked very good sense and reminded me that I was driven by my love of science, that in a real sense I had no other option—there was nothing but science for me!

I did postdoctoral work at MIT, although I hadn't expected to go there; opportunities for women at that level were less available because of the expectation that they would quit. I got the chance because Jon Gallant, a junior faculty member in genetics at the University of Washington, insisted, under interrogation by my postdoc mentor, that I would stick it out. After my postdoc, I took my first academic position, which turned out to be a nightmare. I found myself in a biology department in a university with a medical school, and clearly the nonmedical-school biologists were viewed and treated as second-class citizens. My department was also in a period of incredible flux; we went through six department heads in five years, and the lack of leadership had a terrible effect on the environment. The department was also extremely exploitative of junior faculty: I taught seventy lectures each year, which left very little time for research. Finally, most of the students I taught were premed students, and they had an attitude, which the university did not actively discourage, in which they felt contempt for courses outside the medical school. The department, in the students' minds, had no legitimacy of and for itself. All of this contributed to a very unpleasant situation and, in fact, during this period, anyone who could leave the university did. I set myself a deadline—either to leave the place or get out of science.

Thankfully I found another job, and after five miserable years, I came to Carnegie Mellon University in 1974. I was the first woman faculty member in the Department of Biological Sciences, and twenty years later I am still the only woman faculty member in the department (with the exception of the current dean of the Mellon College of Science, who is also a biologist). At one time we had three women on the faculty simultaneously, but they were not going to get tenure and left before that happened. My colleagues have always treated me like a scientist, so being a woman has never interfered with my work. However, being a woman biologist often produces the expectation that I should serve as a role model for the women students in the department—about 50 percent of our graduate and undergraduate students are women; the college and university have made similar demands. But I can't serve the entire range of role models that are needed; I can't carry all the emotional burden this involves; I can't let this interfere with doing my science; and I refuse to be defined this way.

As a junior faculty member, I spent an enormous amount of time in the lab. As my career has progressed—and partly because of the pneumonia I contracted in 1982, which resulted in lung damage—I spend less time in the lab and more time talking to and guiding students, analyzing data, reading, writing articles, editing journal articles and books, and applying for grants to continue the research we're doing. I enjoy all of these aspects of academic life, although I prefer lab work above all else.

I decided early on that I wanted to do science, not "tag-along" science. I didn't want my career to be determined by having to accommodate someone else. I have remained single, dedicated to science, and very happy with my life.

PRESENT POSITION: Professor of Biological Sciences, Carnegie Mellon University

FIELD: Biology

RESEARCH AREA: Genetics

EDUCATION: B.S. in Chemistry (1960), University of Washington; Ph.D. in Genetics (1964), University of Washington

PLACE OF BIRTH: Seattle, Washington

Elizabeth Jones currently lives in Pittsburgh, Pennsylvania.

INTERVIEW DATE: October 1994

Gretchen Kalonji

Kyocera Professor of Materials Science and Engineering
UNIVERSITY OF WASHINGTON

Initiated into materials science through practical experience in a metals workshop in East Africa, and growing up in an environment of activism and social action, Gretchen Kalonji completed a B.S. and Ph.D. at MIT in just three years. Kalonji works in theoretical materials science and is a major architect of engineering and science education in the United States. In 1994 she received the George Westinghouse Award from the American Society of Engineering Education for her "contributions to the improvement of teaching methods in engineering." She is guided by the Swahili proverb, "Don't travel by someone else's star."

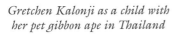

I don't have the kind of story I hear from a lot of scientists who talk about discovering their interest in science "when I was in first grade." I backed into science, one might say, and my path has been far from conventional.

I came into science through a mechanical engineering workshop in East Africa. I had been kicked out of school twice in Hong Kong and once in Kenya. The first time I was kicked out of high school was in Hong Kong during the Cultural Revolution. I was involved in various actions including the siege of the U.S. Embassy and protests against the Vietnam War. After I was kicked out of school in East Africa, I was working on an old bike and a friend of mine offered me a job in his workshop. He was a third-generation Asian Kenyan whose original Indian family name was Lohar, or metalworker. He had an incredible background in metallurgy and was a brilliant engineer, really ingenious, with not a lot of formal training. I began working in his engineering workshop and learned a lot of practical skills such as welding, milling, turning, elementary design and drafting, and then began to segue into the more "science-y" approaches to problems that I would use later on in my career.

We were constrained to make a lot of what

Gretchen Kalonji as a child with her pet gibbon ape in Thailand

we needed because of the unavailability of ready-made parts in East Africa. So, we would be heat-treating metals. There would be all these mysterious quenches (heating and sudden cooling) which he knew by the look of things, by family-based empirical learning. One day, in the streets of Nairobi, I came across a used physical metallurgy textbook, which I got and read. I became quite fascinated by the idea that there were underlying microscopic processes going on in the practical processes we carried out that were responsible for the changes in the properties of the materials.

I never graduated from high school, and I had very little science when I was in school. I had algebra, geometry, and one or two years of sciences, but no chemistry, no physics.

My motivation to pursue formal education in mechanical engineering in the United States, at least initially, was in order to get Kenyan citizenship. I planned to leave Kenya temporarily, get a degree, and then apply for Kenyan citizenship. I had no plans to stay in the United States. Since I was seven, I had only visited the States as my journalist parents moved from India, Hong Kong, Thailand, back to Hong Kong, and then East Africa. But I was quite sure I didn't want to live in the United States, and Kenya was the country where I had lived in the longest.

Then I got married and came with my husband to the United States. When I arrived I had no high school diploma but was accepted as a special student at the University of Maryland. By then my family had also moved back to the States and was living in the D.C. metropolitan area.

When I started taking classes, my baby, Hussein, was four months old. The last time I had been in school was in the tenth grade, seven years earlier. I had been a political activist all my life. I had been interested in subjects like linguistics, political science, and history; I certainly had no idea that engineering was the direction I would eventually pursue. My main interest was in social movements. My pet hope was to study languages independently. My interest in the beauty of linguistic patterns is reflected in my current work, which could be characterized as structural aesthetics of materials.

Realizing I had to start from scratch, I took introductory courses in chemistry and materials science at Maryland. I decided that materials science was a good combination of what I was enjoying in physics and physical organic chemistry. I didn't want an advanced degree in topics with no practical consequences. I went up to MIT to investigate studying engineering.

I saw the admissions director at MIT, a marvelous woman named Julia McCormick. I was accepted and started my undergraduate work at MIT in February 1979, got my B.S. in May 1980, and my Ph.D. in 1982. I am told that I hold the MIT record for completing a Ph.D. in the shortest time. My thesis work was completed in five semesters after my B.S. In the first year of my undergraduate study, I took sophomore courses. I had a cooperative internship at the National Bureau of Standards (NBS, now the National Institute of Standards and Technology, or NIST) in Washington, D.C. John Cahn, my mentor at NBS, was a wonderful person. He had been on the faculty at MIT for thirteen years before going to NBS. He advised me to petition out of most of my courses when I came back to MIT in the fall. In my second semester at MIT, I took only some selected graduate courses, having petitioned out of most undergraduate courses. I started doing theoretical research that formed the basis of my Ph.D. So by the time I matriculated into graduate school in fall 1980, the research for my Ph.D. thesis had been completed with work I did at NBS the second summer.

Things worked well for me during this time, and the main reason was the real vibrancy and excitement of the intellectual community at NBS. I had a lot of fun there and learned a lot very quickly. The coincidence of a couple of courses—one in defects in solids by a marvelous professor (Bob Balluffi) and a series of courses in crystallography by the wonderful Bernie Wuensch—got me started on my current research interest. I was enchanted by group theory, which is the mathematical theory that describes the geometric symmetry of objects such as crystals. I was able to see that there was a class of problems in which I could apply group theoretical techniques to study structural properties of crystalline defects that hadn't been done before. It was a fortunate juxtaposition of the areas of study of two of my early intellectual heroes.

In my research I try to understand how certain disruptions in patterns of atoms in solids affect the way they behave—their mechanical properties, electrical properties, and optical properties. I use a branch of mathematics called color-group theory. In this approach, you can attribute different colors and do mathematical operations in space that correspond to the ways that the atoms are actually arranged in different kinds of situations. Examples of applications could be growing electronic thin films that are used in computer memories, or in materials such as metals or ceramics. Where there is atomic structural change from one arrangement to another, there end up being interfaces inside them and junctions between interfaces. These determine how the structure grows. I use mathematical theory to address questions about how the structure affects properties, also using computer simulations and lab work. The work is fun; I don't require expensive equipment and can do a lot on my own.

Although my original motivation had been to do a practical course of study and go back and live in East Africa, I was quickly enchanted by stuff in the highly impractical side of materials science. That was the most enjoyable time I had. Once we become faculty, life becomes less interesting intellectually because of all the other things we have to do. I worked hard and focused well, but I also remember thinking, "How could this be a Ph.D. thesis?" because it was relatively easy to do. Having a child at the time was essentially a help because it kept me focused.

Perhaps the greatest professional mistake I made was in accepting a faculty position at MIT right after graduation. Midway through my Ph.D. work, I had heard that the department wanted to create a position for me. When I was hired, there were two positions open. One was in polymer physics; the other was a position with industrial support in ceramics processing, specifically in the area of rapid solidification of ceramics. In my first internship with the NBS, I had done some experimental work in rapid solidification of metals and formation of metallic glasses. For my Ph.D. qualifying examinations, I had taken ceramics as a concentration area because I didn't know much about it and was interested in learning. The job was not a good fit, but it was either that or polymer physics. At first the department chair told me I should take the polymer physics position. They would send me to Paris for a year, where I could work with de Gennes, the world-famous polymer scientist, learn about polymers, and come back. But polymers seemed even further from what I was doing. So I took the position in ceramics funded by Norton, a firm specializing in high performance ceramics, because there were some interesting problems and because we had an understanding that I would spend half my time in rapid solidification of ceramics and the other half on what I wanted to do. But by the time I was hired, there was a new department head who expected me to spend 100 percent of my time on ceramics research. He expected me to abandon the research on application of group theoretical techniques to defects in crystals in which I had established an international reputation, an area that really played into my strengths. I had some knowledge of ceramics, but I was really a square peg in a round hole.

It was a very difficult situation, complicated by the fact that Norton had been consulting with the department head for a number of years and he wanted to keep them happy. Norton appeared to believe that they had hired an MIT faculty member to work on their specific problems. They wanted to know how to make better sandpaper, work that never would have led to any kind of research record. Initially I thought that having an experimental component in my research would be good because Ph.D. students in materials science very rarely want to do theory. The culture of the field is that materials science is selected by undergraduates who don't like much math. Theorists in materials science have very few graduate students. It is a field dominated heavily by experimental work.

I accepted the position believing it wouldn't be bad to have a balance between theory and experiment, but it turned out not to be a balance. I was told, "If you publish one or two more theory papers it is all right, but any theoretical work will not count toward your tenure. All that will count is your work on ceramics processing." It was poor advice. You don't take someone out of an area in research in which they are performing well and force them to abandon it and start from scratch. Further, the work was experimental, and I didn't have any lab space for the first two and a half years! My lab space fell into the cracks between two senior professors, each of whom thought I would have a lab in another building. It was a very hostile work environment.

Three years into my faculty appointment, and after intervention from faculty including Millie Dresselhaus [see Mildred Dresselhaus's profile on page 105], the department head said, "You can work on other things if you want to." By that stage, on my own, I had developed a computer-simulation component to my research effort using molecular-dynamics simulation techniques to study the structural properties of crystalline interfaces. I thought that it would be easier to get materials science graduate students interested in doing computer simulation than more abstract theory and that we could assess in a quasi-experimental manner some of the theoretical things that I had been studying. So I had two parallel research efforts and a lot of very good Ph.D. students. While I was at MIT, I graduated six Ph.D.s. Five of my students had offers of positions from other universities. I had the best

record of all the faculty in the department in that regard.

During the same time I became very active in the antiapartheid movement. Together with Willard Johnson, a political science professor and one of the founders of TransAfrica, I led a faculty divestment campaign. I also became involved with students and demonstrations, building shantytowns and working on other projects. In various heated faculty meetings I sponsored resolutions that censured the administration. These activities became a very big component of my life at that time, completely divorced from my technical work. A lot of people told me that I was crazy to continue them.

The other major thing that happened at the same time was that through my work as the AAO (affirmative action officer) of a faculty search committee, I got into a big row with my department head over hiring a black candidate. We had identified someone who seemed to be extraordinarily qualified and whom the majority of the faculty wanted to hire. But all the good things about him were suppressed by the department head in a very unethical way that destroyed his chance of joining the department. I finally went directly to Herman Feshbach, the creator of the Feshbach initiative to hire minority faculty at MIT. Feshbach had said that if one found a qualified minority candidate, he would create a position. My department head got his hands slapped in a mild manner, but he told me that it was his worst week at MIT. It was also the end of my MIT academic career.

Until then, I had received extremely laudatory performance evaluations and very high raises. I had been told informally by the department head that I was a shoo-in for tenure, even that he had been told this by the dean. I had a very highly ranked promotion to associate professor the year before I was to come up for tenure. Now the department head turned on me, and once that happened it was, as my colleague John told me, "like sharks hanging around in the water. Once they see blood, they attack." People who think you are going to be tenured don't say bad things about you at faculty meetings even if they hate you; but once they see a chance to keep you out of the department, all the ugly stuff comes out. In the fall of 1987, my tenure decision came up for the first time. At the meeting, my case was presented by the most scientifically renowned person in the whole department, Professor Balluffi, a person of great integrity. The discussion very rapidly degenerated into a series of allegations against me, including that I took my class to demonstrations, that I told students to read Communist books and watch Communist movies, even that I hid a textbook from students!

I became drawn into a very time-consuming, emotionally draining process of addressing this attack. It began with a very long and protracted involvement with the capricious grievance process at MIT, which ended early in 1991. At the end of it, I was denied tenure. After that, I ended up going to federal court and filing under Title VII on the grounds that the decision had been discriminatory. I went through all the long stages of getting documents out of MIT. I actually got close to the stage of taking interrogatories and depositions, had a judge assigned to my case, and was very close to going to court when it became clear that MIT wanted to negotiate. A senior judge acting as mediator strongly suggested that the provost of MIT and I should talk without anybody else present. After a number of sessions, we came to an out-of-court settlement, the details of which I am not free to divulge. One component I can mention is that MIT agreed to put $250,000 into a program for women and minority faculty development with Judy (J. J.) Jackson as staff. The creation of this program will be the basis of her doctoral thesis in educational administration at Harvard. The process finally ended in February 1995.

While I was fighting MIT, I was also heavily involved in an educational program in conjunction with the African National Congress (ANC). A lot of support for the antiapartheid movement had been mobilized in the Boston-area technical community, but the support

Gretchen Kalonji in a recent photograph
PHOTO COURTESY OF THE UNIVERSITY OF WASHINGTON

didn't have any technical component. I thought it would be a good idea to link that with people's support into programmatic areas in the ANC. So I made a trip to Lusaka, where the ANC headquarters in exile was, and spoke to people there in the Projects Department and the Department of Education. I ended up going to Tanzania to work with some people in the high-tech division of the ANC, to talk about educational development and fundraising for computer science and electronics programs in a school. That school, named Solomon Mahlangu Freedom College (or Somafco) after the first Soweto freedom fighter, became a major component of my life during my last three years at MIT. I made a number of trips each year and was very successful in fundraising, bringing teachers from there back to the States, and getting donations for teachers of all levels. It was a school built on land given by the Tanzanian government, with everything from a crèche to elementary school to secondary school and adult education programs. It was quite broad in scope and a marvelous environment in which to work. This was my first real opportunity to merge the political and the technical sides of my work, and it was very satisfying and exciting. I also met a lot of people who were more familiar with emerging exciting directions in education.

While the MIT struggle was going on, I had an offer from the University of Washington to come as the Kyocera Professor of Materials Science, and I decided to focus on theory and computer simulation. By the time I came to Seattle, the ANC got unbanned in 1990, the expatriate education program was quickly dismantled, and everyone at the school got repatriated.

Shortly after getting here, I got heavily involved with one of the first NSF-sponsored engineering-education coalitions—the Engineering Coalition of Schools for Excellence in Education and Leadership (ECSEL), which had started in October 1990. ECSEL is one of the nine educational coalitions funded by the National Science Foundation. It is a joint effort between Howard University, CCNY, the Massachusetts Institute of Technology, Morgan State University, Pennsylvania State University, the University of Washington, and the University of Maryland.

I spent a lot of my time in outreach programs with the K–12 community, focusing on curriculum development and creating a new materials science course and programs for minorities and women faculty—just a large number of facets of ECSEL work, taking on more and more administrative work, including leading the program at Washington as well as cross-coalition programs in various areas. Now I am one of the codirectors for the coalition, which involves seven universities and scores of faculty, thousands of students taking courses, and hundreds of students actively involved as participants. It is a very complex social dynamic with the twin goals of curricular transformation and equity and access, which combine social justice and technical content. It is difficult work, and I often

wonder if it is worth all the battles I have to fight to keep social justice on the coalition's agenda. It is a lot better now. The coalition has to be renewed every five years, and getting it renewed in 1995 practically killed me. It was a huge, huge amount of work. In all of these NSF-sponsored engineering education coalitions there is a lot of lip service to "diversity issues." But fighting to keep diversity at the forefront can be very exhausting, particularly if there is not equal commitment on the part of your colleagues. I have often wondered whether I should be devoting my time to other things. The coalition has taken time away from other things including my own materials science research. I am beginning to move back more into research that I do on my own and less by proxy using graduate students.

Today I am quite close to doing what I really like, although I would prefer to be able to do creative work both in education and materials science without so much struggle. But that is not realistic when you are talking about the process of political change. Because basically it *is* a struggle. One of the best things about working in the programs in Somafco was the shared vision. Some of the people were very conservative pedagogically, but there was a revolutionary agenda and a sense of collective commitment. The current educational reform in the United States is a fascinating phenomenon because the kinds of pedagogies and learning environments are inherently very revolutionary, or at least many of them are; but people don't think of it as a political process, and there is very little discourse about what it means in terms of the rest of the society's agenda. You can end up with all the resources you need, but it is not quite the same as sharing a committed vision on a broad scale. Sometimes I still feel isolated within the community.

I have always been the kind of person who rushes headlong into a barrier. At my father's funeral, David Halberstam, a close colleague and a friend of my Dad's, told me one of the things my father said about me, "Gretchen doesn't know the meaning of the word *fear*." When you are talking about doing creative work, whether as a scientist or activist, it is the willingness to take risks and to perceive yourself as the creator of something that didn't exist before that is liberating and enables you to do something. When working with students, the most important thing is to help them to recognize themselves as agents in the process of creating knowledge. Confidence is a big—the most important—factor.

For an ideal balance of my energies, I would like to be involved again with educational programs back in Africa because I am tremendously excited at what is happening there. It is one place where I feel optimistic about the future. I think that I could be relatively effective, and I am determined to develop new projects that will allow me to spend part of my time there. But I am also still recovering from my "fighting MIT" era. I am in the process of defining what I want my conventional life to be. Not too long ago, I got a hexagram in the Chinese oracle, I Ching, the gist of which was that one must choose between being a hero and being a scholar. Are you going to be working in the social domain as a leader to move people in a positive direction or withdraw and contribute to scholarly pursuits? I am still rebelling at the idea that I can't do both. I am still trying to find some sort of balance where I *can* do both. And the jury is still out.

PRESENT POSITION: Kyocera Professor of Materials Science and Engineering, University of Washington

FIELDS: Materials science and engineering, engineering education

SPECIALTY: Theory of defects in crystalline solids, atomistic computer simulation techniques, rapid solidification of ceramics; innovations in science and engineering education

EDUCATION: B.S. in Materials Science (1980), Ph.D. in Materials Science (1982), Massachusetts Institute of Technology

DATE/PLACE OF BIRTH: April 13, 1953/Chicago, Illinois

Gretchen Kalonji lives in Seattle, Washington, with her sons, Hussein, Bruce, and Daniel.

INTERVIEW DATE: September 1995

Anna Karlin

Visiting Associate Professor of Computer Science
UNIVERSITY OF WASHINGTON

Anna Karlin was better at math than at most other things so she majored in applied mathematics at Stanford. She didn't feel directed or motivated, however, until a professor suggested that she apply to graduate school in computer science. In computer science she found the perfect blend of mathematical theory with problem-solving techniques. Research and music became her passions. After receiving her Ph.D., Anna Karlin decided to pursue her research at an industrial lab; more recently she has been seeking a future in the academy.

❧

I t doesn't really seem like I ever planned the career path I have taken. I was always just better at math than most other things, though until recently I had no real passion for it. My father is a renowned mathematician. In recent years he has been working on the mathematical and statistical analysis of DNA sequences. He has always thought that molecular biology was the field of the future, and he regularly used to joke that I should do an M.D./Ph.D. and go on to win the Nobel Prize. Actually, I'm not so sure he was joking; he put a lot of pressure on me.

As an undergraduate at Stanford University, I started out in premed but rapidly decided that I hated chemistry and biology. I have always preferred problem solving to anything that involved memorization. By the time I was a senior, I had decided I wasn't going to med school or into biology and, because I had taken a lot of math, my undergraduate degree was going to be in applied mathematics. But I really wasn't driven to

pursue anything. In fact, I was downright unmotivated. I didn't go to classes and did the bare minimum to get by. I guess I was rebelling against my father. Nonetheless, I did reasonably well. By chance, a computer science professor I knew suggested that I apply to graduate school in computer science. I had taken a few computer science courses, but didn't have any particular affinity for the subject. I really couldn't think of anything better to do with my life, so I applied.

Suddenly I found myself in graduate school in computer science. This was the first time that I regretted my lack of dedication as an undergraduate. It was clear to me that the other

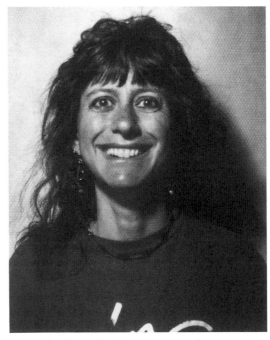

Anna Karlin in a recent photo

graduate students knew much more about computer science than I did. It was rather intimidating. On my very first day, I met a woman who told me that she was going to do theoretical computer science because it was the hardest and most rigorous of the computer science specialties. I was very impressed with her so, during my first year, I decided to get a research internship with one of the faculty who was working in theoretical computer science. A lot of computer science is engineering oriented, but theoretical computer science is really a field of applied mathematics. It was pretty clear to me that my abilities were most naturally suited to this area, and soon I really began to enjoy the research.

My research in theoretical computer science involves figuring out how to solve problems as efficiently as possible. This involves the design and analysis of "mathematical recipes" called algorithms, which describe the operations the computer needs to perform in order to solve a problem. It's very interesting to try to classify problems according to their complexity. The complexity of a problem is how hard it is to solve as a function of the size of the input—that is, how many time units it takes on a computer. For example, suppose I input ten numbers into the computer that I want sorted. The computer uses a unit amount of time to look at each number. In this case, the computer uses at least ten time units to solve the problem, but it turns out it doesn't have to use too many more than that in order to output that same list of numbers in sorted order. We call that an easy problem. On the other hand, suppose I input a list of ten cities into the computer along with the distances between every pair of cities. I request an ordering in which to visit the cities such that the total distance traveled is minimized. This classic "traveling salesman" problem is very complex. There is no algorithm in existence that solves this problem quickly.

I am deeply fascinated by probabilistic algorithms and the probabilistic analysis of algorithms. What a probabilistic algorithm should do is compute the solution correctly

and relatively quickly with high probability. Often there are a lot of possibilities for how to try to solve a problem but only some of them work. If you were to explore each method one at a time, the worst thing that could happen is that you first check all the possibilities that don't work. A probabilistic algorithm avoids this "worst case" by "tossing coins"; depending on the outcomes of those coin tosses, it chooses one of the methods at random. If half the methods are good, and you choose one at random, then you expect to find a good one after two tries. That's pretty good odds. Nobody really understands the power of probabilistic computation. For example, for testing whether a number is prime, there is a randomized, probabilistic algorithm that runs very quickly. But there is no known deterministic algorithm that runs that quickly. Part of what I research is the relationship between probabilistic and deterministic computation.

Lately, I've been working on algorithms for on-line problems. This is when instead of receiving all the input for a problem at once, the computer gets the input in bits and pieces. What we want to do is solve the problem almost as well in this situation as we would if the input was given to us all at once. A classic example of this type of problem is ski rental. Suppose that you're about to go skiing for the first time. Let's assume that renting skis costs forty dollars each time you go, but buying skis costs four hundred dollars. Barring inflation and various other factors, if you knew exactly how many times you were going to go skiing, you would know whether it was more cost effective to rent or buy. Based on our assumed cost estimates, if you are going to go skiing more than ten times, you would minimize your expenditures by buying right at the beginning. But what if you buy the skis and go skiing just a few times? Unfortunately, you don't know ahead of time (usually) how many times you will go. Nonetheless, there is a simple procedure for deciding what to do that is guaranteed to cause you to spend no more than twice the minimum value. You rent until you've paid the cost of buying and at that point you buy. Then no matter how many times you go skiing, you're guaranteed not to spend more than twice what you had to. An on-line algorithm lets the computer make decisions without knowing future requests, attempting to minimize the total cost of solving the problem.

I find it exciting when systems people implement algorithms I've designed. Recently I worked with a colleague and his students on a problem in computer architecture. They wanted an algorithm that had reasonable performance. We created an algorithm and they experimented with it. They found that the performance of this algorithm was much better than what they had been using. It was great fun.

At the same time, theory is my first love within computer science. It's clean and elegant, some might even say beautiful—like pure mathematics. Sometimes the techniques are clever and deep. When you prove a theorem about something, you can say with certainty it is true. Most computer engineering papers don't expose absolute truths. Not everything in theoretical computer science has that flavor, but some things are truly beautiful.

Several professors that I worked with in graduate school deeply influenced the direction of my research and the quality and standards to which I aspire. Professor Andy Yao, in my opinion one of the great computer scientists, was a real role model. Although Andy is very famous, there are others who have played more by the standard academic agenda and received more notice. I appreciate Andy's very idealistic approach. My father views research in a similar way.

After graduate school, I did a postdoc at Princeton. When I looked for jobs, I had quite a few academic offers and a few offers for research labs. I chose to work at the Digital Equipment Corporation (DEC) Systems Research Center. Sometimes I think I chose it because it was my scariest job interview; the people who work there are extremely smart. I also wanted to focus on research and felt that teaching at the same time would be a bit too much for me.

In retrospect, I think I was wrong in expecting that teaching would distract me from research. At DEC, where I had all day to work and think about my research projects, my mind often wandered. There was too much freedom in my schedule, and although I was productive, I wasn't working as hard as I could have been. I had been thinking of switching to academia, so when the University of Washington's computer science (CS) department wrote asking me to apply for the National Science Foundation Visiting Professorships for Women, I was ready to move. Since I've been at the University of Washington (UW), I use my time more efficiently and I've learned an incredible amount by teaching. To explain something to someone, I have to understand it completely. Since I am not naturally articulate, teaching has helped me learn to express myself more clearly and has also improved my problem-solving skills.

I've gone through an interesting evolution since I've been at UW. The incredibly supportive atmosphere of the CS department benefits my work. Colleagues pat me on the back and clearly express appreciation for the work I do, motivating me to do more. DEC was a good place and I learned a lot during the five years I spent there, but it's a very competitive environment. People there are quite aggressive. Although I'm not an aggressive person, I always thought that being under pressure and stress brought out the best in me. I used to believe that I would rest on my laurels if people were positive, but I think now that I was wrong. I've been much more productive in UW's supportive atmosphere.

In the computer science department at UW, 10 percent of the faculty are women, a relatively high percentage for computer science faculties. Generally, the gender representation in my field hasn't bothered me. Because of my father's influence, I never felt that there was something I couldn't do, or that there was anything that I was less good at because I was a woman. If anything, my father expected more of me. What I do worry about is having children. It's very important to me, and it looks as if it's hard to manage. I'm fairly established in my career, so I figure it will work out and be OK. If I was starting out at a university and needed to put in six years before tenure, then it would be a different story. My goal is to be hired as tenured faculty. When an institution reviews you for tenure, they evaluate your research, your teaching, your ability to get grants, and your community service. I haven't followed a traditional path to tenure, but I've kept active in the research community, and because of my two years at UW, I now have a reasonable teaching record as well. I'd love to stay in Seattle because location is important to me, but I'm confident that I'll find a position where I can achieve my goals and still live the kind of lifestyle I enjoy.

Outside of work, my main passion is music. In addition to studying computer science theory in graduate school, I learned how to play the guitar. I had a boyfriend who was in a band. I got really jealous watching him play and wanted to do it too. I had taken ten years of piano lessons as a kid, so I knew a little bit about music. He taught me how to play guitar, and ever since then I've been in a band. I played with a group called Severe Tire Damage. We were the first band to broadcast on the Internet. After I left them, they "opened" for the Rolling Stones on the Internet. When the band I'm in plays a song that sounds good, it thrills me. I love it. I don't play music so that I can perform, I just really enjoy making music. Band practices are much more interesting and fun than performing. Like my research, I find that creating music with a group of people is a total high.

PRESENT POSITION: Visiting Associate Professor of Computer Science, University of Washington

FIELD: Theoretical computer science

RESEARCH AREA: On-line algorithms, probabilistic algorithms, probabilistic algorithm analysis

EDUCATION: B.Sc. in Applied Mathematics (1981), Ph.D. in Computer Science (1987), Stanford University

DATE/PLACE OF BIRTH: March 19, 1960/Palo Alto, California

Anna Karlin currently lives in Fremont, Seattle, overlooking Lake Union and downtown Seattle, with three guitars, a set of drums, and a killer sound system. Her current band has no name. Work, music, and love are important to her. And espresso.

INTERVIEW DATE: August 1995

Betty Lane

Director of Regulatory Affairs
INSTRUMENTATION LABORATORY

Betty Lane was an average student in grade school and junior high until she was turned on to math by a teacher. Her interest and ability led her to major in electrical engineering. She has worked in a number of different jobs over the last twenty-five years, from designing digital systems for air traffic control radar to building a prototype of a heart monitor to managing quality assurance departments.

∽

I always knew I'd go to college and have a career. I grew up with a working mother; she was a medical technician, and my maternal grandmother was a teacher before she married. College goes back quite a number of years in my family: many of my mother's English and Scottish-Irish ancestors were clergy and college educated. And because my mother had to support herself and two children after her divorce, she felt that whether you were a girl or a boy it was important to have a skill and be able to make a living.

I was born in Little Rock, Arkansas, in 1947, where my father was in the Army. My parents divorced when I was three and a half. My father remarried rather quickly, and my mother got a job and moved us to Tulsa, Oklahoma. My brother and I played together a lot as children, and I hung around with the boys in the neighborhood. I always liked sports and, as I got older, loved to take things apart even though I couldn't always get them back together. Because of our family situation, there were a lot of things that we—my mother, brother, and I—learned to do to maintain the house, and I became quite comfortable working with my hands.

I was a pretty average student in grade school, and in junior high I was in the "low group" academically. But I had the same woman math teacher for all three years in junior high, and I credit her for my decision to go into engineering. She was teaching the new math to her "high achieving" class but also introduced some of the concepts to her other math classes. I picked up on the math quite easily and was one of a few students outside her more advanced class whom she invited to take the algebra aptitude test at the end of the seventh grade. I passed and was moved into the advanced track. I loved math,

Betty Lane and partner, Andrea Shirley, in front of their home in Newton, Massachusetts, spring 1994

and my teacher was a wonderful role model; she did not hold any biases that girls can't do math.

In ninth grade, in response to an English-class essay about what I wanted to do with my life, I began to think about the field of engineering. I spent time in the library researching different kinds of engineering, talked with people, and decided that I wanted to pursue aeronautical engineering and become an astronaut. Because I continued to have wonderful and encouraging women math teachers in high school, and continued to excel in math and related courses, I maintained the interest.

I entered Rensselaer Polytechnic Institute (RPI) expecting to major in aeronautical engineering. However, I heard horror stories about the department and the fact that no woman had ever made it through the program. (One woman did complete the program while I was there—in five years, however, not four.) As I began to take physics along with calculus and chemistry, it became more apparent to me that my real aptitude was in mathematics. Aeronautical engineering depends heavily on things like thermodynamics and fluid mechanics, which I didn't grasp as well as the math. So I decided to switch to electrical engineering. My entering class at RPI in 1966 was about a thousand students, only twenty-seven of whom were women. Two years later, there were a lot more; about two hundred women entered as freshmen when I was a junior, and now it's a little higher. At the time I was there, however, there was only one other woman in my electrical engineering classes. And at any given time during my first two years, there were only sixty or seventy undergraduate women at RPI. The advantage was that we all knew each other, and seeing and interacting with successful upper-class women made a real difference in my experience.

RPI had a professional co-op program that combined school with relevant work experience. I enrolled in the program in my sophomore year and interviewed with a number of engineering or engineering-related companies. The expectation was that you would work with the company the fall of your junior year, the summer after your junior year, and the summer after your senior year. Then you would come back to RPI and earn a master's degree. I worked for the Navy in Pennsylvania in the area of systems engineering: first on a simulator for radar (I got to work with some of the first minicomputers), then as a FORTRAN expert (they taught me assembly language), and later on in digital design. The experience helped me to identify what I did and didn't like: I didn't really enjoy building and testing circuits, but I did love programming and digital design. When I finished my master's degree in 1971, I knew I wanted a job doing digital design, designing computers.

I've worked in a number of jobs over the last twenty-five years as my career has progressed. My first job was with Raytheon in Massachusetts, doing digital design of systems for air traffic control radar and missile systems' control displays. I wasn't thrilled about working on missile systems, so I decided to move to the medical field and work on helpful, as opposed to destructive, technology. I took a job with CardioData Corporation, also in Massachusetts, in 1974 and stayed with the company until 1988. I began by building a prototype of a Holter long-term heart monitor—a little tape recorder that records your heart for a whole day—and a system to do the analysis using digital-signal processing. It was a noninvasive diagnostic tool that kept people out of the hospital; it was cost-effective medicine and an interesting technology. I did some of the electrical design and a lot of the mechanical design, I picked all the materials, I hand-wired things together, I did some assembly-language programming for the first prototype, and I worked with the person who did our circuit boards. I even talked to potential customers. CardioData grew from three to fifty-five employees and from zero to $5 million in sales during my fourteen years there. I functioned in a number of different capacities, from production engineer to materials manager to regulatory affairs and quality assurance manager. I grew a lot with the company, although they didn't really see and reward that growth, and I knew that I wouldn't advance beyond where I was.

It's not clear to me whether sexism or homophobia played a role in the company's refusal to promote me beyond a certain level, although it was probably more homophobia. And certainly, if prejudice did play a role, it was only from one or two people. I had come out during the time I was at CardioData. For most people it wasn't a big deal, and for those for whom it was, it was a combination of a little bit of sexism, a little bit of homophobia, and a lot of personality clash.

My next job was with a medical diagnostics company, PB Diagnostics, Inc. I went to work in the operations group for the director of regulatory affairs and quality assurance. I was attractive to the group because of my engineering background and my experience working in instrumentation. The group consisted mostly of chemists, and they wanted someone who could make sure that the engineers were not pulling the wool over their eyes. There I was in a management position where I could hire my own staff. Homophobia was never a problem in my three and a half years with the company.

I was quite happy at PB Diagnostics and wasn't looking for a job when I received an invitation to interview for GENE-Trak Systems. They were looking for someone to come in and set up the entire quality assurance department, which is what I had done at PB Diagnostics. This job was at least one step up in terms of management, so I took it and began to design and later implement quality assurance and to document control systems consistent with the Food and Drug Administration's Good Manufacturing Practice regulations. This included preparing budgets, and hiring and training staff; designing and implementing a software quality assurance system; and designing, implementing, and documenting a formal product development process for reagents, instruments, and disposables. After two years and

some reorganization within the company, I became senior manager for quality assurance for ATC Diagnostics, Inc., the parent company of GENE-Trak. That position included quality assurance responsibilities for two business units, one of which was GENE-Trak. I was responsible for, among other things, combining two existing quality-assurance and document-control systems into a single system, conducting and coordinating vendor audits, and tracking monthly performance reviews and forecasts relative to the yearly budget. Another reorganization in the spring of 1995 resulted in the company's cutting a major project that I was working on and laying off about a third of their employees, including me.

I have been with my partner, Andrea, for twenty-one years. She's a librarian and has been very supportive of my career. She is the one who first realized that CardioData wasn't using my skills to the fullest extent; she pointed out that I had outgrown the position and suggested that I move on. Andrea had two children from a previous marriage, ages four and seven when we first got together, and I've helped to raise them. Peter, the older child, started coming to work with me when he was eight or nine years old; he really loved to play with the computers, and we always hit it off famously. He often introduces me and Andrea as his parents, or his two moms. He's currently working as a computer programmer. Anne, the younger child, graduated cum laude from Smith College, earned a master's in English literature at Rutgers University, and is currently working on a master's in library science at the University of Texas in Austin.

While my career and parenting have taken a lot of time, I've done a lot of other things. I belonged to a lesbian group for a few years that was interested in the access of women to technology, particularly working-class women of color and women who were computerphobic. We did some teaching and demystification of computers. Although our group was lesbian, many of the women who took advantage of the program were not. I was also very active in the women's ordination movement in the Episcopal Church.

Currently I'm in graduate school working on an M.B.A., a result of always looking at people one step above me professionally and seeing M.B.A. beside their names. I think the degree will provide flexibility so that perhaps I can do some consulting in the future. I have always been interested in pushing the glass ceiling, and I hope that earning a business degree will help me to continue to do so. I have also been encouraged to earn the degree by my former boss at GENE-Trak, who is also a good friend; he agrees that an M.B.A. would make me more marketable and indicate that I am serious about a senior management position. Management styles have always interested me. Many of the men I have worked for were what I consider the stereotypical male manager: they believed in competitiveness, they withheld information even when people under them needed that information, and they pitted managers against each other. The women managers I have worked for were stereotypical women managers: they believed in communication, letting people know what was going on, and giving some decision-making power to people who worked for them. Not all men or all women fall into these categories; as both a manager and managee, I believe the open communication style is more motivating and beneficial to both the individuals and the company in the long run.

I have just started a new job, where I am working in an established company in a group that is composed primarily of men. It is a real change for me to come into an established company and not one that is just moving out of the R&D phase. For one thing, the average age of the people is greater; that means many people are older than I am, instead of my being one of the oldest. Because many are older, the men especially, but not exclusively, are less enlightened about sexist language. I have already encountered at least one man in my department who calls the women who work for and around him "girls." He hasn't called me a girl, and I will begin working on edu-

Betty Lane dressed for work, 1995

cating him about his language. However, I am very pleased that my new company distributes in the introductory material given to all new employees the nondiscrimination policy of the company, which includes not only the usual clauses but also nondiscrimination on the basis of sexual orientation. This is the first place I have worked that has had this as a specific written policy. Progress!

PRESENT POSITION: Director of Regulatory Affairs, Instrumentation Laboratory

FIELD: Electrical engineering

SPECIALTY: Systems engineering

EDUCATION: B.S. in Electrical Engineering (1970), Rensselaer Polytechnic Institute; M.S. in Electrical Engineering (1971), Rensselaer Polytechnic Institute; M.B.A. (in progress), Northeastern University High Technology M.B.A. Program

DATE/PLACE OF BIRTH: November 8, 1947/Little Rock, Arkansas

Betty Lane lives with her partner, Andrea Shirley, in West Newton, Massachusetts.

INTERVIEW DATE: May 1995

Frances Lockwood

Vice President of Technology and Product Development
THE VALVOLINE COMPANY

The first challenge Frances Lockwood faced was her own doubt about whether she could do engineering. Fortunately, a high school teacher bolstered her confidence and pointed her toward college. Since then she's successfully taken on many risky challenges, including moving on her own to a new job in a strange city with her six-month-old son and working her way up the corporate ladder.

❧

I was born in one of the last generations where people expected that most women would get married and work in the home; people were always asking me if I wanted to be a teacher or a nurse, as if those were the only alternatives. Getting into chemistry and engineering was about overcoming my own conditioning: I found myself asking, "Am I capable of doing this?" When you've been brought up to think you probably can't do something, deciding "Well, I'll just try it" is risky. I was able to take the risk because I really liked what I was doing.

My early motivation came from my high school mathematics teacher. He felt that I was capable, and he convinced me that I should go to college and study science or engineering. From high school I went to Rensselaer Polytechnic Institute (RPI). I first went into engineering, although I didn't actually know what engineering was. My parents hadn't been to college, and I had never even met an engineer. When I was in college, the engineering curriculum consisted of seemingly unrelated courses; you couldn't be sure what they were leading up to unless you had enough background to give you some overview. As a result,

I found the classes boring, so I dropped out of school and went to work as a laboratory technician. That work experience got me into chemistry, so when I returned to school, I finished in chemistry—a decision made more by default than by design.

I went to graduate school at Penn State because some of the professors at RPI encouraged me to—and because the job market was terrible. As a chemist with just a B.S., I could only expect to work as a glorified technician, and I felt I'd already done that. I passed the candidacy exams in chemistry, but I had trou-

Frances Lockwood in a recent photo
PHOTO COURTESY OF VALVOLINE

ble selecting a project that really turned me on. At that point, I met Dr. Elmer E. Klaus in the chemical engineering department, who was one of the best-known people in the country in the field of lubricants. He sold me on the idea of switching departments and fields and working for him. He was able to pay a better stipend than I was getting in chemistry, and I didn't have to teach to get it.

At the master's level I looked at the physical properties of liquefied coals. This was during the energy crisis of the 1970s, and people were interested in alternative energy sources. However, they were having trouble designing plants without any fundamental information about what liquid coals did at high temperatures and pressures. Later, for my Ph.D. work, I looked at lubricant oxidation. The Air Force was very concerned to have very stable, oxidation-resistant lubricants.

When I finished my Ph.D., I went to work for General Motors in their fluid and lubricants department in the R&D center in Warren, Michigan. I stayed there two years, and then my husband wanted to move. Moving to Michigan had been a compromise because both of us could get jobs there. But he wasn't happy, so we moved to the Washington, D.C., area, where he worked for the U.S. Environmental Protection Agency and I took a job with a major defense contractor, Martin Marietta. They had an interest in the lubrication of different aluminum metalworking processes. I did government contract research developing new lubricants and developing ways to monitor their aluminum fabrication process and improve it. The goal was to work the metal while expending the minimum amount of power and obtaining the best surface finish and shape at the end of the process. You had to know something about metallurgy, something about chemistry, and something about how the lubricants and materials behave under high pressure and elevated temperature. You also needed some understanding of the actual equipment involved in fabrication because sometimes you find an artifact that's produced by an equipment problem or

by water dripping off the roof of the plant. In short, you really need to know everything about a process to make it more efficient.

From Martin Marietta I went to Pennzoil in Houston, Texas. I was "head-hunted" there, and I went as director of their physical sciences group, where I was responsible for testing all of their products. I ran a department that did the laboratory bench testing and looked after their automotive testing programs. I was promoted to vice president after about a year and spent my last two years there as vice president of advanced technology, which involved longer-range product development.

When you first start working in industry, the main thing you need is superior technical skill. You have to be the one who can get the job done and who can answer the question when your boss asks it. You also need to make business and technical contacts that will help you—you have to work the system, not just work on your own. As you move up, a lot of your success depends on your ability to sell your projects to the people who put down real money to support them; the higher you go, the more intense the selling becomes. You still have to have the fundamental technical expertise (and you can't lose that), but you're not going to advance beyond a fairly low level unless you're also good at selling yourself and selling what you're doing. And as you go up, it also becomes more and more important to develop networks and support from your customers.

I am currently vice president of technology and product development at Valvoline. My group looks after the quality of all the products, which include industrial lubricants, passenger car motor oils, commercial motor oils, antifreeze, and other automotive chemicals. We also develop new products—we are typically looking for a new characteristic of the product and trying to select the appropriate chemistry to accomplish that. For example, if we wanted better fuel economy, we would be formulating an oil with special viscosity and special additives.

In my job, my main concern is the future. What parts of our product line will become obsolete? What parts will not experience a lot of growth? What will we do to fill those gaps? Answering these questions requires a knowledge of the larger world: What will General Motors do next? What will Ford do? What's happening in Germany and France and China and in our marketplaces? I spend a lot of time reading and thinking and planning strategy. I also spend a fair amount of time reorganizing processes and the way we do things to try and do a better job for our immediate customers. I try to ensure that the initiatives I've started get completed and bring dollars to the bottom line. Whether it's a product or process monitoring, most of the things I'm doing will either add profits through new products or reduce cost of production. I spend a lot of time thinking about money.

I have an office and I travel a lot. I network with all my resource bases: I may go visit one of our parent company laboratories, or I may go visit a university laboratory. I may phone a professor in a foreign country or someone else I'm trying to work with—they are my resources. Then I might spend time with my immediate customers, people we've got a project going with and who are looking to me for a certain piece of it. I'll call people in my department who are actually doing the work, to keep up to date. I make suggestions if there are roadblocks. If they need something, I'll get it. For example, someone will say, "We're supposed to get this engine test done, but we can't get it done for two months because So-and-So's sick." And I'll say, "Well, that's ridiculous; we can't wait two months." Then I'll make phone calls and get someone in there to get the test running in a week. I delegate projects to various people and, inevitably, these types of roadblocks will develop. My job is to get rid of them. I also sell our work to the upper management: "We need money to do this and here's why."

Being the kind of person I am, I may also take a day to walk into a lab and get my hands dirty. I've done that my entire career. I do it because I think it's fun and also because I think it's important for management to stay in touch with what goes on at the bench. I may spend a day in a quality control lab, working as a quality control technician. Or if I get a new computer system, I'll try it out for hours and actually test out the software. I might go to the laboratory and look at the engine parts. I'll talk to people about how we control the dynamometers and where we've got thermocouples. I don't think of myself as micromanaging: what I try to do is put resources together. If I find out we don't have good temperature control on a particular test, I'll put my people in touch with others who can help improve it.

I like my job. What's motivated me all along is that I fundamentally enjoy what I'm doing, and I'm good at it. Problem solving fascinates me. If we make a product and it does something really great, but it has a drawback, then we reformulate to overcome the drawback so that the product has overall superior performance—it's just fun.

I deliberately married someone who I sensed was not going to have to have things his way all the time, who was not possessive or jealous, who was very independent, and had no problem with my being independent. I got lucky as well. When I first went to Houston, my husband had trouble finding a job there. After staying in Baltimore for some months, he moved down there without a job and stayed unemployed until he found an ideal situation where he works at home. He's made himself flexible in finding his work, rather than having to move for his work choices.

I think one of the biggest challenges women face is having children and working, especially in higher-level positions. The whole system is just unfriendly. It's extremely stressful when you feel obligated to your job and, of course, to your child. Your child will always get sick when you have a meeting with a senior vice president or an important customer. It's difficult to find caregivers whom you're comfortable with, and they always quit when you're least able to handle the problem. If you get to my level and you're still living near your parents or your husband's parents or other family members who might be able to help, it's almost a miracle—most of us aren't.

Fortunately, some companies have the attitude that if you have to be away from work or leave work early to be with your child, you should just do it with no questions asked. I think that's a pretty good way to handle it. I hope that more and more people will start to see working at home part of the time as an acceptable thing to do. It would help all of us if, when our children were sick, we could just take a computer home for the day.

When I moved to Houston, I had to move on my own with a six-month-old baby, to take a new job that had a lot of challenges. After going through that, I feel I can do almost anything. I found child care for him and spent all my hours after work with him. It was hard on both of us. There were compromises and sacrifices. Without help from one of my neighbors, I don't know how I would have done it. When things got really tough, I'd phone her up and say "Would you keep him for a day?" and she did. Without her, it would have been a nightmare.

I remember once I brought my son into work when he was just getting over chicken pox, and we got sent home. My son has spent quite a bit of time reading in my office. I think businesses need to be friendlier to that sort of thing. Most of my younger counterparts seem to feel that they're just going to go ahead and have two or three children and the company will just have to live with it. In my generation, there was more fear. I remember one key executive who, when I mentioned getting live-in help, turned to me and said, "Oh! So then we *can* count on you!" There's still too much concern about that. When someone has a heart attack, no questions are asked, and it usually involves a lot more time off than pregnancy and childbirth.

Most of the time at work, I don't think about being a woman; it's probably negative to spend too much time thinking about it. I just think about getting the job done and working well with the other people I have to work with. But sometimes I see so little diversity in the technical workforce that I think, "This is boring—where *is* everybody?" It's not that the people I work with are boring; they're a lot of fun—it's that it seems there should be more diversity.

At some points, I've felt my gender has been a disadvantage because of the social choices people make about who to go to lunch with or to play racquetball with: men tend to select other men. I don't feel at all that way in my current position. Along the way, I've been in situations where I've felt very good, where there was absolutely no issue with my being a woman, but I've also been in situations where I didn't feel so good. I heard many times, "Gee, you're so good at what you do, I'm really surprised—you're a woman." Some people are just shocked that a woman can do this kind of work, although I don't hear that now as often as I did in the early days. The biggest handicap I think corporate women now face is that some men worry that *other* men will not want to deal with a woman. It's usually, "I recognize your expertise and have no problem working with you, but if I send you to a foreign country or send you to these customers, they may have a problem with it."

Sometimes I think back on my lab technician days before they passed all the rules on sexual harassment. Women, including myself, who went to work as secretaries and lab technicians had no power in their organization, and we had big problems. I really get a big kick out of it when people say sexual harassment is when you tell an off-color joke; back when I started out it was when they pushed you into a closet. For me the problems disappeared for several reasons: I got some real power in the organization, they passed some pretty nice laws, and I'm a lot older.

I'm not sure where young women are today. I hope they start with much higher expectations than I did. They should find something they really, really like to do—because the odds are that if they really like it, they'll be very good at it. I think it's good to become exposed to as many different subjects as possible and then pick something that really excites you.

But what I've found for myself is that I tend to get excited about something when I know a whole lot about it. When someone first said, "Well, work in lubrication," it sounded about as exciting as dirt. But a lot of subjects become more exciting when you start to know a lot about them. At this point, any barriers to thinking that I can do something are gone. I've taken enough risks and been successful enough to build up a lot of confidence.

PRESENT POSITION: Vice President, Technology and Product Development, Valvoline Company

FIELD: Chemical engineering

RESEARCH AREA: Lubrication, friction, and wear

EDUCATION: B.S. in Chemistry (1973), Rensselaer Polytechnic Institute; M.S. (1976) and Ph.D. (1978) in Chemical Engineering, Pennsylvania State University

DATE/PLACE OF BIRTH: June 4, 1950/Passaic, New Jersey

Frances Lockwood lives with her husband, Kenneth Partymiller, and her son, Matthew Partymiller, in Georgetown, Kentucky.

INTERVIEW DATE: April 1995

Vivian Loftness

Department Head and Professor of Architecture
CARNEGIE MELLON UNIVERSITY

Vivian Loftness's work as an architect has spanned the globe: she has studied world climates and their impact on architecture, particularly in the United States, Europe, and Africa; she has designed a solar village in Athens, Greece; and she has worked for the U.S. and Canadian governments on environment quality issues specific to large commercial building. Architecture combines all the things she loves—science, math, and the fine arts. She worked with the American Institute of Architects Research Corporation and with engineering firms in Germany and New York City before finding her way to a university career.

❧

There's quite a debate in the profession today about whether architecture is a fine art, a science, or both. Some people and some universities focus on it as a fine art and pursue the philosophical underpinnings and the materiality of creating a beautiful object. Others recognize that buildings are not just objects but spaces that people inhabit, places in which the fundamental elements of physics are at play—sound, light, temperature. I view architecture as a combination of the arts and sciences; that's what makes it such an exciting profession for me. I became an architect because I loved the fine arts throughout my school years, yet I was also an avid chemist and mathematician. I loved science courses more than anything else during high school. Because I wasn't quite sure what I wanted to pursue in college, I looked for colleges with very strong math and science programs, particularly where the science was married to the

fine arts. To me architecture was a natural—it had to rely on material science, chemistry, physics, and structural engineering. Architecture has these wonderful elements that I could explore in a "fine art" medium. I ended up at MIT, planning to major in architecture but knowing that I could change to a major in math or chemistry if I wanted to. I carried these thoughts and the corresponding courses through the end of my sophomore year, when I finally committed myself to the study of architecture.

Vivian Loftness in her office in Carnegie Mellon University's Department of Architecture

At the time I was a student, the architecture program at MIT was, surprisingly, not a highly technical program. In order to get the technical competence that I felt I needed, I ended up taking courses in material science and chemistry at MIT and courses at Harvard in environmental engineering. I had to "sneak out" to take the courses in other departments and then pretend that I didn't really know this material in my architecture classes. Actually, this is one of the reasons that I took my current administrative position as head of Carnegie Mellon's Department of Architecture. I am really excited by the potential of a university that embraces the marriage of art and science rather than one that sets up a schism. The next generation of architects should have this breadth and rigor, which will lead to more high-quality buildings that perform well for their users.

At MIT, I completed a six-year program in five years, which gave me the opportunity to accept a Rotary International Scholarship to Finland for a year. The MIT program was a four-plus-two degree program—that is, four years for the B.S. degree and two for the master of architecture. About half of the architecture schools in the country have this type of program, and the other half have a five-year bachelor of architecture program. Both programs have their advantages and disadvantages. The four-plus-two program provides students with a broader-based education; you don't usually declare your major until your junior year. But then again you spend six years at a university. The five-year degree requires that you dedicate yourself early on—in fact, in your freshman year, starting immediately with very intense courses in architecture—with the result that you get less diversity in terms of university courses. However, you can take advantage of opportunities for double majors and graduate degrees without excessively prolonging your studies.

The study of architecture provides a stupendous education: it deals with complex problems, indeterminate (no right) answers, multiple client bases, and a need to have an iterative multidisciplinary process. It is a broad-based education, although many architecture students have a limited sense of how capable they are and what it is they can do with their degree. At Carnegie Mellon, we have begun to marry the five-year bachelor's of architecture program with a one-year master's program, building on students' minors during their undergraduate years to offer second degrees in a number of areas, including a master's in urban and regional sustainability jointly with the Heinz School of Public Policy, a master's of science in computation design jointly with the Department of Civil and Environmental Engineering, and a master's of science in advanced technology and building performance. I believe that this type of program benefits the students greatly and provides them with many more career options.

My research interests have always been quite diverse. All of my early work was in energy conservation and natural conditioning strategies, such as passive solar heating and natural ventilation, focusing on climate and architectural regionalism. I worked for about five years with the American Institute of Architects Research Corporation on contract to the Departments of Energy, Housing and Urban Development, and Commerce. My work there focused on the impact of new goals in energy, new goals for natural conditioning, and new goals for regionalism in architectural decision making. In our climate studies, we used thirty years of climate data in computer simulations to evaluate the relation of climate to building design decisions. This revealed the impact that the Southeast climate should have on buildings in contrast to the climates in the Midwest or Northwest. This work resulted in a number of publications, including *Regional Guidelines for Building Passive, Energy Conserving Homes,* which is designed to help home builders in different regions incorporate local materials and regional climate considerations into their designs as a way of providing not only exciting architecture but energy benefits as well.

I focused during those first five years on residential energy conservation and reached a point where I was sure that I wasn't going to uncover any major new knowledge in residential design. So I made a decision to leave the AIA and take a job with an engineering firm in New York that was actively involved in energy design in commercial buildings. I was a liaison between that engineering practice and the architects they were working with. I tried to create a bridge—a common language, common objectives, and early communication so that the architects' decisions would reinforce the engineering understanding. It was a wonderful experience for me because it gave me a lot of insights into commercial building engineering. There was, and still is, very little work on how to make the megamall, the megaschool, or the megahospital a viable, environmentally sound, energy-efficient, and human-friendly high-quality setting.

I have always been lucky in that very few people were doing the type of research I was doing (design and systems integration, thermal comfort, climate data analysis), which provided me with great opportunities. In 1981 the World Meteorological Organization in Geneva contracted me to conduct a study of world climates and the impact they had on architecture, specifically looking at developing countries like those in Africa. Africa has very diverse climates, and studying climate data across the continent was extremely interesting. This study led to conclusions and recommendations on a range of critical early design decisions: building form and organization, building enclosure (materials and wall sections), and opening design.

I've also worked in passive solar research (the use of sunshine for heating without mechanical assistance), and because so few people at that time were trying to apply a science or engineering knowledge-base to architecture, I had another wonderful opportunity to work with the European Common Market in 1980. I was hired by the German government to work on a solar village in Athens, Greece. I lived in Cologne, Germany, and commuted to Athens for a year, which, as you can imagine,

was very exciting. The Lykovrissi Solar Village provides 450 units of energy-conserving homes for low-income people. Year-round comfort was essential since these dwellers did not have beach homes to go to in the summer like the wealthier Greeks did. We couldn't just use the sun to offset all the heating needs in the winter without causing serious discomfort in the summer. The challenge was to optimize the use of conservation—passive solar for winter, and then ventilation and radiant cooling in the summer. There are six different neighborhoods within the village, and each one manifests a different solar energy-conservation technology. The village is being monitored right now by the Common Market. I haven't yet seen the data to know how various buildings are actually performing, although I have my biases about which solar concepts will perform the best over the long term.

I attribute much of my interest in architecture to my early exposure to math, science, and the arts. My father was a nuclear physicist, and my mother was a foreign language teacher. I don't ever remember anyone telling me that math and science were hard, and I always excelled in those courses. Two things probably helped me to excel in math. When I was nine years old, my family spent a year in Paris. I was put into a French school and I didn't know any French. The one course that I understood and did well in was math because the language was the same. The French schools were far ahead of American schools in teaching math—they introduced it much earlier in the curriculum. Because I understood it best, I focused a lot of energy on math. That gave me a big leg up when I returned to the United States. The second opportunity that helped me enormously is a rather telling story, now that I think back on it. I had *the* most wonderful math teacher—an African American woman with a Ph.D. in mathematics who may not have had the range of career opportunities in the 1950s and 1960s that she would have with affirmative action today. Teaching in the public schools was one of the

Vivian Loftness with her husband, Volker Hartkopf, and their children, Sophia, Nicholas, and Alessandra

few career options she had, and she had a passion for teaching. She took our sixth-grade class well beyond algorithms. She made math transparent for me. Between these two opportunities, I came to really love math.

This love of math continued through the first two years of college, until I finally moved into differential equations and numbers disappeared completely. When numbers started to disappear, all of a sudden the allure of math began to disappear. I knew then that I didn't want to pursue abstract mathematics, although I still love applied math.

I remember my days at MIT, when there were eighteen men for every woman. My roommate and I were the only women in the advanced physics class of about 180, so the faculty member knew our names immediately. However, I never felt at a disadvantage because of my gender. I do occasionally find when I walk into a meeting with a group of engineers that they assume that I am there to take notes. Their impression changes when I begin to speak and they realize that I have a body of knowledge and insights to contribute to the discussion. I don't resent that—in the past very few women did enter into these arenas (beyond those who were there to take notes).

A contrasting story occurred when I was on the construction advisory board for Owens-Corning Fiberglass a number of years ago,

when my daughter was just six weeks old. The meeting was in Orlando, Florida, and I wasn't going to be able to go unless my spouse, also an architect, agreed to come along because I needed to be near my daughter but couldn't care for her continuously throughout the meeting. He agreed and came as a "spouse" of the advisory board member. He had the baby strapped to his stomach for most of the four days, and no one ever learned his name. They assumed he had no intelligence in this field. It was quite an experience for him to become the "invisible spouse," an attachment to the real person. It was especially amusing because my husband, Volker Hartkopf, could have easily traded places with me at the meeting because we do similar work.

The only reason I am at a university today is that I married someone who was at a university. I would not have sought out a university setting; I had purposefully decided to pursue a practice-oriented career. I came to Carnegie Mellon in 1981, although shortly after that both my husband and I were contracted by the Canadian government to work for two years at Public Works Canada on environmental-quality issues for large commercial building. They had incorporated a lot of energy-conservation measures in their commercial buildings in the 1970s, and they were having serious failures in the 1980s—air quality and building façade failures. They wanted to know why. So we began to work on what we called *total building performance*—a comprehensive performance agenda that you could use as a design platform for balancing conservation with environmental quality, with building integrity, and with access to views and outdoor spaces. We are interested in the next generation of technology for buildings and how it can be used to accomplish better environmental quality for people. Total building performance emphasizes people—the acoustic, thermal, visual, air quality, and spatial needs of humans, what we should do architecturally and how technology can help to support that. I'm convinced that highrises and megaplexes are environmentally unsafe and nonsustainable, and the technologies that have been designed to support them are not engineered to succeed. I thought, when the World Trade Center was bombed, that we would finally stop the race to build the highest building in the world. It hasn't happened, and that concerns me, especially as we export these nonsustainable solutions to developing nations.

It was really eight years out of my degree program that I began my career as a faculty member. I love what I'm doing now—I teach, do research, and now have added administrative responsibilities. On top of that, I have three children who are three years apart. The secret to balancing all of these commitments is multifold: I have a spouse who pulls his weight, and we've always had a live-in au pair. I work about a ten-hour day and a few hours on the weekend, although mentally I often don't leave work at the end of the day. I also rarely find time for myself; I need to work on that. There are some real myths about academia that I know I believed and that we need to dispel: the myth that faculty members have very relaxed schedules with summers off; that faculty members work alone in an "ivory tower"; and that universities are out of touch with the "real world" of economics, profes-

sional practice, and industrial issues. Instead, most universities are twenty-four-hour campuses, the "real world" drives much of our research, and many of our faculty are actively involved in real projects with teams of faculty from several disciplines. Indeed, I believe that universities are in the forefront of innovation and professional practice and will lead the discussions of sustainability.

My husband and I work very closely together in our research. There are certainly advantages to this: we can travel together to conferences, we can stand in for each other if the need arises, and we always have a ready-made team on whom we can count. But it also means that we never escape our work. It's a real challenge for us not to discuss our work on a Saturday.

I have always enjoyed what I've done at the moment that I'm doing it. I believe that life is not made up of dramatic choices but of natural flows. Almost all of the opportunities I've just talked about were not deliberate actions on my part; rather, they resulted from previous opportunities. I try to live my life according to that philosophy. However, all of these opportunities have been dependent on acquiring the richest knowledge base I could, on continuously building this knowledge, and on becoming a passionate advocate for quality-built environments for people.

PRESENT POSITION: Department Head and Professor of Architecture, Carnegie Mellon University

FIELD: Architecture

RESEARCH AREA: Total building performance

EDUCATION: B.S. in Architecture (1974) and M.Arch. (1975), Massachusetts Institute of Technology

DATE/PLACE OF BIRTH: May 24, 1952/Stockholm, Sweden

Vivian Loftness lives in Pittsburgh, Pennsylvania, with her husband, Volker Hartkopf, and their children, Sophia, Nicholas, and Alessandra.

INTERVIEW DATE: February 1995

Susan Love

Director of the Revlon/UCLA Breast Center
UNIVERSITY OF CALIFORNIA AT LOS ANGELES

In her fight against breast cancer, Susan Love assumes the role of surgeon, oncologist, author, and social activist. She is the author of Dr. Susan Love's Breast Book, *which has been hailed as one of the top books on women's health written in a decade. She and her lesbian partner, Helen Cooksey, were plaintiffs in a Massachusetts Supreme Court case that allowed Helen to become the legal coparent of their daughter, Katie Love-Cooksey.*

❧

I've always liked science and working with people. I don't know exactly when those impulses began coming together as an interest in medicine, but it was sometime in high school. There aren't any doctors in my family, so I didn't really have any role models, but medicine seemed like a way to accommodate my combined interest in science and people.

I began college as a premed chemistry major at Notre Dame of Maryland. After two years, I left and entered a convent in New York City, and the convent sent me to school at Fordham. I still thought I was going to be a doctor; I was just going to do it as a nun. Or, rather, I thought that fleetingly. I really wanted to be out in the world helping people, and the nuns were more interested in saving souls. I left the convent after about five months, but I finished my degree at Fordham.

When I applied to medical school, most places had gender-based quotas and would only admit 5 or 10 percent women. Even the application process itself was a challenge. When I spoke to my premed adviser—who would be writing my recommendations—he said, "If you go to medical school, you'll be killing some boy." The Vietnam War was going on, and men who went to medical school were exempt from the draft. Despite the guilt trip, I applied to medical school, and I got into two or three places. I chose to go to SUNY (State University of New York) Downstate Medical Center because it was the cheapest option and I had to put myself through. It was challenging. This was before feminism had begun to have much of an impact, and many women, myself included, had bought the line that it was a big privilege that we were allowed to study medicine. We still had no sense that we had a right to be there.

When I was halfway through medical school,

Susan Love as an intern in surgery, 1974

the women's movement finally had an impact; admissions were opened up and made sex blind. As a result, the enrollment of women increased to 30 percent. By the time I graduated, medical schools were a little more receptive. I believe four of the five top people in my graduating class were women.

I never expected to go into surgery—I actually thought surgeons were glorified plumbers. But during the third year of medical school, we spent time with different specialties, and surgery was the only one I really liked. Surgery is hands-on, and I like touching things and feeling them and seeing what they are. There's immediate gratification. If you think somebody has appendicitis, you open them up and find out if you're right; whereas in medicine, if someone has a problem, you give them a drug and wait two weeks. I liked using my hands, and I liked the practical approach to problems.

At that time, and even today, surgery was one of the most male-dominated professions. When I was applying for residencies, some people asked me, "What kind of birth control do you use?" The implication was that if I got pregnant, they'd fire me outright. I was only the second woman ever to finish the training program at Beth Israel Hospital in Boston; the first one was just six months or a year ahead of me. At one point there were no on-call rooms in the hospital for women, and there was no designated place for women to shower. The surgeons' locker rooms had big lockers and showers and a lounge; the nurses' locker room, which the women residents shared, was a tiny place with only one toilet. We were definitely breaking new ground, and a lot of people there thought women shouldn't be surgeons. We had to be tougher, better, and stronger than anyone else. I made it by becoming one of the boys. I think some women go through experiences like that in a sisterly or daughterly mode, but I just toughed it out and didn't really stop to think.

When I finished my residency, I had no intention of specializing in breast problems. At that time, and still today, women's health was looked down on as a specialty within medical circles. There was a feeling that only dumb people went into gynecology, and that breast surgery was only done by surgeons who couldn't do anything else, or who were on the verge of retirement and had begun doing easier things. For a woman to choose to be a breast surgeon was capitulating to the stereotype that it was the only thing you could do. I was determined that I was as tough and strong as anyone, that I was trained as well as anyone, and I could do big macho surgery just like anybody else. I wasn't going to let them ghettoize me in breast surgery.

I went into private practice. There were very few women surgeons at the time, and a lot of the patients who were referred to me were women with breast problems; internists didn't send me men with hernias. I quickly realized that the women patients had been treated very badly. Nobody gave them information and nobody explained the options for treatment; they were being treated in a very paternalistic way. There was a clear need to take better care of women with breast problems, and I realized that I could help in a way that a lot of people couldn't; so I decided to specialize.

I became the breast surgeon at the Dana Farber Cancer Institute at Harvard. Before long I was dealing with breast problems almost exclusively. Then the Faulkner Hospital approached me about setting up a breast program. After much negotiation, I agreed to set up the Faulkner Breast Center, which was a center with all women doctors: we had five women surgeons, a plastic surgeon, an oncologist, and a radiation therapist. The program was so successful that we were turning patients away. People from other centers came to see what we were doing to try and mimic it—but they never figured out that the main difference between us and them was simply that we treated our patients as intelligent human beings. We spent a lot of time talking with patients, and we really tried to explain things.

In the meantime, I was getting more and more frustrated that we hadn't made much progress in treating breast cancer. Over the course of time, I had figured out good ways to explain a lot of the issues around breast disease to my patients. I decided that by writing a book, I could take these explanations and put them in a form that would give women around the country access to important information. That way, even if their doctors didn't explain things to them, they could read the book and learn what they needed to know. That would empower women both in terms of their disease and in terms of their interaction with their doctor—they would feel a little stronger and a little more powerful because it wasn't all "medicalese" and they could understand the issues. As I go around the country, women are always telling me how my book was the bible that helped them through the experience. They would read it before they went to the doctor, and it helped to demystify a lot of things.

I met a lot of women on my initial book tour who were very frustrated at the lack of progress with breast cancer. It became clear that the time was ripe to politicize breast cancer, and to really get things moving. I called together a group of people and we started the National Breast Cancer Coalition (NBCC), a national organization of breast cancer groups that works to increase research funding and expand women's role in decision making about breast cancer.

It was partly through my involvement with NBCC, and partly through my increasing notoriety, that I found myself testifying in the Senate next to Dr. Dennis Slamon, a UCLA researcher. At that time UCLA was looking for somebody to help them set up a new breast center, and they called me. I was a little frustrated with private health care and I wanted to do more research and to teach, so it seemed like a reasonable idea. Also, my family and my partner Helen's family are in California, so we moved here.

The breast center here has four surgeons, a nurse practitioner, an administrator, and myself. We also have a part-time oncologist and radiation therapist. As director I operate all day Monday and Tuesday. I see patients all day Wednesday, half of Thursday, and half of Friday. I do research Friday mornings and I do administrative stuff Thursday mornings. On top of that, I try to write papers, fly to Washington to do political work, and spend time with my family.

The current problem with breast cancer research, for prevention particularly, is that we have no mechanism for obtaining intermediate markers, which are chemical or genetic changes that appear in the very early stages of cancer. We've made good progress in figuring out some of the early mutations for colon cancer because there's colonoscopy; we know a lot about cervical cancer because we have the PAP smear. But we have no way of accessing the breast to identify the early, precancerous stages. If you want to do a prevention study, you've got to wait until people get cancer. I want to figure out a way around this problem. We know that most breast cancers start in the milk ducts, so if we could figure out how to access the milk duct, then maybe we could detect early changes. Right now, I'm trying to put a little scope into the milk ducts through the nipple to extract cells to examine for early changes. At this point I can get into the duct, but the challenge is figuring out a way to easily access whatever duct we want and whenever we want to access it. If we can't do that, the process isn't going to work. But I think it will work, and if it does, we will have more options. For example, if we can identify cells in the precancerous stages, we could perhaps squirt something down the ducts and clean them out without resorting to surgery.

The center also maintains a database. We're collecting information on every patient who comes in the door and using this data to study a variety of epidemiological issues. We're also comparing our data to data collected on women in a county facility. We're trying to see what variations appear between different socioeconomic and ethnic groups. We do know that breast cancer is most common in white women of higher socioeconomic status.

I think we need a whole shift in paradigm in treating breast cancer, and I think that it's coming. I think the notion that we have to kill

*Susan Love and family reading
at home*
PHOTO BY STEVE GOLDSTEIN

cancer cells to cure people is crazy. As we start to exploit some of what molecular biology has learned about cells and how they work, the "slash, burn, and poison" treatment we do now will become a thing of the past. People won't even believe that we used to treat breast cancer that way. I believe that breast cancer will be eradicated, or at least become totally curable, within my lifetime.

I didn't really come out of the closet until I finished my residency, so I was pretty old—about thirty-two. When I went into practice, I was ready to settle down. I went on a "find a man" campaign with the idea that it was time to have a husband and a house in the suburbs with a little white picket fence. In the process, I found a man who met all of my requirements, but the idea of marrying him—or even living with him—was more than I could deal with. It became clear to me that the problem was that men weren't really what I was looking for. Later that year, I fell in love with a resident named Helen Cooksey. We went away for a weekend together, and within a week I had moved in with her. We've been together for fourteen years.

Helen wanted a child, and she tried to get pregnant but didn't, so we switched. I got pregnant through artificial insemination with sperm from her first cousin, and we had a daughter named Katie Love-Cooksey. One of our concerns all along was the fact that Helen had absolutely no legal right to *our* daughter. The issue came to a head once when we were going with my family to vacation in Mexico. When we tried to go through immigration, we were told we couldn't take Kate out of the country without a notarized letter from her father. I guess the law was made to prevent people in custody battles from taking kids out of the country, but we had no way around it. When we got back home, Helen was so incensed that she immediately called a lawyer to ask what could be done. We started adoption proceedings so that she and I could jointly, legally adopt Kate. It took several years and lots of money, and finally the case went to the Massachusetts Supreme Court; but we won!

Despite the legal hassles, I think that when you're out, you have fewer problems with homophobia because most people are too polite to be homophobic to your face. When I was recruited by UCLA, I was very clear about my situation and came out during every interview. If it had seemed like it would be in any way a problem, I wouldn't have come here. I think that once you're fairly prominent in your field, your sexual orientation matters less. It's been my experience that socioeconomic class trumps sexual orientation. I think being out is harder when you're not in a professional situation, so I also feel an obligation to be out for all the people who can't. I've never really gotten anything but good reactions from my patients or my colleagues.

I don't balance career and family very well. There's always tension trying to figure out how to do that best. The model for academic surgery is not one that includes any respect for your family. When I came to UCLA, I told the chief of surgery, "Vacation is very important to me, and I take about eight weeks a year." And he said, "I think you get six weeks with this job, but I want you to know that nobody here ever takes their vacation." I replied, "Well, just watch me." We're not good role models to the younger generation in terms of balancing work and personal life. I think it's very important to model that and to take time for your family. If I take time off to go to my child's school, I tell people I'm going to her school; I don't pretend I'm going to the dentist. There's always tension between spending enough time at home and spending enough time at work and spending enough time on the political stuff. I'm always torn, and there's no real way to fix it.

We have more women in medicine now than when I started, but we still need them in the upper ranks. Even now, I'm the only tenured woman in the Department of General Surgery at UCLA. I think you really have to know that that's what you want to do and you truly have to love it. Most of the women I know who went into surgery wound up having psychotherapy either before, during, or after their training. It really is a case of being a round peg hammered into a square hole—all the while being sleep deprived. I say, though, that if you really like it, you just have to push forward and not let anybody get in your way.

PRESENT POSITION: Director of the Revlon/UCLA Breast Center

FIELD: Medicine

RESEARCH AREA: Breast cancer

EDUCATION: B.S. in Chemistry (1970), Fordham University; M.D. (1974), State University of New York

DATE/PLACE OF BIRTH: February 9, 1948/Long Branch, New Jersey

Susan Love lives in Los Angeles with her partner, Helen Cooksey, their daughter, Katie Love-Cooksey, two cats named Sugar and Cream, and a dog named Brownie.

INTERVIEW DATE: April 1995

Sara Majetich

Associate Professor of Physics
CARNEGIE MELLON UNIVERSITY

Sara Majetich grew up in a steel town and coal region surrounded by science and technology. She was fascinated by the striking bands of colored rock—gray, black, red—that were apparent in her home town, and equally curious about its steel mills and coal mines. In an attempt to broaden her interest beyond math and science, her parents stipulated that she could take an advanced math course only if she agreed to take tennis lessons. She took the lessons but stayed with science, earning bachelor's and master's degrees in chemistry and a Ph.D. in physics.

❧

I have always been curious about where things came from. I grew up seeing lumps of coal in everyone's backyard in Pittsburgh. This is a hilly city where road cuts exposed many layers of rock below the earth's surface. I remember wondering what caused bands of gray limestone, black bituminous coal, and reddish iron-containing rocks. I started collecting different kinds of rocks and reading about rocks and minerals at an early age. In elementary school I learned how coal and iron ore were used to make steel. My class visited a coal mine where we donned hard hats with lights on them and went down into the mine. I was fascinated to be underground and actually see the coal seams, the machinery, and how they measured the oxygen level. We also visited a steel mill, and I was impressed with the huge blast furnaces and the terrible noise. Steelmaking was done on a grand scale, and it seemed very important. I remember looking through what I now know is the cobalt glass filter to see the liquid metal that eventually

turned into ingots. I was impressed by how they combined different rocks and created shiny steel.

Like many Pittsburghers, I had relatives who worked in both the coal mines and the steel mills. I'm not sure how much of an influence this had on me, although I remember how dirty my great-uncle was when he came home from working in the mines. I am sure that my interest in coal mines and steel mills

Sara Majetich testing samarium cobalt nanoparticles with a SQUID (superconducting quantum interference device) magnetometer
PHOTO BY KEN ANDREYO

Sara Majetich in her office in Carnegie Mellon University's Department of Physics
PHOTO BY KEN ANDREYO

came less from an interest in "technical" things than from an interest in "Pittsburgh" things, since I knew people who were involved with mines and mills. My parents were confused by this interest in coal and rocks, and for a while they tried to divert my attention to "girl things" like dolls, but it just didn't work. I was never interested in dolls but instead was always asking for things like Tinkertoys or Erector sets (which I never got!).

Even as a child I wanted to do something important, to have a career, and to make a contribution to society. I was drawn to technical fields as a way to achieve my goals. I remember some people questioned my seriousness and the appropriateness of my interest in male-oriented fields, but I never doubted that it was right for me. I also remember a few times when my parents indicated that boys were better at math, despite the fact that my mother is much better at math than my father. I recall similar comments from a few teachers. But I always aspired to high-profile, "male" professions: astronaut, nuclear physicist, chemist. These interests helped to define me. The knowledge that I was good in math and science helped me to persist even when others doubted I would make it, and even when my own self-esteem was low.

By high school my interest in math and science was really strong. One year my parents bargained with me: they would allow me to take an advanced math course if I also took tennis lessons. Although both of them were pretty good athletes, I was never really interested in sports. We still laugh about this incident. Most kids could only play tennis *if* they did their math homework, but for me it was the reverse.

I attended Princeton as an undergraduate and planned to major in chemistry. There were very few women students in the field, and many of my professors asked why I was interested. Some speculated that my interest was in dating the male chemistry students. They couldn't understand that my interest in chemistry was no different from that of my male classmates. Some classmates had equally bad attitudes. It made my college experience less pleasant, but my love of science kept me going. I learned early on that scientists and their personalities do not define science. The work can be beautiful even when done by people whose behavior is not.

I received my master's degree in chemistry from Columbia University. I met my husband while at Columbia, married, and went with him to his first academic position at the University of Georgia. That's when I switched to physics. When I entered the Ph.D. program in physics, I was the first woman in the department. People quite frequently asked why I was there and whether there wasn't a more "appropriate" field for a woman like me. Fortunately, my advisers didn't adopt this attitude. But I do remember one incident when, in response to some difficulty I was having as a new graduate student, someone remarked that "women and Asians just aren't good at that." I made sure, from that point on, that I was good at whatever I did. I knew that I had to be the best to gain respect and success.

Graduate school was the first time I worked in a machine shop. In junior high girls weren't allowed to take shop classes. I realized that being able to use the equipment was important for my success, so I learned how to use machines like lathes, drill presses, and milling machines. I got along fine with the guys in the shop at the University of Georgia. I was such an oddity that I wasn't perceived as a threat, but they were pleasantly surprised when I was at the top of my class.

There were other, less flattering reactions. No single one bothered me a great deal, although they had a cumulative effect. More bothersome were the two men's bathrooms side by side outside my lab with no women's bathroom nearby! Or the fact that people were afraid to give me any feedback because they were terrified that I would run crying to the ladies room (assuming I could find one!). Fortunately, my love of science kept me going, and the hardships made me even more determined to succeed.

Today I am a physics professor at Carnegie Mellon University. My scientific knowledge has increased my appreciation of rocks, and I make my living studying the properties of tiny crystals containing a few hundred to a few thousand atoms. My research in solid state physics is interdisciplinary, overlapping areas of physics, chemistry, materials science, and electrical engineering. I strike a balance between investigating the scientific reasons that small crystals behave the way they do, and designing new materials based on these particles for applications such as xerography, making computer disks, and medical uses like magnetic resonance imaging (MRI). Because of my scientific training, I now understand why one cadmium compound is red while another is yellow, and why some materials are easily magnetized while others are not. I still enjoy hunting for rocks, but now I think of them in terms of what properties they possess and what applications they might be useful for.

Chemists approach their subject by thinking about what happens when a few atoms interact with another few atoms and you have a chemical reaction. Physicists like to think about what happens inside a block of lead with millions and millions and millions of atoms. Since both of these pictures involve atoms, there should be something that describes what happens in between, when you have a few hundred or a few thousand atoms. This science is neither pure chemistry nor pure physics, and that's the area I'm working in—trying to understand how physics and chemistry are connected. My work has many important applications. For example, computers and their components are getting smaller and smaller. Technology is moving toward the point where we will have devices with ten thousand atoms or less, and there's a real need to understand how this works.

In my lab we make and study tiny particles. We examine what happens with their optical properties when they are excited by lasers; we have a fancy apparatus called a SQUID (Superconducting Quantum Interference Device) magnetometer to look at their magnetic behavior. We also have electron microscopes to study the size and type of atoms. We're making particles smaller than the ones that already exist on magnetic computer disks so we can increase the storage capacity. Someday you may rent movies on video disks that contain our magnetic particles.

My research involves working with a large number of people: typically three graduate students, about a dozen undergraduates, other faculty, technicians, and scientists from other institutions. I am a particularly strong advocate of undergraduate research and take on many students in my lab. Working with others is necessary to train new scientists, to gain expertise through collaborations, and to share results. It is also one of the most enjoyable aspects of a technical career. I spend a lot of time in the laboratory talking with students about our research. For me, research is very rewarding and very personal. If you make no effort in research, you go nowhere. When you finish a piece of research, that accomplishment is truly yours. Doing research is also incredibly demanding. An enormous amount of dedication is required, but how many people devote their lives to making something new and better? Researchers are by definition problem solvers. Since there's no shortage of problems in today's world, we're lucky to have people dedicated to research.

Since I am a faculty member, my work involves more than my research. I spend plenty of time in my office writing grant proposals and papers. During the year I also teach and attend many meetings on campus. I travel frequently to scientific conferences or to other universities to talk about our results.

Because my husband was an assistant professor when I began graduate school, I entered my faculty career with a pretty realistic idea of what academic life was like. I remember watching one of my husband's friends help him plan what he needed to set up his lab, and thinking about what I would need if I wanted to do certain types of experiments. As a graduate student I didn't see how much time my professors spent writing research proposals and journal articles, but I got some experience as a postdoc that proved to be wonderful training. Even though I knew it was coming when I took my first faculty job, I was still shocked at how much time it took to write those first few proposals. It gets easier, but it still is very time intensive.

Because I am in a nontraditional field for women, I am conscious of how I differ from my male colleagues and from women in more traditional areas. I have to have a better understanding than my male peers of my goals and specific knowledge of how to reach them. This self-knowledge enables outsiders to become insiders. It took me a while to realize, for example, that when I said "I think . . ." in response to a problem, I was more likely to be right than some men who said "this is . . ." more confidently. Since I have to function in a male-oriented environment, I have learned to speak more like men, projecting authority and interrupting frequently. Sometimes it seems strange, but it has been effective in enabling me to be a successful scientist. In other ways stereotypical female behavior has also helped me to be successful. Traditionally research groups are very hierarchical, with a detached and remote research adviser waiting for graduate students to prove their worth. My group is more like a family unit or a team. There is a lot of give and take. I genuinely expect all my students to become good scientists. Having the flexibility to borrow from different styles to find a solution that works is essential in nontraditional careers.

My husband is still at the University of Georgia, where he is now a full professor. Neither of us is happy living apart, but the job market dictates this separation. I sometimes worry that I'm not a very good role model for my students, but right now there's not much flexibility in the job market. My husband does most of the commuting because he's tenured and has postdocs who can handle the lab as well as some of his classes.

There are a lot of options for careers in science or technical fields. I remember receiving advice from people who meant well but assumed I'd be happier doing something else, but I believe that what is most critical is to know yourself well so that you can make the best choices. What's best for someone else may not be ideal for you. My own judgment hasn't always been perfect, but it's been better than other people's; I have to live with the consequences. When times are tough, it helps to remember I've had a say in what I am doing, and that gives me peace of mind.

PRESENT POSITION: Associate Professor of Physics, Carnegie Mellon University

FIELD: Solid state physics

RESEARCH AREA: Nanoparticles

EDUCATION: B.S. in Chemistry (1979), Princeton University; M.S. in Chemistry (1980), Columbia University; Ph.D. in Physics (1987), University of Georgia

DATE/PLACE OF BIRTH: April 5, 1959/ Pittsburgh, Pennsylvania

Sara Majetich lives in Pittsburgh, Pennsylvania, and her husband, George, lives in Athens, Georgia.

INTERVIEW DATE: September 1994

Luz J. Martínez-Miranda

Assistant Professor, Materials and Nuclear Engineering
UNIVERSITY OF MARYLAND

Luz Martínez-Miranda grew up knowing that science was always going to be in her life. She assumed it would be chemistry, but a top-notch teacher got her hooked on physics. Now she combines her science interests with engineering and has learned that being multidisciplined can lead to interesting results in research.

One of the difficult things about being in academe is that you can very easily become separated from laboratory work and operate mostly from an office. I like being in the lab watching data come in. I started working at a time when funding began to get tight, so I've never managed a large group, as did some of my senior colleagues or contemporaries who started to work earlier than I. Tight fund-

ing allowed me, out of necessity, to remain in the lab; being in the lab allowed me to stay informed about the development of instrumentation and software that makes experimentation easier.

I was trained in condensed matter physics but have worked mostly in engineering departments. There is a fair amount of overlap between engineering and physics, but to do physics in an engineering department you need an engineering department that has matching research interests. Funding agencies view engineering-physics interactions positively, but the fiscal structure of many universities makes it difficult.

My current appointment is in the Materials and Nuclear Engineering Department at the University of Maryland. I came here because I really wanted to teach, and I can split teaching and research equally at Maryland. My de-

Luz Martínez-Miranda and her twin brother, Dr. José-Daniel Martínez-Miranda, at her graduation from MIT, June 1985
PHOTO BY JANET A. ALLEN-FRASER

partment is relatively young. It started as a program within a combined department of chemical and nuclear engineering. Now chemical engineering is a separate department, and our department has twenty-two faculty at present, including four women faculty members. It probably has one of the highest percentages of women faculty in an engineering program in the United States.

I do research in liquid crystals. Liquid crystals have many real-world applications: they can be found in all digital displays that are not LED driven. Liquid crystals are interesting physically because their behavior is between a solid crystal and a disordered liquid and is also concentrated in one-dimensional space. Theoretical physicists and chemists study the liquid crystal system to research theories that deal with one and two dimensions. Because liquid crystals occur naturally, they offer a readily available system that can test those theories. Liquid crystals are responsible for membrane interaction in the body. Over the last decade and a half, researchers from the biological sciences have been doing experiments that were once the sole property of physicists. Both disciplines now look at very similar phenomena.

If there is a chemist on site, the crystals may be synthesized, but typically we buy synthetically grown crystals. We conduct experiments that might run anywhere from just a day to three or four weeks, if it is a highly detailed experiment on phase transitions. The experiment also depends on the stability of the crystal. One of the things that plagued the liquid crystal field in the beginning was that many of the model systems were highly reactive to water, which made it difficult to normalize the crystal. There are now a variety of systems that are chemically stable.

My other projects have involved solid state materials. I'm working with amorphous carbon films and metal clusters. I'm collaborating with a group at Sandia National Laboratories and another group at the Naval Research Laboratories that is working on materials for electrical components with optical applications.

When I was a little girl, I didn't know that I would grow up and go into solid state physics, but I knew one of my primary interests was science. My other major interest was music. Both of my parents are chemists, so I grew up with the image that you went to a laboratory to work. My twin brother and I would line up our toys and pretend that we were in the lab. By the time I entered high school, I knew I wanted to study science and presumed I would study chemistry. High school was a turning point for me. My physics teacher, Mr. Morales, was top notch. He taught from a traditional physics textbook that has been used since the 1950s, but instead of starting with elementary vector calculus and using trigonometry, he started with the section on geometrical optics. It's a more visual section and can be enhanced by laboratory experiments. It had a big impact on me. By the time our class moved from studying optics to solving the problems about the canoe going down the river and across current, I was hooked.

After high school, I went to the University of Puerto Rico and majored in physics. Professor Gómez-Rodríguez, who was head of the department and later became dean of the school and then head of the materials program, was trying to attract students to one of his new physics programs. At that time, you had to take physics without calculus before taking it with calculus. He wanted to bypass that requirement. Since my brother and I had had the opportunity to study advanced math, including calculus, at the University High School, we were able to start in Dr. Gómez's program. We were among the first four students to enter the class at the first-year level, and he was delighted to have us there.

When I was working on my master's thesis at the University of Puerto Rico, I became interested in phase transition phenomena—changes in the physical properties of matter as it changes from a solid to a liquid to gas. I joined one of the two experimental groups in the department and worked with Professor Díaz-Colón. A material can change its appearance when it moves from a liquid phase to a solid phase, but within the solid phase you can also have a rearrangement of the constituent atoms. You can monitor these rearrangements by measuring atom response to an electric field or a magnetic field or by doing X-ray experiments. After my master's degree, I interviewed for doctoral work with several people at MIT who were doing work in phase transitions. Some were even studying critical phenomena. Their research concentrated on exactly what happens inside the atomic system when a material goes from one phase to another, in addition to pinpointing when properties change. A lot of properties change very dramatically through phase transition. I thought Professor Birgeneau was doing very nice work in liquid crystals and decided to pursue my thesis work with him.

My thesis focused on critical phenomena in liquid crystal three-phase systems. I had to map out the liquid crystal system and compare it to the other systems that have been defended in the literature. Our group did the first detailed X-ray study of liquid crystal phase transition, and we compared it with other types of measurements done on phase transitions.

Physicist Millie Dresselhaus [see Mildred Dresselhaus's profile on page 105] was teaching at MIT while I was there, and though I was not her student, two of my closest friends were. She was a wonderful role model. The three of us, and one other theoretical physicist student, created our own internal "girls' network." We did things together and checked on each other's work. I was the first woman to seek a Ph.D. in the lab I was working in as well as the *only* woman in my lab. I used to go to my network for support. I still keep in touch with these women. In addition, I met informally with a group of classmates who were mostly men. We were all in various areas of physics, and it created a support network for us. We developed strong bonds that continue to sustain me.

I experienced a culture change when I left Puerto Rico to attend MIT. MIT is a very high-pressure place, but there were other differences. U.S. culture is much more chauvinistic. At the University of Puerto Rico, if a woman decides to do something, no one presumes that she isn't capable of doing it. There may be resistance from families for other reasons, but pressure not to study a certain discipline just because you are a woman doesn't exist. The American Institute of Physics has done studies that show that the United States is near the bottom in the percentage of women who pursue the field of physics; countries like Brazil, Spain, and Italy rank among the top. Once I had declared physics as a major at the University of Puerto Rico, and proved that I could do it, there was a general acceptance of my ability from my professors. The only resistance I encountered there came from a professor from the States. At MIT it was different, but I used the support of my network to persist.

I'm not very good at balancing my work and my personal life, but one of the things that does help provide balance is music. At MIT I was active with performing groups. There were times that I would break out of lab to go to rehearsal. I play classical piano and the harpsichord. Church events and friends keep me active. I have a commitment to go home every year to Puerto Rico for Christmas. Working in an academic environment is an advantage because I can leave for two or three weeks at the holiday time.

My parents were always supportive of my brother and me. My brother is the musician and I'm the scientist. He helped to balance my interests as we grew up. We were in school together until the first year of college, when he went off to pursue a degree in music at the Eastman School of Music at the University of Rochester. My mother was very careful never to distinguish between what my brother could do and what I could do. My parents never told me that I could not do things because I was a girl. Since both my parents were in science, they never questioned my going into science or seeking a Ph.D. My maternal grandmother was also very insistent about our furthering our education, although she had never gone beyond the third grade. She set the path from one generation to the next.

I was blessed with a family and friends who are supportive and accustomed to encouraging people to pursue science. And while pres-

Luz Martínez-Miranda in the High Resolution X-ray Laboratory at the Liquid Crystal Institute at Kent State University, January 1995
PHOTO BY RENATA MARROUM

sures come from everywhere—in physics people believe that if you are not doing physics twenty-four hours a day, you really aren't committed—I believe there have to be things other than science in people's lives. I work in an environment that lets me teach as well as conduct research. I feel productive and happy.

During my postdoctoral assignment at Berkeley, I went to a miniconference on women in science and engineering. One speaker used the opportunity to mention the flexibility of academic life: the only "set" time is the time when you teach. So while you might be working more hours than many of the people you know, you can distribute those hours as you like. When asked if she had any problems trying to raise her kids when they were small, she said, "Yes, I felt very guilty. But I once asked my children about it, and they said, 'What do you mean? You were one of the only mothers who was able to come to the 3:00 P.M. school play.'" Her story bodes well for my future.

PRESENT POSITION: Assistant Professor, Materials and Nuclear Engineering, University of Maryland

FIELD: Applied physics

RESEARCH AREA: Liquid crystals

EDUCATION: B.S. (1977) and M.S. (1979) in Physics, University of Puerto Rico–Río Piedras; B. Music (1979), Conservatory of Music of Puerto Rico; Ph.D. in Physics (1985), Massachusetts Institute of Technology

DATE/PLACE OF BIRTH: September 8, 1956/ Bethesda, Maryland

Luz Martínez-Miranda is back at the University of Maryland after a leave at the Physics Department and Liquid Crystal Institute as the recipient of a National Science Foundation Visiting Professorship for Women, which she undertook at Kent State University. She plans to resume her musical activities shortly and is delighted to belong to the same parish her parents belonged to when she was born.

INTERVIEW DATE: March 1995

Sue McNeil

Professor of Civil and Environmental Engineering and Engineering and Public Policy
CARNEGIE MELLON UNIVERSITY

Going from a single-sex high school (all female) to a single-sex college classroom (all male), Sue McNeil didn't see much of a difference. She doesn't remember any time during her undergraduate work in Australia or her graduate work at Carnegie Mellon University when she felt alienated, or when people implied that civil engineering wasn't an appropriate profession for women. The first woman tenured in the engineering college at Carnegie Mellon University, she finds that her most productive hours of the day happen after 10 P.M., which is lucky for her because her students, two daughters, and husband keep her quite busy the rest of the day.

❧

Civil engineers have always focused on building new structures and facilities like bridges and dams, but I'm interested in what already exists. I want to know what infrastructure is out there, what condition it's in, how fast it will deteriorate, what we can do to fix the problems we identify, and how much it will cost. To figure these things out, we use economics and engineering, draw on mathematical and computer tools, and utilize technology to collect condition data.

For example, I am particularly interested in what happens to bridges over time. One of the technological tools we use to explore this question is ground-penetrating radar, which helps us to understand what's occurring underneath the surface of the bridge deck—six to eight inches beneath the road surface we drive on. Chloride ions from the salt we use on roads in the winter migrate to the steel reinforcing bar and cause it to corrode. When

the bar corrodes, it expands in volume, pushing out the concrete so that the concrete is no longer attached to the steel reinforcing bar. It "debonds" and causes cracks to propagate at that level, which eventually end up as potholes on the surface. The radar helps to find these problems before they surface, literally, which helps local, state, and federal agencies to forecast when the surface will need serious attention. This process really serves as a planning tool because a planning cycle for surface repairs is typically three to five years.

Once we know what's going on under-

Sue McNeil surveying by the roadside in Australia, April 1976

ground, we can determine the best fix: whether to put the equivalent of a band-aid on the superficial problems—patch the actual potholes when they surface; to do a repair with minimal interruption of traffic—close down one lane, remove the top surface or deteriorated concrete, and resurface; or do a major repair and close the entire bridge for an extended period of time, which is often planned five or six years in advance. One reason you always see road repairs going on is because road surfaces are only designed to last ten or fifteen years. The agencies responsible for fixing roads and bridge decks do stagger the repairs, but you simply can't avoid user delay and aggravation costs.

Part of my interest is also in how to get better information fast so that we can make better decisions more quickly. Our research team has developed software that uses neural networks to interpret data and figure out how bad a problem is and how much time we have until it needs to be addressed. The current output from the radar is very crude and difficult for untrained eyes to read, but this computer system could make a big difference.

My interest in engineering started early. I grew up in Australia, and because my father was a mining engineer, I was exposed to engineering and engineers most of my life. Periodically, I had the opportunity to go down into coal mines and actually see the engineering process. I saw how taking coal out of the mine relates to geology, how coal is formed in beds, and how it behaves before it is mined. In an underground coal-mining operation, you go in with equipment and take the coal seam out; because of the way coal forms, you end up with a very stable layer of rock as a roof, and you leave supports for the roof in the form of coal pillars. Eventually when you finish mining you take out the supports and let the roof collapse behind you. I found all of this fascinating.

My early interest was strengthened by a high school geography field trip. We visited a laboratory for the local water authority, and I saw scale models of dams, spillways, and water treatment works. I remember thinking,

"Wow, this is what engineers do." Even as a child I was fascinated by how you take a large-scale structure and model it.

These exposures prompted an interest in engineering on my part and a tacit expectation on my father's part. My father was always technically oriented, and so we always talked science and math. I remember telling friends in my all-girls high school that I was interested in engineering, and I remember their response: "You can't do that." So I started telling people that I was going to the university to do "something" in math or science. This incident wasn't devastating to me, and it didn't affect my goals or plans. But I remember it.

I was lucky to attend college in Australia in the 1970s because it had a system of traineeships that allowed students to work over the summers and provided tuition and a stipend during the school year. I was hired right out of high school in 1973 by the Department of Main Roads (the equivalent of a state department of transportation). I began working the summer before my first year of college. For the first two summers I worked in a drafting office where I was involved in road design. Usually, they'd give me a problem someone else had already tackled and ask how I would lay out the road. I had to look at standards and what was already out there. It was great exposure. I also did culvert design for a bridge made out of a reinforced concrete box. I had to work out how much water would be going through the culvert in order to determine how big to make the bridge. The third summer I worked with the surveyors, and we actually went out in the field and put in the stakes where the new road was going to go. During the fourth summer I worked with the computing people on bridge design. The fifth and final summer was spent on road construction sites. The traineeship provided me with hands-on experience and the opportunity to see a lot of real civil engineers at work on very interesting projects.

I don't remember any time during my undergraduate work in Australia or my graduate work in the United States when I felt alienated, or when people pointed out or implied that civil engineering wasn't an appropriate profession for a woman. I just went from a single-sex high school (all females) to a single-sex college classroom (all male) and didn't see much of a difference. Perhaps I wasn't a threat to anyone because there was only one of me!

I got married in 1976, at the end of my fourth year of a five-year program of undergraduate work, then moved on to graduate school at Carnegie Mellon. My husband John's background is in electrical engineering, but over the years he has moved away from engineering and into management consulting. We have always experienced the "two-career problem," which involves a complex set of trade-offs. My daughter, Sarah, was born in June 1982, near the end of my graduate work. That was a conscious decision. After I finished my dissertation, we moved to New Jersey because of John's job. I worked as a consultant part-time, and then Emily was born in the summer of 1984. The next year I taught at Princeton part-time. At that point I was starting to get the message that two years out of the academic mainstream was a long time, and so I started looking at academic jobs. I went to MIT for my first academic position and two and a half years later received a phone call suggesting that I might like to apply for a position at Carnegie Mellon. I came to Carnegie Mellon in January 1988 with a three year old and a five year old. I was tenured as a full professor in 1994.

I never really had a role model. My interest in the subject drove me to work toward my Ph.D., and my interest in teaching drew me to academic life. I find teaching a tremendous challenge: figuring out ways to keep students not simply awake but excited about engineering. I enjoy students at different levels for different reasons: seeing the twinkle in the eyes of first-year undergraduates when they finally see the connections among physics, chemistry, math, and engineering; watching graduate students pushing the edge of knowledge and finally discovering their niche; and helping teaching assistants to think through what teaching really means in relation to learning. It's rewarding and very time consuming; I often find little time for other things when I'm teaching. I'm always looking for ways to keep myself fresh and interested when teaching the same material over and over: I search for new examples; I try to create new assignments; I explore new teaching mediums. In 1994 I was awarded the engineering college's Benjamin Teare Teaching Award; it was one of my proudest moments.

Despite my success, I have had and continue to have moments of self-doubt, but somehow I've always managed. I've always focused on what I wanted to do and then done it. Tenure hasn't really changed my life. I still feel an obligation to do all those things I did prior to tenure, plus more. My husband and I recently agreed to serve as copresidents of the PTA at our children's school, something that I believe is important but wouldn't and couldn't have done prior to tenure.

The support network I've had and continue to have is incredible. My parents, my husband, and his parents were supportive not only of a professional daughter/wife/daughter-in-law but also of my interest in earning a Ph.D. in civil engineering. My mother came for the arrival of each child and was enormously supportive. My in-laws spent three months in the States watching my one year old so that I could finish my dissertation because my husband was working out of town in New Jersey. My husband, whose profession gives him much more career flexibility than mine, has moved three times for my job. His support has been vitally important in enabling me to achieve what I have achieved.

It's not easy balancing all the roles and responsibilities I've taken on—researcher, teacher, mentor, committee member, taxicab driver, adoring fan, middle school math tutor—but the flexibility of academic life makes it doable. For example, I'm able to attend many of the children's functions at their school. Also, I'm lucky because I don't need much sleep. I am a night owl, and often my most productive hours of the

Sue McNeil with her husband, John, and daughters, Sarah and Emily, in a recent photo

day are from 10 P.M. to midnight. I relish that time and use it well. Also, we have hired help when we've needed it—nannies, au pairs, someone to clean the house. These people have been invaluable.

My kids have grown up with the university as an extension of our family life. They have come to university functions and classes with me; they've sat through many lectures. I sometimes worry that seeing me do all that I do might backfire—they might decide that balancing a career and family is just too much hard work. We talk about it, but not as much as we should.

The first thing to go in my schedule, when something has to give, is time for me—swimming, exercising. Every so often I get frustrated and wonder, "Why am I doing all this?" And then I think, "What else could I do?" I love what I do—engineering and parenting. And I wouldn't want to be doing anything else.

PRESENT POSITION: Professor of Civil and Environmental Engineering and Engineering and Public Policy, Carnegie Mellon University

FIELD: Civil engineering

RESEARCH AREA: Infrastructure management

EDUCATION: B.Sc. in Mathematics (1975), University of Newcastle; B.E. in Civil Engineering (1977), University of Newcastle; M.S. in Civil Engineering (1981), Carnegie Mellon University; Ph.D. in Civil Engineering (1983), Carnegie Mellon University

DATE/PLACE OF BIRTH: June 17, 1955/Newcastle, New South Wales, Australia

Sue McNeil lives in Pittsburgh, Pennsylvania, with her husband, John, and daughters, Sarah and Emily.

INTERVIEW DATE: September 1994

Sandra Murray

Associate Professor of Neurobiology, Anatomy, and Cell Science
UNIVERSITY OF PITTSBURGH SCHOOL OF MEDICINE

Sandra Murray became interested in biology when a childhood injury temporarily paralyzed her arm. Her family encouraged her interests and helped her gain confidence in her own worth—confidence she needed in graduate school when a prospective adviser turned out to be racist. Realizing that the best revenge was living well, she went on to become a successful professor, balancing research, teaching, and the demands placed on her as one of the few women and people of color at her institution.

⁂

From a very early age, I had an interest in biology that people around me really couldn't satisfy. As a child, I had a broken clavicle, and my arm was paralyzed for a while. In the hospital, I got very concerned with what went on inside that made people move and walk; I especially wanted to know what had happened inside of *me* that made my arm stop working. I would ask questions and the hospital staff would give me old books. There was a surgeon who retired and when he cleaned out his office, I got his old books—picture books that would fold out with diagrams.

My father had a moving company. I was allowed to play with anything that came back on the junk truck, and one of the things that came back was books: science books, biology books, doctors' books. I collected and read those as a small child when I was still recovering from the injury to my arm. Since I could not run out and play, I spent time looking at pictures and trying to figure out what *claidocranial* meant.

I also did science fairs. I thought they were the best things. You didn't have to go to class

for an *entire week*, and if you worked it right, you could tell the teacher you needed another week to prepare. My projects were often over-ambitious—trying to make hard water soft and soft water hard or finding a cure for cancer. They were not patentable things and they never worked, but I had a ball doing them. Since I still had to read background material, whether the project was sensible or not, by the time I got to college, science—especially biology—was very easy for me. So I just continued to do biology until I ended up as a professional research scientist.

Sandra Murray at the International Symposium on Intercellular Junctions (Connexins), Hiroshima, Japan, 1993

My family couldn't have been more supportive. If I had homework to do, then I didn't do any housework. As long as I was reading I didn't have to do chores. Later on they did start to wonder *what* I was reading, but just the process of seeing me read a book made them happy. I had a lot of books to read because of the moving truck "junk": my father collected books that he enjoyed reading, and my mother collected books that matched the decor of the house. There was never a problem finding books to read so I could impress my parents.

I always felt that there was no limitation to being a woman and going into any field that I wanted to go into. I saw my mother do lots of things that I would now classify as "man's work." She would put on coveralls and my father's boots that were too big for her and go outside to do all kinds of work. She worked around the moving company too, and had her own business as part of it. Since I was given anything that came off the moving truck that was a toy, I not only played with discarded dolls but with trucks, Erector sets, and even a broken radio.

I remember once when I said I wanted to be something, my mother asked whether many women were doing it, and my father said, "What difference does it make? Sure she can do that!" I didn't know that there were fields women didn't go into until I got to college. I was *told,* but I didn't really believe it. I remember a high school counselor telling me, "After all, you're a girl and you're colored, and colored girls don't become research scientists." It hurt when she said that, but it didn't really register; I didn't think she knew what she was talking about. By that time I had a job as a laboratory aide at the University of Illinois Medical School and I was participating in science classes at the University of Chicago.

I did my undergraduate work in biology at the University of Illinois and supported myself with my laboratory job and by working in my father's business. I went on to Texas Southern University in Houston and pursued my M.S. while working as a teaching assistant in genetics. When I went to the University of Iowa for my Ph.D., I thought for sure that genetics would be easy for me. I had done my master's thesis on DNA in leukemic animals, so it seemed like a natural progression.

When I started my Ph.D. program at Iowa, I met a man who was a very good geneticist. He taught the genetics course and would have liked to have had me in his laboratory. He was very well known and he published in all the top journals. But he never published what he believed were the implications of his research; he only talked about those in class.

The first experiment he explained to us was that he had taken *E. coli* (bacteria that live in the intestine) and put them in either a nutrient-rich environment or a nutrient-deficient environment for several generations. He then put both sets of bacteria into nutrient-rich environments, and he showed using enzyme chemistry that those coming from the nutrient-deficient environment didn't do as well as the ones that had been in a nutrient-rich environment all along. I remember him saying to me, "So, Sandra, if your mother, and your mother's mother, and your mother's mother's mother were in a slave hut and didn't eat well, you should not expect to sit in this class and do as well as the students who are sitting next to you." As a result, I studied very hard in genetics. If there was anything I was going to get a good grade in, it was genetics. When I got an A in the course, he called me into his office and said, "You know, I'd very much like you to work with me. You must understand, however, that you have done nothing here to disprove my theory." Given my lighter skin, he thought I probably had non-African blood that had allowed me to do well. Or perhaps I had studied much harder than everyone else. Either reason might explain why I could score higher than 90 percent of a class that contained more than a hundred students. It was very important to him to find an explanation for how I could have gotten an A in the course without disproving his theory.

He did another experiment where he put flies of different sizes in a graduated series of chambers where there was a lot of food at one end and the amounts decreased until at the other end there was no food at all. He showed that the small flies spent more time in the chambers without food than the larger flies, to the point that they often died of starvation. According to his theory, it wasn't because the large flies made the small flies go down there; the small flies just did it. "And so, you see," he concluded, "when individuals know they are inferior, they seek out areas where they can expire." And then he told me, "You have to understand that you will probably go away from the center of learning." He was referring to my habit of going away from the department to do my studying. When I studied in my office at school, he would sneak into the room and stand in back of me and watch what I was studying and try to get a feel for how much time I spent studying what and what books I had opened. He needed to see if I was studying more than everyone else so he could prove the other theory.

That was running me nuts, so I stopped studying in my office. And he even equated *that* to the flies. In my office I would have been with other graduate students, and I would have been closer to the library and other knowledge resources. Instead, I was like the little bitty fly, flying off into nothingness in the dorm—where he had also found out I was studying!

There's nothing you can do with people like that except leave them. The best revenge is success. Even though I was very interested in genetics, I realized it was in my best interest to find another department and another adviser, which is what I did. I got my revenge by going on to live well and going on to laugh about it. But I didn't laugh when I was a student. I didn't laugh when I was taking the courses. I didn't laugh when I started graduate school thinking I might like to go into genetics. Fortunately for me, I encountered him late in my education. If I'd met him earlier, he might have sidetracked me. But by the time I was a graduate student, I had a sense of security and a sense of my own worth, so although his treatment of me hurt, I was able to go on.

For the most part my peers have been very supportive, but there are still certain problems with not looking like everyone else. Sometimes a white man's career is nurtured in ways that may not occur with a woman or a minority. It may be neglect rather than hostility. No one is saying, "I want to get Sandra," but often no one is saying, "I want to help Sandra" or "Gee, I wonder why Sandra doesn't know that. After all, we all went up to the racquetball club and talked about it at great length." So the minority or female faculty member can encounter problems with isolation; they forget to include you. And even though it's more a case of forgetting than anything else, the isolation hurts people in academia at all levels. If you don't know where the yellow brick road is, you don't walk it as well as someone who does.

On the other hand, sometimes they remember to include you when it's not always in your best interest. So if there's a committee about anything with "Black," "Woman," or "Minority," and you happen to be one of the few women or people of color in the department or university, you may be called upon and have to say "no" more often than nonminority or male faculty do. Saying no can make you look and feel like you're not a team player, but if you don't say no, you'll end up looking like Swiss cheese. You'll be pulled in every direction and become completely unfocused. The trick is knowing when to say no and when to make sure you're on a committee—the finance committee, as opposed to the committee that decides the color of chairs in the conference room.

You can control the external pressure to help people, but it's harder when there's an internal obligation. You can turn away the external pressure to join some panel, but it's harder when your own conscience is telling you to do it. That little voice inside says, "How can you miss the committee meeting with that student when no one was there for you in the same situation, and you know you really could be there?" If someone asks directly, "Can you do this tomorrow?" it's eas-

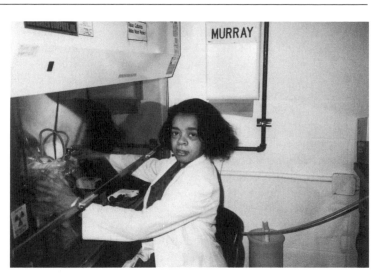

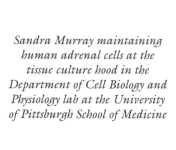

Sandra Murray maintaining human adrenal cells at the tissue culture hood in the Department of Cell Biology and Physiology lab at the University of Pittsburgh School of Medicine

ier to say no if I don't feel I should do it anyway. I am on a lot of committees—there are some things I just feel I should do—but I also say no a lot.

During the day I work in my lab, which is something I enjoy. Unfortunately, the higher I go up the academic ladder, the less time I get to spend in my lab. The more I get funded, the more people I have working for me, and the more research I can get done. I have two postdocs, three graduate students, and usually four undergraduates. I counsel all my students, I look at their experiments and help plan experiments. Each undergrad is assigned to a senior person in the lab, so I don't see them every day that they come in. I have a lab meeting every week where we talk about what did and didn't get done.

I study the capacity of cells to send signals from one cell to an adjacent cell via structures called connexons, which are associated with controlling the function of cells and the rate of cell population growth. I also study signal transduction; that's when one cell gives off a peptide hormone that brings about a response in another cell by interacting with molecules on the external side of the cell membrane. So I use molecular biological, biochemical, and morphological methods to ask, "How do cells function? What brings about normal functions in a cell population? What controls the rate of cell population growth if a normal population has been injured, and how does that compare to the daily process of aging and replenishing in that population? What is different in cancer cell populations?"

I study cells in culture and sometimes human tissue taken from donors; very rarely do I use animals. I have cells lines that originated from tissue, but I can grow them in the incubator and study them just as cells. One reason I wanted to do this kind of research is that you have control over the environment in which the cell lives, and you can limit the number of variables in a way you can't in an organism. You can also do kinetic studies that involve very brief (perhaps a second) stimulation. On a whole tissue you can't do that. Also, I never liked working on animals. Many biologists use rats or some other animal, but that never appealed to me. I never wanted to touch a rat, and I certainly never wanted to hurt a rat. The tissue culture is something easy and pleasant to study. I enjoy coming to work and talking to cells; I don't enjoy going home at night knowing that an animal has been hurt.

I interact with clinicians to look at potential applications of my research. One long-term goal of my work is being able to replace cells in the body. To do that, you have to be able to control the immune systems of the person to whom you are giving the cells.

Ideally, you would give someone their own cells. For example, if you have someone who is at high risk for diabetes, you might take a sample of pancreas cells at birth and store them in cryoprotection. Then when that person is forty and develops diabetes, you can give them the cells. In looking at these kinds of possibilities, I collaborate with clinicians who normally do kidney transplants, and we have a standing meeting where we integrate research. They give us the human adrenal tissue that we use for many of our experiments. Another potential application of my work is to ask, "If this is a tumor cell population, what kind of things can I do that will only affect the tumor cell population and stop it from growing, and not affect the rest of the cells in the body?"

I teach gross anatomy to the first-year medical students. I like it because it recalls the questions that I asked as a little child: "Why does my arm move? What's on the inside?" I enjoy seeing my students see the answer for the first time and watching the discovery. I also give lectures in cell biology and physiology.

I love my work. I think what I do is important. It gives me a feeling of accomplishment, and I feel that it's moving somewhere. The questions I ask in my research are very basic: "What is that cell? What does that cell do? What's in the body? If I put it in the body, what will happen?" I can see where in the next ten years this kind of research will be applied and perhaps even revolutionize medical practice. I see my work as something that's going somewhere. I like the challenge, and it *is* a challenge. To write the next grant that gets funded is *really* a challenge.

I like training students. I like interacting with people, and I have time to do that. I like seeing people who look like me succeed in my field. I tell my students that they have to have the love of a search and be persistent. I tell them, "Don't be afraid of a challenge, but lean into it. If you're uncomfortable, it means you're growing. Don't allow yourself to be isolated; find people who will tell you what you need to know. Most importantly, tell yourself you're good, and more than good—damn good!" I like the feeling that I will someday replace myself. I have a number of graduate students who I feel will sit in my position, but higher; who will walk in my shoes, but farther. It's a good feeling—damn good!

PRESENT POSITION: Associate Professor of Neurobiology, Anatomy, and Cell Science, University of Pittsburgh School of Medicine

FIELD: Molecular and cell biology

RESEARCH AREAS: Role of signal transduction in cell communication, function, and growth

EDUCATION: B.S. in Biology (1970), University of Illinois at Chicago; M.S. in Biology (1973), Texas Southern University; Ph.D. in Anatomy (1980), University of Iowa

DATE/PLACE OF BIRTH: October 7, 1947/Chicago, Illinois

INTERVIEW DATE: November 1994

Nalini M. Nadkarni

Member of the Faculty
EVERGREEN STATE COLLEGE

As a graduate student, Nalini Nadkarni became fascinated by rain forest canopy ecology. Although her advisers were skeptical, her interest was rewarded when she made an important new discovery: tree roots extending from branches in the canopy layer. This find put her on the cover of Science and in a tenure-track position at the University of California at Santa Barbara. However, she realized that a tenure-track position wasn't conducive to her happiness and family life, so she made a few career moves and now shares a position at Evergreen with her husband, Jack.

❧

As a child I loved trees; I was always a tree climber. I wasn't so much interested in science as in nature and just being outside. By the time I started college at Brown, I was pretty set on premed; it seemed like the way to go into science. But during the first two years, I found myself really hating the competitive feeling I got in the courses. I also hated being in a lab all day: I broke a ton of glassware and found myself looking longingly out the window. Fortunately, there was a very inspiring young professor named Jonathan Waage who was a field ecologist. He gave some lectures in an intro biology course and took us on field trips to look at dragonfly behavior. I suddenly realized there was a whole world of people doing this stuff for a living.

I ended up taking a junior-year transfer to the University of British Columbia, which has a very good forestry school. I thought working in forestry might be the way to make a living understanding forests. But by the end of the year, I realized that forestry is mostly about cutting down trees and producing them commercially. So I decided to go back to Brown to get a biology degree and then move on to the next step.

The other thread in my life was modern dance. My parents had given my sisters and me modern dance lessons with a very wonderful teacher. I had studied since I was four years old, and I danced a lot at Brown. I knew—even though it was hard to tell me anything—that dance and biology probably wouldn't go together as a career, so I decided to try each out

Nalini Nadkarni at Otis Smith Farm campsite, spring 1974
PHOTO BY ROBERT PFAFF, JR.

after graduation. I found a year-long research position as field assistant for a biologist in Papua New Guinea. I encountered field biologists in the tropics for the first time and just loved it. Afterwards, I traveled overland through India, visited my father's family for a few months, then went to Paris and found a studio where I could dance full-time. I stayed there living the life of a dancer for six months. Afterwards, I sat down and said, "Well, which was better?" It was very clear to me that although I loved living in Paris and dancing, field biology was the better choice. I didn't like living in a city; I liked being out in a forest, and I felt I could make a longer-term contribution that way.

I started graduate school at the University of Washington in 1979. The critical moment for me was when I took a summer course in tropical ecology with the Organization for Tropical Studies. I thought, "Wow—people are asking these really interesting questions in tropical systems, and some of them are even making a living at it!" It also taught me the process of doing science: not just the nitty gritty of naming a tropical tree or a bird but how you go about posing a hypothesis and collecting data to test it. It was during that trip that I really got excited about looking at forest canopies because the epiphytes (plants that live perched on host trees) and the bird life in the canopies were so rich compared to the forest floor. I recognized that there was a lot we didn't understand about life in the canopy, and I really wanted to understand how it fit into the forest as a whole. I wondered what we were doing on the forest floor when we should be up there, but people were only just beginning to apply mountain-climbing techniques to climb tall trees and examine the canopy. I stayed on after the course ended to learn those techniques.

When I came back to my graduate school committee—who were all temperate-based forest ecologists—they kind of didn't get it. They didn't understand why I was so fired up about the tropics, first of all, and secondly, they couldn't see why I felt I needed to do canopy work. Eventually they said, "Well, if you want to look at the canopy in the rain forest, you should really look at the temperate rain forest here in our own backyard." So I decided to do a comparative study of epiphyte biomass in the temperate rain forest and the tropical rain forest in Costa Rica (where my heart really was). I figured out ways of sampling the material, and extrapolating it to the canopy as a whole, and trying to put that into the context of the entire ecosystem. I was able to pursue this work without the support of my committee because I wrote and received a $50,000 grant from the Man in the Biosphere Program. At that time that was a lot of money for a little graduate student to have, so I was able to go off on my own.

It was during the course of carefully taking biomass samples, cutting out little patches of mosses in the canopy, that I started noticing these roots in the big-leaf maple trees that I was climbing. When I came back down and asked my professors about them, they gave me blank looks: "What roots are you talking about? There are no other vascular plants up in the canopy." When I traced the roots back, I found that they all ended back in the branches or trunk of the maple tree. I sent samples out to root experts all over the world and found that no one had ever documented this before. It wasn't that these roots were hard to see; it was just that I was climbing around up there and taking samples and happened to be the first to notice them. I made the connection that this was a never-before-discovered pathway of nutrient transfer in the canopy. It was something new, and it helped explain why rain-forest ecosystems can function the way they do even though their soils are very often poor.

Anyone who climbed that tree would have made this major discovery, but no one had done it. For me it was a tremendous hit. The paper I submitted to the journal *Science* made the cover, which was nearly unheard-of for a young graduate student. It made people realize that there really is some important stuff going on in the canopy.

Making the cover of *Science* was great. I think I was seen in graduate school as someone who had these goofy ideas about the canopy and why it was important. It was only by sheer will and stubbornness and true passion (as it still is) that I persisted in studying the canopy. I'm not pointing fingers or denigrating my graduate committee; they were trying to help me by saying, "This isn't real science. You're not going to help yourself out by doing this silly research project." But as a message to women or young people, I would say if you do have a strong passion about a particular area of research, as I did, sometimes you just have to forge ahead and stick with it despite the lack of encouragement.

I applied for academic jobs even before I got my Ph.D. officially, and was offered a tenure-track position in ecosystem ecology at the University of California at Santa Barbara. My research took off fairly slowly at first. The National Science Foundation turned down my grant proposals three times before I was awarded an ecology grant. Again, it took hard-headed passion, being convinced that this was important research, and reapplying for the *fourth* time before I got standardized funding; but since then publications have been flowing out and things have taken off.

I was on the tenure track at UC Santa Barbara for five years. They're a fairly high-powered research institution, and so teaching is not regarded as very important. I was feeling really pressured because I like teaching. I started a tropical biology course through their education-abroad program, but I still had to get grants and write papers. Part of the pressure was that my husband was there as a "captive spouse." We had decided when we got married that we were not going to live apart. Whoever found a job first would take it, as long as the other could do research on the side. I ended up getting the first job offer, but UC was not very sympathetic to captive spouses. Jack had a bit of lab space out of my lab, did some teaching, and became director of the education-abroad program in tropical

biology. But he had no real professional status, and it wasn't a great situation for him.

We looked around and found a position at the Marie Selby Botanical Gardens in Sarasota, Florida, a botanical garden devoted to the study of epiphytes—my major research area. It was a smaller place, less high key, less pressure; and Sarasota is Jack's hometown. I was pregnant at the time with my first child, so we decided to move. We were there for about two and a half years and things were going well, except that again Jack didn't have a professional position himself. Then we saw an ad for a position at Evergreen and decided to apply jointly. Evergreen is a teaching college, and we felt with a half-time teaching position each, we could still continue our research. We got the position and came out to Washington about three years ago. It's been great. Jack is really happy and very productive, and I love the teaching and the atmosphere. It's much less competitive than Santa Barbara. Here I'm a "member of the faculty," and there are no distinctions such as assistant or associate or full professor. We're both able to keep up our research in Costa Rica because we have one and a half quarters and the summer off. I think the college is happy with the arrangement too.

It's still a challenge finding a balance—or at least avoiding imbalance—between personal commitments and professional life. Trying to figure out, "Is it really OK to put my son, Gus, in after-school care so that I can have that extra hour and a half every day? How do I feel about that when the other kids in our neighborhood are coming home and their moms are there?" Whenever I go on a field trip, I have to find a phone to call the family while everybody else is still off in heated discussion. Sometimes when I'm tired at the end of the day, I feel like I haven't done anything justice: the kids have been dropped off early at day care and picked up late, dinner was really terrible, and I didn't get much done at the office. But in a better mood I can look at that same day and say, "It was great—look what you did: you had a wonderful bedtime with Erika and Gus, the dinner *was* edible, and you got some things off your desk, so you *are* managing to get several different things done at the same time."

I'm still as passionate about the canopy as I've always been. Today there are all kinds of ways of getting to it: cranes, ropes, hot-air balloons, remote sensing, and aerial photographs. But we still haven't developed good ways of analyzing the data. Tree crowns and forest canopies are spatially complex: they're irregular, they're unpredictable, they're three dimensional. We plant ecologists just don't have the analytical tools to work with that kind of data. So in the last two years I've become very interested in getting those tools, either by creating them or by modifying existing tools. I've been working with a group of database experts and computer scientists and

Nalini Nadkarni climbing in Costa Rica, 1991
FROM THE IMAX FILM *TROPICAL RAINFOREST*. PHOTO COURTESY OF THE SCIENCE MUSEUM OF MINNESOTA

bringing canopy people physically together with database people, who may not know a leaf from a stem but who really know how to deal with data. We're beginning to talk together and realize that we can help each other; we present good and interesting questions and they help provide statistically rigorous analytical tools.

Coupled with that, then, has been my growing interest in trying to effect communication among canopy scientists. For the last decade there have been so few of us that we've all been really isolated: there's one person in Ghana, a few people in Norway, a handful of people in the Northeast. We haven't been able to get together and communicate very easily, so last year a few of us started the International Canopy Network. Our goal is to enhance communication among canopy researchers and to get information about the forest canopy out to other fields and the general public. We've developed a canopy e-mail list that has about 500 members; we write a quarterly newsletter that goes out to about 1,200 people in fifty countries; we're developing educational materials for kids; we give talks and slide programs in elementary schools; we give climbing demonstrations. We're trying to provide avenues from researchers directly to the general public, as well as enhancing conservation efforts.

My work has gotten a fair amount of attention in the popular press, which still feels really incongruous because I came from a pretty insecure base as a graduate student. In some ways, I really enjoy it because I'm extroverted and a natural ham, and it allows me to get the message out. Every time an article comes up in a newspaper or magazine, it means I can talk about the canopy. If I only wrote my scientific papers, I could never get so many people excited about this work. And though I just detest television—I don't even have a TV in the house—I realized in making some educational programs and PBS specials what power it has. I feel like I might as well use it to promote what I feel burningly excited about, which is getting people to think about trees. I think my colleagues sometimes roll their eyes a little and think, "Oh, there's Nalini being shown climbing with her son on her back again." I don't feel too bad about it because I feel confident of my scientific integrity and at the same time I'm publishing papers in scientific journals. But I do admit to cringing when I think about certain extremely academic types reading an article about me in *Glamour*.*

There is a challenge for anyone who tries to be a pioneer. It's hard to have the confidence to say, "I *know* that this is worthwhile science, and I *know* you should give me funding so I can work on these interesting but difficult questions." It's not easy to approach database people, who really don't know much about trees, and say, "Come to this workshop; I can assure you that there will be interesting questions." I'm always sticking my neck out and worrying that I will fall on my face—and I do. I get grant proposals turned down and papers rejected all the time. But there are rewards to these challenges also.

Because I'm hungry to get everything out of life, because I find life so fabulous, one of my biggest challenges is making choices—and knowing that when I make one choice, I close options on another one. The forest ecol-ogy–dance question was a big choice. Whether I'd go to the University of Washington or somewhere else was a choice. Whether I'd stick with canopy work—which everyone was telling me didn't make any sense—or stay with something more standard was another choice. I feel I've made good choices in retrospect, but I still sometimes wonder, "What if I had done this instead?" Now that I'm sort of midcareer and opportunities are opening up in a variety of different ways, the choices are, if anything, more difficult to make.

PRESENT POSITIONS: Member of the Faculty, Evergreen State College; Adjunct Faculty, University of Washington and the University of South Florida; Adjunct Researcher, Missouri Botanic Garden; President of the International Canopy Network

FIELD: Forest ecology

RESEARCH AREA: Understanding ecological interactions in forest canopies

EDUCATION: B.S. (1976), Brown University; Ph.D. (1983), University of Washington

DATE/PLACE OF BIRTH: October 14, 1954/ Bethesda, Maryland

Nalini Nadkarni lives with her husband, John Longino, and their two children, Gus and Erika, in Olympia, Washington.

INTERVIEW DATE: September 1995

*Nalini Nadkarni was featured in the essay "Women Right Now" in the September 1990 issue of *Glamour*.

Lee Park

Assistant Professor of Chemistry
WILLIAMS COLLEGE

Afraid of disappointing her Korean immigrant parents because she didn't want to be a medical doctor, Lee Park was relieved that she loved chemistry. She attended the all-women's college Wellesley, then jumped into the male-dominated, competitive environment of MIT. She has happily found the balance between research and teaching that she loves as a faculty member at a small four-year college.

❧

I have just finished my second year as an assistant professor of chemistry at Williams College, which is a small, undergraduate liberal arts school. The primary focus here is on teaching, but the college also has a strong emphasis on research. I knew that I wanted to be at a school like Williams because I enjoy teaching and working closely with my students. Williams is very much like Wellesley College, where I received my undergraduate degree. I had a wonderful experience at Wellesley and I knew I was interested in coming back to a similar kind of a school. It has definitely been the right choice for me.

I am a synthetic inorganic chemist, more specifically an organometallic chemist. Organometallic chemistry is a branch of inorganic chemistry that deals with metal complexes in which a metal is bound directly to a carbon atom. My research involves the synthesis and characterization of new metal-containing liquid crystalline materials; it's synthetic work with a bent toward materials science. Since beginning my chemistry major in college, my interests have been focused on inorganic chemistry, and I chose MIT for graduate school because of its strong inorganic pro-

gram. I worked with Richard Schrock, a very well known organometallic chemist. I was very interested in doing synthetic work because I like being able to make new compounds and materials and investigate how they behave. Some chemists work on making molecules because they know that a compound will have specific useful properties. For instance, pharmaceutical chemists might isolate a particular compound from some natural source and work on synthesizing it because they know that that compound has medicinal properties. They'll work on creating a synthetic process that is cheap, efficient,

Lee Park at Williams College, summer 1993

and can lead to mass production. But there are other chemists, like me, who like to make new molecules because they like to see what kinds of structures can be made and what new properties can be found. Creating something new and studying it is like solving a puzzle. Synthetic chemistry is really a lot like cooking, something else I've always loved doing. The down side to my work is that it pretty much kills "cocktail party" conversation; as soon as I mention I'm a chemist, people just respond, "Oh." People are eager to ask about the work of doctors and lawyers, but they tend to assume that they won't understand what a physicist or chemist does. This makes it difficult to talk casually about my work, which can be somewhat frustrating since I love what I do and would like to be able to share it.

My parents emigrated from Korea before I was born. My father came to this country for graduate work at the University of Chicago and my mother to go to college at Southern Methodist University in Dallas. I grew up in Berkeley, California. My father is a mathematics professor in the California state university system. My mother is a librarian as well as a teacher of English as a second language; she has master's degrees in both English and library science. My younger sister graduated with a biology major from Williams College about a year before I arrived; she's not in science right now.

When my parents came to this country, they consciously left Korea behind. They did not teach my sister and me to speak Korean. My parents clearly raised us to be American and wanted us to be successful. Certain career choices seem secure, stable, and well respected, and as immigrants my parents wanted those things for my sister and me. There was a fair amount of pressure from my family for me to become a medical doctor, which is fairly common among first-generation Asian immigrants. I spent a lot of energy in high school trying to figure out what to do about that pressure. I'm not sure I ever had the chance to explore the other things I might have been interested in. I remember being aware as early as junior high

school that I did not want to be a medical doctor; but I wasn't able to tell my parents until I was safely in college, three thousand miles away, and it wasn't easy to tell them even then. I was relieved to find that I enjoyed chemistry as much as I did since I knew that my parents would consider it an acceptable alternative to becoming a medical doctor. As much as I love chemistry, I am not sure it's where I would have ended up had I been free of parental influence.

A large part of the reason that I went to Wellesley was because it was far from home. The fact that Wellesley is a women's college didn't play into my decision to go there; at that time, I didn't see being at a women's college as either an advantage or a disadvantage. But in the end, the women's college aspect of Wellesley was probably one of the most important and valuable features of my college experience. Although in my childhood I had never, even in a subtle way, gotten the message that I couldn't do anything because I was female, the support at Wellesley became very important to me. There were many women in my department, my thesis adviser especially, who were good role models for me. This became especially important when I went to graduate school, where there were very few women to act as mentors or role models.

Another effect of moving to the East Coast for college was that it was the first time I realized I was "Korean" rather than just generically American. People actually asked me if I could speak English, a situation I had never encountered in California and that I thought was grossly provincial. I wanted nothing to do with being Korean. The Asian student associations would send me mail and I just refused to participate or identify in any way with the Asian students' groups. Had those organizations been more cultural, I think I might have been interested; I would have liked learning something about my background. But I saw them as primarily social institutions. The Korean community in this country, although large, is very close in some ways, and I saw a lot of matchmaking going on between people's parents. I had Korean friends at Welles-ley who would get phone calls from Korean men at Harvard because the parents had met and exchanged their kids' addresses. I didn't want anything to do with that community.

Now I am more aware that although I was raised as an American, I was also taught certain Asian customs and behaviors. I realize that certain Korean patterns of behavior are ingrained in me. I was raised to respect authority figures and to treat them a certain way. I was taught to approach advisers, teachers, and professors with great deference, especially male authority figures. It was hard for me to learn to be more aggressive. I've never been particularly soft-spoken and I don't know that anyone would characterize me as quiet, but I was always extremely polite and deferential when approaching authority figures. I think this trait hurt me when I first got to MIT. I finally learned that even if speaking up seemed rude to me, it was more important to get somebody's attention. I had a hard time in graduate school for the first couple of years because of this. It took a while before I realized that I had to take charge of things. I felt that I had to learn to behave in ways that were somehow less "Asian" and also less "female." I had been raised to believe you should be modest about your work, and that if the work were good enough it would be noticed on its own merits. But in graduate school I learned that even if your work is good, you still have to go out and "sell" it if you want it to be noticed. I spent my initial years feeling terribly inferior because everyone was telling me how brilliant they were and how important their work was, and I believed them. Finally I came to understand that those people didn't necessarily know much more than I did, but that they did know how to get noticed, and that this ability to "sell" their work was a part of what made them successful. They still had to be able to back themselves with good work, of course, but people who did good work and didn't call attention to themselves didn't necessarily get the credit they deserved. That was

a hard lesson to learn because it went so strongly against the way that I had been raised; it felt almost dishonest to me.

This is one of the reasons I would never be interested in becoming a faculty member at a major research university where the ability to sell yourself and your work is crucial for getting funding and getting graduate students to work for you. You have to present your work as being fundamentally and crucially important or else your research won't be funded and you won't be able to continue your work. I love chemistry and I love teaching and being able to explain to my students how chemistry works, why it works, and what we know. I enjoy being able to do my research—being able to make a new compound and figure out what it does and why, and working with students to discover those things. I love the process of science, the research and discovery and analysis. I'm just much less interested in convincing everyone else that my research is the most important work in the world.

Liberal arts colleges like Williams have, for a number of years now, been placing more and more emphasis on research. I think it would be foolish for a student to be able to graduate with a chemistry degree without having research experience. Williams is a very small school, and I have a lot of contact with my students. My students participate in research with me either by doing a senior thesis or by working in the lab for ten weeks during the summer. I anticipate having student assistants continuously, but since there are no graduate students or postdoctoral fellows here, doing research is very different than at a large university. I am still learning how to balance my research with my teaching. It can be difficult, but it's also a lot of fun.

All of this also takes a great deal of time. I'm lucky that my husband has been very supportive. One of the difficulties in any academic career is that you don't necessarily have the freedom to choose where you live, and I'm fortunate that my husband has been willing and able to move with me. We plan to have a family someday, but not right away. A big is-

Lee Park with two of her students, Amy Prieto and Susan Gillmor, working in the nuclear magnetic resonance lab at Williams College, February 1996

sue for junior women faculty is that the years in which you might like to have children are the same years you're most likely to be working toward tenure. The question becomes, Do you put off one or the other, or do you try to do both at the same time? I have worked with women who have felt pressure to start having kids because they were turning forty. At this moment I don't feel that kind of pressure. I want to try not to let my career decisions affect when we decide to have children.

I was nineteen or twenty years old when I decided to be a chemistry major and get a Ph.D. At that age I was not thinking "it will take me this long to get my Ph.D., and this long to do my postdoc, and this long to get tenure, which means I will be thirty-five when I am done." I wasn't prepared to think about the consequences of being a chemistry major or how going to graduate school would affect when I would be able to have a family. I'm not sure that if anyone had tried to convey those issues to me that it would have made a difference; I might not have been ready to think about them. But I do remember suddenly becoming conscious of those issues while in graduate school, and being sort of surprised that I hadn't considered them before. Now when I talk with women students who are interested in continuing their education, I try to let them know that some of these decisions are going to be different for them than for their male classmates. I encourage students to be as realistic as possible. It doesn't mean they should give up ambition or optimism or whatever dreams they have. When I graduated from Wellesley, I believed that I could do anything I wanted; I just didn't really have any idea what that meant. I still believe I can do anything, but I think I'm more realistic about some of the choices that have to be made. Did I really want to do the things that would be required of me to be on the faculty at a major research university? The answer for me was finally no, given what it would require in terms of my time and my personal life and the person I would have to become.

At MIT I felt that success was defined very narrowly: it seemed to mean becoming a major researcher at a place like MIT. Since I wanted to be successful, I assumed that that was what I wanted. I was very unhappy until it dawned on me that that was not what I wanted. It's hard to learn what it is you want when you're being distracted by what everyone else thinks you should want. It's hard not to get swept up in what everyone else thinks success is. I feel that I'm successful now because I really love what I'm doing. It's a nice feeling.

PRESENT POSITION: Assistant Professor of Chemistry, Williams College

FIELD: Chemistry

RESEARCH AREA: Organometallic materials chemistry

EDUCATION: B.S. in Chemistry (1986), Wellesley College; Ph.D. in Chemistry (1991), Massachusetts Institute of Technology

DATE/PLACE OF BIRTH: May 4, 1965/Lafayette, Indiana

Lee Park lives with her husband, Eric Tiffany, a computer scientist, in Williamstown, Massachusetts.

INTERVIEW DATE: March 1995

Elisabeth Paté-Cornell

Professor of Industrial Engineering and Engineering Management
STANFORD UNIVERSITY

Working in risk analysis for engineered systems gives Elisabeth Paté-Cornell an opportunity to combine her interdisciplinary interests and her desire to see things work. She pioneered the inclusion of human and organizational factors in engineering risk analysis to arrive at practical ways of reducing the risk of technological activities, ranging from operations of the U.S. space shuttles, dams, and offshore platforms to anesthesia in the operating room. She is one of the youngest members elected to the National Academy of Engineering and the first woman faculty member from Stanford to be elected.

≈≈

When I was a teenager I thought that math was fun, and I enjoyed it the way one enjoys crossword puzzles. I was also very attracted to the humanities and literature. The French school system provides a solid theoretical basis, and I had the benefit of a good academic preparation in high school. I was also always interested in making things work. If my clock did not work, I would open it to see why. My father was a career officer of the French Marines and served for several years as the head of one of the French military schools of the Signal Corps. He was very much an engineer and a problem solver. Although he was not always enthusiastic about my choices, he had a definite influence on my decision to become an engineer. In the end he was very supportive.

The real decision came when I left high school. I was torn between the sciences and the humanities, and I was encouraged by teachers on both sides. After a lot of thought, I made a decision to go toward the sciences because it

Elisabeth Paté-Cornell demonstrates to her students how a particular model works, 1984
PHOTO BY CHUCK PAINTER, STANFORD UNIVERSITY NEWS SERVICE

Elisabeth Paté-Cornell, 1993

would give me many more choices. I could always enjoy literature and the opera without being a professional in the humanities myself, but the reverse wasn't true. My undergraduate degree was in mathematics and physics. I then entered the Institut Polytechnique in Grenoble, France, where I received a master's degree in 1970 and, in 1971, an engineer degree in computer science with an electrical engineering component. At the same time, I took most of the courses for a degree in economics but not the final examinations for that degree: I had been teaching math and physics to high school students, there was a schedule conflict, and I had to make a choice between taking my own final exams or being an examiner for my students. I chose the latter.

I came to Stanford in 1971 for a master's in operations research, a field of mathematics dealing with applications as well as theory. This suited me well because I wanted to do something practical and meaningful with

math. After completing my master's, I went back to France. I worked for about six months as an engineer-economist in transportation planning and completed a project for the Paris Metro. But after my M.S. in operations research, I realized that I wanted a field of application that included technical and mathematical analysis as well as social sciences.

I came back to Stanford in 1973 for a Ph.D., this time in the interdisciplinary department of Engineering–Economic Systems (EES). For my doctoral work, I chose to study the mitigation of seismic risk from a public policy viewpoint. I looked at the costs and benefits of reducing earthquake risks in two different ways: the reinforcement of buildings and a long-term investment in earthquake prediction. That study involved pulling together entirely different notions. One was very much engineering oriented—how one actually reduces property damage and human casualties in earthquakes with different levels of reinforcement and for different kinds of buildings. The other involved the reliability of warnings and their use by human beings to reduce risks. I found the fundamental issues extremely interesting, and by then I had a good background to address the interdisciplinary nature of the problem.

During my graduate studies, I had a true mentor in my adviser, Professor William Linville, who was, at that time, the chairman of the EES department. Bill was interested in merging engineering systems analysis and economic analysis to find realistic solutions to actual problems. He encouraged me to combine my diverse intellectual interests, even though his own work was not directly related to risk analysis. He was extremely supportive at a time when there were only a few women in engineering Ph.D. programs. I sometimes had the feeling that he was watching me as one would watch a sleepwalker on the edge of a roof: he made sure that I wouldn't fall, in an environment that I did not know very well, but he did so without restricting me in my work.

After my Ph.D., I first joined the MIT faculty in civil engineering and then the faculty of the Stanford Department of Industrial Engineering and Engineering Management. Since that time, I have pursued two general lines of research. One is the integration of human and organizational factors into probabilistic risk analyses (PRAs) for engineering systems, starting with the optimization of warning systems. Conventionally, PRAs focus on the probabilities of accidents or other events leading to loss of life or property, and on the severity of these losses based on historical data, measurements, and expert opinions. The emphasis is mostly on technical failures. I added to this analysis some human and organizational elements—behavior, judgment, and decision making—and their effects on the reliability of the different components. For example, I have done this type of analysis with Paul Fischbeck for the reliability of the twenty-five or thirty thousand tiles of the heat shield that protects the space shuttle orbiters during reentry. Our analysis showed that about 15 percent of the tiles are most risk-critical (they constitute about 85 percent of the risk) and should receive particular attention for maintenance and repair. I have also applied these methods to the performance of anesthesiologists in operating rooms, and to a diverse set of technical systems including oil platforms in the North Sea, command and control systems for nuclear weapons, and oil and gas pipelines in the Gulf of Mexico. This diversity of topics has given me some perspective by allowing comparisons across different fields. This work combines probability, statistics, organizational behavior, and, sometimes, psychology—and, of course, the disciplines of the specific domains. Since I do not have a formal background in all these disciplines, I have relied on the background literature and to some degree on experts in the different subjects.

Another side of my research has been the treatment of uncertainties in probabilistic risk analysis and the implications of a lack of fundamental knowledge for rational decision making. People have different attitudes toward taking risk according to how much they

know about it. With a couple of my students, we explored the implications of these attitudes for policy making and individual decisions.

I teach several courses related to risk analysis and economics, starting with an undergraduate course in engineering economy to which I have attached a large segment of decision analysis under uncertainty. In my graduate course in risk analysis, I present the theory of probabilistic risk analysis and I use my latest studies as examples to give the students a sense of reality and of ongoing research. After this course, I also teach a project course and a couple of seminars. My six or so doctoral students are an essential part of my research activities. We all meet regularly so that each of them knows what the others are doing and so they can exchange ideas.

There are not many people at Stanford who work actively in my field, and they don't work much together. I have understood from the beginning that I needed to depend essentially on myself. I have come to rely on a network of friends and colleagues in political science, economics, mechanical engineering, civil engineering, and other fields. They are the "friends of the group" and my students can knock at their doors to discuss issues or ask questions.

Public service is another important part of my professional life, although it seems less fashionable these days than working for industry. I am currently a member of the Marine Board of the National Research Council (NRC), and I chair an NRC committee on risk assessment and management of marine systems (for example, offshore platforms). I am also a member of the Army Science Board and of the NASA Advisory Council. These activities allow me to provide inputs from my work that improve systems' safety, and to bring back interesting questions and issues to my research and my students. It also puts me in touch with large organizations that face many operations research problems, and it gives me the opportunity to study uncertainties in real-life decisions. In fact, I see this kind of service as a duty. Even though it is an enormous amount of work and it is hardly rewarded financially, I find it very satisfying.

All these activities are sometimes difficult to combine with a balanced family life. I am lucky to be married to a man who is extremely supportive: I would not be able to do what I do without him. We have two children, a son who is fourteen and a daughter, twelve. Allin is in a field tangential to mine: he is an expert on structural reliability and a research professor at Stanford. We discuss our work, but we decided early not to work together in any official way. We don't coauthor publications, and we don't acknowledge commenting on each other's papers.

I have enjoyed living in two cultures. Growing up in France and coming to the United States to a completely new environment helped me develop new views as an adult. Having studied in two countries, I also find that a great aspect of the U.S. educational system is the opportunities it affords to children and young people to try various and diverse subjects and activities and to explore what works. This system, however, does not always encourage them to challenge some fundamental issues that are conveyed to them as absolute, almost "religious" truths. So we have tried to teach our children to question assumptions.

I think that it is important to find one's own way as long as it is appropriate for the context, and that it is not necessary to follow someone else's pattern. It is certainly possible for women to have a rich professional life in science and engineering, and to enjoy a family, a home, and children as well. You may not have much sleep for a while, but with the right support and with confidence in what you are doing, you can find your own way!

PRESENT POSITION: Professor of Industrial Engineering and Engineering Management, Stanford University

FIELD: Industrial engineering, engineering management

RESEARCH AREAS: Risk analysis, operations research

EDUCATION: B.S. in Mathematics and Physics (1968), Université de Marseilles, France; M.S. in Computer Science and Applied Mathematics (1970), University of Grenoble, France; Engineer Degree in Computer Science and Numerical Analysis (1971), Institut Polytechnique de Grenoble, France; M.S. in Operations Research (1972), Stanford University; Ph.D. in Engineering-Economic Systems (1978), Stanford University

DATE/PLACE OF BIRTH: August 17, 1948/Dakar, Senegal

Elisabeth Paté-Cornell lives with her husband, Allin Cornell, their son, Phillip, and their daughter, Ariane, in Portola Valley, California.

INTERVIEW DATE: June 1996

Donna Rose Peterson

Software Quality Assurance Engineer
CELLULAR TECHNICAL SERVICES

The loss of not one mother but two, complicated by the confusion that comes from being adopted, growing up as a Native American in a predominantly white environment, her gender, her early marriage, and children were never excuses for Donna Peterson in her quest to pursue her goals. All these obstacles contributed toward a vulnerable and sensitive personality, and yet they did not stop her from earning a successful career in the demanding and traditionally male-dominated world of engineering. She believed her parents' wisdom—that her Tlingit heritage gave her strength and that she could be anything she wanted to be.

❧

When I was in high school, there were no computer classes; the field was just beginning to take off. I had no idea that computer science existed until I entered junior college for the second time in my early twenties. I was married and already had a daughter when I took my first BASIC programming class. Based on experiences in this class, I made the decision that this was what I wanted to do for the rest of my life: I'd found my niche. It was an exciting discovery because I'd felt lost not knowing what career I would pursue. I knew this was the field for me because I picked up assignments and finished them easily and quickly while others in my class were lost, bored, and frustrated. When an instructor told me I should go into computer science, I remember saying, "Gosh. Computer science? Are you sure? Me?" It seemed so far out of reach. But I thought, "OK. I'll go for it."

After receiving my A.A. degree, I enrolled in my local college, Humboldt State University, and began working toward my computer science degree in the business department. I'd had my son during the fall quarter and had been there a year when my husband was accepted at California Polytechnic State University for architecture. I also transferred but was rather taken aback to find that computer science at Cal Poly was part of the engineering department. It was a totally different ballgame: lots of calculus, physics, engineering statistics,

Donna Peterson and her daughter, Sarahlynn, 1981

Donna Peterson in the Cellular Technical Services lab, Seattle, 1995
PHOTO BY DMITRY KAPLAN

and electrical engineering. I took it all on. I did it one step at a time, figuring that if it got too hard I could switch over to management information systems under the business department. But the more I got into engineering, the more I was totally excited, and there was no way I was leaving.

I wasn't always so determined. When I was very young, I was teased by other children because I had darker skin than they did. I was insecure. I think part of my problem was that I was adopted at age two and a half. Even though I dearly loved my wonderful new family, I was haunted by a fear that they too would leave me someday. I had nightmares where I would wake up screaming. I wouldn't let my mother or father go out in the evenings, and they had to take me everywhere. By the time I was five my nightmares decreased, but I continued to have them occasionally until my early teens. Then, at seventeen, I had devastating news. My nightmare came true when I returned from a friend's to discover that my adoptive mother had suddenly passed on. I was already in college, but within months I quit to marry Mark, which gave me the security I so desperately needed at that troubling time.

While I was growing up, my parents provided me with experiences that increased and reinforced my self-confidence. My mother wanted me to be a ballet dancer. It was not my favorite activity, but she made me practice daily and I excelled at it. This placed me in the advanced class when I was only eleven, a much younger age than the other advanced students. When I was twelve, I convinced my mother to let me join the AAU swim team, which conflicted with my ballet. I was a latecomer, and everybody was much better than I. At the same time I also wanted a horse. So I made a deal with my mom: I asked her if she would buy me a horse if I made AAA time in any stroke in swimming. I was a C time in all my strokes, which was pretty bad, so she agreed, thinking she was safe. Within eighteen months, however, I had my AAA time in the butterfly, which had been my worst stroke of all—and I got my horse. It taught me that I could do anything I put my mind to. The fact that my mother lived up to her end of the bargain when it was such an enormous bet made me appreciate that there are real rewards for hard work and perseverance.

I certainly needed perseverance to get my engineering degree. When my husband and I both decided to quit our full-time jobs and go to school at the same time with a three-year-old daughter and my son on the way, we knew life was not going to be easy. Every day we struggled to balance our finances and our time for each other and course work. Although my husband, Mark, is a devoted father and has always shared with the housework, there was always an unstated assumption that his degree came first; sometimes he resented that my choice made his life more difficult. Of course, I also resented that I was second just because I was a woman. The fact that we made it through seven years of this together is a testimony to both of us and our ability to work through problems, to see the light at the end of the tunnel, and not to give up. It would have been so easy to quit, but we didn't and I'm really proud of both of us for that.

It would have been hard even if we hadn't had children, but with them it was especially challenging. Our parents, our relatives, our friends, and sometimes even our instructors would try to persuade one or both of us to give up and take care of our children—as if we weren't taking care of them. But we always tried to put the kids first: we staggered our courses and our work hours so that one of us would always be with the children. We didn't have the luxury of popping over to the library or getting into student study groups—all the normal things that help students get through their work. After a day of school and work, we went home and took care of the kids; when they went to bed, we'd start studying. We'd study until one o'clock, sometimes two or three o'clock, and get up for the next day around seven. I felt like I was in a time warp; I was always ragged and tired, but my goal was so important that I was willing to do it.

Cal Poly provided cooperative education experiences where students could take temporary jobs or internships in industry to gain work experience and college credit as well as earn a salary. I participated in three—at McDonnell Douglas Aircraft, Hewlett Packard, and Sealaska—which were invaluable. They allowed me to learn about the real world, earn much-needed money, and then return to the academic world with a different point of view.

Each time I went to another workplace and came back, I was able to apply the lessons with another real-world point of view. These experiences also reinforced my confidence in my career choice.

My internship at Sealaska was in Juneau, and I used the opportunity to track down my birth mother. I discovered that she had passed away when I was two and a half and that was why I'd been adopted. The story of how she died, and how I was subsequently separated from my father and five siblings, profoundly affected me. My birth mother had a weak heart from having scarlet fever as a child, and one night she found herself desperate for medical attention. Heavy snowdrifts prevented car or bus travel, so she had to walk to the hospital. But when she arrived at the nearest "white" hospital, they denied her entrance because she was a Tlingit and told her to go to the "Native" hospital. So she and her young husband walked three miles to the Native hospital, which promptly turned her away because she was married to a white man. She walked back and forth several times, trying to see a doctor; and finally at one of the hospitals, she timidly pleaded, "I simply cannot walk any further." They let her use one of the beds to rest, but they were not going to treat her. My father left to find someone from the church to intervene. She died alone before he returned. She left a bewildered, enraged husband and six young children behind. I was the youngest. My father was unable to bear the grief and left, and the government decided that white families were better suited to care for the children than our Native relatives. I was the only one of six who ended up in a loving white family. My oldest sister was dyslexic, and the government put her in a home for the mentally retarded even though my great-aunt campaigned heavily to keep her. When she was twenty-five, they finally tested her for dyslexia and released her with a letter of apology from the state of Alaska. But it was too late.

Although I dearly love my adopted family and wouldn't trade them for anything, I remain saddened and confused about the fact that my mother's and father's ancestors are not *my* ancestors. And while I've found my birth mother's family and am very fond of them, they really don't know me very well. It's as if my life was shattered and there is no way I'll ever be completely whole again. When I hear men and women I work with swear that discrimination is no longer a factor in our society, I always want to tell them the story of my adoption. It was only about thirty years ago, and its repercussions will last a lifetime. This is one reason I work so hard today, to keep something like that from ever happening to me or my children again.

After graduation, I went to work for Boeing Commercial Aircraft Company, where I stayed for over four years before moving to Cellular Technical Services (CTS). There are tradeoffs between working at a large firm like Boeing and a smaller firm like CTS. Boeing has traditionally had military-style leadership, and I found it difficult to adjust to a place where engineers are expected to give 150 percent to the company and rarely told that they've done a good job. At CTS I found a more open environment, and with it came perks like free soda, coffee, and juice, and flexible hours. In a smaller company they seem to appreciate and respect your knowledge more.

The best part about working at Boeing was that I had the opportunity to work in the 777 simulation integration lab, developed to simulate the high-tech 777, which is Boeing's latest commercial aircraft. We were simulating the airplane on the ground; there was a complete cockpit environment and a pilot to fly the simulated aircraft. There were monitoring devices all around the lab. One of my jobs was to test out the software for the navigation system. I worked with a team of fifteen to twenty people, and we'd each concentrate on monitoring different aspects of the flight test, using headphones to communicate. It was very exciting to be able to use all that technology and work with all those experts in one place doing something that had never been done before. Software had never before been put through an integrated simulation prior to being installed on

a commercial airplane. We really helped to ensure the safety and success of the 777.

CTS is a new, start-up, entrepreneurial company, and our specialty is real-time embedded software systems that help cellular phone companies do their billing. We're developing a product called Blackbird, which will look at incoming cellular calls and determine whether they're good calls from subscribers or imitation calls. At CTS, my work mostly involves understanding software development processes and how to create and manage those processes to develop the best product possible with the least amount of trouble. A development process is how various teams of people work together, what the interactions are between them, and what work one team expects the other to deliver. If you have a group that develops the software, another that tests it, and another that installs it, all of them have to work together smoothly to get the product out the door. That's where I come in, and it is especially challenging with a fast-growth company such as CTS. I work out who hands off what to whom and when. In the past I've been part of a development group, I've been in testing, I've done systems analysis—I need all those skills to do the job I do now.

I still enjoy the work as much as I enjoyed my first BASIC programming course. It's incredible. In the morning, I wake up and I can't wait to get to work. When I'm at work, I sometimes don't want to go home. To me, it's not really a job. I'm having so much fun with what I do that the nice paycheck is just a bonus! I love investigating, putting the pieces of the puzzle together, and the variety of the assignments—every day is different. I also love learning about new technology so that I can write or review software for it. You have to understand the application to develop software. Since I've been in the field, I've had to learn how a nuclear power plant operates, how one computer program can take apart another computer program to give us more information about the original one, how an airplane can sense if the landing gear is up or down, how energy can be directed from an airplane's engines to its batteries, how air can be circulated around an airplane cabin so that the pressure and quality are maintained, how an airplane can tell where it's at in the air and where the runway is. I've even learned how fiber optic cables work and about virtual reality. At CTS I'm learning how the cellular phone industry works and how we can prevent cellular fraud.

Balancing work and family remains challenging. I think Mark and I hoped that once we got through college everything would be magical, but we still face our share of problems. When you have a career and children, you can make a choice to put your career first or your children first, and you live with the choice for a long time. I've decided that since my children are about five years away from leaving the house and going to college, I'm putting them first. So as much as I love my work and think I could advance faster, for now my children take priority.

One thing I have done outside work is to immerse myself in learning about my culture and subsequently helping my tribe. I was nominated to the board of directors of our Native corporation twice. I helped to lead an effort that was very successful in changing some of the unethical practices of the board. In Alaska, the Natives were not given reservations but were set up with Native corporations to manage our land and assets and provide dividends to Native shareholders as payment from the government for taking Alaska and using it for themselves. The problem is that nobody oversees these corporations, and while they were set up to help all Native Alaskans, they sometimes benefit only a very few. So I have involved myself in a fight to remove corruption from the corporation.

And while I have chosen a less active role at present because my family and career need all my energy, I still consult with shareholders continuing the effort. There are elders in our tribe who look to me to become a future leader, and I'm proud and pleased that they would think of me that way.

I believe that once you make a decision, once you know what you want to do, you will pay a price to get there. In my career, I've put in a lot of hours. The first two quarters at Cal Poly I went home and cried myself to sleep at night because I was so overwhelmed. I didn't know if I was going to make it, and I didn't know if it was worth it. I had a sweet little nine-month-old baby who wanted my attention, and I felt that I was being pulled in too many directions. Now I look back and say, I paid a price to get here, but I have what I want. I've been happily married for seventeen years, I have two great kids, I'm able to have a home in the country with horses and a career I really enjoy. When some people look at successful people and think, "I could never do that," I want to tell them that they can. As long as you're willing to pay the price, you can do anything you want to.

PRESENT POSITION: Software Quality Assurance Engineer, Cellular Technical Services

FIELD: Computer science

SPECIALTY: Quality assurance

EDUCATION: A.A. in Data Processing (1983), College of the Redwoods; B.S. in Computer Science (1990), California Polytechnic State University

DATE/PLACE OF BIRTH: March 8, 1959/Juneau, Alaska

Donna Peterson lives in Kent, Washington, with her husband, daughter, and son.

INTERVIEW DATE: August 1995

Arati Prabhakar

Director
NATIONAL INSTITUTE OF STANDARDS AND TECHNOLOGY

Taught at an early age that being different was good, not bad, Arati Prabhakar wasn't upset at being the only Indian child in her grade-school class and the only female in the applied physics Ph.D. program at Caltech. Her challenge came when she realized that her heart wasn't in laboratory research. Viewing the Ph.D. as enabling rather than limiting, and willing to leave the traditional academic career path, she went to work first at the federal Office of Technology Assessment and then at the Defense Department's Advanced Research Projects Agency before being appointed director of the National Institute of Standards and Technology by President Bill Clinton in 1993.

❧

The National Institute of Standards and Technology (NIST) promotes economic growth by building partnerships between industry and government focusing on technologies that matter to the economy. We do the jobs that the private sector won't do by itself—building technology infrastructure and focusing on longer-term and risky projects. The NIST laboratories, which as the old National Bureau of Standards dates back to 1901, are an essential part of the organization. These are the nation's measurement laboratories: they do everything from creating the time standard to assuring that the test methodology for DNA fingerprinting is defined properly. Most of our 3,200 staff work in the laboratories. We have an Advanced Technology Program that funds projects in companies to share the cost of developing high-risk technologies that have broad com-

mercial potential, and a Manufacturing Extension Partnership that helps small and medium-sized companies adopt new technologies. I was appointed director of NIST by President Bill Clinton and took office in May 1993 after the Senate nomination hearings.

I was born in New Delhi, India. My mother was the single most significant influence in my life. She's the one who brought our family to this country. She worked as a social worker in India for several years before I was born and then stayed at home with me for a while. It was

Arati Prabhakar, December 1994
PHOTO BY ROBERT RATHE PHOTOGRAPHY

during that time that she began to look through college catalogues and decided that she wanted to come to the United States to go to school. She brought our family to the U.S. when I was three years old, intending to return to India, but she never did.

My mother attended the University of Chicago and earned a master's degree in social services administration. She raised me to believe that I could do anything I wanted; she herself was an excellent role model of that philosophy. She regularly took me as a child to science museums and plays about science. She wasn't pushing me in that direction; she simply wanted me to know that this was as acceptable as anything else I might want to do. She has always been a woman of vision and drive, two traits she tried to pass on to me.

When I was seven years old we moved to Texas. Growing up as an Indian kid in Texas now is not as big a deal as it was when we moved there. There was not much of an Indian community, and I was the only Indian kid in my class. I was always different, but that didn't bother me because I learned from my mother that it was all right to be different. I think the fact that I was inherently different because I was an Indian made my being the only woman in my engineering classes very easy. I was used to this status and it didn't bother me.

My life and schooling were mainstream middle American. I went through the public school system in Texas and then on to college at Texas Tech University. By then I was strongly committed to engineering and earned a B.S. in electrical engineering in 1979. I've always had a very practical bent; when I was very young I remember telling my mother that I didn't know if I wanted to be a discoverer or an inventor—even then I was struggling with science versus engineering. I finally decided that being an inventor was better because you could create things that helped people; I think that factor was important to me because my mother's work was so centered on helping people.

I always knew I'd go on for a Ph.D. When I was growing up, my mother used to begin sentences with, "When you get your Ph.D. . . . ." I went to Caltech for graduate school and ran into my first brick wall. Like others there who had sailed through their undergraduate programs, I was shocked to find that not only was I not the best person in the class, I wasn't even close. It's very important to come to a point in your life where you have to fundamentally rethink what you're doing: I was planning to get a Ph.D. and go to a university to do basic research for no reason other than that was the traditional academic achievement path. At Caltech I learned that I didn't like doing basic research. It was very tough to leave that path, but it would have been much more painful to follow the traditional road and find myself fifteen years later unhappy in my career.

I was the only woman graduate student in applied physics when I started and the first woman to earn a Ph.D. in the department. Before I started, there had been several women who switched fields or left the school. There was at least one man in my department who, when I was moving into my office, stopped by and said, "Welcome to the group. Women don't seem to last long around here." It was not said with any viciousness; it was just the atmosphere of the department. Fortunately, because of my background, I didn't have any problems being "unusual."

My doctoral research focused on semiconductors. The process of building a semiconductor wafer involves literally a few hundred different steps—cleaning the wafer, putting materials on the wafer, taking materials off the wafer, heating the wafer, and so on. One specific new materials technology that the industry was thinking about in the early 1980s was platinum silicide and some of the other silicide materials. There were several advantages to using this material, but one of the concerns was that if the metal element diffused into the underlying silicon, that could ruin the device performance pretty dramatically. In my thesis research, I used an electronic test methodology to examine whether that kind of device degradation could occur from diffusion of metal impurities into the silicon from the silicide. Essentially I did temperature studies and concluded that as long as you don't anneal the sample above a certain temperature you should be safe.

I completed my Ph.D. in 1984. I had a wonderful thesis adviser who understood that a Ph.D. was an enabling rather than a limiting tool. But neither of us knew quite what to do with me. One day he suggested that I should seek a congressional fellowship, even though neither of us had a clue about what it meant. I applied for several congressional fellowships and was awarded one with the Office of Technology Assessment (OTA). In contrast to most people who come to Washington with a dream of influencing public policy, I came because I was about as far from laboratory research as I could be. My job at OTA was to generate a study on microelectronics research and development to explain to members of Congress and their staffs what was going on in the world of microelectronics and where research was leading. The experience was a tremendous education for me; it gave me the opportunity to call anyone in the country who worked in microelectronics. And the fact that I left the traditional career path and did something completely orthogonal and liked it signaled to me that I wanted to follow a nontraditional path even if there were no road maps.

After OTA I went to work at the Defense Department's Advanced Research Projects Agency (DARPA). For the first time I was doing exactly what I wanted to do. I was a program manager who initiated and managed projects. The first year I managed $12 million in projects. I was responsible for helping to create something greater than the sum of the parts by building the linkages to get money to flow to certain projects and to get those projects connected to people doing related research. My technical knowledge, interest, and strength in seeing the bigger picture made it a dream job. When I left DARPA, which by then had became ARPA, I was the director of the Microelectronics Technology Office with

a budget of $300 million and a staff of eleven. Things had changed a lot in seven years. When I started, my part of DARPA largely focused on research and worked with the traditional defense industries and universities. By the time I left, ARPA had major projects with commercial industries and more of an emphasis on dual use as the approach to addressing the military's needs for electronics. I felt that I had the best job in the federal government at DARPA/ARPA.

My exit was not planned. On the Sunday after President Clinton's inauguration, I was at home when the phone rang. A woman said, "I'm calling for the president and the vice president. We wanted to know if you'd be interested in interviewing for the job as director of the National Institute of Standards and Technology?" At first I thought that one of my friends was playing a prank. Then I realized it wasn't a prank and I said yes, even though I didn't know much about NIST and where it was heading. A week later I interviewed with Secretary of Commerce Ron Brown, and a few months later my nomination was approved. I began work in May 1993; I am the tenth director of NIST since 1901, and the second director to come from outside the organization. I am the first director who was trained as an engineer, which I consider both symbolic and meaningful given what we're trying to accomplish.

I consider my job at NIST a tremendous opportunity. For many years, if you wanted to drive technology in the ways that interest me—that is, to benefit industry and our economy—the only substantial source of funds was through the Department of Defense. I felt very strongly that we needed to make investments deliberately focused on economic outcomes, rather than simply assuming that whatever economic spillover happened from defense research and development was adequate. With global competition so rigorous, we can no longer be satisfied with such an indirect approach, and how well we deal with our civilian technology needs is very important to me—as it is to the country's future.

Recently, a typical day for me might include a speech to industry and government researchers taking part in a technical conference at NIST, followed by meetings with individual company representatives taking part in one of our NIST programs; a tuna sandwich somewhere on Capitol Hill; and visits to members of Congress and their staffs to explain what our programs are—and just as importantly, what they are not. We constantly battle misinformation about our programs. Then I might speak at a meeting with an industry association. I also travel a good deal. The most interesting and valuable part of my job is visiting companies to tell our story, see what our partners are doing, and learn about new directions they are taking. It's also very important to keep open communications with my very large staff and to paint a picture of where we want to go.

I joke with people that when I first started at NIST I felt like the "technology poster child"—young, female, and ethnic. Starting with my first public appearance, I could never, ever be less than 100 percent. It is an added pressure that I think a lot of women in positions like mine feel: You have to deliver, you can't falter, you can't show any weakness, you can't do well 99 percent of the time—it has to be 100 percent. Fortunately, pressure can also be a very motivating thing; it's certainly helped me to be my best.

I have never viewed myself as a role model to young women or Indian women, maybe because most of my own role models were middle-aged white men. They were the only people on the faculty when I was going through school, for example. But it never occurred to me that I couldn't do what they were doing. I realize that a lot of young people look for role models of their own gender or ethnicity, but I think it's good to cultivate the imagination to envision yourself doing all sorts of things even if you don't see someone doing them who looks like you.

I enjoy cooking, reading, and spending time with friends. I'm engaged to Pat Windham, who works on the Senate Commerce, Science, and Transportation Committee; not surprisingly, I met him through work. He is the senior Democratic staffer who focuses on technology issues. In fact, he helped to write the legislation that created NIST in 1988. Work is an important enough part of my life that I want to share it, so it is important to me that the man in my life understands my work and my passion for it.

I believe that an important factor in my life has been my willingness to take risks. When I left Caltech to take the congressional fellowship there were faculty members who worried that I was taking my life and throwing it away. Even my thesis adviser, who had more faith in me than anybody, worried about what I would do next. *I* worried about what I would do next. But each risk I took paid off.

PRESENT POSITION: Director, National Institute of Standards and Technology
FIELD: Applied physics
RESEARCH AREA: Semiconductors
EDUCATION: B.S. in Electrical Engineering (1979), Texas Tech University; M.S. in Electrical Engineering (1980), California Institute of Technology; Ph.D. in Applied Physics (1984), California Institute of Technology.
DATE/PLACE OF BIRTH: February 2, 1959/New Delhi, India

Arati Prabhakar lives in McLean, Virginia.

INTERVIEW DATE: May 1995

Margaret N. Rees

Professor of Geology, Department of Geoscience
UNIVERSITY OF NEVADA–LAS VEGAS

Although she "hated" science in high school, Peg Rees discovered and fell in love with geology when she took a community college class in the subject. She quickly caught up on her math and science requirements, majoring in geology and minoring in physics, and went on to earn a master's degree and a Ph.D. She applies her love for the outdoors and uses her mechanical skills to repair her snowmobile when she spends three months of the year studying sedimentary rocks in Antarctica. As a lesbian scientist at the University of Nevada at Las Vegas, she is developing into a feminist educator.

As a sedimentologist and stratigrapher, I study rocks that were deposited on the earth's surface as sediments like those found in the ocean or across the land. I focus on sedimentary rocks that were deposited between seven hundred and five hundred million years ago, which spans a pretty interesting geological time—the transition between the Proterozoic and the Cambrian. It was during this time period that organisms first developed shells, which are more easily preserved in the rock record than soft-bodied organisms. The advantage of this evolution for geologists is that in Cambrian and younger rocks, we can find in a variety of places similar fossils that represent a particular geological time period. We can also interpret the environments in which the sediments were deposited and determine, for example, if they represent an equatorial or polar region, shallow or deep oceans, rivers, or sand dunes. Slowly we can begin to understand what the world was like during a given period of time millions of years ago.

We know that continents move and grow and ocean basins form and are consumed through plate-tectonic processes. The further back in time that we try to reconstruct what the earth looked like, the more difficult it becomes because the fragments are more dispersed from continent to continent. It is sort of like putting a jigsaw puzzle together of all the continental fragments around the world that represent the same period of time. By working in interdisciplinary groups, geolo-

Peg Rees on Casper Mountain, Wyoming, while working with Union Oil Company, 1974

gists can develop hypotheses about the evolution of the earth and what mechanisms drive the plate-tectonic movements. I look at the sedimentary rock record while other geologists are interested in the igneous and metamorphic rocks or deformational processes related to mountain building. Still others are trying to understand the role of the earth's mantle and core. It is pretty exciting that, by working together, we may begin to understand this earth on which we live. Although most people think of the earth's surface as static, all the volcanoes and earthquakes show us that everything is in motion. Using satellites we can figure out exactly what piece is moving in what direction. We might not see any major changes in our lifetime, but the earth's crust is always changing.

I've worked in Antarctica for eight years out of the past eleven trying to unravel its place in the Cambrian world. I go down about the first of November and come home the first of February. This is during Antarctica's summer, when there is twenty-four-hour daylight and moderately warm temperatures—somewhere just below freezing. We go down to New Zealand on a commercial aircraft, and then from New Zealand to Antarctica we fly on military aircraft because they're the only ones that can transport all the people and supplies and land on the ice. We fly to a small town called McMurdo, which is one of the U.S. bases. We go grocery shopping there and pick up our supplies. All the food and equipment we need were brought there the previous February by ship. The people who work at the base in support of our science investigations are very important; without their help, we could never get our work accomplished. I am privileged to have close friendships with a few of them. Once organized, our field party's gear is loaded into an LC-130, a big military cargo plane with skis on it. We pinpoint the places in the mountains that we want to go, and then they land us on the nearest glacier and push everything out the back door and say, "We'll pick you up in about six weeks."

I've always worked in Antarctica in a team of four that usually consists of myself, another geologist, a graduate student, and a mountaineer. We always take a mountaineer because they are trained to find safe routes on the rocks and along the glaciers, which have large crevasses—which we certainly don't want to fall into! The mountaineer usually is our radio operator and snowmobile mechanic and also helps in all aspects of our work.

Our work consists of hiking through the mountains and examining the rocks that are exposed at the surface and not covered with snow and ice. We map what we observe, take photographs and notes, and collect hundreds of pounds of rock samples to look at with more technical equipment at home. We don't take any technical equipment; we have a hammer, a hand-held magnifying glass, a camera, and a notebook. Recently we have added a hand-held global positioning surveyor to our list of equipment to better locate where we collect samples—the maps of Antarctica are still not very detailed.

Geology is very much an observational science. You're trained to observe carefully in the field, to take pictures, and collect samples that you think are representative to bring home for documentation or further study. I collect a lot of fossils from the field; I don't identify them, but I bring them back for a team of people who can identify them and tell us the age of the sedimentary rocks. We also collect igneous rocks for other people to analyze geochemically. From those results one can interpret how and in what environment a rock formed. We may have only small exposures of the volcanic rocks, but from the chemistry we can tell a lot about their history. From radiometrically dating them, one can also determine their age.

We don't know precisely what we're looking for; we're just looking to see what's there. We have a notion or hypothesis that we are testing and have an idea of what we might find or what we might be looking for. We're trained to observe as many features as we can in order to understand the rock record. We're trained in particular rock types, but if we run across something that we are not familiar with, we just have to do our best. I ask myself, "What observations can be made? What documentation can be collected in order to understand this feature or to convey needed information to somebody else when we get back?" This is particularly important in Antarctica, where we can't bring in large teams of people or revisit a locality.

The people at the University of Nevada–Las Vegas, and particularly those in the geoscience department, are just great; they've been very supportive of my work in Antarctica. We arrange my teaching schedule to make it possible for me to go to Antarctica. For the fall semester, sometimes I coordinate seminars and sometimes I have graduate seminar classes. I condense and intensify the teaching time in the beginning of the semester, and then while I'm away students are writing reports or doing a research project that we have set up ahead of time. When I come back I work with the students individually and do all the necessary grading. In the spring, I carry a heavier teaching load and teach in the more conventional time frame. When I was chair of the department, the associate chair took over the duties for me during my absence. When I come back from Antarctica, I'm pretty much ready for the social interaction of teaching. Once I get back, it's nice to have the comforts of home and technology around me. Since our rocks don't arrive with us (we come back by plane in February, and they come back by ship around April), I spend that time catching up on three months of mail and other work that has piled up.

Having two lives, one at home base and one in the field, is pretty typical for most academic geologists and many industrial geologists, whether they are working in Antarctica or somewhere less remote. Even if they're working in the United States, there tend to be at least week-long periods of time, and probably longer, where they're away doing mapping or collecting.

It's really hard to maintain a "regular life." My work and life cycle has made me reflect on the presentation of the patriarchal history of the explorer. You always hear about the explorer's time in the field, but you never hear about his home life or social relationships. That is really underplayed, but it is an integral part of making life work. It is characteristic of me, and of most geologists, that we find it easy to be gone. If we have partners or families, time away from home has to be an accepted aspect of the relationship and one needs to try organizing work around life. I am a lesbian and both my partner and I have chosen not to have children, which makes traveling much easier. Certainly I know many women and men geologists with children; it's really a balancing act, but they do it and do it well.

In geology there is enormous variation in the demands made on one's time. Some who work in industry have eight-to-five jobs, mostly in the office or the lab, writing reports and sending samples out to be analyzed. At places like the U.S. Geological Survey, up until the budget cuts, people traveled more and spent more time in the field. It's changing now, but at some of the oil companies people would be sent out to wells or other locations and sometimes were away for quite a while. Geologists for mining companies commonly are either stationed in remote locations or traveling between various locations. As academic geologists, we are involved in teaching classes, advising graduate students (which means time in the field with them), doing our own research, and providing service to the community and the university.

My journey into and through science education and a career is probably different from that of most other people because I am not only a woman but also a lesbian. I grew up in Modesto, California, when it was a little farm town in the Central Valley. I was a horrible high school student. I look back now and realize this was in part because I never fit in, had no lesbian role models because all the teachers had to be closeted, and the school environment was structured around a heterosexual culture. I certainly developed low self-esteem during those years and was continually advised

Peg Rees in Antarctica working in the Churchill Mountains of the central Transantarctic Mountains, 1987

orado, a type of course required for every college student in geology. I collected money from every relative I had, and we went to summer field camp in Colorado after my second year in college. The group that taught the camp was from the University of Kansas. We were out mapping and working out of doors every day, which is something I've always loved—I've always skied and hiked. Mapping involves taking topographic maps like the ones people use for hiking, and drawing where the different rock types are and then making some interpretations about how the rocks were folded and faulted. One can either do that in minuscule detail or can cover really large areas. At the time, we were covering fairly large areas, walking well over ten miles a day.

At the camp there was a person from the University of Kansas named Bert Rowell, who was British and had been in the country just a few years. We became friends and still do a lot of research together and copublish. After camp was over, I went back to California and continued my geology studies at Sonoma State College, where my friend and I went after community college. The geology department there was just great, although it certainly was not without its problems. It was a very small department with four white men who were fairly young and dynamic. I didn't feel lost in the crowd, which I think was really important since I hadn't had a very strong high school background. At Sonoma State I started my science and math right at the beginning with prealgebra. At the community college, I had been taking Eastern religion, philosophy, and pottery. In high school I took bookkeeping so I could get a job and put myself through most of school, although my parents helped quite a bit, too. And so I started from ground zero and worked my way through all the sciences I needed and ended up with a minor in physics and almost a minor in math. Although my friend and I went to Sonoma, she did not continue in geology; but we lived together. Luckily, I got along great with the only other female geology student there at the time. Infrequent as it might be, I am still in touch with both of these women.

not to do, or told that I could not do, science and math. I went on to a community college in my hometown. I continued to hate science but had to pass one class in order to graduate. I did poorly in all my attempts at science classes until I took a geology course from a really dynamic teacher named Charles Love. He wouldn't let me drop the course the first day; he told us that whoever wanted to drop the course after two weeks could. By the end of two weeks, I had become friends with another lesbian in the class and found the course itself fascinating. When asked at the end of two weeks if I still wanted to drop, I said, "Hey, this is great. I'm staying in." That course and friend were real turning points for me. We took two more classes from the teacher, and then he encouraged me and my friend to do an eight-week summer field camp in Col-

After earning a B.A. in geology, I couldn't get a job. I had kept up written correspondence with Bert Rowell, and he suggested that I apply for graduate school and for a teaching assistantship at the University of Kansas. It was the only job offer I'd had, so I took it. Some people at Kansas were great, and some were horrible. It was a typical all-white-male department. One professor whom I had planned to work with said that I couldn't work with him unless I wore a skirt: that was not going to happen. I nearly dropped out, but then I received funding from Bert Rowell and another professor, who received a grant that would fund my summer fieldwork in Nevada and Utah for my master's degree. I jumped at the opportunity and learned to love the desert.

I wanted to teach at a community college after I finished my master's degree (and I still have all 250 rejection letters), but instead I got a job with Union Oil Company in Casper, Wyoming. It was during the oil boom of the mid-to-late 1970s. I worked there for a couple of years, during which time I probably was the most depressed I had ever been. I learned that "girls can't sit on the big oil rigs as a geologist or anything else" and that "girls are not welcome to join or even eat at the Petroleum Club." Although I made a few friends outside of work, joined a softball team, and took classes at the community college (woodworking and winter mountaineering), I knew that things had to change in my life. I was extremely lucky that a professor at Sonoma State called me about a job opening at a community college north of San Francisco. I got the job and taught there for four wonderful years. I had plenty of lesbian role models in the college at all levels—from students to administrators—and began a journey of understanding feminism, heterosexism, homophobia, my own internalized homophobia, and racism. With these new insights, I began to develop a stronger and more positive self-image.

During the last year at the community college, I became very ill. The doctors (all male) misdiagnosed my condition and said it was a "woman's illness." They said it was stress related and that I shouldn't continue in my job. Even though it was the best job that I ever had and the best environment that I had ever lived in, I quit my job and decided to return to the University of Kansas for a Ph.D. During the entire time I was teaching at the community college, I had been doing research on the side and in the summers, so I figured being a Ph.D. student wouldn't be too stressful and I could take time off if I got ill.

Finally, four years ago, I was properly diagnosed with a gluten intolerance. I was told not to eat wheat, and now I'm a healthy person. I almost died from the same problem when I was young and had missed time in high school because I was in and out of the hospital. A woman hematologist here in Las Vegas, Heather Allen, figured it out, and to her I will always be grateful. It's ironic that I've had hematologists study me my whole life and was even diagnosed with leukemia once. It took forty years to figure out what was really wrong with me, but now that they have I'm very happy.

Even though I had this disease that made me sick and need to sleep much of the time, both my parents were very supportive of my academic and recreational pursuits. They always told me to go for it. I'm very mechanical; I attribute that to my father, who was a mechanic and always had me helping him work on cars. (My sister tended to do housework.) I can work on snowmobiles in Antarctica and fix cars on field trips if they break down. My father was fairly verbally aggressive, however—a style I also learned and that has hardened me emotionally. But he also taught me confidence and to stand up and speak up for myself. Regrettably, all of these attributes helped me to be successful in the masculinist tradition of geology. It has been a long road to unlearn these ways to be a better feminist teacher of science.

My mother was a nurse, but since I was sick all the time and in and out of hospitals, I didn't have much of an inclination toward her field. But my mother had the patience and the kindness to sit with me for hours to help me with schoolwork when I was missing a lot of school and when it was painfully obvious that I could not spell and read as well as most other children.

With these experiences in hand, as I grew, and continue to grow, as a lesbian feminist scientist, I have begun to recognize how I had to learn the masculinist ways of the science culture and the heterosexual ways of our society to "pass," to succeed. It is a lot of work to be a woman in a man's world and a homosexual in a restrictive heterosexual society. When I moved to my job at UNLV ten years ago, driving from Kansas with my lover in a U-Haul truck, we made the decision to stay out of the closet. Nevertheless, I continue to see subtle ways that I still try to "pass" as a heterosexual. In classes, for example, I may refrain from using any personal examples or explaining who the woman is in the photograph I am using to illustrate a geological feature (although she may appear in many photos). People are presumed to be heterosexual unless they do something overt to change that perception. As a teacher, I feel that I need to learn better how to "not pass" so that students can have positive lesbian role models in their lives. I know just how important those role models were in my development as a scientist and a person, and they still are in my everyday life. Homosexual students, like heterosexual students, need to know where they can have safe and confidential discussions. Recognizing the importance of role models and how the strong heterosexual culture of our educational institutions adversely affects homosexual students, I have chosen to spend my service time at the university and in the community to support gay and lesbian students and our issues. When I was the faculty adviser for the gay and lesbian student organization, the very homophobic responses of some administrators certainly heightened my awareness of the need for tolerance in education and for political action if we ever hope to have social equality for all people. It also made me aware of how grateful homosexual students are to have "out" friends on the faculty who can be their advocate.

In part because of these experiences and because I am a lesbian scientist, I have developed ties to women's studies where faculty development is strongly encouraged and inclusivity is fostered. Through reading, having discussions, attending national meetings, and team-teaching classes in women's studies, I have begun to view my life, my science, and my teaching in a much broader and, I think, more holistic way. I have learned new feminist approaches to teaching, scientific research, and living life. I am in the midst of developing new courses in geoscience and a cross-listed course in women's studies, refocusing my research toward more socially responsible endeavors and living my life in an activist manner.

I advise young women to stay aware of the social world around them. As Sandra Harding, one of the leading feminist scholars of science, might say, don't just be trained as a foot soldier of science. Although most of doing science is putting your head down and working really hard, we must be aware of the social world in which we live, what the relationship of our science is to it, and what we can do to help provide a sustainable future and a more just and humane world for all people.

PRESENT POSITION: Professor of Geology, Department of Geoscience, University of Nevada–Las Vegas
FIELD: Geology
RESEARCH AREA: Sedimentology and stratigraphy
EDUCATION: B.A. in Geology (1972), Sonoma State University; M.S. (1976) and Ph.D. (1985) in Geology, University of Kansas
DATE/PLACE OF BIRTH: December 28, 1949/San Diego, California

Peg Rees lives in Las Vegas, Nevada, with Dr. Maralee Mayberry, a sociologist, at least nine months out of the year. The other time she does research in Antarctica, Southeast China, Australia, or someplace else in the world. Peg and Maralee often enjoy traveling together.

INTERVIEW DATE: May 1996

Nancy Rhoads

Senior Engineer
NORTHROP GRUMMAN CORPORATION

Nancy Rhoads has been fascinated by airplanes all her life. Although she was diverted into humanities as an undergraduate, she later learned how to fly airplanes and then how to build them. After a near-fatal car accident left her paralyzed from the chest down, she has persevered through many challenges to continue pursuing her love of aerospace.

❧

I can't remember a time when I wasn't interested in flying or in science. Part of my interest can be attributed to my father's fascination with airplanes. My dad collected books about World War I biplanes, and, being a carpenter, he used to build model airplanes from scratch using only pictures and the dimensions found in books. These models, made from pine, were roughly a foot and a half in length and often had movable control surfaces. Once he made his own design: a red and white racing biplane with painted dice rolled to the numbers seven and eleven on the side (my birthday is on July 11). But my dad never learned to fly. We didn't have a lot of money, and he was too busy working and raising a family.

Neither of my parents had a college education. They both came from small towns in Iowa at a time when going to college was more of a luxury than it is now. My dad graduated from high school in the midst of the Depression, in 1932, and went into the Navy. He had barely finished his enlistment when World War II began, and he chose to enter the Coast Guard instead of staying in the Navy. Mom was only nineteen when they married in 1941. She went to work in a candy factory in New York City while Dad was away at war. She had to lie to get the job, saying she wasn't married, and she had to take her wedding ring off every day before she went to work. After the war Mom continued to work except when my brothers and I were babies. I grew up believing it was natural for a woman to work full-time. I always planned on going to college and having a career.

Marriage and a family were the last things on my mind the spring day in Iowa in 1972 when I graduated from high school. I had won a scholarship and couldn't wait to get to

Class picture of Nancy Rhoads, 1972

college in the fall. We lived near Iowa State University, and both my brothers attended there. While I was still in high school, I would visit them on weekends and go to the university library to do my book reports, essays, and research. I loved it.

My first experience with my college adviser proved discouraging. He asked what I wanted to major in, and I confidently replied, "Literature and aerospace engineering." After a few beats of stunned silence he said, "Those two subjects don't go together." Then he added, "That would be really hard, a lot of physics and math. Are you sure you can handle that?" I didn't understand his pessimism. My highest scores on my ACTs were in science and math, and I was salutatorian of my high school graduating class. One of my brothers was double majoring in math and computer science, the other had graduated with high honors in electrical engineering. I insisted on pursuing my choice of majors, and the adviser drew up my quarter's curriculum: French, freshman composition, physics, and math.

I was put into a physics class that was already using calculus, although I hadn't taken calculus in high school and really should have taken it first. I can still remember leaving the lecture hall after that first physics class. My brother Doug was sitting in the hall to meet me for lunch, and I collapsed on the bench next to him and burst into tears. I had never felt so stupid in my life. It was the first time I felt that I might not understand the material well enough to pass the class!

When I returned to my adviser with the problem, he merely shrugged and said if basic physics was too hard he didn't know what I was going to do. I quickly got discouraged and fell back on what I knew to be easy for me: literature. Mom had instilled a love of books in me at a very young age. I don't remember reading the typical children's books. Instead I would grab one of Mom's thickest and heaviest books and beg her to read from it. It was a collection of the works of Mark Twain, and Doug and I loved hearing the adventures of Tom Sawyer and Huck Finn.

Writing seemed to come easy to me as well, so majoring in literature was a piece of cake. I guess it was too easy for me. Although I enjoyed it, got good grades, and even went to graduate school for a year, I was restless and bored. Something was missing, although I didn't know what.

My brother was working for Boeing in Seattle, so I moved there too. I spent a year working a secretarial job, I traveled to Europe, and I finally learned to fly an airplane. Then I decided it was time to check out aerospace engineering again, but this time I was more cautious. First I enrolled in a precalculus class, and when that proved ridiculously easy my confidence soared. I found out the requirements for admittance to the aerospace engineering department at the University of Washington: I needed three quarters of calculus and some physics courses. Shortly after my first solo cross-country flight in a small plane, I began my studies at UW. The campus was beautiful, I loved my physics classes, and the calculus was fairly easy. There is a wind tunnel on campus that was used by Boeing and other companies. I applied and got a job there. A wind tunnel is a facility to test airplane models. It consists roughly of a test section in which a model of a plane is mounted in a tubular circuit through which wind, usually generated by fan blades, is blown to simulate flying conditions.

Working at the University of Washington Aero Lab (UWAL) was the best job I'd ever had, and I loved it. We installed airplane models, ran tests, plotted the data, calibrated the balance that measured the data, and did tunnel maintenance. I probably learned more there about practical aerodynamics and what real engineers did on the job than I did in my classes. One time I was so involved in working in the tunnel, I totally forgot to show up for an important test in one of my classes. My whole life revolved around airplanes. During the week I was in class, working at the tunnel, or studying. I practically lived on campus, sometimes not getting home from working at the tunnel until two o'clock in the morning. On the weekends I flew airplanes and hung

Nancy Rhoads, February 1996
PHOTO COURTESY OF OLAN MILLS, INC.

around small airports watching the planes, talking to other pilots, going to air shows in the summer, and traveling from Seattle to the East Coast in a two-seat plane with no radio. Often while traveling cross country in the plane, I would stop in Iowa to visit my folks. It was such a thrill to take my dad up in the plane and let him try flying it. Everything looks so different from up there. You can see so far from an airplane.

Engineering school was nothing like liberal arts or the other classes I had taken. The professors were always extremely busy, and the teaching assistants were often difficult to understand. It was hard and a lot of work. Many times I felt overwhelmed and isolated. Out of my class of around sixty students, there were only three women, including me. Nevertheless, it wasn't as insurmountable as my adviser at Iowa State had predicted. I graduated from UW in 1981 with a B.S. in aerospace engineering. The early 1980s was a high point for the aerospace field, and I had my pick of jobs. I liked Northrop in Hawthorne, California, the best. I didn't know it at the time I ac-

cepted the job, but I was about to begin my career on one of the most interesting and advanced airplanes at the time—the highly classified B-2 Stealth Bomber.

I was assigned to the aerodynamics group and soon found myself in a wind tunnel again. Only this time I was assigned to various tunnels around the country. Though I was traveling for Northrop, the nature of the project prevented me from acknowledging who I worked for or what I was working on. It was an exciting time. I sometimes worked all night in a tunnel and slept during the day in a hotel room. I was completely fascinated by the B-2; the technology was mostly new to me.

After a couple of years in Northrop's Aero Division, I considered working in other areas in the company and became interested in the flutter group. This group deals with the structural dynamics of the airplane. They also conduct wind-tunnel testing, but instead of using a relatively inflexible model whose only motions are essentially pitch and yaw, the flutter models use highly dynamic, flexible fiberglass. Vibrations can literally tear a structure apart if it is incorrectly designed. The test goal is to excite the model—that is, to start it vibrating while it is "flying" in the tunnel to discover at what speed the excitation becomes self-feeding. At that point, if the vibrations are allowed to continue, they may grow and destroy the entire structure. Our job was to find this flutter speed. Based on analytical data, we had a good idea where it was. We had to approach this velocity in the tunnel cautiously. Once it was achieved, the tunnel had to be shut down immediately to avoid losing the model. Occasionally things go wrong, however, and the model literally tears itself to pieces. It's a very interesting type of testing with tense moments as you approach the predicted flutter speed. The test engineer, who is watching both the model and wing-tip accelerometer strip charts, is responsible for stopping the wind. A mistake means losing a model that cost thousands of dollars and took months to build.

Wind-tunnel testing precedes the structural testing of a full-scale structure. The next step is to build the plane, or a piece of it such as a control surface, and do vibration testing. After testing the control surfaces, the flutter group participates in the ground vibrations test (GVT) of the entire airplane. This is no small task in the case of the B-2, with its significant size—the wingspan, or distance from wingtip to wingtip, is 172 feet. Testing for the B-2 took place in Palmdale, California, near Edwards Air Force Base. This meant I had to travel a couple of hours each way to get to work. Then my work was impacted by a tremendous, life-altering event: I survived a near-fatal car accident en route to work on the morning of March 24, 1986, becoming instantly paralyzed from the chest down. The medical term for my paralysis is C6–7 quadriplegia, which means I have good use of my arms but no use of my fingers and, of course, no movement from the chest down. After thirteen months of rehabilitation and a lot of support from the people at work, I returned to my job part-time, but with the new perspective of a wheelchair user. It was, to say the least, not easy to get used to. I had last seen my desk on a Friday more than a year earlier, expecting to be at work the following Monday morning as usual. Now I was in a wheelchair. Not only were there the obvious environmental obstacles—my desk and computer terminal had to be raised, the old bathroom door was replaced by an electric one—but I had to face the more subtle obstacles of discrimination as well. By and large, this discrimination in my workplace wasn't intentional; and fortunately my boss, Dick Tye, was always willing to fight for me. But there were some problems born mainly out of ignorance. For example, during GVT the airplane is in a huge hangar surrounded by computers and equipment, with cables and hydraulic lines running everywhere on the floor. In order for me to get close to the plane, people needed to help me get my chair over all these cables. Someone in the safety department decided this was a hazard for me. In an emergency— say a hydraulic line burst—it would be more difficult to evacuate me than everybody else. I

was told I couldn't be there, which of course meant I couldn't do my job. Dick had to make a few phone calls, but he got it straightened out.

Flight testing was my next big challenge at work. My first one after the accident took place at Edwards AFB, and again I met resistance. There was some reluctance on the part of my immediate manager to send me out to the base. Flight testing requires long hours and always seems to take place early in the morning. Once I made it clear I both wanted and was able to go, I participated in the test program. Again, there were a few instances when my presence in a wheelchair caused some alarm. Once while the plane sat outside and I was sitting under it, examining a particular section of the underbelly with another engineer, someone called my co-worker aside to advise him it wasn't safe for me to be there. I ignored the suggestion that I leave and nothing more came from it. Overall, I enjoyed the flight test program and found my disability to be more of a hindrance in other people's minds than it was to me.

I continue to work part-time due to the constant pain I'm in, which is caused by the incomplete nature of my spinal cord injury. Even though I have no movement from the chest level down, I have some sensation because my spinal cord is not completely damaged. A small part of it is sending signals to my brain that allow me to feel when my legs are being touched. Unfortunately, people with incomplete injuries such as mine tend to be in a lot of pain for which there is little or no treatment. Pain pills make me sleepy and do nothing for the pain, so I basically just have to live with it. Some days staying in bed is about my only option, but I try to use that only as a last resort. Working full-time is not out of the question, but it would have an adverse effect on my home life. Since I have a three-year-old son, I choose to continue working part-time to have the stamina it takes to care for him.

Since my accident I have discovered a lot of different ways to do things at work. The computer is no problem to use: I simply type with what is essentially a one-finger method. Since my fingers can't move, my hands have contracted into a semi-fist shape, which actually works to my advantage. The stiffness of my fingers allows me to type with my thumb or a knuckle, and I am able to grasp things such as a glass. I can operate the mouse on the PCs and get my disks in and out of the disk drives. I modified the handles on my file cabinets and figured out how to open the security padlocks that are required on all cabinets containing classified data. I had lever-type door handles installed on the doors I use at work and an extra pull handle put on the stall door in the bathroom. It is amazing how small and inexpensive changes can make a huge difference in my ability to do things independently.

I think my engineering background has helped me figure out the solution to a lot of little problems both at work and at home. Whenever I am confronted with a new obstacle, I enjoy the challenge of finding a reasonable solution or alternative method of accomplishing my goal. I recently started driving again in a specially modified minivan adapted with hand controls, and my day goes much

like that of any other working parent, starting with dropping my son off at day care on my way to work. I've been up in small airplanes since the accident, but haven't found a way to modify them so I could fly one comfortably. I miss flying a lot but look forward to new adventures. The aerospace industry isn't quite what it used to be, but I'm pretty happy where I am in my career. I'm still involved with airplanes.

PRESENT POSITION: Senior Engineer, Northrop Grumman Corporation

FIELD: Aerospace engineering

RESEARCH AREA: Structural analysis

EDUCATION: B.A. in Literature (1976), Iowa State University; B.S. in Aerospace Engineering (1981), University of Washington

DATE/PLACE OF BIRTH: July 11, 1954/Cedar Falls, Iowa

Nancy Rhoads lives with her son, Justin Douglas, and their dog, Heidi, in Cerritos, California, and hopes someday to return to the Pacific Northwest.

INTERVIEW DATE: February 1996

Evelyn M. Rodriguez

Associate Director for Research and Senior Medical Officer,
Bureau of Health Resources Development
HEALTH RESOURCES AND SERVICES ADMINISTRATION,
DEPARTMENT OF HEALTH AND HUMAN SERVICES

Evelyn Rodriguez credits her desire to become a pediatrician to the wonderful doctor she had as a child and to her younger sister's congenital heart defect. Though some of her neighbors told her that "girls don't become doctors," her mother's encouragement helped her to keep going. Evelyn Rodriguez received an M.D. from Harvard Medical School and a master's degree in public health in epidemiology from the Columbia School of Public Health. She is board certified in pediatrics and public health and general preventive medicine.

❧

I'm a physician epidemiologist, but I identify most with being a pediatrician. My day-to-day work as associate director for research is scientific research, science administration, and health policy. I wear another "hat" as a lieutenant commander in the Commissioned Corps of the U.S. Public Health Service, which serves under the surgeon general of the United States.

As an epidemiologist, I collaborate in studies, analyze data, propose hypotheses to test, publish manuscripts, and help develop health policy. I teach medical students introductory epidemiology in the Uniformed Services University of the Health Sciences. I also see patients and teach at the Bethesda National Naval Medical Center as an assistant professor. My clinical knowledge helps me to propose hypotheses to test. Within my field of medical epidemiology, my specialty includes anything to do with children and, in particular, perinatal epidemiology and HIV/AIDS. Perinatal epidemiology is the study of the risk factors associated with poor birth outcomes, such as cerebral palsy, birth defects, low birth weight, and prematurity.

I became interested in HIV/AIDS research very early in the epidemic and very early in my career. In 1982, when I was a pediatric intern at the Children's Hospital in Boston, I saw children who appeared to have an acquired immunodeficiency that was new, the cause of which wasn't known. We knew they were very sick and that they invariably died, but we could only give them supportive care. It wasn't until 1983 that the HIV virus was discovered as the underlying cause of their illness.

As a pediatric resident at Babies Hospital in New York City, I saw many more babies in-

Evelyn Rodriguez with a mischievous patient, 1995

fected with HIV. As you can imagine, there was a lot of interest in research to combat the disease. I finished my pediatric residency in 1985 and started working at the Kings County Medical Center and the State University of New York Health Sciences Center at Brooklyn, my hometown. As a young attending physician, I taught medical students and residents in the pediatric outpatient clinic and worked in the emergency room. I decided that I wanted to go back to graduate school to get a master's degree in public health with a concentration in epidemiology in order to conduct HIV/AIDS research.

I was initially discouraged from pursuing the degree by some of my professional peers because epidemiology was a very new science. The methodologies are novel and still in the process of being defined. At the time, some of my colleagues believed that "real" research could only be done in a laboratory setting, whereas in epidemiology you can't control the variables that may affect your study because the population is being studied in the "real world." The field of epidemiology is very challenging, but the information that we gather from real-world observations is critical in shaping medical interventions and public health policy.

I decided to return to Babies Hospital and the Columbia School of Public Health, where I knew pediatricians who were conducting epidemiologic research. I became a Mellon fellow at the Sergievsky Center, which is part of the Columbia School of Public Health, where I was supported with a stipend and tuition to get my master's degree in public health. It was while I was doing work for my master's thesis in epidemiology that I became interested in perinatal epidemiology and got the opportunity to become involved in HIV/AIDS research. I was a study pediatrician for a group study of babies born to women infected with HIV and also participated in study design issues.

My master's thesis work developed from my reading literature on perinatal HIV/AIDS. Some investigators in New York City had pro-

posed that children born to mothers with AIDS who themselves developed HIV infection had a fetal embryopathy—that is, they "looked funny" at birth. The geneticists and others who thought these children "looked funny" included drawings in their papers that depicted, to my eyes, normal-appearing African American and Puerto Rican children. What my master's thesis proposed to do was to tease out the effects of race and ethnicity from the effects of HIV; my hypothesis was that the features cited in the literature were normal and not related to the HIV virus.

I am Puerto Rican, born to parents who migrated to the United States in the early 1950s. They met in Brooklyn, married, and raised my younger sister, Maribel, and me. My father worked in a paint factory; my mother worked as a seamstress and embroiderer in the New York City garment district. My parents encouraged me in whatever I wanted to do—especially my mother. They really believed in the American dream—that doors were open for me and that I could achieve my life's dream. When I shared with my mother that I wanted to be a doctor, she said, "You can do it!" When our neighbors said that "girls don't become doctors, they become nurses," she persisted and came to the defense of my dream. She told me, "Whatever you want to do, you can do. Don't let anybody tell you that you can't. Don't let the lack of money get in your way." I took all of that to heart.

When I was young I dreamed of being a pediatrician like the one I had, Dr. Warren Owens. He was in private practice with his wife, who was a nurse. They had a large family, and their office was on the first floor of their home; it was a very warm place to be. When we were unable to pay, he would see us free of charge. He would also give my mother free samples of medicines he thought we needed. He was just wonderful. I often wish I could have thanked him personally for what he meant to me.

My younger sister's congenital heart defect also played a role in my career choice. She had patent ductus arteriosus, which causes heart failure and poor growth. Today this condition rarely requires surgery because medication is administered early in the neonatal period. But in the 1960s the condition invariably meant major heart surgery. I remember it very vividly—she was four years old at the time of her surgery. Now she has a master's degree in communications from the University of Puerto Rico and is applying to law school.

When I was in elementary school, I read everything. I read popular books and the classics. I taught myself how to read and write Spanish in high school. I started out by reading picture *novelas* and then challenged myself until I could read *Don Quixote* in the original Spanish version. My first language was Spanish, and I had learned English in grammar school before the days of bilingual education. Nevertheless, I didn't receive formal training in Spanish until I got into high school.

When I was in high school, students could take the secretarial-business track or the college-bound track, and I chose the latter. The high school administration was generally unsupportive of my "lofty" academic aspirations, but I persisted. As a freshman at my Catholic high school, I was on a half scholarship because in grade school I had been a straight-A student, I had won a regional oratorical contest, and I was a spelling bee champion. Despite my continued straight-A average, the school decided not to offer the scholarship in my subsequent years because of their budgetary constraints. It was very difficult for my mother to pay the tuition. Early in my sophomore year, I told the school that, because my family could not afford the tuition, I wanted to graduate a year early.

I graduated from high school in 1974 at the age of sixteen. I attended Saint Francis College in Brooklyn as the youngest student in my class. I was very fortunate that the college had a small, excellent science department. I graduated summa cum laude with a B.S. in biology in 1978.

After college I decided I would attend a local medical school. By that time I was married. Among other offers, I was admitted as a student at the City University of New York's Mount Sinai Medical School in Manhattan, a city school where the tuition wasn't too high. The school was affiliated with the hospital where my sister had heart surgery. But after I received my acceptance to Harvard Medical School, however, I decided to go there instead.

I have three wonderful sons. Having children while keeping my career going was a challenge. I had my first child, José Luis, the summer before my third year of medical school. When I moved back to New York after medical school, my mother became his primary caretaker while I finished my residency training. After I finished my residency and was a young attending physician at the State University of New York Health Sciences Center at Brooklyn, I delivered my second child, Raphael. He was an infant when I started my master's program at the School of Public Health at Columbia. My third son, Alejandro, is a toddler. In my spare time I enjoy watching my active boys play sports, and I work out at the gym several times a week.

At Harvard Medical School, my role models were Carola Eisenberg, a psychiatrist from Argentina, and Alvin Poussaint, a nationally known child psychiatrist and author. Dr. Eisenberg was very encouraging as a role model because she was a woman who had both a career and a family life. Dr. Poussaint is an African American who was the director of minority recruitment and retention, and he counseled me on academic and career issues.

What I'm most proud of in my career is a recent development—a paper I published in the medical journal *AIDS*, which is the culmination of years of planning, research, consensus building, and collaboration with many colleagues at the National Institutes of Health and universities throughout the country. We report that maternal hard-drug use is a risk factor for two outcomes: mother-to-infant HIV transmission and positive HIV cultures among mothers at the time of delivery. This means that it is important to help women with HIV infection to stop using hard drugs during pregnancy for two reasons: to lower the risk of infecting their babies with HIV, and to lower their personal risk for developing HIV/AIDS.

As an officer of the Commissioned Corps of the U.S. Public Health Service, my goal for the future is to continue population-based research that will improve the health of the American people.

PRESENT POSITION: Associate Director for Research and Senior Medical Officer, Bureau of Health Resources Development, Health Resources and Services Administration, Department of Health and Human Services

FIELD: Medical epidemiology

RESEARCH AREA: HIV/AIDS, perinatal epidemiology

EDUCATION: B.S. in Biology (1978), Saint Francis College; M.D. (1982), Harvard Medical School; M.P.H. in Epidemiology (1990), Columbia School of Public Health

DATE/PLACE OF BIRTH: December 8, 1957/ Brooklyn, New York

Evelyn M. Rodriguez lives with her family in Gaithersburg, Maryland.

INTERVIEW DATE: January 1996

Sue V. Rosser

Professor of Anthropology and Director,
Center for Women's Studies and Gender Research
UNIVERSITY OF FLORIDA

Sue Rosser is a leader in women's health and gender equity in the sciences. She has found a unique way of satisfying her interdisciplinary interests, which originated with a double major in French and zoology from the University of Wisconsin. By combining her research in biology and health sciences and her understanding of the different ways people learn, she designs programs and teaching methods to make a difference for women in science and to bring women's health issues into the classroom.

꩜

People frequently ask how I ever got involved in both women's studies and science, or more specifically how I made the trek from a Ph.D. in zoology to serving as a director of women's studies. It formally happened during my postdoctoral experience in the University of Wisconsin at Madison. I was in the second year of my postdoctoral work and was pregnant with my second child. The faculty member with whom I was doing the postdoc suggested that I might have an abortion because it wasn't a good time in the research to have a baby, that we needed to collect more data so we could get our grant renewed. I was so stunned that I began thinking for the first time about the different expectations we have for women and men in science.

It was 1974–75 and the university was just starting a women's studies program. Ruth Bleier and another person had created a course on the biology and psychology of women built around feminist critiques of research. Since Ruth was on a 100 percent research appointment, she was only able to teach the course once. I was asked to teach the course because folks in the women's studies programs knew that I was a feminist and had been involved in consciousness-raising groups. It was an exciting possibility. Despite the fact that I had had children and earned a Ph.D. in zoology, I did not know very much about my own body, and it was fantastic to learn about women's health and biology in detail as I created the material for the course. At the time the book *Our Bodies, Ourselves,* which later became a classic, was just being

Sue Rosser, March 1996

323

written and was not even available. I was in the first year of one of the older, larger, and better-established women's studies programs. I got to see its beginning and work with all its pioneers. By the end of 1976, I realized that I wanted to get a faculty appointment and stay involved in women's studies.

A position opened up at Mary Baldwin College, a small liberal arts women's college in Virginia. Although I was hired as a biology professor, I had an agreement with the dean to start a women's studies program. My colleagues in biology were quite shocked because they thought they had hired a 100 percent biologist. I began by offering courses on the biology of women and women's health and disease. My colleagues soon saw that my courses attracted a large number of students who ultimately chose to be biology majors. Students who took my women's studies courses found they needed more scientific knowledge to understand the process of menstruation, contraception, childbirth, or whatever had drawn them to the course.

Looking back, I realize that I had always longed for the interdisciplinary experience that women's studies provides. I was never a "biologist's biologist." That is why I was content working in a small liberal arts college and in women's studies at bigger universities. I like the interaction among science, humanities, and social sciences.

My interdisciplinary interests go back to my childhood. I grew up in Madison, the home of the University of Wisconsin, where I had many excellent teachers in secondary school. Many of my humanities teachers were scholars with Ph.D.'s who were in Madison because their spouses and partners were faculty members at the university. This was less true of my science teachers because other options existed for spouses in science-related fields. In those years I thought of myself as a potential humanities or social science major because I did not find science courses exciting. However, it was the post-Sputnik era and since there was a nationwide emphasis on attracting children to math and science, I took

four semesters of high school math, including precalculus.

When I went to the University of Wisconsin, I planned to major in English or French. In my first semester I didn't take any science because I got back late from a summer in Europe, and all the science and math courses were closed out. I ended up with a bizarre assortment of classes—advanced French, Latin, classical mythology, ancient religion and the early church, and honors English composition. Then second semester, I took Genetics for Poets, a course for nonscience majors. I got the highest grade in the class, and the professor asked me to work in his lab. I started that summer and ended up working for him throughout my undergraduate years. He kept pressing me to major in science. I took a number of zoology courses, partially to please him and partially to get him off my back. I got very interested in the material, but I stayed interested in humanities. I ultimately graduated with a double major in French with honors and in zoology.

When it came time to go to graduate school, I was attracted to both French and zoology. Several factors made me decide on zoology. There were more jobs, and I was a little more interested in the subject. Also, I was married, and going to graduate school in French typically meant long periods of study in France, and I thought that might not work. But I was still interdisciplinary in my interests; I was not content with just sciences or just humanities. It is no accident that I do what I do today.

In graduate school, I started out working on fossils. I was fortunate to have a university fellowship and did not have to teach. In my fossil research, I was working on the pineal gland and became interested in seasonal reproductive cycles, which are influenced by this gland. As I was finishing my master's degree, I was lured to the Primate Center to look at endocrinology and reproductive physiology. I thought it would be interesting to study the melatonin output in monkeys because I saw that melatonin, which is produced in the pineal gland, is correlated with the menstrual cycle and thought there was a potential for a contraceptive. I was extracting melatonin from the urine of squirrel monkeys to study endocrinology and reproductive cycles, and I ended up reproducing my first child!

My daughter Meagan was born in the fall of 1971. Shortly after she was born, I attended a seminar where the speaker showed a graph of reproductive cycles. Each point on the graph was a season. I realized to get enough data for my thesis, I would have to have between eight and twelve points on a similar graph, which would take between eight and twelve years. I didn't want to take that long to get my degree, so I returned to paleontology, working on rodent teeth, although John Robinson, my major professor, was a primatologist. But I had a child and the idea of going to Africa to dig up Australopithecines seemed infeasible. So I worked on rodent teeth from the Badlands of South Dakota and on specimens from the Field Museum in Chicago.

After completing my Ph.D., I did something that is not very good for your career but that many women do. Since my husband had not finished his Ph.D., I stayed at Wisconsin for my postdoctoral work. It was an especially bad idea because I had done all my undergraduate and graduate work at Wisconsin. This is a big no-no, although nobody pointed it out to me. No one told me that it was important for your career to gain the multiple perspectives that come from being at different schools.

At the time I was a student and postdoc there were no women faculty in zoology and not many other women graduate students. Very few of them were married. I can't recall any other women graduate student who had a child.

There was no money for fossil research, but there was lots of money for cancer research. Even though that was a very different area for me, I got a fellowship in the lab of a developmental biologist, Dr. Bob Auerbach. My second year I moved to another lab to work under an immunogeneticist. So my postdoctoral

experience coupled with my graduate experience in paleontology, endocrinology, and reproductive physiology gave me a broad background at both the molecular and organismic level. This was relatively rare even at the time. It was after the second year of my postdoctoral experience, when I had my second child, that I got involved in women's studies.

My job at Mary Baldwin permitted me to use my broad background. In a small school you teach some of everything. But there was no time for research, and I did not have the computer facilities to do research, which involved a lot of statistics on data from rodent fossils. I focused more on teaching and noticed that ways of teaching and learning at a women's college were very different from what I was used to. As a postdoc, I had often taught comparative anatomy for summer classes with a lot of premeds. My male students were often very aggressive: because there was such intense competition for medical school, they would move the pins in lab practicals so others would make mistakes. Mary Baldwin was very different. Women students wanted to do well but not at the expense of others. There was a very cooperative environment. I had to modify my teaching to be effective. It made me think about what techniques were useful to attract women to science. This led to a lot of my ideas about female-friendly science.

After my second year at the college, my marriage broke up. Working at a small college involved less pressure to publish, and it was possible to teach, write, and manage alone with two young children. In fact, I received an invitation to go back to Wisconsin as a faculty member in women's studies and geology (my minor for the Ph.D.) but decided not to take that offer. With two little children I thought it would be too hard to work toward tenure with a split appointment and especially as the first woman in the geology department. So I stayed in Virginia.

I began to publish more of my work on women in science, and I received many invitations to give talks on the topic. This was hard to manage at Mary Baldwin because I had no help setting up labs and classes, so I began to look around and in 1985–86 moved to the University of South Carolina as the director of women's studies and professor of family and preventive medicine. Working at a small liberal arts college was good for me at the beginning of my career, and I was able to move to a university environment later because I had published. Some people who start at small colleges end up there forever even if they don't want to because they have no time to publish. Starting in a small college was also good for me because I saw how all facets of the college worked and fit together. I served on lots of different committees and as division chair. As a junior person at a big university I wouldn't have had many of those kinds of opportunities. I went to South Carolina as a tenured associate professor and director of women's studies with a faculty appointment in the Medical School.

At South Carolina my interests in biology and women in science merged in my teaching and my research. For many years I recognized that I was teaching women's studies courses with different methods than my science courses, but I hadn't really thought about how to put them together. In 1983–84, while at Mary Baldwin, I had been invited by Towson State University to participate in a curriculum transformation project. They wanted somebody who had worked in women's studies and biology to run faculty seminars on the new work that was coming out on the biology of women and to teach an introductory biology course infused with women's studies.

I went to Towson as a visiting professor in the fall of 1983. In the spring of 1984, I took a sabbatical. That was the first time I was actually forced to integrate women's studies into biology, and it led to the publication of my first book, *Teaching Science and Health from a Feminist Perspective: A Practical Guide*. I continued to work with the project for three years. My longstanding relationship with the project launched me into consulting with universities trying to integrate women's studies into their science curriculum and/or science into women's studies.

When I went to South Carolina, my first book had just come out. As often happens with women, once I got tenure and some of the pressure to publish was off, I found it easier to write. I started publishing more and more and developed lots of books and article ideas and continued to consult in women in science and women's health. I also built the program at South Carolina. Administering the program was sometimes difficult and very time consuming, but I found it exciting and interesting. It was a venue to get my ideas into courses. Being an administrator of women's studies also gave me connections to other departments and colleagues, which is important to my interdisciplinary interests.

In 1992, I received a National Science Foundation (NSF) grant to take the ideas from my book *Female-Friendly Science* and apply them to assist faculty within the University of South Carolina nine-campus system to integrate women's studies into science, engineering, and mathematics courses. It was a two-year project involving twenty-five male and female faculty members from one research campus, three four-year campuses, and five two-year campuses. As a result of our work we learned that using the methods from *Female-Friendly Science* helped everybody, not only women students. We did three measures of improvement. We looked at confidence, retention, and grades. For both male and female students, all three were raised. For female students, confidence and retention rose more; those were the areas where they had more problems. For male students grades rose more. On average, males tend to have slightly lower grades than females. What this approach really did was take whatever the student was having more difficulty with and improve that area.

In the fall of 1993, I was invited to the University of Wisconsin to be visiting distinguished professor in their Women in Science program. I worked with nine campuses within the University of Wisconsin system doing faculty development on curricular content and pedagogy for an NSF project on integrating women's studies into science curricula. In early 1994 NSF asked me to give a lecture for Women's History Month. I was then invited to be senior program officer for women's programs at NSF.

I went to NSF in January 1995, after the fall elections, and by the time I got there the political climate had changed considerably. More of my time was spent defending the Program for Women and Girls than expanding the program, as I had hoped to do. Before I went to NSF, the University of Florida had invited me to apply for the directorship of their new Center for Women's Studies and Gender Research. In early 1996 I left NSF for Florida.

At NSF and other institutions in Washington, I had been surprised to find that all the "women's health people" I'd known for years didn't know the "women in science people" and vice versa. At the University of Florida there is a lot of interdisciplinary work. Our center and the School of Agriculture have a project on women and gender in developing countries. Individuals going to work in forestry in Africa are made aware of the gender dimensions of their project so that they don't develop a program that hurts women. We've just submitted a proposal with the College of Engineering to develop programs for women in science. I interact with all facets of the campus and use a lot of my science.

My faculty appointment is in anthropology, with affiliated appointments in zoology and the Medical School. The zoology department focuses on problems very different from my interests—reptiles such as alligators rather than mammals. The anthropology department includes about ten people who do gender-related research. It's a large department and one of the top ten in the country, according to the National Research Council. The women's studies program is a combined program that includes interests as diverse as agriculture, medicine, law, liberal arts, and international studies, so anthropology is well positioned for the kind of interdisciplinary work I do.

I am currently working on my seventh book, tentatively titled *Revisiting Female-Friendly Science*. It is not an update of my earlier work but a discussion of what has happened as ideas such as collaborative learning and teaching the history of science have been incorporated into the classroom. Because there is little awareness of the roots of these methods in ethnic and women's studies, some of these methods have been applied in ways that hurt rather than help the students for whom they were designed. For example, in trying to encourage collaboration through group work in a classroom of twenty-five students, five of whom are women, teachers often make groups of five with one woman in each group. This isolates each woman and often has a negative impact on her collaboration and participation.

My two daughters manifest my own interests in their careers; this doesn't seem rebellious enough! Meagan has a degree with a double major in psychology and women's studies from the University of Massachusetts–Amherst. She lives in Boston and works at a hospital as a counselor in a residential treatment facility for women that uses a lot of feminist methods. They recruited her because she had a dual degree in psychology and women's studies. Caitlin just finished her junior year at Harvard in chemistry. She became very interested in women's studies last year after taking a course taught by Alice Jardine, a famous literary critic. She has also worked on women in science. This summer she's in a village in Kenya in a Berkeley-sponsored Peace Corps–like program helping high school students to prepare for their exams in math and science.

Often people ask me how a French degree is useful for someone with a Ph.D. in zoology. As a director of women's studies I find it is very useful to have a background in French. Among other things, it helps me to understand and appreciate my humanities colleagues. I still believe in the broad preparation I had. I also believe in the importance of math and science. It is very important for young women to pursue their studies in ways that keep many doors and options open. Options require staying in math and science long enough to have choices. A career can involve picking many different threads and weaving something new: my own career is an example of that.

PRESENT POSITION: Professor of Anthropology and Director of the Center for Women's Studies and Gender Research, University of Florida

FIELD: Biology, women's studies

RESEARCH AREA: Women's health, women in science, teaching methods

EDUCATION: B.A. in French and Zoology (1969), M.S. in Zoology (1971), Ph.D. in Zoology (1973), University of Wisconsin–Madison

DATE/PLACE OF BIRTH: March 11, 1947/ Springfield, Missouri

Sue Rosser lives in Gainesville, Florida, with her cat, Tiger, who is fifteen years old.

INTERVIEW DATE: June 1996

Vera Rubin

Astronomer and Staff Member, Department of Terrestrial Magnetism
THE CARNEGIE INSTITUTION OF WASHINGTON

As a young girl, Vera Rubin was captivated by the stars. Although she once doubted that she could become an astronomer, she went on to earn her bachelor's, master's, and doctoral degrees in astronomy. Her work has changed astronomers' views of how stars orbit in a galaxy and has also caused scientists to recognize that we live in a universe where most of the matter is dark—that is, not visible by any techniques yet devised. Her work has also earned her the National Medal of Science and election to the National Academy of Sciences. She believes that pursuing a nonestablishment path of working solo most of the time and refusing to listen to discouraging comments helped her make her own way. She is proud of her forty-eight-year marriage, her four children (all with Ph.D.'s), the successes in her career, and of "having pulled it all off."

I've spent most of my professional life devising questions that I wanted to answer—almost always about galaxies and almost always about motions of stars in galaxies. A very important part of my research career has been deciding what I wanted to study. Then I would see what was available—if anyone else had worked on the particular problem, what kinds of observations had been made in the past. Often there was nothing because instruments were just getting good enough for some of the things that I wanted to do. I would figure out how I could get the answers I wanted, and then I would devise an observing program and figure out exactly which galaxies I wanted to study—the trick really being to figure out what I had to do to get an answer. Then I would have to apply for telescope time. If you work in an observatory, you get some guaranteed time; if you don't work at an observatory, you must write a proposal.

Vera Rubin measuring spectra taken at the Kitt Peak National Observatory, 1970
CARNEGIE INSTITUTION OF WASHINGTON

Proposals are usually accepted twice a year for some observatories, once a year for others. You have to know the instruments that are available pretty well to make sure there is an instrument available that can do what you want to do. Observing time is very, very precious; most observatories with the big telescopes are over-subscribed by a factor of two or four applications for every opening.

From about the mid-1960s to the mid-1980s, I would go observing three or four times a year. I would go mostly to Kitt Peak National Observatory, near Tucson, which is funded by the National Science Foundation. Sometimes I would go to Chile, where the United States has a sister observatory, the Cerro Tololo Inter-American Observatory, also funded by the National Science Foundation. The Carnegie Institution, where I work, has the Las Campanas Observatory, also in Chile. I would typically go for about four or five nights, but when I went to Chile it was longer—eight or ten nights. I'd observe all night and would know what I was going to do from the start of every night until the finish. Every minute was planned.

Until the mid-1980s, I would record my data on photographic plates because film was not stable enough dimensionally to measure to the accuracy that was needed. It was hard. I would have to go to the observatory a couple of nights early and, in total darkness, cut the glass plates—making sure there were no slivers of glass—because the spectrograph only took two-inch by two-inch plates and photographic plates are eight by ten inches. At the start of the observing session I'd bake them, generally in dry nitrogen; this was a trick that astronomers learned to make the plates much more sensitive. To maintain their sensitivity I'd have to keep the plates under pressure; every time I'd take a plate out during the night, I'd have to repressurize to prevent their being exposed to air.

I often went observing with a colleague, Dr. Kent Ford, Jr.—the astronomer who built the spectrograph that I was using. We were a good team because he was more interested in the instruments and I was more interested in the galaxies. In addition, there is always a telescope operator at the observatory to help.

Until about 1980 I would spend the whole night in the dome—which is unheated because the telescope has to be at the outdoor temperature so there won't be any distortion—working at the back end of the telescope to keep a star on a cross wire. To guide the telescope, I would first find the object that I wanted to study—that in itself is not trivial because the sky is so big. You have to go with a very accurate chart of the sky. Sometimes I would be observing objects that were actually too faint to see, so I would have a photograph that I had taken earlier and I would measure very, very accurately what I wanted to measure relative to some star that I could see. I would be using a spectrograph, which spreads out the light. I would have to set the telescope where I thought the object was and then move the little eyepiece to where I, without moving the telescope, could find a bright star. And then I'd have a paddle that would move the telescope very, very slowly. I would spend the whole night with my eye to the eyepiece, in total darkness. Sometimes I only took two six-hour exposures; more often it was two or three hours per exposure.

All the nights were like that until the early eighties, when observatories started getting automatic guiders. Then you would sit in a warm room and look at a TV screen. Initially, we would just guide on the TV screen and then, after a while, you wouldn't even guide at all: the telescope would do it. Scientifically, it was an advancement, but all astronomers had prided themselves on their good manual guiding. I had really worked very hard to get beautiful spectra; I thought I was great as a guider. But the very first night I used the automatic guider, I decided that the spectra were better—and I am very critical. Also, it was awfully cold before. My toes would be numb and I'd have to go inside a couple of times during the night, generally to develop the plates (and certainly the first plate of the evening) while someone else took over the guiding. By and large, it was an advance; on the other hand, there was something quite lovely about being in the dome guiding the telescope by hand. Future generations won't get to experience that, but it was quite inspirational. It still is exciting, but it's become differently exciting.

By about 1984 we were not even using photographic plates; we were using electronic digital detectors known as CCDs, charge-coupled devices. Now we just end up with a digital tape that we read into a computer. What we're doing is taking a picture with a detector that records on a thousand by a thousand pixels the amount of light that falls on each of them and gives them a number. It's like a television screen, with a number for each little element on the screen. And then we have a computer program that reads the tape and remakes the image. I used to take the photographic plates back to my office and put them under a microscope that had a measuring device, but now I just carry a tape back and sit at a computer terminal.

I use the best computer screen I can afford, and the screen has excellent resolution. I only look at 512×512 pixels at a time, but most (or all) of the information is contained there. I can enlarge the image so that each pixel is about 4 mm×4 mm, if necessary, but of course then I see less of the whole image. Even with the improved technology, we still need two people. But we're doing much more; we're doing things that weren't possible before. It still is virtually impossible to go observing alone. I generally take a postdoc with me, but occasionally I go by myself. There's an enormous amount of processing that needs to be done. There are really two jobs involved in observing: there's someone who sits and directs the telescope and gets on the object to make sure everything is right and exposed—all of which is done at the computer. The other job is to be working on previous exposures to make sure they're all right and to take out certain distortions. Some of my exposures now can be as short as seconds; some of them are a half hour.

Vera Rubin with her collection of old globes, circa 1985
PHOTO BY MARK GODFREY

I'm now also doing some observing with the Hubble Space Telescope (HST), which is public, just like an observatory; they announce when they will accept applications, and then an astronomer applies for time. Unlike most astronomers, though, I'm doing that almost alone. That means I had to learn enormous amounts. It took me months to read all the manuals and to learn how to write the proposals. After a lifetime of knowing the instruments, I essentially had to start over to learn how to direct this telescope. In my earlier observations, I had discovered that some of the galaxies in the Virgo cluster have very strange motions near their nuclei, and I wanted much higher resolution images to see the details of their structure. I picked a set to observe with the Hubble that were very strange when I measured their motions from the ground. Those HST images were taken for me about a year ago, and the one that was the strangest is an object that I'll be obtaining spectra of with HST later this year. It's hard to do spectroscopy with the Hubble Space Telescope because it's a small telescope with an old detector, but it can get spectra of much greater detail much closer to the nucleus. From the ground it's all blended into one pixel because the earth's atmosphere smears it out.

Currently, I'm trying very hard to find time to do science. That gets harder and harder as you become successful. I really would like to be sitting and measuring my spectra and studying my images. Some days I get to them and some days I don't. It's a real battle because every day I get requests to speak, to visit, and to attend meetings, and I get queries from students and colleagues concerning scientific questions.

I give a lot of talks. I just came back from a four-day cosmology meeting at Princeton, where I had to give the last summary talk. I gave a commencement address at Berkeley in May. I am now reading through the galleys for a book of mine that the American Institute of Physics is putting out. I'm still trying to write up the ground-based work for the Virgo galaxies that the Hubble telescope photographed for me. The Hubble images from last year should have been studied by now, but I am just now starting to study them. I serve on the board of directors of the Association of Universities for Research in Astronomy, the organization that runs the U.S. National Optical Observatories. I'm on the board of directors of Associated Universities Incorporated, which runs Brookhaven National Laboratories and the U.S. National Radio Observatories.

In addition, every four or five years I go off and teach for a term because I like it and I sort of miss it. In addition to other places, I've spent a term at Berkeley, a term at the University of Texas, and a summer at Cambridge, England. I visit several universities a year, spending about a week, and give a few technical lectures, give a public lecture, and generally meet with the women students or anyone interested in discussing women and

minorities in science. I enjoy the interaction with students.

The commitments are endless; but one of the reasons I'm willing to do all these things is that I feel an obligation to the community.

I became interested in astronomy when I was about twelve, by just looking at the sky. I was captivated by the stars. (I also liked playing the piano and building model airplanes.) My parents were supportive of my interest, but my father, an electrical engineer, said I should do something more practical, like mathematics. He didn't think I could support myself doing astronomy. My father, who lived into his nineties and was still enormously alert, later changed his mind about my being able to support myself as an astronomer.

I decided to go to Vassar because there weren't many colleges for women that offered astronomy, and Vassar offered me a scholarship, which I needed. And I knew that Maria Mitchell had taught there. I had read about her when I was a child, about how in 1847 as a twenty-nine-year-old librarian in Nantucket, she had discovered a comet with the telescope her father had installed on their roof. A year later she was the first woman elected into the American Academy of Arts and Sciences, and in 1865 she was appointed director of Vassar College's observatory and professor of astronomy. When I was at Vassar from 1945 to 1948, it was still an all-women's college and I was the only astronomy major. There were only one or two physics majors. Most of the astronomy I learned at Vassar was from books; it was very difficult. In my senior year—I went through in three years—I was the only person in the class. If I hadn't done my homework or if I hadn't done it right or if I hadn't done enough—my being the only person in the class made the personal interaction with the teacher very difficult.

I decided to go to Cornell for graduate school because my husband was there. I married when I graduated from Vassar, and my husband, Robert Rubin, was in graduate school in physical chemistry at Cornell. I had met him the summer before I graduated—our families introduced us. (We have just celebrated our forty-eighth wedding anniversary.) I got my master's while he was finishing his Ph.D. I then got my Ph.D. at Georgetown because my husband had taken a job in Washington, D.C. He had several job offers, but we decided to come to Washington because both of our families were there and because there were more opportunities for me. He's really a mathematician involved in a branch of physics known as statistical mechanics, but during most of his career at the Bureau of Standards he applied his expertise to molecules. Then, ten years ago, he moved to the National Institutes of Health, where he applies his expertise to cells; he studies how viruses fuse with cells. Though he's actually retired, he still works full-time at NIH.

I had our first child right after my master's, the second one while I was working on my Ph.D., and the other two between terms when I was teaching at Georgetown. It's a very complicated situation to have both a family and a career, but my husband offered me continual support and encouragement. I was able to make my own way, though. I was very nonestablishment and it worked. I really believe that there must be both diversity in the way science is done and the way people work. Somehow or other, science must be inclusive of having a family.

All of our four children have Ph.D.'s. The oldest and youngest sons, David and Allan, are geologists; our other son, Karl, is a mathematician; and our daughter, Judy, is an astronomer. [See Judith Young's profile on page 445.]

After I got my degree at Georgetown in 1954, I was offered a job at a local community college teaching one course in physics and one course in mathematics. That was unbelievably wonderful. I taught from twelve to two Monday, Wednesday, and Friday and had a physics lab on Friday afternoon. I had a maid for the first time in my life, and my mother helped out as needed. Our kids hardly knew that I was gone—they ate their lunch and went to nap. We bought a car, we bought a television set. I really learned that it could all work. The next year, I accepted an offer from Georgetown to come back and do research and teach.

My next job was at the Carnegie Institution. I waited until I thought they would hire me, and then I walked in and asked for a job. (The Carnegie Institution of Washington was established in 1902 by Andrew Carnegie and now has five labs across the United States.) At the time they weren't doing optical astronomy; it was really a physics lab, but the spectrograph I ended up using was being built there—that's one of the reasons I wanted to work there. It's a small place, and we're all called staff members. Of our fifteen staff members in the Department of Terrestrial Magnetism, about five of us are astronomers and the others are geochemists and geophysicists. It was not then a place that an astronomer might think of working, but it was an institution that would support you to do your science. I thought it would be a nice place to work. I've been there since 1965.

In 1981 I was elected to the National Academy of Sciences by the members. You don't even know that you're up for election. The same is true with the National Medal of Science, which I received in 1993 in recognition of the work I've done throughout my career. I'm now on the committee to choose new members for the medal.

In my life, I'm most proud of my children and my marriage. In my career, I'm generally proud of having pulled it all off. Just a couple of years ago I made a discovery I am proud of because it came when I was senior and beginning to wonder if there would be any more discoveries and because it came from looking very carefully at spectra. I discovered a galaxy with a disk in which half the stars go clockwise and half the stars go counterclockwise. The spectrum just didn't look normal to me. None of us have good enough equipment to really see something in that detail, so it took me several years to believe it and to prove it. Shortly after my announcement, it was confirmed by a young astronomer who had previously taken spectra of that galaxy. What's really interesting is that it forced astronomers to redesign the way they study motions in galaxies.

On a very real level things have gone very smoothly for me, although early on it was unbelievably difficult. When I was getting my Ph.D., I worked awfully hard, but my husband was enormously supportive. We'd put the children to bed, and then I would work from 7:00 P.M. until 2:00 A.M. Then I'd get up with the children in the morning and spend the whole day with them. It was hard, but it was harder *not* doing astronomy.

After I got my master's, I presented a paper (on the topic of whether galaxies had a motion in addition to their expansion) at the American Astronomical Society. I wasn't a member, and I didn't know anyone there. I also had a three-week-old baby I was nursing, and so I went in, presented my paper, and left. I expect that had never been done before and hasn't been done since, but the next day my paper topic was on the front page of the *Washington Post*.

I always had a doubt that I'd have a career. It was a joke in my family when I was growing up, "Will Vera really ever be an astronomer?" I was never confident that it would work because my path was so unconventional. For better or worse, most astronomers come from a very few institutions where everyone knows each other and everyone knows what's expected of them. Because I was always off by myself, I didn't know any astronomers. Typically, a male graduate student will establish a set of colleagues whom he will know his whole life. I didn't really have that. The male students would pick up the phone to call each other about problems, but no one would pick up the phone to call me. I didn't work on problems that everybody else was working on—I found it very distasteful to have to compete that way. I chose problems that I thought would be of value to astronomy when I had finished.

The other side of the story is that there are challenges if you don't become a scientist. What would you rather spend your day worrying about? I feel this way about nurses and doctors: If you spend your day worrying about medical things, why not be the doctor instead of the nurse? If you enjoy the challenges of learning things that people have never known before and making the decisions about which research you're going to do, you really have to have a Ph.D. There are interesting positions you can get with a bachelor's or a master's degree where you can work for a scientist; you'll be given chores to do that can be very, very interesting, but you rarely have the privilege of choosing the problem and deciding how it should be carried out.

When I was in school, I was continually told to go off and find something else to study or told that I wouldn't get a job as an astronomer. But I just didn't listen. If it's something you really want to do, you just have to go do it—and maybe have the courage to do it a little differently.

PRESENT POSITION: Astronomer and Staff Member, Department of Terrestrial Magnetism, Carnegie Institution of Washington

RESEARCH AREA: Galaxy motions

FIELD: Astronomy

EDUCATION: B.A. (1948), Vassar College; M.A. (1951), Cornell University; Ph.D. (1954), Georgetown University

DATE/PLACE OF BIRTH: July 23, 1928/Philadelphia, Pennsylvania

Vera Rubin lives in Washington, D.C., with her husband of forty-eight years, Robert Rubin.

INTERVIEW DATE: July 1996

Laura Santos

Senior Member of the Technical Staff
SANDIA NATIONAL LABORATORIES

Influenced by television soap operas, young Laura Santos imagined herself a successful doctor. But a summer job with the Environmental Protection Agency after her sophomore year in college changed her career direction. When she returned to Tufts University in the fall, she created her own environmental degree through the civil engineering department. She went on to get a master's degree in environmental health from the University of California–Berkeley, one of only four universities that offered such study at the time. As an environmental-compliance specialist and a diving enthusiast, she often gets to witness the impact of her work firsthand.

&

I graduated from college in 1975, before many of the modern-day environmental disasters occurred. Before that time, environmental concerns had mainly focused on communicable diseases from contaminated wastewater and inadequate ventilation systems in industrial settings. The public was reminded of the need for safety and environmental controls in the late 1970s, when a leak from an old chemical dump site was linked to high rates of birth defects and illness at Love Canal in Niagara Falls, New York. A couple of years later, the worst industrial disaster in history occurred when thousands of people died from a toxic gas leak from a pesticide plant in Bhopal, India. Industry was not taking the precautions needed to protect the environment. Now there are many more people who specialize in what I do: environmental compliance.

Laura Santos being recognized by Saul Levine, then director of the Nuclear Regulatory Commission's Office of Research, on NRC's completion of the two-year internship program, 1979
PHOTO COURTESY OF THE NUCLEAR REGULATORY COMMISSION

I am an environmental compliance specialist at Sandia National Laboratories, a research and development laboratory in California. We work primarily for the U.S. Department of Energy (DOE), which requires that Sandia have programs in place to provide environmental compliance. In California we have major responsibilities for defense, environmentally driven technologies, integrated manufacturing technologies, microelectronics, computer networking, and advanced transportation. Our research, development, and demonstration activities at Sandia-California are focused on several important areas of particular interest to the state, including combustion science and technology, semiconductor manufacturing technologies, advanced information infrastructure, modeling and simulation, advanced manufacturing technologies, and advanced energy and sources.

Our site has a department of approximately twenty-five professional compliance specialists, each with extensive knowledge in a particular environmental or safety area, such as industrial hygiene, fire protection, or hazardous waste. I have worked in several environmental protection areas, including wastewater discharges, hazardous waste management, environmental impact evaluations, and air quality.

My "customers" are the researchers on-site at Sandia. When our researchers begin a new project, they meet with the environmental and safety professionals to explain what the research entails. We discuss what chemicals, equipment, and processes they will be using, the kind of waste they will be generating, the design of their lab, and what kinds of safety hazards may be involved. Although a person may have experience in more than one area, at Sandia they generally will have only one area that they are responsible for; one person could not cover multiple areas and still provide the fast turnaround needed to get the researchers up and going as soon as possible. Every potential hazard gets investigated. When necessary—due to an unsafe situation or one that does not meet the requirements— changes are negotiated and permits and other required documentation are prepared. After the specialists complete their work, they provide the researcher a written summary that explains what regulations apply to his or her research.

The laws are very specific and prescriptive about what has to be done to maintain environmental protection. For example, if you need a hazardous waste storage facility on site, the regulations tell you how much waste can be stored in a given area and how high you can stack the barrels of waste; they stipulate that floors have to be sealed so that waste cannot penetrate the ground if it happens to spill. There is rarely any room for creativity where compliance is concerned. Some people find all these environmental laws to be tedious and difficult to understand, but I am familiar with many of them and actually like working with them. You can't really take a class to learn regulations; I learned them by writing permits and helping develop compliance plans.

What I like the most about this job is having happy customers. The researchers really appreciate that we make their lives easier. I also like the fact that what I do makes a difference: compliance specialists minimize the impact that hazardous chemicals have on people and the environment.

I have a few "customers" other than researchers. I work with auditors from the DOE to show them how Sandia's environmental compliance programs are set up. Regulators representing the State of California or the Environmental Protection Agency (EPA) also make periodic visits. Occasionally, Sandia does work for private companies such as Ford Motor Company. The DOE encourages the lab to work with private companies so that the technologies that we develop are transferred to private industry for different applications. In this way, Sandia performs a service to the country, functioning as a partner with industry and helping to develop new technologies.

Working to protect the environment is fairly common now, but it wasn't when I was young. It wasn't something that I knew I would pursue or even had an interest in. I was born and raised in New York City, where my father was a policeman and my mother returned to work as a junior accountant as soon as my two brothers and I were all old enough to be in school. Although I was always encouraged to go to college, my parents never tried to direct me into a specific career path. I had always been really good at math; it came naturally to me, but I didn't know what to do with my talent. The only thing I can remember clearly influencing me were daytime soap operas on television and the way they glorified nurses and doctors, who were always attractive and energetic and led interesting lives. So the medical profession was the only career I knew to aspire to.

I went to a Catholic high school because the New York City schools had a bad reputation, and my parents were convinced that a more disciplined environment would help their children to get ahead. My school may have been good in terms of discipline, but it didn't offer classes that would help me compete well in college. I couldn't take calculus or other college-prep courses. I did well academically but never felt challenged there and never learned how to study.

Then I went away to Tufts University in Boston for my undergraduate degree. It was the best of the schools that accepted me, and they offered me some scholarship funding so that I was able to afford to attend. At Tufts I planned on majoring in premed, but I did poorly my freshman year. It became clear that if I wanted to survive, I needed to get tutors and learn how to study. I improved my grades dramatically, but to get into medical school you can't blow even one year of your grades. By the time I was a sophomore, I had lost a great deal of confidence and had so much catching up to do. I felt pressure to graduate within four years because Tufts is very expensive and also because taking more than four years to graduate was pretty much unheard of at the time.

But something happened at the end of my sophomore year that made all the difference in the world. The placement office had posted

Laura Santos as manager of Sandia Day, a company open house at Sandia National Laboratories, October 1994
PHOTO BY BARRY SCHRADER

a notice that the Environmental Protection Agency had summer jobs available; I applied and was hired to work in their wastewater permits office in Boston. I liked the environmental field so much that I decided to make it my course of study. I was totally lost before that summer job. I don't think I would ever have gotten where I am without it.

There was no environmental degree at Tufts; the closest thing to it was sanitary engineering, in the civil engineering department. But I was able to work with my professors to structure my own degree program. They were all very supportive. My adviser, Mr. Drummond, was the most helpful and gave me a lot of direction and encouragement. We decided that I had to go to graduate school because I only had two years of education that were environmentally oriented; I needed more. I got accepted to UCLA and UC Berkeley and decided to go to Berkeley. I received a fellowship from the U.S. Department of Health, Education, and Welfare that paid for everything. They had identified the need to educate people in the environmental area because studies indicated there would be a critical shortage of professionals in this field. I took an organic chemistry course and lab the summer before the official start date of the program and then completed my master's degree in one year.

I had a hard time finding a job when I graduated: there weren't very many companies hiring environmental professionals that year. Finally, six months after graduation, I got a position with the Nuclear Regulatory Commission (NRC) in Washington, D.C. My first assignment was working on environmental standards for siting nuclear power plants. I also worked on projects to regulate the handling and disposal of uranium, which required a lot of site visits. I went with a more senior engineer for the first few trips, so when it came time for me to take primary responsibility for a project everyone knew what my role was and I felt I had a great deal of credibility.

The uranium mines and mills I visited were located mainly in New Mexico, Colorado, Wyoming, and Utah. They mine seventy-two parts dirt to get one part of uranium out of the ground, using acids or other solvents to extract the uranium. The mines end up with acres of waste known as tailings. They are radioactive and contain heavy metals and other hazardous contaminants. We were concerned with stabilizing the tailings to protect people, animals, and the environment. Some of the mines were close to farms, and the heavy metals leached out of the tailings and into the groundwater, where they were taken up by the roots of the plants that cows and other animals subsequently grazed on. Migratory birds would land on acid ponds that formed in the tailings and die. Construction companies needing fill materials would use the tailings in their construction; as a result, many new buildings in the area had high levels of radiation. The way the waste was handled sounds so careless now,

but until the hazards became apparent, people didn't know better.

The NRC had us research and develop the best way to stabilize these tailings piles. We developed a way to collect and capture the leachate, the rainwater that permeates through the tailings, underneath the piles. We also designed long-lasting caps that kept migratory birds and burrowing animals out of the piles. We came up with some very basic safety requirements that included signs and fences for preventing children from playing on the piles and construction companies from coming in and taking the dirt. The methods we designed remain the state of the art in the mining field today.

I was with the Nuclear Regulatory Commission for four years. In 1980 I took a position as a licensing engineer with the General Electric Company (GE) in San Jose because I wanted to move back to California. GE is a vendor of nuclear reactors. They felt that my understanding of the NRC's rules and regulations, as well as my knowledge of the people at NRC, would be very valuable to them, even though I didn't really have experience with reactors and reactor systems.

The job was totally different from what I had been trained to do previously. I worked with the utility companies and the NRC to make sure that what GE was delivering to the customers met NRC requirements. After the accident at the Three Mile Island plant in 1979, everything changed in the world of nuclear power. The NRC scrutinized the old reactors as well as the new, and many reactors needed to be reconstructed.

I worked for GE for three years, negotiating licenses for GE customers. Then a company in San Francisco—Bechtel Power Corporation—recruited me to do the same work for them. Bechtel is an architect-engineering firm involved in the construction of nuclear power plants. I worked for them for two years. Both of these jobs required a lot of negotiating skills, and my engineering background was particularly important.

By the mid-1980s, the reactor business in

the United States was grinding to a halt. The cost of retrofitting nuclear reactors was prohibitive; utility companies were having a hard time affording the reconstruction and weren't placing orders for new plants. Bechtel decided to move their business to Los Angeles. I was married by then, and my husband, a lawyer, had his own business. He wasn't able to move and I wasn't going without him, so I decided to go back to doing environmental work, which is what I really wanted to do anyway.

I found an environmental job at the Science Application International Corporation (SAIC) and was able to remain in the Bay Area. Among other things, SAIC provides environmental support services for the DOE and the EPA, which was my client for my first few projects. I was working in the wastewater area again.

The EPA didn't have enough staff to write permits for industries, so they contracted with SAIC to have the permits written. I visited some interesting companies to write permits: an explosives facility in Nevada, an acrylic carpet factory in Virginia, and an aluminum can company in Seattle. I gradually moved away from working with the EPA, and the Department of Energy became my primary client. At various DOE facilities, I prepared permit applications for wastewater discharges and for the handling, treatment, and storage of hazardous waste; and I performed health risk assessments and environmental evaluations. Sandia asked me to develop a program for them that would improve their compliance with air quality regulations. About a year later, they invited me to

join their staff permanently. I started there in 1990.

I got married when I was twenty-nine, just before I left GE. My husband and I have always been preoccupied with work, and neither one of us ever really wanted to have children. I don't even know if I could even handle the added responsibility that having kids would bring.

My husband and I like to take at least two trips each year, most of the time to dive. It's like another world under the water. I love it. I've heard stories about how some areas used to be better for scuba diving but because of accidents or other industrial hazards, they no longer have fish or coral to look at. That's so disappointing for diving enthusiasts. I have a personal investment in protecting the environment, and I know what can happen if we don't. I have a great respect for the work I do; it's a great field for a woman.

PRESENT POSITION: Senior Member of the Technical Staff, Sandia National Laboratories

FIELD: Environmental engineering

RESEARCH AREA: Regulatory compliance

EDUCATION: B.S. in Engineering (1975), Tufts University; M.P.H. in Environmental Health (1976), University of California, Berkeley, School of Public Health

DATE/PLACE OF BIRTH: March 29, 1953/New York City, New York

Laura Santos lives in Fremont, California, with her husband, Wilton, and their two cats, Rosie and Misty.

INTERVIEW DATE: November 1995

Linda C. Shackelford

Head of the Bone and Muscle Laboratory,
Space Biomedical Research Institute
NASA/JOHNSON SPACE CENTER

Linda Shackelford's childhood greatly influenced her choice of a career. She grew up on a Mississippi farm where she developed an interest in and empathy for sick and hurt animals and learned entrepreneurial skills selling eggs and milk from the chickens and cows she owned. She had an uncle and grandfather who were pilots, and a grandmother and aunts who attended college. She eventually hopes to become a member of the astronaut corps and conduct her research in space.

I study bone loss and associated muscle loss in space flight and try to develop countermeasures to limit that loss. In addition to data from NASA's flight records, we NASA researchers have been privileged to analyze cosmonaut data, which Russia has shared with us since 1989. The Russian data is especially helpful because their cosmonauts have spent greater periods of time in space than American astronauts have.

We know that bone loss in flight usually occurs in the lower body and spine, rarely in the upper body. Even though cosmonauts exercise on treadmills and bicycles all the while they're in space, that doesn't stop their bone loss. In the past researchers have used biochemical countermeasures that may decrease the amount of calcium lost from the bone as a whole, but volunteers using these treatments in bed-rest studies still had substantial calcium loss from certain bones in the lower extremities.

We've been doing bed-rest studies to simulate space flight and to see how resistive exercise works. Because we have regional bone loss due to regional decrease in load on the bone, we are developing strategies to treat

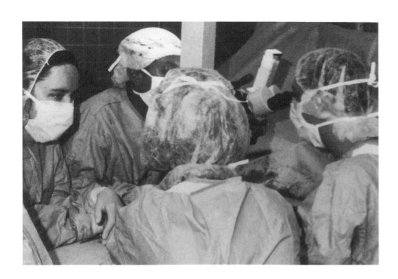

Linda Shackelford replanting a forearm severed in an automobile accident, William Beaumont Army Medical Center, June 1985

that localized decrease. We are able to carry out closely measured exercise programs in space that are difficult to do on the ground. The reason for that is as you start feeling better, you're apt to increase what you're doing in other activities, so it's hard to determine what's really increasing the bone density. In space there's essentially no load on the skeleton unless you're exercising, so we can monitor in flight how the body responds to different load regimens. We've been testing localized countermeasures and some appear highly effective. We need a lot more statistics to determine whether or not this is a true countermeasure.

Besides its use for bone loss in space, this potential countermeasure could also be used to treat osteoporotic women. Currently doctors recommend exercise for such women, but they're not specific about what type of exercise is most effective. Women who don't want to take estrogen after menopause may be able to use the exercise protocol we develop to preserve their bones. This research could identify specific exercises that will help to maintain bones both on earth and in space.

I also assist NASA research scientists and flight surgeons at eight space shuttle landings a year. I monitor astronaut activities and fluid consumption on the crew transport vehicle (CTV), which docks with the shuttle on the landing strip, and I continue monitoring in the clinic for four hours of postflight testing. When needed I monitor the health and safety of the crew and research volunteers in the physiology laboratories at Johnson Space Center.

My interest in medicine and aviation go way back. I grew up in northeastern Mississippi; my family has been there for generations, dating back to the 1700s. Some of my ancestors were Native Americans; most of the region's inhabitants at the time were Native Americans, and there was considerable intermarriage in the 1800s. I'm too far from it to be considered Native American, but the history is interesting. I was born in Mississippi in 1955. My parents were married young; my

mother was still in high school. My father's grandfather was a physician, and some of the men from his hometown offered to send my father to medical school because my grandmother was divorced and didn't have the money. But he wanted to get married and work; so he moved the family to Illinois until I was about five years old, when we moved back to northern Mississippi.

I've always loved animals, and when I was about seven we moved to a farm. I remember wanting to take care of the sick and hurt animals, and it bothered me not to know how to do it. This frustration led to an early interest in veterinary medicine. I also developed an interest in science in second-grade health class. I particularly remember a fifth-grade science teacher who encouraged my interest and applauded my persistence—I would do something over and over again until I could get it to work (which often I couldn't!). I also remember that in the fifth grade I wanted to be an astronaut. There was a cartoon on at the time called "Astro-nut," and that's what my friends called me. But I was serious: This was the time of the *Mercury* and *Gemini* space flights, and I would get up in the middle of the night to watch the coverage on television. I remember pretending to be the science officer on my star ship (actually an old barn behind my house). Other factors contributed to my interest in space, most notably my family history: I had an uncle who was an engineer and flew a T-38 as an instructor pilot for the Air Force. When he'd come home, he'd tell us flying stories that fascinated and excited me. My mother's father was also a pilot; he had his own plane and would take us flying when we visited. My parents even met in an airport. Eventually both my brother and I became licensed pilots, he much earlier than I because I didn't have the money to fly—I was saving all my money for college.

I was quite a businesswoman as a child, and I squirreled away as much money as I could. Around age eight I bought my brother's chicken business, sold the eggs, earned enough and saved enough from my allowance to buy a little heifer calf, and sold the milk. Then my grandfather gave me a registered calf to raise as a show calf. I joined the 4-H club, which provided a lot of wonderful exposure and opportunities for me. The organization as a whole and the county agent with whom I interacted treated girls and boys the same, which I think was important and impressive. Like my other business ventures, my affiliation with 4-H was lucrative: I made money from my winnings in 4-H competitions. By age fourteen I had my own checking account. Even though I was a successful entrepreneur, my interest in medicine never waned.

One of my 4-H friends worked in a hospital, and I started working as a laboratory assistant drawing blood and setting up tests at the age of sixteen. This was done through a high school work-study program. I wanted this job to see if I liked working with people. I had thought about what I wanted to do with my life and how I could serve God, and felt that I would serve better by helping people instead of animals. I found interacting with patients enjoyable and set my sights on medical school. Years later, when I found myself tagging along behind a military veterinarian providing services to farmers in Honduras, I confirmed in my mind what I had grown to know through my experiences in medical school and residency. True service and happiness are not determined by what you do but come from doing work you enjoy and knowing you do it well. The question of what brings happiness is the theme of King Solomon's book, Ecclesiastes. I read this book frequently in my late teens and twenties, and still read it occasionally now.

I always wanted to go to college. Because my parents married young, I had aunts and uncles in college and went to their college graduations. I was interested in going to Mississippi State for agriculture, but my family had a history with Mississippi University for Women ("the W"): my maternal grandmother and two of my aunts had gone there. One aunt graduated as a medical technician and the other as a mathematician. She taught

math at my high school, and I remember those courses well. I loved the way she taught logic. To this day I call her with problems because she has such a clear way of thinking.

My father wanted me to go into medicine, although I never knew that until years later. My maternal grandmother didn't want me to become a physician because she thought it would interfere with marriage; she wanted me to become a medical technician like her daughter. So my mother discouraged my father from encouraging me to go into medicine. But I always sensed his approval for my decision to pursue it. I think the father-daughter relationship is very important to a young woman's future profession—if a father encourages a daughter to do what she wants to do, it's more likely she'll make it in a man's world.

In the end I double-majored in biology and chemistry at the W, winning a full scholarship and finishing in three years. I'm glad that I went to the W because we all got a lot of attention, attention that I don't think we would have gotten at the time in a co-ed school. Also, women took leadership roles and no one considered us overly aggressive for doing so. However, I always preferred being around guys, even in grade school. Girls just wanted to talk about who was dating who, whereas the guys talked about who was doing what. I remember in third and fourth grade we'd line up to go to lunch, and I always tried to get to the back of the line because if it cut off at a certain point when a table was filled, I'd get to sit with the guys. Despite there being no men at the W, it was a valuable and wonderful experience.

My experience at the University of Mississippi School of Medicine was very different from the W; I encountered something I had never encountered before—sexual harassment. Since then, and throughout my training and career, I have witnessed and received unfair treatment. I have seen people justify unfair or unkind treatment with the attitude that "I've paid my dues, let them pay theirs." I have tried to stop the cycle by treating others as I wish to be treated. Sometimes I've failed in this out of my own weakness. I hope those I failed can forgive me. I have to work at forgiving others, as I tend to hold grudges. The past cannot be changed, but forgiveness is important in freeing energy to change the future.

I started medical school thinking I'd go into internal medicine because my grandfather died of a heart attack when I was a freshman in college. But as I participated in a program where first-year students followed a senior medical student around on weekends to learn a little bit of clinical stuff, I met a woman medical student in neurosurgery who worked in trauma. During my observation of one case, I picked up a very subtle skull fracture in an X-ray that no one else had noticed. Everyone was impressed, and my interest was piqued. After that I followed the neurosurgeons around and began assisting them in the operating room, which I loved. I spent all my extra time in the operating room. I decided then that I was going into surgery, even though earlier on I had made a conscious decision not to do so because the lifestyle didn't seem conducive to having a family.

I started going on early-morning surgical rounds as a first-year medical student even though it was typical to begin doing this in the third year. It was here that I observed Dr. James Hardy, one of the finest men I've ever met. He had a lot of women in his resident program and treated them the same as the men. Dr. Hardy had four daughters and no sons, and I'm convinced that men with daughters are often more apt to recognize women's potential and help them achieve it.

Besides Hardy, several other people, all women, stand out in my mind as role models. Rhea Seddon was an inspiration to me as a first-year medical student. She grew up in Tennessee not far from where I grew up and was in her residency when she was accepted into the astronaut program in 1977. Another was a woman pediatric surgeon who interviewed me for medical school. I was impressed with her professional credentials but equally impressed that she had a family and outside interests, which she encouraged others to have. I also remember reading inspiring biographies of women aviators as a child. The example these women set no doubt helped me to realize my own accomplishments.

The Army paid for my medical school education, so I used the money I'd been saving for medical school to earn my pilot's license. My flight instructor, an old buddy of my grandfather's, said I was almost as good as my brother, whom he considered the best pilot he'd ever taught (and he had taught World War II aviators). Later I learned to fly a helicopter in the Army Flight Surgeon course. I tied for second place in my class for piloting skills. I would have loved to have gone to the Air Force Academy after high school, but they didn't allow women at the time and my mother would never have agreed to it if they had.

I owed the Army four years after medical school: I spent six months in Honduras, two years in Germany, and one and one-half years at Lysterr Army Hospital in Fort Rucker, Alabama, as an orthopedic surgeon. After completing my required service, I requested an assignment in aeromedical research. I was assigned to the U.S. Army Aeromedical Research Laboratory in Fort Rucker as chief of the biomechanics branch, where I served from 1989 to 1991. I had a very fair and supportive division director, Col. Dennis Shanahan, M.D., and worked with excellent engineers (I always enjoy the company of engineers) and biomechanics, an area I loved. This new job at USAARL suited my interests, and I thoroughly enjoyed my assignment. The only thing missing was the mission. I still wanted to work with physiology of space flight. Seventeen years prior I had received a recruiting brochure from the Army and had answered with a letter requesting information on opportunities to research human physiology in space flight. At that time they had no offerings. Then in 1990, at an aerospace medical meeting, I made the proper contacts with a NASA research physician, now an astronaut, which led to my current position.

I was listening to a talk by Bernard Harris, who at the time was in charge of exercise countermeasures, and afterwards I went up to ask him a few questions. As I was waiting to speak with him, a doctor from Kennedy Space Center was asking some questions about stress fractures. I had dealt with a lot of overuse injuries and stress injuries as well as trauma when I was with the Army, so I began to answer some of his questions. Harris turned and asked if this was my area of research, assuming that I was a physiologist. I said, "Actually, I'm an orthopedic surgeon," and he asked if I needed a job. I wanted to stay in the military, so I arranged with the Army to come to NASA, but then Desert Storm intervened; they weren't letting doctors leave the Army at that time. In the meantime, the people at NASA decided it would be better if I were a civil servant because Army tours of duty are only three years and they wanted me around for a longer time. Eventually I left the military for NASA, although I joined a reserve unit and still remain active. I really miss doing orthopedics, which I still love, and so I do it in the summer during my two weeks of active duty.

In 1987 I married a medevac pilot who instructed a flight medic course during the same time I attended the flight surgeon course at the same school; we divorced in 1993. We had a son in 1989, James Taggart, and he is the light of my life. He is already determined to be a pilot and flies the little flight simulator we have on a computer at home. It's funny— as kids my brother and I would go out in the backyard, get two by fours and nail them together, and put tin cans on for instrument panels—that was our airplane. The toys change from one generation to the next, but the play often stays the same. James is pretty good at the simulator, and why not, given his family's history in aviation! My brother and I bought the airplane we learned to fly in, and now my son has tried his hand on those same controls. He is a pretty good little pilot!

I plan to complete my current objective of providing a countermeasure to the musculoskeletal losses due to weightlessness. I am delighted to get some hands-on laboratory work doing microsurgery with some engineers in the orthopedics department at the University of Texas Medical Center. I would love someday to work in the laboratory of the space station we researchers at NASA and in the scientific community are now designing.

One thing I have learned is that I cannot control all the circumstances around me, nor can I control all outcomes. I can make the best of circumstances and I can hope for better. Faith in God and love for my fellow man cannot be changed by circumstances; those come from within. I do not define success for myself and others in what is achieved. Success is in doing a job to the best of my ability and in facing new situations with courage. The final success will be in believing in the Creator on my last day on Earth, when medicine and science and I myself have failed me, and with that faith journeying into an existence far beyond our present knowledge.

PRESENT POSITION: Head of the Bone and Muscle Laboratory, Space Biomedical Research Institute, NASA/Johnson Space Center

FIELD: Medicine

RESEARCH AREA: Countermeasure development for bone and muscle loss in space

EDUCATION: B.S. in Biology and Chemistry (1976), Mississippi University for Women; M.D. (1980), University of Mississippi School of Medicine; Residency in Orthopedic Surgery (1985), William Beaumont Army Medical Center

DATE/PLACE OF BIRTH: November 25, 1955/ Baldwyn, Mississippi

Linda Shackelford lives with her son in Houston, Texas.

INTERVIEW DATE: July 1995

Cheryl L. Shavers

General Manager, Advanced Technology Operation,
Technology and Manufacturing Group
INTEL CORPORATION

As a child, Cheryl Shavers found solace in books. Reading addressed her curiosity and provided escape from her surroundings, as did a school where her background and race didn't matter to teachers, only her interest and enthusiasm. Her willingness to take risks and her attitude that she can win over anyone who has ignorant ideas with her accomplishments have contributed to her success.

❧

Societal myths tell us that if someone is brought up in a disadvantaged environment, their odds of success in life are greatly reduced. At best this distorts our appreciation for those who make it despite the odds. At worst it can cause some of the disadvantaged to believe that they are destined for failure. In reality, the truth is somewhere in between. As a child growing up in a disadvantaged environment and limited by a respiratory ailment, I found my key motivator was education through reading. Reading was available to everyone, knew no boundaries, and limited no one. It was through this means that the world opened up to me.

But despite this new view of the world, it was a struggle to transcend my environment. In fact, an event that occurred early in my life was instrumental in my interest and ultimately my career in the sciences. The unfortunate murder of a woman in our neighborhood spurred my interest in the process and methods of criminal investigation. My perpetual curiosity, even at the young age of eleven, led me to many hours in the library and many talks with my teachers to learn about careers associated with police science. From this came the realization that working in a crime lab would become my goal, even if it meant earning a chemistry degree to get there!

If I had been a cat, curiosity would have killed me by now. Regardless of the subject, my interests always went far beyond what was presented to me or even expected of me. It was always fun to surprise the teacher when one of my many projects produced not only a paper or talk on the subject matter but a working model to boot! Whether building looms in art class or creating a replica of an

Cheryl Shavers in a recent photograph

Edison film machine for an American cinema course, I was motivated by the desire to gain an in-depth understanding of the process surrounding the subject. Soon these traits captured the attention of several educators, and to my surprise I found that my background and race didn't matter to them—my motivation and initiative did.

After I won a scholarship to attend college, my journey toward a degree in chemistry caused me mixed emotions and at times downright trepidation. High school was easy, but college presented new challenges altogether. The first was the lack of cultural diversity in the sciences, and the second was the predominately male environment. The challenge here was finding common ground, and this proved to be the skill of artful communication. By embracing the differences in others, we discovered the commonality among us. Thus I learned to lead with my personality by becoming a good listener and communicator. As a result, my accomplishments and abilities were what my peers chose to judge me by, and the ease I felt in high school soon returned.

Close to my graduation at Arizona State University, I found a summer internship that placed my dream in sight. I worked at the Phoenix Police Department crime lab, which was one of the first to develop and use electrophoresis blood-type matching in police investigations. Lab personnel were just starting to explore the technique, and my first assignment was as a criminalist trainee. The experience was exciting and illuminating. However, I also discovered that life's lessons don't end when you reach your dream. It became apparent to me that not everyone you encounter during your journey will necessarily be your cheerleader. In the crime lab that I learned more about myself than I learned about the motives of others. The experience turned from one of reaching a childhood dream to one of making a serious career decision. Looking back on it now, I most definitely made the right decision to leave the police field. But struggling through it then made me

question systems based on inflexible rules and regulations, which ultimately stifle creative and intuitive individuals.

Graduate school had not been in my plans, and when Motorola offered me a position in their engineering program after I left the police department, I took it. One of Motorola's requirements was that I take some graduate classes while rotating among several job assignments over the course of a year. Since any graduate courses would suffice, I ended up taking business courses by default. Unfortunately, the subject came too easy to me, and I found myself craving the familiar challenges offered in the sciences. A clandestine thermodynamics class exposed me to a series of professors who ultimately submitted my name for a stipend. The day I received notification of the stipend award and of my admittance to graduate school was a turning point in my life. Opportunity did not have to knock twice; I was ready. Instead of resigning from Motorola, I took a leave of absence, decided to skip the master's degree program, and went straight for a doctorate in three and a half years. What a challenge!

I've learned to take advantage of every opportunity presented to me. Opportunities are all around you, but you must be ready to see them and act on them quickly. Put yourself in a position where other people can see you and want to help you. Opportunities will open up.

After I received my doctorate, my first assignment was with Hewlett Packard as a process development engineer. The assignment involved front-end oxide development for 64K RAM and ROM technology, leading to work in the metallization thin films area. It was there that I first realized working style does not necessarily transcend cultural style. In an environment of many different cultures with many different styles, good communication became even more critical to my ability to conceptualize, formalize, and introduce new methods and techniques for semiconductor manufacturing to the engineering staff. While other engineers, as well as my managers, felt that the only way to learn a science was to live with the science, my concept was the only way to learn a science was to understand the science—that understanding being gained by challenging the status quo. It was an unpopular stance at the time but a necessary one in the innovative process. Quite honestly, it was a bumpy road, but it forced me to think about impossibilities and how to make them real. This ultimately led me to an assignment in the technical legal department and a decision to pursue a law degree and patent attorney status at Hewlett Packard.

The first hurdle was passing the patent agent examination in the Library of Congress and getting admitted to law school. The second was making sure law school was really what I wanted to do. I passed my first hurdle within the first year to become a registered patent agent and subsequently was admitted to three law schools. But was this the right path?

Many hours of sitting alone with my thoughts, deciphering technology, writing patent applications, and contemplating four years of law school soon became mindbending. What was I doing? I craved the challenge of something new, but science and technology were my great love; this was where I wanted to make a difference. Thus, two weeks before law classes were to start at Santa Clara University, I relinquished my place and simultaneously resigned from Hewlett Packard to accept an opportunity in manufacturing management. I have never regretted that decision.

The skills I learned while in the technical legal department are still with me today, and I continue to practice as a freelance patent agent.

Looking back on it now, I realize that the move from Hewlett Packard was a risky one, but I've always believed that anyone can pursue their interests and loves successfully if they feel comfortable and confident in their own decisions. Moving from a well-respected Fortune 500 company to a small company of only one hundred employees granted me the opportunity not only to get a taste for management but also to push my technical skills to their limit. Wiltron Company, a microwave device manufacturer, entrusted me with the task of turning around a product line from design all the way to manufacturing. But a turnaround also means dealing with existing people issues. Since people are the key ingredient for success within any organization, the first step was to show my employees how to take risks—to embrace risk, calculate it, have fun with it. This was simple to me, but I had to find a way to teach what I knew.

In order to teach others, they must believe in you. For that reason I spent a lot of time on the manufacturing floor learning the process, learning the machines, and learning about the employees—struggling alongside them until a level of respect was established among all of us. That's when my employees caught the fire to succeed. Risks became challenges, challenges became goals, and goals became reachable.

If there is any one thing I would teach my child, it would be how to make a decision. It is critical to know how to analyze choices in life. Most of the time when I set goals I have no idea how I'm going to reach them, but I know I will. I always figure out several options to choose from in case my goals change. If you set a high enough goal, each time you accomplish some small portion of it you enhance your own self-confidence and self-esteem. I don't need a pat on the back from my manager when I do a good job—I know when I've done well!

It was a sad day when Wiltron decided to relocate out of the area. Rather than go with them I accepted a position as an engineer at Varian Associates, a semiconductor equipment company. Some people told me that I had taken a step backwards. But oftentimes you must learn about the products, technology, and culture of a company from the bottom up before you can set achievable goals within that organization. Within a short time I was promoted to engineering manager of the Thin Films Development Laboratory, turning my step back into a major leap forward. However, the promotion came at a time when the lab was struggling. Management wanted a home run but would settle for a triple. However, they underestimated the talent within the lab, which proved to be to my benefit. Through communication with engineering, manufacturing, marketing, and customers, the lab was able to develop processes on site, on demand. We continued to do so well that eventually Varian started to sell equipment directly from the lab. Now, that's pretty high pressure!

Among my many customer interactions I eventually met and worked with engineers from Intel Corporation. A debate about technology trends and practices between me and a fellow from Intel ultimately resulted in my joining Intel as a senior member of the technical staff. The one thing I remember about that debate is that I was determined to debate the issues, not the emotions. Afterwards, a friend who was present said, "I have never heard someone who argued so hard against getting a job at Intel!"

For a while at Intel, things went rather slowly. I worked on thin-film research for submicron interconnect technologies and alternative metal systems for the effects of electro- and stress migration. For Intel, this group was somewhat laid back, not a good fit for an overachiever. But I used that time to understand Intel's culture and technology and my role in it. When I was ready, I laid my strategy and transferred to another organization within Intel.

With two promotions in nine months, I recognized that I would not have been given these opportunities if I had not laid out a plan to create the opportunities. I believe that if you deserve a raise, you need to go get the raise. If you want more responsibility, you need to ask for it. You must make the choices and not blame others if you don't reach your goals. Establish your own reward system, know your comfort zone, and pay attention to your surroundings. For myself I always say, "This is my life, my career, and my responsibility. If I'm unhappy with it, then I need to change it!"

As general manager of Advanced Technology Operation (ATO), I have responsibility for the business operations and technical investigation of future-generation devices for PC platforms. Along with a Pentium™ processor, which is the brains of a computer, there are a number of chipsets of all types of devices that make the Pentium™ processor work to its full capability. ATO engineers look at technologies that will bring all those chipsets and devices together on PC platforms so that we can meet future manufacturing needs. The assignments are high-risk, short-term, matrix-managed programs that typically impact revenue dollars.

The success of my people ensures my success. It is my job to make sure that my employees see their accomplishments as successes as well. Providing an infrastructure in which everyone from the newest to the most senior employee has an equal say ensures that those who work for me are, in fact, making their own decisions. As a manager, *you* are the company to that employee and thereby carry the burden of leading by example. In my department, everyone is equal; they have different skill sets but equal say. Your job must be someplace that you want to go to, not away from. So if a problem arises, I pay particular attention to it and find a way to solve it.

The glass ceiling looks more like the sky to me. Sometimes it is very clear and sunny. I know where to go and how to get there. Other times it is gray and cloudy, showing me that a storm is approaching and that I should be cautious. But rarely is the storm so heavy as to prevent me from venturing out for fear of being struck by lightning.

I refuse to carry societal baggage about any form or means of discrimination—I'm just too busy trying to make a difference. It isn't that I haven't faced some of the same issues other women and minorities face, I just don't accept them. Complaining about these issues is a cancer. It destroys from within, paralyzes you, and eventually consumes others around you. Being proactive keeps me moving and motivates those around me.

When I look back now I see how far I've come and applaud those who have come with me along the way.

PRESENT POSITION: General Manager of Advanced Technology Operation, Technology and Manufacturing Group, Intel Corporation

FIELD: Management, business/technology operations

RESEARCH AREAS: Physical and chemical vapor deposition, thin films

EDUCATION: B.S. in Chemistry (1976) and Ph.D. in Solid-State Chemistry (1981), Arizona State University

PLACE OF BIRTH: San Marcos, Texas

Cheryl Shavers resides in Santa Clara, California, the heart of Silicon Valley, where she has worked in the semiconductor industry for more than fifteen years.

INTERVIEW DATE: March 1995

Mary M. Shaw

Professor of Computer Science
CARNEGIE MELLON UNIVERSITY

Although she has found being a woman a barrier as a consumer in the world of finance and health care, Mary Shaw has never found her sex to be a barrier in her professional life. She earned a B.S. in math from Rice University and a Ph.D. in computer science from Carnegie Mellon. When not at her computer, she can be found with her husband flying, scuba diving, cross-country skiing, bicycling, or canoeing.

From an early age my father treated my younger brother and me like intelligent human beings. I didn't realize this was anything special until I was fifteen or sixteen and noticed that other adults wouldn't pay any attention to me because I was a kid, even though I had a fact base that was every bit the equivalent of what the adults had. For example, we raised show dogs and I knew all the pedigrees and bloodlines. People who came to look at our dogs would ignore my answers to their questions but accept the same exact words when they came from my father.

As a child I was not driven to conformity; I never ran with the pack. I collected stamps and did science fair projects. I never took things apart, but I did do "number stuff." I remember grappling with long division long before I was taught it at school. I also remember creating an incredible amount of hassle for my seventh-grade teacher because somewhere I had learned to extract square roots manually and I wanted to learn to extract cube roots the same way. I couldn't understand why she didn't want to teach me to do it. I realized in retrospect that this was not the sort of thing very many people knew, but I did not understand that at the time.

My father was trained as a civil engineer but worked as an economist for the Department of Agriculture. The year before I took algebra, my father brought home the IBM programmer aptitude test that they were giving to employees. The Department of Agriculture was starting to develop a computer group, and they were giving one of those puzzle-and-game kinds of tests—at least that's the way I viewed it. I did it once under the time limit and then, at the be-

Mary Shaw, circa 1986

hest of my father, did it again without a time limit. The reason I remember it is because once I took algebra the next year I recognized some of the problems as things that I could now solve directly instead of working through them informally. Incidentally, my father reported to me that I had done better on the test than most of the programmers.

When I was fifteen my father gave me Polya's book *How to Solve It,* a book everyone should read at that age. There were no advanced-placement courses in math when I was in high school, but there were advanced science courses, so I took them. I also became involved in an activity program once a week run by an IBM employee, George Heller. He taught us how computers worked and sparked my interest. I realize now that we did very primitive things, but it was a big deal then. We even went to the IBM Space Computer Center in Washington, D.C., one Saturday morning so that we could run our programs, which were about a page long. This was a thrill because there were only a small number of computers in use in the late 1950s and early 1960s, and we received special permission to work on the computers at IBM.

I was also involved in a summer program during my high school years sponsored by Jean Taylor at the Johns Hopkins University Operation Research Office. They believed that you ought to get kids in their teens to do some kind of science analysis to spark their interest. They created groups of six high school kids with an undergraduate college student as the group leader, and they gave each group a problem to solve. The basic premise was that education has its place but basic smarts and common sense were also pretty important. I actually had an argument with my mother because I wanted to interview for this program the first summer, and she had planned to teach me to "keep house" that summer. We agreed that I would interview for the program and go if I was accepted, but if I wasn't accepted, I would not seek other summer employment but learn how to keep house instead. I didn't learn to keep house that summer.

This program, like many other science and math programs during the late 1950s and 1960s, was a reaction to Sputnik, the first space satellite, which was launched by the Russians in 1957. The spirit of the times was "learn math or learn Russian"—that is, if we didn't catch up in the space race our country would pay dearly. Sputnik really did have a galvanizing effect on science and math education in this country, although I didn't fully understand the politics at the time.

My going to college was an unquestioned assumption in my house, and in 1961 I went off to Rice University in Houston, Texas, to major in topology. Topology is a branch of mathematics that deals with intrinsic properties of shapes—what happens if distances don't matter. Although this was my initial interest, it lasted only thirty seconds after I opened my first topology book. It became clear that topology was really tough abstract math, not just fun and games, and it wasn't as fascinating as computers. The only real computing being done on campus at that time was at the Rice Computer Project, and so I wandered in sometime during my sophomore year and asked what was going on. Jane Jodeit handed me the reference manual and suggested that I read it first and then come back and ask questions. I thought she was being encouraging, so I read it and went back. I figured out later that she was probably saying, "Shoo, kid, go away." But Jane, Marty Graham, and later John Iliffe started giving me programming tasks, and I worked part-time with the Rice Computer Project for the rest of my undergraduate years.

In my junior year I met Alan Perlis, a professor at Carnegie Mellon University, at a summer program sponsored by the University of Michigan. I was captivated by him and his work. When I went back to Rice, I thought about graduate school but wasn't sure if I really wanted to do it. People around me, especially Alan Robinson, said, "Go ahead, apply; that doesn't mean you have to go." I learned later from one of my mentors that many of those around me were "scared to death" that I wouldn't go to graduate school. I entered the newly formed Department of Computer Science at Carnegie Mellon in 1965. I wanted to go to Carnegie Mellon because at other places, like MIT for example, computer science was part of electrical engineering, and I knew I wasn't interested in electrical engineering.

In the mid-1960s, the computer science graduate students worked and played with the Computation Center staff. I met Roy Weil in this group my first year in graduate school. We grew closer and closer over time, and we finally married in 1973. Roy is my best friend as well as my husband—we share many interests, and he's incredibly flexible about accommodating my professional needs.

I received my Ph.D. and started my first job as a faculty member at Carnegie Mellon in 1971. I was the first woman faculty member in the department, and I am currently one of two tenured women in the department. Being a woman has never had a serious negative impact on or been a serious barrier in my professional life—at least that I was aware of—although in the world of finance and health care I have been and continue to be appalled by treatment I receive because I am a woman. For example, when I married in 1972 most of the banks in Pittsburgh would not consider my salary in the mortgage application. Also, credit card companies would not issue credit cards to a married woman in her own name if she chose to keep her name. Since I planned to keep my own name when we married, I collected all the credit cards I thought I'd ever need and just didn't report to them that I had married.

I've done research in an assortment of areas and with a variety of people. One of the things I've enjoyed most is stumbling into collaborations with people with common interests. The thread that has run through my research is trying to help people develop better software more effectively. In the 1960s, the work I did with programming languages, including my thesis, was directed at understanding the interaction between programming language design and the cost of compiling the resulting

program. This abstract data type work, which took up most of the 1970s, was a way of stepping up a level. It was an enduring collaboration with Bill Wulf, Ralph London, and others. Progress in programming language design often takes the form of simple constructs that capture larger, more complex computations. The abstract data work did this language support for algorithms and data types. During this period I also worked with Joe Traub and Jon Bentley on algorithms topics. At some point I realized that this business of abstract data types provided a good way to organize software for one class of problems, but didn't seem to solve all the problems available. I wanted to look at other patterns, like user interface design; for a while I did that and generated some interesting results.

In 1984 I switched gears to help create the Software Engineering Institute at Carnegie Mellon. I served as chief scientist of the SEI until 1987, at which point I decided what I really wanted to do was research in software "architecture." I had picked up the thread that there are not only interesting ways to organize software but different approaches for different problems. There are lots of advocates for particular architectures, each claiming his is best for all problems. My preference is to help designers decide which one among these architectures actually fits the problem at hand. To do this, I must describe the architectures and their properties precisely. I am interested in figuring out what it is about a problem that requires its own software organization. This is what I call software architecture. It sounded to me like what I was trying to do was discover an engineering structure for software. I thought it would be useful if I understood what the structure of an engineering discipline was, so I spent time reading the history of engineering fields and came away with a model of how engineering fields developed. That helped to shape what I've done in software architecture. Currently I'm working with David Garlan and others to try to better understand the shared folklore about the architecture of software systems and how the various components of the systems (boxes) and the way they interact with each other (lines) are represented in box and line diagrams. These representations are totally informal and totally idiosyncratic, but they are accepted based on shared folklore. We want to make this folklore explicit, put it on display, and support it in order to help software developers.

I have also been involved in educational activities, which are vitally important to the field of computer science. Because computer science is growing rapidly, contributions to education have considerable leverage on the development of the field. For many years the computer science department at Carnegie Mellon offered undergraduate courses but no undergraduate degree. In 1981 the department began considering the possibility, and I formed a group of faculty and graduate students to design a suitable curriculum. We decided to do a complete design for modern computer science rather than attempting incremental improvements on existing courses. The result of this group's effort is a curriculum design suitable for consideration by many universities, not just mine.

I have also worked on exporting these ideas directly to industry. Among other things, I have worked with IBM's Information Systems Division on an in-house curriculum that relies heavily on a fundamental course derived from one we created at Carnegie Mellon. This course has been offered to IBM ISD people from all over the country.

Someone once asked me, as he was preparing to introduce me at some function, what nugget of good advice I would give to all the young students in the audience about how to make a successful career. My response was "ignore all pieces of advice given in this form." I say that somewhat jokingly because I never had a deliberate or concrete plan. As a young faculty member, I didn't pick up on how the game was played as fast as some people do. I haven't focused or controlled my research plan tightly, maybe because I'm easily diverted, but as a consequence I have a richer collection of things that I can draw on.

Mary Shaw and her husband, Roy Weil, with their mountain bikes

I realized during graduate school that I actually get more done working six days a week than seven (on average, working about ten hours a day). On that seventh day, I indulge in many different hobbies. In the late sixties my husband and I began canoeing; in the early seventies we took up bicycling; then came flying, scuba diving, and cross-country skiing. Canoeing season is from snow melt through sometime in June or July; bicycling season is from whenever the rivers dry up until it gets too cold; and cross-country skiing season is whenever there's enough snow on the ground. That covers most of the year! As a matter of fact, my husband, Roy Weil, and I have edited the last two editions of *Canoeing Guide to Western Pennsylvania and Northern West Virginia.* We also wrote *FreeWheeling Easy in Western Pennsylvania,* a guide to easy bicycling and walking trails that are closed to motor vehicles. This guide sold so well the first year, and trails developed so much, that we are already revising. These hobbies have been an important and ongoing part of my life.

PRESENT POSITION: Professor of Computer Science, Carnegie Mellon University

FIELD: Computer science

RESEARCH AREA: Software engineering and architecture

EDUCATION: B.A. in Mathematics (1965), Rice University; Ph.D. in Computer Science (1971), Carnegie Mellon University

DATE/PLACE OF BIRTH: September 30, 1943/ Washington, D.C.

Mary Shaw lives with her husband, Roy Weil, in Pittsburgh, Pennsylvania.

INTERVIEW DATE: October 1994

Bonnie Shulman

Assistant Professor of Mathematics
BATES COLLEGE

As a teenager, Bonnie Shulman shocked adults around her by hitchhiking across the country instead of going to college. She ended up in Boulder, Colorado, studying beat poetry, writing, and living on welfare as a single mom. On her thirtieth birthday, she realized that she wanted to go back to school to study science. She went straight through her B.A. and M.A. degrees to a Ph.D. in mathematical physics. She deliberately chose work at a small teaching college and has turned her focus to feminist critiques of mathematics.

❧

I didn't actually begin college until I was thirty. I went to high school at Bronx High School of Science and was therefore on the fast track in math and science. I graduated in 1968 and did not go to college, which was a big scandal for many concerned adults around me. I think that the reason I didn't continue with school was that I wanted a life. I was tired of being the only girl in all my classes, and all I'd seen was the nuclear science track and "Build Better Bombs." I had this picture of science that didn't really include girls, and I had no idea what kind of career I could have in science that would be compatible with my ethics. Instead, I hitchhiked back and forth across the country, lived in a commune for a while, and had many other interesting experiences, including becoming pregnant and having a daughter when I was twenty-one.

One summer I traveled to Boulder, Colorado, in a broken-down black 1951 van with a boyfriend, two dogs, and my three-year-old daughter. I ended up as part of the Naropa Institute, which was just beginning and had just started a poetry program (later dubbed the Jack Kerouac School of Disembodied Poetics). The beat poets had been my heroes, and I was very interested in writing, in part because my mother is an English teacher. The two-culture split between the sciences and the arts, which C. P. Snow talked about, was inside me as well, and the first thing I pursued in my life was writing. I studied poetry with Alan Ginsberg and many of his cohort—it was a very exciting time; things were in flux and there was a lot of intellectual stimulation. I ended up staying in Boulder with what was in my pack; I never went back to New York, to all my stuff or my life.

I put an ad up on a board and found another single mother with a child and we got a place together. Eventually, a rather large group of single mothers who were writers and artists and

Bonnie Shulman at age twenty-two with daughter, Hatha, age eight months

musicians came together, and we formed a kind of salon that met at our different houses. We had all kinds of wonderful activities, but we were always pretty broke; we lived on welfare and supplemented it however we could. I typed for a living and did secretarial work, transcribing tapes for the poets and other people. I also published my own poetry and even had a printing press for a while. In fact, at one point I lived in the mountains and had this press in a cold, wood-heated basement; it was very romantic but not money producing. I also got some experience working with people and teaching: I worked in prisons and mental health institutions, and I did poetry in the schools and gave creative writing workshops.

Around the time I turned thirty, it all began to get to me. People had been telling me for years to go back to school, but they all thought I would go into English because that's what I was doing. However, I had one friend who had gone back to school in geology. We had lived together for a while in a teepee back in the woods. He was still living in the teepee, but I had seen amazing and good changes in his life as a result of going back. One night around the kerosene lantern, I was looking over his shoulder while he was doing some calculus homework, and I said, "Oh! No, no, no. It doesn't go like that—it goes like this." He turned around and said, "How do you know?" I sort of shame-facedly replied, "Well, shucks, I guess I must have taken calculus in high school." I had never admitted to any of my friends that I had this background, but now he knew.

So when I turned thirty, I was having this great identity crisis, and he and I went to the top of a mountain for my birthday. I said, "What am I gonna do? What am I gonna do?" and he said, "You know, science. It's the only thing that makes any sense to go back to school in." And for some reason that just took, like a seed in a well-prepared garden. Within a month, like a hurricane, I was down the mountain at the University of Colorado at Boulder. I registered, did all the paperwork, had everything taken care of, and that September I started school.

By then I had all the confidence in the world. I had done all of these difficult things, struggled, lived on my own, lived back in the woods, hauled water, and raised my daughter (then nine) all by myself. School seemed like it would be easy compared to all that, and I remembered that I had always been good in school. I had a very different attitude than I would have had if I had gone back earlier—certainly different from any of my peers who were beginning at around the same time. My confidence and its momentum carried me through until my junior year. At that point it finally occurred to me how difficult a task I had chosen, but by then I was hooked.

When I started school, I went through the course catalog and found this really neat course on cosmology and the origins of the universe, and it just captured my imagination. I was and am an avid fan of science fiction, and I thought, "Oh cool, I'll understand how all this stuff works, and maybe I'll become a science fiction writer." I took the course, loved it, and then thought I'd be an astrophysicist, so I took all of the undergraduate astronomy courses. While I continued to be very good in math, it seemed to me like a lesser task. I thought anyone could do math—because I could—that it was physics that was really hard and really mattered. The math, I thought, was just a tool.

I had started out as a freshman knowing that I was going all the way through for my Ph.D. I figured there was no point in doing things half-way. I had always gone for the biggest goal I could get; I'd gotten my black belt in karate, and I knew I was going to graduate school. There was a woman who taught astrophysics and who served informally as my mentor during my undergraduate years. She had a very theoretical approach to her work, but she told me that I was even more theoretical than she was. During my senior year, she said to me, "I think that you are a mathematician, and that's what you should major in and go to graduate school in." When she, of all people, said that, I listened. I ended up getting a degree in mathematics; with a few more courses I would have had a second major in physics, but I figured it was unnecessary.

I stayed at the University of Colorado to do my graduate work. I had gotten some grants and scholarships at other places, and at the time I really wanted to go to some hotshot school, but my daughter did not want to move. She was a teenager then, and I figured she wouldn't be in the house very much longer. I knew there would be time later in my life to make decisions based just on what I wanted to do, and so I decided to make this decision with her. I felt like she had gone to school with me and deserved some of the benefits that would accrue when I completed my degree. I did make that decision in favor of family over career, but in hindsight I don't feel that my career suffered.

The same woman who had suggested I major in math ended up becoming my graduate adviser. Sometimes I think she was rather canny. She wanted a mathematician, so she sent me off to get trained and then hired me on as her graduate student in mathematical physics. I worked on a mathematical model of solar coronal loops and, in particular, the magnetic fields in and around the loops. A simple model of a solar loop is to think of it as a long cylinder bent into a ∪. You make an assumption that a magnetic field has some large value inside the cylinder and a smaller value outside. This is called the "sharp boundary model," and it assumes a sudden, discontinuous change in the magnitude of the magnetic field. I figured that in nature it's probably not like that, and that there's probably a transition region where things change, so I decided to look at a continuous model. I extracted out the mathematics, massaged that, and worked on it for a while and then turned back around and saw what implications my mathematical results had for the physics.

This kind of translation process between math and physics—making those connections between abstract mathematical structures and reality—has always fascinated me. Even though I've come up with lots of explanations as to why that should work, it still remains mysterious and magical; it's what keeps me engaged in mathematical physics.

It was tough, though, being an older, nontraditional student; and although I wasn't the only one on campus, we were few and far between. I didn't know anyone else like me in the sciences. I was somewhere in age between my professors and the students, and in some ways I related to my professors more easily. They often had children the same age as mine or younger, and they would ask for parenting advice. That kind of interaction enabled me to be a bridge between students and faculty, and that kind of bridging became a theme for me. I was bridging math and physics, I was bridging generations, and I was bridging gender by being a woman in a male-dominated field. In some ways it gave me an advantage, but more often than not people thought of me differently. They saw me not only as a woman but as a single mom and someone who'd been on welfare, and they wondered what I was doing. I was just different, and the way people thought of me because of that worked on my self-image.

There were a couple cases of sexual harassment. As a mature student, I'd had ten years of consciousness raising, and I could be clear in my own mind that the professors involved were the problem, not me. That didn't mean the incidents weren't also damaging. In both cases I chose not to report it, although if there had been some of the mechanisms that are in place today, I might have. At that time, pressing a complaint was a difficult process to go through, and there was little hope of actually changing anything. I also decided not to follow through—and it turned out I was right—because either or both of the professors involved could have had an important say in my future. One of them ended up sitting on my thesis committee. You have to weigh these things carefully when deciding what to do, and it's extremely important to talk it through with others so you can be certain you're not crazy. I did get the word out among certain professors to warn their students about these men.

Another challenge was just balancing my

*Bonnie Shulman
delivering a talk at the
Annual Winter
Mathematics Joint
Meetings, 1992*

academics and personal life. Many of my friends from the poetry and arts community were shocked by my decision and a little dismayed by my lack of availability. They didn't really understand the demands that being a student—particularly a graduate student in the sciences—put on me. I lost some of those friends, but the ones that I kept were truly my good friends and supported me even when they didn't understand things. I felt that I was making a lot of sacrifices in my personal life for school, and perhaps that I even compromised some of my values. My value was that people came before almost anything, and it was a real switch for me to put my career first. I was really ambitious. I wanted this career, and I wanted the Ph.D. It bothered me, however, that I made choices that in another part of my life I would not have approved of. I promised myself that I would do this only to get the union card, only to get through graduate school, because this was something I really wanted and this was what I had to do to get it. I racked my brain to find another way to do it, and it really seemed that there wasn't one. I had to make those sacrifices. I did not maintain a relationship during that whole time. Boyfriends came and went, mostly be-

cause I just wasn't available a lot of the time; what energy I had went to my daughter.

My professors, who were mostly men, did encourage me to go on in research, but somehow I never heard about, nor was I asked to apply for, the biggest and hottest hotshot kinds of grants and programs. I wasn't in that network. In the end it turned out OK because it became clear to me that the career path I wanted was exactly the kind of job I have now; I really wanted to teach. That wasn't a secondary career goal for me but really a primary one. I valued teaching and didn't want to sacrifice it to be on the fast track in research and to publish papers or perish. I would have chosen to do what I'm doing, but I didn't get to make the choice completely freely.

In the end I just said, "I will sacrifice to get this degree, but no longer. I am *not* going to continue like this after graduate school." I told this to some of my professors, and one of them said to me, "Don't kid yourself. It's not going to change after graduate school; then there'll be tenure and other hurdles. It's always like this." I remember looking at him and saying, "Not for me. I just won't." I am pleased to report that I have been true to that.

Part of it was my stubborn choice of job. I

teach at Bates College, a small liberal arts college in Maine; we have about fifteen hundred students, all undergraduates. We're expected to balance our time between teaching and research, which, for our purposes, is defined more broadly than publishing papers, although that's important. General scholarship, participating in conferences, giving talks, and doing expository writing also count as research. There's a big emphasis on teaching; we pride ourselves on the quality of teaching here, and good teaching is rewarded. This contrasts with the average research institution where, although the balance may be shifting, research is definitely stressed more than teaching. My Ph.D. adviser had envisioned me going to Princeton or another prestigious research institution, and perhaps I could have done that. I still sometimes doubt myself because I took this kind of job over a research job. There's an ethic within academe that says that the real scholars, the smart ones, don't settle for a job at a small college because there isn't enough time for research, which is all that really matters. When I think about it, I know I could have succeeded on the fast track—not Nobel Prize level, but I certainly could have survived. However, I don't think I would have thrived in that world, and it's not what I wanted. Part of my being true to myself was sticking up for and choosing this career.

I spend a lot of time with students, and that's one of the great delights of my job. This is a largely residential college, and I participate very fully in the living situation; I spend a lot of time interacting with students outside of class. I have an ideal of helping to give back in ways that I was given to, and more than that, in ways that I wish I had been given to. I remember what it's like to be a student, and I try to make that experience as fruitful, positive, and growth inspiring as I can. I'm very involved in the math education reform movement, so when I prepare for class, I work at coming up with interesting problems and exercises that will help students to discover the things I want them to know rather than my

just telling them those things. My preparation also involves planning group work and thinking about the dynamics of the groups and how they are and aren't working. I am well trained for this from my earlier experiences in working with different populations in teaching writing.

I've made other decisions to do what I want to do with my life. One of them is that I jumped tracks in my research. I still have more things I would like to look at someday with my solar coronal loops, but I am now on pretenure leave for the year and I have put my mathematics research on hold. Currently, I am doing feminist critiques of science and in particular mathematics. This was a great love of mine even before I started school, but until now it was only an avocation. I'm now asking questions like, "What do we mean by 'science works'? If all 'science works' means is that we can do what we set out to do, what would happen if we set out to do different things?" Feminist critiques have made some inroads into biology, but physics and math have been largely immune. There's been a great cry in the literature for people within these disciplines to extend feminist critiques into these as well, and it seemed to me that I was uniquely positioned to do so. I don't find it plausible that the critiques should no longer apply after a certain point. To me the question of scientific objectivity is really, "How well is human agency hidden? How hard is it to find the footprints?"

Again, this work is a bridging. I'm trying to see what desires and motivations led to the set of assumptions that we use in math. I'm looking for the junctures where choices were made and trying to find the roads not taken. This is a very mathematical thing to do. It involves uncovering implicit lemmas (or preliminary propositions) and exploring the consequences of changing your axioms. I'm looking at foundations in mathematics and trying to find the blood behind seemingly bloodless structures. I work at applying feminist critical methodologies to mathematics not because I hate math but because I love it, and I want to better understand what we as mathematicians do and why. I had to choose to do this research instead of the other because I knew I couldn't do both. Although I may go back someday, I've just decided to do what I want to do, to pursue ideas that excite me. I hope that it flies with my tenure decision, but if it doesn't then at least I will have had a good time and been committed to what I was doing along the way.

I do see science and mathematics as agents for social change. That's why I want to understand how who we are and what we want to do affects how and what we know. We need to understand that dynamic in order to change things. I don't believe my critiques will be ultimately successful unless they affect practice, and that is what I'm after although I don't know if I will be successful. One problem is that as soon as you start to have some kind of effect, you lose your credentials. People start questioning whether you're still a mathematician because you're questioning methods and practice. However, I am leading the kind of life that I wanted. When I was in graduate school, it wasn't clear if it was going to be worth it. I suffered a lot. But I empowered myself by keeping the promise I made about following my heart after graduate school, and the union card did empower me to do what I want to do.

PRESENT POSITION: Assistant Professor of Mathematics, Bates College

FIELD: Mathematical physics

RESEARCH AREAS: Feminist critiques of science and mathematics; special functions; plasma physics

EDUCATION: B.A. in Mathematics (1985), M.A. in Mathematics (1988), and Ph.D. in Mathematical Physics (1991), University of Colorado at Boulder

DATE/PLACE OF BIRTH: February 8, 1951/ Champaign, Illinois

Bonnie Shulman lives with her old gray cat in Lewiston, Maine. Her partner, Don, lives in New York; her daughter, Hatha, lives in Portland, Oregon.

INTERVIEW DATE: December 1995

Ellen Kovner Silbergeld

Professor
UNIVERSITY OF MARYLAND MEDICAL SCHOOL

Ellen Silbergeld, one of the nation's foremost experts on lead poisoning, holds several faculty positions in the environmental health and environmental policy fields. But she avoided science even through her undergraduate education at Vassar. It wasn't until she held a staff job at the National Academy of Sciences that she realized that she wanted to help clean up the environment and that studying engineering and medicine would help her to do that. She has been instrumental in changing environmental policy, from getting the lead out of gasoline to convincing McDonald's to replace foam packaging with paper. In 1993 Ellen Silbergeld was awarded a John D. and Catherine T. MacArthur Foundation award in recognition of her work.

❈

My field is environmental health and environmental policy. Once a year, I teach a full course at the Johns Hopkins School of Hygiene and Public Health, where I have three graduate students. At the University of Maryland Medical School, I teach a full course, teach three or four other courses to the medical students in pharmacology, and have three graduate students and two postdoctoral fellows there. I teach in two courses at the University of Maryland Law School, one on lead poisoning and one on risk assessment.

I also spend a fair amount of time as a consultant toxicologist with the Environmental Defense Fund (EDF), after working there full-time for almost ten years. In my work with the EDF, I've had a significant impact on public policy. I was instrumental in convincing the federal government to phase out the use of lead in gasoline. I was one of a group of environmentalists who fought a move to water down the federal government's standards for control of carcinogens such as dioxin, asbestos, and formaldehyde. I was also a member of the EDF team that worked with McDonald's to make the switch from foam to paper packaging. Recently, I've focused international attention on the Amazon River basin, where miners use mercury to extract gold from soils and sediments.

I identify research topics in three ways: things that I know and know how to do, things that are intellectually exciting and challenging, and problems that are significant in terms of their severity or pervasiveness of impact. My current research involves two major

Ellen Silbergeld using molecular techniques to study the effects of environmental chemicals on early development, 1995

projects: one in environmental exposure and infectious disease, conducted primarily in Brazil; the other on endocrine disruption, where I'm looking into chemicals like dioxin that affect reproduction and development.

A few years ago, I came up with a new lead-screening test. Because it is extremely low cost and provides instant feedback, I hope the test will make it possible to have very widespread screening in other countries or places where an expensive, laboratory-based test is very difficult. Right now laboratory tests cost fifty to sixty dollars and require taking blood to a laboratory, getting an analysis, and going back and finding the person screened. In Baltimore, with kids in many inner-city neighborhoods, that's very hard to do. The new test could be done at home, but mostly it would provide instant feedback from clinics, schools, or other settings where screenings are done. The patent has been awarded and now they've sold the license, but it seems like it's taking a long time to get to a marketing stage. The delay is frustrating.

In the meantime, I've also invented a method for detecting mercury. The mercury test's primary use will be out in the field for ecological studies. Mercury analysis is extremely difficult because mercury vaporizes at room temperature, so collecting samples, preserving them, and analyzing them is very difficult.

I have enjoyed collecting things since I was a child—especially rocks and insects, although my collecting didn't translate into an interest in science. In fact, I used to actively avoid science. I'm not really sure why. Of course to a certain extent, I was the victim of female stereotypes, including my own. I loved math and was good at it, but by my senior year in high school in Washington, D.C., I had gone through two years of calculus and was one of only two girls left in the class. I was also the victim of the very poor way that science was, and often still is, taught at the lower levels. I became thoroughly convinced not just that I wasn't very good in science but that it wasn't very interesting. It's usually not until you get

to the very high levels of science that you begin to see opportunities for creativity. I think education has it backwards: I think we ought to be throwing kids into situations where they can exercise creativity and later—once they become excited—teach them why learning chemical reactions is important, rather than making them learn chemical reactions first, which is unbelievably boring.

When I was younger, I was influenced by some very inspirational teachers in languages and in history, but not by math or science teachers because they were not that great. But I was most influenced by a number of very, very intelligent and strong women, including my mother and others in my parents' circle of friends. My parents didn't know many scientists. My father was a lawyer and my mother had a variety of positions. She started as a journalist and ended up as an administrator at the Corcoran Art School. However, both my parents were very committed and involved in social movements; I'm sure that's why environmental issues eventually attracted me.

As an undergraduate at Vassar, I continued to avoid science and carried a double major in history and English. After I graduated, I enrolled in an economics program at the University of London, although I left after one semester. I realized that I didn't want to dedicate my life to mere commentary; I wanted to actually *do* something. So I moved back to Washington, D.C., and got a job as a file clerk, the only job I could find. When I refused to file, they fired me.

Then I made a critical move: I took a job at the National Academy of Sciences as a staff person for various committees. That's where I became interested in environmental science. It was the current of the times, the time of the first Earth Day. Environmental science had a sense of urgency—these were new, exciting, uncharted areas, and the work could make a difference. I decided I wanted to learn how to clean up the environment and looked for a graduate program in the D.C. area.

When I walked through the door of the School of Engineering at Johns Hopkins, I had no scientific background. A friend advised me to take a biochemistry course at the medical school rather than at the graduate school. I sat in class with a dictionary on my lap because I didn't know what the words meant. I had never heard of eukaryotic cells or mitochondria. But once I got through that course, I decided I loved it. After I finished my Ph.D., I did my postdoc at the Johns Hopkins School of Hygiene and Public Health, where I worked with a truly outstanding toxicologist, Alan Goldberg, and Julian Chisolm, one of the world's leading authorities on the clinical manifestations of lead poisoning. By that time, I had decided that I wanted to focus on the impact of the environment on biological systems. Goldberg and another postdoctoral student were looking at the effects of lead— exactly what I wanted to explore.

What interested me about lead was that it was a truly important problem and no one had the faintest idea why it was toxic. There were many, many children with lead poisoning, and people didn't seem to be paying much attention to it. I was fortunate to be in Baltimore, where there has been a long tradition of concern about lead poisoning. Baltimore was the first city in the United States to look for lead poisoning and to do something about it.

When I look back on my education, I realize I faced sexism in both the engineering and the medical school. At the time, I mostly ignored it. It wasn't until later in my career that I confronted these sexist attitudes. I believe that one of the most important influences for change in attitude in the United States is when men realize their daughters are having a hard time, when they look at their behavior and say, "My god, I'm putting down women in my class and *this* is what my daughter is complaining about." I've had several male colleagues tell me that it is an extraordinary experience to see your behavior through the eyes of someone you love. But the way I handled it at the time—the way an awful lot of women did—was to work very, very hard to excel. The men might not have liked me but they couldn't put me down.

Today, a great number of people involved in the environment, particularly at the community level, are women. It's an issue that women take very, very seriously. They may be motivated by concern for their own families and children, or for people in general.

Children are certainly an important motivation for me. But I don't think it is easy for anyone to be a scientist and have a family. My husband, Mark, is with the Consumer's Union. We met in Washington right before I went to graduate school and got married when I was in my second year of graduate school. Our daughter, Sophia, is fifteen, and our son, Nicholas, is eleven. I had my children toward the middle of my career, when I had finished my degree and was working as a scientist at the National Institutes of Health. But I do not think there is a "good time" to have kids, and certainly I don't think it's easy for anybody to raise children—whether you stay at home or work. I do think the absolute essential is to have a partner who respects what you're doing and raises the children with you.

Some of the most interesting experiences I've had have been when people called me for help. I once got a fax from a small group in the Amazon, and this got me involved in my work on mercury. I once got a call from the National Trust in Bermuda to help with their trash problem; that's how I got involved in the whole incineration issue, first there and then in the United States. And I got involved in the Missouri dioxin episode when a reporter from a small gay newspaper in St. Louis called me to ask questions. The Missouri dioxin episode began in 1983 when, at the height of controversies involving the EPA's mishandling of abandoned hazardous waste sites, people became aware that there were several places with high concentrations of dioxin in soils. Altogether, over half a dozen separate places, including the town of Times Beach, were eventually evacuated and closed off by the government. But it took courageous and persistent citizens to get the government to act.

Overall, I'm most proud of convincing the

federal government to get lead out of gasoline, but I'm also very pleased to have worked with groups like the small group of citizens in Binghamton, New York, who were very concerned when the state government office building there caught fire in 1984. The fire started when a large electrical transformer failed and caught fire. The transformer was filled with PCBs (polychlorinated biphenyls). Although Congress had expressly banned PCB manufacture and use with the Toxic Substances Control Act of 1976, the EPA had allowed PCBs already in use to remain in place, including in thousands of electrical transformers. When PCBs are burned, they can generate dioxins and other toxic byproducts. The state wanted to reopen the building the next day, but the citizens who worked there were very concerned about what had happened. I'm proud of the fact that together we kept that building closed for many years until it truly was cleaned up. As a consequence of this fire, and the millions of dollars it cost to clean up the building, I was able to persuade the EPA to change its policy on leaving PCB-containing electrical transformers in place around the country. I'm proud of the fact that, with the example of Binghamton, I was able to persuade the EPA to change a very bad policy.

In 1993 I received a $290,000 fellowship from the John D. and Catherine T. MacArthur Foundation in recognition of my work. I've used the money to seed a broad range of research projects and to start my students on work before they get strong funding. Chiefly I've used it to support my work in Brazil.

I think that it's very important to have a passion for what you do. It seems strange to me that as scientists we never think of it as bad to have a passion for understanding molecular genetics but that we are sometimes embarrassed to have a passion for the social outcomes of our work. I have many passions for my work. I'd like to see environmental health become the bedrock of medicine and public health. I'd like to see everything related to environmental health focus on prevention rather than mopping up messes. I think it will happen, and it's that thought that helps to keep me going.

PRESENT POSITIONS: Professor, Departments of Pathology (Toxicology) and Epidemiology and Preventive Medicine, University of Maryland Medical School; Affiliate Professor of Environmental Law, University of Maryland Law School; Adjunct Professor, Department of Pharmacology and Experimental Therapeutics, University of Maryland at Baltimore; Adjunct Professor, Departments of Health Policy and Management and Environmental Health Sciences, Johns Hopkins School of Hygiene and Public Health

FIELD: Environmental health

RESEARCH AREA: Lead and mercury toxicity

EDUCATION: A.B., Modern History (1967), Vassar College; Ph.D., Environmental Engineering Sciences (1972), Johns Hopkins University

DATE/PLACE OF BIRTH: July 29, 1945/Washington, D.C.

Ellen Kovner Silbergeld lives in Baltimore with her husband, Mark, and their children, Sophia and Nicholas.

INTERVIEW DATE: July 1996

Barbara Smuts

Professor of Psychology and Anthropology
UNIVERSITY OF MICHIGAN

At age thirteen Barbara Smuts read her first article about Jane Goodall's work with wild chimpanzees and decided this was her life's ambition. Her early work focused on female olive baboons and their friendships. For two years she spent twelve-hour days, often seven days a week, with a troop of 120 olive baboons. Recently she's also become interested in bottlenose dolphins, a group with sixty million years of independent evolutionary history.

❦

I am a primatologist—I study nonhuman primate social behavior. Off and on for six years I studied a troop of 120 olive baboons living in the Eburru Cliff area in central Kenya. I focused on the evolution of intimate relationships, particularly female friendships. Like males in many species, male baboons sometimes use aggression to exert leverage on females. Since female baboons are so much smaller, they have developed ways to counter male aggression, and one of those counter-strategies is making friends with other males. These friendships help protect females, and often the male friend forms a very close bond with the female's infants. Prior to my research, many believed that paternity was the primary factor in forming these relationships; the data from my study disprove this. As is the case for humans, it takes time and energy to develop and maintain friendships, but the benefits are well worth it.

For the first two years of my study, I spent twelve hours a day, seven days a week with this troop of baboons, which included eighteen males and thirty-five females. I would rise at about 5:00 A.M. and go out and find the troop where I had left them the night before. The troop would trek anywhere between three and nine miles a day, and I would trek along with them until they settled in another set of cliffs for the night. During most of the time I

Barbara Smuts rests under a tree with several members of her baboon troop in 1977. The juvenile female to her right and the adolescent male in the tree behind her are napping. An adult male, to her left, rests. The fact that some of the animals have fallen asleep indicates how comfortable they are in her presence.
COPYRIGHT 1977 BY BARBARA SMUTS/ANTHROPHOTO

was doing my study, another graduate student, Nancy Nicolson, was doing a simultaneous study of mother-infant relations in the same troop. We shared a house but worked independently, and often went for hours without seeing one another as we tracked different females.

Like Jane Goodall, I combined an anecdotal, qualitative approach, based on intuition derived from hours and hours of unstructured observations, with a more rigorous, quantitative approach that allowed me to draw certain conclusions quite firmly. Both before I started collecting systematic data on the baboons and throughout my study, I spent many hours in unstructured observation; I tried to empty my mind of all preconceived notions and let the baboons tell me what was important in their lives. This led to many intuitions on my part about friendship among baboons, which I could test using quantitative scientific methods.

To do this, I used objective criteria for distinguishing friendly male-female pairs: grooming and proximity. Grooming involves picking through a companion's fur to remove dead skin and ectoparasites, and previous research had indicated that it is a good measure of social bonds. Proximity was simply who was observed near whom when the group was foraging, traveling, or resting. When I compared favorite grooming partners and frequent companions, they overlapped almost completely. So I created a formal definition of friendship: any male that scored high on both grooming and proximity measures I considered a friend. My data indicated that most females had just one or two male friends, but for males the number of female friends varied from none to eight. I also noted that older females tended to be friends with older males and younger females with younger males, although there were occasional May-December relationships in which the female was considerably older than the male.

In order to study these phenomena, I focused on one female at a time and kept track of her activities for thirty minutes; I did this for every female in the troop and then began the cycle again. I wrote down every exchange between a male and the female, and noted every movement she made toward or away from a male. My observations indicated that females were wary of most males in their troop, no doubt because these males sometimes attacked them. Many times I observed an adult male defend a female or her offspring against another troop member. In most cases, the defender was a friend. In about half the friendships I documented, the male was likely to be the father of the female's most recent infant, but in the other half he was not.

At first the baboons all looked alike to me, but after I had been immersed in their world for a while, they emerged as distinct individuals. I gave each baboon a name, most of them drawn from Greek and Roman mythology. It only took a few months to be accepted by the troop so that I could collect data systematically. It was a very gradual habituation, and some animals warmed up more quickly than others. I think part of the reason it was easy to habituate them was that the country was so open and they could see me from a huge distance. I'm also convinced that baboons get used to women much more quickly than they do men. I think they recognize and distinguish women from men and generalize from their own species. I can't prove this, but it's my strong feeling.

I found the work very intense, requiring a lot of concentration, but very relaxing at the same time. I loved wandering around in nature. I never had to decide where to go; I just followed their lead. The baboons were constantly taking me to new places, and I really got to explore the African savanna in the company of experts. It was paradise. This site was very safe because there were no lions or elephants, but virtually all the other game was present to enjoy. What a backdrop to my work!

For as long as I can remember I was drawn to the natural world. I always viewed animals as kindred spirits; I knew that on the inside they were just like me. I loved watching them; I wanted to know what they were doing and why. I grew up on Long Island, and my family moved to Michigan when I was ten. My parents were both intellectuals and trained as historians (as is my only brother); they were the first generation in each of their families to go to college. My father had a degree in history from Columbia University, and my mother worked on a master's in sociology, also from Columbia. As a child I was surrounded by books and intellectual discussions and taken to museums, concerts, and other cultural events from an early age. Every summer from the time I was two years old my family camped for a month; the first three or four years we camped on an island in Lake George, in northern New York, and often we were the only people on the island. So my parents appreciated and enjoyed the natural world as well as the intellectual and cultural worlds.

When my father retired early from his career in public relations at Ford Motor Company, he went back to graduate school in evolutionary biology. He and I have discussed our mutual interests for many years, and recently we published our first paper together. He says if he knew growing up what he knows now, he would have become a scientist. My mother stopped working full-time when she had children, but she went back to school when I was in high school and began working on a master's in history. Then she went on for a Ph.D., which she earned in 1995 at the age of seventy-four. She's publishing a book with Yale University Press on the emergence of the science of child development. She's been quite a role model for me.

In fifth grade I had a wonderful biology teacher who inspired me further. I would stop by the neighborhood butcher's shop on the way home from school and come home with any leftover animal parts they'd give me, and I would sit and dissect sheep's eyes and cow hearts in the kitchen while my mom cooked dinner. She was very tolerant. I was always involved in science projects, and my parents were encouraging. My dad and I spent many happy hours in my room growing crystals.

At age thirteen I read my first article about Jane Goodall's work with wild chimpanzees in

National Geographic. It was at this point that my fantasy of living with animals became an ambition, which I achieved eleven years later when I joined Goodall's research team in Tanzania. All of my decisions after age thirteen revolved around this ambition. I went to Harvard in 1968 intending to major in biology because of my interests and goals. Each freshman was assigned an adviser, and my male adviser cautioned me against biology because I was a woman. He told me I would have a hard time competing in biology because it was very quantitative and really tough, and he suggested that I think about majoring in something "softer." I didn't know any better and, like many other freshmen at Harvard, I was intimidated, so I switched to anthropology. In retrospect this turned out to be a very good move, although it was made for all the wrong reasons.

In anthropology I got to know Irven DeVore, who was a primatologist (trained as a cultural anthropologist) and one of the very first people to study baboons in the field. He studied primarily nonhuman primates but also did a lot of work with foragers like the Kalahari bushmen. He became one of my mentors and was immensely supportive, as was Robert Trivers, a graduate student in biology at the time. Trivers became one of the three or four most prominent theorists in the twentieth century on the evolution of social behavior. He was a teaching assistant in some of my courses when I met him, and he was writing a series of critical and very influential papers and sharing them with us. Trivers gave me the intellectual framework to translate my fascination with nonhuman primates into scientific inquiry. I was fortunate to have both men as mentors.

My decision to go to Stanford for a Ph.D. in behavioral biology was driven by my desire to work with Jane Goodall. My primary mentor at Stanford was David Hamburg, a psychiatrist interested in the biological basis of human behavior. I started my work with Goodall at Gombe in Tanzania in 1975, just about eleven years to the day after I read her first article. I went to Gombe to do a two-year study on the behavior of female chimpanzees, but two months after I arrived I was kidnapped along with three others. The kidnapping was politically motivated: I was released after a week to bring the demands to the American, Tanzanian, and Dutch governments. The other three were held a few weeks longer. It was a very stark immersion into the reality of African politics, poverty, and oppression. The kidnapping made me much more aware of and sensitive to the people of Africa; prior to that I hadn't thought much about them because I was so focused on the wildlife. After this incident the field station was closed for many years to outsiders, although the Tanzanians continued to work there.

My interest in female nonhuman primates came from my interest in feminism, which developed in college. I read Simone de Beauvoir's *Second Sex* as a sophomore, and I instantly became a very committed feminist. It became my goal to integrate a feminist perspective into my scientific work, and it was natural for me to focus my research on females: they had been studied less than males, and I was one of them. I was particularly influenced by a dissertation by Richard Wrangham, who is now a professor of anthropology at Harvard. Richard was a few years ahead of me, and he completed a study of male chimpanzees in 1975, the year I set out to study female chimpanzees in Tanzania. Essentially I hoped to do for females what he had done for males—to supply the complementary piece of the puzzle. Due to the kidnapping and subsequent interruption of my work, I never completed that study, and to this day we know less about female chimps than we do about adult males.

For me the most serious consequence of the kidnapping was the disruption of the work I had been aiming at for so long. It was hard to imagine what I would do if I couldn't study female chimpanzees with Jane Goodall. At that time there really weren't any other viable chimpanzee study sites for American students, so after several months in which I considered many alternatives, I decided to join one of DeVore's graduate students, who was

starting a baboon project in Kenya. I went to Masai Mara National Park to study baboons. But that fell through after only seven months because some of the Kenyans involved in running the research stations were corrupt and had been poaching wildlife; it was a very uncomfortable situation for us. It was also not a great study site because I couldn't leave the vehicle and follow the baboons on foot.

However, as the cliché goes, the third time was a charm. Thanks to Shirley Strum, another baboon researcher, I was able to study the same species of baboons at another Kenyan site, near the small town of Gilgil, which is northwest of Nairobi. It was a much better study site because I was able to work on foot.

I have always had great confidence as a primatologist because watching and thinking about animals is second nature—it feels like home—to me. When I began my work I didn't fully realize how risky my approach was for someone just starting her career—relying on the anecdotal, intuitive approach as well as the more rigorous quantitative approach. It just seemed second nature to communicate what I had learned in ways that made sense to me, even though including lots of stories in scientific publications wasn't common at the time. Goodall and Diane Fossey did this, but they were always a little bit outside the academic mainstream; and they were so special and so unique that they could get away with it. I, however, was very much inside the system, trying to do something similar and make it legitimate.

I want my work to have a much greater impact than it has had. I have published mainly in academic journals, and that has been limiting. I'm in a transition phase of my career right now and thinking about how I could best have a wider impact on the public. I believe that one day we will look back on our treatment of animals in captivity and view it with the same horror that we now feel when we think about human slavery. The public will realize that these animals are thinking, feeling beings with emotions and awareness of who they are and what they are doing. I have seen baboon mothers become inactive and dazed when they lost infants; one mother called out every time the troop passed the site of her infant's death. It doesn't make sense to cling to the assumption that baboons and other nonhuman primates are fundamentally different from us.

I'm committed to writing more articles for the public, and I'm also seriously beginning to explore the use of video to help people better understand nonhuman primates. A few years ago I spent four and a half months in Gombe, where I hadn't worked since the kidnapping, studying the baboons and recording most of my observations on videotape. I now have about a hundred hours of tape focusing on dyadic interactions—greetings between two individuals. These greetings capture in a nutshell the essence of the relationship between two animals, just as human greetings do if you look at them carefully. I'm hoping that a picture is really worth a thousand words as I make a series of videotapes to communicate very directly to people the sentient nature of these animals. I want to start with baboons, but I'm interested in doing this kind of presentation for other animals as well.

I did the study and videotaping in Gombe with my long-time partner, David Gubernick, who is also a researcher in animal behavior. It is often difficult to integrate a family with extended fieldwork in faraway places, although many women primatologists have done so. Most of the women primatologists I know who are married and have children are married to men in the field, and it is a partnership both professionally and personally.

Recently I have turned my attention to bottlenose dolphins. I supervised some graduate students who were studying them, and I went out to visit them at their study site in Western Australia and instantly became drawn in. I was struck by the parallels with primates—not so much specific behavioral parallels but the deeper level of their individuality, the strength of the personalities, the social intelligence, and the complexity and nuanced nature of their social relationships. This would have been interesting to me if I'd seen it in another primate, but it was particularly striking in dolphins because they are an unre-

Barbara Smuts, 1990
PHOTO BY DAVID GUBERNICK

lated group with sixty million years of independent evolutionary history. Several important hypotheses that have been generated from primate studies, about the nature of social relationships and the relationship between intelligence and sociality, can now be tested in a second kind of organism. Until recently only primates were known to show that level of social sophistication. That's the reason I became so interested in the dolphins. Although my affinity is still stronger for primates, this lends an exciting new dimension to my work.

PRESENT POSITION: Professor of Psychology and Anthropology, University of Michigan

FIELD: Primatology

RESEARCH AREA: Nonhuman primate social behavior

EDUCATION: B.A. in Social Anthropology (1972), Harvard University; Ph.D. in Neuro- and Biobehavioral Sciences (1982), Stanford University Medical School

DATE/PLACE OF BIRTH: November 9, 1950/New York, New York

Barbara Smuts lives in Ann Arbor, Michigan.

INTERVIEW DATE: November 1995

Tami I. Spector

Associate Professor of Organic Chemistry
UNIVERSITY OF SAN FRANCISCO

As a woman and a lesbian, Tami Spector felt somewhat out of place in the male world of graduate school in organic chemistry. She discovered a love of teaching through her work as a teaching assistant, and decided to pursue a career in academia rather than industry. She based her postgraduation career moves not only on potential for strong professional development but also on her desire to live where there was a viable lesbian community. She and her partner now live in northern California, where Tami was the first woman hired in physical science at the University of San Francisco.

As a young woman in college I chose science over music for the practicality, and chemistry over biology for the challenge. Undergraduate school was fun and affirming. My adviser was an inspired teacher who could see talents in me that I couldn't see; he said that while I was a late bloomer as a chemist, out of my class of all-male chemistry majors, I would be the one to achieve a Ph.D. With this encouragement I received my undergraduate degree and began my search for doctoral programs in organic chemistry.

Applying to graduate school was a study in my naïveté and provincialism. I did not want to leave New England, and after I'd been accepted into a number of graduate schools with a full scholarship, my parents set about convincing me that I would not be happy living in the brutal winter climate of Buffalo, the New York school my adviser was pushing for. The appropriate choice, they convinced me, was an Ivy League school with an air of New England prep-school masculinity. At Dartmouth I had a choice of three male organic chemists to mentor me.

Tami Spector at home in San Francisco, 1995

Upon my arrival at Dartmouth I plunged myself deep into my work, each day attending classes and each night crossing the Connecticut River into Vermont, a refugee at the dining room table, to study until I went to sleep. Each day repeated the cycle of the one before; each morning I bolstered myself to enter the Ivy League and male world of chemistry. I took qualifying exams, cumulative exams, oral exams, and did original research on the side. I ate, drank, and slept chemistry.

Every day I sat with my fellow students in the first-year chemistry graduate student office debating the ins and outs of chemical reagents and discussing who had achieved the highest score on the most recent exam. Although I was friendly and collegial, I kept my distance, in part because I am a lesbian. Other students quite naturally created their social structure from people within the department, but I didn't want to talk about departmental gossip or chemical reactions in my few precious hours away from school; rather I sought to make like-minded friends outside of my professional environment. I came to believe that I had to separate my professional life from my personal life, that it was not necessary to be friends with the people I worked with, that I didn't even have to like them, let alone agree with them socially or politically. Eventually I did make friends whom I hold dear to this day, forming special bonds based on the commonality of not fitting in. And although this strategy allowed me to hold onto my identity, I missed out on much of the networking that runs the professional world of science.

My goals changed as I worked my way from my bachelor's to my doctorate in chemistry. In college I wanted to pursue a career in industrial pharmaceutical chemistry, my interest influenced by my undergraduate mentor's large enthusiasm for natural product chemistry. In graduate school, at a distance from my persuasive undergraduate adviser, I became fascinated by the beauty and theory of physical-organic chemistry. Choosing this as my field of doctoral study, I worked on the NMR energetics of perfluorinated cyclooc-tatetraenes. NMR stands for nuclear magnetic resonance, a way of studying molecules. I used this method to study these complex organic molecules and their internal energy and changes in structure.

I was inspired by the work ethic of my doctoral adviser. It wasn't unusual to find him sitting in his office writing grants at 7:30 in the morning when I arrived and photolyzing perfluorobenzene when I left at 7:00 in the evening. His joy and enthusiasm for the beauty of chemistry were palpable. Each day I arrived at my lab bench ready to achieve and hoping that things would go well: that I wouldn't spill the contents of a flask that had taken two months to prepare, and that my molecule—a beautiful white crystalline solid that my research adviser called a "delicate flower"—would perform as I commanded rather than turn black as charcoal. This unfortunate and all-too-common event would return me to square one, a multitude of steps back for a single step forward. I would stand in my stained lab coat, absorbing solvents and reagents through my skin, and force those little molecules to behave.

In graduate school in chemistry, the choosing of a research project involves selling yourself to a potential adviser in exchange for a preconceived original idea for which they have already accrued funding. You work in their laboratory, on their ideas, for their money. Ultimately you place yourself in the hands of someone who has more knowledge about chemistry than yourself, a person with enough experience and expertise and sense to know if a project has the wherewithal to go forward. It is not uncommon, however, for first-year chemistry graduate students to fall prey to an adviser's overly ambitious ideas, ideas that the older and wiser third- and fourth-year students wouldn't touch.

Unfortunately, I was one of those unlucky first-year students who found herself working for three years on an unsuccessful research project. After immense frustration, self-depreciation, and a talk over lunch with an expert in my field who told me I deserved the

Nobel Prize if I succeeded in what I set out to achieve, I walked into my adviser's office and announced that I wanted a different research project. He complied and gave me a new project involving the valence isomerizations of perfluorocyclooctatetraenes, molecules that, through a variety of advanced NMR techniques, I watched and recorded as they tumbled through their dynamic dance. Perhaps because I had been technically well prepared by my first three years of toil, this new project went smoothly, and in a year and a half I completed the experimental part of my doctoral degree.

My first three years as a teaching assistant were, by contrast, more successful. I enjoyed interacting with the undergraduate chemistry students. I took my obligations as a teaching assistant seriously and was rewarded with the Teaching Assistant of the Year Award in 1985. This experience led me to shift my career choice from industrial to academic chemistry. Toward the end of my doctoral program I spoke to my research adviser about possibly becoming a college professor. As I stood in his office discussing my future in rolled-up jeans, green high-top sneakers, and a T-shirt with a image of Popeye proclaiming "I yam what I yam," to my surprise and delight he expressed confidence in my choice.

I chose my postdoctoral position based on the following criteria: that I wanted to work with a highly recognized "strained-ring organic" chemist in a city relatively open to my lesbian life. Thus limited, I wrote to a variety of prospective physical organic chemists and was offered and accepted a postdoctoral position at the University of Minnesota. I lived in Minneapolis close to the university, where I happily started a life with a new openness toward my own sexuality.

During my postdoctoral appointment I carried out research on photochemically induced single-electron transfer reactions of strained-ring hydrocarbons, while simultaneously working as a lecturer at the University of Minnesota and Hamline University in St. Paul. I loved lecturing to a classroom of stu-

dents and interacting with them during my office hours. I gained added confidence in my teaching abilities and was rewarded with positive feedback from my students. As a researcher I worked in a large group under the guidance of a research adviser who was significantly less available than my Ph.D. adviser had been. Fortunately, as a postdoc I already had enough chemical knowledge to work on my project without a senior scientist prodding me along. In addition, because the group was composed of six other postdocs and many senior-level graduate students, I had plenty of people to converse with scientifically.

By the time I finished my postdoctoral appointment and began my tenure-track job search, I had a long-term relationship that greatly influenced my professional decisions. As a couple we decided to limit my job applications to schools in midsized to large metropolitan areas. In doing so we could accommodate my partner's desire to attend graduate school, and both of us would have access to a gay community where we would feel comfortable. My postdoctoral adviser tried to push me to apply for jobs in other localities, but I told him honestly that I wasn't willing to live in such places. My stubbornness was unusual for a chemist and particularly so for an academic chemist, for whom tenure-track jobs can be hard to secure. Most of my heterosexual peers were willing to move for a job, but after living for five years in northern New England, where I felt alienated as a lesbian and a Jew, I decided that locale was a high priority in my life. Once I was certain about this, I felt more comfortable with my position despite the disagreement of some of my professional colleagues and mentors. Bolstered by my own convictions and assured by my postdoctoral adviser and colleagues at Hamline that I could maintain my current employment status for another year if my job search failed, I applied to several schools and was offered a job at the University of San Francisco, a private Jesuit school located in the heart of San Francisco.

For my first five years there I was the only

Tami Spector at home in San Francisco, 1995

organic chemist; I had replaced a professor who was long in need of retirement. Until 1994, when a second organic chemist was hired, I taught the entire organic chemistry curriculum—a one-semester course for pre-dental, pre-physical therapy, and biology majors; a full-year organic chemistry course for chemistry majors and pre-professional health majors; and all of the associated laboratories. It was exhilarating, fun, exhausting, and frustrating. My first real teaching experience had been lecturing to hundreds of organic chemistry students at the University of Minnesota, an experience that cemented my desire to become a professor. At the University of Minnesota my enthusiasm for chemistry and openness to the students had carried me through, and six years later these are still the things that I believe are most important: a willingness to interact with students and to respect them, and to be enthusiastic and knowledgeable about chemistry.

I was the first woman ever hired in the physical sciences at the University of San Francisco, and at times it has been a struggle to assert myself and be heard. This year we hired another organic chemist, and she has added a much-needed dimension to my life as a professor in the department. We are remarkably compatible, although of distinctly different personalities. I am assertive with col-

leagues and slightly reserved with the students; she is more outgoing with the students but less assertive with our colleagues. The balance works. We share more in common about teaching philosophy than most of our male colleagues and are notably less competitive about our achievements and scientific status.

Besides my normal teaching duties my work involves the managing of a research lab in physical organic chemistry. At any one time I have three or four master's students and undergraduate students participating in collaborative research with me. Initially, the experience of running a research group was overwhelming. As graduate students and postdocs, chemists typically concentrate on their own specialized research with the guidance and financial support of a research adviser. Having responsibility for providing funding and thesis topics for my own research students was not something I was well prepared for. The mentoring of a research group, which involves motivating, inspiring, and teaching, is an aspect of being a Ph.D. scientist for which I was insufficiently trained. Fortunately, through my six years of running a research group, I have gained enough experience to feel more confident in my abilities and over time have developed a management style that works for my research students and me. The majority of my collaborative experiences with students have been scientifically successful and have led to my students gaining entrance into the Ph.D.-granting institutions of their choice or to employment in industrial chemistry.

Throughout my graduate schooling and postdoctoral appointment, my lesbianism has led me to keep my professional and private life separate. By the time I became an assistant professor, I was more comfortable with my own sexuality and was much more willing to talk about my personal life in the normal course of collegial conversation. This has impacted my workaday life significantly in the last few years, and recently I have, for the first time in my professional life, formed close friendships with people in my work environment. This has been quite important to me because I spend a significant amount of my life at work, and it is an alienating experience to feel personally distanced from my colleagues. Interestingly, I still have a preference for keeping my professional and private life separate and so have not really developed close friendships with other scientists at the University of San Francisco; instead I've developed a closeness with colleagues in the humanities. Letting myself integrate more of my personal life with my professional life has taught me that I have little to lose and much to gain by revealing my lesbianism.

From where I stand now, as a woman professor in the chemistry department at a small liberal arts school, I believe that my presence makes a difference in the world of science, that by being a woman I alter the perceptions of my students, presenting them with a different view of a chemist. I want to teach students to approach scientific problems through their own intuition and experiences in the physical world rather than perpetuate the myth that science is disconnected from our daily lives and available only to the smartest and most analytical. By honestly expressing to them my journey through the world of chemistry I strive to make science a human rather than a manly endeavor. When I stand in front of a room full of students, at least half of whom are young women and who may be dreaming of becoming doctors, teachers, and chemists, I want to be their role model. I want to speak the truth of my experience so that they can go forward to challenge themselves and the world.

PRESENT POSITION: Associate Professor of Organic Chemistry, University of San Francisco

FIELD: Organic chemistry

RESEARCH AREA: Synthesis and spectroscopy of strained-ring organics

EDUCATION: B.A. in Chemistry (1982), Bard College; Ph.D. in Chemistry (1987), Dartmouth College

DATE/PLACE OF BIRTH: July 27, 1960/Flushing, New York

Tami Spector lives in San Francisco with her partner and their cat.

INTERVIEW DATE: October 1995

Donna Spiegelman

Associate Professor of Epidemiology and Biostatistics
HARVARD SCHOOL OF PUBLIC HEALTH

Early in her career, Donna Spiegelman realized that although she enjoyed computer programming, she would never be happy working in a for-profit environment. She began working in the Occupational Health Program of the Harvard School of Public Health, which enabled her to take graduate classes at Harvard. She eventually earned a doctorate in biostatistics and epidemiology and now works on developing statistical models for epidemiological research. She is a lesbian mother.

✑

As a child I was very, very interested in nature and science. I was one of those kids who had a chemistry set, a microscope, and a telescope. I went to museums, looked at the stars and planets at night, and kept frogs and mice in the basement. I *loved* science, and I was a straight-A student. As I got older, I was hit by the adolescent culture that dictated that girls weren't supposed to do well academically, especially not in math and science. If you wanted to be popular and well liked, you couldn't do those things. I basically accepted the whole deal—hook, line, and sinker; I completely lost interest in science and math. I retained some interest in the humanities, but I started not doing well in school. The only reason I got into Brandeis as an undergraduate was that I managed to do very well on the SATs.

At Brandeis I didn't go to classes, and I did term papers the night before they were due. I was in college from 1973 to 1977, and even though it was the tail end of the sixties era, there was still enough of a tail in Boston and at Brandeis to have a profound influence on me. I really wasn't sure what I wanted to do, and when I finished school I found it hard to consider careers and work when I was im-

Donna Spiegelman and daughter, Nessarose Schear, working at home, February 1993

PHOTO BY ELAINE SCHEAR

mersed in thinking about politics, personal identity, sexual identity, and feminism. I explored many different areas and took classes in many fields, including basic science and computer science. My father encouraged me to do the latter. He worked for IBM and believed that computers were the wave of the future. I taught myself FORTRAN one summer when I was working as a parking-lot attendant and discovered that I liked it. Although I took some programming classes when I went back to school, I never really planned to pursue the subject.

When I got out of school I tried to find a human-services job at a time when even minimum-wage jobs in that field were extremely difficult to get. I ended up, by default, getting a computer programming job at a high-tech company near Boston. I was very good at programming, and I did well. I transferred to another company and got a higher salary, and found myself making more than twice the amount of money that any of my friends made. But even though I enjoyed the challenge of solving puzzles and the logic and structure of programming, I wasn't truly satisfied. I've always had a very strong social consciousness, and I didn't like working on things that I didn't view as socially useful. I consider myself a socialist, and I wasn't comfortable working in a for-profit firm.

So I applied for jobs in the health sector and ended up working at the Harvard School of Public Health in the Occupational Health Program. They were doing research on the health effects of workers' exposures to various substances in the workplace. I loved the work, the programming, and the science. I remember thinking, "This is my future; this is for me."

One of the benefits we had as Harvard employees was taking courses at the school without having to go through the admissions process or pay the (hefty) tuition. So I began to take classes, got to know some of the professors, and subsequently decided to go to graduate school. I had a hard time deciding whether to pursue epidemiology or biostatistics, but I was advised that since epidemiology

was a profession dominated somewhat by physicians, and since I had an aptitude for biostatistics and computing, I would probably fit in better and make a larger contribution as a biostatistician. So I decided to pursue the program in biostatistics.

I needed four semesters of calculus for admission to the program. I had taken two semesters' worth in high school ten years earlier and hadn't looked at it since. I got a review book and went through it chapter by chapter, and then took the third and fourth semesters at Harvard College. I really paid for not having taken math in college, but I was able to overcome that obstacle. The biostatistics program was very difficult for me because I had a weaker math background than most of the others in the program, nearly all of whom had been undergraduate math majors. (I had majored in psychology, although by my third year of college, I had lost interest in the subject.) I didn't do terribly, but I wasn't the star student either. I did have one advantage from my years of work: I could see the bigger picture and understand the ways in which biostatistics fits into epidemiological research.

While I was a doctoral student, I did almost nothing but work on my thesis seven days a week from morning till night. It was really a strain on my relationship with my lover, Elaine. I had to beg her to put up with me and promise her over and over that it wouldn't last forever. My friends all thought I was a workaholic, but I always knew that I wasn't; I just needed to finish my thesis. Nobody believed me, but I think they've come to see that it was true, and I think Elaine has too.

By the time I got my doctorate, I was thirty-five years old and just not interested in doing a postdoc for twenty thousand dollars per year for the next two years. Given my age and the fact that I already had about ten publications, I felt ready for a faculty position. My first job was in Tufts University's Department of Community Health. Once I started at Tufts, I was in a less competitive environment, one where people lived more balanced lives. Work is important to people at Tufts, but things outside of work are also important. It's a supportive environment. The university covered more of my expenses and needs through hard money, and I had to cover less of them through soft money. However, as I secured more of my own funding and become more involved in collaborations with other researchers, the pace started to pick up a bit. Once you have your own studies and your own staff, you have people who constantly need to know, "What do I do next? Will you look at this program and tell me if it's OK?" They're sitting in the next room, and every time you walk by they look at you because they want to get on with their work and they can't take the next step until you look at what they've done so far; meanwhile, you have a hundred other things to do.

After three years at Tufts, I was offered a position at Harvard, where I am now, working as an associate professor of epidemiology and biostatistics, a position I was promoted to in 1995 from the level of assistant professor. I came to this job five months pregnant, and when my daughter, Nessarose, was born, I took a three-month maternity leave, during which I didn't come into work once. However, for an established researcher in academia, the logistics of maternity leave are not so simple—what are your staff and students supposed to do for three months? Even if your institution is completely supportive and pays you, nobody else can supervise your staff or work with your doctoral students. So once a week I would have them come to my house, and I would sit there with the baby, hold her in my arms, give her a bottle, change her diaper, or whatever needed to be done. That way those who needed to could meet with me; they brought me my mail and my messages, although I returned very few calls and answered almost no mail. I met with them so they could keep their work going, and thereby kept my own work going.

Once I went back to work, Nessarose first had an in-house baby-sitter and later joined a family day-care center. Elaine gets up with Nessarose in the morning, gets her dressed, gives her breakfast, and takes her to day care. I get up at 6:00 and try to leave by 7:30. I need to leave work at 5:00 so I can arrive at the day-care center by 5:30 sharp, because they fine us twenty dollars for every five minutes that we're late. So I can work five days a week, forty hours a week. When I'm at work it's a fever pitch, and I don't stop from the second I walk in until the second I leave; but there are limits on how much I can do and still be there for my family. A lot of my colleagues, especially my male colleagues, claim that they work sixty to eighty hours per week. That's who I'm competing against, but there's no way I could do more than these forty hours a week; that's just the way it is.

My work involves developing statistical methods for epidemiological research. To measure the effects of potential environmental hazards on health, you need to use fairly sophisticated mathematics in the form of statistics and statistical models. You also need good data, and some of the data that you need is difficult, and very expensive, to get. For example, it can be difficult, if not impossible, to measure accurately how much of a certain substance someone has eaten over the course of their life. When these things are not measured well, our estimates of their effects are biased, usually because we fail to detect adverse effects. In other words, we may miss real associations that we could see if we had better measures of the exposures that we're interested in. What I do is develop statistical methods to get better measures in an economically feasible way, and then use those methods to correct our estimates of health effects in relation to substances in our environment for the biases generated by measurement error.

This involves sitting down with pencil and paper and working through formulas, equations, models, and likelihood functions, deriving variances, and coming up with possible approaches. It can be very time consuming. I come up with ideas that look good on paper and then try them, and often they don't work well. Sometimes it's a numerical problem, or something that I didn't consider at first that

*Donna Spiegelman and
family at home*
PHOTO BY RHODA SPIEGELMAN

becomes more apparent as the work evolves and needs to be factored in. The theories can be relatively easy to work out, but then you have to implement them by writing computer programs to fit the models to real data. All of the models are nonstandard; we don't use any commercial software. Everything has to be programmed from scratch, and we have to work out all the usual bugs. Then we start working with the actual data and try to get coherent, realistic models that actually fit the data and have desirable numerical properties and, ultimately, desirable statistical properties. We investigate this either through simulation studies based on probable situations given our knowledge of various data or through examples with real data. It takes time. I have three master's-level programmers who work with me. They're extremely smart, skilled, competent people who help with the programming and getting the examples and the simulation studies done.

As is common at the graduate level in biomedical sciences, I have a relatively light teaching load: one seven-week course per year, which involves two lectures per week, given mostly by me, and one two-hour lab per week, guided by teaching assistants. The course generally has about ninety students, but I've been teaching it for three years, so I have a pretty established collection of lecture notes and prob-

lem sets. I am also on ten students' committees, and I have one doctoral student. I spend a fair amount of time helping them with their work. As a statistician, I'm also involved in collaborations with a number of other researchers in the Boston area. Right now I'm working on a long-term study of a hundred thousand nurses that looks at the health effects of diet, reproductive factors, and lifestyle factors; another study of the effects of diet on estrogen metabolism; an intervention study of vitamins A and E as possible preventive agents for the progression of HIV infection among women and their children in Tanzania; and a study of HIV and nutrition in a cohort of five hundred women and gay men. Working on those projects involves meeting with the other investigators once or twice a month to advise them about data management and analysis. I get very involved in the grant-proposal preparation by helping them design studies to maximize the amount of information they can get for the lowest cost.

Right now, I'm finishing up an analysis of a study that was done at numerous hospitals around the country looking at possible adverse health effects of occupational exposure to anticancer drugs among pharmacists and pharmacists' aides. The primary exposure assessment method was a questionnaire, which asked people to estimate how many times each week they mixed a list of about twenty different anticancer drugs. A 10 percent subsample of these eight hundred pharmacists kept a log at their bench where they wrote down exactly what they did every day for one to two weeks. For that sample and time and for those people, we know exactly how many drugs they mixed per week. Using this information, we can model the relationship between true and estimated exposure. We then use that model to correct for our estimates of the health effects of the exposure. The prevalence of fever among pharmacists who were mixing anticancer drugs was originally estimated as being increased by about 3 percent. After we correct for measurement error, the estimate increases twofold to about 7 percent. It makes quite a big difference, and can have an impact on policy in terms of determining what the maximum permitted exposures are, either in the workplace or in the environment as determined and enforced by the EPA and other regulatory agencies.

My work should have a closer relationship to policy setting, but it's a long road. I publish in two places. One is in statistical journals where I present some of the models I've developed and some of the methodologies I've worked out; it's all totally theoretical in terms of equations, and at the end there's an illustrative example. The other place I publish is in scientific journals, primarily epidemiological journals, where I try to demonstrate to other scientists that these methods are useful for adjusting measurement error and misclassification in their work. This is a long way from people actually using my models in original analyses that might then be used for policy and regulation. To date that hasn't happened. But I'm just now in the fifth year of my postgraduate career, and I think that I will eventually be more involved in those kinds of activities. It's a matter of establishing your credibility and reputation, of getting recognition among colleagues for quality work. It takes some time before people are comfortable with new ideas and are willing to consider them in terms of realistic applications as op-

posed to appreciating interesting theory from a distance.

If I could work more hours, I could probably get papers out more quickly. In this sense, men who can stay late and whose wives will make them dinner and let them go back to work afterwards have an advantage. At Harvard we're all essentially independent entrepreneurs, so nobody really cares whether I work twenty, forty, or eighty hours a week. But when I'm judged, they'll judge me on the quantity and quality of my work. I don't anticipate any problem with the quality, but there may be a problem with the quantity, and nobody will be interested in any excuses. It's considered a level playing field; and I guess there really is no equitable way to factor the extent of family commitments into promotion, tenure, and award decisions. Or perhaps there is a way and I'm just not creative enough to figure it out. There's no question that many men have support structures that enable them to work eighty hours a week; perhaps if men actually did half the work involved in caring for a family and running a smooth household, that would level the playing field.

Being in a same-sex relationship makes this much easier. If I were living with a man, I might have somebody doing one-tenth the work instead of a full half. I think that perhaps heterosexual women can compensate because their male partners often make more money and are further along in their career paths. There's more money in the household, so a lot of these people hire help to do the things Elaine and I do ourselves, although we do have some hired help: a woman comes in and cleans once a week, and Nessarose goes to her day-care center four days a week.

Being a lesbian hurts a little bit socially. I've experienced little overt homophobia, but I do encounter more subtle forms of discrimination. I think people are sometimes reluctant to include me and Elaine in social plans because they're uncomfortable with a lesbian couple. Work relationships are sometimes furthered socially, new ideas developed and new collaborations formed; I may be somewhat excluded from this social networking. But this is a fairly small thing. Being a lesbian also affects my relationships with my male colleagues. I rarely experience any advantage in terms of being considered a potential sex object for a man, but since that kind of interaction hurts women as much if not more than it helps them, I don't mind that people don't relate to me in that way. My strategy is to focus as exclusively as I can on doing the best job I can in the time I have to do it, and hope that there is enough of a meritocracy out there that when the time comes to judge me, my accomplishments will receive their due recognition.

All young women need to believe that they have as much right to math and science as boys and men do. And mothers of girls, by believing their daughters are brilliant and can do anything they set their minds to, like mine did, can help give their daughters the self-esteem they'll need to hang in there with dogged determination when the competition heats up. Girls can become incredible, brilliant mathe-maticians and scientists. There is exciting and important work to be done that women and girls will find immensely satisfying and fulfilling for a lifetime if only they follow their hearts and continue with their interests.

PRESENT POSITION: Associate Professor of Epidemiology and Biostatistics, Harvard School of Public Health

FIELD: Biostatistics and epidemiology

RESEARCH AREA: Developing new statistical methods for epidemiological research

EDUCATION: B.A. in Psychology (1977), Brandeis University; M.S. in Biostatistics (1985) and joint Sc.D. in Biostatistics and Epidemiology (1989), Harvard School of Public Health

DATE/PLACE OF BIRTH: August 30, 1955/Perth Amboy, New Jersey

Donna Spiegelman lives with her lover, Elaine Schear, and their two-year-old daughter, Nessarose Schear, in Boston, Massachusetts.

INTERVIEW DATE: October 1994

Lois Steele

Acting Director, Division of Health Services System Development, and Research Medical Officer, Division of Medical Systems Research and Development
INDIAN HEALTH SERVICES, TUCSON, ARIZONA

Lois Steele is a member of the Fort Peck Assiniboine-Sioux Tribes, and she was raised on the Fort Peck Reservation in Poplar, Montana. She began medical school at age thirty-four, and her current research focuses on cervical cancer, one of the leading cancers of American Indian and Alaskan Native women. She views research as a way of life: when she observes things, she needs to check them out. She has danced all her life and currently performs with the "Hot Flashes," an over-fifty tap-dance group.

⤜

I see patients and do epidemiological research for the Public Health Service at the Indian Health Service (IHS) in Tucson, Arizona. I also do ethical reviews—especially if a tribe requests them—on research that involves the IHS, especially in regard to their records or money.

My current research focuses on epidemiology, and specifically on risk factors for cervical dysplasia, a precancerous condition of the cervix. Cervical cancer is one of the leading cancers of American Indian and Alaskan Native women, and I'm interested in knowing why. It doesn't make sense for our population here in the Southwest to have this high incidence of cervical cancer when you look at the accepted risk factors such as multiple sex partners. Some work would indicate that our high incidence could be connected to a dietary folic acid deficiency. If it is dietary, we may be able to correct it. We are exploring other risk factors as well.

I also work with the IHS national Institutional Review Board (IRB), as well as the In-tertribal Council Review Board, to ensure that the research done with our people is ethical and that the research subjects understand what they are answering or allowing to happen. Trying to make sure people are not hurt by research is very complicated. When good things come out of the research, however, it can be very rewarding.

Most of my work involves the other doctors, researchers, statisticians, and health-systems experts at the IRB. Together we are responsible for the bulk of the research programs. One colleague is the AIDS coordinator for the area,

Lois Steele, age twenty-eight, as a schoolteacher on the reservation at Fort Peck, Poplar, Montana

one is the psychiatrist, another the clinic director. Because my work is largely epidemiological, most of my research involves analyzing patient charts and outcomes.

For me, there is no typical day, but I spend a lot of time teaching. The term *physician* is closely associated with the word *teacher,* and I consider what I do most days to be teaching: I visit tribes and teach about disease states and risk factors and what can be changed; I also speak at conferences and give presentations. No day is the same: on some days, I start out in the clinic seeing patients and reviewing Pap smear and biopsy reports. Sometimes we work on issues for budget requests—things most likely to generate questions during congressional hearings; these types of jobs always seem to have to be done within a day at IHS! Variety is work as usual.

As a member of the Fort Peck Assiniboine-Sioux Tribes, I was raised on the Fort Peck Reservation in Poplar, Montana. When I was born, my father worked for the Bureau of Indian Affairs and was assigned to Washington, D.C. My parents divorced. My mom then remarried but divorced again, and raised six of us by herself on a shoestring budget on the reservation. She didn't worry one way or another about education. She didn't push us to go to school, and she didn't discourage it. She let each of us be his or her own person. Luckily, the reservation had a good library—and a great librarian—and all six of us became fairly well educated. All but one has finished college, and he's the smartest of the bunch. A brother and sister each have their Ph.D.'s, another brother has a master's in social work, and I have an M.D. Another sister was pre-veterinary but could not go on; now she runs a boys' club for inner-city kids.

Growing up in Montana, I had a good sense of women as risk takers and explorers. The first woman congressperson, Jeanette Rankin, came from Montana; she was legendary when I was growing up. I always had a sense that women from Montana were different. I remember the story of how my grandfather once made the mistake of telling my grandmother how to herd horses; she told him where to put the horses and rode off. Of course, he lost the herd. Maybe I'm not qualified to speak for white, middle-class America, but I do know that women in Montana in the 1940s and 1950s had to be risk takers; otherwise they wouldn't survive on that prairie.

I got married very young. Not many Indians went to college in the middle to late fifties. Very little federal grant money was available at the time. Nevertheless, my husband and I both left the reservation for college because he had a football scholarship and I got an academic scholarship and student-teaching assistantship. I got my bachelor's degree in zoology and returned to Rocky Mountain College in Billings, Montana, to teach in the Health and Physical Education Department. Right after graduation I tried graduate school but for personal reasons returned to Montana and to public-school teaching for ten years. I didn't have much money, so I earned my master's degree in biology at the University of Montana in the summers while I was teaching. Mostly I taught math and coached, although I liked to teach science. I could always get a job coaching at a college because I was good and they needed women coaches. But my real love was teaching biology, and I had to fight to teach it. I didn't begin medical school until I was thirty-four, but I always had an interest in research. I first did research my senior year in college, and then again for my master's degree in biology, but medical school really opened the research door for me. I think some of us live research our whole lives, no matter where we are or who we associate with; when we observe things, we feel the need to check them out. This is research that goes beyond test tubes; it is a way of life.

Something I've always conveyed to my own children is that they need to be their own people. I have two daughters, three granddaughters, and a grandson. Throughout my career my kids were very good. If one needed more attention, the other one just rolled with it and seemed to understand. What was important to them, I tried to make important; and what was important to me, they tried to make important. As a single mother, I could set priorities, and that often meant the floors got vacuumed every two weeks instead of every other day. Today, my girls both have careers they care about, and I am happy for them. I believe you should enjoy what you are doing, not because it is going to get you anywhere but because you want to do it. That's what my mother taught me and what I taught them.

I know I have been discriminated against at times in my career. I think any minority woman who says she hasn't been is either trying to gloss over it or isn't watching what's happening. Discrimination is real in schools, in industry, and in government. I've taken a low-key approach when it has happened to me because there was little I could do without my career suffering. But if it happens to anyone else, and if I have the power to make a change, I make the change. I sit on the Committee on Women in Science and Engineering of the National Academy of Sciences, and we think a lot about how to make science better for women at all levels. I believe we need to reach girls very young if they are to consider science careers. If women only understood that every good cook who experiments with recipes is doing research, we'd have more women in science and more men cooking!

I urge young women—if they have an opportunity—to first visit an undergraduate or graduate school they are interested in attending and talk to the women faculty. If there are no strong women on a faculty, then women students aren't going to be treated well. The best way to evaluate a potential mentor is to consider whether he or she really looks at you as another person, not just as a token minority or woman, or as a student whose labor can be used. All people, but especially women, need mentors who truly appreciate them as people. Mentoring is so critical and so underplayed.

When I consider who helped me make it, I remember the women: Rosalie Wax, an anthropologist who taught a summer course I took at the University of Colorado, was in-

Lois Steele at age fifty-six in her Hot Flashes T-shirt

strumental in my finishing college; Nancy Furstenberg, a physician at Henry Ford Hospital in Michigan, taught me about medical school administration; and I was fortunate to work at medical school with Judy Demers, who later became a state senator in North Dakota. I have had real support from both men and women who are now lifelong friends. A number of men have also believed in me: John Williams, John Vennes, Jim Bouldger—who was the dean of students at the University of Minnesota Medical School—and Charlie Erickson, who is my supervisor right now. My friends continue to be very important to me.

I've danced all my life and now perform with the "Hot Flashes," an over-fifty tap-dance group. It is fun to be with these lively women— one member of our group is eighty-six years old. We dance at state fairs, reviews, and competitions all over town. I think it is important to be comfortable with being a woman, and I have been lucky to meet many strong women. Tap dancing helps keep things in perspective, so I don't take myself too seriously.

I truly love my work. I am a curious person, and my curiosity has always motivated me. I've always known you can learn from anyone and from anything you do, and that the key is to continue to learn. If I characterize how I was different from the girls who grew up around me, it was that I really wanted to know answers, and I really didn't give a damn what anyone else thought. I guess I still pretty well fit that mold.

PRESENT POSITIONS: Acting Director, Division of Health Services System Development, and Research Medical Officer, Division of Medical Systems Research and Development, Indian Health Services, Tucson, Arizona

FIELD: Family-practice medicine

RESEARCH AREA: Epidemiological research

EDUCATION: B.A. in Zoology and Sociology (1961), Colorado College; M.S. in Biology (1969), University of Montana; M.D. (1978), University of Minnesota

DATE/PLACE OF BIRTH: November 27, 1939/ Washington, D.C.

Lois Steele lives in Tucson with her grandson, Hunter, and is an enrolled member of the Fort Peck Assiniboine-Sioux Tribes on Assiniboine rolls.

INTERVIEW DATE: July 1995

Olga Victoria Taller

Manager of Infrastructure for the Internet and
International Systems Development Department
PRODIGY SERVICES COMPANY

Growing up Jewish in the USSR, Olga Taller was never a stranger to adversity. She had few options or opportunities until she and her husband and daughter arrived in the United States as "refugees," and she suddenly had to adapt to her new home: finding jobs and child care, as well as learning a new language and culture. She's learned how to make decisions, stand up for her ideas, and manage diverse groups of people—skills that have brought her through the ranks at Prodigy to her present entrepreneurial post.

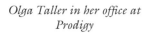

I believe that it is very important to understand your own strengths and weaknesses, and to try to live within your environment but also know when you must move on. This philosophy has helped me personally and professionally throughout my entire life. I was born in Moscow in 1957. One of the first people to

be honest with me was my high school tutor; she was the first person to tell me what anti-Semitism was about in the Soviet Union. Most Jewish children had tutors in the tenth grade, especially in math and physics, to help them prepare for college. My tutor oversaw five girls, three Russian and two Jewish. She was especially strict with us Jewish girls because we were under code no. 5, a Russian law requiring Jews to take harder tests in their precollege exams. She was relentless in terms of my studies, but she knew what I would be facing.

I finished high school at sixteen and then attended the Moscow College of Economics and Statistics in the evening. Even with tutoring, the college entry tests were extremely difficult, and I was only able to qualify for night classes. Because of this, I was required to have a daytime job, which made me eligible to attend evening college. Fortunately, my father was director of a technical school and worked

Olga Taller in her office at Prodigy

with statistics. A good friend of his who worked for the Central Statistical Agency of the Russian Republic helped get me a daytime job as a computer operator in an area related to my studies. My schooling was paid for by the government, and the pay helped with my living expenses.

Anti-Semitism shaped my life in Russia. At nineteen, while I was still in college, I went for a job interview at the Research Institute of Russia, part of the Central Statistic Agency of the Soviet Union. My interviewer was particularly nasty, and even though I knew anti-Semitism was a government policy and not necessarily a personal antipathy, she made me cry. Nonetheless, I was hired and earned 120 to 130 rubles per month—which I called "unemployment money" because the pay was so low. The Research Institute presented me with my first real computer programming assignment. It should have been stimulating, but, in reality, we were re-creating programs already invented in the United States. The job was limiting, and while I was able to use my academic knowledge, I didn't have the opportunity to gain any real business savvy.

Shortly after joining the Research Institute I met Alex Taller, a very bright computer programmer who was later to become my husband. Alex was a Muscovite who because of government rules was no longer able to live in Moscow. His wife had been from Moscow, but when I met him, he was in the midst of getting a divorce. Even today, to live anywhere in Russia you must have a *propiska*. This is a permanent assignment to live in a certain city or town; you get one by being born there or marrying someone who lives or has a job there. Once divorced, Alex no longer had legal permission to live in Moscow. As you can imagine, many people ended up marrying for legal reasons, but Alex and I married for love.

Times were difficult, and after several years of marriage Alex and I made the very tough decision to emigrate from the Soviet Union. If you were Jewish and refused to join the Communist Party—a description that fit both of us—there were no long-term careers in

Russia. The government wasn't concerned with whether you were a man or woman but rather focused on where you were born and on what your status was. Alex was ten years older than I and had reached his career ceiling; there was no place for him to go. While I was only twenty-two when we made the decision, it was clear the future would hold the same for me.

Although it was very difficult, Alex and I told my family about our plans to emigrate. My father was very much against it; my mother, who was less political, was more or less neutral. My father had been a member of the Communist Party since 1942. He had helped build the party and dedicated his life and health to it—he was mesmerized by communism. He had a Ph.D. and was a professor of the political economy of Marx, Engels, and Lenin. Our decision had far-reaching consequences. Because of our emigration plans, my father was ashamed of me. He moved out of the house, divorced my mother after seventeen years of marriage, and reported to the committee director of the local Communist Party. By promising us a two-room apartment, which was very luxurious, he tried to convince us to change our minds and stay in Russia. But we had made our decision, which became even harder because the government made us wait two years to leave the country.

During that long delay I graduated from college; but because of my plans to emigrate, I received a "B" rating on my diploma, rather than an "A" for six years of honors work. I also came under pressure to quit my job with the Research Institute and was expelled from the Young Communist League, where I had been a member since age fourteen. Our emigration date became indefinite. With months and possibly years ahead of us, Alex and I made the decision to start a family. In March 1981 our daughter, Anya, was born. Finally by January 1982 the government let a small number of Jews out of Russia—only about two thousand for the year—and we were given three weeks to leave. At the time I was twenty-four years old.

Before we left, I went to visit my father, who was ill and in the hospital. He had severed his ties with us, but I had to say goodbye. It was the last time I would ever see him. After that visit, the only way he could stay in touch with what we were doing was to meet my mother in the park, where he secretly read my letters. Alex and I could only correspond with our mothers in Russia because no one else wanted to be associated with us. For many years my mother did not tell anyone we had emigrated—especially at work—because she would have lost her job and many of her friends.

We began our journey by going first to Vienna, Austria, and then to Italy, where we were considered refugees and could apply for an interview at the American embassy. I still remember our daughter, Anya, taking her first steps there. To help us financially, we brought things from our home to sell later. On April 6, 1982, we finally arrived in the United States. We lived in Queens, New York, for a few months, and then moved to Parkchester. Russian friends helped us adjust to the United States, and after three months Alex got a job as a programmer.

When I look back and reflect on all of this, it was in the United States that I really began to grow up. In Russia there had been no decision making; everything was predetermined. For the first time I had to look for a job myself, which was very difficult because I had not really worked for four years. I was also surprised to discover that child care was much harder to find in the United States than in Russia or Europe.

Thankfully, no language difference existed in computer programming, so in some respects that made it easier for me to get a job. I started working for Merrill Lynch in New York City as a consultant. I was on my own for the first time in my life, and my first shopping experience for career clothes was overwhelming. I was even scared to go into Woolworth's because it was so big. In some ways, growing up as an only child, I had not been exposed to many hardships or challenges.

Now I had to change dramatically—and learn to make decisions—in my first year in a new country. As a computer programmer, I also grew up five years in one.

My role model at Merrill Lynch was a fifty-year-old black woman. Mildred was everything I needed and wanted to be: technical, extremely smart, logical, and very pleasant. In Russia there were no blacks, and they were either portrayed as oppressed or as muggers and robbers. Mildred was a hard worker, and she took care of her whole family, including nieces and nephews. She really changed my life: she showed me I could achieve something, no matter what my background. She helped me to discover *who* I was.

Soon after we arrived, my family and I moved to White Plains. The commute into New York City meant leaving before eight in the morning and getting home at seven or even later. It seemed like I never saw Anya. When we began thinking of having a second child, I decided I needed a job closer to home. I got one at Lincoln Savings Bank, a warm, friendly place to work. I must admit I was a snob when I first got there because I had worked in New York City. I started as a programmer in a data processing department of twenty to thirty people and quickly became the database administrator. I went to Dallas for training—my first travel in the United States. I also had my second child, Arnold, and went back to work part-time when he was seven-and-a-half months old. I worked at Lincoln another year, but it was not challenging enough for me.

About this time, I learned of a job opening at Trintex—now Prodigy Services Company—and wrote my first résumé by hand to get the interview. My employment agent typed my résumé for me! Trintex hired me as one of its first full-time staff mainframe programmers. As the job and the company progressed, I built several technical systems myself, which helped bring the output of the content creation tools into a form ready to be delivered or transferred to the central database. This allowed information to be accessed by Prodigy service members. In technical terms, I "owned" these systems, and some of them still exist within the Prodigy® architecture.

At Prodigy I really learned to think and design, but I also began to stand up for my ideas. All my bosses were male, and at first I thought they were always right and I could never be like them. A number of them saw that I had potential and respected what I could do. I discovered a hidden talent—getting my technical people to work well with the creative staff: the artists, writers, and application designers. This was the point at which I started to realize how very important it is to understand one's own strengths and weaknesses. I had to figure out how to deal with all the smart, opinionated guys on my staff—and I did. Some of my bosses didn't care about or understand what my group and I were doing, but I could go to a few of them to brainstorm, increase my own knowledge, and then apply what I learned on the job.

Over a period of several years, I moved up to advisory programmer analyst, then manager of advanced connectivity, and today manager of infrastructure for the Internet and International Systems Development Department. At first, I was frightened to be a manager, but now I have managed other managers and because of my entrepreneurial management style have creative, senior-level technical people working for me who have skills on the leading edge of technology. My group has always been ahead of the company technically, a source of pride and joy to me. I oversee one of the most desirable technical groups at Prodigy; people come to me wanting to be hired.

I've come a long way from Moscow, thanks to my employees' creativity and their willingness and drive to test the unexplored. My group came up with several ways to take the Prodigy® service into the future, which included developing the technology for a new generic electronic gateway. This achievement was never assigned to us but was designed for our own local use in the department. It became one of the hottest designs in the company and an integral part of the Prodigy® ar-

chitecture. Now every new client application can be live on the service in just two months, rather than two years. We used our technology to add such popular clients as the *Los Angeles Times* and *Newsday* to the service. The work represented a whole new future for Prodigy®.

Our gateway development also enabled us to build Prodigy® "Chat" and to connect the Prodigy® service to the expansive world of Internet services. My technical people were the ones to highlight for the company the importance of the Internet. Long before it was mainstream, we convinced the marketing department of the value of a connection with the Internet. Marketing's prediction for our Internet mail gateway release was 8,000 pieces of mail a month; in about six months we were processing 1.5 million pieces per month. Two years later we are processing 3.5 million pieces of mail each month. My group also convinced the business side of our company to bring in another Internet service called USENET newsgroups, an Internet-wide bulletin board system. Early on, my technical people realized the importance of the Internet influence on the industry as a whole, and they were right on target.

I was recently promoted to manager of infrastructure for the Internet and International Systems Development. My department is building a new type of business within the Prodigy company walls. I've been able to break out of the confines of the legacy system, and my new group will be building a venture that is affiliated with Prodigy® but will not be the same as that service. I'm the first manager on this new venture, so Prodigy has shown real faith in me. The task is entrepreneurial, and I'm bringing in a new group of employees to do the work.

From time to time, our Human Resources Division has recommended that I employ a woman or minority, but I remind them that when I have a job opening I'm looking for a particular set of skills. I have always wanted people to hire me because of my strengths, knowledge, and experience—not because I am a woman. I was not raised with a male/female prejudice, and I've learned that if you stand up for what you believe in, and what you really want to do most, anyone can be a success.

PRESENT POSITION: Manager of Infrastructure for the Internet and International Systems Development Department, Prodigy Services Company

FIELD: Computer science

SPECIALTY: Internet systems development

EDUCATION: B.S. (1980) in Computer Science, College of Economics and Statistics, Moscow

DATE/PLACE OF BIRTH: August 23, 1957/ Moscow, Russia

Olga Taller lives in Hartsdale, New York, with her husband, Alex, and their two children, Anya and Arnold.

INTERVIEW DATE: January 1996

Sonja Teraguchi

Curator of Invertebrate Zoology
CLEVELAND MUSEUM OF NATURAL HISTORY

Sonja Teraguchi's mother taught her a love of problem solving and a sense of independence. She grew up observing the flora and fauna of her native British Columbia, so it wasn't surprising that zoology became her mania. After a brief stint as a stay-at-home wife, she enrolled in a Ph.D. program. Today, as a curator at a museum of natural history, Dr. Teraguchi has been able to fulfill her greatest goal—contributing to the preservation of nature.

❧

I never had a notion that I would become a scientist. Growing up, I didn't know any scientists. Women didn't do those sorts of things in the 1950s in British Columbia. I was taught that my role in life was to be a selfless helper: that's what women did. But my very independent mother passed on her resentment of being told what to do, so I've always tried to avoid what I was "supposed to do" as a woman. Still, that selfless-helper image has been hard to shed. My mother also taught me to find delight in problem solving. She never had science in school, but she had a very scientific approach to solving problems. She made observations, made guesses about what could have caused the things she observed, and tried various ways to determine which of her guesses was accurate. I now know that's science. Given my mother's influence, it isn't surprising that I became a scientist.

As a child, I spent a lot of time at our family's fishing camp on Shuswap Lake and fell in love with nature. I didn't know it at the time, but all of the things I observed—the eagles, the butterflies, the fish—became a big part of my psyche. When I was about ten years old, I found and caught a horse that had gotten away from its owner. I was devastated when the owner came to claim it. At that moment, I decided I was going to be a veterinarian so I could look after animals. I sent away to the traveling library and got some old books on being a veterinarian. The books offered practical tips about what to do if your cow should get sick. One book said that if a cow gets bloated for some reason, to help her you must stick a knife into her abdomen to let the air out. I couldn't imagine doing that to any poor animal, so that put an end to my first career choice.

By the time I got to high school, my future path was still uncertain. Many of my peers

Sonja Teraguchi on her graduation from the University of British Columbia, 1962

chose to go to two-year schools to become teachers, nurses, or secretaries. Some of them got pregnant and dropped out of high school. Fortunately, I had a math teacher, Mr. McKie, who encouraged me. I began thinking I would be a mathematician because I seemed to do math very well. Mr. McKie convinced me that I could do whatever I wanted to do. He helped me get into the University of British Columbia, and that was all it took. I majored in two subjects: zoology because I loved it, and math because of Mr. McKie.

More opportunities came along for me in zoology than in math. Jeffrey Scudder, a young entomologist from Oxford, joined the faculty in our department. He hired me to work for him while I was still an undergraduate. He was doing very interesting things—going to lakes out in the Caribou to study the insects. I got very interested in trying to figure out why things were. It became a mania—it was so exciting to figure something out. I found that I had a weakness for the animal world, and the minute there was an opportunity to study it, I dropped everything else.

When I graduated, I felt I had to follow the old prescription of having a husband and helping him. I married someone who was also a zoology student. Fortunately, I had the luck of the draw. Anybody who wanted to could have taken advantage of this helper training I'd had, but my husband was a very independent person; he didn't need a clinging vine, nor did he want one. He loved fish and studied things in fresh water, so we moved to the University of Wisconsin in Madison so that he could study to be a limnologist. But when I got a job to earn money to buy my husband a car and I baked him bread, it drove him nuts. It soon became obvious to both of us that being a helper wasn't for me. In the meantime, I had met a number of women who were normal and caring people—not selfish, horrible witches—and they had Ph.D.'s. It was the first time I had met female professional academic role models. It was truly wonderful. I applied to the University of Wisconsin to get a Ph.D. in zoology.

Two experiences have turned out to be really important in my current work. As I was growing up, I saw the destruction of the Shuswap Lake area. Houses were built in all the special places I used to go. I saw a bulldozer rip down the cliffs where calypso orchids grew. I saw nature losing out, and it became a fundamental issue for me. Also, the people of the First Nations that I knew while growing up were being treated very poorly. They had a low view of themselves. My grandparents were homesteaders and would never have survived without the help of the Salish in the Squamish Valley. I knew the Salish to be clever, helpful people; but just like the natural habitats that I loved, they were losing out. I became interested in what happens to people of the First Nations when their culture clashes with newer populations. These experiences influenced what I studied and the job I eventually took. They also influenced my drive to do science.

My first daughter was born soon after I started graduate school. People were very tolerant and very accommodating. My department gave me a tiny room to use for my experiments and for nursing my newborn. The lecture hall had a projection booth that I would sit in when I needed to take my daughter with me to a lecture. My thesis was on the *Chaoborus* larva, a fly that hangs in water and regulates its buoyancy. It was an insect physiology problem that I just had to figure out. To do fieldwork, I would strap my baby on my back and take her with me. I started my Ph.D. in 1968, in the midst of the antiwar movements. We had guards on campus because of the riots. There was an Army math research center right below my lab; and because some students believed that the research being done there was contributing to the war, they blew up the building. All I could think of was how my experiment was going to be ruined. A snow fence had been installed to keep people out of the area. Even though I was like a little pumpkin at eight months pregnant, somebody boosted me over the fence, and I sneaked into the building to see if my aquarium had been broken. The windows had been blown out of the building but my experiment was still intact.

When my husband graduated, he left for Cleveland to take a faculty appointment at Case Western Reserve University. I wasn't quite finished with my degree but followed about a month later and finished my thesis there. After I got my degree, I couldn't leave Cleveland to pursue a career; I needed to stay with my family. My first job was doing an insect survey of a local watershed. Then I got a job as a half-time lecturer and was eventually hired on as faculty at Case Western. It was OK, but I soon realized that a faculty position wasn't really what I wanted. When a position opened in the Museum of Natural History in 1980, I accepted. The job gave me the opportunity to work on environmental issues in addition to working on different scientific problems involving insects.

In my work as a curator at the Museum of Natural History, I'm responsible for the collections and objects related to invertebrates at the museum. This includes shells, insects, and spiders. In addition, I do some teaching of college students and give lectures to people of all ages, from little children to senior citizens. We teach science in a much broader sense than it's taught in college. The museum's mission is to teach people about science and so pass on an appreciation of natural history and the natural world. I also have research projects that involve solving problems that I want to pursue. I have freedom to research what I want, although I have to write proposals to get the funding. Even with the freedom I have, when I chose a project, I keep in mind the mission of the museum.

My latest project is on the population dynamics of insects, whose numbers go up and down continuously. If it's a pest, it causes concern because it eats up the grain or is a hazard in some other way. But if it is an insect like the monarch butterfly, we need to know if their numbers are just naturally fluctuating or if they are dying out. Studies on population re-

quire at least ten years of quantitative data in order to do a mathematical analysis, but fifty to a hundred years would improve accuracy. I'm in my last year of a ten-year study of moths that come to lights in deciduous forests in northeast Ohio. At the eight sites that I have been monitoring, I've documented eight hundred species. I've collected and identified about twenty thousand moths each year, and then computerized the findings by building a database. This data will allow me to identify which species' populations fluctuate, which other species are moving in and becoming abundant, and which species are dying out.

One of the reasons I chose moths is because they come when they are called. I don't have to climb a tree or run around with a net: a light trap does all the work. Some moths live in the tree canopy, some live in leaf litter, and some live in tiny plant stems. I try to determine what is driving down the population of the moths living in the canopy of older trees. In some cases, a decline in population follows a drought or other natural occurrence, but sometimes the decline seems to have no cause. This is a clue that there is something causing a deterioration in the canopy that is affecting the populations of species that live there. Science always leads you from question to question. In this case, I ask what is going on in the canopy that isn't going on elsewhere. In this part of the world, we know that the older trees are not being replaced. We're down to forest remnants, so the trees are aging, but they are also affected by diseases, new insect populations, human-made contaminants, and the quality of the precipitation and the air. The moths can tell us what's going on in the environment; they are indicators of the larger world.

In the early 1970s, I used to go to nearby Resthaven Park to study leafhoppers because I was interested in their migration. Hanging from the red milkweed were these wonderful butterflies with big silver spots on them. Then one year I realized I didn't see any. Although everyone could remember seeing a lot of

Sonja Teraguchi collecting moth specimens in Lake County, Ohio, near the Grand River, 1993

them fifteen years ago, no matter how hard we look, we can't find any in this area now. There are about five species of insects that for some reason—and it may be mostly habitat destruction—we know don't exist in Ohio anymore. By the time we realized they were missing, it was too late. Many endangered species have died out this way. We usually don't have any idea why a species' population has declined, so we make a lot of silly choices when trying to strengthen their numbers. I hope to contribute data that the scientific community can use to make better decisions for protecting species.

I tell as many people as I can about what I learn. On this current project, I am working with the U.S. Forest Service, and they have provided me with funding. Since they are charged with managing pest insects in the forest, they need to know what's going on and what's going to happen. I also publish in entomological and ecological journals because people are interested in what drives the population fluctuations. Occasionally the local government will call me for reports on my findings of the local ecology. They want to hear the truth so if something is being affected by industrial waste or habitat destruction, they have a chance to make changes before it's too late.

My two daughters are grown and are pur-

suing careers in different medical professions. My husband died in 1991. I truly miss him. If I had married a different person, I might not have been able to pursue my work. He was a seven-day-a-week scientist and never noticed if I didn't comb my hair. We never got mad at one another if one of us had to go out at six o'clock on a Sunday morning to do fieldwork. Often we would take the girls and go together. We helped him measure fish, and they helped me sort the insects.

You can't do science unless you have a mania for it. It takes so much work, you can't just do it nine to five; you have to put your body and soul into it. How far you get, how deep you get, how comprehensive your problem solving is—all of these depend on whether you're immersed in it. If you suddenly remember that you forgot to pick up your child and now she's late for her music lesson, those distractions make it much harder. It wasn't possible for me to take the traditional route of just staying home with the kids; on the other hand, it never occurred to me not to have children.

I was very influenced by the prescriptions of my youth. Often I felt caught in the middle—not doing my "womanly duties" properly and not fulfilling my scientific calling to its full potential. I felt guilty. But now I know that women shouldn't feel guilty about their dual callings. There are many levels of participation in problem solving and each level is okay. Whatever choice you make, just do it to your fullest.

PRESENT POSITION: Curator of Invertebrate Zoology, Cleveland Museum of Natural History

FIELD: Zoology

RESEARCH AREA: Insect ecology

EDUCATION: B.S. in Zoology and Mathematics (1962) and M.S. in Zoology (1964), University of British Columbia; Ph.D. in Zoology (minor in Biochemistry) (1972), University of Wisconsin, Madison

DATE/PLACE OF BIRTH: May 13, 1941/Kamloops, British Columbia

Sonja Teraguchi lives in Cleveland Heights, Ohio, with her oldest daughter, who is in medical school at Case Western Reserve. Her other daughter is studying to be a physiotherapist in Miami.

INTERVIEW DATE: November 1995

Karen Uhlenbeck

Professor and Sid W. Richardson Foundation Regents Chair in Mathematics
UNIVERSITY OF TEXAS AT AUSTIN

Karen Uhlenbeck is an avid lover of nature, a mathematician, and a member of the American Academy of Arts and Sciences and the National Academy of Sciences. Her interest in math arose, in part, from her preference to work alone, her natural bent for abstraction, her love of ideas, and her lack of success in undergraduate physics. Although she faced blatant sexism early in her career, she never took it personally, realizing that prejudice treats a person as a member of a class or group instead of as an individual.

❧

M y first love is the outdoors—I enjoy mountain climbing, backpacking, hiking, canoeing, swimming, and bicycling. Many of these interests I inherited from my parents who, at age eighty-three, are still hiking and backpacking. I am at home in nature, and when I can't be out in the wilderness, I can often be found in my garden at my home in Austin. That's the real me. My day-to-day life is something very different.

I am a mathematician. Mathematicians do exotic research, so it's hard to describe exactly what I do in lay terms. I work on partial differential equations, which were originally derived from the need to describe things like electromagnetism; but they have undergone a century of change in which they have come to be used in a much more technical fashion to look at even the shapes of space. Mathematicians look at imaginary spaces constructed by scientists examining other problems. I started out my mathematics career by working on Palais's modern formulation of a very useful classical theory, the calculus of variations. I decided

Einstein's general relativity was too hard, but I managed to learn a lot about the geometry of space-time. I did some very technical work in partial differential equations, made an unsuccessful pass at shock waves, worked in scale-invariant variational problems, made a poor stab at three manifold topology, learned gauge field theory and then something about applications to four manifolds, and have recently been working in equations with algebraic infinite symmetries. I find that I am bored with anything I understand. My excuse is that I am too

Karen Uhlenbeck in her office in the Department of Mathematics at the University of Texas at Austin, 1995

poor an expositor to want to spend time on formal matters.

As a young academic I worked by myself a lot. In fact, that was one of the attractions of mathematics for me. I am the eldest of four children, and I consider dealing with my siblings the hardest thing I've ever done in my life. That had a great impact on my choosing a career—I wanted a career where I didn't have to work with other people. I've always been competitive, but I find it difficult to cope with the attitudes of people who lose. It is still attractive to work in an area where I compete only with myself and don't have to deal with the negative aspects of competition. As my career advanced, however, I found I had a lot to learn from other people of all sorts. I have found it very rewarding to deal with younger mathematicians, and I now truly enjoy collaborative projects.

I can't say that I was really interested in mathematics as a child or adolescent, mostly because one doesn't really understand what mathematics is until at least halfway through college. As a child I read a lot. I read everything, including all the books in our house three times over. I'd go to the library and then stay up all night reading. I used to read under the desk in school. My whole family were and still are avid readers; we lived in the country, so there wasn't a whole lot else to do. I was particularly interested in reading about science. I was about twelve years old when my father began bringing home Fred Hoyle's books on astrophysics. I found them very inspiring. I also remember a little paperback book called *One, Two, Three, Infinity* by George Gamow, and I remember the excitement of understanding this very sophisticated argument that there were two different kinds of infinities. I read all of the books on science in the local library and was frustrated when there was nothing left to read.

I grew up in New Jersey, and since there wasn't a state university at the time, I went to the University of Michigan. Both of my parents were in the first generation of people in their families to go to college—my father was

an engineer, my mother an artist—so there was never a question that I would go to college. I wanted to go to MIT or Cornell, but my parents decided that those institutions were too expensive and the University of Michigan was affordable. I was lucky enough to get into the honors program at Michigan. I had very advanced courses as a freshman and received a superb education. I had a junior-level math course that I found very exciting. I had intended to major in physics but decided to change majors when they started taking attendance in the physics lecture. I also had trouble with labs—I could not learn to look up answers in the back of the book and fudge the experiments. I could never seem to get the labs to come out right. So I switched to math and have been interested in it ever since.

There are three women Ph.D. mathematicians from my freshman honors class at Michigan. Some people at the University of Michigan have a theory to explain this phenomenon of success rates of women from their honors program during this time period: bright women were not being sent to expensive private colleges, so they came to places like Michigan with honors programs. If we had been bright men, they suggest, our fathers would have forked out the money to send us to Ivy League schools.

After undergraduate school I spent a year (1964) at New York University's Courant Institute, but then I married a biochemist who was going to Harvard, so I switched to Brandeis. I had a National Science Foundation graduate fellowship at that time, so four years of my graduate school were paid for at a very luxurious rate. I was one of the people who benefited from Sputnik. There was a handful of women in my graduate program, although I was not close friends with any of them. It was evident that you wouldn't get ahead in mathematics if you hung around with women. We were told that we couldn't do math because we were women. If anything, there was a tendency not to be friendly with other women. There was blatant, overt discouragement, but also some subtle encouragement. A lot of people appreciated good students, male or female, and I was a very good student. I liked doing what I wasn't supposed to do; it was a sort of legitimate rebellion. There were no expectations because we were women, so anything we did well was considered successful.

I have always known that I was a really good mathematician. I have a natural bent for abstraction, and I love ideas of all sorts. I value time to be by myself and think about math—or other things; it doesn't matter. The noise of the world is a difficult thing for me to deal with. I have always had a hard time handling external stimuli.

My first husband's parents were older European intellectuals, and my father-in-law was a famous physicist. They were very influential in my life. They had a different attitude toward life than Americans. I remember my mother-in-law reading Proust and giving me her English version when she learned to read it in French. My in-laws valued intellectual things in a way that my parents didn't; my parents did value such things, but they believed that making money was more important. I don't think I would have survived at that stage of my career without the encouragement I got from my first husband's family.

After graduate school I had two temporary jobs. I taught for a year at MIT while my husband was finishing his Ph.D. in biophysics at Harvard, and then I went for two years to the University of California at Berkeley during the Vietnam War. I was not the only woman in my department in either school, and I must say that all of these women (my contemporaries) succeeded spectacularly, probably because they had made up their minds to do what they chose.

I'm still processing a lot of what happened during those years. I think that the lack of sympathy for feminism of some older women came in part from the fact that many of us were going along fine in our careers, and then somebody started shouting that you were nobody and you weren't supposed to be there. But there you were, and suddenly there was all this fuss about women. And now they *had* to hire women. It bewildered many of us. It's nice to know that maybe some of the roadblocks have been removed, but I bet that what actually happened was not very useful to anybody.

I was told, when looking for jobs after my year at MIT and two years at Berkeley, that people didn't hire women, that women were supposed to go home and have babies. So the places interested in my husband—MIT, Stanford, and Princeton—were not interested in hiring me. I remember being told that there were nepotism rules and that they couldn't hire me for this reason. When I challenged them on this issue years later, they didn't remember saying those things, and, interestingly enough, there were no nepotism rules "on the books." I would have rather they'd been honest and said they wouldn't hire me because I was a woman. Conversely, I would have been just as offended if they'd hired me *because* I was a woman. I want to be valued for my work as a mathematician, not because I'm a member of a particular group.

At that time people were saying all kinds of things about women, most of which had nothing to do with me personally. Prejudice is very rude because it treats you as a member of a class or group instead of as a person. People were tremendously rude.

I ended up at the University of Illinois in Champaign-Urbana because they hired me and my husband. In retrospect I realize how remarkably generous he was because he could have been at MIT, Stanford, or Princeton. I hated Champaign-Urbana; I felt out of place mathematically and socially, and it was ugly, bourgeois, and flat. I was lucky to receive a Sloan Fellowship, and instead of doing something mathematically useful, I took time off from teaching to rearrange my life. I had already met Lesley Sibner, who has since served me for many years as role model and adviser. I also started to work with Jonathan Sacks and was taught Teichmueller theory by Bill Abikoff. These were my first close mathematical contacts. I moved to Chicago, established what has proven to be a long-term relationship with Bob Williams (a somewhat older mathematician), and taught temporarily at Northwestern and then at the University of Illinois at Chicago Circle. I also became friends with S. T. Yau, whom I credit with generously establishing me finally and definitively as a mathematician.

I moved from Chicago Circle, with some regrets, to the University of Chicago in 1982, the same year I received a MacArthur Fellowship. It has been a struggle for me to come to grips with my own success. By looking around me at the fate of other women who wanted to be mathematicians, I can intellectually, if not emotionally, understand that this is not so surprising. Not that the fate of other women is surprising, but I really don't understand my success.

I think what has changed today is that people are tremendously more subtle, so that you don't know what it is you're up against. This is true not only for women but for a lot of young people. Young people today are up against the fact that most of the young scientists are coming from abroad, and so most of the people coming into academia are being trained somewhere other than the United States. No one ever talks about this phenomenon of who is actually succeeding in the sciences and engineering, which is foreign-born men and women. I try to talk about this with my students. It's difficult, however, because you're not supposed to talk about it. In the large classes of engineering students I teach, I'm seeing a lot more diversity—women, Hispanics, African Americans. Engineering and science can be done, not just by white, Anglo men.

I am currently at the University of Texas in Austin, and there are three women in the math department—two full professors and one associate professor. I run a relatively new mentoring program for women in mathematics. I am aware of the fact that I am a role model for young women in mathematics, and that's partly what I'm here for. It's hard to be a role model, however, because what you really need to show students is how imperfect people can be and still succeed. Everyone knows that if people are smart, funny, pretty, or well-dressed they will succeed. But it's also possible to succeed with all of your imperfections. It took me a long time to realize this in my own life. In this respect, being a role model is a very unglamorous position; partly it means showing people all your bad sides. I may be a wonderful mathematician and famous because of that, but I'm also very human.

PRESENT POSITION: Professor and Sid W. Richardson Foundation Regents Chair in Mathematics, University of Texas at Austin

FIELD: Mathematics

RESEARCH AREA: Partial differential equations

EDUCATION: B.S. in Mathematics (1964); University of Michigan; M.A. in Mathematics (1966), Brandeis University; Ph.D. in Mathematics (1968), Brandeis University

DATE/PLACE OF BIRTH: August 24, 1942/Cleveland, Ohio

Karen Uhlenbeck lives on ten acres in the hill country west of Austin with her partner, Bob Williams, who is also a mathematician, and with three cats, who are not mathematicians.

INTERVIEW DATE: February 1995

Judith R. Vergun

*Director, Native Americans in Marine Science Program; Program and Research Associate,
College of Oceanic and Atmospheric Sciences; Teaching Faculty, College of Agricultural Sciences*
OREGON STATE UNIVERSITY

*Judith Vergun has had three careers: she left
college to work as a high-fashion model and
followed that career through fifteen years and
two marriages. In her late thirties she went
back to school, supporting herself and her three
daughters by working as an equine
reproductive specialist. She's now an ecologist
with the philosophy that if you pursue "what
you have a burning desire to do, you'll be
successful and happy."*

❧

I'm an ecologist. I work with natural and
cultural resources, particularly on Native
American tribal lands, including ceded lands.
Indian tribes are sovereign nations. During
the 1800s, American Indians reserved small
portions of land for themselves ("reservations") and ceded large portions of land to the
U.S. government, under treaty agreements
stipulating that Indians would continue using
the ceded lands in "usual and accustomed"
ways. In theory these stipulations allow Indians to continue fishing, hunting, and gather-
ing in the traditional ways for sustenance and
harmony. In practice, non-Indian settlers on
ceded lands have plowed native plants under,
cultivated other crops, clear-cut timber, allowed animals to overgraze the rangelands,
dammed the rivers, and disallowed Indians
most of their treaty rights. Nevertheless, the
status of ceded lands is important in understanding Native people's rights and traditional land management practices. My natural
resource work involves Native people and
lands in the Pacific Northwest and Alaska.

I mostly study plant ecophysiology in natural systems—how particular plants survive
and interact in their own ecosystems. Right
now my research focuses on huckleberries
(*Vaccinium membranaceum*). Huckleberries
grow naturally in mountainous areas and have
traditionally been a very important food
source for people in the Pacific Northwest,
first Indians and eventually other settlers. My
associates and I look at what constitutes an
appropriately balanced ecosystem to provide
these plants an opportunity to grow and produce in a sustainable way. We have observed
that this plant, along with many others, is often out-competed in some ecosystems because of certain recent management practices.
One of these is the suppression of fire.

The impacts of fire suppression have been

*Judith Vergun during her modeling days, circa
1966*

a research interest of mine for some time. Fire is a natural event that initiates regeneration. It's a healthy part of the way natural systems work: fire helps clear underbrush, recycle nutrients, and stimulate healthy growth. In systems where huckleberries are found, we've suppressed fire because the areas are also timberlands and the priority has been to manage for timber. Now we're realizing that such a narrow focus is detrimental to other things in the system. Most systems have a natural fire-return cycle that is essential for their long-term health. If you let relatively healthy systems do what they're supposed to do by themselves, they usually regenerate in wonderful ways. We're trying to determine what happened naturally and what we need to do to reproduce natural cycles.

One location for our huckleberry research is on the Warm Springs Indian Reservation. Indians managed these systems for thousands of years. Systems that looked wild and natural really had many different kinds of treatments applied in special ways by Indian people who understood them and in particular the role of fire. In the huckleberry system, for example, we have investigated records and asked elders what the rotations were and which systems were managed in these ways. We're finding that some Native people employed a rotational burn of about every seven years in huckleberry fields.

We use the information provided by the tribes in conjunction with Western scientific techniques. For instance, we look at carbon dating in our existing vegetation to see how often fires went through, we perform assays in the lab to determine foliar and soil nutrients during plant growth and reproduction, and we monitor moisture regimes to determine how moisture (or its lack) impacts plants. We hope to combine "pure scientific" information with information based on traditional Indian practices to determine exactly what we can do to bring these systems back into a more sustainable balance. This will contribute to management for healthy biodiversity rather for only one product, like timber.

There are many unique challenges in this work. Indian people have proprietary rights to cultural information, and to do these studies we need to establish trust among everyone working on the project. Our work is a partnership between Indians and non-Indians: natural resource specialists, educators, scientists, community members, tribal elders, and culture and heritage committee members. Those of us doing Western science must understand what pieces of information are appropriate to publish and what details are considered sacred tribal information that it is not our place to reveal. Details of ceremonies and private cultural practices don't need to be in our research report, although information about those practices may be accessible through requests to the tribes.

One of my goals is to demonstrate that to have a successful program of any kind we need to include the stakeholders in the design of that program. I use this approach in my teaching as well. I'm specifically concerned with systemic reform in education: creating applied research participation opportunities for all students, encouraging students to use critical thinking skills, and designing culturally appropriate, nondiscriminatory curricula and curricular materials. I am a university member of the Oregon Indian Education Coalition of Post-Secondary Education (OIECPSE), a coalition of education specialists from nine tribes in Oregon.

I've recently developed a new class centered on these concerns. The class, Ecosystem Science of Pacific Northwest Indians, was designed by a group of American Indians and Alaska Natives to show what kind of science class could be offered at a university that would fit their notions of appropriate education. The instructors include an American Indian graduate student, Native people from the Pacific Northwest and Alaska who have been chosen by their people to participate, and myself. As far as I know, this is the first time a class like this has been offered anywhere. It provides each student an opportunity to challenge her or his prejudices and biases by looking at different views of the use of natural resources and attitudes about our global ecosystem. We look at whether we want to push our systems to ultimate production for capital gain or whether we want to manage our systems for balance and sustainability. Comparing traditional Indian views to Euro-American views on natural resource management is an interesting way to discuss these issues. Oregon State University (OSU) administrators and the College of Agricultural Sciences have been particularly supportive of this effort.

Quite frankly, I'm amused at myself when I realize that I've chosen to be part of a university system. I hated school from the time I was in third grade, for what I think were some very good reasons. It was mostly very boring. In the 1940s and 1950s, public education was quite different from what it is today, and largely militaristic. Students were told what to do and what to think, lectured at, and made to memorize lots of "facts" that in retrospect have turned out not to be facts at all. Critical thinking skills were not emphasized. Things are changing somewhat, but we're not there yet! Some time ago, I realized that to effect a change, complaints are not enough. One needs to become part of the work and change things from inside the system. One of the reasons that this is important to me is that I have three daughters; I want life to be different for them, and for all young people, both educationally and professionally. We have lost many valuable, creative thinkers and new ideas because students haven't fit with the system.

When I was in high school, I did the least possible amount of schoolwork and pursued my own outside interests. I grew up near some wonderful mountains in Utah and spent a lot of time in the forests. I'd skip school to go there. I would observe how things changed through the seasons, what plants grew, and what little insects were there. I made my own notes and enjoyed how it felt to be learning. I liked to draw, and I made many sketches of systems and changes through seasons. I didn't realize that I was doing what I call science to-

day: observing changes over time, recording them, then seeing how often the cycle replicated itself.

Another thing that took me away from school was work. My family was close, but we didn't have much money; so it was important for me to be gainfully employed, and I was happy for any excuse to miss school! I went to a university for one year following high school and just wasn't interested. Since I didn't belong to the dominant religion, I didn't much like living in Utah, and when I had the chance to move to San Francisco, I took off! I had an offer to do something that had never been a real interest or dream for me: the chance to spend a summer working for Christian Dior and other high-fashion designers to present their collections. A friend of mine was a high-fashion model, and she invited me to "do the season" with her. She said, "You're just the size, shape, and type they're looking for, and it will be a fun summer." The job lasted fifteen years.

It was during this time that I married my high school sweetheart, mainly because I was pregnant. Unfortunately, my first child, a son, died during his first week of life because of a heart condition. According to my medical doctor friends, this would be a relatively simple problem to repair today because of advanced technology. The loss of my son and the violent death of my father a few years later have been the two most devastating events in my life. When things like this happen, it seems that one has two choices: to let them ruin the rest of your life, or accept what has happened, be stronger for it, and get on with your life. I chose the latter. Eventually, my sweetheart and I divorced. I think that I was ready to accept the responsibilities of marriage, but he wasn't. How many twenty-two-year-olds are? Later I married a Russian man, and I now have three children from that marriage.

I found modeling to be a relatively easy but demanding job. I traveled around the world and was successful. I found it funny sometimes because all of my life I had very little interest in clothes. I preferred to find a comfortable outfit and wear it weeks at a time, with washings in between, eliminating the chore of deciding what to wear each day. I still don't like changing my clothes during the day, and shopping for clothes is more work than fun; but I really appreciate artful design, beautiful fabrics, texture, and color. After some years as a model, I started making television commercials, and eventually I worked behind the scenes in production.

All the years I worked in the fashion advertising industry, I was very unhappy with the way women were (and are) represented and looked at. It's always interesting to me that when I talk about my past as a high-fashion model in Paris, New York, and San Francisco, certain people assume that I'm not very smart. In fact, I don't talk about it much because I feel that it diminishes my credibility in science. Certainly, these attitudes are not fair, and I often think about how this paradigm is created by the way the advertising world depicts women: as objects, as sex kittens, and not as intelligent individuals. This remains a serious national problem.

During the sixties and seventies, I was active in the anti–Vietnam War movement and the Civil Rights movement, and other work on social change. I helped with publicity because of my work experience. I began thinking about going back to school. After fifteen years I thought, "I've been on top of my agency for many years and done almost everything in this field; it's been interesting, but I'd like to do something else."

Because I was particularly interested in the environment, I decided that I'd like to move to a quiet community with a more ecologically responsible perspective, and Oregon seemed like a good place. I had divorced my second husband a few years earlier. The marriage hadn't worked out for many reasons: he had some traditional ideas of the wife's role and didn't support my going back to school. He didn't see any reason for me to get an education beyond the little I already had. I was interested in many different things and really wanted to pursue them before I was too old

to do so. But the most important reason for the divorce was that while being well educated and respected professionally, he was ill tempered and abusive at home and favored the company of prostitutes and call girls. This was not my idea of a great marriage. Those were difficult times. There was no support for women in abusive circumstances, and, like many women, I had put on a happy face for the outside world. In my late thirties, I left my husband and some high-paying job opportunities to return to school. I earned my undergraduate, master's, and Ph.D. degrees all at Oregon State University because I didn't want to move my family again until we all finished school. Getting an education, spending time with my daughters, and supporting their educational goals was the focus of my life.

During this time, I began my second career—as an equine reproductive specialist. My undergraduate studies included an emphasis on reproduction and horses. For ten years, I worked with people who raise working and show horses. My job included training stallions to ejaculate into artificial vaginas so that I could collect the semen and artificially inseminate mares just prior to ovulation. A lot of people find this funny or awkward to talk about—and certainly, a lot of funny things happened. But for me it was a serious job, and it kept me afloat financially. My girls worked with me and learned that reproduction is an interesting and natural part of life. They helped me evaluate sperm cells under a microscope and learned about palpating mares' reproductive tracts to locate follicles on ovaries. They were present during foaling and assisted when necessary. They did all of this before reaching the age when human-sexuality classes were taught at school, so for them there were few surprises when it came time for that.

After earning my Ph.D. in ecology and science education, I started my third career as a university professor. Getting there wasn't easy. While earning my Ph.D., I encountered a couple of "good old boys." Institutional mechanisms and machinery are still not completely favorable to women in science, and I

Judith Vergun (center) with Treva (Peterson) Olivas (Navajo), program assistant, on left, and Georgi Zamora (Tsimpsian), undergraduate participant, Native Americans in Marine Science Program
PHOTO BY JONG WONG

experienced all the nightmares along the way. I've had to deal with sexual harassment and outright discrimination. I saw many younger women experiencing the same things who just said, "Who needs this? I'll go do something else." We lose a lot of good women because the system is not yet built to support them. If I'd been younger, I probably would have quit too, but I had too much invested. Also, my major professor (the third one—I dismissed the first two) was wonderfully supportive, as were many others. There really are *more* than "a few good men." In fact, there are many. One needs to seek them out, along with good women mentors for a balanced perspective.

During my doctoral quest, I took on people and injustices to the very small degree that I could, considering my limited position of power. But you're just not on an equal power basis with a department head, especially one who has no respect for a divorced woman who disagrees with his worldview. I had an airtight lawsuit against him and two of his buddies for discrimination, sexual harassment, and plagiarism but chose not to pursue it. While I most likely would have won the suit, it would have consumed all my time and energy, and I wouldn't have been able to finish my degree. I felt that I needed to finish, then become part of the system, to help create changes so that these things don't happen to others. I made

that choice deliberately, swallowed my pride, and continued in his department to a successful finish. There were other faculty members in the department and throughout the university who recognized and supported the value of my work, so I was able to ignore the oppression to some degree. For anyone in a similar position, I recommend finding a large support group of people who understand the decisions you're making and who acknowledge your academic and professional direction.

The work I was doing was innovative, which was a real threat to some people. Many women in science find this to be true. Also, gender issues enter the picture in many ways. If a woman has a great sense of humor and enjoys laughing at life's little absurdities while doing serious science, she is often described as "flip" and judged to be incapable of high-level scientific endeavors. Men who behave the same way are "great guys," good-natured scientists with clever senses of humor. There are many attitudes and behaviors that can threaten to pull the rug out from under you during your exhausting quest for the almighty Ph.D. My advice is to stick with it and finish. It's worth it.

My three daughters, Shannon, Sasha, and Anna, are my family and my best friends. They are very supportive. I gave up a relatively big income to return to school, and that dramatically affected our family lifestyle. My daughters were part of that choice. They got to vote about whether we would make the move. They were always included. I took them with me, and we did whatever it was together. They learned about intellectual curiosity, looking through microscopes, doing farmwork, and working with nature and natural systems. We agreed that even though we were living in a small community, we would travel as much as possible so that we wouldn't become too provincial. All three daughters have studied in different parts of the world and speak several languages. We really put each other through school. They also have earned interesting degrees: Shannon works in art direction and set design on major films; Sasha is a great comedian in television commercials and an entrepreneur in a couple of small businesses; Anna just earned her bachelor's degree from Smith College, where she graduated cum laude in chemistry, and she's considering medical school.

I've had three very different professions so far, and I've loved them all. I've learned that if you pursue your dreams—what you have a burning desire to do—you'll be successful and happy. I've learned to temper everything with a sense of humor because things happen that you don't expect. If you can see them as funny rather than devastating, it's a saving grace. You always need alternative plans so that if something doesn't work out, you just go on to the other meaningful thing you were think-ing of doing anyway. Flexibility is important; the process may be more important than the outcome. Find good people to work with; if you can work with people with whom there is a mutual respect, you have it made. My life has been fun, exciting, and sometimes exhausting. I look forward to what comes next. I've worked hard throughout my life to effect one kind of change or another, and now that I'm fifty-four it's rewarding to see that many of my goals have been realized. It just takes patience, tenacity, good friends, a sense of humor, good red wine, and a lot of love.

PRESENT POSITIONS: Director, Native Americans in Marine Science Program; Program and Research Associate, College of Oceanic and Atmospheric Sciences; Teaching Faculty, College of Agricultural Sciences, Oregon State University

FIELD: Ecology and science education

RESEARCH AREAS: Plant ecophysiology in natural systems

EDUCATION: B.S. in Reproductive Physiology/General Agriculture (1987), M.S. equivalent in Rangeland Resources (1991), Ph.D. in Ecology and Science Education (1993), Oregon State University

DATE/PLACE OF BIRTH: January 14, 1941/Salt Lake City, Utah

Judith Vergun lives on a small farm in Monmouth, Oregon, with various farmmates: raccoons, skunks, deer, squirrels, wild turkeys, and bats.

INTERVIEW DATE: February 1995

Lydia Villa-Komaroff

Associate Vice President for Research Administration and Professor of Neurology
NORTHWESTERN UNIVERSITY

Lydia Villa-Komaroff comes from a long line of strong Mexican American women: her maternal grandmother raised three children on her own and sold chemical toilets on horseback; her paternal grandmother was a curandera, *a healer; her great aunt was a schoolteacher; and her mother worked as a social worker, teacher, and registrar at a community college. Her father's encouragement of her mother's career and her husband's encouragement of hers were critical in Lydia Villa-Komaroff's own development. She learned early to "act confident even when you're not because then people perceive you as confident, and that makes a big difference." Confidence, ability, and family role models helped her earn a Ph.D. from MIT, a faculty position at Harvard, and her most recent post as associate vice president for research administration at Northwestern.*

❧

I am interested in the question of development: how you get from a single cell—the fertilized egg—to a person, where all of the tissues are in the right place and each organ knows what to do and when to do it. That whole process is a remarkably complicated and beautifully orchestrated series of events. The small part of this process that I'm concentrating on at the moment is the role of a particular protein (called insulin-like growth factor II, or IGF-II) in brain development. Proteins are the machinery of cells that do all the work—proteins make up our skin, proteins carry out the enzymatic reactions that make other proteins, and proteins build the cells. Proteins are really a critical component

of life. The particular protein I'm studying—together with the people in my laboratory—is one that we believe helps to determine how many cells an organism has. The number of cells will affect how big and how tall a person will be when they become adults. Too many or too few cells in the brain can lead to mental retardation or epilepsy.

The "we" that I'm referring to includes four

Lydia Villa-Komaroff holding a mouse that is 60 percent the size of a normal mouse. The mouse, which lacks a gene for a growth factor that acts primarily during gestation, is used to study the regulation of growth.

postdocs (advanced researchers) with Ph.D. or M.D. degrees, one graduate student, some undergraduates, and, at times, high school students. This work cannot be done by one scientist alone—too much knowledge and too many techniques are required. These days most scientists work in teams.

I am a molecular biologist by training. That means that my particular focus is on the flow of information in the cell. DNA in the nucleus of a cell has all the information needed to specify all the parts of an organism. It's like a library, and, like a library, the information is not much use until someone reads it. So the information in the DNA is copied into RNA, which is the molecule that carries the information out to the cytoplasm where it is "read" by the cells' machinery and turned into proteins. The flow of information from DNA to RNA to protein and the biochemistry of those molecules is what a molecular biologist studies.

We use a variety of techniques to ask questions. For example, we do cell culture, where we take cells from a human or mouse brain, grow them in dishes in a controlled environment where we can, and ask about their response to IGF-II or whether they make IGF-II. We can also look for both the RNA message for IGF-II or other proteins or for the proteins themselves in different regions of the brain to ask what kind of cell has the protein and when is the protein that cell. That's the first step—if you want to know what something does, it's often helpful to know where it is and when, because if you have an idea of what's going on at the time then you at least know what things you should look at.

One of the marvelous things you learn as a biologist is the unity of all life. So mice, both in their development and in the way their brains are put together, are remarkably similar to humans. They provide an excellent model for study and a reminder that all life is pretty wonderful.

I always wanted to become a scientist, even as a very little girl, although I'm not sure that I really understood then what a scientist was. I always wanted to find things out, and I knew

that scientists did that. I was raised in New Mexico, the eldest of six children, three boys and three girls. Both of my parents were the first people in their respective families to go to college. My mother always worked—as a social worker in the welfare department, as a teacher, as a registrar at a community college, and at a state agency that dealt with abused children. I come from a long line of strong and professional women. My grandmother worked and raised three children by herself. We were regaled with stories of how she sold chemical toilets on horseback up in the mountains of New Mexico. Later she worked in the welfare department in Las Vegas (New Mexico, not Nevada), and as a child I sometimes went to work with her. She told stories about herself and my great aunt, who were schoolteachers in their early years in little towns in New Mexico.

This wonderful family history of strong women role models really begins with my great-grandfather (my maternal grandmother's father), who must have been a remarkable man. He educated his two daughters because he didn't want them to marry cowboys. His sons, he felt, only had to know how to write their names and learn enough math so that they wouldn't be cheated. But the girls needed more, so he sent them to school through high school, which was very unusual at that time.

My father's mother was also a strong woman. She was a *curandera*, a healer. My father bought us books. I remember when I was five he brought home the *World Book Encyclopedia*, and he said that everything I wanted to know was in those books. I was very excited by that notion. He bought the books and my mother read to us—that's one of my earliest and warmest childhood memories. My parents appreciated each of the six of us as individuals and encouraged all of us to do whatever it was we thought would be satisfying. One sister is a lawyer, the other a banker; one brother is in law enforcement, one is a teacher (formerly a missionary), and one's a music teacher. We assumed we would attend college

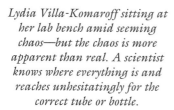

Lydia Villa-Komaroff sitting at her lab bench amid seeming chaos—but the chaos is more apparent than real. A scientist knows where everything is and reaches unhesitatingly for the correct tube or bottle.

in my immediate family, although this assumption was not shared by most of my very large extended family. (My father has eleven siblings and I have 115 first cousins!)

My background is Mexican American, and so the fact that my father recognized, appreciated, and encouraged strong women and supported my mother in her endeavors was critically important in my development. In the Mexican American family, what papa says goes, so it's clear that his support made a difference in my life. What's also amazing is that my parents fully accepted and supported my decision to go far away to college—first to the University of Washington in Seattle and then to Goucher College in Maryland. In the southwestern Chicano culture that I came from, many parents, consciously or unconsciously, discourage children from pursuing higher education because they are afraid that it means a kind of disloyalty to the family. They are afraid that education will change their children—that the children will be lost to them. But I really wanted to get out of New Mexico and away from my family, and my parents didn't hold me back. I continue to see, even now, many Mexican American students whose parents do not want them to go far from the family, especially girls and especially eldest daughters. They really want to keep the family strong and therefore close by.

I think it's incumbent on people like me to convince parents that they won't lose their child to education, but that it will enrich the child and thus the family. I was quite lucky to have the parents I had.

I started as a chemistry major at the University of Washington but was told by my adviser, whose name I cannot even remember now, that women didn't belong in chemistry. I switched majors several times until I ended up in the biology department. I took an incredibly exciting developmental biology course that included both lecture and laboratory work. At one point in the course, we slept in the lab in sleeping bags because we were watching frogs develop over time—we watched them every hour over a forty-eight-hour period. This hands-on experience with developing frogs and chickens crystallized my interest in development and molecular biology. I did not complete my undergraduate years at the University of Washington—I moved to the D.C. area because my future husband was doing his public health service there. I asked one of my professors where I should go, and he suggested Johns Hopkins, but Hopkins wasn't accepting women at the time. Since Goucher was their sister college, I went to Goucher and finished my undergraduate degree.

Tony and I were married when I finished my degree, and he was going to Boston to do his internship and residency. So I applied to graduate schools in the Boston area and ended up at MIT. My graduate class was small, but about one-third of it was women. The department was very supportive, and it was a fabulous place to be a graduate student. There were some people who didn't think women belonged, but the other women graduate students and I simply avoided them. I must say that I was pretty oblivious to the attitudes of others about my being a woman in science. I guess that was a blessing because I never felt I didn't belong or shouldn't be pursuing something that I loved. I learned early on that it's a very good ploy to act confident even when you're not because then people perceive you as confident, and that makes a big difference.

As a graduate student I wanted to do research in developmental biology, but the people who were doing it were not the people with whom I wanted to work. So I decided I should learn more about the field of molecular biology, and I found that the best work in molecular biology was being done using viruses. Consequently, my graduate work focused on poliovirus. After graduate school I did a three-year postdoc at Harvard University, where I first worked in one lab on the development of the silk moth eggshell and then in another lab on making proteins in bacteria. For one of those years—1976—I had to move to a laboratory at Cold Spring Harbor on Long Island. The Cambridge, Massachusetts, city council, due to the controversy around recombinant DNA technology, had banned certain experiments there, and so we had to do them elsewhere. The fear some people had was that if we took genes from one organism (a human) and put them into bacteria, we might somehow create a supergerm, a new disease. Early in 1977 the city council relented somewhat and instituted a set of rules and conditions under which the experiments could be done at MIT. But that year on Long Island was a frustrating and lonely time for me.

My first independent academic position was at the University of Massachusetts Medical School in Worcester. I was there for six years and was granted tenure, shortly after which I left to go to Harvard. I often work seven days a week, from about 7:30 A.M. to 7:00 P.M., but for me there is no difference between work and play because I love what I do. Besides doing research, I teach in the medical school, I advise graduate students, and I sometimes teach in an ethics course. I spend a lot of time in the lab troubleshooting, talking to people about their data and results, and figuring out what we need to do next. I don't spend as much time in my lab as I'd like to.

My husband and I decided not to have children—in part because we both work so hard and neither of us wanted to slow down. We're lucky, however, because there are a lot of children in our lives—fifteen nieces and nephews and three godchildren—and we thoroughly enjoy them. My husband and I both like photography and we both like to ski, and we do these when we travel together at least once or twice a year. I love to read, especially mysteries, and I spend a fair amount of time reading.

I've been lucky to have had options in my life, and I encourage young women to keep their options open. That, combined with hard work, has paid off enormously for me and resulted in an exciting and completely satisfying life. I've been pretty fortunate to be involved in some very exciting findings that received a lot of press, and I really would like to be one of the people who lay the groundwork for understanding how the brain works.

PRESENT POSITION: Associate Vice President for Research Administration and Professor of Neurology, Northwestern University

FIELD: Neuroscience and endocrinology

RESEARCH AREA: Brain development

EDUCATION: B.S. in Biology (1970), Goucher College; Ph.D. in Cell Biology (1975), Massachusetts Institute of Technology

DATE/PLACE OF BIRTH: August 7, 1947/Las Vegas, New Mexico

Lydia Villa-Komaroff lives in Chicago, Illinois, and Brookline, Massachusetts, with her husband, Dr. Anthony Komaroff.

INTERVIEW DATE: January 1995

Salome Gluecksohn Waelsch

Professor Emerita of Molecular Genetics
ALBERT EINSTEIN COLLEGE OF MEDICINE

Salome Waelsch came to the United States in 1933 after her first husband, a young professor at a German university, was dismissed following Hitler's pronouncement of his anti-Semitic laws. She worked at Columbia University for nineteen years without a faculty appointment, teaching genetics and doing research analyzing the effects of mutations on development. In 1955 she joined the faculty of Albert Einstein College of Medicine, a new school that went out of its way to hire women and other victims of discrimination and persecution. Although she is officially retired from her position at Albert Einstein, Dr. Waelsch works in her lab every day.

☙

I work in developmental genetics at Albert Einstein College of Medicine, with a focus on the mammalian species and with the mouse as my model system. For many years I have studied mutations—specifically, genetic changes in the mouse that cause birth defects. My colleagues and I have used these systems to analyze development because the mechanisms by which abnormalities arise indicate the corresponding normal mechanisms that are affected in the mutants. In operations on both mammals and amphibians, we have studied developmental mechanisms through transplantations and explantations of tissues. The abnormalities resulting from these experimental approaches could be analyzed in terms of mechanisms that existed normally but were disturbed by these genetic mutations.

When I look back at my career, it is exciting to realize the number of times I've been able to achieve results and interpretations that have contributed greatly to the knowledge of developmental mechanisms operating in mammals. I have applied that information to the analysis of birth defects in humans, where defects also arise from disturbances of the same developmental systems. My work contributes to the basic knowledge of biology, and particularly of developmental biology.

For many years I have worked with technicians and collaborated with other professors at Albert Einstein and at other universities. I have published more than 125 papers in col-

Salome Waelsch in her office in the Molecular Genetics Department at Albert Einstein College of Medicine, Yeshiva University

laboration with colleagues including L. C. Dunn, Vernon Bryson, Helene M. Ranney, Betty F. Sisken, Gertrude C. Moser, and Anna C. Pai. In addition to institutional recognition through status or title, I have received various academic rewards: I am a member of the National Academy of Sciences, a fellow of the American Academy of Arts and Sciences, an honorary life member of the New York Academy of Sciences, and a fellow of the American Association for the Advancement of Sciences. In 1993 I was awarded the National Medal of Science, and I've recently been named a fellow of the Royal Society in London.

My past explains a great deal about me. I come from a family of Jews who early in this century moved to Germany from Russia and suffered many prejudices. My parents, who were very conscious of the importance of schooling, did their utmost to inspire their children with the desire to get and make use of a good education. This was to help me more than I could have imagined, because later I became a Hitler victim, as did my husbands.

As a young student in Germany, I was interested in old languages, and the Humanistic Gymnasium inspired me very much. From there I went to the University of Berlin to study Greek and Latin, and as a result of the growing anti-Semitism in Germany, I became an active Zionist. At the time I thought I wanted to live in Palestine—now Israel—to teach Greek and Latin. But friends told me they would be very surprised if people in Palestine were interested in learning those languages. That made sense to me, so I decided to study something more universal. Chemistry and biology lectures, in particular the work on experimental embryology at the University of Berlin, so excited and inspired me that I decided biology would be my life's work.

After receiving my certificate of graduation from the University of Berlin—bachelor's degrees did not exist in Germany at the time—I earned my Ph.D. at the University of Freiburg. In Germany it was quite customary to move

from one university to another; in fact, it was desirable. I did my doctoral work under Hans Spemann, a famous professor at Freiburg who was later awarded the Nobel Prize in medicine for his work in developmental biology. Spemann had a definite prejudice against women, myself included. He assigned boring, pedestrian work to me that served mainly to support the studies and work of one of his male students.

I didn't give up; I learned much from Conrad Waddington, who had come to Spemann's laboratory in 1931 as a student from Cambridge. Waddington opened my eyes to the biochemical and molecular problems inherent in inductive interactions between cells, and taught me about the involvement of genetic mechanisms in developmental phenomena. I also was influenced by Victor Hamburger, whom Spemann assigned to oversee my dissertation research. Hamburger introduced me to the principles of genetics. He later became one of the founders of modern neuroembryology. I stayed alert and learned as much as I could. Spemann himself inspired me with his work, despite his prejudices, and provided a tremendous amount of knowledge about the dynamics of early prenatal development in vertebrate systems. I later applied to mice what Spemann had learned from amphibians. He operated on the early fertilized egg, and on later stages of the embryo. My contribution, since it was not possible to operate on the mammalian embryo or the fetus at that time, was to make use of gene mutations that affect development. I analyzed their effects and their results and then drew conclusions about the normal development of the embryo and fetus.

In prewar Germany, life for Jews began to change drastically. My first husband, Rudolf Schoenheimer, was a young professor at a German university. On April 1, 1933, when Hitler pronounced his anti-Semitic laws, Rudolf was immediately dismissed. Although very young, he was known in the United States for some very exciting work he had done in biochemistry, so immediately he was offered a job by Columbia University in New

York. We came to this country early in 1933. We were very lucky.

In 1936, I met L. C. Dunn at a social event with my husband, and I began working at Columbia University. Dunn was looking for a developmental biologist, and, although he had no research support to pay me a salary, he agreed to teach me genetics in return for using my knowledge of experimental embryology in the analysis of the effects of mutation on development. At Columbia I was finally able to combine the causal analysis of development with aspects of physiological genetics, which was to become my lifelong work. Although I stayed at Columbia for nineteen years and was a major contributor in the Department of Zoology, I was never given a faculty appointment. Numerous times I brought to the department chairman's attention the fact that young men who had been "growing up" around me had gained professorial appointments, but I hadn't even been put on the lowest rung of the faculty ladder. At that time, they could tell me in so many words, "You are a woman—no chance!" For almost twenty years at Columbia I was merely a research assistant and then a research associate. It's ironic—in May 1995 Columbia awarded me an honorary doctorate in science at commencement.

In 1955 I was asked to join Albert Einstein College of Medicine and was one of the first people appointed to the faculty of this totally new school. At that time, genetics was not yet being taught, and Albert Einstein was the first institution to offer real courses in genetics for medical students. I came to the school as an associate professor, but was promoted through the years to professor of anatomy, professor of genetics, professor and chairman of genetics, and professor of molecular genetics, which I am today.

The two people largely responsible for the college's liberal policies were Ernst Scharrer, professor of anatomy, and Marcus Kogel, dean of the college, who went out of their way to appoint women and other victims of both discrimination and persecution. In 1955,

when Scharrer approached me at Columbia, he was very much interested in recruiting an expert in genetics to the department and knew I was available. During his life, he was founder and creator of the field of neuroendocrinology. He discovered that nerve cells not only conduct stimuli but also produce and secrete endocrine substances, or hormones. Berta Scharrer, his widow and a good friend to me, came here at the same time I did, never having had an academic position even though she published and worked closely with her husband. Berta is still at Albert Einstein, and if Ernst had lived, I think together they would have received the Nobel Prize.

My second husband, Heinrich Waelsch, was also extremely supportive of my desire to remain in science, contribute to it, and hold an academic position. I met him in my upper Manhattan neighborhood while still at Columbia, and he encouraged me to continue what was to become my life's work. To quote from a paper I wrote called "The Development of Creativity" for the *Creativity Research Journal* in 1994, "Heinrich Waelsch was the person who made me realize the importance of developing my own career rather than continuing the typical female role of remaining another scientist's associate for the rest of my life." While that paper discusses the concept that adversity may have very positive effects on creativity, which I believe was quite true in my own life, Heinrich was an inspiration to me and my career.

At Albert Einstein today, my colleagues and I talk a lot about the lack of opportunities in science for young people. It is very difficult altogether because funding has been reduced. Personally, I never did and would not now give a woman a different piece of advice than I would give a man; I make that clear to my students. I consider my particular field very promising today. In many ways it is a relatively young area, and there's still a lot to be done, particularly on the molecular level. Mammalian developmental genetics and its molecular aspects are very promising areas right now.

When young people come to see me, I frequently advise them to study medicine because it provides an excellent basis for any biological specialization they might later want to go into. At the same time, it offers a kind of safeguard; if a student finds out that science, research, and the more abstract aspects of biology are not the right choice, then they can practice medicine. In the past I have seen young people who study medicine and then go into biological research do particularly well. I also recommend that students attend bigger institutions. I believe restrictions and prejudices have more of a chance to be enacted in smaller institutions, and that opportunities and choices are greater at bigger schools.

PRESENT POSITION: Professor Emerita of Molecular Genetics, Albert Einstein College of Medicine

FIELD: Developmental genetics

RESEARCH AREA: Role of genes in the course of prenatal development of the fetus

EDUCATION: Certificate of Graduation, University of Berlin; Ph.D. in Biology (1932), University of Freiburg, Germany

DATE/PLACE OF BIRTH: October 6, 1907/Danzig, Germany (now Gdansk, Poland)

Dr. Waelsch is a widow. Her husband was Heinrich Waelsch, a professor of biochemistry at Columbia University. She has two children: a daughter, Naomi Barbara Kerest, a teacher in the New York area; and a son, Peter Benedict Waelsch, who is married and has two children and works as a teacher and career counselor at Boston University.

INTERVIEW DATE: October 1995

Katrina D. Washington

Assistant Resident Engineer
NORTH CAROLINA DEPARTMENT OF TRANSPORTATION

Katrina Washington was first attracted by the "hands-on" nature of civil engineering and by being able to see her projects progress. Though wearing a hard hat and supervising several highway inspectors are a natural fit for her, she looks forward to the day when no one will be surprised to find a woman in charge at a construction worksite.

☙

I have been an assistant resident engineer for the North Carolina Department of Transportation in the Charlotte area for two years. My job is to monitor the progress of new highway construction projects. The Department of Transportation assigns inspectors to monitor the progress and quality of the work of the highway contractors, ensuring that it conforms to North Carolina highway specifications. I go out in the field to supervise the inspectors on projects that I'm assigned to and evaluate how well the contractor is progressing. On the status reports I send to the state construction headquarters, I estimate the cost of the contractor's monthly progress. These reports are used to determine how much the contractor will get paid that month. I also monitor the overruns and underruns on the job, to ensure that we complete the project close to budget.

Most projects don't run smoothly from beginning to end. For example, on my current project, the ground has been wet and is delaying construction. Besides having wet ground to contend with, we have to consider whether the existing soil composition will be suitable to use when it's dry. If not, we will have to remove and replace it or modify it in some way. We may stabilize it with lime, cement, or a stone-based material called aggregate. In any case, I will need to work up an estimate for the additional cost on whatever alternative method I recommend and submit it to the resident engineer for approval.

If contractors fall behind schedule, they are notified in writing by the engineer responsible for monitoring the project. Falling too far behind puts the contractor in jeopardy of being taken off the state projects bid list. This means they won't be permitted to bid on any more state construction projects until they can prove that they are capable of performing the

Katrina Washington just after her senior year in high school

work on time and within budget. The contracts also have a liquidated damages clause. If, for example, the contractor negotiated a completion date of November 30, for each day past November 30 that the job is not completed, he or she is charged a penalty fee. The Department of Transportation views the incomplete project as a loss to the state: that's one more day the public cannot use that road.

Some projects include additional incentives for early completion. Our contracts also include a provision for compensating the contractor for extra work because of something unforeseen, like wet material. There are several options for a contractor if something unforeseen occurs during construction. If certain contracted tasks overrun their cost by more than 100 percent, the contractor has the right to renegotiate the contract price. Additional work can be negotiated through a supplemental agreement separate from the original contract. Because I monitor each project closely, I can verify or contest whatever the contractor tries to negotiate. I draw up all the documents for the agreements we contract on projects I supervise. I do a lot of paperwork—a lot of filing, a lot of letter writing.

There are fourteen divisions in the Department of Transportation in North Carolina. I'm in the tenth division, which consists of five counties and six resident engineers. Each resident engineer is responsible for all of the projects in his or her jurisdiction. Overseeing the resident engineer is a division engineer and a division construction engineer. Projects within each division are divided among the assistants, who do the field work and supervise the project inspectors. On my current project, I am supervising three inspectors. The number of inspectors on a job depends on the type of work that needs to be done and the phase the project is in. Some projects require seven or more inspectors because there is construction being done twenty-four hours a day, seven days a week. All the letters and documents regarding the projects are written by the assistants, then proofed and edited by the resident, who is ultimately responsible for signing everything. All of the preconstruction

operations such as design, development, and hydraulics planning take place at our headquarters in Raleigh, the state capital, where the office of the Secretary of Transportation is located.

All new engineers are hired as transportation engineer associates and are considered trainees. Trainees spend eighteen months in a rotation schedule that gives them work experience in various departments. In North Carolina, trainees spend four and a half months in construction and another four and a half in maintenance; they split the remaining months among the units of their choice, such as traffic engineering, roadway design, hydrology, planning, and environment. As trainees approach their eighteenth month, they start looking at the posting board for a permanent position within the Department of Transportation. Trainees are then promoted to transportation engineer level one, which is what I am. If no positions are open, the person stays in rotation as a trainee until something becomes available. Because there's an increase in salary to move into a permanent position, most people don't want to remain trainees.

In high school, I loved science. I've always performed best in math and science. I come from a large family with lots of cousins. My father, who is a minister, and my mother, who had always worked, both have college degrees, but it was my older cousins who influenced my decision to major in engineering. When I was a freshman in high school, my focus was on computers. One of my cousins asked, "Why settle for programming computers—why not be an engineer and design computers?" The question turned on a lightbulb in my head, and I started to look into engineering programs. My parents had always enrolled me in some kind of summer program, so during the summer after my sophomore year in high school, I spent one week at the University of South Carolina and two weeks at Clemson University. Clemson's program was for two summers: during the first summer, students spent two weeks studying general topics; the following summer, they spent three weeks focusing on a specific area. I concentrated in engineering. Because of my positive experiences at Clemson, I chose to attend college there and decided to major in computer engineering.

Clemson is structured so that students don't enter into a specified engineering major as freshmen. During my first year and a half, I found that I really wasn't interested in computer engineering. After my sophomore year, I did a summer internship at South Carolina Electric and Gas. I spent most of the summer talking with a civil engineer, and it piqued my interest. The next year, I took a few civil engineering courses and decided that was what I liked. Civil engineering is a "hands-on" discipline. You can touch what you've designed; you can see a building as it goes up, or a road as it's constructed. At each point you can see progress.

During my freshman year at Clemson I was stressed out all of the time. If I didn't earn an A, I got really upset. Fortunately, the Minorities Engineering Program was very supportive, and I became close to the director, Sue Lasser. Sue helped me keep my schoolwork in the proper perspective and to open up. When I started at Clemson, I was very quiet and kept to myself, but after working with Sue and the Minorities Engineering Program, I started coming out of my shell. Today she laughs, "Now I've got you talking and you won't shut up."

During my sophomore year, a recruiter from Exxon called and asked Sue if she had a civil engineering major with at least a 3.0 grade point average for a salaried internship and a $2,500 scholarship. Sue called me in and said, "I have some good news." Then she told me about Exxon. The internship was in Baton Rouge, Louisiana. They arranged for me to fly in for an interview and paid for my mother to go with me. I took the internship.

Baton Rouge was a nice town. It's the capital of Louisiana, but not fast paced at all. It was a fun place for a nineteen-year-old to live for the summer. I rented a one-bedroom townhouse, and there was always something to do with the other interns. Exxon had several social gatherings—weekend trips to New Orleans and Houston, picnics and pool par-

Katrina Washington, 1996
PHOTO BY DANNY FISCHER

ties—and there was always just going over to someone else's apartment. It was like a family of interns, and I didn't feel isolated at all. Also, the employees at Exxon were very good at taking us under their wing and showing us around.

The internship was at an Exxon Chemical Company plant. I did planning, scheduling, and cost estimating for one of the units at the plant and decided that I really liked the project control area. Most people in this area had advanced degrees. After I finished my internship, I went back to Clemson with my mind made up to continue for a master's degree immediately after my bachelor's degree. I knew it would be too hard to give up a salary and go back to doing homework and taking tests in graduate school if I went to work first. I continued straight through and got my master's of engineering degree in civil engineering at Clemson. After my first year of graduate school, I had a summer position in project control at Enron Corporation, a natural gas company in Houston, Texas. But immediately after getting my master's degree, I went to work for the state.

My next goal is to get my professional engineering license. After I completed my undergraduate degree, I took an eight-hour initial exam for the credential of "engineer in training." The licensing board requires four years of experience before an engineer can take the licensing exam. The board counts graduate school as one year of experience, but requires three years in the field. I need one more year of work experience before I can sit for the exam. If I pass it, I'll be a registered engineer and will be able to design and authorize my own documents and another registered engineer won't have to sign off on my work. Most governmental engineering positions don't require the license, but it's preferred. I want to have the authority to confirm that what I've designed or recommended meets the standards without getting someone else's approval.

Construction—whether private or government—is a traditionally white-male field. In my work I've had people disagree with me or just not come to me and then go over my head if there was something they didn't like. I'm not quite sure if it's a racial issue—some people just have a problem taking directions from someone who's not like them. But I haven't had anything blatant happen.

Something that I've found incredibly inconvenient and embarrassing is having to go to the rest room while on a job site. I tell them that I'll be right back; then I get in my vehicle and drive down the road until I find a McDonald's. But I've never been harassed. The men are usually very professional. One time I was asked out, but I just told him, "I don't date people I work with. This is a professional atmosphere; I'm not here to socialize." I didn't have many problems because I started my job with a "strong" attitude. I knew that I could always soften later. Everyone knew that I meant business.

What bothers me most is when I make a decision and a supervisor reverses it without consulting me or telling me why. It's disheartening because I have to determine for myself what I did wrong or what I should do differently the next time. Many times I just can't tell. There are times when I feel that I can't voice my opinion to my boss—even when I'm pretty sure I'm right—because I might be blackballed or not get the promotion I want. If my work environment gets to me, though, I call my mom or talk to some of my friends to get over it. And sometimes I do go back and speak my mind.

What sustains me at my job is my determination. There are always going to be people who put you down, try to discourage you, or make you change your mind, but if you have the determination and drive, you can do just about anything you put your mind to. You have to be able to put petty things aside and to block out the negative in order to reach your goal.

On the first day of my internship at Exxon, I experienced something that I now find funny, although I didn't appreciate it at the time. The Exxon plant was protected by high-security measures, and anyone entering had to have an employee pass or visitor pass. I approached the guard station and said, "Today is my first day and I'm reporting for work." The guard asked me if I was a "Kelly Girl." And I asked, "What's a Kelly Girl?" (I've since found out that they're temporary secretaries.) I just told him, "No, I'm an engineering intern." Even now, when people who don't know me come to my project site and ask, "Who's the guy in charge?" I just smile, shrug, and say, "I am"—and hope that someday it's not going to surprise people that a woman is in charge.

PRESENT POSITION: Assistant Resident Engineer, North Carolina Department of Transportation

FIELD: Civil engineering

SPECIALTY: Construction management

EDUCATION: B.S. in Civil Engineering (1991) and Master of Engineering in Civil Engineering (1993), Clemson University

DATE/PLACE OF BIRTH: August 13, 1969/ Chattanooga, Tennessee

Katrina Washington lives in Charlotte, North Carolina. She visits her parents in the Charleston area once a month.

INTERVIEW DATE: September 1995

Joanne Westin

Senior Instructor in Biology
CASE WESTERN RESERVE UNIVERSITY

Growing up in an academic household, Joanne Westin was not at all surprised to end up in academia herself. In college she discovered a particular interest in cockroach neural mechanisms. She pursued this interest through graduate school and beyond, marrying another cockroach expert. She followed her husband to Case Western Reserve University and accepted a position as instructor when he started on the tenure track. For many years she continued doing research in his lab, but has since turned her full attention to teaching, which allows her to share her infectious enthusiasm for biology with nearly three hundred students each semester.

❧

I got into biology because of the exquisiteness of living things—especially small ones. I had no lofty ideals, no plans to cure a devastating disease or save the planet from environmental destruction. During the time when I was growing up, there was a feeling that infectious diseases were conquered, and no one thought much about what happened to the garbage or the sewage once it was out of sight. Although I have been involved in many causes over the years, what I still love most about science is its discovery of things like ants that tend their own fungus like tiny farmers; orchids that look and smell so much like female wasps that they trick male wasps into pollinating them; and female fireflies that mimic the flashes of other species to lure male fireflies into serving as their dinner.

I grew up in the rather idyllic setting of a boys' prep school campus in New England. My best friend, Jody, and I spent hours in the woods, collecting wildflowers and making villages out of trees. My father was a beloved physics teacher and my mother was a librarian, so it's not too surprising that I ended up in academia.

When I began high school in 1960, DNA was still new. My freshman biology course tended more toward dissection and classification than anything molecular or physiologi-

Joanne Westin's senior picture, Wellesley College, 1968

cal. I remember getting excited about one laboratory where we dissected grasshoppers—it was so amazing to me that all those tiny, intricate organs could actually produce a working grasshopper. I still possess a cellophane envelope labeled "grasshopper ovaries" in an old scrapbook. I didn't decide that I would be a biologist until later, however. In high school I was also quite partial to French: I spent my senior year at Le College Cevenol in France and began college with vague intentions of majoring in either French or a science.

At Wellesley I continued to enjoy both French literature and biology. The course I loved most (and that probably clinched the biology major) was human physiology taught by Mrs. Fiske and Mrs. Harrison. They managed to make it clear how the kidney or the visual system work without losing sight of how incredibly complex they are. Although we did some very flashy lab experiments, such as regulation of blood pressure in live cats, the lab that I found the most intriguing involved recording the activity of giant interneurons in the cockroach. To write the lab report, we had to read part of a book called *Nerve Cells and Insect Behavior* by Kenneth Roeder; I quickly read the whole volume. I thought it was fascinating that scientists could actually record the neural activity that produces the escape behavior of a cockroach. There were a few juicy stories in that book as well—including one about the praying mantis, which bites the head off her prospective mate. Apparently, removal of the brain releases inhibition of mating behavior so she ends up mating with a headless male.

Not long after that cockroach lab, Dr. Roeder came to give a seminar at Wellesley. I think that was the first time I was brave enough to actually talk to a seminar speaker, and he was very nice and encouraging. He even invited me to come visit his lab, which I did. I ended up doing a senior project on learning in cockroaches and got some tips from a graduate student who was working with Dr. Roeder. My project seems rather silly in retrospect. There had been a report of

transferring memory from one planarian to another by grinding up the brains of trained planarians and feeding them to untrained ones. I thought I would do the same in cockroaches, which could learn very nicely to raise their legs to avoid shocks. Of course I never got any transfer of memory, but I did learn a lot about how to teach things to cockroaches!

My cockroach supplier while I was at Wellesley was Dr. Lou Roth at the Natick Army Laboratory. I never figured out exactly why the Army was paying him, but Lou Roth had traveled all over the world collecting cockroaches and was quite an expert on their evolution and natural history. Every time I went to replenish my stocks, I ended up spending at least an hour listening to him tell about his travels and seeing any new specimens he had collected. He first introduced me to the hissing Madagascar cockroach, *Gromphadorhina portentosa* (which, literally translated, means "ominous snout of an old sow") and first told me of cockroaches flying around the lampposts in exotic tropical countries. I know most people loathe cockroaches, but he really loved them, and I started to think they were neat too.

Most of my friends at Wellesley were premedical students, and I considered that option as well. I could see the intrigue of making diagnoses and the satisfaction that must come from helping people; but I thought my personality was better suited to teaching and research. I thought it would be more fun to play with bugs in a lab, and talk about how superbly designed they are, than to listen to sick people all day.

From Wellesley I went to Cornell University, largely because a friend of Mrs. Harrison's named Jeff Camhi was there, and he was working in neurobiology of insects. After several false starts, I ended up studying nerve regeneration in cockroaches. I wondered about the cues used by nerves both in development and in regeneration to get to their appropriate targets. There was some very interesting work on growth of optic neurons into the frog's brain suggesting that nerves might be responding to some sort of chemical gradient. I wondered if there might be a segment-specific chemical cue attracting nerves toward the appropriate leg in cockroaches. So I did a variety of leg transplants, discovering serendipitously that a single limb transplanted in an abnormal orientation would produce supernumerary limbs. (After I observed it, I found that it had been documented before.) Anyway, my results favored mechanical cues and/or recognition of a target once it is attained rather than chemical cues exerting an effect over distance. The cockroach nerves tended to grow into whichever leg was closest, and they seemed to get to the right muscles in any leg.

While I was at Cornell, I had the privilege of taking a course from Dr. Tom Eisner, who made every lecture an adventure into the behavioral adaptations of some small creature. Eisner worked on things like the patterns that bees can see in flowers because of their ultra-violet vision; the mechanisms that allow a type of beetle to accurately direct a caustic spray at a predator; and the receptors and chemicals involved in attraction of male moths by female moths over incredible distances. He once said that he did this type of research because it was fun, it didn't cost very much, and it didn't hurt anyone. I find it a little sad that research funds are less and less available for this sort of research—that funding agencies seem to be looking for practical benefits from every research dollar.

I took a position teaching at Russell Sage College, a small college in Troy, New York, even before I finished my Ph.D. My adviser had encouraged me to work toward a more research-oriented position; however, I wanted a break from long hours in the laboratory and looked forward to more interaction with people. Russell Sage was a good school with very friendly, nonjudgmental students—a nice place to start out teaching. I will never forget the terror of walking into my first class to see fifty young women with pencils poised waiting to write down *what I was going to say*!

I returned to Cornell after my first year of teaching to take my Ph.D. exam and to teach summer school. I very quickly got into an ar-gument with a new postdoctoral fellow named Roy Ritzmann, who had taken over *my desk* and then had the temerity to complain when I left a few cockroach legs on it. We ended up going out for a beer, and about a year later we got married. We continued to live four hours apart for another year while I kept teaching at Russell Sage. Since Roy had not found a job in that year, I gave up my teaching job (and the title of assistant professor) and came back to Cornell to do postdoctoral research in Jeff Camhi's lab. The focus of the lab was now on the cockroach escape system. I had always wondered why there were so many giant neural fibers, so that was the problem I explored. Jeff was doing some behavioral experiments showing that the escape was oriented in the opposite direction from wind puffs from an attacking predator; and others had shown that different rows of spines on the cerci (the stubby antenna-like projections at the posterior end of the insect) respond preferentially to different wind directions. My project involved recording responses to wind puffs from individual giant interneurons to find out if they might be conveying directional information from the spines to the neurons directing leg movements. I worked with an undergraduate named Jonathan Langberg, and we showed that at least some of the giants did show directionality. These findings were the basis of studies still going on in at least three different laboratories.

The next year my husband got a job offer from Case Western Reserve University (CWRU). After finding that Cleveland was a nice place to live, we moved here. The chairman of the biology department, Dr. Norman Rushforth, has always been concerned with helping the spouses of new faculty in whatever way he can, and he offered me a position as an instructor.

I started out teaching labs, the norm for instructors. Soon my husband and I agreed that we would share teaching labs in "my" physiology lab course, and also share giving the lectures in "his" physiology lecture course. This worked out so well that I eventually started

Joanne Westin lecturing on environmental cycles to her Principles of Biology class, Case Western Reserve University, 1994
PHOTO BY ROY E. RITZMANN

giving the lectures in the introductory biology course, and someone else took over the introductory labs. My Principles of Biology course now has nearly three hundred students in two separate sections. My physiology lab now has five sections; and in addition to teaching three of the sections, I oversee two graduate students who handle a section each, plus five undergraduates who help out. I still share the physiology lectures with my husband.

In spite of being "off" the tenure track, I continued to do cockroach research in my husband's lab for many years—mostly studying the role of other neurons besides the giant interneurons in the escape system. As I became busier and busier with other duties, I had less and less time for research. However, my position has evolved into one that is very comfortable for me, and at the moment I am just as happy not to be involved in research.

I have had a very satisfying career remaining an instructor all these years. I was able to work part-time the semester after my oldest daughter was born, and I took off a whole semester (with pay for most of it!) when my twins were born. I have found family life and a non-tenure-track position an ideal combination. In spite of being busy, I am never so overwhelmed (with grant deadlines, for example) that I can't take an occasional day off

to go skiing with the kids during their vacation, or a few hours in the middle of the day to attend a school concert.

I really enjoy teaching. I learn something new every year, and it is always fun when a new discovery is announced at precisely the time my class is studying the system or genetic disease that's in the news. I still delight in the same things that I tell about every year in physiology—the adaptations of the camel that allow it to delay and then endure an incredible degree of dehydration; the huge lungs of the pronghorn antelope, which allow it to run at 60 mph for an hour; the circulatory features that pump blood all the way to the head of a giraffe but keep blood vessels from bursting when the head is lowered for a drink. It is rewarding when the students find these things as awe inspiring as I do.

In my principles of biology course, major themes are evolution, particularly emphasizing that humans are latecomers in life's history, and ecology, especially the intricate and delicate balance of natural ecosystems that we latecomers are threatening. My personal bias toward saving the rain forest has more to do with saving exquisite tiny frogs than preserving future sources of food, medicine, or energy, although perhaps the global climatic consequences outweigh either of these concerns.

I have always been open to new teaching techniques and have tried various cooperative and investigative methods. The mechanics of teaching, however, are secondary to the students' experience of actually seeing a frog heart beating, of watching fertilization and division of a sea urchin egg, or of recording data, graphing it, and finding that there really is a relationship between the independent and dependent variable. Just one "This is really neat!" from a student is worth all the preparation, animal care, and equipment maintenance involved in each experiment.

I like interacting with students. All of the students at CWRU are bright, most of them work hard, and each one has a wonderful story with many chapters yet to be written. I am proud to have a fleeting role in helping some of them find or confirm an interest, choose a career, or become more appreciative of and concerned about the world around them. Since I devote considerable energy to teaching, I was happy to receive the Undergraduate Student Government Teaching Excellence Award in Mathematics and Natural Sciences in 1992.

Besides teaching, some of my other duties include running the department's summer research program, overseeing the yearly Michelson Morley undergraduate research competition, coordinating the selection of students for various honors and scholarships, and writing a monthly newsletter for the biology department. Also, every year it is my great honor to help judge the Mr. CWRU competition— a chance to see ordinarily quiet and studious young men act silly while a sorority raises money for charity.

I can't advise someone how to achieve a position like mine—it simply evolved from a unique situation. It is difficult to find non-tenure-track positions with security, outstanding students, and freedom to lecture about topics that you enjoy! Marrying someone whose research is very close to yours can make the job hunt daunting, but I have heard of couples who have shared one position, or found two positions at the same university. It has definitely been a plus for both of us to share a common enthusiasm for physiology and for small creatures—though, contrary to what the students believe, we don't discuss Fick's law over dinner every night.

PRESENT POSITION: Senior Instructor in Biology, Case Western Reserve University

FIELD: Neurobiology

RESEARCH AREA: Neural basis of escape behavior in insects

EDUCATION: B.A. in Biology (1968), Wellesley College; Ph.D. in Neurobiology (1974), Cornell University.

DATE/PLACE OF BIRTH: August 11, 1946/Proctor, Vermont

Joanne Westin lives in Cleveland Heights with her husband, Roy Ritzmann, who is a professor in the biology department at Case Western Reserve University. They have three daughters: Jennifer, age sixteen, and Cassie and Katie, both age twelve.

INTERVIEW DATE: February 1995

Sheila Evans Widnall

Secretary of the U.S. Air Force

Sheila Widnall is the first woman ever to head a branch of the U.S. military. She is an aeronautical engineer and was a member of the MIT faculty for twenty-eight years before leaving her position as associate provost to become Secretary of the Air Force. She credits her father for fostering her interest in math and science and her working mother for showing her that women can manage a career and a family. She is a member of the National Academy of Engineering, the International Academy of Astronautics, and the American Academy of Arts and Sciences.

I was born in Tacoma, Washington, the oldest of two girls. My mother worked as a juvenile probation officer and social worker. My father had a more complex career. He started out as a rancher in Colorado during the Depression and, like many others, lost his ranch. So he went out into the world with a horse and a saddle, working as a ranch hand and riding in the rodeo; he eventually wandered into Tacoma and met my mother. My mother always wanted to be married to a college man and sent him to college. He worked as a foreman in the shipyards while attending college and then afterwards until he went to work at Boeing. Later he earned a master's degree in business administration and taught at a vocational school and a local junior college. In my father's eyes, I substituted for the oldest son, so we did a lot of projects together, like building, painting, rewiring, and pouring concrete. I'm sure that those experiences with my father fostered my interest in science and math and that my "working

mother" influenced my decision to pursue a career *and* a family.

I attended a Catholic girls' school from elementary through high school. I maintained my interest in science and math and no one ever discouraged me. I entered MIT in 1956 as a freshman in a class of about nine hundred. I was one of twenty women, of whom only ten graduated. That was culture shock—up to that point I had never been part of a minority. At MIT I majored in aeronautics, which thrilled my father because he had always wanted to be

U.S. Air Force Secretary Sheila Widnall, 1993

an engineer. By my junior year I'd decided to pursue a Ph.D., particularly because many wonderfully supportive teachers urged me to go on. Many of these people turned out to be mentors to me and remain my friends and colleagues today. I have had about nine mentors throughout my career—all men—who have been very important influences on my life.

I stayed at MIT for graduate study. I had my first child six months before I finished my Ph.D. and my second child four years later. My husband and I were lucky because there were a lot of graduate students' wives who were looking for employment; we never had a problem finding good daytime child care. I could never have done all that I've done without a supportive husband—that's been absolutely essential.

My field is aerodynamics: I study fluid dynamics, specializing in aircraft turbulence. I have always been interested in the relationship of fluid mechanics to practical engineering problems. My Ph.D. thesis dealt with wing theory, complex wing structure (unsteady and steady), and cavitating hydrofoils. The application is to flutter analysis of dynamic flows, where the wing sheds vortices from both the wingtips and trailing edge, and these vortices affect the entire flow field. My career has involved four or five major interconnected fields. The defining thread through all my research has been unsteady flow—whether I'm studying turbulence, stability, or acoustics. For example, I've studied the effects of wake turbulence of one airplane on another in flight. I've also done a fair amount of research in aircraft noise: unsteady flow is the fundamental cause of noise in aircraft due to things like turbulence or the inherent unsteadiness of a particular flow like helicopter blades. My work has been analytical, experimental, and computational.

I received my Ph.D. in 1964 and became an assistant professor at MIT. I was hired fairly soon after universities began accepting women for faculty positions. There's no question that I benefited from a change in attitude: before, no matter how good you were,

if you were a woman you were not considered for a faculty position. At the time I was hired and for quite a while after, there was only one other woman engineer at the university. Now things have changed: there are twenty-eight women on the engineering faculty; about 40 percent of undergraduate students at MIT are women; and women are in the majority in six engineering departments, including civil and chemical engineering.

I decided to stay in the academic world after earning my Ph.D. instead of heading out into industry for a couple of reasons: I really love teaching, and I enjoy the autonomy of faculty life—I like being totally responsible for setting my own agenda. Along with that comes the responsibility to fight for funding for projects that you believe in, but that's never bothered me; it comes with the territory.

I think both science and engineering provide wonderful careers for women. The fields are very interesting, they usually pay pretty well, they often provide a lot of autonomy, and one's contributions can be measured. There's not much subjectivity in the evaluation of one's work in many areas of science and engineering, which is important for women. I actually believe that engineering is a better career for women than science because it offers a broader range of opportunities, all the way from industry to government, and at different career levels from a bachelor's or master's degree to a Ph.D.

People often comment that it is unusual to do undergraduate and graduate work at the same institution and then stay on as a faculty member. My husband is also an aeronautical engineer, specializing in guidance control. We married during my senior year in college. We experienced the "dual career couple syndrome" and simply have much less mobility than individuals or single-career families. There were times when I was tempted to go somewhere else, either for graduate school or a sabbatical, but my husband was in the middle of something and couldn't leave. And there were times when he wanted to move, but I was in the middle of something and couldn't

424 Sheila Evans Widnall

leave. The net result was that we stayed put. We did both go to Washington in 1974 for a year—I worked in the Department of Transportation and he worked for Congress. Other than that we stayed in Boston until 1993, when I became Secretary of the Air Force.

I was tenured in 1974, became division head of Fluid Mechanics in 1975 and director of the Fluid Dynamics Research Laboratory in 1979. Along with my research and teaching responsibilities, I also served as the faculty chair for a year and chair of MIT's Committee on Academic Responsibility for a year. I became associate provost in 1992 with responsibilities in several academic areas, including federal relations, promotion and tenure, and international educational programs. As my career progressed I became more involved in public policy, government, and science and technology issues through national committees, boards, nonprofit organizations, and the American Association for the Advancement of Sciences (AAAS). I spent a fair amount of time in Washington as president and chair of the AAAS and as a member of the National Academy of Sciences' Panel on Scientific Responsibility. I testified before Congress and interacted with many individual members of Congress. I was involved with the Air Force before becoming secretary as a member of the Board of Visitors for the U.S. Air Force Academy from 1978 to 1984 and the board's chair from 1980 to 1982. I also served on an advisory committee to the Military Airlift Command and Wright Patterson Air Force Base. So I was not a new face in Washington or in the Air Force when I was appointed secretary, and my background prepared me well for the job. I knew the five previous secretaries very well—they were all men in my field, and we shared technical knowledge and expertise.

As Secretary of the Air Force I do a variety of things. I set major policies, but another part of what I do is representational: I visit bases, interact with the larger community, with local and national media, and with members of Congress. Currently women represent about 17 percent of Air Force personnel—al-

though, as in the field of engineering, those women tend to be concentrated among the more recent entrants, and so the distribution across ranks is uneven. My world now is not vastly different from my world in academe; there are more parallels than most people would think. Because I was associate provost at the time I took the leave of absence from MIT, I was used to dealing with a lot of policy concerns, government relations, and international issues. One of the primary modes of working in a university and in government is building consensus. The skills I honed in this area at MIT easily transferred to my work in government. I also have a whole office full of young colonels and majors with whom I work on a variety of projects, including writing papers, so it very much parallels the type of interactions I had and enjoyed with graduate and undergraduate students at MIT.

There's no question in my mind that women face barriers in professional life; there are benefits as well, but on balance it still constitutes a challenge. I've been able to overcome a good number of barriers due to a combination of things: the confidence I have in my own ability, my drive to succeed, my love of engineering, and the support I received from family, teachers, mentors, and colleagues. I also believe that all the attention on the role of women has been a positive force: universities and other organizations have been encouraged to look for qualified women and have found them. I have clearly benefited from that.

My being the first woman Secretary of the Air Force has given this organization a lot of visibility. Everyone within the organization has been incredibly supportive. When I first came in, the Air Force chief of staff, General Tony McPeak, went out of his way to make me feel welcome and to support me, especially behind the scenes. He made it clear to others that my appointment was not a controversial issue, that I was fully qualified, and that he was pleased with the decision. Consequently I got off to a really good start.

I interact with the Secretary of Defense frequently, about three times a week, because he is the cabinet member to whom all branches of the military report. I often see President Clinton at social functions at the White House and at times travel with him on *Air Force One*. I joke with colleagues that while everyone else on the plane is vying for time with the president, I'm trying to figure out how I can get up front to fly the plane.

During my sophomore year of college, Professor Stark Draper told me that it was important to have fun with whatever career you choose. That was actually a pretty radical idea to me, but throughout my career I've followed his advice. I've always done what excites me, and the details have always taken care of themselves. I never had a life plan, and I still don't. When opportunities have arisen, I've taken advantage of them.

PRESENT POSITION: Secretary of the U.S. Air Force

FIELD: Aeronautical engineering

RESEARCH AREA: Fluid dynamics

EDUCATION: B.S. in Aeronautics and Astronautics (1960), M.S. in Aeronautics and Astronautics (1961), Ph.D. in Aeronautics and Astronautics (1964), MIT

DATE/PLACE OF BIRTH: July 13, 1938/Tacoma, Washington

Sheila Widnall and her husband, William S. Widnall, live in Arlington, Virginia.

INTERVIEW DATE: April 1995

Carol Wilson

Technical Staff
HEWLETT PACKARD

Carol Wilson didn't feel challenged in her studies until she entered graduate school at Berkeley. Then, she found out that what she had thought was a reading difficulty was actually a learning disability. With determination and support from her peers, she completed a Ph.D. in mechanical engineering. Today, she works as a scientist in a research laboratory in a major electronics corporation.

I grew up in a small town in West Virginia. It was a nice place which promoted family unity; however, I felt there were greater opportunities elsewhere. I knew I needed a college degree in order to achieve the type of life I desired. My parents did not have the chance to go to college; in fact, my older brother was the first person to attend a place of higher learning. As I prepared to enter college, my primary focus was to have the ability to "find a good job." However, choosing a specific career (major) was difficult. My father was a banker, and my brother was in business, so a trend was set there. On the other hand, my mother thought I should try nursing, but I faint at the sight of blood. I was interested in music, and my math and science skills were strong, so I decided to use my strengths. I chose engineering as my major, and I worked my way through school with music, playing the string bass, electric bass, and drums with local night club bands. I wish I had been able to concentrate more on physics and math, both in high school and college. These fundamental disciplines would have provided a great foundation for graduate school.

As I progressed through school, I continually had problems with reading, writing, and concentrating on my studies. When I was an undergraduate at West Virginia University, my

Carol Wilson playing the guitar as an undergraduate

technical writing professor suggested that I stop by the reading and writing lab on campus. The instructors at the lab were very helpful; they couldn't diagnose my problem, but they did show me ways to deal with my difficulties. Since I still had good grades, none of this was a "big deal" to me.

After graduation, I got a job with IBM in Charlotte, North Carolina, developing printheads for wire matrix printers. I had a variety of tasks: designing/drafting components and being responsible for their production; negotiating with the manufacturing group to implement engineering changes required for improved performance; analyzing the strength and rigidity of the components; and testing certain aspects of the devices such as heating and cooling cycles during operation.

After a while, I noticed that people with only a bachelor's degree were somewhat limited in their career growth and development. The work that people were hired to do was very much based on the level of their education and experience. The people who had Ph.D.'s did the most interesting work—the kind of work that I wanted to do. So, after four years at IBM, I decided to go back to school to get a Ph.D.

I applied to the three best schools for mechanical engineering and one other that I felt was a "sure thing." All the schools admitted me; but I chose Berkeley, because it had a strong program, a good financial package and an attractive location (I wanted to live on the West Coast). After I started, I realized that I had overlooked an important selection criterion. I should have chosen an individual adviser to work with—regardless of that adviser's university—whose field was directly related to my interests. Most situations similar to mine will work out fine, but it is really helpful to have someone to collaborate with who is interested in your work. When you just choose a school, the selection of advisers is more limited, and you have to take whomever is available for the entire time that you're in graduate school.

Everyone at Berkeley was very smart and

competitive, and they all worked very hard. Suddenly my strengths—math and science—were everybody's strengths. For the first time, I had real problems, because of my learning disability. By far, my worst experiences were taking tests. I would build up so much anxiety that it was literally impossible for me to read and understand the exams. My professors suggested that I get help at the Disabled Students Association. The association had me tested, and the test results showed that there was a big difference between my basic intelligence and my reading comprehension and writing abilities. The counselors told me that I had a learning disability and recommended that I get some assistance from the school.

The major area where the school/professors assisted me was to allow me extra time for taking tests. Once I knew I had more time, I could relax and concentrate on the test questions. Also, I used a tape recorder to record lectures, then play them back to fill in the gaps in my notes. I learn better if I hear something than if I just see it and read it. Most people were understanding, but there were a few who, when they found out I had a learning disability, jumped to the conclusion that I was stupid. All of my professors were very cooperative in helping me when they learned of my disability.

While the professors were supportive, most of them were busy. Therefore, my peers turned out to be my best support group, especially the people in my lab. Despite the competitiveness of the environment, we worked together to learn and to get through the program. If someone in the group was taking a qualifying exam, everyone else would take time out to help that person study. I was the only woman in the lab group, but I wasn't uncomfortable in that situation. There were some specific activities that were for women; for example, the graduate women had an informal organization that we called GWE (Graduate Women of Engineering). There weren't many of us at the time, so it was easy for us to get together and talk about mutual interests and issues. However, most of the problems we were having the guys were

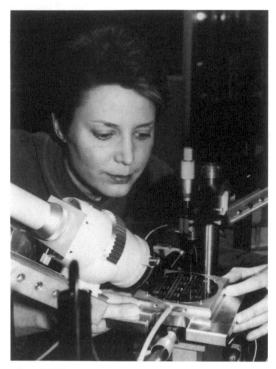

Carol Wilson setting up experimental hardware to acquire measurement data at Hewlett Packard Labs in Palo Alto, California, 1996

having too, so there wasn't a need for any gender-related distinctions.

My Ph.D. is in mechanical engineering, specifically dynamics. I wrote my thesis on what happens when tiny structures, used in data storage systems, oscillate. These structures were at most three-thousandths of an inch thick by three-tenths of an inch long by one-tenth of an inch wide. To do the analysis, I had to develop an experimental system that could work with tiny structures. After developing the system, I had to apply it to something to test its effectiveness. Most research at universities is driven by funding availability, and my adviser had funding to work on disk drives. I focused my research on some of the smallest components found in disk drives, even though my testing system was a global application and not just for data storage.

Working on my Ph.D. was a challenge, and it was very important to me to complete my degree. I've always worked hard for what I wanted, but I never had to work so hard as I did to obtain this degree. Hard work leads to good grades which leads to good jobs, but most of all I felt that I pushed the fringes of knowledge and actually found things that other people hadn't been able to measure. The thrill of new discoveries, no matter how small, is a very rewarding experience. The total experience has shown me how to approach and solve many problems; it has opened some doors and closed others (for example, jobs for which I am over-qualified); it has made me realize the vast amount of "stuff" that I don't know; but primarily, it has given me pride and confidence that I can accomplish such a hard task made even more difficult by my disability. It was the one graduation ceremony I attended.

After graduation, I took a job nearby in one of Hewlett Packard's research laboratories. HP makes personal computers, workstations, printers, and other electronic devices. The work I do for HP isn't directly related to the research I did at Berkeley, but there is some overlap. My job is to look at new materials to see how they will affect the design of different components used in devices that store data electronically, like computer disk drives. Our project's main customer is the HP plant in Boise, Idaho. We try to help them improve the understanding and performance of their disk drives and, in general, improve profitability in the data storage arena.

HP emphasizes team work, so my duties include attending meetings, consulting with people and supervising summer students, but I focus primarily on material and component characterization and analysis. First, I request that sample components be manufactured using whatever material I'm evaluating. When I get the sample components, I examine them under a microscope, then test their performance characteristics. If our lab can't perform a specific test, I have to develop a method to do it. Sample components can't be sent to outside labs for testing because of the risk that competitors might discover what materials and designs we're investigating. Because HP's work is proprietary and the disk drive industry is very competitive, HP develops all the required expertise in-house. While I do most of the analytical work, student interns and/or contractors (temporary people) do the testing, so that I have time to look at the results of the test data. One of the down sides of industrial research is that sometimes the things we work on do not get implemented in a product which could contribute revenue to the company. It's a good feeling to know you're making a contribution.

One of the differences between academic and industrial research is that there are more time constraints in industry. We have to make a product and ship it out the door or, as in the labs, we have to develop the technology and transfer it to the division so they can make a profit. Consequently, I haven't achieved the thrill of new discovery that I had when I worked on my dissertation. This is a little disappointing, because I have high aspirations of improving my work and knowledge base. Nonetheless, I am able to publish portions of my work. In addition, I attend conferences to "keep up-to-date" in my field, but since conferences usually ask for specifics, I can't present on a topic unless it is information that HP has already released.

On occasion, I do some work with professors at Stanford and Berkeley. The most recent interaction I had was with a visiting professor from China, who was extending my work at Berkeley. I am happy to have the opportunity to collaborate with him. It is nice to work with someone who is interested in the same things that I am.

I think I would like to try teaching at a college or university, but I'm not sure that I want to leave industry. A job at a company can be more secure than an academic job. My mechanical engineering career has been somewhat unusual, because I haven't chosen the most ideal companies for my background. HP and IBM are great companies, but they're electronics companies, and opportunities for mechanical engineers are limited. The automotive or aerospace industries would have more applications for dynamics and vibration, though perhaps not so much for tiny structures. Someday, I may investigate those opportunities.

Discrimination or harassment have not been a big problem for me; I've been able to take care of it myself. It usually happened not because of my gender, but because I was young and "wet behind the ears." Reverse discrimination bothers me more. After completing my bachelor's degree, I interviewed for the same job as one of my male classmates. He really wanted the job and I told the particular company that I wasn't interested in it. Nonetheless, two days later they offered it to me and not him. They had a quota to fill, so they needed a woman. That disturbs me. I want my opportunities to be based on my qualifications, not on my gender. Yet, society is always changing—checks and balances are always in place.

Even though I pursued my practical inclinations to be an engineer, I never lost my interest in music. But I developed tendinitis in my left wrist and elbow and, after being in and out of casts and getting cortisone shots for over a year, I decided that I had to give it up. Though my music was more than a hobby, it wasn't my career. It wasn't worth the continuous pain. But there was a positive aspect to that decision. My music interest used to prevent me from playing sports out of fear of injuring my fingers. Now I play softball and volleyball and I've also taken up "dare-devil" sports such as scuba diving, white water rafting and kayaking. I also enjoy traveling.

I try to work toward a balance in life—to try and get the most out of each aspect of life, not just work. Family and friends are all important. It is easy to get caught up in working sixty to eighty hours a week on a project. Sometimes you have to let the work go—it will be there tomorrow and the next day. I try to never be in the position to say, "I wish I had taken the time to. . . ."

PRESENT POSITION: Member of the Technical Staff, Hewlett Packard Laboratories

FIELD: Mechanical engineering

RESEARCH AREA: Dynamics of small structures

EDUCATION: B.S. in Mechanical Engineering (1983), West Virginia University; Ph.D. in Mechanical Engineering (1993), University of California–Berkeley

DATE/PLACE OF BIRTH: May 13, 1961/Fairmont, West Virginia

Carol Wilson lives in Santa Clara, California.

INTERVIEW DATE: October 1995

Susan Wood

Vice President and Director
SAVANNAH RIVER TECHNOLOGY CENTER
DEPARTMENT OF ENERGY SAVANNAH RIVER SITE

A native of England, Susan Wood was surprised by the focus on the difference between men's and women's abilities in technical fields when she emigrated to the United States. She studied physics as an undergraduate and metallurgy and materials engineering as a graduate student. She has spent her entire career at Westinghouse, moving among its various units, and she credits her willingness to take risks as part of the secret to her success. While she admits she's not a clone of her senior management peers—she has a Ph.D., she's female, she's not married, and she doesn't golf—she doesn't believe that being a woman has ever limited her opportunities.

❧

T he future looks bright for young women in technical fields. Management is becoming much more conscious about the value of diversity; many believe that building a team of clones is not as productive as building a team with different kinds of people. Women and other minorities will benefit from this realization, as will industry and business.

I was born in the small village of Snainton, Yorkshire, close to the moors in northern England. My father was a farmer and did not have much formal education. My mother was a nurse; she died when I was a child. I had one brother who was fifteen years older than me; we were essentially a generation apart. Both of my parents were very supportive of education and believed that my brother and I should use our brains to improve ourselves and get along better in the world. They did not distinguish between males and females in terms of encouragement and career plans; I was given the same type of encouragement as my brother when I expressed interest in going to university. The culture in England was very different from the culture in the United States. There did not seem to be the differentiation in focus on what

Susan Wood working at the transmission electron microscope in the Remote Metallographic Facility at the Westinghouse Research and Development Center, circa 1983

431

women could and could not do that I observed when I emigrated to the United States.

My brother was the first person of that generation in our extended family to go to university. At that time, England had a scholarship system that enabled good students who were from poor families to receive full support for tuition and room and board. My brother received a scholarship and pursued a chemistry degree. He was my first role model and mentor; fifteen years later I decided to go into physics, largely influenced by him. I was also greatly influenced by our family's situation; after my mother died, my father remarried, became ill, left the farm, and bought a business that did not do well. We became very poor during my teenage years. I decided quickly that I did not want to be poor, and I knew from my brother's experience that you could escape poverty by using your brain. I truly believe that one of my main motivators early on was poverty.

When I was growing up, the English school system was very different from the United States school system. In my last two years of what Americans call high school, I only studied pure math, applied math, and physics in preparation for A-Level examinations. (A Levels are the advanced-level public exams in the English system.) Then I went to Victoria University of Manchester. I chose Manchester because it is a northern school and more closely aligned with the culture I had grown up with. I began my bachelor's study in October 1966. Again, as the English university system is different from the American one, I studied only physics and math during my three years there. There were 4 other women students in the physics department at my level out of a class of about 125, and there were no women faculty members; but this unequal representation was not an issue for me. It never occurred to me, even though there weren't many women in physics, that women should not be there. The English culture did not overtly differentiate in that way, neither did my parents, and neither did I.

I came to the United States because of my brother. He went into the army after he received his chemistry degree, learned electronics, and developed it as his profession. He moved around the world and finally emigrated to the United States to work for Westinghouse Electric in Pittsburgh, Pennsylvania. I spent two summers with him in 1968 and 1969, when I was an undergraduate, and worked at the Westinghouse Research Center. That introduced me to life in the United States and the career opportunities that were available. I decided that I wanted to go to graduate school and entered a graduate program at the University of Pittsburgh in January 1970. I earned a master's degree in metallurgy and a Ph.D. in materials engineering. I did not pursue a graduate degree in physics because I wanted to do something more applied as a result of my experience at Westinghouse. I had done a little work in electronic materials and enjoyed the practical and applied nature of the work.

There was absolutely no commonality between my educational experience of undergraduate school in England and graduate school in the United States. The department at Pitt was very small, it had a large percentage of foreign students, and I was their first female Ph.D.-level graduate student. For the first time I became conscious that being a woman in this field was considered a bit odd. Some faculty members did not believe that women should become metallurgists, but there were young faculty members who did not differentiate between the sexes. They taught most of my graduate classes, and I interacted with them a lot. The chairman of the department was very supportive, and overall my experience in graduate school was very positive. My research, which I really have not used in my subsequent work, focused on corrosion mechanisms in lead glasses. At that time, there was a resurgence of concern about lead poisoning potential from glazes. I won a special fellowship from IBM to support this work.

My brother was still living in Pittsburgh at the time, but he did not approve of my going to graduate school; he saw it as a ploy to get out of working. I think that sibling competition was a factor here. While my father was supportive of girls being educated, he definitely believed that my brother was more intelligent than I was. I was determined to go forward with my doctoral studies, in part to prove to my father that I was technically competent. My father, however, did not really understand what graduate education was and thus did not understand my decision to pursue a Ph.D. Though I did not have family support, I did have several mentors throughout graduate school—the younger faculty members, my thesis adviser, and the department chair—who provided encouragement and practical advice.

I finished my Ph.D. in 1976 and took a job as a senior engineer with Westinghouse Research and Development Center, in part because my significant other was behind me in graduate school and I wanted to stay in Pittsburgh until he finished. It was a default choice, but not a bad one. When I began at Westinghouse, there were a few difficult personnel situations that I took a strong stance on and managed well; this provided good visibility with management. The department manager recognized my potential and became my mentor. He drove my early years of growth and helped me into a managerial position after only four years of professional work. I balked at first at being pressured in this direction, but again it was not a bad decision. I became manager of Reactor Materials Research and, with the continued support of my mentor, managed several other groups within Westinghouse, including Services and Advanced Materials, Physical Metallurgy Research, and Materials Analysis. The relationship with my mentor was mutually beneficial because every group I managed improved in performance. Once problems were solved and the programs were under control, he would move me into another group to do the same thing. It was challenging and interesting work, and by the time I was thirty-five I had an enormous amount of managerial experience for a technical person.

I did not experience any hostility because I was a woman or a very young manager, perhaps because there were a lot of foreign-born professionals (including many British) in the labs I managed; perhaps because I had an advanced technical degree; or perhaps because there were a number of younger people used to seeing women in the workplace. The professional environment within the R&D Center was also a contributing factor. There were conflicts with peers over technical or managerial issues, but no sexism or ageism; these simply were not on my radar screen.

After being a first-level manager for seven years at the Westinghouse R&D Center, which changed its name to the Science and Technology Center, I became the first woman department manager and subsequently the first woman general manager. By this time, I had a new mentor who was the vice president of the Science and Technology Center, and I began to think seriously about where I wanted my career to go. I was in my early forties and had twenty-five productive years ahead of me. I had decided around the age of thirty that I wanted to be the leader of a technology center, but it is very hard in the commercial world to plan a career path. Where you move in your career depends upon a lot of parameters such as your performance, who is around you, what opportunities arise, and whether you are growing professionally. You have to seize the opportunities and take risks, then rely on your own capabilities to survive. You have to put yourself in "stretch" situations—jump into something new even though it is uncomfortable—and then perform. I opted to do just that—I always took those opportunities when they were presented to me, which happened in part because of my mentor. But when I got to the position of division general manager at the Science and Technology Center, I took a more proactive role and decided I did not want to be in that job for the next twenty years. I knew I would never grow beyond where I currently was, so I needed to take a risk. I also knew that I liked leading a large organization—interacting, managing, and directing as well as doing technical things. I enjoy being a manager of technology. I have no desire to be an administrative manager.

With the help of my mentor, I moved to a business unit of Westinghouse—the Electronic Systems Group in Baltimore—and moved into manufacturing. The job combined technology, management, and product development within the manufacturing division. This opportunity gave me a great deal of exposure to transitioning technology into a product that you can sell to make a profit for the company. Customers' expectations drive deadlines and cost. It was very different from being isolated in a central R&D facility because of the close proximity to product and customer. In one sense R&D is at the front end of product development whereas manufacturing receives the fruits of the process. Close cooperation between the two is essential to ensure design productibility. Despite a downsizing environment within the business unit, my responsibilities grew to encompass product transition and testing during my four-year tenure. Then another opportunity arose that brought me to my current position. Westinghouse Savannah River Company is the Westinghouse subsidiary that manages the Department of Energy's Savannah River Site. Savannah River is the part of the Department of Energy's nuclear weapons complex whose primary mission was the production of tritium. It is still an active production site but now focuses on materials stabilization, tritium recycling, and environmental management and restoration. Thus, the core technology support base required by this site is broad and varied. It includes environmental technologies, sensors, remotization and robotics, tritium technologies, vitrification and waste stabilization technologies, waste and liquid chemical processing, and nonproliferation techniques. I am the vice president and director of the Savannah River Technology Center (SRTC). I am responsible for the strategic planning of the center—deciding where it's going and moving it in that direction. I am also responsible for leading and

managing 1,350 scientists, engineers, and technical support personnel. My job involves diverse internal and external customer interactions as well as teaming relationships with universities, industry, and other national laboratories. We're responsible for transferring some of our technologies to the commercial marketplace; we have to develop partnerships with companies so that we can do that effectively. We also need to leverage university resources both to perform relevant basic research at the lowest cost and to enhance the capabilities not available at the site but that we need to support the site effectively.

The technical activities of the SRTC support the High Level Waste Division, the tritium facility, solid waste and environmental remediation activities, separations processing, and spent nuclear fuel storage. The tritium mission supports the downsizing of the U.S. nuclear weapons stockpile, which is occurring as a result of the end of the Cold War era, in addition to keeping the remaining weapon inventory operational. The Savannah River Site (SRS) recycles tritium reservoirs, one essential component within a nuclear weapon. Since tritium has a relatively short half-life, about twelve years, the reservoirs must be periodically replenished with new tritium. To maintain the stockpile, the reservoirs are shipped back to the SRS, emptied, and replenished with new gas. Those reservoirs that are no longer required go to disposal, after the gas contents are removed and stored. SRTC provides a wide range of technical support for these production processes.

The High Level Waste Division manages the 34 million gallons of liquid high-level radioactive waste stored in the tank farms at the Savannah River Site. This waste has been accumulating since the 1950s from the processing of nuclear materials for national defense, space, medical, and research programs. About 3.5 million gallons of that 34 million gallons is thick sludge, while the remainder is in a water-soluble salt form. SRS has a specially designed process called in-tank precipitation (ITP), which removes the radionuclides from

Susan Wood, circa 1992

the salt solution. It produces a small amount of highly radioactive precipitate and a decontaminated salt solution or filtrate that constitutes more than 90 percent of the total volume of waste. This greatly reduces the amount of high-level waste to be vitrified. Following ITP, the high-level precipitate will be subjected to one last washing/filtering step before being processed into glass in the Defense Waste Processing Facility. Here both the precipitate and the sludge waste are immobilized by mixing them with borosilicate glass frit, melting the mixture at 2,100°F, and pouring the resultant glass into ten-foot-tall stainless steel canisters. The low-level filtrate is stabilized in a solid, cement-based waste form that is pumped into above-ground engineering vaults where it becomes solidified.

The entire process flow is supported by the technology center. SRTC developed specific glass compositions tailored for SRS waste, supported the selection and implementation of the glass melter and subsequent modifications, designed off-gas systems to ensure all gaseous species are removed, and developed the ITP processes.

Another piece of the SRTC mission is related to spent-fuel storage. SRS has facilities to receive and store spent nuclear fuel. Control of fuel basin water chemistry is critical, and SRTC performed extensive work to de-

termine optimal compositions. We are also involved in fuel basin monitoring, including corrosion assessments and diagnostics. SRTC also has extensive capabilities in environmental remediation technologies that are focused toward the cleanup of soils and groundwater. We have, for example, developed bioremediation techniques that effectively use naturally occurring soil bacteria to "remove" organics such as trichloroethylene.

The current mission of the Nuclear Materials Stabilization and Storage Division is focused toward using SRS facilities to stabilize legacy materials. These materials include both the residuals that remain within our facilities after nuclear materials processing ceased at SRS in 1992 and materials that exist at other sites within the DOE complex. SRTC has developed vitrification processes for americium and curium (valuable for medical applications) and plutonium. These technology achievements provide the basis for new mission opportunities at the SRS.

Basically, SRTC provides most of the technology development support for the site. We support existing processes, develop technology to make them more cost effective, and develop new processes. As the SRTC director, I have ultimate accountability for everything the technology center develops.

I have always been driven; I still am. My

early resolve to escape poverty included a decision not to have children. My partner and I have been together for twenty-one years, and I could never figure out how to manage a career and children without association with an extended family. Managing a lifestyle with two careers is difficult enough. My partner also has a Ph.D. in materials engineering, and he has stayed on the technical track. He was extraordinarily helpful early in my career as I struggled to understand the American culture and the American male. He taught me some of the lingo, what the handshakes meant, all the little things that made a difference. He has also been tremendously supportive of my career. There was a considerable amount of time when he worked for me; neither of our egos got in the way, and the situation was never problematic.

The SRTC is predominantly male, particularly in the technical area, and most of the men have very conventional lifestyles. I have made no secret of the fact that I am not a clone of my senior management peers. I have a Ph.D., I'm female, I'm not married, and I don't play golf. But being a woman has never limited my opportunities. I gain respect because of my knowledge base, my personal style, and my willingness to roll up my sleeves and work in the trenches when needed. I've never been caught up in sexism, maybe because it was infrequent or perhaps because I just didn't recognize it, given my personality. The key question is, "Have I hit the glass ceiling now?" I don't know the answer. I sense that the next step will be more difficult, but I continue trying to grow as a professional. I read a lot to learn what's going on in technology and management, and think about how I can bring new ideas to bear on my current responsibilities. That is an important lesson I learned early on—you can't retire on the job. You have to constantly change to meet the needs of the environment; nothing is static, and you have to move and grow with the changes around you. I attribute much of my success to this philosophy.

PRESENT POSITION: Vice President and Director, Savannah River Technology Center at the Department of Energy's Savannah River Site

FIELD: Materials engineering

RESEARCH AREA: Materials diagnostics/radiation effects

EDUCATION: B.S. in Physics (1969), Victoria University of Manchester, England; M.S. in Metallurgical Engineering (1973), University of Pittsburgh; Ph.D. in Materials Engineering (1976), University of Pittsburgh

DATE/PLACE OF BIRTH: January 13, 1948/Snainton, England

Susan Wood lives with her partner, James Greggi, in Aiken, South Carolina.

INTERVIEW DATE: July 1995

Lilian Shiao-Yen Wu

Research Staff Member
IBM Thomas J. Watson Research Center

Lilian Shiao-Yen Wu is an applied mathematician who builds mathematical models that estimate risk in order to optimize profit. Her work helps IBM plan rational solutions to the problem of the short life cycle of expensive personal computers. She was born in Beijing, China, and lived in New Zealand, Hong Kong, and Taiwan until she came to college in the United States. Because all of her previous studies were in Chinese, she gravitated toward mathematics because it is a universal language. For her it has been a good career choice.

❧

At IBM I work closely with our personal computer division, which has its own particular forecasting and planning challenges. Personal computers are like fashion items—they have very short life cycles, approximately six months, yet there's a long lead time before you actually get any information on how well the item will sell in the marketplace. This is the forecasting and planning problem we face.

Many other companies dealing with short-life-cycle products face a similar problem, but because personal computers are also very expensive, IBM's investment in a product line is significant. In my job I use mathematics to think about this problem and to help plan rational solutions. In personal computers we characterize a product based on how confident we are in forecasting the volume to be sold and its profit margin. Given the characteristics of the product, we try to balance the risk of excess inventory against the possibility that demand will exceed the actual supply. We build mathematical models that take into ac-

count these two kinds of risk in order to optimize profit.

Mathematics is an excellent language for describing certain events that happen in the world. Often I enter into business situations that are chaotic. When I cast the problem in mathematical language and put down all the assumptions and objectives on how I want to frame it, the solution falls into place. I then systematically work toward what is best for running the business. My decisions are deliberate and made with foresight and understanding. I find a great deal of satisfaction in

Lilian Wu during high school

Lilian Wu, 1995
PHOTOGRAPH BY RANDY MASSER

helping business people with a situation that's difficult to deal with—in using mathematics first to bring order and then to develop a framework for action. In the process, I get to talk to all kinds of people, and I see my work make a difference in their thinking and in how they deal with the future. Deliberate planning pays off, and at the same time it's a lot of fun talking to people in finance, manufacturing, and many other arenas. Applied mathematicians experience that type of excitement. What we do makes a difference.

My work environment in many ways is like a university, but with a lot more interaction between colleagues. I have a lot of personal responsibility in deciding what I do. I'm very independent, pick my own problems, and interact with a lot of high-quality people. I can always go to another colleague's office, bounce off an idea, and see whether he or she thinks it makes sense. I don't work in isolation; often I work in groups with people from research, manufacturing, and marketing, and with programmers. Mathematical solutions are not static; after analyzing a set of products, we build a model that captures the essence of

how actually to plan those products, and we build personal computer programs based on those mathematics. We then give our computer programs to planners to use in the development of new products. Programs make our mathematical models more accessible and useful.

At IBM, we have very few staff meetings. It's very casual. We write our own progress reports and agendas, which puts a lot of responsibility on a young person coming into a research lab like ours. He or she must find a good problem to work on, with challenging intellectual content that will also be of significant interest either to IBM or the mathematics community. As an applied mathematician, I also interact with people outside of IBM, at the university; it's all part of what I do to contribute to science as well as to IBM. I have taught at the New York University Business School and am a director of the International Institute of Forecasters, a group that represents academia and industry. We get together once a year at an international conference, discuss what we're currently working on, give talks, and exchange ideas. A typical day in my life varies. I talk to people, do research, compute, write, and publish papers. For me, research involves sitting in my office, deriving a formula or analyzing some sales data, trying to make sense out of it, devising a model to describe the data sensibly, and deriving consequences of the model.

As a member of President Clinton's Committee of Advisers on Science and Technology, I've spent the past three months thinking about fusion. Seven of us wrote a report on the state of fusion in the United States and recommended the direction we think fusion should go in the next five years. This work, which was done for Congress and the Department of Energy, was varied and satisfying because it enabled me to tackle national problems. I went for site visits to the Princeton Plasma Lab and to San Diego to examine their fusion reactors. I spent quite a bit of time reading background material, writing it up, and discussing it with members of the committee. That's another aspect of a scientist's life; once we become more experienced, we are invited to work on committees, to use our abilities to think and analyze broader problems. It gives us, as scientists, a chance to give back something of value to society. I've been extremely lucky—I've gotten a great deal out of my career and really like to give back to society. Working on national problems has been a way to do it.

Probably one of the most important people in my life is my mother, Betty Wu. She is not a scientist but a painter. She instilled in me a sense of being no different in abilities than a boy, and gave me a belief that science was a good field for me—that anything was possible. My mother is the kind of person who asks lots of questions, and so I've learned that no question is a stupid question. She influenced me a great deal, giving me a full world to think about in terms of what I would like to do.

I'm the oldest of four children, and my family has always been a source of strength for me. We lived in New Zealand until I was seven, and then moved to Hong Kong. Later my father, Wen-Hui Wu, felt it was very important for me to learn what it meant to be Chinese. So when I was ten my family moved to Taiwan, where I went to an all-girls junior high and high school. I certainly did not have the pressures in Taiwan that a young girl might experience here today—pressures of dating, of female versus male professions. None of that existed for me or for any of my friends.

In high school I wasn't certain what interested me. I originally thought I wanted to specialize in plant diseases because at the time Taiwan was very agricultural, and I felt that would be the best way to help my country. However, when I came to the United States to attend college, all my previous studies had been in Chinese, and microbiology was impossible for me because I had to translate everything from Latin into Chinese. I gravitated toward mathematics, which is a universal language; it has been a good career choice.

Very few women specialize in my field. I'm trying to figure out if it's because the environment is hostile to women or because they haven't been encouraged. Mathematics may not interest women who prefer to work on problems that give them more contact with people. But this is a misconception: while pure mathematics may include very little work with others, applied mathematics—like my daily work—allows interaction with all kinds of people. It's not as if someone hands me a super-hard homework problem, I stay in my office and work on it for weeks, maybe months, and then emerge from my office with the answer. I'm very much part of defining and solving problems, and teamwork enhances the job.

At times it has been difficult trying to combine my personal life with my professional life—making the two work best for me has been a big challenge. At different stages of my life I would have liked more flexibility in apportioning my time—for example, to be able to work three days a week instead of five, as I was able to do for half a year recently at IBM—and still be accepted as a serious researcher. Many people still believe that unless you dedicate yourself 100 percent to your job, you're not committed. That kind of attitude is not very healthy and is going to be a big challenge as more women enter the workforce. We must help women experience a good family life along with a rewarding professional life. The profession would be much better off if it accepted varying degrees of balance between personal and professional life.

I think women should take as much math as they can. They will use it in surprising ways, even if they don't plan to be mathematicians. It's a powerful language, and more and more jobs in the future are going to be technical, so it will enhance their careers to have better technical backgrounds. Mathematics has a lot to say about our lives, and it helps us understand what goes on around us. For example, being able to organize the large sets of numbers we gather on surveys gives us a better description of who we are and of the changes that would help people who are less privileged.

Many decisions based on quantitative information provide much better solutions to real-life problems. We don't convey that enough to our young people, so math simply becomes homework problems without a connection to anything that's real. Mathematics takes practice, just like reading; you have to do it over and over again. Young girls are shortchanging themselves if they decide mathematics is too hard for them before they give it a chance, and a lot of practice.

I am a member of the National Research Council Committee on Women in Science and Engineering, which studies why there are so few women in different science disciplines or professions. The committee is made up of women and men in industry as well as academia. It meets just a couple of times a year, but we stay in contact over e-mail, hold conferences, and publish reports that come out of the National Research Council. I believe women need more role models. There's a tremendous psychological difference between being the only woman to do something and seeing that others are doing it. Having more women in the profession and allowing young

people to work in jobs that use mathematics would be very helpful.

While much of my life is devoted to my work, in my free time I like to ski. Although I'm not an artist myself, I also enjoy art because of my family background. When my schedule was less busy, I was a docent for art exhibits at the Katonah Art Museum, a local gallery in New York. My sister tells me to think of art like I think of mathematics: if everybody can do math, then everybody can draw!

PRESENT POSITION: Research Staff Member, IBM Thomas J. Watson Research Center; Member, President's Committee of Advisers on Science and Technology; Member, Committee on Women in Science and Engineering, National Research Council

FIELD: Applied mathematics

RESEARCH AREAS: Mathematical modeling and statistical analysis in business; bridging the gap between forecasting practitioners and researchers; population biology

EDUCATION: B.S. with High Honors in Mathematics (1968), University of Maryland; M.S. in Applied Mathematics (1972), Cornell University; Ph.D. in Applied Mathematics (1974), Cornell University

DATE/PLACE OF BIRTH: July 6, 1947/Beijing, China

Lilian Wu lives in Chappaqua, New York.

INTERVIEW DATE: June 1995

Rosalyn Sussman Yalow

Senior Medical Investigator Emeritus
VETERANS ADMINISTRATION HOSPITAL, BRONX, NEW YORK

Rosalyn Yalow, the first American-born woman to win a Nobel Prize in Science, was awarded the prize in 1977 for her work with Solomon Berson in developing radioimmunoassay. A medical physicist, she spent most of her career at the Veterans Affairs Medical Center in the Bronx, and most of her professional associations were with men. She attributes her success to timing (starting graduate school during World War II and coming of age when research on isotopes was just beginning), an outstanding colleague (Berson), and a husband who fully supported her career.

&

Neither my mother nor father had much education: my father left school following the eighth grade, my mother completed sixth grade, and both went to work. But no one would ever have thought that they had so little formal education: my father read the *New York Times* daily and eventually had a business in which he did the bookkeeping; my mother read all the books I ever brought home from school, including ones from college. I also had a brother who was five years older than I. He went to college at night during the Depression and then got a job in the post office.

I started to read before I went to kindergarten. Like other children in my Jewish neighborhood, I joined the library at age five—as a matter of fact, I joined on the day I turned five—and from then on made weekly trips. Both my parents encouraged this intellectual endeavor. My parents were always supportive of whatever I wanted to do, including my pursuit of a Ph.D., even though they had no idea

what that was all about. A Ph.D. in physics didn't mean anything to them. Yet I never got the message from them, or anyone else, that there were certain things that girls couldn't do.

When I was growing up, New York had a gender-segregated public school system. I went to all-girls' schools beginning in junior high, continuing through high school, and then Hunter College. My career plan, set during high school, was to become a schoolteacher, an aspiration many of my Jewish female friends

Rosalyn Yalow in her lab at the Bronx VA Medical Center
PHOTO COURTESY OF BRONX VA MEDICAL MEDIA

shared. A high school chemistry teacher introduced me to the joys of working with my hands as well as my mind, so when I entered college I was planning to major in chemistry. However, when I took college physics in my sophomore year, the department became interested in me and suggested that I major in physics. Hunter had an outstanding physics faculty and it was a small department, much smaller than the chemistry department in which no one took a personal interest in me. At that time Hunter College did not have a physics major, so I had to take one course at City College to finish the major. I graduated from Hunter College in 1941 as the first physics major.

I wanted to go to graduate school to pursue physics, and I thought that I would have to work my way through school. I was prepared to work as a secretary in the lab of one of the country's leading biochemists, Dr. Rudolf Schoenheimer. I had taken typing courses in college, studied German, had some lab experience, and had promised to take stenography. I was prepared to do this in order to enter science through the back door. However, the world was already at war, and although the United States wasn't yet a part of it, men with my qualifications were being drafted; so I received a graduate assistantship at the University of Illinois. I was the first woman graduate assistant in the physics department since World War I. The year I began was also the first year the University of Illinois accepted Jewish graduate students. The university wasn't anti-Semitic: they simply couldn't get Jewish students jobs afterwards, and so they thought that it didn't make sense to educate them. I taught eight hours a week and, because the war was in full swing and men were hard to come by, was promoted in my third year. I became an instructor and, while doing my thesis work, taught fifteen hours a week. I have always enjoyed teaching and I'm pretty good at it. I remained the only woman in the physics department throughout my entire graduate education.

I completed my Ph.D. in January 1945. The war was still on, and I got a job as a sort of electrical engineer at the Federal Telecom-munications Laboratory, which was affiliated with the International Telephone and Telegraph Corporation (ITT) research laboratories. I was the first woman engineer at ITT. They needed women in many industries because of the war, and so I never felt any particular prejudice. On the contrary, I felt needed. The research unit where I worked collapsed at the end of the war because the Jewish-French engineers returned to France.

I went back to Hunter College, this time as a faculty member. Hunter had no research facilities, so my job was to teach. I stayed on at Hunter for an extra year because I had an outstanding student, Mildred Dresselhaus, whom I couldn't abandon at that point in her career. [See the profile for Mildred Dresselhaus beginning on page 105.] I wanted to teach her because she had so much potential. Like many other young Jewish women, she planned on being a teacher, and I helped to convince her to major in physics. She eventually became the first tenured woman in enginering at MIT and a member of the National Academy of Sciences and the National Academy of Engineering. Students like her don't come along every day, and good teachers try to encourage good students. I was a good teacher.

My husband and I had been graduate students together, and we married two years after I completed my Ph.D. My son was born in 1952 and my daughter in 1954; I was already working at the Veterans Affairs Medical Center in the Bronx when they were born. At that time, either the federal government or the VA had a rule that you had to resign in the fifth month of pregnancy; but they needed me because I was one of very few people in my area of expertise, so I wasn't forced to resign, although other women were. Everyone simply pretended it wasn't happening: I've always joked that I had the only eight-pound, two-ounce premature baby. I never had difficulty working and raising children. In those days maids were easy to come by, and my mother came over every day to make sure that the maid was taking proper care of the children. I had always planned to have a family and a career; it never entered my mind that I couldn't have both.

I worked many, many hours during those years. Before things were automated, I often went back to work in the middle of the night to change counters. I don't think I ever slept. On Sundays I used to bring the children to my lab because the maid was off, although they didn't find it particularly exciting or interesting.

My Ph.D. was in nuclear physics, but I had done no research during my time at Hunter because they didn't have research facilities. My husband worked at Montefiore Hospital during that time, and so I knew about the existence of medical physics. He urged me to explore this field. Through him I met Dr. Edith Quimby, the leading woman medical physicist in the country. She introduced me to the "dean of the medical physicists," Dr. Gioacchino Failla. We met and talked, and then Failla called the head of radiotherapy, who was setting up a radioisotope unit at the Bronx VA and said, "I have somebody with me, and if you want to get isotopes you have to hire her." In 1947 I was hired part-time at the Bronx Veterans Administration Hospital because I was still teaching part-time at Hunter College. I give a lot of credit to the VA for recognizing that the use of radioisotopes in medicine was a combined clinical and research function. From this recognition and work the medical specialty of nuclear medicine developed.

Initially our research measured the rate of disappearance of radioactivity injected in the skin. Soon after, in the summer of 1950, we were joined by Solomon Berson, an internist. Medical physics required an interdisciplinary approach, and we complemented each other beautifully. We moved into a number of areas: we did twenty-four-hour iodine uptakes like everybody else, but our first contribution was to do a half-hour uptake, which made for better separation between thyroid function and the effects of renal excretion. We did the first thyroid clearance test; we did blood volume determination. We believed that the future lay in understanding human physiology. Sol and I were perfect workmates: he loved physics though he never formally studied it, and I loved medicine though I never formally stud-

ied it. But I learned medicine—biology, physiology, and anatomy—from Berson, and he learned physics, chemistry, and mathematics from me. We complemented each other in many ways. We worked together until his death in 1972.

The work we did that eventually won the Nobel Prize was radioimmunoassay (RIA). We developed RIA as an offshoot and extension of some research on insulin. We were using radiolabeled insulin—insulin tagged with a radioactive molecule—to look at how long it took people to process the molecule. We would inject the labeled insulin and then take blood samples over a period of time and measure the amount of radioactivity—hence, the amount of insulin—remaining in the blood. We found that, contrary to expectation, injected insulin took *longer* to process in diabetics than in nondiabetics who hadn't had insulin injections before. Since it wasn't immediately obvious whether the effect was caused by the insulin or the diabetes, we looked at a third group, nondiabetic schizophrenics who'd had insulin shock therapy. These patients also retained the insulin longer, so we realized that the effect was related to whether someone had been previously treated with insulin, and we concluded that they must be manufacturing antibodies to injected insulin molecules. Insulin bound to antibody is effectively inactivated and thus is harder for the body to process.

Today insulin given to diabetics is genetically engineered and is identical to human insulin, but back then we were using animal insulin, which was just different enough to trigger an immune response in some people. Few people at that time believed that the insulin molecule was large enough to trigger an immune response, and we had some difficulty getting this important result published.

Although the result about insulin was important, we realized there might be something even more valuable in modifying the technique we used to measure it in the blood. What we were really interested in was how much hormone was in a quantity of fluid from the body, and we designed RIA to measure that. Simply put, if we took a known quantity of antibody to a hormone, a known quantity of radiolabeled hormone, and a sample containing an unknown quantity of unlabeled hormone from a patient and mixed them together, the labeled and unlabeled hormone would compete with each other to bind to a finite number of sites on the antibody molecule. After incubating the mixture for a while, we could measure how much radiolabeled hormone had bound to the antibody, and then calculate how much unlabeled hormone must have been present in the sample to compete with it.

RIA lets you test for incredibly small concentrations of a molecule, and it also lets you perform the test on very simple samples. With RIA, you can do a blood test on a diabetic using only a drop of plasma, about one one-thousandth of what you needed before. RIA enabled doctors to diagnose all sorts of conditions caused by changes in hormones. It aided the diagnosis and treatment of disorders like diabetes, dwarfism, underactive thyroids, insufficient sex hormones, and spina bifida in fetuses.

I was awarded the Nobel Prize in 1977 for the work Berson and I did on RIA. By then it had become very clear that it had revolutionized endocrinology and made possible the study of neuroendocrinology (hormones are often found as neurotransmitters). They don't award the Nobel Prize posthumously, which is why Berson wasn't included, but the prize represents our work together. The big question at the time was, "Would the woman survivor get it?" It was clear that if I had died Sol would have gotten the Nobel Prize; but it wasn't clear, with his death in March 1972, that I would get it. Five years later I did.

Throughout my career, most of my professional associations were with men: first male professors in the physics departments at Hunter and the University of Illinois, then with male physicians at the VA. That was never a problem for me or for them. I never interacted with another female scientist, and the only female role model I ever had was Marie Curie. Like many young women who read her biography (written by her daughter) when it was first published in 1938, I wanted to be like her.

The world has also changed enormously in my lifetime. Many prejudices no longer exist. It's now easier for women who work hard to move up. Men are still in senior positions, but I believe women will eventually get there. I did.

I attribute my career success to several factors: I began my career at a time when, because of the war, I was given opportunities that enabled me to prove myself; I had the good luck to come to work at the VA at an opportune time when the research on isotopes was just beginning; I had the good fortune to be joined by Sol Berson; I had a great husband who understood what I was doing and was never threatened by the fact that I was more professionally prominent than he was; and I had a wonderful maid who cared for my children.

When I reached seventy, I became an emerita and moved away from research toward public education. There is now such fear among the public about radiation, particularly radon. After all, there were practically no lung cancer deaths in 1930; it was only 3 percent or 4 percent of what it is now. But radon has always been around, so what's causing all the lung cancer deaths? I believe it's smoking. What I attempt to do now is to educate people about radon and lung cancer.

Looking back over my life, there's nothing that I would change: I chose the right subject, the right graduate school, the right professional career, and the right husband. I have been fortunate in many ways.

PRESENT POSITION: Senior Medical Investigator Emeritus, Veterans Administration Hospital, Bronx, New York

FIELD: Medical physics

RESEARCH AREA: Medical use of radioisotopes, radioimmunoassay

EDUCATION: B.A. in Physics (1941), Hunter College; Ph.D. in Nuclear Physics (1945), University of Illinois

DATE/PLACE OF BIRTH: July 19, 1921/New York City

Rosalyn Yalow lives in New York City.

INTERVIEW DATE: March 1995

Judith S. Young

Full Professor of Physics and Astronomy
UNIVERSITY OF MASSACHUSETTS

In high school Judy Young thought that she would pursue a career in biochemistry. But when her astronomer mother, Vera Rubin, taught an astronomy course at her high school, the lecture on black holes turned her interest to astronomy. The academic freedom she has now as a full professor in the Department of Physics and Astronomy at the University of Massachusetts has allowed her to rekindle her love of biochemistry: when she's not studying star formations in galaxies, she conducts cancer research.

❧

I do many things, but as a faculty member at the University of Massachusetts, my primary responsibility is teaching. I teach one class per semester, and I advise and guide students doing research. I teach astronomy to undergraduate nonmajors about three semesters out of four, and the rest of the time I teach graduate students who are pursuing Ph.D.'s in astronomy. When I'm teaching, it takes up most of my time for that semester—partly by choice but also because a lot of time is involved in preparing lectures, handouts, and problem sets, in helping students, and in grading.

I love teaching astronomy. While I know I'm a good teacher at all levels, I feel that I make the biggest contribution teaching the people who don't know anything about astronomy by just getting them turned on to what's out there in the universe. The undergraduates in my classes have a wide range of interests and abilities. Some of them are very attentive and work very hard, but my impression is that the majority of them don't like to think

or resent being challenged too much. And for some people, astronomy is one challenge and thought-provoking problem after another. That part makes it difficult, but there are always some people who really enjoy the class.

The little bit of time left after teaching is generally spent being a member of the department—attending colloquia and faculty meetings, reviewing articles, and guiding students who do research under my supervision.

Judy Young discussing galaxies in her office in the Department of Physics and Astronomy at the University of Massachusetts at Amherst, 1989
PHOTO BY STEVE LONG

445

I have a little bit of time to conduct my ongoing research, but that gets done more in the summer, when I don't teach. For about the last fourteen years, I've been studying star formation in galaxies. I'm most interested in spiral galaxies because that's where most of the stars are seen to be forming today and because they're so beautiful. I study galaxies using two different types of telescopes. Using a radio telescope, I measure the distribution and the amount of matter in the cold gas clouds that are the fertile sites where stars will form in the future. And then, using optical telescopes, I measure the quantity of hot gas that's produced when a young star first forms and is ionizing the hydrogen nearby. With these techniques, I determine both the quantity of young stars and the quantity of gas from which they form, and that allows me to measure the efficiency with which stars are forming in galaxies. It's a lot like the fuel efficiency of your car: how many stars you get per so many kilograms of hydrogen, or how many miles you get per gallon of fuel.

One of the questions I ask is, What makes galaxies different? Why do some galaxies appear to be ten times more efficient at converting their gas into stars and other galaxies seem to be plodding along merrily but forming stars at a much lower rate, like our galaxy does? One of the things we've learned over the last five years or so is that when galaxies collide with each other, the collision itself makes them much more efficient in converting whatever gas they have into stars.

As a young girl, I was much more interested in chemistry than anything else. Through junior high and the early years of high school, I wanted to go into chemistry, and by my senior year of high school, I decided that biochemistry would be interesting. Then, in my senior year of high school, I asked my mother to teach an astronomy course at my school; being in a rather flexible position at the Carnegie Institution, she agreed. The day that she described black holes, I was so amazed that I decided I wanted to study astronomy. From that day, I decided I was going to be an astronomer, and I have never changed my mind. [See Vera Rubin's profile beginning on page 329.]

I grew up in northwest Washington, D.C., and went to public school. I have three brothers; two are geologists and one's a mathematician. We were always encouraged to think and to reason; if we had questions about math, there was always someone who was willing and able to explain it.

Our family loved to spend time outdoors. We would go camping in the summer, and I remember sleeping out in the open and watching the beautiful night sky. We didn't have a telescope at home, so I was never an amateur astronomer who used telescopes—I just loved looking at the sky. I loved lying out in August in the fields to see the meteor showers. I loved, and still do, watching eclipses, and I have gotten some really spectacular photographs in the last few years of some lunar and solar eclipses.

In high school, I applied to Radcliffe, Princeton, and Yale. I was accepted by Radcliffe and Princeton, but not Yale. I visited both Radcliffe (Harvard) and Princeton and distinctly remember being turned off by the student at Princeton who gave me a tour—he was really not used to dealing with women. Princeton had just begun accepting women, and I realized that being in one of the first classes of women there would be uncomfortable, so I went to Radcliffe. Harvard and Radcliffe still had separate admissions, but all the classes were together. Men could live at Radcliffe after the first year, and women could live at Harvard after the first year. But because the Harvard College Observatory is right around the corner from Radcliffe, it was ideal for me to live at Radcliffe, where I had access to the library and all the classes that were at the observatory. Even though Harvard is big, the astronomy department was small, and Radcliffe was smaller than Harvard, so I didn't feel lost at all.

The ratio of men to women in the astronomy major was eight or ten to one, but my largest stumbling block came from male faculty in an advising role. In my junior year, one faculty member said to me that the best I'd probably be able to do was to get a teaching position at a junior college and maybe I should just get married. Things were said to me that weren't said to the male students. One day in my freshman seminar we were rehearsing the talks that we would be giving, and the faculty member in charge turned to me and asked me to go get the tea for everyone. That was 1970. That same year, a visiting professor from Caltech met with our freshman seminar and said that at Caltech when graduate applications came in from men and women, they automatically downgraded the ones from women because they would just drop out and get married. These comments were made overtly, like it was the natural state of things and there was nothing you could do about it. But the situation is changing. Today such comments are not made, at least not in my department at the University of Massachusetts and among colleagues I know.

After Radcliffe, the first challenge I faced was that I didn't get into the graduate schools I had applied to. Although I had graduated with honors, my grades weren't good enough. The summer after I graduated from college, my parents suggested several other places to apply for graduate school: Minnesota was one, and I got in. I was admitted in astronomy, in the Department of Physics and Astronomy, and I had to pass a physics qualifying exam. My physics grades weren't that great, and I surprised everyone when I was one of four of our entering class of thirty physics students who passed the exam our first year.

Then the astronomers turned their backs on me when I got married. Members of the department, who were themselves married, told me I should leave with a master's degree. But rather than following their advice, I changed advisers—out of astronomy into physics. I knew that if I had stayed in astronomy, when it came time for the oral qualifying exam, they could easily flunk me. It wasn't until many years later, after I had succeeded, that the head of the astronomy program apologized to me. I just worry about

Judy Young in a recent photo
PHOTO BY STEVE LONG

all the women who get discouraged and diverted by all the roadblocks and the negative advice, and who don't have alternative routes to their goals.

There was one woman faculty member in the physics department at Minnesota, Phyllis Freier, who was working in an area bridging physics and astronomy. Her work involved launching telescopes in balloons to rise above the atmosphere and measure the cosmic ray nuclei that come from the galaxy; then she would analyze the different elemental isotopes. It was actually a combination of chemistry, physics, and astronomy, and working under her was an enjoyable way for me to get my Ph.D., although I still wanted to do more astronomy when I was done. My thesis was on "The Isotopic Composition of the Cosmic Rays Neon through Nickel." Because the balloon was first launched successfully right after I started working, I wasn't involved in the design or the flying of the experiment, but I was the one who did the analysis of the data. The data came back on twenty-seven magnetic tapes, and there were thirty thousand different events or particles that had entered the telescope, and I had to carefully analyze each one. Phyllis was a real inspiration as an adviser. Actually, she had been on the Minnesota faculty for over twenty-five years, but I was the first Ph.D. student she had advised.

At the time I was finishing my degree, my thesis adviser was on a space science board in Washington with the director of the observatory at UMass. When my adviser told him that she had a student finishing up, he said that they were looking for a postdoc and that I should apply. I applied for the job and was accepted. My postdoc involved using a telescope, the largest radio telescope of its kind in the United States. In fact, at the time it was the largest of its kind in the world. Since then, a number of other telescopes have been built, but what distinguished this telescope through the 1980s was its large aperture and very sensitive receivers. This combination allowed me to study the gas in galaxies that no one else had been able to detect previously. Other people were beginning to use some other telescopes to do this, but because I had the telescope here, I could get much more time on it than anyone else at a national facility or in another country. For the first five years of my postdoc I spent one week per month at the telescope, plus other single nights that were available. Radio telescopes can operate even during the day, so it was exhausting work, being awake twenty out of twenty-four hours, seven days in a row. I can't do that anymore—I get too tired. But my hard work paid off.

The UMass Department of Physics and Astronomy has about fifty faculty members. The astronomy program has about fifteen faculty, and the radio astronomy group is a subset of six faculty. As a postdoc I did very well; my observations were successful, and I wrote papers. I had come from physics, where the mode of doing things is very different. There would be a big experiment with a lot of peo-

ple, and you would reduce the data and then, after many years, publish it. In astronomy observations can be taken much faster than most people can physically analyze, digest, and write about them. For the first five or six years, I was publishing four or five papers a year in the *Astrophysical Journal*. In 1984 the person who was my mentor at UMass was hired at Caltech, and his position was filled by two junior people, I being one of them. I was hired as an assistant professor but had actually done some teaching as a postdoc (at my request) and got one year of tenure credit. I came up for and received tenure in 1989.

In 1986 I got the Maria Goeppert-Mayer Award from the American Physical Society. This award was given to a woman in the early stages of her career. Selection was worldwide, and I was really honored to be the first recipient, to be selected as the best young woman physicist in the world. The award required that I give talks to encourage other women in science. One of the talks was at General Electric in Schenectady, New York, since they funded the award. When I got to GE to give the talk, there were several hundred men and only a few women in the audience. I started to laugh. I wondered what I was going to say to these men that would encourage women in science. So I told them that when women are in the physical sciences—and especially physics and some of the engineering fields, where there are mostly men—it is important that the women be accepted by their male colleagues. I said that it was very important for them to encourage the women in their lives—their wives, sisters, and especially their daughters—and to tell them it's not OK not to do well in math. They *can* do it.

I never questioned that I would do anything other than having a career, although not necessarily in science. I've seen a very strong correlation between girls who are encouraged by their fathers in math and science and those who succeed. My father is a physicist. When I was in college, there were four women in my physics class, and all of our fathers were physicists. That was the first time I realized how important fathers are to their daughters' success. If your father isn't supportive of you using your intelligence, I think it's more difficult to make it in a male-dominated field. Of course, women role models are also very important. There are just fewer of us. I myself was very lucky to have an encouraging father, a great teacher and role model for a mother, and a Ph.D. adviser who believed in me.

I've been divorced for seven years. My ex-husband is a scientist and has several master's degrees in the sciences, but he never was interested in pursuing a Ph.D., and my success got in the way for him.

My daughter, Laura Rose, was born in 1983. She's twelve and a half. She's a delight and a bright and gifted child. She's very artistic. If I had to make a prediction, I'd say she's not going to be a scientist. But then, at least when I was in elementary school, my parents didn't think I'd become a scientist either. I liked to do a lot of different things when I was younger; I loved sewing and playing the piano; I remember writing poems. My daughter does painting and drawing and a lot of writing and reading; she would make a good teacher. She was born the year after I got my tenure-track position. There's never an easy time to have children; for me, it was just when it happened. I did most of the child care. I would take Laura to school in the morning and put in my full day. My husband came home in the afternoon, after picking her up from preschool, so I could do my afternoon departmental duties. I would come home, make dinner for the family, put her to bed, and then do whatever other work I had to do.

I could not have the lifestyle that I do in any area other than academia. I can go home at three if I need to for my daughter, and I can stay home in the morning if the bathtub drain is clogged. I am very lucky to have the flexibility available in academia. I am also free to travel around the world to use telescopes and to attend meetings.

My career has blossomed while I've been at UMass. By the time I was promoted to full professor in the fall of 1992, I had spent thir-teen or fourteen years on my studies of galaxies; I had accumulated the largest set of data in the world on the subject and was well known in the field. I was proud of what I'd done, but at age forty I also realized that I didn't want astronomy research to be all I did for another forty years. I felt that as a scientist I have the ability to contribute more than just what I do in astronomy. Thanks to two acquaintances, I found myself sitting in on a class here at the university entitled "The Biology of Cancer and AIDS," which brought me back to my original interest in biochemistry. I got an idea for a cure for cancer, and I have just been having the time of my life teaching myself what I need to know to do laboratory studies of cells. I do the cancer research on Fridays and the rest of the week I do my studies of galaxies—which is part of the academic freedom one has in becoming a full professor. The only requirements are my teaching and to continue doing research; there's really no requirement specifying what that research needs to be. I love astronomy, and I am also enjoying the possibility that I can end up making some other contributions as well.

Another project that I am very excited about is in the area of astronomy education for the general public. The university has given me the approval to build an outdoor exhibit that I call a Sunwheel. It's a mini-Stonehenge, with standing stones that line up with the rising and the setting of the sun at the solstices and the equinoxes. It's a structure that can be built anywhere in the open with a good view of the eastern and western horizons. Ours is going to be in an open field on the south side of campus. I just observed the summer solstice sunrise and sunset, and next winter I'll view the winter solstice sun to determine the locations of the standing stones. The scale is 120 feet across, and the stones are old sections of granite curbing. The stones are ten feet long, and we're going to stand them on end, sunk about five feet into the ground for stability, standing five feet tall—that's how tall I am. I'm going to have my astronomy students visit the Sunwheel to watch the sunset several times during the semester. And anyone who visits the Sunwheel will be able to see the magnitude of the variations in where the sun rises and sets during the year. I am now on my way to Colorado to build a Sunwheel near Mesa Verde, on land that's been given to me for this purpose. This Sunwheel will be located at Indian Camp Ranch in Cortez, Colorado. Bringing astronomy down to Earth is very exciting for me!

PRESENT POSITION: Full Professor, Department of Physics and Astronomy, University of Massachusetts

FIELD: Extragalactic astronomy

RESEARCH AREAS: Star formations in galaxies; cancer research

EDUCATION: B.A. with honors in Astronomy (1974), Harvard University; M.S. in Physics (1977) and Ph.D. in Physics (1979), University of Minnesota

DATE/PLACE OF BIRTH: September 15, 1952/ Washington, D.C.

Judy Young lives in Amherst, Massachusetts, with her daughter, Laura, her partner, Gene, their golden retriever, Shadow, and a rabbit, a parrot, two turtles, and five fish.

INTERVIEW DATE: May 1996

Bibliography

Abir-Am, Pnina G., and Dorinda Outram, eds. *Uneasy Careers and Intimate Lives: Women in Science, 1787–1979*. New Brunswick, N.J.: Rutgers University Press, 1987.

Adelman, Clifford. *Women at Thirtysomething: Paradoxes of Attainment*. Washington D.C.: U.S. Department of Education, Office of Educational Research and Development, 1991.

Aldrich, Michele L. "Review Essay: Women in Science." *Signs: Journal of Women in Culture and Society* 4, no. 1 (1978): 126–35.

Alic, Margaret. *Hypatia's Heritage: A History of Women in Science from Antiquity to the Late Nineteenth Century*. Boston: Beacon Press, 1986.

Arnold, Lois Barber. *Four Lives in Science: Women's Education in the Nineteenth Century*. New York: Schocken Books, 1984.

Astin, A. W. *What Matters in College? "Four Critical Years" Revisited*. San Francisco: Jossey-Bass, 1993.

Astin, H. S., and L. J. Sax. "Developing Scientific Talent in Undergraduate Women." In *The Equity Equation: Women in Science, Engineering and Mathematics*, ed. C. S. Davis et al. San Francisco: Jossey-Bass, 1996.

Baenninger, Maryann, and Nora Newcombe. "The Role of Experience in Spatial Test Performance: A Meta-Analysis." *Sex Roles* 20 (1989): 327–43.

Benjamin, Marina, ed. *Science and Sensibility: Gender and Scientific Enquiry, 1790–1845*. Cambridge, Mass.: Basil Blackwell, 1991.

Briscoe, Anne, and Sheila Pfaffin, eds. *Expanding the Role of Women in the Sciences*. New York: New York Academy of Sciences, 1979.

Broome, Taft. "Heroic Woman Engineer." In *Bridging the Gender Gap in Engineering and Science: Conference Proceedings*, ed. Anne M. Humphreys. Pittsburgh: New Image Press, 1996.

Brush, Stephen G. *The History of Modern Science: A Guide to the Second Scientific Revolution, 1800–1950*. Ames: University of Iowa Press, 1988.

———. "Women in Science and Engineering." *American Scientist* 79, no. 5 (1991): 404–19.

Christie, John, and Sally Shuttleworth. *Nature Transfigured: Science and Literature, 1700–1900*. Manchester, England: Manchester University Press, 1989.

Clewell, Beatriz C., and Bernice Anderson. *Women of Color in Mathematics, Science, and Engineering: A Review of the Literature*. Washington, D.C.: Center for Women Policy Studies, 1991.

Curie, Eve. *Madame Curie*. Trans. Vincent Sheean. New York: Doubleday, 1938.

Daniels, Jane Zimmer. "Population and Pipeline." In *Bridging the Gender Gap in Science and Engineering: Conference Proceedings*, ed. Anne M. Humphreys. Pittsburgh: New Image Press, 1996.

DeBoer, G. E. "Perceived Science Ability as a Factor in the Course Selections of Men and Women in College." *Journal of Research in Science Teaching* 23 (1986): 343–52.

Dweck, C. S. "Motivational Processes Affecting Learning." *American Psychologist* 41 (1986): 1041–48.

Dweck, C. S., et al. "I. Sex Differences in Learned Helplessness." "II. The Contingencies of Evaluative Feedback in the Classroom." "III. An Experimental Analysis." *Developmental Psychology* 14 (1978): 268–76.

Eccles (Parsons), J., C. M. Kaczala, and J. L. Meece. "Socialization of Achievement Attitudes and Beliefs: Classroom Influences." *Child Development* 53 (1982): 322–39.

Etzkowitz, Henry, et al. "Athena Unbound: Barriers to Women in Academic Science and Engineering." *Science and Public Policy* 19, no. 3 (1992): 157–79.

Etzkowitz, Henry, et al. "The Paradox of Critical Mass for Women in Science." *Science* 266 (1994): 51–54.

Fennema, Elizabeth, and J. A. Sherman. "Sex-Related Differences in Mathematics Achievement, Spatial Visualization, and Affective Factors:

A Further Study." *Journal for Research in Mathematics Education* 9 (1978): 189–203.

Fox, Mary Frank. "Women, Academia, and Career in Science and Engineering." In *The Equity Equation: Women in Science, Engineering and Mathematics,* ed. C. S. Davis et al. San Francisco: Jossey-Bass, 1996.

Fox, Robert, and Anna Guagnini. "Classical Values and Useful Knowledge: The Problem of Access to Technical Careers in Modern Europe." *Technology and Culture* 116, no. 4 (1987): 153–71.

Gacs, Ute, et al., eds. *Women Anthropologists: A Bibliographical Dictionary.* New York: Greenwood, 1988.

Giese, Patsy Ann. "Women in Science: 5000 Years of Obstacles and Achievements." *Appraisal* 25, no. 2 (1992): 1–20.

Glazer, Penina Migdal, and Miriam Slater. *Unequal Colleagues: The Entrance of Women into the Professions, 1890–1940.* New Brunswick, N.J.: Rutgers University Press, 1987.

Grayson, Lawrence P. "A Brief History of Engineering Education in the United States." *Engineering Education* 68 (December 1977): 246–68.

Green, Judy, and Jeanne LaDuke. "Women in the American Mathematics Community: The Pre-1940 PhDs." *The Mathematical Intelligencer* 9, no. 1 (1987): 11–22.

Hafter, Daryl M. "International Conference on the Role of Women in the History of Science, Technology, and Medicine in the Nineteenth and Twentieth Centuries." *Technology and Culture* 26, no. 2 (April 1985): 262–67.

Harding, Sandra, and Jean F. O'Barr, eds. *Sex and Scientific Inquiry.* Chicago: University of Chicago Press, 1987.

Harris, Barbara J. *Beyond Her Sphere: Women and the Professions in American History.* Westport, Conn.: Greenwood, 1978.

Hartmann, Susan M. "Prescriptions for Penelope: Literature on Women's Obligations to Returning World War II Veterans." *Women's Studies* 5 (1978): 223–39.

Heim, J. A., and W. D. Compton, eds. *Manufacturing Systems: Foundations of World-Class Practice.* Commissions on Foundations of Management, National Academy of Engineering. Washington, D.C.: National Academy Press, 1992.

Helly, Dorothy O., and Susan M. Reverby, eds. *Gendered Domains: Rethinking Public and Private in Women's History.* Ithaca, N.Y.: Cornell University Press, 1992.

Herzenberg, Caroline L. *Women Scientists from Antiquity to the Present: An Index.* West Cornwall, Conn.: Locust Hill Press, 1986.

———. "The Participation of Women in Science during Antiquity and the Middle Ages." *Interdisciplinary Science Reviews* 15, no. 4 (1990): 294–97.

Herzenberg, Caroline L., and Ruth Hege Howes. "Women of the Manhattan Project." *Technology Review* 96, no. 8 (November/December 1993): 32–40.

Herzenberg, Caroline L., Susan V. Meschel, and James A. Altena. "Women Scientists and Physicians of Antiquity and the Middle Ages." *Journal of Chemical Education* 68 (February 1991): 101–5.

Hollenshead, C. S., et al. "The Graduate Experience in the Sciences and Engineering: Rethinking a Gendered Institution. In *The Equity Equation: Women in Science, Engineering and Mathematics,* ed. C. S. Davis et al. San Francisco: Jossey-Bass, 1996.

Howes, Ruth Hege, and Michael R. Stevenson, eds. *Women and the Use of Military Force.* Boulder, Colo.: Lynne Reiner, 1993.

Huston, A. C., and P. H. Mussen, eds. *Sex-Typing, Handbook of Child Psychology.* Vol. 4, *Socialization, Personality, and Social Development.* New York: Wiley, 1983.

Johnson, Thomas Cary, Jr. *Scientific Interests in the Old South.* 1936. Reprint, Wilmington, Del.: Scholarly Resources, 1973.

Kahle, Jane Butler, ed. *Women in Science: A Report from the Field.* Philadelphia: Falmer, 1985.

———. "Opportunities and Obstacles: Science Education in the Schools." In *The Equity Equation: Women in Science, Engineering and Mathematics,* ed. C. S. Davis et al. San Francisco: Jossey-Bass, 1996.

Kahle, Jane Butler, and M. K. Lakes. "The Myth of Equality in Science Classrooms." *Journal of Research in Science Teaching* 20, no. 2 (1983): 131–40.

Kass-Simon, Gabrielle, Patricia Farnes, and Deborah Nash, eds. *Women of Science: Righting the Record.* Bloomington: Indiana University Press, 1990.

Kein, Jenny, and David Kassidy. "The History of Women in Science: A Seminar at the University of Regenberg, FRG." *Women's Studies International Forum* 7, no. 4 (1984): 313–17.

Keller, Evelyn Fox. *A Feeling for the Organism: The*

Life and Work of Barbara McClintock. New York: W. H. Freeman, 1983.

———. *Reflections on Science and Gender*. New Haven, Conn.: Yale University Press, 1985.

Kelly, Alison. "Women in Science: A Biographical Review. *Durham Research Review* 7 (1976): 1092–1108.

———. "Gender Differences in Teacher-Pupil Interactions: A Meta-Analytical Review." *Research in Education* 39 (1988): 1–23.

Keynes, Harvey B. *The University of Minnesota Talented Youth Mathematics Project: Recruiting Girls for a More Successful Equation*. Minneapolis: University of Minnesota Institute of Technology, 1989.

Kirkup, Gill, and Laurie Smith Keller. *Inventing Women: Science, Technology and Gender*. Cambridge: Open University Press, 1992.

Koblitz, Ann Hibner. "Science, Women, and Revolution in Russia." *Science for the People* 14, no. 4 (July/August 1982): 34–37.

———. "A Historian Looks at Gender and Science." *International Journal of Science Education* 9, no. 3 (1987): 399–407.

Kohlstedt, Sally Gregory. "In the Periphery: American Women in Science, 1830–1880." *Signs* 4, no. 1 (Autumn 1978): 81–96.

———. "Science, Women and the Russian Intelligentsia: The Generation of the 1860s." *Isis* 79 (June 1988): 208–26.

Kosheleva, Inna. *Women in Science*. Moscow: Progress Publishers, 1983.

Kramarae, Cheris, and Dale Spender. *The Knowledge Explosion: Generations of Feminist Scholarship*. Athene Series. New York: Teachers College Press, 1992.

LaFollette, Marcel C. "Eyes on the Stars: Images of Women Scientists in Popular Magazines." *Science, Technology, and Human Values* 13 (1988): 262–75.

———. *Making Science: Our Own Public Images of Science, 1910–1955*. Chicago: University of Chicago Press, 1990.

Lazarus, Barbara, and Indira Nair. "An Immodest Proposal for a Women's Institute in Engineering." In *Proceedings of the Women in Engineering Conference 1991*, ed. Jane Daniels. N.p.: Women in Engineering Program Advocates Network, 1991.

Lee, Valerie, Helen Marks, and Tina Byrd. "Sexism in Single-Sex and Coeducational Secondary School Classrooms." *Sociology of Education* 67 (1994): 92–100.

Lewis, Michael. "Parents and Children: Sex Role Development." *School Review* 80 (1972): 229–40.

MacLeod, Roy, and Russel Moseley. "Fathers and Daughters: Reflections of Women, Science and Victorian Cambridge." *History of Education* 8, no. 4 (1979): 321–33.

Manthrope, Caroline. "Science or Domestic Science: The Struggle to Define an Appropriate Science Education for Girls in Early Twentieth-Century England." *History of Education* 15 (1986): 195–213.

Marsh, H. W., et al. "Multidimensional Self-Concepts: Relations with Sex and Academic Achievement." *Journal of Educational Psychology* 77 (1985): 581–96.

Mason, Joan. "The Admission of the First Women to the Royal Society of London." *Notes and Records of the Royal Society of London* 46 (1992): 279–300.

———. "Women in Science: Breaking Out of the Circle." *Notes and Records of the Royal Society of London* 46 (1992): 177–82.

McGrayne, Sharon Bertsch. *Nobel Prize Women in Science: Their Lives, Struggles, and Momentous Discoveries*. Secaucus, N.J.: Carol Publishing Group, 1992.

Meece, J. L., et al. "Sex Differences in Math Achievement: Towards a Model of Academic Choice." *Psychological Bulletin* 91 (1982): 324–48.

Merchant, Carolyn. *The Death of Nature: Women, Ecology and the Scientific Revolution*. New York: Harper and Row, 1980.

Meyer, Gerald Dennis. *The Scientific Lady in England, 1650–1760: An Account of Her Rise, with Emphasis on the Major Roles of the Telescope and Microscope*. Berkeley: University of California Press, 1980.

Miller, C. L. "Qualitative Differences among Gender-Stereotyped Toys: Implications for Cognitive and Social Development in Girls and Boys." *Sex Roles* 16 (1987): 373–88.

Miller, Gordon L. *The History of Science: An Annotated Bibliography*. Pasadena, Calif.: Salem Press, 1992.

Montgomery, Sy. *Walking with the Great Apes: Jane Goodall, Dian Fossey, Biute Galdikas*. New York: Houghton Mifflin/Davison, 1991.

Morantz-Sanchez, Regina M. "The Many Faces of Intimacy: Professional Options and Personal Choices among Nineteenth- and Twentieth-Century Women Physicians." In *Uneasy Careers and Intimate Lives: Women in Science, 1787–1979,* ed. Pnina G. Abir-Am and Dorinda Outram. New Brunswick, N.J.: Rutgers University Press, 1987.

Mosedale, Susan S. "Science Corrupted: Victorian Biologists Consider the Woman Question." *Journal of the History of Biology* 11 (1978): 1–55.

Mozans, H. J. [John Augustine Zahm]. *Women in Science*. Notre Dame, Ind.: University of Notre Dame Press, 1991.

Mullis, I. V. S., and C. B. Jenkins. *The Science Report Card: Elements of Risk and Recovery*. Princeton, N.J.: Educational Testing Service, 1988.

Naples, Larisa Marie. "Outcomes-Based Evaluation for Education Programs in Engineering: A Focus on the Construction Industry's Needs." Ph.D. diss., Carnegie Mellon University, 1996.

Nelson, Lynn. "Bibliography: Gender, Race, Class and Science, Transformations." *New Jersey Project Journal* 1 (Spring 1990): 43–51.

Noble, David F. "A World without Women." *Technology Review* 95, no. 4 (May 1992): 522–60.

Noble, Iris. *Contemporary Women Scientists of America*. New York: Messner, 1979.

Ogilvie, Marilyn Bailey. *Women in Science: Antiquity through the Nineteenth Century*. Cambridge, Mass.: MIT Press, 1986.

———. "Marital Collaboration: An Approach to Science." In *Uneasy Careers and Intimate Lives: Women in Science, 1787–1979*, ed. Pnina G. Abir-Am and Dorinda Outram. New Brunswick, N.J.: Rutgers University Press, 1987.

O'Heran, Elizabeth M. *Profiles of Pioneer Women Scientists*. Washington, D.C.: Acropolis Books, 1985.

Opfell, Olga S. *The Lady Laureates: Women Who Have Won the Nobel Prize*. Metuchen, N.J.: Scarecrow, 1986.

Outram, Dorinda. "Fat, Gorillas, and Misogyny: Women's History in Science." *British Journal for the History of Science* 24, no. 82 (September 1991): 361–68.

Parke, R. D. "Family Interaction in the Newborn Period: Some Findings, Some Observations, and Some Unresolved Issues." In *The Developing Individual in a Changing World*, vol. 2, ed. K. F. Riegel, and J. A. Meacham. The Hague: Mouton, 1976.

Phillips, Patricia. "Science and the Ladies of Fashion." *New Scientist* 95, no. 1318 (August 1982): 416–18.

———. *The Scientific Lady: A Social History of Women's Scientific Interests, 1520–1918*. New York: St. Martin, 1990.

Reed, Elizabeth. *American Women in Science before the Civil War*. Minneapolis, Minn.: Published by the author, 1992.

Richter, Derek, ed. *Women Scientists: The Road to Liberation*. London: Macmillan, 1982.

Rosser, Sue V. *Teaching Science and Health from a Feminist Perspective: A Practical Guide*. New York: Pergamon Press, 1986.

———. *Biology and Feminism: A Dynamic Interaction*. New York: Twayne, 1992.

———. "Educating Women for Success in Science and Mathematics." Columbia, S.C.: Division of Women's Studies, University of South Carolina, 1994.

———. *Female-Friendly Science: Applying Women's Studies Methods and Theories*. New York: Teachers College Press, 1995.

Rossi, Alice. "Women in Science: Why So Few?" *Science* 148, no. 3674 (1965).

———. "Report of Committee W 1970–71." *AAUP Bulletin*, Summer 1971.

———. "Seasons of a Woman's Life." In *Authors of Their Own Lives: Intellectual Autobiographies by Twenty American Sociologists*, ed. Bennett M. Berger. Berkeley: University of California Press, 1990.

Rossiter, Margaret W. "Women Scientists in America before 1920." *American Scientist* 62 (1974): 312–23.

———. "Women's Work in Science, 1880–1910." *Isis* 71, no. 258 (1980): 381–98.

———. *Women Scientists in America: Struggles and Strategies to 1940*. Baltimore: Johns Hopkins University Press, 1982.

———. "History, Women, and the History of Scientific Communication." *Journal of Library History* 21 (1986): 39–59.

———. *Women Scientists in America: Before Affirmative Action 1940–1972*. Baltimore: Johns Hopkins University Press, 1995.

Rowe, Mary. "The Saturn's Rings Phenomenon: Micro-Inequities and Unequal Opportunity in the American Economy." In *Proceedings of NSF Conference on Women's Leadership and Authority*. Santa Cruz: University of California–Santa Cruz, 1977.

Rudolph, Emmanuel D. "Women Who Studied Plants in the Pre–Twentieth Century United States and Canada." *Taxon* 39, no. 2 (May 1990): 151–205.

Sadker, Myra, and David Sadker. *Failing at Fairness: How America's Schools Cheat Girls*. New York: Charles Scribner's Sons, 1994.

Sax, L. J. "Predicting Gender and Major-Field Differences in Mathematical Self-Concept during College." *Journal of Women and Minorities in Science and Engineering* 1, no. 4 (1995): 291–307.

Sayre, Ann. *Rosalind Franklin and DNA*. New York: W. W. Norton, 1975.

Schacher, Susan. *Hypatia's Sisters: Biographies of Women Scientists*. Seattle: Feminists Northwest, 1976.

Schiebinger, Londa. "The History and Philosophy of Women in Science." *Signs* 12 (1987): 305–32.

———. *The Mind Has No Sex? Women in the Origins of Modern Science*. Cambridge, Mass.: Harvard University Press, 1989.

———. *Nature's Body: Gender in the Making of Modern Science*. Boston: Beacon Press, 1993.

Serbin, L. A., and J. M. Connor. "Sex-Typing of Children's Play Preferences and Patterns of Performance." *Journal of Genetic Psychology* 134 (1979): 315–16.

Seymour, E., and N. Hewitt. *Talking about Leaving: Factors Contributing to High Attrition Rates among Science, Mathematics, and Engineering Undergraduate Majors*. Final report to the Alfred P. Sloan Foundation. Boulder: University of Colorado, 1994.

Sherman, Julia. "Factors Predicting Girls' and Boys' Enrollment in College Preparatory Mathematics." *Psychology of Women Quarterly* 7 (1983): 272–81.

Shteir, Ann B. "A Connection Link: Women, Popularization, and the History of Science." *RFR/DRF* 15, no. 3 (1986): 38–39.

Shult, Linda, Susan Searing, and Elli Lester-Massman, eds. *Women, Race and Ethnicity: A Bibliography*. Madison: University of Wisconsin System Women's Studies Librarian, 1991.

Sigworth, Heather. "The Legal Status of Antinepotism Regulations." *AAUP Bulletin*, Spring 1972.

Slack, Nancy G. "Nineteenth-Century American Women Botanists: Wives, Widows and Work." In *Uneasy Careers and Intimate Lives: Women in Science, 1787–1979*, ed. Pnina G. Abir-Am and Dorinda Outram. New Brunswick, N.J.: Rutgers University Press, 1987.

Sloan, Jan Butin. "The Founding of the Naples Table Association for Promoting Scientific Research by Women, 1897." *Signs: Journal of Women in Culture and Society* 4, no. 1 (Autumn 1979): 208–16.

Sonnert, Gerhard, with the assistance of Gerald Holton. *Gender Differences in Science Careers: The Project Access Study*. New Brunswick, N.J.: Rutgers University Press, 1995.

Spanier, Bonnie B. "Women's Studies and the Natural Sciences: A Decade of Change." *Frontiers* 8 (1986): 66–72.

Stockard, Jean. "Sex Inequities in the Experience of Students." In *Sex Inequities in Education*, ed. Jean Stockard et al. New York: Academic Press, 1980.

Tee, G. J. "The Pioneering Women Mathematicians." *The Mathematical Intelligencer* 5, no. 4 (1983): 27–36.

Tidball, M. E. "Baccalaureate Origins of Recent National Science Doctorates." *Journal of Higher Education* 57 (1986): 606–20.

Tolman, Ruth, "Some Work of Women Psychologists in the War." *Journal of Consulting Psychology* 7 (1943): 127–31.

Trecker, Janice. "Sex, Science, and Education." *American Quarterly* 26, no. 4 (October 1974): 352–66.

Trescott, Martha Moore, ed. *Dynamos and Virgins Revisited: Women and Technological Change in History*. Metuchen, N.J.: Scarecrow, 1979.

Vare, Ethlie Ann, and Greg Ptacek. *Mothers of Invention: From the Bra to the Bomb: Forgotten Women and Their Unforgettable Ideas*. New York: Morrow, 1988.

Vetter, B. M. "Myths and Realities of Women's Progress in the Sciences, Mathematics, and Engineering." In *The Equity Equation: Women in Science, Engineering and Mathematics*, ed. C. S. Davis et al. San Francisco: Jossey-Bass, 1996.

Walton, Anne. "Attitudes to Women Scientists." *Chemistry in Britain* 21, no. 5 (May 1985): 461–65.

Warner, Deborah J. "Science Education for Women in Antebellum America." *Isis* 69, no. 246 (March 1978): 58–67.

———. "Women in Science in Nineteenth Century America." *Journal of the American Women's Medical Association* 34, no. 2 (February 1979): 59–66.

———. "Women Inventors at the Centennial." In *Dynamos and Virgins Revisited*, ed. Martha Moore Trescott. Metuchen, N.J.: Scarecrow Press, 1979.

Widnall, Sheila E. "AAAS Presidential Lecture: Voices from the Pipeline." *Science* 241 (September 30, 1988): 1740–45.

Wilson, Jane S., and Charlotte Serber, eds. *Standing By and Making Do: Women of Wartime Los Alamos.* Los Alamos, N.M.: Los Alamos Historical Society, 1988.

Wilson, Joan Hoff. "Dancing Dogs and the Colonial Period: Women Scientists." *Early American Literature* 7, no. 3 (Winter 1973): 225–35.

Wolfe, Alan. "Hard Times on Campus." *The Nation,* May 25, 1970, 623–27.

Wupperman, Alice. "Women in 'American Men of Science': A Tabular Study from the Sixth Edition." *Journal of Chemical Education* 188 (March 1941): 120–21.

Yost, Edna. *American Women of Science.* Philadelphia: Lippincott, 1955.

———. *Modern Women of Science.* 1955. Reprint, Westport, Conn.: Greenwood, 1984.

Zeitz, Baila, and Lorraine Dusky. *Best Companies for Women.* New York: Simon and Schuster, 1988.

Zuckerman, Harriet, and Jonathan Cole. "Women in American Science." *Minerva* 13, no. 1 (Spring 1975): 82–102.

Zuckerman, Harriet, Jonathan R. Cole, and John T. Breur, eds. *The Outer Circle: Women in the Scientific Community.* New York: Norton, 1991.

Field Index

(Indexed by current and past fields)

Employment Sector Index

(Indexed by current and past employment sector)